DATE DUE

AN INTRODUCTION TO

TAXATION

1988 EDITION

RAY M. SOMMERFELD
University of Texas at Austin

HERSHEL M. ANDERSON
North Texas State University

HORACE R. BROCK
North Texas State University

JAMES H. BOYD
Arizona State University

SILVIA A. MADEO
University of Missouri—St. Louis

G. FRED STREULING
Brigham Young University

HARCOURT BRACE JOVANOVICH, PUBLISHERS

San Diego   New York   Chicago   Austin   Washington, D.C.
London   Sydney   Tokyo   Toronto

ISBN: 0-15-546331-4
Printed in the United States of America

Preface

The 1988 edition of *An Introduction to Taxation* marks another important turning point in the history of tax texts published by Harcourt Brace Jovanovich, Inc. In brief, the Tax Reform Act of 1986 has necessitated changes in both the approach and organization of this text. We hope the following details of those and other changes will interest instructors who teach an introductory tax course in any business-oriented college environment.

Conceptual Approach

Enactment of the 1986 Act proves, beyond any reasonable doubt, the need for a conceptual textbook for the introductory course. Only by understanding the historical and theoretical issues behind the 1986 legislation will students be able to make sense of its complex provisions. And only by beginning to build their conceptual understanding in the introductory course will students receive the full benefit of subsequent course material.

Ironically, this more conceptual approach returns *An Introduction to Taxation* to the purity of its origins. The original idea of Professors Anderson, Brock, and Sommerfeld was to provide a tax text with heavier-than-usual emphasis on basic tax concepts, rather than on the more typical tax compliance detail. We stated our basic tenet clearly in the preface to our first edition (1969), as follows:

> [W]e have attempted to place current tax law in its historical and economic setting and to examine each major provision of the 1954 Internal Revenue Code, its rationale, and the way it actually functions. We propose thereby to give students a sound base for understanding the complexities of the Code, the vagaries of judicial and administrative rulings, and future changes in the law.

Although we never deviated far from that original objective, subsequent editions saw a greater emphasis on the details of current tax provisions and on the taxpayer compliance process (including the use of IRS forms). Now, more than ever, instructors wishing a greater emphasis on the procedural detail of taxation are directed to *The HBJ Federal Tax Course*. The intended distinction between the two texts should be clearer now that the latter book has a separate team of authors (John O. Everett, Richard Boley, William A.

Duncan, and Robert W. Jamison). In contrast, the authors of *An Introduction to Taxation* remain committed to the premise that a conceptual understanding of taxation is imperative if students are to become true professionals —and not mere technicians.

Topical Reorganization

The most important difference between this edition and its immediate predecessor (the Tenth Edition) is a complete reorganization of nearly all of the topical content. It would, of course, have been simpler to merely update the prior text to reflect the massive 1986 changes. But we all agree that the old organization of topics would have somewhat distorted student understanding of the current tax environment. It is our aim to capture the significance of the behavioral changes unleashed by the Tax Reform Act of 1986. We hope, at least, to have traced the broad outline of the most significant changes in both personal and business behavior attributable to the 1986 legislation.

A quick review of the table of contents will show that we have divided 25 chapters into seven main parts. The general areas of coverage are (1) economics and history; (2) basic concepts; (3) the typical individual taxpayer; (4) deductions for trades or businesses; (5) property transactions; (6) tax planning; and (7) tax process and research.

Contrary to other tax texts, our introductory coverage includes the basic rules for corporate and fiduciary taxpayers, as well as those for individuals. We believe that it is important for students to understand from the very beginning that there really is only one federal income tax; not two separate taxes. The more traditional approach misleads students into believing that there is an individual income tax that is somehow separate and distinct from a corporate income tax. In Parts Two and Six, we emphasize the fact that taxpayers typically consider one federal income tax as an important variable in selecting the business form in which to operate. That selection—and its relationship to a "corporate income tax"—are particularly important after the 1986 Act; hence, our coverage of that topic has been considerably expanded in this edition.

We also believe that there is good reason to include a relatively thorough coverage of tax research methodology in an introductory course. We have, therefore, included a three-chapter part at the very end of the text for those who are so oriented. Obviously, this material can be covered at any point in the course, or can be entirely omitted, without doing damage to the integrity of other topics.

Although Part One—on economics and history—is equally independent of all remaining chapters, we believe that it generally should be assigned, and that it should be covered in some detail early in the first course. Speculation concerning possible future changes in our federal tax laws—a topic included at the end of Chapter 2—is an especially timely issue. It may also prove to be very important to tax planning for the years after 1988.

Many of the more conceptually oriented professors may elect to omit Chapter 17 entirely. It covers a few of the details related to the taxation of capital gains and losses (Section 1231, 1245, and 1250 among others) that remain in the Code, but which will be of only limited significance to most taxpayers after 1987.

Our text was designed to be covered in either one semester or two quarters. Our general assumption is that all students will have completed at least one course in financial accounting before enrolling for this course.

Pedagogical Features

As in previous editions, each chapter concludes with a number of short-answer questions that provide specific illustrations of how a general tax rule applies in the real world. Many new figures, charts, and drawings are used to help students comprehend important concepts. The *Instructor's Manual* presents solutions to the end-of-chapter problems and alternative course outlines.

A New Future for *An Introduction to Taxation*

Joining Professors Sommerfeld, Anderson, and Brock in this edition are James H. Boyd, Arizona State University; Silvia A. Madeo, University of St. Louis—Missouri; and G. Fred Streuling, Brigham Young University. The new authors have worked closely with the returning authors to ensure a uniform approach to a myriad of tax topics. It is our renewed goal to once again publish an annual edition of a conceptual tax text that can be used for both accounting and nonaccounting majors in a business school environment.

Our publisher is committed to publishing this entry in an annual edition. Thus instructors adopting the textbook this year can be assured of a completely updated text for each following year. It is gratifying to think that *An Introduction to Taxation* will be providing new generations of students with the deep understanding required of those who would be participants—as opposed to spectators—in the evolution of tax legislation in the United States.

And yet we must acknowledge a trade-off in bringing this edition to press. We suspect that we are not the only tax professionals who wish they had had more time to better digest the intricate details of the massive changes set in motion by Congress' enactment of the 1986 Code. In our case, the demands of publication left us four months to attempt to comprehend and articulate the impact of the 1986 tax law. As a result, there are likely to be more "rough edges" than we would ordinarily tolerate. A successful and smooth text necessarily involves field testing of draft manuscript—a luxury not permitted by existing time constraints. Little comfort can be derived from the fact that authors of competing textbooks have operated under the same constraints— or that few, if any, of those authors have been willing to negotiate the conceptual underpinnings of the new law. At the very least, we view our 1988 edition as an important stepping-stone to the best of tomorrow's introductory tax texts.

We were fortunate to have some assistance in our task. The authors wish to thank the following reviewers, whose comments have helped smooth a number of the rough edges alluded to earlier: Valerie C. Milliron, Charles Enis, and Tim Fogarty, all of Pennsylvania State University. The errors that remain are the responsibility of the authors.

Finally, the authors will be revising this text during the fall of 1987 and the spring of 1988. We urge all adopters to communicate their suggestions for improvement (as well as their identification of errors) to any one or all of the authors—or to our publisher, in care of Kenneth W. Rethmeier, Executive Editor, Harcourt Brace Jovanovich, Publishers, 1250 Sixth Avenue, San Diego, CA 92101-4311.

Assuming continued support from the marketplace, we hope that this textbook will continue to pave the way to more complete understanding for students in the years and decades to come.

Ray M. Sommerfeld
Hershel M. Anderson
Horace R. Brock
James H. Boyd
Silvia A. Madeo
G. Fred Streuling

Contents

PART ONE

Economics and History

Taxes are what we pay for civilized society. . . .
Justice Oliver Wendell Holmes, Jr., Compania de
Tabacos v. Collector *(1927)*

Has he not also another object, which is that they
may be impoverished by payment of taxes, and
thus compelled to devote themselves to their daily
wants and therefore less likely to conspire against
him?
Plato, Dialogues

CHAPTER 1

The Economics of Taxation

> *The schoolboy whips his taxed top—the beardless youth manages his taxed horse, with a taxed bridle, on a taxed road;—and the dying Englishman, pouring his medicine, which has paid 7 percent., into a spoon that has paid 15 percent.—flings himself back upon his chintz bed, which has paid 22 percent.—and expires in the arms of an apothecary who has paid a license of a hundred pounds for the privilege of putting him to death. His whole property is then immediately taxed from 2 to 10 percent.*
> *Sydney Smith,* Statistical Annals of the United States of America *(1818)*

What is a tax? Why do governments collect taxes? If governments decide to impose taxes, what should they tax? How should they tax those things—proportionally, regressively, or progressively? Although a thorough understanding of possible answers to these and many other questions is not mandatory to the determination of a particular tax liability, such an understanding often makes intelligible what otherwise appears to be a wholly arbitrary tax provision. Furthermore, such an understanding should be a hallmark of distinction between those who simply make their living because of a tax law and those who constantly strive to improve the law while being concurrently engaged in a tax-related job. Part One of this book attempts to provide tentative answers to these questions for business and accounting students. Hopefully, it also will encourage some students to enroll for further study of the economic aspects of taxation.

Part One consists of two chapters. In the first chapter we define the word tax; identify the most common tax bases; consider alternative ways of taxing those items and events; and note briefly the criteria used in the selection of a tax base. In the second chapter we examine the overall U.S. tax system in historical perspective; review the development of the federal income tax; and assess major recent events of importance to taxation.

THE WORD "TAX" DEFINED

In the first several pages of this text, we will try to define that simple but elusive three-letter word, tax. Many students and professors alike will question the wisdom of our initial effort. It would be much easier, and certainly much more comforting, to simply "get on with it"; that is, to start learning the nitty-gritty details of our unbelievably complex federal income tax law. To do so, however, would be grossly misleading. For those few students who would become true tax professionals, rather than mere tax technicians, much of their eventual professional challenge will be derived from the constant need to define new technical words and phrases in an operational way. Those few students will eventually discover that mere examples, no matter how numerous or lengthy, can never define in a way that permits anyone to express a valid professional opinion (or even an educated guess) in a truly challenging engagement. The apparent security of the definition-by-example is wholly illusory. It frequently leads us to believe that we totally comprehend something which, in fact, we do not really understand at all. Therefore, the authors believe that it is much better to learn at the outset how difficult and frustrating the task of definition can be, because that path will better prepare us for the truly interesting challenges that can be found in the constantly changing world of taxation.

To begin, let us assume that the word tax can be defined meaningfully as *any nonpenal yet compulsory transfer of resources from the private to the public sector, levied on the basis of predetermined criteria and without receipt of a specific benefit of equal value, in order to accomplish some of a nation's economic and social objectives.* To understand this definition, we must consider several phrases in greater detail.

"Nonpenal"

A tax should be distinguished from a criminal or civil penalty (or fine), at least in a crude way. Nearly always, a penalty is devised solely to dissuade a person from engaging in some specific act deemed detrimental to society. For example, a government may impose a fine of $10,000 on the willful failure to file a tax return, the mere possession of a specified drug, or the striking of a police officer. In these instances, the government demands a relatively large exaction for a single act. Ultimately, of course, the government may have no real interest in prohibiting a specific act—for example, the act of possessing (as opposed to consuming) a drug is in and of itself of very little consequence —but it may consider the act detrimental to maintaining general order, to maintaining a healthy populace, or to some other broad objective deemed of primary importance.

Taxes, on the other hand, generally do not have such a specific objective, even though they are often intended to influence more general behavior patterns. They typically provide for lesser exactions for more general behavior that ordinarily is not considered detrimental to society. Thus, for example, a relatively small tax increase may be devised to discourage spending (or, more accurately, to decrease aggregate demand), even though spending per se certainly is not considered an undesirable activity. Alternatively, a relatively small tax may be imposed to discourage, say, the consumption of alcohol or tobacco products. If the consumption of these items is considered sufficiently antisocial, the tax may be increased to the point that it would be more accurate to label it a penalty.

In summary then, the major differences between a tax and a penalty are (1) the relative size of exaction demanded and (2) the specific objective behind it. The larger the exaction and the more restrictive the objective, the more likely that the exaction should be classified as a penalty rather than a tax.

But the line is not clear-cut. Certainly "penalty taxes" have been enacted and imposed in the United States. A good example is the tax on personal holding companies. That tax is imposed to discourage individuals from significantly reducing their personal income tax liabilities on income derived largely from passive investments through the use of a corporate entity. The rate is set in such a way that the "undesirable" action is more expensive than the "desired" action. Penalty taxes have also been imposed in other countries. For example, a few years ago the Canadian province of Ontario enacted tax laws intended to restrict sales of Canadian vacation land to foreigners. Ontario imposed a 20% land-transfer tax on sales of vacation properties to aliens. In addition, it imposed a 50% tax on any profit made on the sale of a vacation property to an alien.

Historically the United States has preferred to influence behavior through the granting of tax privileges rather than the imposing of penalties. The wisdom of this alternative has sometimes been questioned, especially with regard to the issue of pollution control. For example, the federal government has granted certain businesses an income tax credit for the purchase and installation of certified pollution control devices. Some individuals believe that pollution control could better be achieved by the imposition of taxes on those who pollute our air and water. The literature written by environmental economists in the early 1960s tried to distinguish between penalties and taxes by referring to these as *effluent charges* rather than *penalty taxes*.

"Yet compulsory . . . without receipt of a specific benefit of equal value"

The phrase "without receipt of a specific benefit of equal value" is typically the most difficult phrase to understand in our definition of the word *tax*. By using this phrase, we are trying merely to distinguish between (1) a *price* that must be paid before anyone may receive a private good and (2) the value associated with a public good. Private goods and services are defined as those that can be rationed or allocated among all would-be benefactors solely by means of a price mechanism; that is, by operation of the laws of supply and demand. In a purely competitive economy, the decision on how to spend one's wealth is entirely up to the individual. If an individual elects to purchase product A and to forgo the purchase of product B, he or she automatically receives the full benefit of product A but gets no benefit whatsoever from product B. Only those who are willing and able to pay the market price can benefit from a private good or service. Public goods, on the other hand, are defined as those goods and services that *cannot* be allocated by means of a price mechanism. In other words, public goods are both nonrival and nonexcludable. For example, it is impossible to allocate the benefits of a good police force or a legal system by means of a price mechanism. Everyone benefits from the mere existence of a public good, whether or not he or she directly consumes that good or service. Stated another way, society generally considers it improper to spread the cost of, say, a good police force or a fair legal system over only those few who have direct need for that particular public service in a given year because everybody—user and nonuser alike —benefits from its mere existence.

On the other hand a government, like a private business, can and often does engage in transactions that are completely optional and involve the imposition of a user's charge, or *price*, approximately equivalent to the value of the good or service rendered by the government. For example, the charge imposed on the user of the postal services and the price paid for TVA-produced electrical energy cannot be described accurately as taxes because (1) the payer receives a good or service proximate in value to the charge imposed; (2) the decision to use the service, or receive the good, is an elective rather than a coerced decision; (3) persons not paying the charge are unable to receive the good or service; and (4) supposedly the price paid is not significantly different from what it would have been had the same good or service been provided by private enterprises. They are, therefore, not public goods even though they are "publicly provided" goods.

Public goods and services, distinguished from private goods and services, are those items for which a reasonable price and an optimum output level cannot be determined or maintained by the market forces of supply and demand. The national defense force, the legal system, public educational institutions, and the network of highways are services that cannot be parceled out to a nation's populace in any *acceptable* manner by a free-market mechanism. Society has deemed it imperative that such goods and services be equally available to everyone, whether or not they are used directly and without regard for the degree of use.

Nevertheless, politicians often attempt to justify a genuine tax on some "benefit-received" principle. These politicians will argue that the tax is realistically nothing more than a reasonable price paid for a given benefit received. For example, the federal and state excise taxes on gasolines, lubricants, and tires are sometimes justified as constituting a reasonable charge for the use of public highways. Any thorough study of this proposition, however, reveals innumerable loopholes in logic. Nearly everyone benefits from the mere existence of the highways, regardless of how much he or she uses them directly and, therefore, regardless of personal gasoline, oil, and tire consumption. A motel owner conceivably might never drive on a highway; yet to deny that he or she benefits from the existence of the highway would be absurd.

The notion that certain taxes are really nothing more than a reasonable price paid for a good or service received is enhanced by the practice of channeling those taxes into specified government "funds" or "accounts" from which expenditures are restricted. This practice is known as *earmarking*. Thus, gasoline tax receipts are often channeled into a Road-Use Tax Fund that can be used only for building or improving public highways. This benefit principle is reinforced further when nonhighway users of gasoline—for example, a farmer who uses gasoline in a tractor or a student who uses gasoline in a water-ski rig—receive a refund of the gasoline tax. A fairly common practice in the past quarter century, earmarking taxes has both advantages and disadvantages worthy of separate study by anyone seriously interested in taxation. On balance, the disadvantages—including unnecessary confusion—probably outweigh the advantages. Theoretically, at least, it would be better to put all tax revenues into a single general revenue fund and to make all expenditures from that same general fund. Certainly that practice would be more honest than the present system.

Whatever may be the merits of earmarking tax revenues, this bookkeeping procedure does not in some occult manner transform what is realistically a tax into a charge that is even roughly equal to a free-market price. In short, a compulsory transfer of resources, *unless specifically related to a definite and roughly equivalent benefit received,* is sufficiently different in purpose and result from a voluntary transfer that the one (a tax) should be distinguished clearly from the other (a beneficiary's charge, or market price). Ideally, everyone would know when and how they are being taxed.

"From the private to the public sector"

Since the definition specifies a compulsory transfer of resources, perhaps it is redundant to add "from the private to the public sector." Obviously no person or group of persons acting privately can, in the absence of a legal debt, compel any other person to transfer resources to him or her except under conditions of duress. This power of compulsion is restricted to the public sector—that is, to a sovereign government. The phrase "from the private to the public sector" simply excludes the possibility of labeling as a tax any intragovernmental transfer of funds. Thus, if the administrators of a Road-Use Tax Fund were ordered by a higher governmental authority to transfer funds to a General Fund, the transfer would not be a tax.

"Predetermined criteria"

A tax may be distinguished from an outright confiscation of resources, because a tax is levied on the basis of predetermined criteria and on a recurring basis. Predetermined criteria should make a tax more equitable than confiscation. In free-world countries, taxes must generally have a socially acceptable result, since the government setting the tax criteria is itself subject to expulsion without revolution. Except during national crises, few countries have used outright confiscation to achieve the nation's nonmilitary objectives, and no country has used it on a recurring basis.

"Economic and social objectives"

At least between 1940 and 1986, taxes were a major tool by which the federal government directed and influenced the reallocation of resources necessary to achieve U.S. economic and social objectives. Whether or not taxes *should* have been used in this manner is a topic of some controversy and of major political significance, but that they were being so used is unquestionable.

RAISING REVENUES   In one sense, taxes are to governments what incomes are to businesses and to individuals. For all nonfederal levels of government, this characterization is essentially accurate; most taxes at the state and local levels are imposed solely for the purpose of raising revenues—that is, to provide the governmental unit with an income. The federal government, however, is wholly unlike state and local governments, private businesses, and individuals. Theoretically, the federal government can expend any amount of money it wishes without ever collecting any taxes, because the federal government alone controls the power to create money. Most people wish that somehow this were not in fact the case, and therefore, they often reject the notion as ludicrous. To understand U.S. federal taxation between 1940 and 1986, however, it is absolutely essential to understand what governments may seek to accomplish through taxation. Economist Abba Lerner expressed this same idea clearly when he wrote:

> First, there is never any need for the government of a well-established sovereign state to raise an amount of money by taxes just because it needs the money, if it does not wish to bring about the actual effects of the tax on the economy. If there is merely a need for money it is easier to borrow it and much easier to print it. . . . A rational taxing policy is directed at the

effects from the taxpayers' having to pay the money and not at the government's gain in getting it.[1]

Even a brief review of our federal government's operations over the past half century supports the contention that governments, unlike persons, can continually expend more than they receive. Between 1926 and 1986, the federal government operated with a deficit in 48 years and a surplus in 13 years. The net deficit, in excess of $1 trillion, demonstrates that the federal government found it unnecessary to tax just because it needed money.

Until the mid-1940s, it was difficult to cite any comparable evidence to support the contention that tax policies were in fact being used to achieve any objectives other than "raising revenues."[2] In the next 40 years, however, the changes enacted in the U.S. income tax laws increasingly supported such a proposition.

ECONOMIC PRICE STABILITY   Perhaps a government's most fundamental reason for taxing its citizens is to provide a reasonable degree of price stability within the nation. Whether the government does this for the benefit of its citizens or for self-preservation is a moot question. If a government purchases any substantial amount of goods and services without taxing, and there are few underemployed resources, aggregate spending by the public and private sectors can generate a strong excess demand and, therefore, an inflationary bias in the economy. The closer the nation is to a full-employment equilibrium position without government spending, the greater will be the inflationary pressure created by government spending without taxation.

The subtle difference between taxing to pay for government purchases (that is, to raise revenues) and taxing to achieve economic price stability is an important difference that goes a long way toward explaining many changes in our federal tax law. Certainly our federal government each year relates aggregate revenues to aggregate expenditures when it considers a budget proposal. At the all-important margin—at least prior to the Gramm-Rudman Act of 1985—it did *not* accept or reject any single expenditure proposal on the grounds that it does or does not have the wherewithal to pay for the project. Rather, the U.S. government traditionally commited the nation to selected projects with only limited or secondary concern for the source of payment; then it *separately* set the tax policy for the next year, duly considering both the expenditures budget that had been approved and the

[1]Abba Lerner, *The Economics of Control* (New York: Macmillan Co., 1959), p. 233.

[2]This is true of actually implemented policy, but in 1942, the Treasury Department apparently considered an expenditure tax to reduce consumption, promote savings, and discourage inflation. See Richard E. Slitor, "Administrative Aspects of Expenditures Taxation" in *Broad-Based Taxes: New Sources and Options,* Richard A. Musgrave, ed. (Baltimore: Johns Hopkins University Press, 1973), especially pp. 258–63. See also Richard A. Musgrave and Peggy B. Musgrave, *Public Finance in Theory and Practice,* 3rd ed (New York: McGraw-Hill, 1980), p. 456, which reported that this proposal "was given little consideration."

economic milieu in which it had to operate. Although Gramm-Rudman has not really changed the basic strategy, it has caused politicians to spend more time and words explaining how each new program is supposed to be financed. Politicians and citizens alike harbor honest differences of opinion over what part of federal spending can and should be decreased, and ultimately the decision concerning the amount of federal spending must be made in the political arena. Once that decision is formulated, the government then is ready to set tax policy. In this way, taxation is the residual buffer that regulates private demand to keep private plus public demand more or less in line with output.[3] Taxation can therefore be a primary method of contributing to the reasonable price stability of a nation. Obviously, tax policy is not the only weapon against inflation available to a government; monetary policy can also promote or hinder price stability.

ECONOMIC GROWTH AND FULL EMPLOYMENT   The federal government has determined that, in addition to maintaining reasonable price stability, it should promote the near full employment of all resources and ensure a satisfactory rate of economic growth. Collectively, economic growth with full employment and reasonably stable prices was the raison d' être for most of the monetary and fiscal policies implemented between 1945 and 1985. Taxation, as part of fiscal policy, was generally accepted as one of the more potent tools available to the government for achieving those economic goals.

Traditional economic theory calls for either an increase in government spending or a decrease in taxes, or some of each, during any period in which aggregate demand is inadequate to maintain the desired level of economic activity. The Reagan administration would decrease both government spending and taxes under these circumstances, believing (1) that increases in *private* demand sufficiently stimulate the economic growth and employment necessary to restore an equilibrium position, and (2) that government spending is not well directed. In brief, the Reagan administration differs from the typical Keynesian approach in its concern with the supply side and incentives.

ECONOMIC DEVELOPMENT   A goal closely allied with economic growth is the attainment of economic development. The governments of the third world nations want to improve economic and social conditions within their countries. A common problem for these nations is that the portion of the nation's income devoted to investment is too small, whereas the portion devoted to consumption is too large. The tendency to consume nearly all the GNP is inevitable when a large and growing population is located in an economically poor country. Yet some savings and investment are essential if the country is ever to break out of the poverty cycle. Carefully selected forms of taxation can help rectify this shortcoming by reducing private consump-

---

[3]Of course, a change in the tax provisions also causes much controversy. No one wants his tax bite increased, and everyone thinks his should be the first to be reduced. Thus spending decisions ultimately trigger revenue decisions that can be of major political significance.

tion. Obviously, however, this is only half a solution; for any net decrease in real consumption and any corresponding increase in real investment, the government must ensure that its spending programs, whether or not they are supported by tax collections, are devoted to investment purposes. Sometimes these nations must even ensure that the investment is of the particular type—usually called infrastructure—that is a precondition to further private investment. For example, large public investments in roads, harbors, bridges, and education may be necessary before private investment in business enterprise can be successful.

WEALTH REDISTRIBUTION   A few of the objectives associated with tax policies are as much social as they are economic. Wealth redistribution, for example, may be sought either because of a social value judgment that excesses in the distribution of private wealth are undesirable or because of an economic judgment that wealth redistribution is required for a desired level of economic health. The latter argument typically assumes that large concentrations of wealth and income tend to reduce aggregate demand below a satisfactory level since high-income earners spend a smaller proportion of their incomes than do persons with lower incomes. One noted student of income taxation forcefully argued that the progressive rate structure associated with our personal income tax prior to 1987 could be rationalized satisfactorily *only* on the basis that progressive income taxation contributed to a more equal distribution of a nation's wealth.

In summary, the sooner a student becomes accustomed to the idea that taxes can be used to accomplish economic and social objectives, as well as raising revenues for government purchases, the sooner he or she can anticipate correctly at least some of the changes in the tax law. Randolph Paul, a noted tax authority and lawyer, commented on this reemphasis in taxation as follows:

> The point is that taxes, wholly apart from their revenue-producing qualities, may achieve desired effects on particular occasions. This is more than inquiring into effects when imposing taxes. It puts effects first, and taxes in the role of means to desired ends. It recognizes that the highest function of taxes is to accomplish positive social or economic objectives beyond the revenue. They then become more than exactions to defray the cost of government; they reach the higher level of operation as instruments of human welfare.[4]

For whatever reason it has done so, the U.S. government has in fact diverted a substantial proportion of our national income or wealth away from the control of the private sector to the control of the public sector via taxation. Table 1-1 suggests the extent to which taxes do restructure the flow

---

[4]Randolph E. Paul, *Taxation in the United States* (Boston: Little, Brown and Company, 1954), p. 652.

TABLE 1-1

TAXES AS A PERCENTAGE OF GROSS DOMESTIC PRODUCT
FOR SELECTED COUNTRIES IN 1984

Country	Percentage
Sweden	50
Denmark	48
Belgium	47
Norway	46
Netherlands	46
France	45
Austria	42
Italy	41
United Kingdom	39
Germany	38
Finland	36
Canada	34
United States	29
Japan	27

SOURCE: Adapted from Revenue Statistics of OECD Member Countries, 1965–1985, Table 1, p. 82.

of several nations' incomes. Most U.S. citizens probably would be surprised to learn that our country is well down the list of developed nations in terms of the percentage of gross domestic product diverted by taxes. This suggests, of course, that as a nation we are *not* overtaxed. As will be noted later, however, not all countries depend equally on the same tax bases to produce their revenues.

COMMON TAX BASES

The list of possible tax bases—that is, the item, event, or value on which any tax is imposed—is limited only by the boundaries of human imagination. For example, if a government elected to do so, it could impose a tax on the value of all the rings worn on all right hands. In that case, the value of any ring worn on the right hand would constitute a *tax base*. A few of the historically more important tax bases are discussed in this chapter so that the student may appreciate the multiplicity of taxes that exist today in most complex economies.

Income Taxes

An income tax can be imposed in various forms. The most common form is, of course, a tax on *ordinary taxable income*. In relatively rare circumstances it may also be imposed as a tax on *excess profits*. A decision to tax income also necessitates an identification of the basic entities that are to be subject to this

TABLE 1-2

RATIO OF INCOME AND PROFITS TAXES TO TOTAL TAXES IN 1984

Country	Income Taxes / All Taxes
Denmark	56
Finland	50
Japan	46
Canada	43
United States	42
Sweden	42
Belgium	41
Norway	40
United Kingdom	38
Italy	36
Germany	33
Netherlands	27
Austria	26
France	17

SOURCE: Adapted from Revenue Statistics of OECD Member Countries, 1965–1985, Table 7, p. 85.

tax. In the United States the three taxable entities are individuals, corporations, and fiduciaries (estates and trusts).

Ignoring for the moment the important details of income taxation, we may generalize that the ordinary incomes earned each year by individual persons, corporations, and fiduciaries have since 1913 been a common tax base in our country. For all levels of government in the aggregate, more revenues are generated from income taxation than from any other tax. This predominance of income taxation is perhaps a major distinguishing characteristic of U.S. taxation: many other countries rely relatively more on other tax bases. Table 1-2 illustrates this heavy reliance on income taxation.

An excess-profits tax has appeared in the United States during major military crises, including World Wars I and II and the Korean conflict. The definition of *excess* profits as a tax base is particularly troublesome. The usual solution has been to define *normal* profits (or income) as either (1) some average of an entity's prewar profits, or (2) some arbitrary percentage of invested capital. The difference between the actual income earned in a given war year and normal income (as defined above) is then designated as an excess profit taxed at a higher than normal rate. The rationale used to justify the excess-profits form of the income tax is the notion that no one should profit from the increased incomes induced by wartime production.

VAT: The Value-Added Tax

The value-added tax has never been widely utilized in the United States; however, it was once imposed by the state of Michigan, and it is currently imposed in several countries of Europe. In a way, the value-added concept approximates the income concept used in national income accounting. In that branch of economics, *income* is defined as the sum of consumption, investment, and government spending—or, alternatively, as the market value of the goods and services produced within a nation during a given time period. As a tax base, *value added* may be defined alternatively as (1) a company's "sales to customers less purchases from all other companies that are themselves subject to the tax and also less any federal excise tax or state and local sales or excise taxes"[5] or (2) the algebraic sum of "wages, interest, rent, profits, and any other payments to factors of production."[6] This definition of value added obviously departs significantly from the more traditional micro-income concepts in that companies operating at a loss could still have a substantial value-added tax base, since they too add to the value of the output of the entire economy.[7] Because the value-added taxes ultimately have national income as their base, they are generally classified among the *broad-based* taxes.

Numerous individuals and various organizations have, from time to time, suggested that the United States should adopt some form of the value-added tax. Although that has not yet happened, there is growing reason to believe it could happen in the not too distant future. The very large federal deficits that we have experienced for the past six years are directly related to the major reductions in income taxation that have occurred during President Reagan's term in office. The general electorate seems to be pleased with the reduction in income taxes, but there is a growing concern about the large deficit. If further reductions in government spending prove increasingly difficult to achieve, Congress will have to accept the large deficits on a continuing basis or increase revenues significantly. The latter could be achieved either by once again increasing income tax revenues or by instituting some new form of taxation. VAT is the most likely candidate for the latter alternative simply because it can produce so much revenue so easily. Estimates are that each 1% of a national value added tax would produce approximately $20 billion. Obviously, however, such a significant change in taxation could not be achieved without a major political struggle. As is implicit in Table 1-3, increased taxes on goods and services almost seem predictable if the experience of other countries has any implication on what is likely to happen in the United States.[8]

[5]Committee for Economic Development, *A Better Balance in Federal Taxes on Business* (New York: CED, 1966), p. 25.

[6]*Ibid.*

[7]For this reason, some persons undoubtedly would insist that the value-added tax be discussed with sales or excise taxes rather than with income taxes. The authors would not quarrel with such a reclassification; they include the discussion here only to emphasize the fact that the usual definitions of income can be substantially altered if one defines income from a macro viewpoint.

[8]For a further discussion of VAT, see articles by Charles E. McLure, Jr., John F. Due, and Carl S. Shoup in Musgrave, *op. cit.*, and *The Value-Added Tax: Lessons from Europe*, Henry J. Aaron, ed. (Washington, DC: The Brookings Institution, 1981).

TABLE **1-3**

RATIO OF TAXES ON GOODS AND SERVICES TO TOTAL TAXES IN 1984

Country	Taxes on Goods and Services / All Taxes
Finland	38
Norway	36
Denmark	35
Canada	33
Austria	33
United Kingdom	30
France	29
Germany	27
Italy	26
Belgium	25
Netherlands	25
Sweden	25
United States	18
Japan	15

SOURCE: Adapted from Revenue Statistics of OECD Member Countries, 1965–1985, Table 7, P. 85.

Employment Taxes

In a limited sense, employment taxes could also be included in a discussion of income taxes. Because employment taxes are typically imposed only on some portion of a wage or salary earned,[9] however, and because they are often viewed as a contribution to a retirement fund, they really cannot be equated to more comprehensive income taxes. Additionally, they sometimes are imposed, at least in part, on the employer who pays a wage or salary rather than on the person who earns it. In that case, the employment taxes have virtually no connection to the income of the *taxpayer,* who is the employer.

For purposes of this introduction, therefore, it is most useful to divide employment (or social insurance) taxes into two major groups—those imposed on the self-employed and the employee and those imposed on the employer. The former—which would include the contributions by both the self-employed and the employee to the Federal Insurance Contributions Act, or FICA, program—could be classified conceptually with the income taxes. The latter, including the employer's contributions to the FICA program as well as to various unemployment programs, could be classified conceptually with the transactions taxes. Alternatively, if we could prove that the employee ultimately pays the employer's share of these taxes through lower wages, then the entire amount could be classified as part of the income tax.

[9]Effective January 1, 1987, the FICA tax base for employees, employers, and the self-employed consists of only the first $43,800 of earned income per year. Amounts earned in excess of $43,800 are exempt from these taxes.

Wealth (or Ownership) Taxes

Wealth taxation, like income taxation, has various forms. Selective forms of wealth taxation—such as taxes on the ownership of real property or certain personal properties—are far more common than is a comprehensive net-wealth tax. The beginning student of taxation should understand that a tax on wealth technically does not duplicate an income tax. A wealth tax is a levy on an aggregate accumulation of net wealth at one moment in time—hence, a *stock concept*—whereas an income tax is a levy on the net increase in wealth during a given period of time—hence, a *flow concept*. The accounting student should immediately recognize the parallel between these two tax bases and the two basic financial statements—the balance sheet (or statement of financial position at one moment in time) and the income statement (or statement of profit and loss for a given period of time).

Real property is generally defined for tax purposes as land, buildings, and other assets that are permanently attached to the land. Because of the impossibility of moving realty and the difficulty of concealing ownership, real property has been a primary tax base for many years. The major problem in the taxation of real estate has been the difficulty of determining accurately and equitably the fair market value of real estate on any given date. The less frequent the sales of comparable realty in any geographical area, the greater the difficulty in estimating value.

One interesting aspect of the tax generally imposed on this country's real estate is the nearly universal practice of taxing the owner of the property on the *gross* value of the realty "owned." Thus, a taxpayer who owns outright a piece of realty valued at $100,000 would presumably pay no more real property tax than another taxpayer in the same jurisdiction who owns realty valued at $100,000 but whose property is mortgaged for $80,000, even though the second taxpayer obviously has only a $20,000 equity interest in the property owned. Thus, the tax on real estate cannot be equated even roughly to a true net-wealth tax, since it (1) considers only one form of wealth (realty) and (2) taxes it on a gross (rather than net) basis.

Ownership of certain personal property is also a common tax base in the United States. The most common is the tax on automobile ownership. In some jurisdictions, this tax is levied on market values alone, whereas in other jurisdictions such factors as age and/or weight of the automobile are also considered in determining the tax liability. Other common forms of selective personal property taxes include taxes on boats and business inventories. Because of the administrative problems associated with valuing assets and enforcing the law, the personal property taxes on property other than automobiles are rapidly disappearing from the American scene.

A tax based on aggregate net wealth would be far more equitable than the typical selective wealth taxes because the former tax would apply equally to all forms of wealth and only to the net excess of the fair market value of property owned over debt owed. Nevertheless, net wealth never has been popular as a tax base. Its unpopularity must be attributed to the administrative difficulties of valuing a multiplicity of assets at frequent time intervals as well as to the ease of concealing ownership of many assets. For most persons, the largest single asset they "own" is their ability to work. Thus, a truly comprehensive net-wealth tax might even necessitate the valuation of a human life—that is, assessment of the value of the personal services the individual might render—based, perhaps, on the discounted value of an estimated earnings stream. The administrative difficulty in estimating income streams and in selecting a discount rate is apparent. Similar valuation problems apply to many more conventional forms of wealth.

Wealth-Transfer Taxes

In addition to the various taxes on selected forms of ownership per se, governments frequently impose a tax on the *transfer* of an individual's ownership interest to anyone other than a bona fide purchaser. For example, the federal donative transfers tax and the state inheritance taxes are based on the gratuitous transfer of an ownership interest.

The Tax Reform Act of 1976 combined what previously had been two separate wealth-transfer taxes—the federal gift tax and the federal estate tax—into a single donative transfers tax. Conceptually this tax is relatively simple. If in any year during the donor's life he or she makes a taxable gift, then that donor must pay a tax determined by applying the tax rates to the *aggregate* value of all taxable gifts made since birth, less a tax credit (similarly determined) for all taxable gifts made in *prior* years. In this manner, current gifts are taxed at progressively higher marginal tax rates. At the donor's death, a similar tax calculation is made, as follows:

Compute the value of the *taxable* estate	$XXX
Add aggregate value of *taxable* gifts made during life	$XXX
The sum equals the donative transfers tax base	$XXX
Compute the gross tax on the above value (this tax rate schedule is printed in Appendix C)	$XXX
Subtract an aggregate gift tax based on all gifts made during life (also using the tax rate schedule in Appendix C)	$XXX
The remainder is the federal estate tax payable at death	$XXX

The estate tax is payable by the executor from the assets left by the deceased person. Observe that this estate tax is equivalent to a true net-wealth tax because it is based on the excess of the fair market value of the decedent's assets over the debts owed (plus certain other special exemptions written into the law). Technically, however, it is considered a wealth-transfer tax (based on the value of the assets transferred) rather than a net wealth tax. As noted above, the law contains a long list of special provisions (or exceptions), most of which were enacted either to allow smaller estates to escape taxation or to make the law's administration feasible.

Most estates wholly escape the federal estate tax because of a $192,800 tax credit. This means that a person dying with an estate of less than $600,000 will pay no estate tax because a $192,800 credit will negate the tax otherwise payable on an estate of exactly $600,000. In addition, a decedent may leave any amount of property to his or her spouse free of the estate tax. Because of these generous exemptions, one expert estimates that only one half of 1% of the estates of all persons dying after 1986 will be subject to the federal donative transfers tax.[10]

The gift tax is made administratively feasible by allowing every individual to make gifts of $10,000 per year to as many donees as he or she wishes without incurring a gift tax. In other words, the law provides that no *taxable* gift occurs until a person gives more than $10,000 to one person in one year. In addition, gifts to charity are excluded from the gift tax base. Without these exemptions and deductions, the I.R.S. would face the truly Herculean task of discovering small gifts among family members and exacting a tax from the donor for each gift.

On the other hand, because of the generous deductions, exemptions, and credits, little revenue is obtained from the donative transfers tax. That fact might suggest that the expenditure of time, effort, and money required to enforce the law is greater than the benefit received from it. Such a conclusion is doubtful for two reasons. First, and most important, the donative transfers tax has the primary objective of wealth redistribution; that is, this tax is specifically intended to redistribute wealth from the wealthiest segment of our society to the poorer segments. Second, because of the combined effects of our realization criterion and certain "basis rules," which are explained later in this book, the appreciation in value that occurs between the time a taxpayer acquires a property and the time he or she dies is never subject to an *income* tax as long as the property is not sold or exchanged in a taxable transaction. This means, of course, that a significant amount of income—at least as that word is defined by economists—wholly escapes income taxation. Many theorists believe that the donative transfers tax partially makes up for this failure to impose an income tax on unrealized appreciations in value. In any event, relatively few persons will ever be fortunate enough to have to pay tax on a gift or an estate.

Transactions Taxes

Numerically, the most frequently encountered tax is that imposed on the consummation of a retail sale. In classifying the various tax bases, the retail sales tax can logically be grouped with other taxes that are levied on the occasion of a specified transaction. Under this classification scheme, it is possible to distinguish (however hazily) between taxes imposed on specific commodities (usually called excise taxes) and taxes imposed on all commodities (inevitably subject to a list of exceptions) that enter into a specified transaction.

The sale transaction undoubtedly is the one most often singled out for tax purposes. A study of sales taxation, however, reveals that even it is

---

[10]Estimates suggest that 75% of the wealth in the United States is owned by the top 20% of all wealth owners; 24% is owned by the top 1%. See Musgrave and Musgrave, *op. cit.*, p. 474.

complicated, since not all sales are subject to the sales tax. Generally speaking, governments have tried to tax sales only at one of three levels—the manufacturer's level, the wholesaler's level, or the retailer's level. Retail sales taxation is further complicated by the frequent exclusion of the sale of such items as services, food (when not consumed on the premises), and selected medicines and drugs.

Exclusions, such as those suggested in the preceding sentence, require comprehensive definitions. What, for example, is a *retail* sale? Is the sale of one ream of 20-lb. bond paper to a business, which will use the paper as stationery in routine correspondence, a retail sale? Is the sale of the same paper to a student who is writing a research paper on taxation a retail sale? Finally, if the end use of the paper determines its tax status, how does the clerk who completes the sale know from whom to collect the tax? Equally troublesome questions can be raised about the definitions of *food, medicine,* and *services.* For example, under Texas law, candy sold by Campfire Girls is not "food," while cookies sold by Girl Scouts *are* "food."

Other transactions or events that have been the basis for a tax include stock transfers, severance of natural resources from the earth, and official registration of selected legal and business papers. Thus, in certain jurisdictions, the transfer of stock ownership from one party to another, whether or not by sale, has been a taxable occasion. In other jurisdictions, the separation of a natural resource from the earth (for example, natural gas, petroleum, and iron ore) is a taxable event. In yet other jurisdictions, a stamp tax is imposed on the registration of a deed, the notarization of a document, or the filing of a business paper. As noted earlier, the payment of a wage or salary is usually the base for one or more of the social insurance (employment) taxes. In each of these instances, the amount of the tax is usually determined by application of the tax rate to the dollar amount involved in the specified transaction. For example, the sales price of a stock transaction might be made the base for the stock-transfer tax. Similarly, the value of any unrefined natural gas removed from the earth could constitute the base for a severance tax. The dollar amount of all salaries paid could be the base for an employment tax.

Excise Taxes

The manufacture, sale, or consumption of various commodities has also been singled out as an appropriate base for taxation. Taxes imposed on only *selected* commodities are widely referred to as excise taxes. The taxes on alcoholic beverages, tobacco products, and highway fuels are perhaps the most common. They are by no means, however, the only items selected for special tax treatment. Many students may be surprised to learn that the following items (along with many others not listed) are bases for federal excise taxes in the United States: fishing equipment; pistols and revolvers, shells and cartridges; tires; truck parts; telephone and teletypewriter service; wagers and the occupation of accepting wagers; sugar; narcotic drugs, as well as opium for smoking; white phosphorous matches; adulterated butter; filled cheese; cotton futures; machine gun transfers; and transportation of persons by air.

Finding a common rationale for the taxation of this diverse list of commodities and services is indeed difficult. Several of the excise taxes are allegedly imposed to regulate the use of items that are or may be dangerous to society. There is considerable question, however, about precisely how the taxation of alcoholic beverages, opium, or machine gun transfers helps to control abuse of these items. Perhaps the most that can be said for taxes on these commodities is that they afford yet another basis for prosecution in some criminal cases.

On *a priori* grounds, two other rationalizations for the existence of certain excise taxes seem more plausible. First, many excise taxes may exist simply because they are "good revenue producers"; second, other excise taxes undoubtedly exist because some legislators consider them to be something of a beneficiary's charge.

Historically, many taxes have been considered good taxes as long as they produced substantial amounts of revenue every year without fail. *Using that criterion,* commodity taxes on those items for which a relatively large and inelastic demand exists would produce a *good* tax. For this reason, taxes have been imposed on matches and on salt (especially prior to the days of refrigeration and in relatively underdeveloped nations).

The idea that the (immediate) highway user ought to pay for the cost of the highways via taxes on gasoline, tires, lubricants, and so on was considered earlier. The same basic idea, with slight modification, is sometimes used to justify the excise taxes on air fares (to pay for the government's investment in air terminals), alcoholic beverages (to pay for police protection necessitated by alcohol abuse), and wagering (to pay for the policing of legalized gambling). Obviously, this justification presumes that the incidence of these taxes rests with the person who receives the benefit from the government expenditure or with the person who makes the expenditure necessary in the first instance.

Other Miscellaneous Taxes

The preceding discussion is by no means a thorough cataloging of all tax bases. Among the more important or interesting tax bases not already mentioned are import and export taxes (customs duties), head taxes, franchise taxes, and the expenditures tax.

Import and export taxes closely resemble excise taxes in that they are imposed only on selected items imported into (or exported from) a sovereign state. Sometimes these taxes become so universal that they approximate a transactions tax—that is, a tax on the *transaction* of importing and exporting, regardless of the commodity involved. Under these circumstances, customs duties resemble sales taxes more closely than they do excise taxes. On the other hand, the historical, economic, and political rationales for customs duties more often parallel the rationale for excise taxes than that for sales taxes. In both third-world and developed countries, import duties typically suppress the importation of only those foreign products that can, at least theoretically, be made domestically. The hope is, of course, that this protection encourages the development of the local industry. Export duties are fundamentally a method of increasing government revenues, used primarily by countries with little economic diversification. Thus, the country whose economy has been heavily dependent on the production of one product—for example, coffee, sugar, or tin—has often relied on an export tax as the primary source of government funds.

For even less developed countries, the head tax (a flat tax on each human) has produced substantial revenues. As countries develop, the head tax often evolves into a crude form of income taxation, as the amount of tax "per head" may vary with some crude measure of income. In our own early Virginia Colony, the amount of the head tax was reportedly dependent on personal apparel worn to church.

A franchise tax is a tax on a right granted by a sovereign government. When a government grants one or more persons the right to do something that they would otherwise not have the authority to do, the granting government often imposes a special yearly tax on the recipient of the right. A common form of the franchise tax is the one imposed for the privilege of conducting a business as a corporate entity. The actual tax base for the franchise tax has varied widely and included, among other measures, the dollar amount of sales, earnings, dividends, par or stated value of capital issues, and tangible assets owned by the corporation.

The expenditures tax is a novel idea that, to our knowledge, has been implemented only very rarely (in India and Sri Lanka) in the last 200 years. Crudely stated, the idea is that progressive income taxation imposes as great a burden on those who save and invest (and who thus make possible even greater national incomes) as on those who spend their entire incomes on consumption. The expenditures tax would turn this around by taxing total consumption during a given period and exempting from taxation any portion of income not spent on consumption items.[11] A few Washington politicians are suggesting that we seriously reexamine this tax if we must increase taxes anytime soon in the United States.

The purpose of this discussion of alternative tax bases has *not* been to provide students of elementary taxation with a comprehensive discussion of the merits or shortcomings of any particular tax or even to acquaint them with all the taxes known to humanity. Rather, it has been simply to demonstrate the ubiquitous nature of taxation. We dismiss any detailed consideration of the various taxes mentioned, not because they are nonexistent or unimportant, but because they are overshadowed in U.S. taxation by the giants—the personal and corporate income taxes. Before turning our attention to these giants, however, a few more economic aspects of taxation ought to be considered.

Following an initial selection of tax rates and tax bases, most governmental units seem to spend a disproportionately large amount of time and effort

---

[11]For details, see Nicholas Kaldor, *An Expenditure Tax* (London: Allen and Unwin, 1955).

discussing the advisability of modifying the rates. These bodies may, from time to time, increase or decrease an existing tax rate, but they seldom switch from one basic rate structure to another. Similarly, though they frequently make minor modifications of existing tax bases, they only rarely delete an old tax or add an entirely new one. During their deliberations, however, legislators, their constituents, lobby groups, and the general press frequently refer to the proportional, progressive, or regressive nature of the various taxes in force and the new ones being considered. As an integral part of the emotional political dialogue, the references often confuse the issues because they fail to define the terms they use in this dialogue. We will, therefore, begin with the definition of the words *proportional, progressive,* and *regressive* as they apply to taxation.

DEFINITION OF TERMS

In the simplest way, a tax can be defined as the product of the tax base and the tax rate. In equation form, this definition is

$$T = B \times R$$

where T stands for tax, B for tax base, and R for tax rate. By elementary algebraic manipulation, this equation can, of course, be rearranged to read

$$R = \frac{T}{B}$$

Procedural Definitions

Proportional, progressive, and regressive can be defined readily in terms of the preceding equation. If the ratio T/B remains constant for all possible values of B, then the tax rate R is *proportional.* If the ratio T/B increases as B increases and decreases as B decreases, then the tax rate R is *progressive.* Finally, if the ratio T/B increases as B decreases and decreases as B increases, then the tax rate R is *regressive.*

In other words, a tax is proportional if one flat rate applies equally to every measure of the tax base. Most of our common taxes are in this category. For example, sales, real property, personal property, customs, and excise taxes are generally imposed with a proportional tax rate. If, on the other hand, a higher tax rate is applied to increasingly larger values of the tax base, then the tax is progressive. Income, estate, and gift taxes are typically imposed with a progressive tax-rate structure.

Limitations of These Definitions

The preceding definitions are based on the premise that the appropriate comparison is between the tax paid and the tax base itself. Thus, for sales taxation, only the amount involved in a *taxable sale* is included in the denominator of the ratio *T/B;* for income taxation, only *taxable income* is included. In the popular press and in political propaganda, however, the terms proportional, progressive, and regressive are not defined in this manner. Rather, they are defined, albeit loosely, by the following ratio:

$$\frac{\text{Aggregate tax liability over some time period}}{\text{Some measure of ability to pay, frequently personal income}}$$

If the ratio above is even roughly constant for most values of, say, personal income, common usage of the terms would classify the tax as a proportional tax. If the ratio tends to decrease with increasing values of personal income, then the tax is alleged to be regressive. Although this alternative definition lacks the precision of the earlier one, it may be the more meaningful of the two. Without doubt, it is the definition implicit in virtually all nonacademic discussions of tax matters. Unfortunately, it is a very crude measure for several reasons.

Incidence Problems

The first major problem encountered in any precise application of the popular definition of tax-rate structures is our inability to determine who *finally* pays most taxes. The assumption made by the general public is that the tax is assignable to (borne by) the person who pays it. For example, the retail sales tax is assumed to be borne by the purchaser of the taxed good or service; the corporate income tax is assumed to be borne by the corporation paying the tax.

Several questions can be raised about the validity of this common assumption. Suppose, for example, that a man decides to purchase a new automobile. Because of the current competitive nature of the market, he arranges a deal whereby the car dealer agrees to "pay the sales tax" via a reduction in the price of the car. Instead of paying, say, $10,000 plus sales tax, the buyer effectively pays $9,500 plus a $500 sales tax. If we could establish that the market price for the car in question actually was $10,000, exclusive of the tax (a difficult question to establish in fact), the *initial* effect of the transaction would be to shift the retail sales tax from the car buyer to the car seller, even though the tax was legally and technically imposed on the buyer. Even then we cannot safely conclude that the sales tax has simply been shifted from the purchaser to the seller of the car. To reach an accurate conclusion, we would have to determine if the car dealer could possibly shift the tax to labor, via substandard wages; suppliers of capital, via reduced interest payments; other less-informed purchasers, via higher prices; or some other party, in some other manner. Obviously an accurate answer to these questions remains largely out of reach because of our necessarily limited knowledge of the real world. The complexities of measuring all the pertinent variables make such measurements practically impossible.

Given the state of relative ignorance in which we live, it is not surprising that tax experts are in less than complete accord on their assumptions about tax incidence.[12] Unfortunately, far too many persons make decisions about taxation based on totally erroneous premises about the incidence of many, if not most, taxes. We may often read statements suggesting that property owners are somehow injured by unduly heavy taxes on real property. The premise behind these statements rests squarely on the assumption that the real property tax is borne entirely by the landlord. Most renters probably pay some of their landlord's property taxes, even though the form of the rent payment camouflages this fact.

If we accept the "popular" definition of proportional, progressive, and regressive as applied to taxation, we must understand that our conclusions can be no more valid than our data are accurate. One of the most complicated and unresolved issues in all of taxation is the determination of the final incidence of any tax. Observe that we must determine who finally must "bear" each tax before we can accurately determine the numerator of the ratio

$$\frac{\text{Aggregate tax liability over some time period}}{\text{Some measure of ability to pay, frequently personal income}}$$

Ability to Pay

The second major problem encountered in any precise application of this popular definition of tax-rate structures lies in our failure to find a truly adequate measure of ability to pay taxes. Progressive–regressive notions achieve their greatest application in statements related to welfare economics. For example, it is frequently argued that retail sales and (most) excise taxes are regressive because they require a greater relative contribution by the poor than by the rich. A poor person must spend a greater percentage of income for consumer items (which typically are subject to either sales or excise taxes, or both) than a person with a large income.

If the assumptions about spending and taxing patterns are valid, then, of course, the conclusion of regressivity is also valid. Many persons unwittingly go one step further and presume that regressivity necessarily fails to conform to generally accepted notions of ability to pay. This last conclusion requires at least one further assumption—that personal income is a meaningful measure

[12]For example, see Edgar K. Browning, "The Burden of Taxation," *Journal of Political Economy,* 86(4), August 1978, pp. 649–71; Joseph Pechman and Benjamin Okner, *Who Bears the Tax Burden?* (Washington, DC: The Brookings Institution, 1974); Richard A. Musgrave, Karl E. Case, and Herman B. Leonard, "The Distribution of Fiscal Burdens and Benefits," *Public Finance Quarterly,* July 1974, pp. 259–311. See also Don Fullerton, A. Thomas King, John B. Shoven, and John Whalley, "Corporate Tax Integration in the United States: A General Equilibrium Approach," *American Economic Review,* 71(4), September 1981, pp. 677–91; William H. Oakland, "A Survey of the Recent Debate on the Short-Run Shifting of the Corporation Income Tax," *National Tax Association Proceedings* (1969), pp. 525–47; and Marian Krzyzaniak and Richard A. Musgrave, *The Shifting of the Corporate Income Tax* (Baltimore: The Johns Hopkins Press, 1963).

TABLE **1-4**

THE PROGRESSIVE EFFECT OF THE PERSONAL EXEMPTION

	Taxpayer 1	Taxpayer 2	Taxpayer 3
Income earned	$500	$1,000	$1,500
Less $500 exemption	500	500	500
Taxable income (tax base)	$ 0	$ 500	$1,000
Times tax rate	0.10	0.10	0.10
Equals tax liability	$ 0	$ 50	$ 100
Effective tax rate (tax income)	$0/$500 = 0%	$50/$1,000 = 5%	$100/$1,500 = 6⅔%

of the ability to pay taxes. Without a doubt, annual income is one of the major ingredients of a person's ability to do anything of a financial nature, including the payment of taxes. However, it is certainly not the only ingredient. The amount of a person's accumulated wealth and his or her prospect of earning equal or greater sums in the future are two other items of major significance. Finally, the taxpayer's age, marital status, health, and number of dependents are usually of real importance. In short, before we can determine whether a tax *is* regressive relative to the taxpayer's ability to pay, we must find some comprehensive measure of taxpaying ability.

Several considerations deemed pertinent to the ability-to-pay concept have been incorporated in the Internal Revenue Code's definition of *taxable income* in an attempt to make the income tax more equitable. Unfortunately, these modifications add one final complication to the definition of the terms proportional, progressive, and regressive as applied to taxation.

This complication can be readily understood in terms of an illustration common to much of the literature that has accompanied the progressive tax controversy. Many writers carefully point out that including a provision for a standard deduction or a personal exemption makes a progressive tax of an otherwise proportional income tax.[13] The arithmetic of their conclusion is simple. Suppose, for example, that country A imposes a (flat) 10% tax on all income in excess of $500 per year earned by each of its citizens. The progressive nature of this otherwise proportional tax is shown in Table 1-4. In other words, this tax is a proportional (constant 10%) tax on *taxable income* (defined as all income over $500) but a progressive (increasing percentage) tax on total income. Whether this tax is judged to be proportional or progressive depends on which income measure is used as the denominator of the ratio to determine the effective tax rate. The only important point of the illustration is simple: The meanings of the terms proportional, progressive, and regressive, as applied to tax-rate structures, are often elusive, and persons who use the terms to advocate a particular position frequently fail to articulate the assumptions implicit in their analysis. This failure, in turn, often results in misapplication, misstatement, and general misunderstanding.

[13]For example, see Walter J. Blum and Harry Kalven, Jr., *The Uneasy Case for Progressive Taxation* (Chicago: The University of Chicago Press, 1953), p. 4.

In conclusion, the student should be aware that in most discussions about progressive and regressive taxation, the writer often assumes both (1) that the tax is not shifted—that is, the tax is presumably borne by the party it is legally imposed on—and (2) that the appropriate measure for determining progressivity (or regressivity) is some vaguely defined but apparently "generally accepted" notion of personal income. From this frame of reference, it is commonly believed that the U.S. personal income tax and the estate and gift tax are progressive, whereas most other taxes (those typically imposed at a uniform rate) are regressive.

MARGINAL, AVERAGE, AND EFFECTIVE RATES

Other distinctions in tax-rate structures are the differences among marginal, average, and effective tax rates. First, we distinguish between marginal and average rates; then we consider the differences between the nominal-average and the real- or effective-average rate.

Marginal–Average Distinctions

The *marginal* tax rate is the rate that would be applicable to the incremental unit of the tax base. For any tax that is proportional, in a technical sense, the marginal tax rate is (obviously) the basic tax rate. For any tax that is either progressive or regressive, in a technical sense, the marginal tax rate can be determined only if we know both (1) the rate structure and (2) the aggregate measure of the tax base before considering any incremental amount. The *average* tax rate is simply an arithmetic expression of an aggregate tax liability divided by a given amount of a tax base.

To demonstrate the difference between the marginal and average tax rates, let us consider the 1988 U.S. income tax on single individuals. The apparent tax-rate structure applicable to single taxpayers appears to consist of only two tax brackets: that is, a 15% bracket applicable to a taxable income of less than $17,850 and a 28% bracket to any taxable income in excess of $17,850. Thus, a single (unmarried) individual who reports a $15,000 taxable income in 1988 can be said to have a marginal tax rate of 15%; this means, of course, that an increase in taxable income of, say, $100, would result in the taxpayer's paying $15 of that additional $100 to the government in personal income tax. A $100 increase in the taxable income of a single taxpayer reporting a $30,000 taxable income in 1988 would result in the taxpayer's paying $28 of that additional $100 in personal income tax because he or she is in the 28% marginal tax bracket. On the other hand, the average tax rate of the former individual would be 15% (that is, $2,250 tax liability divided by $15,000 taxable income), whereas the average tax rate of the latter individual would be approximately 20% ($6,079.50 divided by $30,000). Obviously, the marginal tax rate is always greater than the average tax rate for any progressive tax after the first step in that progression.

It is important for the student to grasp the significance of the marginal tax rate early in studying taxation, because the marginal rate determines how knowledgeable taxpayers will act in many circumstances. In an important sense, the marginal tax rate is to business what the law of gravity is to physics: tax bases tend to seek their lowest level just as water does! In other words, taxpayers tend to arrange their financial affairs so that any tax base is subject to tax at the lowest possible marginal tax rate. Relative to the income tax, financial affairs should generally be arranged to report incremental units of taxable income at such times and/or in such ways as to allow the application of the lowest possible marginal tax rates, other things being equal. On the other hand, incremental units of deductions and losses should be reported at such times and/or in such ways as to allow the application of the highest possible marginal tax rates, other things being equal.

Nominal-Average and Real-Average Distinctions

The preceding discussion of average tax rates is based on the premise that the pertinent comparison is that existing between the aggregate tax liability and the tax base determined in a technical way; that is, using a technical rather than a popular definition of the tax base. As explained earlier in this chapter, the popular descriptions of various tax rates are often significantly different from the technical definitions. In the same manner, average tax rates are frequently computed using a popular surrogate for a more technical tax base. The average rate determined in a technical sense might be better labeled the *nominal-average* rate.

For certain purposes, such as making a social value judgment about our existing tax provisions, an average tax rate might be better determined by dividing the aggregate tax liability by an adjusted tax base. The appropriateness of the adjustments depends on the purpose of the calculation. For example, if we wanted to know an individual's income tax based on a real or economic measure of income—rather than on a technical tax base called taxable income—it would be appropriate to divide the individual's aggregate income tax liability by his or her economic or real income.

To illustrate the notion of a real-average (some tax scholars prefer to call this an effective-average or an actual-average) tax rate, consider the calculation pertinent to a single individual who in 1988 receives a $40,000 salary and $100,000 in tax-exempt state bond interest each year. Ignoring any additional details, and simply assuming that this individual's $40,000 salary is equal to his or her $40,000 taxable income, we could readily determine that the nominal-average tax rate was 22% (that is, $8,944 aggregate tax liability divided by $40,000 taxable income). On the other hand, this same individual's real- or effective-average tax rate would be closer to 6% (that is, $8,944 aggregate tax liability divided by $140,000 real or economic income).

The selection of both tax rates and tax bases has, in past, proceeded more on political than on economic grounds. As the objective of taxation shifts away from simply raising revenues and toward accomplishing specified economic objectives, the selection of both tax rates and tax bases becomes increasingly important. The intelligent selection of both is complicated because (1) we cannot determine with any precision the ultimate incidence of most taxes (that is, who *really* pays the tax); (2) tax objectives often conflict, and no ordinal ranking of their importance has been stipulated; and (3) the distribution of tax bases does not always coincide with the distribution of needs. Although the number of possible combinations is large, governmental units must choose among them. It is most unfortunate, therefore, that there has been so little attention given to the criteria that might be used in setting tax rates and in selecting tax bases.

CRITERIA USED IN THE SELECTION OF A TAX BASE

One of the earliest attempts to identify the criteria for selecting a tax base is credited to Adam Smith, who, in 1776, suggested that a "good" tax ought to be equitable, convenient, certain, and economical.[14] He called these criteria the "canons of taxation." A review of the current literature shows that Smith's criteria are still considered today. As you may by now suspect, however, the terminology used is less than crystal clear.

Equity

Tax equity is commonly defined as the equal treatment of similarly situated taxpayers. The obvious problem with this criterion is that the definition fails to provide a method or basis for measurement to determine under what conditions two or more taxpayers are "similarly situated." The phrase "tax equity" as used in the literature and in political discussions seems to imply that the appropriate measure is implicit in the tax base. In other words, a tax imposed on the purchase of a given commodity is assumed to be equitable as long as all purchasers of the identical commodity (with possible modification for quantity, quality, price, or intended use) have to pay an equivalent tax. By this same standard, a tax imposed on taxable income is deemed to be equitable as long as two persons earning the same taxable income during a given time period pay the same amount of income tax.

The larger problem is, of course, that this standard considers only one dimension of the total taxpayer (the standard is best categorized as unidimensional *horizontal equity*), and in many cases the dimension considered is not the most significant one for purposes of taxation. The problem can be demonstrated easily as follows: suppose that each of two taxpayers purchased, for personal consumption, a 60-cent loaf of bread on which there is imposed a sales tax or an excise tax of 4 cents. Since each purchaser paid an identical tax on an identical purchase, the tax may be said to be equitable. If we expand the number of variables considered to include incomes, wealth, marital status, physical condition, or any of hundreds of other possible factors

---

[14]*The Wealth of Nations*, Book V, Chapter II, Part II (New York: Dutton, 1910).

common to these two taxpayers, then we may decide that the tax is not truly equitable in any meaningful sense. The 4-cent tax on the loaf of bread may be grossly inequitable *in a social sense* if one purchaser is married, has 10 dependent children, and spends his or her last dollar to purchase this loaf of bread and feed the children, whereas the other purchaser is single, independently wealthy, and buys the bread to feed the swan.

To expand this simple concept of horizontal equity, a related but not necessarily equivalent tax criterion—that of *ability to pay*—has been equally popular. The latter criterion can be referred to as *vertical equity.* Prior to the 1986 act, vertical equity seemed to suggest that unequally situated taxpayers should be treated differently. Specifically, it suggested that those who had a greater tax-paying ability should pay a larger part of the total taxes so that, in the aggregate, the tax collections were "equitably" distributed among all taxpayers. This was generally achieved through the use of a progressive tax-rate structure. The 1986 Act appears to provide a new definition of vertical equity, at least in general terms; it suggests that all people should pay the same tax rate except at the lowest income level.

In applying this criterion, two further problems are readily apparent. First, the concept is again unidimensional as applied; that is, in application a single measure is often used as an appropriate index of ability to pay. Unfortunately, no single measure is really adequate. The most frequent measure utilized this way today is income; the next most frequent is wealth; and the vehicle used to achieve what is presumed to be vertical equity is the tax-rate structure.

A second major problem in vertical equity existed prior to 1987 in that there was no really satisfactory method of determining just how differently unequally situated taxpayers ought to be treated. Even if we had been able to measure each person's ability to pay, we still faced the problem of determining how much more the most able should pay than the least able. This problem led to frequent changes in the tax rate structure—almost always in the name of equity—but with little consensus on the correctness of the result. Fortunately, the three other tax criteria proposed by Adam Smith are somewhat easier to explain and are therefore less subject to the wide differences of opinion that exist on the subject of tax equity.

Convenience

Both taxpayers and tax administrators place great stock in administrative simplicity, and in practice this tax criterion is often controlling. Any tax that can be easily assessed, collected, and administered seems to encounter the least opposition. Thus, for example, the retail sales tax is popular in many jurisdictions at least partially because most taxpayers find it relatively convenient to pay 4, 5, or 6 cents per dollar of purchase. Individually these small sums seem immaterial; no formal tax return must be completed by the purchaser; and few additional records must be maintained by the vendor.

Even the income tax, which is generally conceded to be a most inconvenient tax, has been made more tolerable by the creation of the standard deduction, withholding, and tax tables. Some experts argue, of course, that we are willing to pay too high a price for convenience as opposed to other criteria. Those experts may contend that inconvenience would be a better criterion for tax policy; in other words, a good tax may be one that hurts! A majority of the taxpayers, however, would probably not agree with that conclusion.

Certainty

Certainty, like convenience, is high on most taxpayers' lists of criteria for a "good" tax. Most citizens like to know, with a reasonable degree of certainty just what their tax bill will be, given any set of circumstances. Obviously the existence of certainty also permits a maximum of advance planning. The major problem with using certainty as a criterion for the selection of tax policy is the fact that different economic and social conditions may demand different tax provisions. Therefore, to the extent that taxation is used to achieve nonrevenue objectives, the criterion of certainty must diminish in importance—at least from the government viewpoint.

Tax administrators have attempted to increase the certainty of some aspects of income taxation by providing detailed instructions, advanced rulings, regulations, and other interpretations of the law. Property taxation often is made more palatable by widespread publication of annual tax rates, infrequent property reappraisals, and provisions for review boards. These and other efforts to increase the certainty of many taxes have added measurably to their general acceptance in America.

Historically, the term *certainty* has also meant consistency in the amount of revenue collected. For many years, taxes that produced widely fluctuating amounts of revenue were considered undesirable, whereas those providing stable amounts were favored. Government administrators solely dependent on revenue collections to conduct their operations were particularly concerned about this kind of tax certainty. For the last four decades, however, the notion that tax collections should vary with the economic cycle has been increasingly accepted as the desirable alternative to certainty of collections. This change, obviously, necessitates nontax sources of revenue (including debt financing).

Economy

Undoubtedly, a good tax should involve a minimum cost for compliance and administration. Like many cost studies, however, attempts to quantify the cost of the various taxes have not been particularly successful because of the difficulty of measuring the pertinent data. Press releases about the "cost" of collecting a dollar of any given tax usually refer only to the efficiency of the tax collector's operation. An accurate statement of the cost of a tax would, of course, include the cost of taxpayer compliance, as well as the cost of collection and enforcement. It might include even the social costs of mental and emotional strain associated with many tax decisions. The federal income tax is generally considered one of the "cheapest" taxes to collect. However, these statistics include only the government's cost of administration, and the complexity of the income tax makes compliance costs very high. The total "cost" of the income tax, or any other tax, is anyone's guess.

Productivity

Although Adam Smith did not include the ability to produce large amounts of revenue as one of the canons of taxation, this factor is given much consideration by politicians today. Generally, taxes that cannot produce a significant amount of revenue are not popular even if they are equitable, convenient, certain, and economical. As a practical matter, most taxes could not have limited productivity and still be economical. A relatively unproductive tax is typically as expensive to enforce as a much more productive one. Many state and local governments are currently examining their tax structures in an attempt to delete the less productive taxes while increasing other already productive ones. The only tax on the horizon that is not already used, but which could be highly productive, is the value-added tax, mentioned earlier in this chapter.

Social and Economic Effects

Between 1940 and 1986, the federal income tax was frequently used to reallocate resources for the achievement of specified economic and social objectives. Those who approved this use of taxation also recognized a new tax criterion—that is, did the tax (or tax provision) contribute to the rapid and efficient attainment of the economic or social goal stipulated for it? The opponents of this criterion alleged that deliberate intervention with free-market forces through taxation was wholly improper. To this latter group, the proper tax criterion was one of nonintervention. The tax that disrupts the free-market mechanism the least is, for these individuals, the one considered the most desirable tax. The latter group seems to have won the battle, at least for now, if the Tax Reform Act of 1986 is any basis for judging.

During the past decade, economists have also become increasingly interested in efficiency as a tax criterion. Studies have been undertaken to determine, for example, the distortion caused by taxes on labor, taxes on capital, excise taxes, and inflation.[15] The relationship between interest rates and large federal deficits has also been a source of growing controversy.[16] Except for these final considerations, however, the criteria for selecting tax rates and tax bases have changed relatively little since the days of Adam Smith.

[15]For example, see David N. Hyman, *Public Finance: A Contemporary Application of Theory to Policy* (Chicago: Dryden Press, 1983), p. 400. See also *How Taxes Affect Economic Behavior*, Henry J. Aaron and Joseph A. Pechman, eds. (Washington, DC: The Brookings Institution, 1980).

[16]See Michael J. Boskin, "Taxation, Saving, and the Ratio of Interest," *Journal of Political Economy*, 86(2), Part 2, April 1978, pp. 523–27; and Martin Feldstein, "The Welfare Cost of Capital Income Taxation," *Journal of Political Economy*, 86(2), Part 2, April 1978, pp. 529–51.

PUBLIC OPINION

If public opinion surveys are a fair measure of taxpayer sentiment, our current tax structure might be considered in need of change. Possibly the best surveys are those conducted each year since 1972 by the Opinion Research Corporation of Princeton, New Jersey, for the Advisory Commission on Intergovernmental Relations (ACIR).[17] By asking the same question for a period of years, the ACIR can observe trends in attitudes; by asking different questions, they can serve as a sounding board for new tax ideas. Three of their many interesting findings are summarized below.

In 1983, over 1,500 individuals were asked the following question: "If the federal/state/local government had to raise taxes substantially, which would be a better way to do it?" The response shows overwhelming support for additional sales taxes at all levels of government. The specific results are summarized as follows:

Tax	Level of Government		
	Federal	State	Local
(Individual) Income	24	23	12
Sales	52[a]	57	45
Property	—	—	19
Don't know	25	20	24

[a]This option was worded as follows: "A New National Sales Tax on All Purchases Other Than Food."

The federal income tax has been identified as the "worst" tax each poll for the past nine years. The long-term trend for that dubious distinction is implicit in the comparison below of the responses to the following question: "Which do you think is the worst tax—that is, the least fair?"

Responses	Percent Selecting in					
	1986	1983	1981	1979	1977	1975
Federal income tax	37	35	36	37	28	28
State income tax	8	11	9	8	11	11
State sales tax	17	13	14	15	17	23
Local property tax	28	26	33	27	33	29
Don't know	10	15	9	13	11	10

To determine how people feel about the overall level of taxes and government services, the ACIR asked the following question in its 1986 poll: "Considering all government services on the one hand and taxes on the other, which of the following statements comes closest to your view?

[17]The annual reports for each year are available from the Advisory Commission on Intergovernmental Relations, Washington, DC 20575.

1. Decrease services and taxes.
2. Keep taxes and services about where they are.
3. Increase services and raise taxes.
4. No opinion."

Approximately 51% of the individuals polled identified option 2—the status quo—while 31% picked option 1; 9% option 3; and 9%, option 4.

Students interested in making further comparisons between our tax structure and taxpayer preferences are encouraged to consult the annual reports of the Advisory Commission on Intergovernmental Relations.

AUTHORS' CONCLUSIONS

Based on the best evidence available, the authors have reached three major conclusions about the U.S. tax system today. First, as a nation, we are not "overtaxed." This important conclusion is based both on comparative economic data (such as Table 1-3) and on public opinion surveys (such as the third ACIR finding, noted above). Second, we probably depend too heavily on the income tax; legislators should begin to look elsewhere for additional revenues. This second conclusion is also supported by both comparative economic data (see Table 1-2) and public opinion (see both the first and second ACIR findings cited above). Our third conclusion is that any major tax increases should probably come from new and/or additional taxes on goods and services—quite possibly, from a federal value-added tax. This final conclusion is also based on both comparative economic statistics (see Table 1-3) and public opinion (again, see the first two ACIR findings cited above).

PROBLEMS

1. Citizens frequently make payments other than taxes to governmental units. Write a short essay distinguishing taxes from penalties (or fines), from charges for goods or services (or beneficiary's charges), and from confiscation.

2. FICA (Social Security) has often been described and justified as old-age insurance. Are payments made to the government under this act beneficiary's charges or taxes? Why?

3. An increase in any federal tax is often justified as "necessary to pay for a war." How adequate is this explanation? Why? If Congress refused to enact a requested tax, how would the United States pay for various government programs, including a war?

4. Which of the following payments would you classify as a tax? How would you classify the other payments?
   a. Payment for automobile registration (that is, license plates)
   b. Payment for a hunting or fishing license
   c. Payment for a "safety sticker" on an automobile

    d. Payment for parking on a "metered" street

    e. Payment for federal stamps required on transfer of a real estate deed

    f. Payment for riding a city-owned and -operated bus

    g. Payment for a bottle of liquor purchased in a state-owned store

5. In what significant way are the "fiscal resources" of the federal government significantly different from those of state and local governments?

6. Is the price paid for postage more accurately classified as a "price" (beneficiary's charge) or a "tax"? Explain your answer.

7. Assume that a city requires that every dog be licensed and that the fee for this annual license is $5. Assume further that the money collected in this way is put into a special fund used to pay the cost of the city dog patrol operation. Is this $5 fee better labeled a "price" or a "tax"? Explain your answer.

8. "The primary purpose of federal taxes may be significantly different from the primary purpose of state or local taxes." Discuss.

9. Write a short essay supporting the idea that mandatory military service is a form of progressive taxation.

10. Must taxes involve the transfer of money? Under what circumstances might you expect a government to impose a nonpecuniary tax?

11. Politicians seldom increase their popularity by advocating a tax increase. Nevertheless, in spite of the fact that the U.S. federal government does not "need" to collect taxes before it can spend, no federal politician has ever advocated the end of all tax collections at the federal level of government. Explain the apparent contradiction.

12. Section 164(a) of the Internal Revenue Code (the basic statutory authority for the U.S. federal income tax) authorizes a taxpayer to deduct certain taxes in the determination of taxable income. That subsection reads, in part, as follows:

> Except as otherwise provided in this section, the following taxes shall be allowed as a deduction for the taxable year within which paid or accrued:
> (1) State and local, and foreign, real property taxes.
> (2) State and local personal property taxes.

Based on the authority of Sec. 164(a)(2), taxpayers in some states can deduct the cost of their automobile license plates, whereas taxpayers in other states cannot claim that same deduction. How might you explain the apparent conundrum?

13. What good reasons might a free-world government have for imposing a fee of, say, $20 on a pack of cigarettes? If that were done, would it be correct to refer to the $20 charge to the consumer as a "tax"? Explain briefly.

14. Early in the 1960s, a new national party, the Constitutional Party, was formed. Its principal platform was elimination of the federal income tax and substitution of a general sales tax and beneficiary's charges. On what grounds could such a movement be criticized?

15. Large cities often impose a heavy tax (for example, 10%) on the cost of hotel and motel rooms. What good reasons can be given in support of such a tax?

16. Two objectives of the U.N. are peaceful settlement of international disputes and encouragement of cultural and economic intercourse between nations and peoples. Under its present charter, the U.N. has no taxing power. Assume that

everyone agreed that the U.N. should have the power to tax the citizens of member nations. What problems would arise in selecting a tax base?

17. Some states have recently tried lotteries to raise revenues. Relate the use of lotteries to the states' objectives and to the problem of selecting a tax base.

18. Governmental units in the United States depend primarily on property, income, and sales taxes to raise revenue. Rate each of these tax bases in terms of Adam Smith's canons of taxation.

19. In the recent past, personal property taxes—that is, taxes on the value of bank accounts, stocks, bonds, furniture, television sets, refrigerators, and similar personal assets—have been disappearing from the list of tax bases used by state and local governments. Why are these particular taxes disappearing despite the fact that almost every state and local government is currently looking for new sources of revenue?

20. Forty-six states now impose an income tax. What practical problem does this present for businesses engaged in interstate commerce? What comparable problem exists with the federal government?

21. The federal estate tax allows a tax credit for a limited amount of inheritance tax paid to a state government. Most states impose an inheritance tax equal to the maximum credit allowed against the federal tax, but only a few states impose additional state inheritance or estate taxes. Why should this be true?

22. Some tax scholars have noted that as the economy moves from the very primitive to the highly industrialized state, tax systems typically evolve from poll taxes, to property taxes, to flat-rate income taxes, to graduated income taxes. Furthermore, these scholars suggest, at the various stages of economic progress each of these taxes can be said to approximate some social measure of "ability to pay."
a. Explain how a poll tax or a property tax might reflect an ability to pay.
b. What sociological factors augur well for this sequence in tax systems?

23. Proposals to eliminate the federal income tax have been made. For each of the alternative bases listed below, indicate briefly the major political and economic problems that would arise in shifting to such a base at the federal level.
a. Wealth tax
b. Employment taxes
c. Excise taxes

24. Define both horizontal and vertical equity.

25. If taxpayer X has a taxable income of $10,000 and pays an income tax of $2,000 and taxpayer Y has a taxable income of $50,000 and pays an income tax of $8,000, what statement can you make concerning horizontal equity in that taxing jurisdiction? concerning vertical equity?

26. What do salt, white phosphorous matches, motor fuels, tobacco, and alcoholic beverages have in common as far as a tax base is concerned?

27. If the retail sale of marijuana is legalized in the United States, what good reason(s) do you have for predicting that it will become a common tax base?

28. People who own their own homes have strongly different views from those who rent their homes when it comes to the best method to increase state revenues in times of need. Which group, owners or renters, would you expect to be the stronger supporter of the sales tax? Why?

29. Our educational background seems to influence how we feel about different taxes.

Which of the following groups of persons do you suppose consider the state sales tax as the *fairest* of all? Give reasons for your choice.
a. Those with less than a high school education
b. High school graduates with no college education
c. Those with some college education

30. Congress made "buttlegging," or smuggling large quantities of cigarettes across state lines, a federal crime in 1978.
    a. Why do people "smuggle" cigarettes?
    b. Why was buttlegging made a federal crime?
    c. What broader implications do these facts portend for tax policy generally?

31. The maximum wage or salary subject to Social Security taxes, as well as the maximum Social Security tax payable by an employee, has increased dramatically over the past 50 years, as demonstrated in the following table:

Year	Maximum Base	Maximum Tax
1937	$ 3,000	$ 30
1959	4,800	120
1972	9,000	468
1979	22,900	1,404
1982	32,400	2,171
1984	37,800	2,533
1987	43,800	3,132

Those maximums will increase even more in the next few years. Explain these increases. What political response do you predict for further changes?

32. Do you think that most Americans would prefer lower taxes (for themselves) to a grossly simplified tax system? Comment on the significance of the option you deem to be the more popular. Can you locate any evidence to support your conclusions (that is, are your opinions shared by many other people)?

33. Consider the taxes normally paid by consumers in the United States. Make a list of the ones that have some characteristics of a penalty; make a separate list of those that have some characteristics of a beneficiary's charge.

34. Imagine that you are the minister of finance in a small third-world nation. What features might you incorporate in your tax program to encourage economic development?

35. Prepare three graphs representing tax *payments* under proportional, progressive, and regressive tax systems. Record the amount of taxes paid on the vertical scale and the tax base on the horizontal scale.

36. Prepare three graphs representing tax *rates* under proportional, progressive, and regressive tax systems. Record the tax rates on the vertical scale and the tax base on the horizontal scale.

37. a. Taxpayer Kane earned a total income of $10,000 in 19x1. Only $6,000 of his income, however, was included in the tax base for the income tax. Kane paid a tax of $1,200 during 19x1. What nominal-average tax rate does Kane pay? What real- or effective-average rate does Kane pay?
    b. In 19x2, Kane had taxable income (tax base) of $8,000. That year he paid a tax of $1,700. Assuming that the tax-rate structure was not changed by the government unit imposing the tax, what marginal tax rate did Kane pay on the additional income of $2,000 in 19x2? What nominal-average rate did Kane pay in 19x2?

38. In a technical sense, is the present FICA (Social Security) tax progressive, proportional, or regressive in relation to income? Explain with a simple diagram.

39. Taxpayer A, a single individual, has a total income of $50,000. Taxable income for the current year, however, is only $40,000. Using the 1988 tax rates
   a. Determine A's marginal tax rate.
   b. Determine A's nominal-average tax rate.
   c. Determine A's real- or effective-average tax rate.

40. Assume that your state legislature enacted, and your governor signed, a new law that imposed a tax on the sale of all new and used gasoline engines at the following rates:

0 to 50 horsepower	—		$5 per horsepower
50 to 100 horsepower	$250	plus	$4 per horsepower over 50
100 to 150 horsepower	$450	plus	$3 per horsepower over 100
150 to 200 horsepower	$600	plus	$2 per horsepower over 150
over 200 horsepower	$700	plus	$1 per horsepower over 200

   a. If A purchased a Buick with a 175-horsepower engine and B purchased a Ford with a 90-horsepower engine, who would pay the greater tax, A or B?
   b. Who would be in the higher marginal tax bracket, A or B?
   c. What would A's nominal-average tax rate per horsepower be?
   d. In a technical sense, would this new tax be progressive, proportional, or regressive?
   e. If the new tax applied only to gasoline engines, what should happen to the price of diesel-powered automobiles? Explain briefly.

41. The government of Neverneverland, a small, strange, island republic in the middle of the Ancient Ocean, imposes two taxes on its citizens and resident aliens. One monthly tax is based on the size (measured in cubic feet) of the taxpayer's residence, an igloo, according to the following rates:

First 3,000 cubic feet	¢10 per cu. ft.
Next 3,000 cubic feet	¢18 per cu. ft.
Next 6,000 cubic feet	¢34 per cu. ft.
Nest 12,000 cubic feet	¢62 per cu. ft.
Remainder	¢100 per cu. ft.

(Note: the basic monetary unit in this imaginary country is the cube, or ¢.)

The second tax is a tax of ¢5 per ounce of wonderdrug, which is made and distributed by a secret agency of the government. Neverneverland, you see, is a very strange country indeed: humans can live there only if they take exactly one ounce of wonderdrug on the first day of each full moon. If they fail to take this drug at the prescribed time or in the prescribed amount, they will die within 20 hours.
   a. In a technical sense, is the tax imposed on igloos progressive, proportional, or regressive?
   b. In a technical sense, is the tax imposed on wonderdrug progressive, proportional, or regressive?
   c. In a popular sense, is the tax imposed on wonderdrug progressive, proportional, or regressive?
   d. Fred Jidair's home in Neverneverland contains 9,000 cubic feet of space. Is the

nominal-average tax paid by Fred on his home less than, equal to, or more than ¢34 per cubic foot?

e. If Fred decides, after the birth of his seventh child, to expand the size of his igloo from 9,000 to 12,000 cubic feet, would his marginal tax rate be less than, equal to, or more than ¢34 per cubic foot?

42. Sam Sharp lives in the Empire of Konform, which is ruled by King Kon. Sam, an employee of King Kon, earns an annual salary of $20,000 (his only source of income). The income tax in Konform is determined according to the following rate schedule:

$0–$1,000	—	5% of income
$1,001–$5,000	$ 50 plus	7% of income in excess of $1,000
$5,001–$100,000	$330 plus	10% of income in excess of $5,000

In addition, any relative of King Kon may deduct 50% of his or her salary in the calculation of income tax base; any employee of King Kon may deduct 10%.

a. Technically, should the income tax in Konform be classified as proportional, progressive, or regressive?

b. Determine Sam's nominal-average tax rate.

c. Determine Sam's real- or effective-average tax rate.

d. Determine Sam's marginal tax rate.

43. What can be done to make a sales tax (relatively) more progressive in relation to income? Explain.

44. If a government desired to decrease consumption spending and increase investment, other things being equal, you would expect it to advocate regressive rather than progressive taxes. True or false? Explain briefly.

CHAPTER 2

The History of U.S. Taxation

The income tax . . . must be viewed primarily as a regional victory of the South and Middle West over the Northeast, part of the same sectional movement that produced the Interstate Commerce Act in 1887, the Sherman Antitrust Act in 1890, and the unsuccessful campaign for bi-metallism.
Boris I. Bittker, Federal Income, Estate, and Gift Taxation (1964)

The tax system of every country is in a constant state of flux, and the United States of America is no exception to this somewhat evident observation. In this chapter we review the major ways in which the overall U.S. tax system has changed during the past 80 to 100 years before we examine the most important changes in our federal income tax in somewhat greater detail. At the end of this chapter we attempt to assess the most important recent changes in U.S. taxation and consider the impact of those changes on the future of taxation in this country.

Among the more interesting future issues is that of intergovernmental fiscal relations. Because a relatively few taxes produce the vast bulk of all tax revenues collected, two or more levels of governments sometimes impose and collect taxes on essentially the same tax base. For example, our federal government, most state governments, and a growing list of municipal governments all utilize an income tax. Most states and more and more city governments now impose a retail sales tax, while at least a few government officials consider the possibility of a federal value-added tax. This tendency to rely on overlapping tax bases raises numerous important questions at every level of government. For example: Should two or more governments consolidate their separate taxes if they are imposed on essentially a single tax base? If so, which level of government should have the responsibility of collecting that tax? How can the proceeds of a consolidated tax best be redistributed without the recipient becoming unduly beholden to the distributor? In the face of such complex future issues, the nostalgia associated with somewhat simpler times is inviting.

EVOLUTION OF THE PRESENT SYSTEM

Less than 60 years ago, our country's tax structure was dominated by locally collected taxes, and total tax collections were relatively small, both absolutely and as a percentage of national income. After the Great Depression of the 1930s, and especially during World War II, this picture changed drastically. By 1945, our tax structure was dominated by a rather sizable federal tax. Table 2-1 clearly demonstrates these changes in our tax structure.

In reviewing these data, the student should note that even though state and local taxes decreased as a percentage of total tax collections between 1934 and 1960, they continued to increase significantly in absolute amounts. In addition, state tax receipts increased rapidly; they now have resumed roughly their depression position relative to total tax receipts. The increasing claims on tax funds at all levels make intergovernmental fiscal relations an important issue today.

TABLE **2-1**

FEDERAL, STATE, AND LOCAL TAX RECEIPTS* FOR SELECTED FISCAL YEARS, 1902–1984

| | Receipt (in millions) | | | | Percentage Distribution | | | |
Year	Total	Federal	State	Local	Total	Federal	State	Local
1902	$ 1,373	$ 513	$ 156	$ 704	100.0	37.4	11.4	51.3
1913	2,271	662	301	1,308	100.0	29.2	13.3	57.6
1934	8,854	2,942	1,979	3,933	100.0	33.2	22.4	44.4
1942	22,962	13,351	4,979	4,633	100.0	58.1	21.7	20.2
1950	54,799	37,853	8,958	7,988	100.0	69.1	16.3	14.6
1960	126,678	88,419	20,172	18,088	100.0	69.8	15.9	14.3
1970	274,996	185,670	50,486	38,840	100.0	67.5	18.4	14.1
1980	727,984	492,846	148,691	86,447	100.0	67.7	20.4	11.9
1984	975,043	634,352	217,422	123,269	100.0	65.1	22.3	12.6

NOTE: Because of rounding, detail may not add to total. Data for 1984 is estimated.

SOURCE: Data for 1902–1984 from Tax Foundation, Inc., *Facts and Figures on Government Finance,* 23rd ed., 1986, Tables A14 and A15, pp. a16 and a17.

*Includes social insurance taxes.

Tax Base and Level of Government

During the past 50 years, state and local governments in the United States depended heavily on property and sales taxation, whereas the federal government increasingly relied on personal and corporate income taxes. Table 2-2 reveals the distribution of tax collections among the various tax bases, by level of government, in a recent year.

This table demonstrates clearly that the income tax is indeed the most productive tax utilized today. Of total tax collections, *excluding* social insurance taxes, almost 60% came from income taxes alone. At the federal level, about 85% came from the personal and corporate income taxes combined. At the state level, nearly 50% came from sales and gross receipts taxes. At the local level, over 75% came from property taxes. Our current national tax structure is summarized below:

	Level of Government		
Tax Base	*Federal*	*State*	*Local*
Income	Primary	Secondary	
Property			Primary
Sales and excise		Primary	Secondary
Social Security	Secondary		

Forget for the moment the distribution of tax bases by government levels and try to comprehend the sheer magnitude of the numbers involved. The statement that our federal, state, and local governments collect more than $700 billion in taxes each year does not really mean much to most of us. We can comprehend the number 700, but we really cannot sense the meaning of

TABLE **2-2**

TAX REVENUES BY TAX BASE AND LEVEL OF GOVERNMENT, FISCAL YEAR 1983
(IN BILLIONS)

Tax Base	Total	Federal	State	Local
Individual income	$344	$289	$ 50	$ 5
Corporate income	51	37	13	1
Sales and gross receipts	145	44	84	16
Property	89	—	3	86
Motor vehicle and operator licenses	7	—	6	1
Death and gift	9	6	3	—
All other	21	5	12	4
Total	$666	$381*	$171	$113

NOTE: Because of rounding, detail may not add to total.

SOURCE: Adapted from Tax Foundation, Inc., *Facts and Figures on Government Finance,* 23rd ed., 1986, Table A11, p. a13.

*Excluding social insurance taxes.

one billion, let alone 700 billion. To put these magnitudes in perspective, consider the fact that roughly one billion *seconds* ago we were engaged in the Korean War. Christ died slightly more than one billion *minutes* ago. And a billion *hours* ago, man lived in caves! Then recall that our governments collect about two billion dollars in tax revenues every single day of the year! And taxes are only a part of total government revenues.

Each level of government also receives funds from nontax sources. For example, all levels of government receive substantial sums from various insurance trust funds and from miscellaneous charges. Most state and local governments receive funds from the federal government, and several of them also operate utility companies, liquor stores, and so on. For these reasons, total tax receipts are always less than total governmental revenues. If we expand the data for the federal government to include social insurance taxes and nontax revenues, both the growth in Social Security taxes and the decline in corporate income taxes are obvious. (See Table 2-3.)

Because of the growth in Social Security taxes and a concurrent reduction in income taxes, especially for individuals in the lower income classes, about one half of the U.S. population currently pays more in Social Security tax than in federal income tax. The decline in corporate income taxation revealed in Table 2-3 was, in all probability, ended by the changes enacted as part of the 1986 Tax Reform Act.

Intergovernmental Transfers

The issue of intergovernmental transfers is of genuine importance to state and local governments. President Reagan has attempted to transfer the fiscal responsibility for some social welfare programs from the federal to lower

TABLE **2-3**

TOTAL GOVERNMENT REVENUES BY MAJOR SOURCE, VARIOUS YEARS
(PERCENTAGE DISTRIBUTION)

Major Source	Fiscal Year			
	1960	1970	1980	1983
Individual income taxes	28.2	30.3	30.7	29.1
Corporation income taxes	14.8	11.0	8.4	4.3
Social insurance taxes	8.9	12.6	16.6	17.9
Property taxes	10.7	10.2	7.3	7.5
Sales and gross receipts	16.0	14.6	12.0	12.2
Death and gift	1.3	1.4	0.9	0.7
All other	2.9	2.4	2.3	2.4
Total taxes	82.7	82.4	78.2	74.3
Nontax revenues	17.3	17.6	21.8	25.7
Total revenues	100	100	100	100

SOURCE: Adapted from Tax Foundation, Inc., *Facts and Figures on Government Finance*, 23rd ed., 1986, Table A13, p. a15.

levels of government. Many of those governments might be willing to assume additional responsibilities if they were assured of either new or additional sources of revenue. The administration's plan provides only limited resources for state and local governments during a transition period and additional promises to return certain tax bases—most notably, the excise taxes on products such as gasoline, alcohol, and tobacco—to the exclusive domain of the lower levels of government. Prior to the Reagan administration, there had been a steady trend toward larger and larger federal collections of taxes along with increasing intergovernmental transfers from the federal to state and local governments. This trend has now been reversed. Just how far and how quickly the "new federalism" will progress remains to be seen. Whatever the solution, if the tax imposed on any one tax base is to be increased significantly, or if an entirely new tax such as VAT were to be introduced by some future administration, that change would be of more than passing interest to state and local government authorities.

Regardless of what might happen in the future, there can be no doubt today that the income tax dominates the federal tax structure. The largest single federal tax is the tax on individual incomes; the second largest is the Social Security tax; and the third largest is the tax on corporate incomes. Because of this dominance and because the tax liability is so amenable to modification, we will restrict most of our attention in the remainder of this text to the federal income taxes.

Before we examine the details of our present income tax provisions, however, let us consider the general development of those provisions in broad historical context. Although income taxation has conceptual roots that are over 2,000 years old, most of the current rules have evolved in the past 75 years. In the next part of this chapter, we will divide our discussion into two major periods—that prior to the Sixteenth Amendment (1913) and the years after that constitutional change. The latter period is further divided into five periods that can be distinguished from each other by the kind of legislation that dominated those years.

INCOME TAXATION PRIOR TO 1913

Historians suggest that elementary forms of income taxation were imposed by the Roman Empire even before the birth of Christ. Indeed, the fact that Christ was born in the city of Bethlehem could be attributable to some form of "income" taxation. Saint Luke relates the events in this manner: "There went out a decree from Caesar Augustus, that all the world should be taxed. . . . And all went to be taxed, everyone into his own city. And Joseph also went up from Galilee, out of the city of Nazareth, into Judea, unto the city of David, which is called Bethlehem; (because he was of the house and lineage of David) to be taxed with Mary his espoused wife. . . ."[1] Although no details

Luke 2:1-5 (King James Version).

concerning this tax are available, the fact that the taxpayer was required to respond to the tax personally and with his family suggests that it may have been some form of the poll or head tax as well as a census mechanism. A poll tax with graduated tax rates—often called a *faculties tax*—constitutes the most elementary form of the income tax. Essentially, a faculties tax is a tax on *estimated* income. This form of income taxation is not uncommon today in preindustrial societies.[2]

Other early traces of income taxation may be seen in the Florentine Republic in Italy in the fourteenth and fifteenth centuries.[3] What began as a tax on property evolved into a tax on income. By 1451, much income and wealth could be attributed to established industry and commerce rather than to the more traditional forms of property. Consequently, the value base for taxation became a capitalization of the earnings stream. Because of administrative complications and political favoritism in the earnings calculations, this early income-based tax fell into disrepute and was largely replaced by indirect taxation on consumption.

The Colonial Faculties Taxes

The earliest variant of the income tax in the United States appeared in 1643 in the colony of New Plymouth as a tax based on "a person's faculties." Although no measurement techniques were provided in this law, the appointed assessors were supposed to base the tax on "personal faculties and abilities."[4] Three years later (1646), the Massachusetts Bay Company enacted a similar tax based on the "returns and gains" of artists and tradesmen. Early in the eighteenth century, faculties taxes based on estimated incomes were commonplace among the New England colonies, and the definitions of the tax base slowly became increasingly comprehensive definitions of income. This gradual expansion is attributed to recognition that taxation based only on selective forms of property does not adequately recognize every citizen's tax capacity or ability to pay. Thus, income taxation began in this part of the world as a supplement to more traditional forms of property taxation.

The colonial faculties taxes had largely disappeared by the middle of the nineteenth century, to be replaced by partial income taxes in a few of the new Southern states, including Virginia, North Carolina, and Alabama. These newer forms of income taxation can be traced to England, where, under the leadership of William Pitt, the first "modern" income tax was adopted in 1799. Generally, the Northern and Middle states avoided income taxation before the twentieth century, although during the Civil War the federal (Union) government did utilize such a tax.

---

[2]The "progressive poll tax" is still used today in some African countries. See John F. Due, "The African Personal Tax," *National Tax Journal*, XV (December 1962), pp. 385–98.

[3]The authors owe a considerable debt to Professor Edwin R. A. Seligman for much of the early history of income taxation. Persons interested in additional details should see his book, *The Income Tax*, published by Macmillan in 1911 and again in 1914 in an enlarged and revised edition.

[4]*Ibid.* (1911 edition), p. 368.

The Civil War Income Taxes

The first U.S. federal income tax was enacted into law on August 5, 1861, to raise revenue in support of the Civil War. Although this law was never enforced, the 1861 tax was extended by a law adopted on July 1, 1862, and limited collections were made under the latter act. The law imposed a 3% tax on most incomes between $600 and $10,000 and a 5% tax on all income in excess of $10,000. Enforcement of the law was greatly confused, and evasion was widespread.[5] The 1863 tax return form is of historic interest, and a copy appears in Figure 2-1.

The 1864 Revenue Act revised the earlier income tax rates and provided a maximum tax rate of 10%, applicable to incomes in excess of $10,000. The rate structure was again revised in 1865 and in 1867. The latter change instituted a flat (proportional) tax of 5% on most incomes in excess of $1,000. All Civil War income taxes lapsed in 1872, when the need for war financing was eliminated.

Although the Civil War income taxes were not an overwhelming success, they did illuminate some important aspects of income taxation. First, although the income tax never challenged the dominance of the tariff duties during this period, it was a major revenue producer. During the 10-year period that they were enforced, the Civil War income taxes provided the federal government with $376 million. The largest single year was 1866, when approximately $73 million (of a total of $490 million of federal revenue) was collected in income taxes.

A second important lesson learned during that decade was that a detailed taxpayer guidance system is essential to successful income taxation. Major administration problems were encountered. Surprisingly, perhaps, these early laws did provide for withholding at the source on wages and salaries, interest, and dividends. But other aspects of the administrative machinery were not so advanced. For example, it remained for the state of Wisconsin to demonstrate (in 1911) the importance of a central tax commission, autonomous from local officials.

Perhaps the most surprising fact of that decade of income taxation is that the tax functioned as well as it did. Richard Goode, an economist with special competence in tax matters, once suggested that there are six prerequisites to a successful income tax: (1) a money economy, (2) general literacy, (3) minimum accounting records, (4) acceptance of the idea of voluntary compliance with tax laws, (5) political acceptance of an income tax, and (6) an efficient administrative machine.[6] Considering the situation in the United States in 1872 with regard to each of these six criteria, it is not surprising that the income tax was permitted to lapse once the pressure for war financing ended.

---

[5]The first Commissioner of Internal Revenue, George S. Boutwell, was appointed by President Lincoln in 1862.
[6]Richard Goode, "Reconstruction of Foreign Tax Systems," *Proceedings of the Forty-Fourth Annual Conference of the National Tax Association* (1951), pp. 212–22.

The Constitutional Question

Even many educated persons are surprised to learn that the U.S. government imposed and collected an income tax prior to 1913, for the common belief is that this form of taxation was unconstitutional prior to the ratification of the Sixteenth Amendment. This belief, however, is only partially accurate.

Article I, Section 9, Clause 4, of the Constitution reads as follows: "No Capitation, or other direct, Tax shall be laid, unless in Proportion to the Census or Enumeration herein before directed to be taken." Since incomes are not equally distributed between people or states, an income tax cannot be divided among states in proportion to population. When the Civil War income tax was tested in the Supreme Court, the question the Court decided was, therefore, a straightforward one: Is an income tax a "direct tax" as that term was understood by those who drafted the Constitution?[7]

The most important early decision of the Supreme Court on this question was in the 1880 case of *Springer v. United States,* and the decision was unanimous and negative—that is, the income tax was deemed to be an indirect tax. The Court said, "Our conclusions are, that *direct taxes,* within the meaning of the Constitution, are only capitation taxes, as expressed in that instrument, and taxes on real estate; and that the tax of which the plaintiff in error complains is within the category of an excise or duty."[8] Fourteen years later, the Court changed its mind.

Between the *Springer* decision in 1880 and the Revenue Act of 1894, income taxation was a political football. Generally, the states of the West and the South favored the income tax, whereas the Eastern states opposed it. The income tax was part of the Populist program, along with railroad regulation, expanded currency, and the direct election of senators. This was the program of an "oppressed" agrarian midland, revolting against the Eastern bankers and industrialists—in short, a program for the poor against the rich.[9] No less than 14 income tax bills were introduced into Congress between 1873 and 1879, but none of them gained the majority necessary to become law. Finally, on August 28, 1894, such an act was made law, without the signature of President Cleveland. By this date, the lines were well drawn and a final political showdown was inevitable.

Once the income tax had found its way through the halls of Congress, the battle was transferred from the legislative arena to the judicial, with the executive standing by. *Pollock v. Farmers' Loan and Trust Co.*[10] was instituted by a stockholder (Pollock) to restrain the corporate officers from paying a tax

---

Here we are discussing only the legal (or constitutional) meaning of the phrase "direct tax." Actually, the phrase is originally one adopted from the economics literature. For a discussion of that matter see C. J. Bullock, "Direct and Indirect Taxes in Economic Literature," *Political Science Quarterly,* XIII (1898), pp. 442–86.

[8]*Springer v. United States,* 102 U.S. 602 (1880).

[9]See Richard Hofstadter, *The Age of Reform* (New York: Vintage Books, 1955), for a most informative history of this politically tumultuous period. The Populists were never successful as a party, but their program was certainly successful after it was adopted by other reform groups.

[10]157 U.S. 429 (1895); 158 U.S. 601 (1895).

FIGURE **2-1**   Pages 2 and 3 of the Income Tax Form Used in the 1860s

DETAILED STATEMENT OF SOURCES OF INCOME AND THE AMOUNT DERIVED FROM EACH, DURING THE YEAR 1863.

☞ Gross Amounts must be stated. ☜	AMOUNTS
1. Income of a resident in the United States from profits on any trade, business, or vocation, or any interest therein, wherever carried on	
2. From rents, or the use of real estate	
3. From interest on notes, bonds, mortgages, or other personal securities, not those of the United States	
4. From interest on notes, bonds, or other securities of the United States	
5. From interest or dividends on any bonds or other evidences of indebtedness of any railroad company or corporation	
6. From interest or dividends on stock, capital, or deposits in any bank, trust company, or savings institution, insurance or railroad company, or corporation	
7. From interest on bonds or dividends on stock, shares or property in gas, bridge, canal, turnpike, express, telegraph, steamboat, ferry-boat, or manufacturing company or corporation, or from the business usually done thereby	
8. From property, securities, or stocks owned in the United States by a citizen thereof residing abroad, not in the employment of the Government of the United States	
9. From salary other than as an officer or employee of the United States	
10. From salary as an officer or employee of the United States	
11. From farms or plantations, including all products and profits	
12. From advertisements	
13. From all sources not herein enumerated	
TOTAL	

DETAILED STATEMENT OF DEDUCTIONS AUTHORIZED TO BE MADE

	AMOUNTS
1. Expenses necessarily incurred and paid in carrying on any trade, business or vocation, such as rent of store, clerk hire, insurance, fuel, freight, &c	
2. Amount actually paid by a property owner for necessary repairs, insurance, and interest on incumbrances upon his property	
3. Amount paid by a farmer or planter for—	
(a) Hired labor, including the subsistence of the laborers	
(b) Necessary repairs upon his farm or plantation ...	
(c) Insurance, and interest on incumbrances upon his farm or plantation	
4. Other national, state, and local taxes assessed and paid for the year 1863, and not elsewhere included	
5. Amount actually paid for rent of the dwelling-house or estate occupied as a residence	
6. Exempted by law (except in the case of a citizen of the United States residing abroad.) $600	600	00
7. Income from interest or dividends on stock, capital, or deposits in any bank, trust company, or savings institution, insurance, or railroad company, from which 3 per cent. thereon was withheld by the officers thereof	
8. Income from interest on bonds, or other evidences of indebtedness of any railroad company or corporation, from which 3 per cent. thereon was withheld by the officers thereof	
9. Salaries of officers, or payments to persons in the civil, military, naval, or other service of the United States, in excess of $600	
10. Income from advertisements, on which 3 per cent. was paid	
TOTAL	

SOURCE: Income Taxes 1862–1962, *A History of the Internal Revenue Service, I.R.S. Publication No. 447 (Washington, D.C.: U.S. Government Printing Office), p. 9.*

the stockholder deemed unconstitutional. The issue in the case was almost identical to that raised in the earlier *Springer* case. However, slight factual differences did exist. In *Springer,* the income in question involved income from personal property and from professional earnings; in *Pollock,* the income was derived from land. The plaintiff argued that if a tax on real estate is a direct tax, then a tax on the income from real estate must also be a direct tax. The first *Pollock* decision was a 6–2 decision, holding that the 1894 Act was unconstitutional to the extent that it taxed income from real estate (as well as income from municipal bonds).[11] Because so many other aspects of income taxation were unanswered by this decision, the counsel for the appellants requested a rehearing, which was granted.

On the rehearing, the nine justices on the bench reaffirmed the earlier decision in a second opinion by a scant 5–4 vote. Interestingly, the reports do not reveal the name(s) of the vacillating judge(s). This second opinion extended the earlier decision to income derived from personal property and, for all practical purposes, to all income.

Today, most historians would concede that the decision was heavily influenced by the political and social tenor of the times. Although Chief Justice Fuller's words were clear, they had a hollow ring. He noted that "the distinction between direct and indirect taxation was well understood by the framers of the Constitution and those who adopted it."[12] Justice Field, in a long concurring opinion, concluded his statement with more telling words:

> Here I close my opinion. I could not say less in view of questions of such gravity that go down to the very foundation of the government. . . . The present assault upon capital is but the beginning. It will be but the stepping-stone to others, larger and more sweeping, till our political contests will become a war of the poor against the rich; a war constantly growing in intensity and bitterness.[13]

It is hard for us today, when the income tax is an accepted part of economic and political life, to comprehend the political heat generated by the issue in 1895. The following quotes from editorials in the popular press at the time of the *Pollock* decision seem to come from a different world:

> *The St. Louis Post Dispatch:* Today's decision shows that the corporations and plutocrats are as securely entrenched in the Supreme Court as in the lower courts which they take such pains to control.

> *The New York Tribune:* The great compromises which made the Union possible still stand unshaken to prevent its overthrow by communist revolution. The fury of ignorant class hatred, which has sufficed to

---

[11]The latter portion of the decision is not particularly germane to the immediate discussion and is, therefore, dismissed. Later statutes have carefully exempted this income from tax, although many persons are now prepared to argue again the constitutionality question.

[12]*Pollock v. Farmers' Loan and Trust Co.,* 157 U.S. 429 (1895), p. 573.

[13]*Ibid.,* p. 607.

> overthrow absolute power in many lands . . . has dashed itself in vain against the Constitution of the United States, fortified by the institutions which a free people have established for the defense of their rights.

In short, the issue of income taxation at the turn of the twentieth century was as controversial as, say, abortion is today.

Edwin Seligman's analysis of the constitutional issue is both more thorough and more convincing than the analysis offered by the bench. After a lengthy study, Seligman concludes:

> With this general uncertainty as to the use of the older terms, it need not surprise us to find that there was no agreement at all as to the use or meaning of the newer term, "direct tax." As a matter of fact, the term was scarcely employed at all before 1787. We have found only one instance of its use in the United States before that date, namely, in a Massachusetts act of 1786.
>
> . . .
>
> From the above review of the origin of the direct-tax clause it is clear that it was due simply and solely to the attempt to solve the difficulty connected with the maintenance of slavery. But for that struggle Gouverneur Morris would never have introduced the term "direct tax," and there would have been no reason to introduce it anywhere else.[14]

The battle for the income tax did not end with the Supreme Court. The friends of the tax decided that a constitutional amendment would provide a surer route to acceptance than would a new statute and another judicial review. Thus, in 1909 the Congress was persuaded to pass a joint resolution that on February 25, 1913, was ratified as the Sixteenth Amendment to the U.S. Constitution. It states that "[T]he Congress shall have power to lay and collect taxes on incomes, from whatever source derived, without apportionment among the several States, and without regard to any census or enumeration."

The 1909 Corporate Income Tax

Even before ratification of the Sixteenth Amendment, the income tax had reappeared in a limited form. In 1909 Congress enacted, and President Taft signed, a bill that imposed a 1% tax on all corporate incomes in excess of $5,000. In 1911, this tax was tried again on constitutional grounds, in *Flint v. Stone Tracy Co.*[15] This time the Supreme Court found that the tax on corporate incomes was not a direct tax but rather a special form of excise tax on the privilege of doing business.

This special corporate tax was short-lived, for the 1913 revenue measure included provisions for both personal and corporate income taxes. During the

---

[14]Seligman, *op. cit.*, pp. 555, 561.
[15]*Flint v. Stone Tracy Co.*, 220 U.S. 107 (1911).

next half-century, the income tax was transformed from a levy of minor importance to the position of preeminence it holds today.

THE U.S. INCOME TAX SINCE 1913

The history of the federal income tax from 1913 to the present is a mirror reflecting the economic and social environment of the times. Like the Civil War, World War I necessitated vast changes in federal fiscal operations. Income tax collections rose from some $35 *million* in 1913 to nearly $4 *billion* in 1920. With the end of the war, tax collections decreased, but they never returned to prewar levels. In 1930, the combined individual and corporate income tax collections totaled approximately $2.5 billion, slightly more than half of total federal receipts. This pace of taxation was roughly maintained until World War II. During the years 1941–1945, income tax collections averaged nearly $20 billion annually, representing approximately two thirds of total federal receipts. The Cold War, the Korean conflict, and the Vietnam involvement have all contributed significantly to the maintenance of record-level tax collections since 1945. Income tax collections today exceed $400 billion annually, which is approximately 40% of total government receipts. The sheer magnitude of these numbers makes any meaningful comprehension difficult. In 1913, however, the income tax was not so difficult to comprehend.

The Period 1913–1939

The 1913 income tax was a modest affair. The tax applicable to individual incomes began at 1% on taxable incomes in excess of $3,000 and increased to a maximum of 7% on taxable incomes in excess of $500,000. The $3,000 exemption was increased to $4,000 for a married taxpayer who lived with a spouse. The tax imposed on corporate incomes was a flat 1%, with no exemption provisions. Withholding was provided at the source for interest, rents, salaries, and wages but not for domestic dividends.

The 1913 law, and particularly the progressive nature of the tax, was subject to judicial review in the case of *Brushaber v. Union Pacific Railroad Co.*[16] Counsel for the plaintiff argued that the progressive rate structure was tantamount to an arbitrary abuse of power and therefore violated the due process clause of the Fifth Amendment. The Supreme Court, however, disagreed, and since 1916, progressive income taxation has never really been threatened, either by the legislative or judicial branch of the government.

The legislative branch has, of course, frequently modified earlier statutes. In 1916, for example, the tax rates were increased to range from 2–12% (on incomes in excess of $2 million). That year also ushered in the first U.S. war-

---

[16]240 U.S. 1 (1916).

profits tax on munitions manufacturers, which was broadened into an excess-profits tax in 1917. The withholding provisions were eliminated in 1916.

A limited dependent's deduction ($200 for one child) was introduced in 1917 and was extended (to $200 for each dependent) in 1918. The Revenue Act of 1918 also introduced "discovery-value depletion," the predecessor of percentage depletion. Special provisions for "capital gains" were introduced in 1921—a modification that has provided more complexity than any other single provision ever enacted—and provisions for loss deductions were frequently modified during the period 1918–1934. A graduated corporate income tax was introduced in 1936.

Between 1913 and 1939, some 17 income-tax-related laws were enacted by Congress. Although the language of each act tended to reflect closely the earlier provisions, a single codification, to unify these many laws, was deemed desirable. By the joint efforts of the Justice Department and the Bureau of Internal Revenue, this desire was realized with the enactment of the Internal Revenue Code of 1939. All revenue acts passed between 1939 and 1954 were integrated into the 1939 Code. Thus the framework of the 1939 code was used until 1954.

The Period 1939–1954

In 1939, less than 6% of the U.S. population was required to pay a federal income tax. Just six years later (1945), more than 74% of an enlarged population had to pay that same tax.[17] As a mass tax, the income tax is a relative newcomer to our country. Its drastically increased coverage is attributable largely to a major reduction in exemptions during a period of rapidly rising personal income and inflation. Wide coverage was facilitated by the reintroduction of withholding provisions in the Current Tax Payment Act of 1943. To avoid the "doubling up" of two years' tax liabilities in a single year, the federal government in 1943 forgave 75% of the lower of the 1942 or 1943 tax liabilities.

During the period 1940–1954, several changes were enacted to simplify the administration of the income tax laws. For example, the optional "tax table," now familiar to every taxpayer, was introduced in 1941 and extended to larger incomes in 1944, when the exemption and dependent rules also were simplified. The administration of the law was further improved by the reorganization of the Bureau of Internal Revenue in 1952. The old Bureau operated through 64 "collectors," who were political appointees. The new Internal Revenue Service operated through 9 regional commissioners and 64 district directors selected on a merit system.

Social and economic "equity considerations" also weighed heavily in the income tax modifications enacted between 1939 and 1954. For example, a deduction for personal medical expenses was first introduced in 1942. A

---

[17]For more details of this growth see Richard Goode, *The Individual Income Tax* (Washington, D.C.: The Brookings Institution, 1964), pp. 2–4.

special exemption for the blind was granted in 1942; another for old age was permitted in 1948. Income splitting, to equalize the federal tax treatment of incomes earned in community- and noncommunity-property states, was also enacted in 1948. A "head-of-household" provision was adopted in 1951 to give single persons with family responsibilities some of the tax advantages that previously existed only for married couples. By 1954, Congress decided to reorganize and rewrite the 1939 Code.

The Period 1954–1969

The Internal Revenue Code of 1954 constituted a comprehensive revision of the 1939 Code. It rearranged many of the old provisions in a more logical sequence; deleted much obsolete material; sought to make the language of the Code more understandable; and instituted numerous substantive changes.[18] All revenue measures modifying the income tax between 1954 and 1986 were incorporated into that codification.

The dominant objectives of the revisions between 1954 and 1969 were economic, although matters of equity and administration received considerable attention. In the former category, two innovations deserve special comment. The investment credit provisions—introduced in 1962, liberalized in 1964, suspended in 1966, reinstated in 1967, deleted in 1969, reintroduced in 1971, further liberalized in 1975 and 1978 and repealed in 1986—had as their primary purpose the stimulation of *investment* spending. The second major innovation of economic significance enacted between 1954 and 1969 was the general tax reductions of 1964 and 1965, which were granted to stimulate *consumption* spending. The proponents of the tax reductions argued that the cut in taxes would even reduce the budget deficit by stimulating the economy to the point that more income taxes would actually be collected at the lower rates than would have been collected at the old, higher rates. This experiment is now generally conceded to have been successful.

Income-averaging provisions were enacted in 1964 and liberalized in 1969 to reduce the tax inequity that can result from the combined forces of an annual income period and a progressive rate structure. Without income averaging, the taxpayer whose income varied widely from year to year often paid more taxes in the aggregate than a person who earned an equivalent income at a constant rate. (Incidentally, the income-averaging provisions were repealed as part of the 1986 Act.)

Experiments intended to improve tax administration took various forms. Perhaps the greatest advance was the computerization of much tax information by the Internal Revenue Service in Regional Service Centers. In

---

[18]The objectives of the 1954 revision are stated clearly in both the House Ways and Means Committee Report [H.R. Rept. No. 1337, 83d Congress, 2d Session 1 (1954)] and the Senate Finance Committee Report [S. Rept. No. 1622, 83d Congress, 2d Session 1 (1954)].

addition, a Small Claims Division of the Tax Court was introduced to handle informally the adjudication of many small tax disputes without much cost to the taxpayer. Finally, a revised tax form was devised to help simplify the reporting process.

The Period 1969–1978

Historical "periods" are, of course, arbitrary classifications. Additionally, the closer in time an observer is to the events, the more difficult it is to determine whether a change of such magnitude has occurred that it is meaningful to speak in terms of a new period. We believe, however, that the Tax Reform Act of 1969 marked the beginning of a distinctive period in U.S. tax history, which ended with the Revenue Act of 1978. That period was characterized by periodic and systematic attacks, supported by well-documented studies, on the tax provisions that had permitted large-scale tax avoidance in prior years. The same theme seemed to reoccur in 1986, thereby leaving the years 1978–1986 as either an aberration to a longer period (1969 to present) or a separate and brief period of its own.

Clearly, the effectiveness of many notorious tax avoidance schemes was seriously curtailed between 1969 and 1978. The relative advantage of specified capital gains was substantially reduced; major avoidance opportunities in charitable contributions and private charitable foundations were eliminated; the ability to claim a deduction for losses from oil and gas properties, motion pictures and video tapes, vacation properties and certain farm-and-ranch operations, citrus groves, and livestock operations was sharply limited; percentage depletion allowances were drastically cut; the early deduction of prepaid interest was eliminated; the deduction of investment interest was also limited; and the minimum tax on tax preferences was significantly increased.

The Tax Reform Act of 1976 also made major changes in the federal gift and estate taxes. Major revisions to those two taxes had been promised for many years, but not until 1976 was something finally done to correct many well-known shortcomings of the prior law. President Jimmy Carter campaigned strongly for still greater tax reforms, and shortly after taking office, Treasury Secretary Blumenthal announced the new administration's support of a drastic simplification proposal.

The Carter administration's support for additional reforms and drastic simplification in income taxation was short-lived. By midsummer 1977, the president had given up on the more dramatic tax changes initially considered. Even with a large Democratic majority, there was little chance of getting further tax reform measures approved by Congress. Furthermore, public opinion surveys revealed that the general public would neither understand nor fully appreciate many of the recommended tax law changes that had great theoretical merit. In summary, President Carter quickly accepted the political realities that had constrained many prior administrations in making tax reform proposals.

The Period 1978–1986

Instead of continuing the trend of tax reform started in 1969, the Revenue Act of 1978 was, in many ways, a direct reversal of the recent past. Most importantly, it made major cuts in the taxation of capital gains (effectively returning them to their pre-1969 preferred position); deferred the effective date on the carryover basis rules for inherited property (which had represented a hard-fought victory for reform proponents in the 1976 Act); and reduced the minimum tax on tax preference items in at least two significant ways. Although the 1978 Act did include a few reform-type provisions, those provisions were clearly of minor significance. The reasons for this dramatic turn of events are not entirely clear. It was, perhaps, a combination of political and economic concerns. That is, Congress may have interpreted the success of the property tax revolt in California—commonly known as Proposition 13—as a harbinger of general dissatisfaction with high taxes and decided that it was time to lower federal taxes as well. Coupling these political concerns with a growing interest in the need for greater capital formation, Congress possibly reversed its field and once again gave economic considerations top billing.

A provision in the 1979 Windfall Profits Tax Bill went on and made permanent the originally temporary deferral of the 1976 carryover basis rules for inherited property. President Carter had previously threatened to veto *any* bill that included a provision to modify carryover basis. However, the proponents of repeal knew that Carter wanted the Windfall Profits Tax too badly to veto that bill to achieve a lesser objective. Thus the opponents of carryover basis adroitly achieved a major reversal of one tax reform that had looked certain just four years earlier.

The shift away from the concerns of tax reform and the supremacy of economic impact was accelerated with the election of President Ronald Reagan in 1980. Reagan campaigned hard on promises to make major reductions in both personal and business income taxation. To the surprise of many, he quickly made good on both promises with the passage of ERTA (the Economic Recovery Tax Act of 1981). It appears that the tax revenue increases, which followed the 1964–1965 tax reductions noted earlier, had made a lasting impression on those who recommended tax policy to Reagan, including economist Arthur Laffer.[19] Laffer, a former chief economist in the Office of Management and Budget, observed that a reduction in the effective income tax rates does not necessarily reduce government revenues. He noted that at both a zero tax rate and at a 100% rate, income tax revenues should be nonexistent.[20] The shape of the rest of the curve, however, is

---

[19]The 1964 "Kennedy" tax cuts are viewed by many as demand (rather than supply) stimulants. For one such analysis, see Walter Heller, "The Kemp–Roth–Laffer Free Lunch" in *The Economics of the Tax Revolt: A Reader,* Arthur B. Laffer and Jan P. Seymour, eds. (New York: Harcourt Brace Jovanovich, 1979), pp. 46–49. In fairness, however, the 1964 cuts did lower the highest marginal tax brackets and provide investment incentives; hence, supply-side effects may be relevant.

[20]A tax rate of 100% produces no tax revenues, because people would find no reason to engage in productive efforts if the government took all of the income generated.

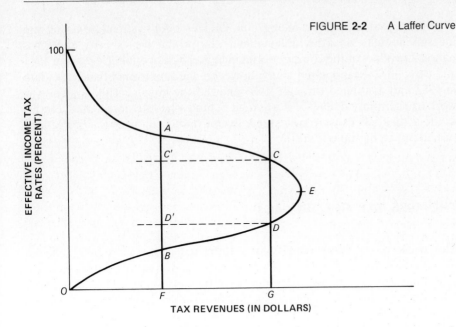

FIGURE **2-2**   A Laffer Curve

unknown.[21] One possible curve might be shaped as in Figure 2-2. In this curve, tax rates *A* and *B* both produce the same total tax revenue (represented by distance *OF*); so do tax rates *C* and *D*. Point *E* is, of course, the effective income tax rate that produces the maximum tax revenue.

If, in Figure 2-2, the vertical distances *AC'* and *D'B* are equal, a reduction in the tax rate equal to that distance could either increase tax revenues from distance *OF* to distance *OG*, or decrease tax revenues from *OG* to *OF*. If, before the tax reduction, the effective tax rates were at point *A*, a reduction equal to distance *AC'* would, of course, increase tax revenues. On the other hand, if before the tax reduction the effective tax rate was at point *D* on this curve, an equal reduction in rates would decrease tax revenues from distance *OG* to distance *OF*.

One problem with tax policy is that no one knows either (1) the general shape of the real Laffer curve or (2) exactly where we are on that curve at any time. The widely divergent opinions on these two unknowns were implicit in some of the early estimates of the federal budget deficits that would attend the passage of ERTA. The following three comparisons are illustrative:

	Early Estimates of ERTA-induced Budget Deficits by		
Year	*Reagan Administration*	*House Budget Committee*	*Chase Econometrics*
1982	$43 billion	$ 85 billion	$118 billion
1983	35 billion	110 billion	144 billion
1984	23 billion	120 billion	162 billion

[21]For an interesting and scholarly discussion of the Laffer curve, see Charles E. Stuart, "Swedish Tax Rates, Labor Supply and Tax Revenues," *Journal of Political Economy*, 89(5), October 1981, pp. 1020–38; see also Don Fullerton, "On the Possibility of an Inverse Relationship between Tax Rates and Government Revenues," *Journal of Public Economics*, 19(1), 1982, pp. 3–22.

The Reagan administration alleged that ERTA would so stimulate saving and investment that, via a multiplier effect, the productive capacity and gross national product of the country would increase. The economic events of 1981 and early 1982 disappointed many; however, the turnaround that began late in 1982 and continued through 1986 renewed the hope that the system was working as promised, even if it was a bit behind schedule. Incidentally, so far as the actual deficits were concerned, even Chase Econometric's projections turned out to be too optimistic.

THE 1986 TAX REFORM ACT

The concern for fundamental tax reform that died so quickly and so unceremoniously in the last year or two of the Carter administration was somewhat surprisingly revived in President Reagan's second term. This time, however, the tax bill proposed an irresistible blend of old-fashioned tax reform *and* new-style economics.

Tax reform was to be achieved through the technique introduced in the 1969 Act; that is, the systematic elimination of the many Code provisions that allowed some taxpayers to reduce their federal income tax liability to little or nothing, even though they earned a substantial amount of income in both economic and financial accounting terms. These were, of course, largely the very same provisions that had been highly recommended just three or four years earlier by both Congress and the administration as necessary economic stimuli. The list of the now-targeted-for-extinction provisions included, among others, the capital gain incentives; the investment credit; ultra-rapid depreciation; and loss deductions generated by tax-sheltered investments. In order to keep the revenue estimates neutral—that is, this proposed tax bill, unlike most, was to neither increase nor decrease overall federal tax revenues—many other tax-reducing Code provisions also had to be either eliminated or severely curtailed. That hapless list included the deduction for state and local sales taxes; personal interest (other than home-mortgage interest); income averaging; individual retirement account (or IRA) deductions (for at least some individuals); medical expenses; miscellaneous itemized deductions; and many others too numerous to mention here.

Economic stimulus was to derive under the new law from significantly lower marginal tax rates. For example, the top marginal rate for individuals would drop from 50% to 28%; that for corporations, from 46% to 34%. Furthermore, because of the elimination of many tax-advantageous provisions, there was to be a "more level" economic playing field that would minimize tax factors in what should be essentially economic decisions. As part of this proposal, approximately $120 billion in income taxes over five years was also shifted away from individual taxpayers to corporate taxpayers. The ultimate incidence of this significant shift in taxes was never seriously debated. Instead, Congress was trying, in this effort, to put permanently to rest the public embarrassment caused by periodic news releases noting that some of the largest corporations in America paid less in federal income tax than did the proverbial widow in Dubuque.

The Driving Force

The driving force behind the 1986 Act was very clearly the quest for lower marginal income tax rates. Early proponents of major tax reform in 1985 and 1986 rallied around a new term—modified flat tax—that was confusing to many old-time tax scholars. To at least some of those individuals, it appeared that the new term was inherently contradictory: income tax rates could be either flat (that is, proportional) or progressive, not both. To think in any other way was as intellectually unsettling as contemplating a round cube. And, since the very earliest days, progressive tax rates had always been an accepted part of income taxation. The very notions of both ability to pay and vertical equity, examined in Chapter 1, were inherent in the progressive tax rate schedule and, therefore, in federal income taxation.

The struggle surrounding passage of the 1986 Act would make a classic study in political compromise. Eventual enactment required the active support of such amazingly diverse political bedfellows as President Ronald Reagan, a champion of Republican conservative causes, and Congressman Dan Rostenkowski, a leader of liberal Democrats and chairman of the powerful House Ways and Means Committee. The one aspect of the 1986 act that obviously brought these politically diverse individuals together was the dramatic reduction in the top marginal tax rates of both individual and corporate taxpayers, an issue of substantial political significance.

In addition to reducing tax rates, the 1986 Act went on to implement what, after all, can most accurately be described as a modified flat tax! Essentially the new law imposes one flat (or proportional) tax rate on all corporate taxpayers and another flat rate on all individual and fiduciary taxpayers. To politically achieve this major modification to income taxation, however, a somewhat lower rate had to be provided for both individual and corporate taxpayers earning lower levels of income. The eventual compromise reached in the 1986 law can be illustrated with a relatively simple conceptual diagram as shown in Figure 2-3. In other words, our new tax law basically imposes only one flat tax rate (B) on all taxpayers in the same general category. That rate is currently 28% for individuals, estates, and trusts and 34% for corporations. Taxpayers earning less than some minimum amount of taxable income (represented by distance OX in Figure 2-3) are, however, subject to one (or more) lower marginal rate(s). For individuals, estates, and trusts, there is but one (15%) lower rate (illustrated as tax rate A); corporations are subject to two lower rates, of 15% and 25%, at different levels of taxable income. The *apparent* tax advantage associated with a lower level of taxable income is, however, partially or fully "recaptured" from all taxpayers reporting a taxable income in excess of some stipulated amount (represented by distance OY). This recapture is achieved by increasing the basic tax rate (from rate B

FIGURE **2-3**

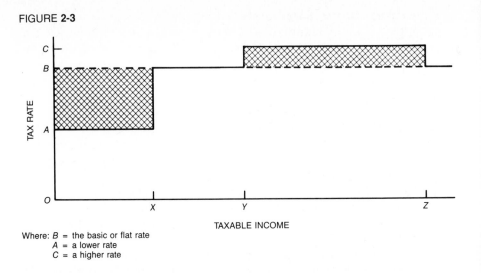

Where: B = the basic or flat rate
       A = a lower rate
       C = a higher rate

to rate *C*) over a limited range of income (that is, from income level *OY* to *OZ*). The difference between rates *B* and *C* is currently 5% for all categories of taxpayers. The two crosshatched areas in Figure 2-3 are (generally) equal in size.

Thus, one of the conceptual underpinnings of our new tax law is that all taxpayers earning more than some given amount of taxable income (represented by distance *OZ* in Figure 2-3) should effectively pay one (flat) rate on their entire taxable income. Although a few of the details associated with the new tax law, as you will discover in later chapters of this text, will prove that the conclusion expressed in the prior sentence is not entirely accurate, the essential truth of that conclusion is indeed the present reality. Stated in another way, the 1986 Tax Reform Act effectively redefined vertical equity for the United States. Prior to 1986, vertical equity meant that those who earned more should pay *relatively* more tax than those who earned a lesser taxable income. After 1986, vertical equity in U.S. income taxation apparently means that those who earn more should pay *the same proportion* of their additional incomes in taxes when compared to those who earn a somewhat lesser taxable income. Although it is extremely doubtful that the average voter actually understands this somewhat esoteric tax premise, it could prove to be one of the most significant victories of conservative thought during the Reagan years.

Primary Benefits of the New Law

Although it may be years before anyone can make a really fair general assessment of our new federal income tax law, it is not too early to identify some of the primary benefits that should flow from the most recent changes that were made. Most importantly, the new law ought to increase the degree of horizontal equity that exists, particularly for people in the upper-middle income classes. Prior to the 1986 Act, for example, individuals who earned a real economic income of between $100,000 and $500,000 per year often paid very different effective tax rates. The range of tax paid was from nearly 50% of income (for about 5% of the group) to little or nothing (for 2–3% of the same group). Under the new law, nearly all of those same individuals are now expected to pay somewhere between 25% and 28% of their real income in taxes. This change should put an end to the popular media stories about those few people who earned large incomes but paid no federal income taxes. Unfortunately the frequency of those stories misled the general population into believing that, under the old law, few, if any, "rich people" ever paid very much federal income tax. The truth of the matter was that the above-average income earners had always paid the lion's share of our federal individual income tax before 1987. That established fact was not, however, comprehended or accepted by the average voter. Because the average person believed that the rich paid little or no income tax, there was a strong incentive for those individuals to cheat on their own tax returns. Hopefully the new law will reverse this incentive, even if the old perception was based on total misinformation.[22]

A second primary benefit that should follow from the new tax law is the end of a massive misallocation of economic resources into buildings. ERTA, the 1981 tax act, provided an almost irresistible array of tax benefits for high-income taxpayers who were willing to invest in developed real estate. Although the new tax law may represent a classic case of legislative overkill, it clearly should cause future investors to acquire and build developed realty primarily for economic rather than tax reasons. Unfortunately it may take several years for the real estate industry to return to normalcy and for many of the new commercial buildings to be occupied in many sections of our country.

A third and final benefit of the new tax law is the removal of many low-income taxpayers from the income tax roles. Reasonably generous increases in both the standard deduction and the personal exemption will serve to remove our poorest citizens from all federal income tax liability. For others, earning only slightly more, these same changes will serve to simplify compliance with the new law. For the more fortunate taxpayers with higher incomes, however, the new law adds an almost draconian degree of complexity. This added complexity will be a major detriment of the 1986 Act for about 30% of all individual taxpayers and nearly all corporate taxpayers.

The Achilles Heel

If the Tax Reform Act of 1986 has an Achilles heel, it must be the uncertainty of the revenue estimate. As noted earlier, the bill was intended to be revenue neutral. That is, it is supposed to provide the same total amount of income tax

[22]For a further description of the horizontal inequity that existed under prior law, see U.S. Treasury Department, *Tax Reform Studies and Proposals,* Part 1, February 5, 1969. For a further statement concerning the actual payment of taxes by high-income taxpayers prior to the 1986 act, see John Schreiner, "Wealthy Are Doing Their Share to Satisfy Uncle Sam's Appetite," *Los Angeles Times,* July 20, 1986, Part IV, pp. 3, 8.

revenues for the federal government as would have been provided under prior law. Even though the total was not to change, relatively more was to come from the corporate income tax and relatively less from the individual income tax.

Predicting federal revenues is, unfortunately, a very inaccurate business under the best of conditions. For example, the Congressional Budget Office (CBO) and the Office of Management and Budget (OMB) are both required by law to predict annual federal deficits or surpluses every August, with revisions every February. According to a 1987 Congressional Service Research Report, their record on even these short-term forecasts is not very good. During the 10 years from 1977 to 1987, 75% of those forecasts underestimated the real federal deficit by an average of $35 billion; the other 25% overestimated the real deficit by an average of $18 billion. Projecting economic impact over a longer term, and following such massive tax law changes as those included in the 1986 Act, makes the CBO/OMB task look like child's play. Although the attempt to keep the bill revenue neutral was honest, that task is quite probably beyond human capacity, at least in today's world.

We must now, therefore, simply sit back and await the results. The way the bill was written, there is good reason to believe that the results for 1987 will be positive. That is, we can reasonably expect an increase in federal income tax revenues in the first year following the new act. Thereafter, however, the estimates are much more "iffy." At least one of the coauthors of this text would not be surprised if an unanticipated deficit of between $100 and $200 billion were to materialize in the second or third year out. If that dire prediction were to materialize in 1988, a presidential election year, it is very likely that the only reaction would be to increase the federal debt (via a large deficit) accordingly. Following the elections, however, the issues of tax reform would once again occupy center stage in the theater on the Potomac River.

If a large unanticipated deficit does materialize in 1988, or shortly thereafter, the next ideological fight in tax reform will very likely take place between (1) those who would go back and increase the marginal income tax rates on both individual and corporate taxpayers to pre-1987 levels and (2) those who would support VAT to provide the needed but missing revenues. Issues of regressivity and overlapping jurisdiction (that is, state versus federal issues) would dominate the debate. Matters of complexity in tax compliance would also be discussed, but, like always, those concerns would eventually take short shrift in the end.

On the other hand, if the Tax Reform Act of 1986 proves indeed to be revenue neutral, we may enjoy a somewhat longer period of relative tranquility in tax reform. Nearly everyone—politician, taxpayer, businessperson, and tax adviser alike—is tired of the constant change that has characterized the U.S. federal income tax law for the past 25 years. Just perhaps it will be possible for both tax students and taxpayers to learn the details of a tax law before it becomes obsolete.

In Part One, we have touched only the surface of some complex subjects. Some of you may be sufficiently stimulated by this brief introduction to make a more exhaustive examination at another time. The remainder of this book is concerned exclusively with income taxation because that is the dominant form of taxation in today's economy. Bear in mind throughout, however, that the income tax is but one part of a complex tax structure. As taxpayers and tax practitioners, we must be concerned with how much tax must be paid in a given situation. As citizens and students of taxation, we must also strive to gain an appreciation of the place of the tax laws in the social, economic, and political fabric of our time.[23]

PROBLEMS

1. How would you characterize the major changes in the federal income tax between 1913 and 1939? between 1939 and 1954? between 1954 and 1969? between 1969 and 1977? since 1978?

2. If the income tax was truly unconstitutional prior to the ratification of the Sixteenth Amendment in 1913, how could the United States actually impose and collect an income tax for approximately 10 years in the 1870s and 1880s?

3. What is a direct tax? What is an indirect tax?

4. The federal income tax on individuals did not become a "mass tax" until about 1942. Explain what this means and what was necessitated by the transition from a "select tax" to a "mass tax."

5. Is it likely that either the personal or the corporate income taxes will be repealed in the near future? Explain briefly.

6. Between 1861 and 1872, several revenue acts passed by Congress included an income tax.
   a. Was the constitutionality of these acts ever tested before the U.S. Supreme Court? If so, what did the Court find?
   b. List four reasons why these early experiments in income taxation may be considered significant for subsequent income tax laws.

7. How did Congress and the administration achieve the dramatic reduction in the marginal income tax rates of individual taxpayers in the Tax Reform Act of 1986 without, supposedly, precipitating a major decline in the overall federal tax revenues?

8. Assuming that the U.S. federal income tax law accurately reflects the collective value judgment of the average citizen, how would you define vertical equity
   a. after 1986?
   b. before 1987?

9. How much federal income tax do you believe each of the following four persons *should* pay on the income they earn? (Note: this question is asking for your personal opinion, not what the current law demands.)

[23]The following intermediate level public finance texts can provide additional insight into the economics of taxation: Michael J. Boskin, ed., *Federal Tax Reform* (San Francisco: Institute for Contemporary Studies, 1978); Robin W. Boadway, *Public Sector Economics* (Cambridge, MA: Winthrop Publishers, 1979); Edgar K. Browning and Jacqueline M. Browning, *Public Finance and the Price System,* 2nd ed. (New York: Macmillan, 1983); Musgrave and Musgrave, *op. cit.* (footnote 2, Chapter 1); and Hyman, *op. cit.* (footnote 15, Chapter 1).

Person	Income	Occupation
Andrew	$ 25,000	Factory worker
Beverly	150,000	Medical doctor
Calvin	300,000	Football player
Diane	600,000	Actress

10. Compare your answer to question 9, above, with that of all your classmates and determine how the majority would define vertical equity.

11. Using the daily newspapers or weekly news magazines available in your library, determine if any major changes in tax laws have been proposed or enacted within the past six months. If so, what reasons have been given in support of these new provisions?

12. The estimated budget effects of the 1986 Act on federal tax revenues were, per the Conference Committee, as follows:

Fiscal Year	Surplus	Deficit
1987	$11.4 billion	
1988		$16.7 billion
1989		15.0 billion
1990	8.1 billion	

The CBO's February 1987 estimate of future federal deficits were as follows:

Fiscal Year	Deficit
1987	$176.2 billion
1988	134.4 billion
1989	117.1 billion
1990	77.9 billion

How accurate were these predictions? What are the tax implications of any major errors in these estimates?

13. The Gramm-Rudman Act set the following deficit targets in late 1985:

Fiscal Year	Deficit
1987	$144 billion
1988	108 billion
1989	72 billion
1990	36 billion
1991 and thereafter	None

How close is the federal government to achieving these Gramm-Rudman goals? What will happen if they fall short of their objectives?

PART TWO

Basic Concepts

I guess you will have to go to jail. If that is the result of not understanding the Income Tax law I shall meet you there. We will have a merry, merry time, for all of our friends will be there. It will be an intellectual center, for no one understands the Income Tax law except persons who have not sufficient intelligence to understand the questions that arise under it.
Elihu Root, quoted in Randolph E. Paul, Taxation in the United States

. . . it is probable that the income tax has come to stay. Let us be thankful that it has come in such a shape, and let us look forward with hopeful anticipation to a future in which the income tax, improved and amended, will play its important part in bringing about greater justice in American taxation.
Edwin R. A. Seligman, The Income Tax *(1914)*

CHAPTER 3

Income: General Concepts

> *The first nine pages of the Internal Revenue Code define income; the remaining 1,100 pages spin the web of exceptions and preferences. The average taxpayer rarely gets beyond the nine pages.*
> Senator Warren Magnuson, Congressional Record *(1966)*

The determination of an *income tax liability* quite obviously must begin with an operative definition of the income concept. Unfortunately for everyone concerned, few concepts in the history of economic thought have been more widely debated than the income concept. To make matters even more difficult, as we move from a conceptual plane to the pragmatic and often political world of taxation, no logical explanation of the many distortions to the basic concept can be offered as guidance to either the serious student or the confused taxpayer, who was of special concern to Senator Magnuson in the headnote to this chapter.

Conceptually, computation of a taxpayer's net income tax payable is a simple matter and can be easily reduced to a formula:

  Income broadly conceived
− Exclusions
  ────────────────
= Gross Income
− Deductions
  ────────────────
= Taxable income
× Applicable tax rate

= Gross tax liability
− Tax credits and prepayments
= Net tax payable

The apparent simplicity of the general income tax formula is deceiving because its correct application depends on myriad classifications, definitions, distinctions, and exceptions contained in the Code and the closely related administrative and judicial interpretations. These authoritative interpretations sometimes give common words used in the Code a special meaning for tax purposes. Furthermore (and most important), to understand tax provisions, a person often must understand not only the literal wording of the Code but the social, economic, and political forces that motivated its enactment, the administrative considerations that attach to a particular interpretation of it, and the personal opinions of the individuals assigned the responsibility of interpreting it. Justice Learned Hand stated this conclusion most explicitly and colorfully when he said

> . . . as the articulation of a statute increases, the room for interpretation must contract; but the meaning of a sentence may be more than that of the separate words, as a melody is more than the notes, and no degree of particularity can ever obviate recourse to the setting in which all appear, and which all collectively create.[1]

Part Two of this text attempts to explain the fundamental tax equation in broad terms. The first three chapters provide an overview of the taxable income taxation. Chapter 3 begins with a discussion of the income concept, broadly conceived. It then compares the income concept used in economics, in financial accounting, and in taxation. Chapter 4 contains an overview of the tax concept of deductions that are made to arrive at taxable income. In Chapter 5 permissible accounting periods and accounting methods are explained.

Whether any income tax is payable for an entity and, if so, how much, depends in part on the type of entity involved. The nature of various types of taxable entities and their tax status are reviewed in Chapter 7.

One major difficulty with Part Two is the need to include both general concepts and specific rules. In studying these materials, always keep this fundamental distinction in mind. The conceptual portions should be viewed as comparable to a globe; that is, these discussions give you only the broad outline of a tax geography. The detailed rules considered in other portions are comparable to a city map; that is, they must be followed with great precision if you are to end up in the correct place. In a few instances, the discussion in Part Two lies somewhere between the globe and the city map; that is, some of the most important tax provisions are introduced briefly in the

[1]*Helvering* v. *Gregory,* 69 F.2d 809 (CCA-2nd, 1934).

conceptual materials along with a cross-reference to other portions of this text where those same rules are considered in much greater detail. To begin, let us consider the basic income concept.

INCOME CONCEPTS

There is no single universally accepted definition of the word "income." Rather there are many definitions, often based on the uses to be made of the definition. Each definition depends on concepts and assumptions that may not be totally acceptable for other uses. In this chapter we will examine some of the fundamental issues underlying the problem of income definition and measurement. We will begin with major distinctions in the concepts of income found in economics, accounting, and taxation, especially with the conflicts between the accounting and tax concepts of income.

The Income of Economics

A traditional starting point is to analyze the definitions of income given by Robert M. Haig and Henry C. Simons. These men were two of the early scholars of tax theory who were well versed in economics. Haig's definition of income is simple and straightforward: "Income is the *money value of the net accretion to one's economic power between two points of time.*"[2] A similar definition is given by Simons: "Personal income may be defined as the algebraic sum of (1) the market value of rights exercised in consumption and (2) the change in the value of the store of property rights between the beginning and end of the period in question."[3]

Professor Harvey Brazer has restated the concept of income held by Simons and Haig (and even before them by the German economist George Schanz and others) in easily understood terms: "Under this concept income is equal to the algebraic sum of consumption plus the change in the individual's net worth during the year or other accounting period. . . . It asks simply, how much could this individual have spent for consumption during the year while remaining as well off in terms of net worth at the end of the year as he was at the beginning of the year."[4] Perhaps the most important aspect of Simons' definition of income, at least from the accountant's viewpoint, is his suggestion that consumption and the net change in the individual's store of claims

---

[2]Robert M. Haig, "The Concept of Income—Economic and Legal Aspects," *The Federal Income Tax* (New York: Columbia University Press, 1921), p. 7.
[3]Henry C. Simons, *Personal Income Taxation* (Chicago: University of Chicago Press, 1921), p. 50.
[4]Harvey E. Brazer, "The Economics of Tax Reform," *Proceedings of the Fifty-Sixth Annual Conference* (1963) *of the National Tax Association*, p. 47.

ideally are "both evaluated at market price, with the latter [increase in store of claims] computed on an accrual rather than on a realization basis."[5]

The major difficulty in using this definition for such practical purposes as taxation is in obtaining reliable measures of net worth and consumption. In other words, the problem is one of valuation. Unfortunately, only a relatively insignificant portion of total assets has easily ascertainable and accurate market values. The "value" of most assets is a subjective characteristic that depends on someone's estimate of the satisfaction to be derived from the object in question in comparison with the expected satisfaction that could be obtained from other objects that might be purchased as an alternative.

Another problem arising from this economic concept of income is in distinguishing between *monetary* income and *real* income. This difference refers to the familiar problem caused by changes in the value of the monetary unit—in accounting, the problem is commonly called the *price-level problem*. The changing price level does not cause a serious problem in measuring consumption, but it may be very important in measuring the change in accumulation in value during the year if the price level has changed markedly. Most economists stress *real* capital accumulation, measured by the increase in command over scarce resources. Presumably, "gains" that are due merely to an increase in price level can be approximately eliminated by deflating by an index of consumer prices.

A broad economic view of income would presumably include *all* receipts from *all* sources, including such gratuitous receipts as gifts, inheritances, and bequests—mainly on the basis that including such items eliminates the need to differentiate among an individual's receipts according to the intentions of other parties and that it makes the definition simpler, more precise, and more definite.

Another concept of income advocated by some economists is based on consumption. Under this concept, generally associated with the name of Professor Irving Fisher, realization is ultimately represented only by *consumption,* because only when an item is consumed is there a logical stopping place among the sequence of economic relations.[6] From this viewpoint, income represents satisfaction derived from consumption and is measured in monetary terms by the amount spent on consumer goods "consumed" during the period—for example, the imputed use value derived from an owner-occupied home. The source of what the individual consumes (and only individuals can consume) is immaterial. Obviously the computation of

[5]Melvin I. White, "Consistent Treatment of Items Excluded and Omitted from the Individual Income Tax Base," *1959 Compendium,* p. 318. (The complete reference is *Tax Revision Compendium: Compendium of Papers on Broadening the Tax Base,* submitted to the Committee on Ways and Means, beginning November 16, 1959. This three-volume collection of papers on income taxation is one of the modern classics and is quoted frequently throughout this text. To simplify the footnotes, all subsequent references simply cite the *1959 Compendium.*)
[6]See Irving Fisher, *The Nature of Capital and Income* (New York: Macmillan, 1906); "Income in Theory and Income Taxation in Practice," *Econometrica,* 5, No. 1 (January 1937), pp. 1–55; and (with Herbert W. Fisher), *Constructive Income Taxation* (New York: Harper, 1942).

imputed income is highly subjective; however, the failure to include imputed income in any income tax base inevitably decreases the (theoretical) equity of the tax.

An income tax based on a consumption definition of income would, for all practical purposes, be an expenditures tax. Although the consumption–expenditures approach to taxation is interesting from an academic viewpoint, it has relatively little significance in the present tax structure of most countries. The most thorough statement of this approach to taxation is attributed to Nicholas Kaldor, an English economist.[7]

The Income of Accounting

Major discrepancies exist between the broad definition of income discussed in the preceding section and the computation of income under generally accepted accounting principles. The primary difference is the complete absence of any "realization" criterion in the economic view of income.

Generally accepted accounting principles suggest that income should be measured on the basis of completed transactions. Note the importance of this distinction: Economists define income in terms of *value,* depending essentially on expectations about the *future.* Accountants define income basically in terms of the *past,* expressed in money measurement. They are concerned with the flow of transactions of the enterprise because completed transactions—presumably at arm's length—provide independent judgments of "value" on which accountants can rely. Accountants consider the economists' concept too impractical and difficult to apply and too lacking in objectivity and accuracy to be a basis for measuring periodic income in the accounts. The recognition of unrealized gains or losses requiring detailed annual listings and subjective valuations of assets and liabilities is frightening to many accountants, who are steeped in the virtues of practicality and conservatism and who are saddled with legal liability for the accuracy of the financial statements they certify.

The student of accounting may be surprised to discover that economists frequently fail to understand the reluctance of accountants to use subjective valuations to the extent that they are used by economists. Professor Simons, for example, once charged that accountants prefer to sacrifice relevance for accuracy. On the other hand, he admitted that "outright abandonment of the realization criterion would be utter folly; no workable scheme can require that taxpayers reappraise and report all their assets annually; and while this procedure is implied by the underlying definition of income, it is quite unnecessary to effective application of that definition. . . ."[8]

The contrast between economic and accounting concepts of income can be seen easily from a grossly simplified example. Suppose that on January 1,

[7]See Nicholas Kaldor, *An Expenditures Tax* (London: Allen and Unwin, 1955).
[8]See Simons, *op. cit.,* pp. 207–208. This conclusion was reaffirmed by Professor Simons in his later book, *Federal Tax Reform* (Chicago: University of Chicago Press, 1950). Both books are excellent reading for the serious tax student.

19x1, John Glover, a young accountant fresh from the university, took inventory of his financial condition. His only assets consisted of a bank account and his clothing. On that date, he took a job with an accounting firm. He also decided to invest $1,000 of his bank account in a new highly speculative mining company, leaving him a bank balance of only $500. During 19x1, he earned a salary of $20,000; he also was allowed to prepare a few tax returns for friends outside the firm, for which he received fees of $2,000 and incurred expenses of $400. Glover's mother made a gift to him of $2,000 cash in 19x1. In addition, the mining company discovered uranium and was highly profitable; he received dividends of $900 on the shares, which increased in value so that they were worth $9,800 on December 31, 19x1. Glover was not frugal, however, and on December 31 his only asset, other than the shares of stock, was a bank account of $400; the remaining $24,600 cash that he had available during the year was spent purely for consumption items.

Using the general ideas previously described (but ignoring price-level changes), the economist would compute Glover's income as $33,300, as follows:

	Value at Beginning of Year	Value at End of Year	Increase (or Decrease)
Cash	$ 500	$ 400	($ 100)
Shares of stock	1,000	9,800	8,800
Increase in "net worth"			$ 8,700
Plus: Consumption expenditures			24,600
Total "economic" income			$33,300

The accountant, on the other hand, would compute Glover's income as $22,500, as follows:

Salary		$20,000
Fees from outside returns	$2,000	
Less: Expenses	400	
		1,600
Dividends		900
Total "accounting" income		$22,500

Note that the accountant includes only *realized* income, deducting the applicable expenses that can be matched against that income. A gift generally is not considered by the accountant to be income. Even more important, the increase of $8,800 in the value of the stock is disregarded by the accountant because it has not been "realized" through sale or exchange, and consumption expenditures are also disregarded.

Accountants have developed a comprehensive and well-defined body of literature that contains concepts and specific rules for measuring income.

Almost all of these rules are based on the realization concept and the matching concept. Although this concept is examined in detail in Chapter 17, its importance in determining a taxpayer's gross income for a period warrants a brief review at this point.

THE REALIZATION CRITERION IN ACCOUNTING   *A Dictionary for Accountants* defines *realize* as follows:

> To convert into cash or a receivable (through sale) or services (through use); to exchange for property which at the time of its receipt may be classified as, or immediately converted into, a current asset.[9]

Thus, the accountant generally considers income to be realized when assets are converted into other property that has a high degree of *liquidity* and *measurability* or when services are rendered resulting in the acquisition of such property.

However, the last pronouncement of the American Institute of Certified Public Accountants on the matter of realization is somewhat different from that quoted above (and comes reasonably close to the tax position). In its *Statement No. 4,* the Accounting Principles Board assigned the concept of realization the position of a pervasive measurement principle and then described it as follows:

> Revenue is generally recognized when both of the following conditions are met: (1) the earning process is complete or virtually complete, and (2) an exchange has taken place.[10]

This statement seems to differ from definitions offered earlier, with less emphasis placed on the liquidity of the asset received and more emphasis on the completion of the earning process. Nevertheless, accountants continue to hold that generally income has not been realized until a transaction has been consumated and a measurable liquid asset received.

THE RECOGNITION CONCEPT IN ACCOUNTING   The adjective *recognized,* when used to modify income, means simply that the income item is to be admitted or acknowledged for the purpose at hand. Income recognized for accounting purposes is simply income that is included in the appropriate financial statement(s) prepared for that accounting period. Generally, this is the period in which realization occurs. In limited circumstances, for financial accounting purposes income may be recognized prior to realization. For

---

[9]Eric L. Kohler, *A Dictionary for Accountants,* 2nd ed. (Englewood Cliffs, NJ: Prentice Hall, 1957), p. 407.
[10]*APB Statement No. 4,* "Basic Concepts and Accounting Principles Underlying Financial Statements of Business Enterprise," (New York: American Institute of Certified Public Accountants, 1970), p. 59.

example, when a product has an assured market at a fixed price, it might be argued that income should be recognized when the product is completed.

Similarly, in some cases recognition may occur after realization. For example, if income is prepaid, it is generally recognized later in the period(s) in which it is earned.

The Income of Taxation

We have seen that the income of economics is far too subjective to be used by the accountant in measuring income for financial reporting purposes. It is also far too subjective to be used generally as a basis for determining income taxes. Nevertheless, the all-inclusive approach to income measurement attributed to Simons and Haig approaches a method used, albeit infrequently, by the I.R.S. to reconstruct the income of taxpayers who are without adequate and accurate accounting records. This is the *net-worth method,* which relies heavily on the basic assumption that all inflows of wealth are taxable unless specifically excluded by law. Essentially, this method of measuring income compares the taxpayer's net worth at the beginning and end of a period. The change in net worth is then combined with estimated consumption expenditures for the period to get an estimate of total income.

Although the method is subject to criticism on the grounds that the taxpayer has the burden of proving that any portion of the computed income was derived from excluded sources, it is sometimes the only realistic alternative available to the I.R.S. The possibility of its use certainly encourages gamblers, prostitutes, and others to keep a set of reasonable financial records for tax purposes, if for no other reason.

The net-worth method of estimating income for tax purposes yields different results than would the economic concept of income we have been discussing. This is so largely because of the exclusion under tax law of certain types of income, the use of the realization criterion for tax purposes, and the allowance of certain specified deductions in arriving at taxable income. For example, assume that a taxpayer whose tax return is audited has almost no records. The I.R.S. agent determines the taxpayer's net worth at the end of the tax year as follows:

Cash	$ 400
Stock in mining company (at fair market value)	9,800
Total assets	$10,200
Liabilities	0
Net worth	$10,200

Based on the taxpayer's living standards and circumstances, examination of the few records available, and discussions with those familiar with the taxpayer's activities, the agent estimates the taxpayer's consumption expenditures at approximately $24,600. Further examination leads to the conclusion that the taxpayer's net worth on January 1 was $1,500. The agent thus concludes that the taxpayer's income in the broad economic sense was approximately $33,300.

Increase in net worth during the year	$ 8,700
Consumption expenditures (estimated)	24,600
Total "income"	$33,300

To continue the illustration, suppose that the taxpayer can show that the shares of stock were purchased during the year for $1,000 with cash on hand at the start of the year. The increase in the stock's value is not taxable. In addition, the taxpayer can prove that during the year his mother gave him $2,000 as a gift. Based on these additional data, the taxpayer's gross income for tax purposes is an estimated $22,500.

Total income in economic sense		$33,300
Less: Unrealized increase in stock value	$8,800	
Tax-free gift from mother	2,000	
		10,800
"Income" for tax purposes		$22,500

By now you should have observed that the data in this example are identical to those previously given for John Glover. Observe that even though the *procedure* used under the net-worth method to reconstruct the initial measure of income is almost identical to the "economic" income computation, the final *result* in this example is identical to the accounting measure of income.

Although the measurement of income as computed under generally accepted accounting principles comes much closer to yielding a basis on which income taxes can be computed—yielding in the above example an identical measure—there are still many differences between income determined under generally accepted accounting principles and income computed for tax purposes. These differences are created by the many factors that enter into and influence the federal tax structure. Primary among these factors are the underlying body of economic, social, and legal philosophies of the people and the Congress; the (proper and improper) exercise of power by groups and lobbies with vested interests; the variation in interpretations of laws and regulations by the courts (which often conflict because of opposing values and ideologies of those handing down the decisions and because of changing "public policy"); and the increasing use of tax policy as an instrument of social and economic planning and control.

Before examining some of the specific items that are to be included in taxable income and some that are to be excluded, let us consider the major reasons why differences exist between accounting income and taxable income.

WHY ACCOUNTING INCOME AND TAXABLE INCOME DIFFER

For our purposes we can attribute differences between income as measured for tax purposes and income as measured for financial accounting purposes to four concepts in taxation that often outweigh the correctness or logic, or both, of financial accounting. These are:

1. Wherewithal to pay
2. Realization and recognition
3. Ease and consistency of administration
4. Social and economic objectives

Wherewithal to Pay

The phrase "wherewithal to pay" suggests that the levying of the tax should occur at a time when the taxpayer can most readily pay the tax and the I.R.S. can most readily collect it. The concept may be expressed simply as "get the tax when the taxpayer has the money to pay it."

The requirement that, generally, unearned revenues be reported as taxable income in the year received regardless of the year(s) in which they are actually earned is a classic example of application of this concept. For example, the lessor who receives rent paid in advance for future years must report the entire prepayment in the year it is received rather than in later years when it is earned. This requirement, the subject of much acrimonious debate, is designed to provide maximum possible assurance that the tax will be collected, presumably because the taxpayer has the cash available for paying the tax in the year the prepayment is received, whereas he or she may not have the cash available to pay taxes in later years when the income is actually earned. Alternatively, the taxpayer may still have the cash at the later date, but may be outside the jurisdiction of the U.S. tax authorities.

Although the unearned income rule is frequently cited as a deviation from generally accepted accounting principles that is unfair to the taxpayer, the concept of wherewithal to pay more often works to the taxpayer's advantage. For example, generally a taxpayer defers the tax recognition of the entire or partial gain on an installment sale until he or she receives the cash, even if financial accounting would report the entire gain in the year of the sale. A taxpayer may similarly defer the recognition of taxable gain in many barter-type transactions, in the event of an involuntary conversion of property, in the sale of a personal residence, and in many transactions between the taxpayer and a related business entity. These and other illustrations of tax provisions related to the wherewithal-to-pay concept are discussed in detail in subsequent chapters. Suffice it to note here that these rules often are of tremendous benefit to a taxpayer.

Realization and Recognition for Tax Purposes

REALIZATION IN MEASURING TAXABLE INCOME   The realization concept in income taxation is similar but not identical to the accounting concept just reviewed. Most of the differences between them are best explained by practical constraints—that is, by the accountant's legal liability for accurate statements on the one hand and by the objectives and administrative considerations common to income taxation on the other.

The importance of the realization concept to the taxpayer can be readily seen. A mere increase in the value of an asset—even if easily measurable and readily convertible into cash—is not taxed. For example, the taxpayer who purchases shares of stock for $1,000 and finds, at the end of the year, that the stock has a quoted market value of $1,500 has no income to report because none has been realized; that is, there has been no change in the assets held. Only when the shares are sold or exchanged for other assets is the gain recognized.

Similarly, the taxpayer who, to his good fortune and surprise, discovers under his land valuable oil and gas reserves worth millions of dollars recognizes no income until this increase in value is realized through conversion into other assets through sale or exchange.

On the other hand, the concept may also work to the disadvantage of a taxpayer. Declines in asset values generally are not recognized until they are realized through disposition of the asset, no matter how real the decline seems to be. (Some minor exceptions to this rule exist—notably in accounts receivable and merchandise inventory.) Thus, the taxpayer who purchases shares of stock for $1,000 and finds that the stock is worth only $300 at year-end has no deductible loss until realization takes place through conversion of the shares by sale or exchange. (Losses on securities that are *completely worthless* may be recognized even though the securities are not disposed of.)

A major reason for the rather strict adherence to the realization concept (in addition to the notion of wherewithal to pay already discussed) is the need for a high degree of objectivity and certainty in the tax computation. Tax authorities are even more wed to the concept of objectivity than are accountants generally. This is not surprising, since there must be at least one specific point at which the amount of tax can be computed and levied with reasonable certainty and accuracy. As previously observed, abandonment of the realization criterion would result in considerable subjectivity, making the tax dependent on the whims of personal judgments. This would mean constant litigation and dispute and an administrative nightmare.

It is important to note that the realization concept does not dictate that assets must be converted into monetary claims for gain to be recognized, even though that requirement would result in greater objectivity and easier tax administration. For example, if the taxpayer exchanges shares of stock for land, a gain or loss must generally be recognized. The amount of the gain or loss depends on the basis of the stock given up and the fair market value of the land (or other asset received). Obviously, subjectivity is immediately introduced in this situation; that is, the determination of the value of the land or other asset is often not a simple or objective process. It is also apparent that unless realization is deemed to have taken place at the time of the exchange, a rather simple device for tax avoidance (the barter transaction) would have been introduced. Thus, even though the I.R.S. would prefer to use only objective data, it is nevertheless required to establish market values in many cases even when it retains the basic realization criterion.

RECOGNITION FOR TAX PURPOSES   *For tax purposes, income generally must be recognized in the same accounting period that it is realized.* However, a number of exceptions to this general rule exist. For tax purposes, income recognition only rarely precedes realization, but it quite often follows realization. This significant difference in income measurement techniques between accounting and taxation can be explained by the *wherewithal to pay* concept. This concept suggests that under many circumstances "the income tax shall impinge at whatever time the taxpayer has the funds with which to pay the tax." In numerous situations, wherewithal to pay seems to outrank in importance more sophisticated refinements of income measurement that would cause income to be recognized at a time other than when the funds are readily available. Perhaps the outstanding example is the taxation of certain unearned revenues at the time of receipt. As previously discussed, there are numerous situations in which recognition is deferred until periods after realization because under the circumstances the taxpayer has no wherewithal to pay the tax. These situations are discussed in detail in Chapter 17.

Ease and Consistency of Administration

Closely allied to the realization concept is the "administrative need for a taxable event to be fixed with adequate certainty in order to avoid disputes between the I.R.S. and the taxpayer as to the occurrence of the event or the amount involved."[11]

This goal often creates a distinct conflict between what is generally accepted in financial accounting and what is required for tax purposes. The conflict occurs more often in relation to expense items than in relation to income items because expenses frequently are estimated for financial accounting purposes even though they may not be deductible on the tax return. To quote former Commissioner Cohen:

> It is often proper or even necessary to reflect future events of a contingent nature, such as potential losses or pending lawsuits, in a financial statement. However, an attempt to reflect this type of transaction in the

---

[11]Sheldon S. Cohen, "Accounting for Taxes, Finance and Regulatory Purposes—Are Variances Necessary?" speech before the 19th Annual Tax Conference, The University of Chicago Law School, October 1966. Reprinted in *Taxes,* 44, No. 12 (December 1966), p. 784.

computation of a tax liability could result in protracted controversy between the government and the taxpayer over the likelihood of the occurrence of the event and the amount potentially involved. The tax accounting rule is easier to administer because it involves fewer subjective judgments and estimates.

Similarly, tax requirements stricter than generally accepted accounting rules are often justified because they are easier to administer and produce more uniform results among different taxpayers. In short, administrative convenience is frequently important in explaining differences between taxable income and accounting net income.

Social and Economic Objectives

Finally, tax laws often result from a desire to achieve stipulated social or economic goals. Frequently, tax laws are changed to secure full employment, to combat inflation, to relieve social pressures, or to attain other goals of the national administration or the Congress. As a matter of fact, many critics today complain violently that tax laws have become little more than economic tools, whereas others, of course, think that's just what they should be.

As a result, many items that would be viewed as income for both economic and financial accounting purposes are excluded from taxation, or items that would not be considered in computing economic income or financial accounting income are allowed as tax deductions. For example, in 1982 and 1983 taxpayers were permitted to exclude from taxable income a limited amount of interest on "all-savers" certificates of deposit issued by financial institutions in order to stimulate savings that could be used largely in making loans for home purchases. Clearly this interest represents both financial and economic income to the recipient even though it was not taxable. Similarly, the Accelerated Cost Recovery System (ACRS) enacted in 1981 authorizes a taxpayer to deduct the cost of plant and equipment used in business significantly faster than is allowed for any other income measurement purpose. The purpose was to stimulate investment in productive assets.

There are dozens of other special rules in the Revenue Code that are designed to achieve economic or social goals deemed by the Congress to be desirable. These "exceptions" are especially prevalent in provisions related to deductions and will be discussed throughout this text. Much of the complexity in our tax laws can be traced directly to these efforts to achieve economic and social goals through tax incentives and disincentives. Typically, the portion of the Code written to achieve the objective is quite simple, but the provisions necessary to prevent unintended results and abuses are most complex. For example, in the 1986 Tax Reform Act the Congress enacted a very complicated provision designed to limit benefits to investors in "tax shelters." Tax shelters represent activities or ventures that take advantage of tax rules to offer investors deductions and credits, often exceeding the real economic costs or losses currently borne by the taxpayer, in excess or in advance of income from the shelter.

In explaining the reason for the complex limitations on "passive activity losses," the Senate Finance Committee stated:

> . . . [W]hile the bill reduces or eliminates some tax items that the committee believes do not provide social or economic benefits commensurate with their cost, there are many preferences that the committee believes are socially or economically beneficial. This is especially true when such preferences are used primarily to advance the purposes upon which Congress relied in enacting them, rather than to avoid taxation of income from sources unrelated to the preferred activity.[12]

GROSS INCOME FOR TAX PURPOSES—STATUTORY INCLUSIONS AND EXCLUSIONS

The general concepts of gross income for tax purposes that have been discussed in this chapter stem in part from the Internal Revenue Code, in part from administrative interpretations of the Code, and in part from decisions of various courts. A cursory examination of the statutes reveals that they contain relatively few sections devoted to defining gross income.

Section 61 of the Code purports to define gross income. Although the definition it provides—gross income means all income—does not tell us much, it clearly suggests that any doubtful items are included within the definition. This conclusion is supported by three other phrases in Sec. 61(a), which, in its entirety, reads as follows:

(a) General Definition. Except as otherwise provided in this subtitle, gross income means all income from whatever sources derived, including (but not limited to) the following items:
   (1) Compensation for services, including fees, commissions, fringe benefits, and similar items;
   (2) Gross income derived from business;
   (3) Gains derived from dealings in property;
   (4) Interest;
   (5) Rents;
   (6) Royalties;
   (7) Dividends;
   (8) Alimony and separate maintenance payments;
   (9) Annuities;
   (10) Income from life insurance and endowment contracts;
   (11) Pensions;
   (12) Income from discharge of indebtedness;
   (13) Distributive share of partnership gross income;
   (14) Income in respect of a decedent; and
   (15) Income from an interest in an estate or trust.

[12]Senate Report No. 313, 99th Congress, 2nd Session (Washington, DC: U.S. Government Printing Office, 1986).

The four statutory phrases that support an expansive interpretation of "gross income" for tax purposes are:

1. *Except* as otherwise provided . . .
2. Gross income means *all* income . . .
3. From *whatever* source derived . . .
4. Including (but *not limited to*) . . .

In view of the all-inclusive nature of Code Sec. 61(a), the taxpayer must look to the phrase "except as otherwise provided" as a basis for omitting an item from gross income. The statutory exceptions are collectively identified as exclusions. In other words, *any item of income that is not included in gross income is known as an exclusion.* The words of Sec. 61 clearly suggest that all exclusions must have a statutory base and that these provisions must be found within Subtitle A of the Internal Revenue Code. In fact, a few exclusions do not have statutory bases, but they are so widely accepted that no one seriously challenges their validity today. Perhaps the best known exclusion based solely on administrative authority is that formerly extended to Social Security benefits. These benefits were excluded from taxation by a Treasury Department ruling in 1941. Although various proposals were made from time to time to revise the statutes to include Social Security Benefits within the income tax base, none of those proposals was enacted by the Congress until 1983, when a portion of Social Security benefits was made taxable in certain cases.

A careful examination of a detailed table of contents of the Code might suggest that all of the exclusions are neatly contained within Part III of Subchapter B of Chapter 1. The title for that part of the Code reads "Items Specifically Excluded from Gross Income." Part III includes Secs. 101 through 133, the titles of which read as follows:

Sec. 101. Certain death payments.
Sec. 102. Gifts and inheritances.
Sec. 103. Interest on state and local bonds.
Sec. 103A. Mortgage subsidy bonds.
Sec. 104. Compensation for injuries or sickness.
Sec. 105. Amounts received under accident and health plans.
Sec. 106. Contributions by employer to accident and health plans.
Sec. 107. Rental value of parsonages.
Sec. 108. Income from discharge of indebtedness.
Sec. 109. Improvements by lessee on lessor's property.
Sec. 110. Income taxes paid by lessee corporation.
Sec. 111. Recovery of tax benefit items.
Sec. 112. Certain combat pay of members of the Armed Forces.
Sec. 113. Mustering-out payments for members of the Armed Forces.
Sec. 114. Sports programs conducted for the American National Red Cross.
Sec. 115. Income of States, municipalities, etc.
Sec. 116. Partial exclusion of dividends received by individuals (repealed).
Sec. 117. Qualified scholarships.
Sec. 118. Contributions to the capital of a corporation.

Sec. 119. Meals or lodging furnished for the convenience of employer.
Sec. 120. Amounts received under qualified group legal services plans.
Sec. 121. One-time exclusion of gain from sale of principal residence by individual who has attained age 55.
Sec. 122. Certain reduced uniformed services retirement pay.
Sec. 123. Amounts received under insurance contracts for certain living expenses.
Sec. 124. Qualified transportation provided by employer.
Sec. 125. Cafeteria plans.
Sec. 126. Certain cost-sharing payments.
Sec. 127. Educational assistance programs.
Sec. 128. Interest on certain savings certificates.
Sec. 129. Dependent Care Assistance programs.
Sec. 130. Certain personal injury liability assignments.
Sec. 131. Certain foster care payments.
Sec. 132. Certain fringe benefits.
Sec. 133. Interest on certain loans used to acquire employer securities.
Sec. 134. Certain military benefits.

The seemingly clear list of 15 inclusions provided in Sec. 61(a), coupled with the specific exclusions located in Part III of Subchapter B, may give the student who is unfamiliar with the myriad controversies surrounding the nature and measure of income a false and unwarranted sense of security about his or her understanding of income. As you will discover throughout the remainder of this text, these few specific items of inclusion and exclusion are but the tip of a very interesting iceberg.

Some of the exclusions contained in the Code Sections listed above—for example certain of the exclusions in Secs. 101, 102, and 103—apply to all types of entities. Many of the exclusions, for example Secs. 104, 105, 106, and 107, apply only to individuals. Most of these exclusions are explained in Chapter 7.

SUMMARY OF THE INCOME CONCEPT FOR TAX PURPOSES

The preceding discussion of the income concept for federal tax purposes can be summarized briefly. Before any taxpayer must report the receipt of income for federal income tax purposes, he or she must answer three fundamental questions—*all* in the affirmative. Those three questions are:

1. Did the taxpayer have any income?

2. Was that income realized?

3. If income was realized, must it be recognized immediately?

Perhaps the best possible test for the presence (or absence) of income is the one suggested by economists: Did the event under consideration for the potential taxpayer cause *either* an increase in net worth *or* in consumption? If the answer to this first question is yes, we ordinarily should presume that income is present. The conclusion that income is present, however, is not sufficient to trigger the income tax. To be taxable, income must also be both realized and recognized.

Realization usually requires *both* (1) a change in the form or the substance of the taxpayer's property (or property rights) and (2) the involvement of a second party. Income is most commonly realized when a service has been rendered; a property has been sold or exchanged; or a property belonging to the taxpayer has been used by someone else. Thus, the receipt of any form of payment for a service rendered—whether it is received in cash or in noncash property—is generally sufficient to cause the realization of income; so is the exchange of one property for another. Not every item of realized income is, however, subject to an immediate income tax. Realized income must also be recognized for federal income tax purposes.

In general, income must be recognized for tax purposes in the same accounting period that it is realized. There are, however, many exceptions to this general rule. Tax nonrecognition, when it occurs, may be either permanent or temporary. Permanent nonrecognition is typically due to an exclusion provision inserted into the Code by Congress. Temporary nonrecognition may be attributed either to (1) specific accounting methods (or conventions) or (2) special nonrecognition provisions put into the Code by Congress, usually to provide for income taxation at the time that the taxpayer has the wherewithal to pay a tax. (Tax accounting methods and fiscal periods are discussed in Chapter 5.)

CLASSIFICATIONS OF INCOME

There are many ways in which income may be classified for tax purposes because different classifications are used for different purposes. Two examples of these classification schemes are (1) the historically important distinction between capital gains and other types of income and (2) the distinction under the 1986 Tax Reform Act between "income from passive activities" and other types of income.

Capital Gains Versus Other Types of Income

The federal tax laws have traditionally placed great emphasis on the distinction between "capital gains" and other types of income because of the unique preferential treatment given to income realized in the form of capital gains. Any gain realized on the disposition of property is income and is generally included in gross income. However, prior to January 1, 1987, an individual taxpayer who reported a net capital gain in a given year was allowed a deduction equal to 60 percent of such gain. Thus, in effect only 40 percent of the income realized in the form of a net capital gain was taxable.

Capital gains of corporations were also given preferential treatment, being subject to a tax rate not to exceed 28%, even though the maximum corporate rate on other types of income was 46%. These extraordinarily beneficial rules were a powerful motivation for taxpayers. A major goal of tax planning was to ensure that the maximum amount of income was realized in the form of capital gains. On the other hand, a corporation could not deduct any part of a net capital loss, and an individual could offset only $3,000 of net capital loss against other types of income each year. (The capital loss limitations remain unchanged by the 1986 Act.)

For gains recognized after 1986, the 60 percent deduction is no longer applicable, so that capital gains are included in taxable income in the same way as all other taxable income. However, for 1987 the maximum tax rate on capital gains of both corporations and individuals is limited to 28%, even though other income may be taxed at a higher rate. Thus, there is still an incentive to have income classified as capital gain. The rules relating to capital losses are unchanged from those prior to the Tax Reform Act, so it remains necessary to separate capital gains and losses from other types of income. (In addition, the Act requires that taxpayers continue to make the distinction because the law may be changed again in the future.)

While the detailed rules governing net capital gains are not covered until Chapter 15, briefly a net capital gain arises from the sale of exchange of a capital asset that has been held for more than six months. The usual capital assets are those assets held for investment, such as corporate stocks and bonds and undeveloped land, as opposed to ordinary assets that are held for use in a trade or business.

Passive Activity Income Versus Other Income

As previously discussed in this chapter, the Tax Reform Act of 1986 included complex provisions designed to curb the perceived abuse of beneficial tax rules. An especially important provision in that Act, intended to curb the use of tax shelters, is the disallowance of net "passive activity" losses.

In any taxable year the deduction of losses (negative income) from passive activities is limited to profits from other passive activities. The nuances of this provision result, in effect, in a four-way classification of income for individuals, trusts, estates, and certain corporations that are classified as closely held or as personal service corporations. These categories of income are:

1. Income from passive activities
2. Income from nonpassive activities
3. Portfolio income
4. Compensation

Although the details of these classifications and their significance are discussed in later chapters, a brief overview will indicate the nature of each category and the importance of properly classifying income and losses.

PASSIVE ACTIVITY INCOME OR LOSS   Passive activity income or loss arises from a business activity in which the taxpayer is an investor but is not involved in operations on a regular, continuous, and substantial basis. (The question of what constitutes a trade or business is discussed in Chapter 7.) Thus, generally a limited partner in a limited partnership will have income or loss from a passive activity. (However, if the limited partner is paid, by way of salary, guaranteed payment, or allocation of partnership profit for performing services, such payments are not passive activity income.) Even a sole proprietorship would have passive activity income if the proprietor did not have regular, continuous, and substantial involvement in the operations of the business. Generally, income or loss from rental activity is passive activity income or loss for this purpose. Gains and losses on sales of investments in assets, income from which is treated as passive activity income, are themselves classified as passive activity income for purposes of applying the passive activity loss rules. A net loss from one passive activity can be offset against the net income from other passive activities, but generally it cannot be offset against nonpassive activity income, portfolio income, or compensation.

NONPASSIVE ACTIVITY INCOME   This income classification represents income earned in a trade or business in which the taxpayer "materially participates." Material participation involves taking part in operations, including management, on a regular, continuous, and substantial basis. Thus, the typical sole proprietor who runs a business will have income or loss from a nonpassive activity. Also, a general partner who takes an active continuing role in a partnership will likely be deemed to have nonpassive activity income from the partnership.

PORTFOLIO INCOME   Portfolio income generally includes interest, dividends, and royalties. It also includes gain or loss attributable to disposition of (1) property that is held for investment (and that is not an investment in a passive activity) and (2) property that normally produces interest, dividend, and royalty income. Losses from a passive activity cannot be offset against portfolio income.

COMPENSATION   Compensation represents salaries, wages, commissions, and so on, received for rendering personal services to an employer. Losses from a passive activity cannot generally be offset against income from compensation.

To illustrate the importance of proper classification of income, assume that during 1987 an individual taxpayer received interest and dividends of $50,000 on corporate investments. This income was classified as portfolio income. Her share of loss from a limited partnership in which she took no active role was $26,000, and her share of income from rental property was $16,000. The taxpayer may offset $16,000 of the loss from the limited partnership against her rental income of $26,000 because both of these are passive activities. However, the remaining $10,000 of loss from the partnership cannot be offset against her portfolio income. Prior to 1987 the entire passive activity loss could have been offset against her portfolio income. As discussed in Chapter 4, any passive activity loss not allowed in the current year can be forwarded to future years.

As you will see in later chapters there are numerous other ways in which incomes and losses are classified for tax purposes, often in contradictory ways.

PROBLEMS

1. What are the major obstacles to using the economic concept of income as a measure of income for accounting and for tax purposes?

2. Briefly describe the "consumption expenditures" approach to income measurement. Is it suitable as a basis for taxation? Explain.

3. Imagine that you are a special agent from the I.R.S. investigating the tax affairs of a notorious gambler. You have decided that the net-worth method must be used. Develop a list of the information you would need and the sources of such information.

4. It has been suggested that businesses should be permitted to "deflate" their reported income by "price-level" adjustments. How would this action affect the relative tax burden of wage earners as opposed to businesses?

5. Explain the "wherewithal-to-pay" concept.

6. Define the word "realization" as it is used in *accounting*. Now define the word as it is used in *taxation*.

7. What are the major factors that cause differences between accounting income and taxable income?

8. What is meant by the term "recognition" in taxation?

9. Is *realization* necessary for *recognition* of income for tax purposes?

10. In general, what income is to be included in gross income for tax purposes?

11. How does the wherewithal-to-pay concept affect income recognition for tax purposes?

12. Why is "administrative convenience" important in the definition and measurement of gross income?

13. What is the rationale underlying the general rule that prepaid income is taxed in the year of receipt, even for an accrual-basis taxpayer?

14. Explain the rationale that exclusion of some amount—for example, $500—of interest each year would increase the rate of savings by individuals.

15. Rosman does a lot of baby-sitting while attending college. During the current year, Rosman received the following for baby-sitting services rendered:

Cash	$3,000
Clothing	500*
Room	1,200*

*Estimated fair market value.

What amount of income has Rosman realized for federal income tax purposes?

16. What special tax problems do employee perquisites create? Consider, for example, such prequisites as a company car; airline employee passes; health, accident, and life insurance coverage; the executive jet; and club memberships.

17. Taxpayer B borrowed $5,000 cash from City National Bank. What income, if any, has taxpayer B realized? Explain briefly.

18. Taxpayer L found a $100 bill on a New York City street. Does L have any income because of his "find"? If so, has that income been realized?

19. Corporation DEF discovered a large oil deposit (worth $20 million) on its lands. Does DEF have any income? If so, has that income been realized? (Assume that DEF has *not* extracted any of this oil.)

20. From your general knowledge of current income tax developments, do you think federal tax laws passed in the last two years have reflected economic goals? Explain.

21. The local independent school board pays individual W $10 per week to transport her children to school in her own car because the school's bus does not pass anywhere close to W's home. Does W have any income? If so, has that income been realized?

22. In recent years, much has been written about the "underground economy." What is meant by this term? Why has the underground economy been created?

23. It has been suggested that homeowners should be required to include in gross income the rental value of their homes. What practical and theoretical arguments can be given against this proposal?

24. What is meant by the term "completed transaction"?

25. Why do "tax shelters" exist? How do they affect tax laws?

26. Tom T. Mouse, a university student 22 years of age, lives with his parents who provide Tom a room, food, laundry, etc., free of charge (although these items have a fair market value of $6,500) during 19X7. Tom earned $1,000 in cash from a part-time job. Also, in return for setting up a set of accounting records for a neighbor's business, Tom was given a television with a fair market value of $450. Tom received no cash for this work and did not expect to receive anything for it. During the year Tom's uncle gave him 100 shares of C corporation stock. On the date of the gift, the stock had a fair market value of $32 per share. Later in the year, the uncle died and Tom inherited property worth $64,700.
   a. What is the amount of Tom's "economic income"?
   b. What is the amount of his income for taxation purposes?

CHAPTER 4

Deductions: General Concepts

As explained in Chapter 3, the income tax is levied against taxable income, a statutory and legalistic quantity determined by subtracting authorized deductions from gross income. These deductions are spawned by such diverse forces as accounting concepts, common sense, tradition, politics, social justice, and administrative convenience, and they are as complex as the forces that created them. The advocates of new deductions inevitably forecast, as in the headnote to this chapter, the dawn of a new and better world if Congress will but grant their request.

The term *deductions*, as used in federal income taxation, can be defined only procedurally—for example, as those items that collectively constitute the difference between the quantity called *gross income* and the quantity called *taxable income*. A few considerations implicit in this purely procedural definition are, however, important. Note that the two quantifications—gross income and taxable income—describe purely legalistic quantities; outside the realm of federal income taxation, neither quantity has particular meaning. It is a widely accepted notion in federal income taxation that *nothing is deductible unless authorized by the Code or the regulations.*

At this point, a well-grounded student of accounting is apt to have misgivings. Apparently, income is itself a net concept, generally conceded to be the difference between properly matched revenues and expenses for some arbitrary time period. Thus, we imply that all "properly matched expenses" must be "deductions" for purposes of determining income. Ignoring possible differences in timing—that is, ignoring the accounting refinements common to the "matching concept"—the accounting student's intuition is only partially correct for matters of federal income taxation. In general, most of the items that would fall into the accountant's "expenses" classification are also "deductions" for tax purposes; in addition, however, the Code provides for many other deductions in the calculation of taxable income. Thus, the term *deduction* is a much broader, more generic and legalistic term than *expense*. This is especially true for the individual taxpayer, although the comment also has limited relevance for the corporate taxpayer.

The deductions allowed a corporation are all considered to be business deductions and are roughly comparable to the expenses that appear on its annual income statement prepared in accordance with generally accepted accounting principles. This generalization also applies to the computation of taxable income from a sole proprietorship or partnership. There are, however, numerous and major exceptions to the general rule. Some of these exceptions relate only to differences in the timing of deductions; others involve the aggregate amount deducted in the long run. In this chapter, we examine some of the more important differences between "tax deductions" and "accounting expenses." In addition, a general discussion of the deductions granted to individual taxpayers is presented, although detailed consideration of such deductions is deferred until later chapters.

The allowable deductions may be grouped into three broad categories:

1. Deductions applicable to a trade or business, including an employee's business-related expenses

2. "Nonbusiness" deductions related to production of "nonbusiness" income

3. Purely personal deductions specifically provided for individual taxpayers

THE BASIC AUTHORIZATION: THE REVENUE CODE

In order to deduct any item, the taxpayer must be able to point to some provision of the Code that authorizes the deduction. It is not necessary that the statute list the specific item by name, but the item must clearly fall under one of the provisions of the law. In this regard, a mere reading of the Code may not reveal whether or not an item is deductible, because Treasury Regulations, Revenue Rulings, and court decisions constantly interpret the meaning of the statute. The knowledge of these *interpretations,* therefore, constitutes the real stock in trade of the tax practitioner.[1]

The Code provides for a multitude of deductions for very dissimilar items, including losses, expenses, and "special" items not necessarily involving monetary outlays. These provisions can be usefully divided into two major categories—the general (or universal) provisions and the specific deduction authorizations.

The General Provisions

Two Code sections that serve as the general basis for deductions are Sec. 162, Expenses of Carrying on a Trade or Business, and Sec. 212, Expenses for Production of Income. In addition, as discussed on page 4-7, Sec. 165 permits a deduction for losses incurred in a trade or business or in any transaction entered into for a profit. The importance of these sections warrants a closer examination of the three provisions.

EXPENSES OF TRADE OR BUSINESS   The broadest provision pertaining to deductions—and, incidentally, the provision that comes closest to approximating the expense concept in accounting—is located in Sec. 162(a), which reads in part as follows:

> (a) In General.—There shall be allowed as a deduction all the ordinary and necessary expenses paid or incurred during the taxable year in carrying on any trade or business, including—
> (1) a reasonable allowance for salaries or other compensation for personal services actually rendered;
> (2) traveling expenses (including amounts expended for meals and lodging other than amounts which are lavish or extravagant under the circumstances) while away from home in the pursuit of a trade or business; and
> (3) rentals or other payments required to be made as a condition to the continued use or possession, for purposes of the trade or business, of property to which the taxpayer has not taken or is not taking title or in which he has no equity.

Although these general words may suggest to the unsuspecting taxpayer (or student) that virtually every "business expense" is deductible, an investigation of the interpretation given these words by tax administrators and courts would not support such a conclusion.

The definitional boundaries of a "trade or business," although they are of particular importance to the individual taxpayer, are as elusive as the

---

[1]Every would-be tax advisor should be thoroughly familiar with one or more of the excellent loose-leaf tax services, which are the only way to maintain a complete and current compilation of the changing legislation and of new court interpretations. These services are discussed in Chapter 23.

definitions of "ordinary" and "necessary." The intention to make a profit is necessary; the actuality of a profit is not. On the other hand, the intention to make a profit is not a sufficient condition. Many transactions and business ventures are profit-oriented, but they may not constitute a trade or business for tax purposes. Rather, some personal effort of an entrepreneurial nature must exist before any income-producing activity can be said to constitute a trade or business. This distinction is particularly difficult to draw with relatively passive investment ventures. Thus, the ownership of a single rental unit has been found not to constitute a business.

A second major problem arises in determining whether a particular venture constitutes a trade or business or whether it is a hobby. Many taxpayers, particularly those of financial means, enjoy such expensive endeavors as building racing automobiles, breeding racehorses, and feeding beef cattle. Obviously, such endeavors may be sound and profitable business ventures. When a taxpayer consistently reports losses, however, the tax administrators suspect that the real motivation is purely personal enjoyment rather than a desire to conduct a profitable business. Whenever the I.R.S. can prove its suspicions, a host of otherwise deductible expenses is lost. These cases are obviously difficult ones and are often brought to the courts for adjudication. Section 183 prohibits a net loss deduction from a "hobby."[2] Further, it provides that, unless the I.R.S. establishes to the contrary, an activity is presumed to be engaged in for profit if the gross income for three or more out of five consecutive tax years (two out of seven years if the activity is horse breeding, racing, showing, and so on) exceeds the deductions attributable to the activity. However, if the gross income from the activity does not exceed expenses for at least three out of five consecutive years, it is *not* automatically presumed that the activity is not engaged in for profit. Even for a hobby, expenses are generally deductible to the extent of the gross income from the hobby.

A few employee expenses also are allowable as deductions under Sec. 162. Generally, the employee must be able to demonstrate that any business expenses deducted are directly related to the performance of duties or are required by an employment agreement. Nonreimbursed costs of special clothing not suitable for off-duty wear, union dues, tools of trade, and membership dues of professional employees in professional organizations are typical examples of such employee expenses. Travel, transportation, and entertainment are also frequently encountered employee business expenses. The Code and the Regulations are rather precise in describing the purpose and nature of costs that may be deducted as travel, transportation, and entertainment, and the Regulations specify the nature of records that must be maintained when such expenses are claimed. Entertainment expenses in particular are often held to be personal expenditures and therefore not

---

[2]Of course, some expenses such as taxes are deductible even though the activity is considered a hobby. Other expenses of a hobby are deductible only to the extent that the gross income from the activity exceeds the expenses, such as interest and taxes, otherwise deductible.

deductible. Although the I.R.S. requirements are frequently criticized, when it comes to travel and entertainment there is obviously a fine line between bona fide business costs and personal expenditures by either an employee or a self-employed individual. Again, the tests of reasonableness, necessity, appropriateness, and "direct business connection" are crucial in deciding whether an item is or is not deductible.[3]

Obviously, the difficulty created by allowing deductions of this type lies in the rather arbitrary distinction between what constitutes a cost of earning income and what constitutes a personal expense. It might be argued, for example, that every person employed outside the home incurs extra costs because of his or her job. The cost of commuting to work, the extra expense incurred in eating restaurant meals, the additional costs of wearing appropriate clothing and of personal grooming all result from the taxpayer's employment, but they are all considered personal expenses.

In Chapter 13, the distinction between business-related expenses and nondeductible personal expenditures is examined in some detail.

EXPENSES FOR PRODUCTION OF INCOME   As already explained, many business-oriented activities do not qualify as a trade or business for tax purposes because no personal effort of an "entrepreneurial nature" is involved. Until the Revenue Act of 1942, taxpayers were frequently denied deductions for expenses related to these income-producing activities because they did not qualify as a "trade or business." For example, in 1941 the U.S. Supreme Court found that expenses incurred by a wealthy taxpayer to maintain an office for the purpose of managing his securities and real estate were not those of a trade or business and were, therefore, nondeductible personal expenses.[4] Following this decision, Congress enacted the first two paragraphs of the current Sec. 212. (The third paragraph, relating to deduction of expenses related to taxes, was incorporated later by the Revenue Act of 1954.) The current section reads as follows:

> Sec. 212. Expenses for Production of Income.
> In the case of an individual, there shall be allowed as a deduction all the ordinary and necessary expenses paid or incurred during the taxable year—
> (1) for the production or collection of income;
> (2) for the management, conservation, or maintenance of property held for the production of income; or
> (3) in connection with the determination, collection, or refund of any tax.

This section makes many income-related expenses deductible even though not incurred in a trade or business. For example, an expense attributable to the renting of a single property may not be deductible under Sec. 162 because

---

[3]The "directly related to business" tests are prescribed for entertainment expenses in Code Sec. 274 and Reg. 1.274-2.
[4]*Higgins v. Commissioner,* 312 U.S. 212 (1941).

such limited rental activity does not constitute a trade or business. Nevertheless, Sec. 212(2) authorizes such a deduction. The Regulations help delineate what is meant by "production of income." Regulation 1.212-1(b) states in part:

> The term "income" for the purpose of section 212 includes not merely income of the taxable year but also income which the taxpayer has realized in a prior taxable year or may realize in subsequent taxable years; and is not confined to recurring income but applies as well to gains from the disposition of property. For example, if defaulted bonds, the interest from which if received would be includible in income, are purchased with the expectation of realizing capital gain on their resale, even though no current yield thereon is anticipated, ordinary and necessary expenses thereafter paid or incurred in connection with such bonds are deductible. Similarly, ordinary and necessary expenses paid or incurred in the management, conservation, or maintenance of a building devoted to rental purposes are deductible notwithstanding that there is actually no income therefrom in the taxable year, and regardless of the manner in which or the purpose for which the property in question was acquired. Expenses paid or incurred in managing, conserving, or maintaining property held for investment may be deductible under section 212 even though the property is not currently productive and there is no likelihood that the property will be sold at a profit or will otherwise be productive of income and even though the property is held merely to minimize a loss with respect thereto. . . .

Section 212 is the primary authority for the deduction of such expenses as safety deposit box rental and investment counsel fees that relate to investments in securities that produce taxable income. Many other expenses associated with property or an activity intended to produce income are also deductible under Sec. 212. In determining whether any expense is deductible, the major consideration is whether it is related to an activity entered into with the hope of making a profit or merely engaged in for pleasure or personal reasons.

DEDUCTIONS FOR LOSSES   The general authorization for the deduction of losses is found in Sec. 165(a), which reads as follows:

> There shall be allowed as a deduction any loss sustained during the taxable year and not compensated for by insurance or otherwise.

Subsection 165(c), however, restricts the general provision for individual taxpayers as follows:

> In the case of an individual, the deduction under subsection (a) shall be limited to—
> (1) losses incurred in a trade or business;
> (2) losses incurred in any transaction entered into for profit, though not connected with a trade or business; and
> (3) losses of property not connected with a trade or business, if such losses arise from fire, storm, shipwreck, or other casualty, or from theft. . . .

Again, we observe the same three-way classification of losses incurred by an individual taxpayer: that is, a loss may be (1) incurred in a full-fledged trade or business, (2) incurred in a "nonbusiness" but profit-oriented transaction, or (3) incurred in a purely personal connection. In the event of losses to purely personal properties, no deduction is allowed unless the loss is attributable to a casualty or a theft.

Unfortunately, each set of facts is to some extent unique, and to determine whether or not any particular loss is deductible it may be necessary to determine the taxpayer's intent and motive for entering into a particular transaction. This is a difficult, if not impossible, task in many cases. Limited application of this often troublesome Code provision is examined in later chapters. A few special rules, however, should be noted at this early juncture. For example, the I.R.S. generally maintains that many anticipatory expenditures cannot be deducted as losses unless a taxpayer has already established himself or herself as being "in business." Thus, expenditures for travel incurred by a taxpayer to investigate the possibility of opening a *new* business may be denied. However, to confuse the issue, the I.R.S. has ruled that if a person attempts to acquire a *specific* business or investment and the attempt fails, expenses related to the attempt may be capitalized and deducted as losses. (Further, the taxpayer may, under Sec. 195, elect to capitalize "start-up" costs that would otherwise be deductible and amortize them over a period of not less than 60 months.) Losses of anticipated gains are similarly denied; only actual losses sustained (measured by the adjusted "cost" of the property) can be deducted. Losses must be those of the taxpayer before a deduction can be granted. The other subsections of Sec. 165 are of less general interest, although they, too, deal with deductible losses.

GENERAL PROVISIONS: POSITIVE CRITERIA   In both Secs. 162 and 212 (but not in Sec. 165), the terms "ordinary" and "necessary" are used. In addition, Sec. 162 contains a "reasonableness" test. The meaning of each of these words in income taxation differs somewhat from customary usage. An expense need not recur frequently to be *ordinary*. In fact, an expenditure may be labeled an ordinary expense for tax purposes if no more than, say, one in 100 taxpayers ever incurs the expense and if he or she incurs it only once in a lifetime. The essence of the ordinary criterion seems to be that it would be commonplace among other taxpayers who find themselves in comparable circumstances. In the usual meaning of the term, the "comparable circumstances" may indeed be extraordinary. In the case of *Welch v. Helvering*, the Court, struggling with the meaning of the word "ordinary," said that "the decisive distinctions are those of degree and not of kind. One struggles in vain for any verbal formula that will supply a ready touchstone. The standard set up by the statute is not a rule of law; it is rather a way of life. Life in all its fullness must supply the answer to the riddle."[5]

[5]290 U.S. 111 (1933), pp. 114–15.

To be *necessary,* an expense must be capable of making a contribution to a trade or business. Fortunately for the taxpayer, the courts and tax administrators do not insist that necessity be determined on an *ex post* basis; it is sufficient if the expense appeared to be necessary when it was incurred. The courts generally do not second-guess business people on the necessity of making expenditures. As a practical matter, therefore, this positive criterion is probably the least significant of those considered. When invoked, it frequently relates to illegal activities. For example, fines paid for overweight trucks were found to be unnecessary, to frustrate public policy, and therefore to be nondeductible.[6]

Finally, even an ordinary and necessary expense incurred in a trade or business or in connection with the production of income must be *reasonable in amount* before it can be deducted for tax purposes. Technically, this requirement is stated in Sec. 162(a)(1) only in relation to compensation, but the courts have found that "the element of reasonableness was inherent in the phrase 'ordinary and necessary.'"[7] As a practical matter, the reasonableness criterion is important most frequently for related taxpayers. For example, a corporation may attempt to pay its sole stockholder–executive (or his or her children) an unreasonably large salary, interest, or rental payment. If allowed, these expenses could disguise payments that in reality are dividends —a result of particular importance since dividends, unlike business expenses, are not deductible to the corporation paying them. Therefore, the I.R.S. constantly screens transactions between related parties to determine their reasonableness.

GENERAL PROVISIONS: NEGATIVE CRITERIA   In addition to the positive criteria, there exist four negative criteria that must also be satisfied before any unspecified expense may be tax deductible. Any expenditure not specifically authorized as a deduction is disallowed if it is *purely personal,* a *capital expenditure, related to tax-exempt income,* or *contrary to public policy.* The Code sections pertaining to nondeductible expenses in general include:

> Sec. 262. Personal, living, and family expenses.
> Sec. 263. Capital expenditures.
> Sec. 265. Expenses and interest relating to tax-exempt income.
> Sec. 162. (Expenses contrary to public policy.)

In addition, many other Code provisions prohibit such specific expenses as selected taxes (Sec. 275). As explained earlier, our concern at this point is limited to the provisions of more general application.

Personal, living, and family expenses.   Section 262 states that "except as otherwise expressly provided in this chapter, no deduction shall be allowed for personal, living, or family expenses." In light of the earlier discussion, all

---

[6]*Hoover Motor Express Co., Inc. v. United States,* 356 U.S. 38 (1958).
[7]*Commissioner v. Lincoln Electric Co.,* 176 F.2d 815 (6th Cir., 1949), p. 815.

expenses must be categorized as either (1) directly related to a trade or business, (2) related to a profit-making venture that is not a trade or business, or (3) incurred without any intention of profit. Only the last category, the purely personal expenses, are categorically disallowed unless some section of the law specifically provides for their deduction. The difficulty in everyday tax practice, of course, comes in categorizing actual expenses. The problem of hobby losses is again pertinent.

Capital outlays. Section 263(a) states that

> No deduction shall be allowed for—
> (1) any amount paid out for new buildings or for permanent improvements or betterments made to increase the value of any property or estate. . . . [or]
> (2) any amount expended in restoring property or in making good the exhaustion thereof for which an allowance is or has been made.

(The omitted portion of Sec. 263 recognizes that other Code provisions specifically authorize the immediate deduction of a number of expenditures that could be classified as capital expenditures and requires capitalization of specific items.) Any student acquainted with intermediate accounting is well aware of the practical difficulties in determining whether or not a particular expenditure is a "capital expenditure" or a "revenue expenditure." In general, the tax solutions to such riddles parallel the accounting solutions; therefore, no detailed consideration of them is presented here.

However, the mere fact that a capital outlay is not deductible at the time of the outlay does not prevent its recovery (deduction against income) at a later date through depreciation, amortization, depletion, or other cost-recovery techniques.

Expenses related to tax-exempt income. Section 265 disallows a deduction for any interest or other expense that is paid or incurred in order to realize tax-exempt income. This provision closes a loophole that would otherwise exist for persons in high tax brackets. Without this provision, a person in a top tax bracket might, because of income taxation, actually obtain a positive cash flow by borrowing high-interest money and investing it in low-interest state or local obligations. To illustrate, let us assume that a taxpayer in the 38.5% marginal tax bracket borrowed $1 million at 12% and invested the proceeds in a 10% state bond issue. The annual interest expense would amount to $120,000, which without Sec. 265, would reduce the borrower's tax liability by $46,200 (38.5% of $120,000). The tax-exempt interest earned on the state bonds would amount to $100,000, thus producing a net positive cash flow of $26,200 per year to the taxpayer. As stated above, Sec. 265 prevents this kind of tax legerdemain.

Expenses contrary to public policy. Prior to the 1969 Tax Reform Act, no statutory authority specifically disallowed such "expenses" as bribes, kickbacks, and fines. Nevertheless, the courts frequently disallowed such expenses on the grounds that allowing the deduction would frustrate public policy, and taxpayers were frequently required to go to court to determine whether various items were contrary to public policy. Now, Sec. 162 specifies several types of expenditures that controvert public policy and are disallowed:

1. Fines or penalties for violation of law.
2. Illegal bribes or kickbacks paid to public officials.
3. A portion (usually two thirds) of treble damages paid under antitrust laws in criminal proceedings.
4. Payments such as kickbacks and bribes other than to government officials and employees if such payments are illegal under any generally enforced United States or state law providing for a criminal penalty or loss of license or privilege to engage in trade or business.
5. Any kickback, rebate, or bribe under medicare or medicaid.

Kickbacks, bribes, and so on, other than those specified above, would still be deductible if ordinary and necessary. Payments to foreign government officials are not deductible if such payments violate U.S. laws.

However, the addition of these provisions does not solve all the questions involving public policy. The boundaries of this prohibition are particularly difficult to specify because the courts have consistently held that expenses are deductible even if the income that the expense produces is illegal. For example, the expenses incurred by a gambler are deductible for tax purposes even if the gambler operates his business in a state that prohibits gambling. In a way, this is only equitable, because the illegal income is fully taxable. On the other hand, the granting of the deduction does make the activity more profitable (after taxes) and to that extent serves to controvert the laws of the state.

In sum, then, an expense is ordinarily deductible in the computation of taxable income if it either is authorized by a specific Code section or satisfies eight general criteria. An unspecified expense may be deducted if it is

1. Ordinary
2. Necessary
3. Reasonable in amount
4. Incurred in connection with a trade or business or in the production of income

and if it is *not*

5. A capital expenditure
6. A personal expenditure
7. Related to tax-exempt income
8. Contrary to public policy

The Specific Provisions

In addition to the general provision under Sec. 162 discussed above, Part VI of Subchapter B authorizes almost 30 specific deductions in Secs. 163–191. Some of these are of general importance; for example,

Sec. 163. Interest.
Sec. 164. Taxes.
Sec. 167. Depreciation.
Sec. 168. Accelerated cost recovery systems.
Sec. 170. Charitable, etc., contributions and gifts.

On the other hand, several sections apply to very few taxpayers; for example,

Sec. 184. Amortization of certain railroad rolling stock.
Sec. 186. Recoveries of damages for antitrust violations, etc.
Sec. 188. Amortization of certain expenditures for child-care facilities.
Sec. 192. Contributions to Black Lung Benefit Trust.

Most deductions are like the expenses appearing on published financial statements. On the surface, then, there is apparently little problem in determing either the nature or the amounts of items that may be deducted as business expenses. Unfortunately for the student, this is not always true. A detailed examination of each Code section in Part VI of Subchapter B would yield the usual list of exceptions, exceptions to exceptions, limitations, and special definitions. Many of these specific deductions will be examined in detail in subsequent chapters of this text.

LIMITS ON DEDUCTIONS AND LOSSES   Section 162 states that there "shall be allowed as a deduction ALL the ordinary and necessary expenses paid or incurred . . . in carrying on a trade or business," Section 212 provides that ALL ordinary and necessary expenses related to nonbusiness income shall be deductible. And Section 165 ostensibly makes possible the deduction of "ANY loss sustained during the taxable year and not compensated for. . . ." However, one should not be misled by this seemingly *all*-inclusive language. As we have already seen, some expenses, even though they are incurred in trade or business, are disallowed entirely. In addition, there are many limitations on individual deductions, groups of deductions, and losses, even though the items involved meet the general requirements for deductibility. Representative limitations are illustrated below.

Limitations on specific deductions.   Both the Code and Regulations place limits on the amounts that may be deducted for certain individual items. Often these limitations in effect specify the maximum amount considered "ordinary and reasonable." A few important examples are given.

1. Corporations may deduct charitable contributions only to the extent of 10% of taxable income determined before the contributions deduction and certain other deductions. For example, if a corporation had taxable income of $100,000 before deducting charitable contributions and during the year had made charitable contributions of $25,000, a contributions deduction of $10,000 would be allowed for the year. The excess $15,000 not allowed could be carried forward to the five succeeding years and treated as contributions made in those years.

2. Deductions by employers for contributions paid to employee pension and profit-sharing plans are limited to a percentage of salaries and other compensation paid to "covered employees" during the year. For example, the

deduction for contributions to profit-sharing plans is generally limited to 15% of compensation. (Prior to the 1986 Tax Reform Act, the employer could contribute up to 25% of compensation to the plan and any excess of contributions made over the amount deductible could be carried forward to future years. This is no longer permissible after 1986.) Thus, if a corporation had covered compensation of $1,000,000 during a tax year and made contributions of $200,000 to a profit-sharing plan, only $150,000 would be deductible. The remaining $50,000 could be carried over and added to contributions made in the succeeding year. There is no limit on the number of years that such excesses can be carried forward.

3. For years after 1986, generally only 80% of business-meal and business-entertainment expenses will be deductible under the 1986 Act. This includes the cost of meals furnished by an employer to employees on the employer's premises as well as costs of meals for employees traveling away from home. The 20% disallowed is never deductible.

4. A limit is placed on the amount of "investment interest" that can be deducted by a noncorporate taxpayer. For our purpose, investment interest can be defined as interest related to all income-producing activities of the taxpayer that (1) are not subject to the passive-activity loss limitation and (2) are not trade or business activities in which the taxpayer materially partici-pates. For years beginning in 1991, the investment interest deductible will be limited to the amount of "net investment income" (income from investments to which investment interest applies, minus deductible expenses related to that income). For example, if in 1991 the taxpayer paid investment interest of $45,000 and had net investment income (disregarding interest) of $9,000, only $9,000 of the interest would be deductible. The taxpayer would be allowed to carry forward the disallowed interest of $36,000 and treat it as investment interest incurred in subsequent years.

For years prior to 1987, the amount of investment interest deductible in a year was limited to the total of net investment income plus $10,000. For tax years 1987 through 1990, there is a rather complex phasein of the new limits, discussed in Chapter 10.

Limitations on losses.   There are limits on several specific types of losses. One of these provisions, which has been in the law for many years, limits the amount of net *capital loss* deductible by an individual taxpayer to only $3,000 per year. In other words, only $3,000 of net capital loss can be offset against other types of income in a year by an individual. Any net capital loss not used up in achieving the net deduction of $3,000 may be carried forward to subsequent years until exhausted. (Corporations are not permitted to offset any net capital loss against other income. A net capital loss may be carried back three years and then forward for five years by a corporation.)

Several limitations have been established to curb taxpayers from taking unintended benefit of special tax provisions that were designed to encourage taxpayers to engage in certain types of activities, usually to encourage investment in business or income-producing assets. Two of these limitations deserve special mention because they affect many taxpayers.

The first of these limits the loss that a taxpayer may deduct from specified activities to the amount that the taxpayer has "at risk" in an activity. The second is the general prohibition of a deduction for a net loss from passive activities. These two limitations are reviewed below.

The "at-risk" limitation.   In 1976 Congress enacted Sec. 465 containing the "at-risk" rules, designed to limit the deduction allowed to individual taxpayers for losses incurred from certain "tax shelters." The intent was to eliminate artificial tax losses resulting from the use of nonrecourse debt. Nonrecourse debt is a liability secured only by the underlying property in the activity for which the debt was incurred; the debtor has no personal liability for payment of the debt. The original law listed five types of activities (motion picture production and distribution, farming, leasing of personal property, oil and gas exploration and production, and geothermal exploration and exploitation) to which the limitation applied. For years after 1978, the at-risk rules were extended to other trade, business, or income-producing activities, other than real estate rental. The 1986 Act extended the at-risk rules to real estate rental activities.

The amount at risk, which limits the loss deductible from the activity, is generally the amount of money and property contributed by the taxpayer to the activity plus amounts borrowed with respect to the activity, for which the taxpayer is personally liable or which is secured by the taxpayer's property outside the activity (to the extent of the fair market value of such property). The at-risk amount does not include (except in specific circumstances in the case of real estate) amounts secured only by property used in the activity.

For example, suppose that a taxpayer purchased a rental building for $1,000,000, paying the seller $50,000 in cash as a down payment. The remaining $950,000 was secured by a mortgage on the building, payable to the seller. The purchaser had no personal liability for the debt, and no other assets were pledged as security. During the first tax year of ownership, the purchaser incurred a net loss of $80,000 from operating the building. The amount deductible as a loss by the taxpayer that year is limited to $50,000, the amount at risk. The $30,000 not allowed as a deduction that year can be carried forward and treated as a loss allocable to the building in the succeeding year. There is no limit on the number of years the loss can be carried forward.

There are complex rules for determining the amount of loss deductible by partners in partnerships and by shareholders in "S corporations" (which are taxed as partnerships) under the at-risk rules when the partnership or S corporation suffers a loss.

Disallowance of net passive loss.   In Chapter 3, it was pointed out that the 1986 Tax Reform Act disallows ("suspends") the deduction of a net passive loss by individuals, estates, trusts, and certain types of corporations. As a result, it is essential that income be properly classified. For purposes of the passive loss limitation income can be classified into four categories: passive activity income, nonpassive activity income, portfolio income, and compensation for personal services. A net loss from one passive activity can be offset against net income from another passive activity, but a net passive loss cannot be offset against any of the three other types of income. On the other hand, net losses from any source other than a passive activity can be offset against any other type of income.

For example, suppose that in 1987 an individual taxpayer had a loss of $50,000 from one passive activity, a net profit of $32,000 from a second passive activity, and income of $300,000 from salary. The taxpayer may offset $32,000 of the loss from the first passive activity against the $32,000 of net income from the second passive activity. However, the $18,000 of net passive loss cannot be offset against the gross income from salary. It may, however, be carried forward to 1988 and treated as a passive loss in that year or in subsequent years.

On the other hand, if in the above example the taxpayer had a loss of $50,000 from a nonpassive activity, a profit of $32,000 from a passive activity, and income of $300,000 from salary, the taxpayer could generally offset the entire $50,000 loss against the passive income and the salary.

As discussed in Chapter 3, a passive activity is one that involves the conduct of a trade or business in which the taxpayer does not *materially* participate. However, a rental activity is considered to be a passive activity regardless of whether the taxpayer materially participates. In order to be considered materially participating, the taxpayer must be involved in the *operations* of the activity on a regular, continuous, and substantial basis. In considering whether the taxpayer is materially participating, such factors as whether the activity is the taxpayer's principal business activity, how often the taxpayer is at the place where the activity is conducted, and the extent of the taxpayer's knowledge and experience in that type of activity will be considered. Intermittent involvement in management decisions is not considered to be material participation.

Even though rental activities are defined as nonpassive activities, a taxpayer can offset against income from nonpassive sources each year up to $25,000 of net losses from rental of real estate if the taxpayer is *actively* engaged in the activity. Active participation is less demanding than *material* participation. It does not require regular, continuous, and substantial participation. However, it does require that the individual participate in the making of management decisions, such as approving new tenants, deciding on rental terms, approving capital outlays, approving repairs, and so on.

To illustrate these rules, assume that a taxpayer owns and manages three rental buildings. In 1987 the taxpayer incurred a loss of $21,000 on the first building, a loss of $82,000 on the second building, and a profit of $60,000 on the third building. In addition, the taxpayer had gross income from nonpassive business activities of $60,000. The taxpayer can deduct $25,000 of the net real estate rental loss against his other income for the year. The remaining $18,000 of the net rental loss will be suspended in the same way as other passive activity losses.

The $25,000 exception for rental real estate losses is phased out beginning at the point at which the taxpayer's adjusted gross income is $100,000. The amount deductible is reduced by 50% of the amount by which the taxpayer's adjusted gross income from nonpassive sources exceeds $100,000. If, in the above example, the taxpayer's adjusted gross income from nonpassive sources had been $134,000 instead of $60,000, only $8,000 ($25,000, minus one half of $34,000) of the net rental real estate loss would have been deductible against other income in 1987.

If a taxpayer who qualifies for the $25,000 offset for rental real estate losses does not have enough other income against which to offset the $25,000, the otherwise allowable loss is treated as a net operating loss (NOL) arising in that year and can be carried back to prior years and forward to future years in accordance with the rules for NOLs, discussed later in this chapter.

In the year in which a taxpayer's entire interest in an activity is disposed of in a fully taxable transaction, all suspended losses applicable to the interest are recognized and are allowed against any other type of income. Special rules apply when the activity is transferred by gift, death, or in some other nontaxable transaction.

CARRYOVER OF DISALLOWED DEDUCTIONS AND LOSSES   Most of the limitations imposed on specific deductions and losses provide that amounts not deductible in one taxable year can be carried forward (or, in a few instances, back) to other years and deducted in those years. Sometimes the disallowed amounts can be carried to an indefinite number of future years. In other cases there is a limit on the number of years to which the item can be carried; if the amount carried over cannot be fully deducted during that limited carryover period, any unused amount simply expires.

For example, in the preceding discussion of limitations and disallowances of deductions and losses we have seen that charitable contributions made by corporations in excess of the amount deductible in a tax year may be carried forward for only five years, and, if the carryover is not used in that time, the unused amount expires. Similarly, a corporation that has a net capital loss for a year may take the loss back to the three preceding years and offset the loss against any net capital gains in those years. If the loss is not used in full in the three prior years, it may be carried forward to the five years following the loss year. At that point, any unused loss simply expires.

On the other hand, there is no limit on the number of years that disallowed investment interest, excess contributions to a profit-sharing plan, or disallowed passive losses may be carried forward.

One other very important carryback and carryover is of interest at this point. Under Code Sec. 172, a "net operating loss" (essentially the net loss from the taxpayer's trade or business) can be allowed as a deduction against income of other years. The NOL is carried back and offset against income of the third year preceding the year in which the loss occurred. Any amount not used in the third prior year is then offset against income of the second year and then against income of the first year preceding the loss. Any amount of loss still unused is then carried forward, generally for up to 15 more years, in order, after the loss year. Thus, the net operating loss of a tax year can affect a total of 18 other years. The taxpayer may, however, elect (irrevocably) to relinquish the carryback right and only carry the loss forward for 15 years.

DEDUCTIONS: PERSONAL DEDUCTIONS FOR INDIVIDUALS

Earlier in this chapter, we noted that deductions allowable under the federal income tax laws may be classified into three groups:

1. Expenses and losses incurred in a trade or business
2. Expenses and losses related to nonbusiness production of income
3. Personal deductions for individuals

The general characteristics of the first two groups have been explained in the preceding discussion. In the remainder of this chapter we briefly review the general types of purely personal deductions allowed to individual taxpayers. You are urged to resist the temptation to become enmeshed in details at this point. The detailed provisions are examined in much greater depth in subsequent chapters.

1. Large, unusual, involuntary personal expenditures
2. Deductions that amount to subsidies to specific groups
3. Taxes paid to local and state governments
4. Personal and dependent exemption deductions

Large, Unusual, Involuntary Expenses

The tax laws recognize that unusually large expenditures or losses beyond the control of the taxpayer effectively reduce available income and, thus, wherewithal to pay a tax. Equity suggests that consideration be given to these expenditures in computing the tax liability by permitting deduction of that portion of the expense or loss deemed to be unusual or excessive. Perhaps the two most meaningful applications of this concept are the deductions for medical expenses and casualty losses.

Unreimbursed medical costs paid by the taxpayer for himself or his dependents generally are deductible only to the extent that they exceed 7.5% of "adjusted gross income." (Adjusted gross income, commonly called A.G.I., is a technical concept examined in Chapter 9.) Medical costs include such items as physicians' charges, dental care costs, hospital charges, the cost of nursing care, hospitalization insurance premiums, costs for travel necessary to obtain medical care, and the costs of insulin and prescription drugs and medicines.

The 7.5% rule related to medical costs presumes that a limited amount of such items constitutes normal living costs of a personal nature and that only the abnormal or unusual costs in excess of this norm should be deductible.

A similar provision applies to losses of the taxpayer's property from fire, storm, or other casualty, or from theft. Unreimbursed loss in excess of $100 from each such involuntary conversion may be treated as a casualty loss. The total of all such excesses over $100 for each casualty may be deducted only to the extent that the total exceeds 10% of the taxpayer's adjusted gross income for the year.

Two problems encountered in allowing the deduction of such expenses and losses immediately become apparent. First, which of the many possible losses shall be made deductible? Second, what amount shall be considered "normal"? These questions are examined in Chapter 10.

Deductions That Amount to Subsidies

A number of deductions of a personal nature have been introduced into the Code to achieve desired economic, social, and other objectives. In effect, these deductions provide subsidies for specific groups. Two of the more important of these deductions are for charitable contributions and for interest paid.

Section 170 provides that contributions, up to 50% of the taxpayer's A.G.I., made to qualified organizations—primarily organizations formed for religious, charitable, scientific, or educational purposes; veterans' organizations; and governmental units—may be deducted. Obviously, this provision is intended to encourage giving to worthwhile groups, but it is also in effect a subsidy to the donee organization because a part of the gift represents an amount that would otherwise have been paid as income tax.

Similarly, until 1987 the taxpayer could deduct almost all interest paid on money borrowed for business, investment, or personal purposes. The major exceptions were the disallowance of interest on money borrowed to purchase tax-free securities and the limit on "investment interest," mentioned earlier. For years beginning after 1986, no deduction will be allowed for a part of "personal interest" paid or accrued during the year except, within specified limits, interest on a debt secured by a mortgage on the taxpayer's principal residence or second residence. For 1987, the portion of personal interest disallowed is 35%. This percentage increases each year until it reaches 100% in 1991. Personal interest is essentially all interest other than that paid or incurred in connection with the conduct of a trade or business (other than as an employee), investment interest, and interest taken into account in computing the taxpayer's income or loss from passive activities.

The allowance of a deduction for interest paid on the taxpayer's residence has been criticized as inequitable because it permits the homeowner to deduct a large portion of his or her monthly mortgage payments as interest but allows no deduction to the tenant, whose monthly rental payments include an interest factor. Thus, in effect, it grants the homeowner a subsidy. The more general argument regarding personal interest is that in many cases interest is a voluntary personal expense incurred solely because the taxpayer is willing to pay interest in order to obtain goods or services—which leaves little reason to treat it as a deduction. The move in the 1986 Tax Reform Act to disallow a deduction for personal interest reflects this general argument. The survival of the allowance for home mortgage interest is probably due in large part to the political influence of the real estate industry, to the continued perception that home ownership is desirable for society, and to the fact that many members of Congress own two homes.

Taxes Paid to Local and State Governments

Certain state and local taxes (primarily property and income taxes) are allowable as personal deductions, largely on the basis that they help the smooth functioning of the federal system of government by making nonfederal taxation less costly to the taxpayer. Prior to 1987, state and local retail sales taxes were also deductible.

Standard Deduction

Beginning in 1987, individual taxpayers are permitted a *standard deduction,* which can be taken *in lieu of* the allowable itemized personal deductions, the deductions permitted under Sec. 212 related to "nonbusiness" income and the nonreimbursed employee expenses allowed under Sec. 162. The amount of the standard deduction depends on the taxpayer's marital status, age, and certain other factors. For 1987 the amounts are generally $3,760 for a married couple filing jointly and $2,540 for a single individual. These amounts are scheduled to increase in 1988 and to be adjusted for inflation after 1988.

For example, if an unmarried person had itemized deductions for taxes, contributions, interest, and so on for 1987 of only $920, he or she would nevertheless be able to deduct the standard deduction of $2,540. On the other hand, if an unmarried person had actual itemized costs of $6,000, the entire amount would be deductible.

The standard deduction existed in the tax law prior to 1977 but was replaced in that year (and until 1987) by the *zero bracket amount,* which achieved the same result by applying a zero tax rate to a specified amount of income (equal to a standard deduction amount.) At the same time, only those itemized deductions in excess of the zero bracket amount were deductible.

For example, in 1986 a single taxpayer with itemized deductions of $6,000 would actually deduct only $3,520 ($6,000 − $2,480, the amount of taxable income subject to a rate of zero for a single person in 1986) in arriving at his or her "taxable income." However, since in 1986 the tax rate was zero on the first $2,480 of taxable income for a single person, the taxpayer was in effect deducting this amount in addition to the $3,520 technically deducted.

On the other hand, if the single taxpayer's itemized deductions were only $920 in 1986, he or she could deduct no part of these costs in arriving at taxable income because they were less than $2,480. Because the first $2,480 of taxable income was subject to a rate of zero in that year, however, the taxpayer was in effect getting the benefit of a $2,480 deduction.

The 1986 Tax Reform Act abolished the zero bracket amount and restored the standard deduction, which is a concept generally easier for both taxpayers and return preparers to understand.

The standard deduction (as well as the zero bracket amount in prior years) provides a tax benefit to low-income taxpayers and to those with small amounts of itemized deductions. It helps relieve many relatively low-income taxpayers from the requirement to file a tax return, thus reducing the administrative burden on both taxpayers and the I.R.S.

Personal Exemptions

In addition to the "itemized" personal deductions or standard deduction just discussed, individual taxpayers are permitted to deduct a specified amount

($1,900 for 1987) for each personal and dependent *exemption.* Conceptually, the personal exemptions permit a basic tax-free living allowance for the taxpayer. The number of exemptions to which an individual is entitled depends on the taxpayer's family situation and other factors. This deduction is discussed in detail in Chapter 7.

The student who pursues a study of taxation will discover that much of the controversy in this field revolves around (1) identifying or selecting the costs that should be deductible in computing taxable income and (2) determining just when these costs should be deductible. In the remaining chapters, we examine several of these problems in detail.

PROBLEMS

1. Section 262 of the 1954 Internal Revenue Code specifically disallows the deduction of "personal, living, and family" expenses. Yet many persons may deduct a purely personal contribution to a local charity. Explain the apparent contradiction.

2. It is conceivable that the cost of a taxpayer's subscription to the *Wall Street Journal* would be tax deductible, whereas the cost of a subscription to the *New York Times* would be disallowed. Explain the fact circumstances that would lead to such a situation. Explain other fact circumstances that might justify the deduction of the cost of a subscription to the *New York Times.*

3. List and explain the general criteria (positive and negative) that may be applied to determine whether many expenditures are deductible or nondeductible.

4. What advantages would accrue to taxpayers if the government would accept as a proper tax deduction any item that could be treated as an expense for financial accounting purposes? What disadvantages to taxpayers would result from such a law?

5. One of the social costs associated with multiple deductions is the complexity of the tax laws. What social advantages accrue to offset this social cost?

6. A number of expenses—for example, estimated guaranty and warranty costs —are estimated and deducted by many businesses in measuring financial income. These items generally may not be deducted on a tax return until they are actually incurred. Accountants often criticize the tax restriction on the grounds that it "mismatches" revenues and expenses. What reasons might be given to support this tax requirement?

7. Some of the most significant (in terms of dollars deducted) "personal deductions" of individual taxpayers are criticized as inequitable subsidies to specific groups. Perhaps the most notorious of these are the deductions for state and local real estate taxes and the deductions for interest paid on home mortgages. Explain why each of these two deductions might be considered inequitable. Why might they be considered desirable?

8. What is meant by the terms *reasonable, ordinary,* and *necessary?*

9. In what fundamental way do the deductions allowed individual taxpayers differ generally from the deductions allowed corporate taxpayers? What forces explain this difference?

10. Distinguish between a tax-deductible "nonbusiness expense" and a nondeductible "personal expense."

11. a. What tax treatment is given expenses of a "hobby"?
    b. How do we distinguish between a hobby and a business venture?

12. Do the "claim of right" and "constructive receipt" doctrines have their counterparts in the rules governing expense deductions? Explain.

13. Distinguish between a "trade or business expense" and a "nonbusiness expense related to income production."

14. The amount of interest deductible on money borrowed to purchase investment property is limited. What is the likely reason for this restriction?

15. What is the likely reason for the existence of the standard deduction?

16. A taxpayer who owns a textile manufacturing plant in New York is visited by an important customer. The taxpayer "wines and dines" this customer and his wife during their stay in New York. Total cost of this entertainment is $900. Is this a reasonable, ordinary, and necessary business expense?

17. Which of the following expenditures do you think would be potentially deductible?
    a. Cost of entertaining customers at a private club by an outside salesperson.
    b. Fines paid by a trucker for inadvertently exceeding the state's maximum weight laws.
    c. Current research and development expenses related to business.
    d. Cost of a personnel director's meals while entertaining prospective employees.
    e. Advertising intended to help defeat specified legislation proposed to the state legislature.
    f. Estimated costs of warranty on products sold during the year.

18. a. Indicate whether or not each of the following expenditures would be potentially deductible by a corporate taxpayer:
    (1) Cost of prizes given away by a television manufacturer as part of a sales contest.
    (2) Cost of uniforms and equipment for company-sponsored baseball team.
    (3) Assessment for benefits paid to union employees during periods of illness.
    (4) Fee paid to speaker to address employees about the importance of voting in an upcoming election.
    (5) Fee paid to speaker in support of a particular candidate in an upcoming election.
    (6) Estimated charge for self-insurance program in lieu of commercial insurance coverage.
    b. Indicate whether or not each of the following expenditures would be potentially deductible by an individual taxpayer:
    (1) Contribution to purchase gift for employee's supervisor.
    (2) Cost of keeping watch in good repair. (Taxpayer is a registered nurse.)
    (3) Penalty for late payment of federal income taxes.
    (4) Interest associated with late payment of federal income taxes.
    (5) Cost of subscription to *Journal of Accountancy* (Taxpayer is employed by local CPA firm.)
    (6) Wages paid caretaker of former residence that is currently listed "for sale or rent."

19. Indicate whether each of the following items is potentially deductible. If only part is deductible, indicate the amount to be deducted.

a. Taxpayer operates a truck on a contract basis. While hauling gravel under a contract, she was stopped for speeding. She paid a fine of $25 for speeding and a fine of $30 for carrying an overweight load.

b. Assume the same facts as in part a, except that the taxpayer is an employee instead of an independent contractor. She was not reimbursed by her employer for either fine.

c. Agnew operates a contracting business. During the year, he gave a member of the city council a new watch, which cost $200. Agnew hopes that the council member "throws some city business" his way.

d. A gambler won $45,000 during the year. To earn this income, however, she incurred expenses for travel and other items totaling $10,200.

20. Indicate whether each of the following items is potentially deductible. If only part is deductible, indicate the amount to be deducted.

a. Stinchcomb, who is an attorney, also operates a farm. During each of the past five years, his expenses on the farm were $9,000, and farm income was only $4,000. During the current year, he has income of $4,800 and expenses of $9,200.

b. Toledo owns 60% of Ace Corporation's outstanding stock. During the current year, Ace Corporation paid Toledo a salary of $82,000. Executives in similar situations earn about $40,000 per year.

c. Black borrowed $50,000 from the First State Bank and used the money to buy City of Blanksville bonds. She paid interest of $4,200 on the borrowed funds. Interest received on the bonds was $3,500.

d. White purchased a piece of land for $45,000 for his new office building. However, he has to tear down an old building on the property, paying $3,200 to a demolition company for clearing the land.

e. Benson is married and has three children. Normal living costs for the home, utilities, food, and clothing total $12,000 for the current year.

21. Xavier is a self-employed manufacturer of electronics equipment. During the year, she had the following expenditures that she thinks may be somewhat questionable when preparing her tax return. Indicate whether each is potentially deductible or is nondeductible.

a. Trip to Washington, D.C., to testify before congressional committee holding hearings on proposed legislation to restrict foreign imports of electronics equipment. Xavier is very interested in curtailing imports and asked to be heard. Transportation, $280; lodging, $260; meals, $108.

b. Cost of telephone calls, letters, and telegrams to members of Congress from her state urging them to vote for the import restrictions bill recommended by the congressional committee, $118.

c. Contribution to electronics manufacturing association to help pay for television campaign to urge public support for anti-import bill, $1,200.

d. Gift to Congressman Doe (a new color television set costing $600). Xavier expects Doe to support the anti-import bill.

e. Kickbacks to purchasing agents of companies who buy substantial amounts of Xavier's products, $4,000.

f. Kickbacks to purchasing agents of four cities buying Xavier's products, $2,000.

g. Cost of television ads purchased for an opponent of Congressman Doe, who after all did not support the anti-import bill, $1,000.

22. a. The president of Unlimited Aviation Corporation traveled to a foreign country to talk to a group of military officers in that country about purchasing military aircraft manufactured by Unlimited. The officers hinted that a "gift" to them

might increase the likelihood that Unlimited would receive the contract sought. The president authorized payment, and the company paid $500,000 to each of the six officers (a total of $3,000,000). Are these payments deductible by Unlimited?

b. During a severe cold wave in 19X1, Randolph Company paid $50,000 to officers of a natural gas pipeline company to ensure that gas supplies to the company were not curtailed. Although supplies to Randolph's competitors were greatly reduced, Randolph had no curtailment. Can Randolph deduct the $50,000 payment?

23. Samantha Wilson, an appliance dealer, included the following expenses in computing her income for financial accounting purposes in 1988.

a. Estimated loss from bad debts, $1,200. This amount was based on assumed losses of one fourth of 1% of net sales.

b. Estimated expenses arising from guarantees and warranties, $4,000. This amount was based on experience showing that, normally, future service costs amount to about 2% of the sales price of certain products sold under guaranty and warranty. During 1988, these sales totaled $200,000.

c. Estimated repair expense, $800. To prevent large fluctuations in income resulting from the fact that major repairs to buildings and equipment tend to occur at irregular intervals. Wilson estimates the average annual repair expense and deducts this amount each year.

d. Amortization of advertising costs, $3,000. In 19X0, the company spent $15,000 for large magazine advertisements and expected to benefit several years, Wilson decided to defer the cost and charge it off over a five-year period.

Indicate whether each of the above items could potentially be allowed as a deduction on the tax return. If the item is not deductible for tax purposes, indicate how the amount should be handled on the tax return. (Disregard the question of whether the procedures followed were "generally accepted" for financial accounting purposes.)

24. The 1986 Tax Reform Act imposed a "floor" under "miscellaneous itemized deductions," including most unreimbursed employee expenses such as travel, transportation, and entertainment. That is, such costs are deductible only to the extent they, in total, exceed 2% of the taxpayer's adjusted gross income. Why, in your opinion was this "floor" imposed by the 1986 Act?

CHAPTER 5

Accounting Periods and Methods

This result gives me much puzzlement. Without the receipt of any money or of any property equaling the petitioner's investment in the mortgage notes, the petitioner is held liable to income tax upon a large amount of accrued interest which he did not receive. In the words of Nicodemus, "How can these things be?"
J. Smith, dissenting Nichols v. Commissioner 1 TC 328 (1942)

This concept renders realization devoid of any special meaning; realization is made merely a synonym for recognition. *According to this concept, all amounts appearing in financial statements are necessarily deemed to be realized by virtue of their appearance there.*
Robert T. Sprouse, "Observations Concerning the Realization Concept" (1965)

The amount of taxable income reported by a taxpayer in specific circumstances depends in part on the method of accounting used by the taxpayer and on the starting and ending dates of the taxpayer's taxable year. In this chapter we examine the fiscal periods that may be chosen and the accounting methods most commonly used. In addition, we discuss the problem of identifying the taxpayer who should report income in certain circumstances.

THE ACCOUNTING PERIOD

The concept of income is meaningful only if we know the *accounting period,* or the period of time to which the income applies. The basic period for measuring taxable income is a year. Section 441(a) states that "Taxable income shall be computed on the basis of the taxpayer's taxable year."

The Calendar Year

Generally, any taxpayer may use the *calendar year,* ending December 31, to report income. Most individuals—almost all individuals whose income is from salary, wages, interest, and dividends—do use the calendar year. Prior to 1987, any taxpayer who maintained adequate records could elect to use a *fiscal year* instead of a calendar year.[1] However, as discussed later, the Tax Reform Act of 1986 now requires certain types of taxpayers in specific circumstances to use the calendar year.

The Fiscal Year

A fiscal year may be any 12-month period ending on the last day of any month except December (for example, the period beginning May 1 and ending the following April 30). Alternatively, a taxpayer can adopt a fiscal year ending on the same weekday that last occurs in a calendar month (for example, the last Tuesday in November) or on the same day of the week occurring nearest the last day of the calendar month each year (for example, a fiscal period that ends on Thursday occurring nearest to February 28 each year.)[2] In both of the last two cases, some accounting periods will contain 52 weeks, while others will contain 53 weeks.

For years beginning after 1986, partnerships are required to use the same tax years as their owners unless they are able to show that a business purpose exists for using a different taxable year. In general, a partnership must use the same tax year as that of the partners who own a majority interest in partnership capital and profits. If partners owning a majority interest have different taxable years, the partnership must adopt the same tax year as its "principal partners" (all of those who own at least a 5% interest.)[3] If the principal partners have different tax years, then the partnership must use the calendar year.[4] Since individuals usually use a calendar year, a partnership with only individuals as partners will generally be required to use the calendar year.

---

[1]Reg. Sec. 1.441(b).
[2]Reg. Sec. 1.441-2(a).
[3]IRC Sec. 706(b)(1).
[4]*Ibid.*

For years after 1986, an S corporation must generally use a calendar year, unless it can show that a business purpose justifies the use of a fiscal year, and all trusts, except tax exempt trusts and wholly charitable trusts, must use the calendar year.[5]

Choosing the Taxable Year

The taxpayer's initial selection of a taxable year is determined by a timely filing of the initial tax return. Thus, an individual electing a calendar year must file the first return by April 15 of the second taxable year, or a corporation electing a fiscal year ending on March 31 must file the first return by June 15 of the next fiscal year. It is important for corporate taxpayers to determine exactly when the company's first year begins under state law so that a timely return can be filed; the period covered by a return can never exceed a year.

The accounting period initially chosen must be followed in all subsequent years unless prior approval is obtained from the I.R.S. Generally, the I.R.S. will not grant permission to change the tax year unless a valid business reason exists for the requested change. The conformity of the tax year with the "natural business year" (generally ending when merchandise inventory quantities are low) was, prior to 1987, accepted by the I.R.S. as a valid reason for changing tax years.[6]

Changing the Accounting Year

A change of accounting periods always creates an interim tax year of less than 12 months. For example, a calendar-year taxpayer who decides to switch in 19X6 to a fiscal year beginning July 1 must file a short-period return for January 1 through June 30, 19X6. Subsequent returns will be for fiscal years beginning July 1 and ending June 30.

The tax liability for a short period caused by a change in accounting period must be computed by an annualization procedure.[7] Basically, this procedure calculates an annual tax based on the assumption that the same rates of short-period income and expenses are incurred throughout a 12-month period. This annual tax is then apportioned to the short period, based on the fraction of a year covered by the short period. The annualization procedure is designed to eliminate any incentive for taxpayers to take advantage of the lowest marginal rates (that is, start at the lowest rates in the tax rate schedule twice within the same 12-month period.)

---

[5]The calendar year requirements for S corporations are found in Sec. 1378 and those for trusts in Sec. 645.
[6]Rev. Proc. 74-33, 1974-2 C.B. 489.
[7]IRC Sec. 443.

Where a change in the tax year is required by the I.R.S., special procedures for handling the changeover may apply. For example, as we have seen, S corporations, personal service corporations, and partnerships may be required under the 1986 Tax Reform Act to change their taxable years. An entity required to change its tax year as a result of this provision must file a return for a short tax year that begins with the first day of its old tax year beginning after December 31, 1986, and ends on December 31, 1987.

For example, if a partnership that has been using a fiscal year ending March 31 is required to change to a calendar year in 1987, it will be required to file a short-period return for the period April 1 through December 31, 1987. The first calendar-year period will be January 1 through December 31, 1988.

In order to prevent bunching of income in the year of transition, a special transition rule is provided for S corporations and partnerships required by the 1986 Act to change taxable years. Under this provision, partners in a partnership or stockholders in an S corporation may *elect* to take income from the short period (required in order to change to a calendar year) into account over a 4-year period.

THE METHOD OF ACCOUNTING

The taxable year in which an item is to be included in gross income or is to be deducted in arriving at taxable income may depend on the *accounting method* adopted.

Subchapter E of the Internal Revenue Code contains the ground rules for accounting periods and methods. Section 446 provides the specific rules for tax accounting methods:

(a) General Rule. Taxable income shall be computed under the method of accounting on the basis of which the taxpayer regularly computes his income in keeping his books.

(b) Exceptions. If no method of accounting has been regularly used by the taxpayer, or if the method used does not clearly reflect income, the computation of taxable income shall be made under such method as, in the opinion of the Secretary [of the Treasury], does clearly reflect income.

(c) Permissible Methods. Subject to the provisions of subsections (a) and (b), a taxpayer may compute taxable income under any of the following methods of accounting—

  (1) the cash receipts and disbursements method;

  (2) an accrual method;

  (3) any other method permitted by this chapter; or

  (4) any combination of the foregoing methods permitted under regulations prescribed by the Secretary.

(d) Taxpayer Engaged in More Than One Business. A taxpayer engaged in more than one trade or business may, in computing taxable income, use a different method of accounting for each trade or business.

(e) Requirement Respecting Change of Accounting Method. Except as otherwise expressly provided in this chapter, a taxpayer who changes the method of

> accounting on the basis of which he regularly computes his income in keeping his books shall, before computing his taxable income under the new method, secure the consent of the Secretary.

Although Sec. 446, quoted above, seems to give the taxpayer great flexibility in choosing the basis of accounting, Sec. 448, enacted as part of the Tax Reform Act of 1986, denies to certain types of business entities the right to use the cash basis of accounting. (This restriction will be examined later in the discussion of the cash basis.) Additional and more specific procedural requirements on detailed accounting provisions are spread throughout the Code.

The Cash Basis

Most individual taxpayers, especially wage earners and individuals in the professions, use the *cash basis* of accounting. The cash basis is not only simpler, in that it requires less record keeping than other methods, but it also gives the taxpayer limited control over the timing of expenses by accelerating or deferring cash receipts and cash payments.

TIME FOR REPORTING INCOME   A taxpayer on the cash basis *generally* reports income when it is received in cash or a noncash equivalent and deducts expenses when they are paid; however, there are many modifications and exceptions to these two basic rules.

The "cash-equivalent" concept.   Most individuals are prudent, and if taxed only on *cash* receipts they could easily avoid the tax by arranging to receive noncash property for services rendered. To eliminate this tax-avoidance ruse, the concept of *cash equivalent* has been developed. Essentially, the cash-equivalent concept suggests that whenever a taxpayer receives noncash property in a transaction, the fair market value of the property received serves as a measure of the cash equivalent realized from the transaction. Thus, income is realized on the exchange of services for a noncash asset even in the case of a cash-basis taxpayer, as made clear in the regulations that state that gross income

> . . . includes income realized in any form, whether in money, property, or services. Income may be realized, therefore, in the form of services, meals, accommodations, stock, or other property, as well as in cash.[8]

Thus, if Steele, a barber, agreed to shampoo and cut Giese's hair every two weeks of the year in return for which Giese agreed to mow the grass on the lawn of Steele's residence during the spring and summer months, and if the fair value of the services provided by each during 19X1 was $320, each party would have income of $320 from the exchange.

---

[8]Reg. Sec. 1.61-1(a).

A mere right to receive income is not taxable until actual or constructive receipt occurs. For this reason, a cash-basis taxpayer selling merchandise or services on "open book account," which represents a right to receive income, has no actual or constructive receipt of income. However, if the customer gives the seller of the merchandise or service a negotiable note for the balance, the fair market value of the note will be taxable to the seller immediately. The negotiable feature is the equivalent of constructive receipt of income by the seller.

Constructive-receipt doctrine.   Another doctrine intended to reduce the opportunity for the cash-basis taxpayer to defer income by not taking cash, even though he or she could do so at will, is the concept of *constructive receipt*. This doctrine finds clear and explicit expression in Regulation 1.451-2(a):

> Income although not actually reduced to a taxpayer's possession is constructively received by him in the taxable year during which it is credited to his account, set apart for him, or otherwise made available so that he may draw upon it at any time, or so that he could have drawn upon it during the taxable year if notice of intention to withdraw had been given. However, income is not constructively received if the taxpayer's control of its receipt is subject to substantial limitations or restrictions.

Obviously this rule is designed to prevent cash-basis taxpayers from deferring *receipt* of cash, and thus deferring the income tax in order to take advantage of the "present value" of money or to avail themselves of lower tax rates in later periods of lower income. Nevertheless, it is possible for cash-basis taxpayers to make limited deferrals of income simply by deferring billings for services in some circumstances. The doctrine has little application to accrual-basis taxpayers, since they ordinarily report income when it is earned in any event.

As noted in the quotation from the Regulations, the doctrine of constructive receipt is applied whenever a taxpayer has control, without substantial limitations or restrictions, over the amount involved. In addition, it is often held that for an amount to be constructively received, the payer (1) must have credited or set aside that amount for the payee, and (2) must have been able to make payment. Some of the common applications of the rule will suffice to show its scope and importance:

1. Amounts of interest credited to a depositor's account in banks, credit unions, and so on, are taxable when credited even though not withdrawn by the depositor until a later year.

2. Dividends on corporate stock are constructively received when unqualifiedly made subject to the demand of the shareholder. This has been interpreted to mean that if dividend checks are mailed late in the year and are not received by the shareholder until the following year, then they are not taxable until the latter year.

For example, assume that on December 28, 19X1, Argyle company issued a check in payment of services rendered by its accountant. However, because

Argyle was overdrawn at the bank, the company's manager asked Argyle not to cash the check until January 5, 19X2. There would be no constructive receipt in 19X1 because the issuer had insufficient funds to pay the debt.[9]

Claim-of-right doctrine. One additional concept needs to be mentioned at this point even though it is applicable to both cash-basis and accrual-basis taxpayers. The *claim-of-right doctrine*—a judicial concept—holds that an amount is includible in income when actually or constructively received (or, in the case of an accrual-basis taxpayer, is accrued) if it appears from all the facts available in the year of receipt that the taxpayer had an unrestricted right to such item even though the taxpayer might be required to repay the amount at some future time. Money received by a taxpayer and treated as his or her own, under a claim that it is his, or hers, will be taxable to the taxpayer even though the claim is disputed.[10] Thus, the accrual-basis taxpayer who receives prepayments of income will generally be required to report the income in the period the prepayment is received even though it is earned in a subsequent period.

Some examples of funds held to be taxable income to the taxpayer under the claim-of-right doctrine are:

1. Bonus in year of receipt even though it was computed in error and had to be repaid in a later year[11]

2. Contingent legal fees that must be repaid in the event of reversal by an unfavorable court decision

Generally, if a taxpayer is required to repay amounts previously included in income, the taxpayer is entitled to deduct, in the year of repayment, the amount repaid. If the inclusion and subsequent repayment resulted from the claim-of-right doctrine, a special provision, designed to alleviate the adverse effects of the inclusion, is available if the amount of the deduction exceeds $3,000.[12] This special rule is available to the taxpayer in most cases to ensure that the tax benefit in the year of deduction is as great as the increased tax liability in the prior year.

For example, assume that in 19X1 an attorney agreed to represent a client in a lawsuit. Under terms of the engagement, the attorney's fee was contingent on successful defense in the suit. In 19X1, the case was decided by a lower court in favor of the attorney's client, and the client paid the contingent fee of $50,000. In 1987, however, the lower court's decision was overturned by an appeals court, and the attorney returned the $50,000 fee under the terms of the engagement.

The attorney would be required to report the $50,000 as income in 19X1, but she will be entitled to a deduction in 19X2 for the $50,000 repaid. In

---

[9]See *L. M. Fischer*, 14 T.C. 792 (1950).

[10]See *North American Oil Consolidated v. Burnet*, 73 S. Ct. 671 (1953), for the basic doctrine of claim of right.

[11]*U.S. v. Lewis*, 71 S. Ct. 522 (1951).

[12]Sec. 1341.

addition, she will recompute the tax liability that would have resulted in 19X1 if the item had not been included. The difference in 19X1 taxes is then compared with the reduction in tax in 19X2 resulting from the deduction in that year. The larger of these two amounts is the tax benefit allowed the taxpayer.

The claim-of-right doctrine does not generally apply if the taxpayer knows at the time of receipt that income that might otherwise fall under the claim-of-right doctrine is subject to an absolute obligation for repayment by the taxpayer. For example, if the owner of an apartment house requires each tenant in the apartment house to make a "damage deposit" of $250, with the provision that any amount not necessary to repair damages is to be refunded when a tenant vacates an apartment, such deposits will not constitute income under the claim-of-right doctrine.[13]

TIME FOR DEDUCTING EXPENSES   Regulation 1.461-1(a) further explains how to determine the year in which a deduction is to be taken by a cash-basis taxpayer.

> Under the cash receipts and disbursements method of accounting, amounts representing allowable deductions shall, as a general rule, be taken into account for the taxable year in which paid. Further, a taxpayer using this method may also be entitled to certain deductions in the computation of taxable income which do not involve cash disbursements during the taxable year, such as the deductions for depreciation, depletion, and losses under sections 167, 611, and 165, respectively. If an expenditure results in the creation of an asset having a useful life which extends substantially beyond the close of the taxable year, such an expenditure may not be deductible, or may be deductible only in part, for the taxable year in which made. . . .[14]

Note that the payment must actually be made; there is no doctrine of constructive payment equivalent to the doctrine of constructive receipt, which was explained above. (However, a deduction may be allowed for a payment made with a noncash asset.) When payments are made by mail, the usual rule is that mailing constitutes payment because the postal system is deemed to be the agent of the addressee as well as the mailer, but there are conflicting court decisions on this point.

Questions are frequently raised about prepayment of expenses. Ordinarily a prepayment, such as a purchase of supplies, can be deducted in the year of payment even if the supplies are not used until the following year. If the payment creates an asset extending substantially beyond the end of the year, however, only that part used up in the current year is deductible. There are conflicting decisions over the proper period for deduction of prepaid rent and insurance by cash-basis taxpayers. As a generalization, however, it can be

---

[13]See *John Mantell*, 17 T.C. 1143 (1952).
[14]Reg. Sec. 1.461-1(a).

said that such prepayments must be allocated over the period for which payment was made if to do otherwise would result in a material distortion of income. The I.R.S. has argued frequently that prepaid insurance and prepaid rent must be allocated in almost every case. In a 1980 decision, the Ninth Circuit Court of Appeals held that rent prepaid for 11 months beyond the close of the tax year was deductible in the year paid. In that case, the court specified a 12-month period beyond the end of the tax year as being a period for which prepaid rent is deductible.[15] However, the amount involved in that case probably would not be considered material. Code Sec. 461(g) requires cash-basis taxpayers to deduct prepaid interest over the period of the loan, except for points on home (personal residence) mortgages, which, as discussed later in this chapter, generally can still be deducted on a current basis.[16] "Tax shelters" using the cash basis of reporting generally are allowed to deduct prepaid amounts only if the related economic performance (providing of the services or property involved) occurs within 90 days after the close of the taxable year.[17]

Deposits made in advance on goods or services are deductible in years when the goods or services are received.[18] Obviously, expenditures for capital assets such as equipment must be capitalized and depreciated, even by the cash-basis taxpayer. Deposits on inventory goods also become a part of the cost of the goods acquired.

LIMITATIONS ON USE OF CASH BASIS   For years beginning after 1986, Sec. 448 severely restricts the ability of certain types of entities engaged in most activities to use the cash basis.

> Sec. 448 Limitation on Use of Cash Method of Accounting
>   (a) General Rule.—Except as otherwise provided in this section, in
>   the case of a—
>   (1) C corporation
>   (2) partnership which has a C corporation as a partner, or
>   (3) tax shelter,
> taxable income shall not be computed under the cash receipts and disbursements method of accounting.

Although Sec. 448(b)(1) goes on to exclude any "farming business" from the prohibition in Sec. 448(a), most corporations engaged in farming were already, and continue to be, required to use the accrual basis of accounting because of Sec. 447(a). Under Sec. 447(a), the taxable income of a corporation engaged in the trade or business of farming, or of a part so engaged if a corporation is a partner in the partnership, must be computed under the accrual basis. However, if the trade or business is that of operating a nursery

---

[15]*Zaninovich*, 616 F.2d 429 (CA-9, 1980).
[16]Sec. 461(g).
[17]Sec. 461(i).
[18]*G. R. Shippy*, 308 F.2d 743 (CA-8, 1962).

or sod farm or the raising or harvesting of trees (other than fruit and nut trees), Sec. 447(a) does not apply. Thus, for example, a corporation engaged in operating a nursery may continue to use the cash basis of accounting.

Sec. 448(b) also permits "personal service corporations" (corporations whose activities are substantially all in providing services such as legal, accounting, and so on) and corporations that qualify as "small businesses" to continue to use the cash method of accounting.

A small business is, for this purpose, one that for "all prior taxable years beginning after 1985" meets a $5,000,000 gross receipts test. Under this rule, a corporation (or a partnership with a corporate partner) is deemed to have met the $5,000,000 gross receipts test for a prior year if the average annual gross receipts for the three taxable years ending with such prior taxable year does not exceed $5,000,000.[19]

For example, assume that a corporation had gross receipts as follows:

1984	$4,000,000
1985	4,900,000
1986	5,200,000
1987	5,400,000

For 1987, the corporation could use the cash method. The only "prior year beginning after 1985" is 1986. The average sales for the three-year period ending in 1986 is $4,700,000 [($4,000,000 + $4,900,000 + $5,200,000)/3].

The corporation in the above example will not be eligible to again use the cash method of accounting for any year after 1987 because its average sales for the three-year period ending December 31, 1987, is $5,166,667 [($4,900,000 + $5,200,000 + $5,400,000)/3].

The Accrual Basis

TIME FOR REPORTING INCOME   A taxpayer on the *accrual basis* generally reports income when it is earned, even though not yet received, and deducts expenses when they are incurred, even though not yet paid. Income is deemed earned "when all the events have occurred which fix the right to receive such income and the amount thereof can be determined with reasonable accuracy."[20] In general, the rules of measuring gross income for an accrual-basis taxpayer are similar to those that would be used in financial accounting. The accrual basis *must* be used to account for sales, purchases, and inventories by a taxpayer with inventories of stock in trade,[21] although such taxpayers may use the cash basis in accounting for expenses and other revenues. In addition, as previously discussed, after 1986 corporations must generally use the accrual method.

[19]Sec. 448(c)(1).
[20]Reg. Sec. 1.461-1(c)(2)(i).
[21]Reg. Sec. 1.446-1(c)(2)(ii).

One rule of special importance to accrual-basis taxpayers (although it applies to cash-basis taxpayers as well) is the one governing tax treatment of prepaid income. Under the claim-of-right doctrine, as a general rule income received in advance is wholly taxable when received rather than over future years when earned. However, an accrual-basis taxpayer, but *not* a cash-basis taxpayer, may defer recognizing income from *services* (but not interest, rents, warranties, or guaranties) applicable to services to be rendered in the first tax year *after* the year of receipt *if* all the services will be performed not later than that next tax year. If *any* services are to be performed *after* the next year, *all* of the advance receipts are taxable when received.[22]

For example, if a taxpayer received $24,000 on September 1 of the current year, representing 16 months' rent on property owned, the entire $24,000 would be taxed to the taxpayer in the current year under either the cash or the accrual basis of accounting.

The rules regarding guaranties and warranties are somewhat confusing. If a prepaid guaranty or warranty is related to products manufactured or sold by the taxpayer, no deferral of income from receipts of such prepayments is permitted under either the cash basis or accrual basis.[23] If, however, the warranty or guaranty is not related to products manufactured or sold by the taxpayer, an accrual-basis taxpayer (but not a cash-basis taxpayer) may defer recognizing income if all the services will be performed in the first tax year after receipt, under the general rule discussed earlier.[24]

For example, assume that Whitlock, an appliance dealer, offers purchasers of appliances an opportunity to acquire for $10 a warranty under which Whitlock agrees to provide all labor and parts free of charge to the customer for any repairs necessary within one year from date of sale. Since the warranty is related to appliances sold by Whitlock, all amounts received under such warranties are taxed in the year of receipt.

On the other hand, assume that Araf is in the appliance repair business and does not sell appliances. During the current year Araf sold service warranty contracts, with total receipts of $30,000. At the end of the current year an analysis of prepayments showed the following:

Contracts that expire during the next taxable year		$4,200
Contracts that extend beyond the next taxable year:		
Portion applicable to next year	$7,000	
Portion applicable to subsequent years	1,000	8,000

Since the prepayment does not relate to appliances sold by Araf, he may defer the $4,200 until the following tax year. However, all of the $8,000 applicable to contracts that extend beyond the next year must be reported as income in the current year.

In addition to the deferral of prepaid income in limited cases provided in Rev. Proc. 70-21, the Code provides for deferral by accrual-basis taxpayers in

---

[22]Rev. Proc. 70-21, 1976-2 C. B. 549.
[23]Rev. Proc. 70-21, Sec. 3.10(5).
[24]Rev. Proc. 70-21-3.10(4).

a few other specific instances. Code Sec. 455 permits publishers to prorate certain subscription income over the period of the subscription. Code Sec. 456 likewise permits certain "membership organizations" to prorate dues over the membership period. Finally, Reg. Sec. 1.451-5 contains complex rules that permit the seller of goods to defer prepaid income until the year in which the payments are properly accruable under the method of accounting used for tax purposes (but not later than the year in which the payments are recognized as income for financial accounting purposes) if certain tests are met.

TIME FOR DEDUCTING EXPENSES   The Revenue Code does not contain a concise statement of when expenses are deductible under the accrual method. The most commonly quoted general rule is found in Reg. Sec. 1.461-1(a)(2), which states:

> Under an accrual method basis of accounting, an expense is deductible for the taxable year in which all the events have occurred which determine the fact of the liability and the amount thereof can be determined with reasonable accuracy.

Thus, until Sec. 461(h) was added to the Revenue Code in 1984, the general rule was that an accrual-basis taxpayer was entitled to a deduction whenever a fixed and determinable liability was incurred. (If there are substantial contingencies or no reasonable estimate of the amount of expense can be made, there is no deduction.) Sec. 461(h) added one more critical test for determining whether the all-events test has been met—the requirement that "economic performance" has occurred.

> (h) Certain liabilities not incurred before economic performance—
>   (1) In general.—For purposes of this title, in determining whether an amount has been incurred with respect to any item during any taxable year, the all events test shall not be treated as met any earlier than when economic performance with respect to such item occurs.

Sec. 461(h)(2) explains the time at which economic performance is deemed to have occurred:

> (2) Time when economic performance occurs.—Except as provided in regulations prescribed by the Secretary, the time when economic performance occurs shall be determined under the following principles:
>   (A) Services and property provided to the taxpayer.—If the liability of the taxpayer arises out of—
>   (i) the providing of services to the taxpayer by another person, economic performance occurs as such person provides such services,
>   (ii) the providing of property to the taxpayer by another person, economic performance occurs as the person provides such property, or
>   (iii) the use of property by the taxpayer, economic performance occurs as the taxpayer uses such property.

(B) Services and property provided by the taxpayer.—If the liability of the taxpayer requires the taxpayer to provide property or services, economic performance occurs as the taxpayer provides such property or services.

However, the taxpayer is allowed to deduct items for which economic performance has not occurred at the end of the year in certain limited circumstances. If the liability has been fixed and is determinable, but performance has not yet occurred, the taxpayer may accrue the item provided that:

1. Economic performance with respect to the item occurs within a reasonable period (not to exceed 8½ months) after the close of the tax year.
2. Such item is recurring in nature and the taxpayer consistently treats the item as incurred in the taxable year in which the requirements are met, and
3. Either the item is not "material," or the accrual of the item reflects a more proper matching against income than would deduction in the year of performance. (The treatment of such items in the taxpayer's financial statements is to be considered in this test.)[25]

Section 461(f) permits the deduction of a liability paid under protest, but any amount refunded to the taxpayer in a subsequent year must be recognized as income to the extent the refund represents an amount that resulted in a tax benefit in the year deducted.

The requirement that an expense can be reasonably estimated effectively eliminates for tax purposes the use of "reserves" for estimated expenses. Although such practices are common in financial accounting, no provisions are now found in the Code for such reserves. Prior to the Tax Reform Act of 1986, accrual-basis taxpayers were permitted to use the reserve method to account for bad debts, but for years beginning after 1986 only the "direct charge-off method" for bad debts will be allowed.[26]

The prohibition of reserves is justified primarily as a means of administrative convenience, since the use of subjective estimates would create practical audit difficulties for the I.R.S. However, the 1986 provision eliminating use of the reserve for bad debts was also designed in part to increase tax revenues by deferring the time at which taxpayers could take bad debt deductions.

There are many provisions in the Internal Revenue Code affecting the time for deducting specific items. For example, individuals cannot deduct charitable contributions until the year in which payment is made or in which the amount is charged on a bank credit card even though the taxpayer is on an accrual basis.[27] Similarly, medical expenses are deductible only in the year paid.

[25]Sec. 461(h)(3).
[26]Sec. 166(a).
[27]Reg. 1.170A-1(a)(i) and Rev. Rul. 78-38, 1978-1, C.B. 68.

The Hybrid Basis

Although Reg. Sec. 1.446-1(c)(2) generally requires that the accrual basis be used to account for inventories and sales and purchases of inventory items (gross profit), a taxpayer may nevertheless use the cash basis in computing all other items of income and deduction. This procedure is quite commonly followed by owners of small businesses and is called the *mixed* or *hybrid basis* of accounting. If the cash basis is used in computing gross income, however, the cash basis must also be used in computing deductions.

Inventory Methods

As discussed previously, Reg. Sec. 1.446-1(c)(2) requires that taxpayers use the accrual method to account for inventories. Section 471 suggests that "the use of inventories is necessary in order clearly to determine the income of any taxpayer." To calculate inventory costs for a specific accounting period requires an understanding of two main elements, the valuation of inventories and the flow of their costs through the business.

VALUATION   To satisfy the condition of Sec. 471, that a taxpayer's income be clearly reflected, Reg. Sec. 1.471-2(c) permits the use of either (1) the cost method or (2) the lower-of-cost-or-market method. Under the cost method, the term "cost" depends on whether the inventory is purchased or manufactured. The cost of purchased inventory typically includes the invoice price plus adjustments for discounts, transportation, and other acquisition costs. In the case of manufactured inventories, the inventory costs include the price paid for (1) raw materials, (2) direct labor, and (3) all related indirect costs. To what extent indirect expenses should be considered a period cost (deducted in the year incurred) or a product cost (charged to the inventory and deducted in the year the inventory is sold) has always been an item of contention between taxpayers and the I.R.S. Congress tightened the rules considerably in the 1986 Tax Reform Act, requiring that significantly more indirect costs be considered as product costs. Under the rules of new Section 263A, added in 1986, items such as payroll costs for purchasing and warehouse personnel, some pension and profit-sharing costs, warehouse rent, and all depreciation and insurance attributable to storage facilities will now be treated as product costs rather than period costs. Taxpayers who purchase rather than manufacture inventory consisting of personal (not real) property and whose gross receipts have not averaged over $10 million during the preceding three years, are exempt from the stricter capitalization rules. Farmers and taxpayers using the lower-of-cost-or-market valuation method are likewise exempt from the new provisions.

The lower-of-cost-or-market valuation method is also permitted under Reg. Sec. 1.471-2(c). "Market" for purchased inventory means the current bid price prevailing at the date of the inventory in quantities usually purchased by the taxpayer. For manufactured inventory, "market" is the total reproduction cost at current prices. (Reg. Sec. 1.471-4). The use of the lower-of-cost-or-market method is quite tedious, since the comparison of cost with market must be made on a product by product basis rather than in the aggregate.

INVENTORY FLOW   To accurately price inventories as they flow through a business requires using the specific identification method for valuing inventories. However, in many businesses inventory items are so numerous that specific identification is not economically feasible. Thus, inventories are usually valued based on some assumed inventory flow concept rather than the actual flow through a taxpayer's system. Three specific flow concepts are acceptable for that purpose, namely average cost, FIFO (first-in, first-out), and LIFO (last-in, first-out). The election to use the LIFO method is conditioned on the requirement that LIFO also be used for financial statement purposes. Typically, LIFO produces a lower taxable income. Thus, the condition that it must be used for book purposes as well often discourages the use of LIFO by some taxpayers.

OTHER BASES

In addition to the cash, accrual, and hybrid methods of accounting, a taxpayer may sometimes use either the installment method or one of the long-term construction contract methods. The installment method effectively spreads the gain (or gross income) realized on the sale of goods or property over the years during which the seller receives payment for the asset sold. This method is discussed in Chapter 17.

A long-term contract is a contract involving the production, manufacture, building, installation, or construction of property that is not started and completed in the same year. For manufacturing contracts to qualify as a long-term contract, the manufactured item cannot be included in the finished goods inventory and should take more than twelve months to complete.

Three methods are available to account for long-term contracts. The *completed contract method* defers recognition of gain or loss from the contract until the period when the contract is completed. Advance payments received from customers and costs applicable to the contract are accumulated until completion of the project. Because this method provides a potential to defer income from a long-term contract for several accounting periods, the Tax Reform Act of 1986 has limited its availability for large taxpayers. The completed contract method may now be used only by taxpayers with annual gross receipts of $10 million or less—and then only if the contract is expected to be completed within a two-year period. The *percentage-of-completion method* is still available for all taxpayers regardless of size. This method requires that a portion of the total gross profit be recognized based on the estimated work completed on the contract during each tax year. To the completed contract method and the percentage-of-completion method, the Tax Reform Act of 1986 added a new method called the *percentage-of-completion–capitalized cost method* available to taxpayers in lieu of the percentage-of-completion method. This method requires that for 40% of the contract the percentage-of-completion method be used and for the remaining 60% the taxpayer use his regular accounting method. The practical application of this provision is to treat each long-term contract as two separate contracts accounted for under two different methods.

Changing Methods

A taxpayer who desires a change in tax-accounting methods must generally obtain the prior approval of the Commissioner.[28] Form 3115, an application for change in accounting method, is used to seek approval. Such a change often necessitates an adjustment to avoid the duplication or omission of certain items of gross income or deduction. Under some circumstances these "adjustments" may be reported by a taxpayer over a period of up to 10 years, as opposed to total recognition in a single tax year. In still other circumstances the Commissioner may not approve a request for a change in accounting method unless the taxpayer agrees to use the new method for financial accounting as well as tax purposes. And in yet other circumstances, the Commissioner may insist that a taxpayer change his or her accounting method to reflect income more clearly. Obviously, the details of each of these "special circumstances" cannot be investigated at this point in our study of income taxation. It will suffice to observe that, in general, a taxpayer is relatively free in the initial selection of an accounting method but may be more restricted in electing to change that method at a later date.

TAX ACCOUNTING VERSUS FINANCIAL ACCOUNTING

In this chapter and the two preceding ones we have seen some of the ways in which accounting rules that must be followed for tax purposes differ from accepted accounting principles used in financial reporting. These differences may conveniently be classified into two categories for purposes of discussion.

1. Some variations merely represent differences in the *time* (year) or reporting income or expenses on the tax return and in the financial accounts. Tax rules may require (or permit) income or expenses to be reported on the tax return in one period, whereas they should be recognized in a different period in accordance with generally accepted accounting principles. An excellent example of timing differences is the previously noted tax rule that

---

[28]Sec. 446(e).

income received in advance is usually taxable in the year received regardless of when earned. Financial accounting principles demand that unearned revenue be recognized as income only in the period when actually earned.

2. Other variations represent *permanent* differences between income reported on the tax return and that reported in accordance with financial accounting. These variations redistribute the burden of taxation among taxpayers and may affect the total amount of taxes collected by the government. The permanent differences take various forms. For example, certain items of income are wholly or partially excluded from taxable income; specific groups of taxpayers are wholly or partially excused from paying an income tax; special deductions may be allowed other taxpayers; and selected deductions may be limited or denied to specified taxpayers.

Differences in Timing

Mere timing differences do not generally have a significant effect on the total income ultimately reported, or on the aggregate tax liability eventually paid, by any taxpayer. Because of the time value of money, however, these provisions may be extremely important to the taxpayer. As a general rule, a taxpayer would much prefer to pay a $1,000 tax liability five years hence than to pay the same amount today.

The tax and financial accounting variations that result from differences in timing can be subdivided into four categories:

1. Gross income is taxable in a period before it is recognized for financial accounting purposes (for example, income received in advance for services to be rendered in a later period by the taxpayer must be recognized for tax purposes in the year received even though under financial accounting principles the income must be recognized only as the services are rendered.)

2. Gross income is taxable in a period after it is accrued for financial accounting purposes. For example, the profit on sale of merchandise or property sold under an installment contract must generally be recognized at the time of sale for financial accounting purposes. For tax purposes, however, the gain may be deferred and recognized as cash collections are made on the installment contract.

3. Expenses or losses are deducted for tax purposes before they are deducted for financial accounting purposes. The most common example of this timing difference is in the charging to expense of the cost of "depreciable assets." For tax purposes, accelerated cost recovery may be used, permitting the taxpayer to charge off the cost of assets over a short period on an accelerated basis. For financial accounting purposes, however, accelerated cost recovery is not acceptable, and, instead, the cost must be charged off over the asset's actual economic life, often on a straight-line basis.

4. Expenses or losses are deducted for tax purposes in a period after they are deducted for financial accounting purposes. As an illustration, under financial accounting principles an accrual-basis taxpayer should estimate bad

debts and charge the estimated amount to expense in the year of the sale. Under tax rules after 1986 the taxpayer is not allowed to use the "reserve" method but, instead, must charge off bad debts only as individual accounts become worthless.

Most of the timing differences can be explained by such underlying tenets of taxation as wherewithal to pay, objectivity and realization, administrative convenience, and the desire to encourage or discourage specific activities in an effort to achieve certain social or economic goals. Many of the differences related to deductions are created because it is frequently permissible, or even preferred, to estimate future costs relating to goods or services sold and to deduct these as expenses of the period in which the corresponding revenue is recognized. In fact, the estimating process is required by the matching concept of financial accounting. This procedure is rarely permitted for tax purposes, however; instead, most expenses are deductible only when paid or when the exact liability can be computed with mathematical accuracy and legal certainty.

Permanent Differences

Some permanent differences between taxable income and financial net income occur because items are specifically excluded from gross income, although they are properly included in income for financial accounting purposes. For example, interest income received by a taxpayer on investments in bonds of state and local governmental units are not taxable but should be included in income in the financial statements. Conversely, other differences are created because specific items are not deductible in arriving at taxable income even though they should be treated as expenses in the financial reports. Interest paid by the taxpayer on money borrowed to purchase or carry tax-free state and local bonds cannot be deducted in the tax return, although it is a proper expense item in the financial reports.

On the other hand, the tax laws permit taxpayers to take several deductions that would not be considered as proper expenses under generally accepted accounting principles. For example, a corporation that receives dividends on shares of stock that it owns in other corporations is permitted to take a deduction equal to 80% of the dividends received. As another example, a taxpayer who receives income from mining or producing minerals and ores is entitled to a deduction on the tax return for percentage depletion, expressed as a percent of gross income. For financial accounting purposes, percentage depletion is not acceptable as an expense; depletion must be based on an allocation of cost as the minerals or ores are produced.

Other differences exist because the tax laws require items to be included in gross income even though they are not properly treated as income under generally accepted accounting principles. Many of the existing timing and permanent differences will be examined in subsequent chapters in this book. As they are examined, the student of accounting will frequently question whether the differences are justified or if it would be desirable to eliminate them.

SHOULD TAX RULES CONFORM TO GENERALLY ACCEPTED ACCOUNTING PRINCIPLES?

It is often suggested that rigid tax requirements be changed so that income is computed in accordance with generally accepted accounting principles. Section 446(a) of the Code is frequently cited as proof that this was the intent of Congress. That section states:

> (a) General Rule.—Taxable income shall be computed under the method of accounting on the basis of which the taxpayer regularly computes his income in keeping his books.

There are numerous other instances throughout the Code that tie tax treatment of items to the financial accounting treatment accorded the item by the taxpayer.

The primary argument for conformity (certainly from the viewpoint of accountants) is that generally accepted accounting principles lead to a realistic, accurate, and meaningful yearly net income measurement. There is also a compelling practical reason for having tax and financial accounts that agree: conformity leads to ease of computation and helps avoid intolerable record-keeping costs to the taxpayer. Keeping different records for tax purposes and financial accounting purposes is both confusing and costly.

On the opposite side is the opinion that such tax tenets as wherewithal to pay, objectivity, ease of administration, and social and economic objectives are far more important than matching revenues earned with the costs of earning them. In addition, it is frequently pointed out that accounting principles are in such a state of flux and accounting rules are so flexible (with many alternative accounting methods available), that they do not offer a consistent and equitable basis for determining tax liability.

The alternative suggestion sometimes advanced—that whatever accounting methods are followed for tax purposes should also be required for all other purposes—would surely be rejected by most accountants. This would be tantamount to the assumption by Congress of the responsibility for developing accounting rules. It is also likely that most accountants would reject the idea of "requiring" the taxpayer to follow generally accepted accounting principles in preparing a tax return.

Tax law changes in recent years have been ambivalent in their effects on conformity between tax rules and financial accounting. Some provisions, such as the law and regulations involving partnerships, have tended to force financial accounting into line with tax requirements. Other provisions, such as the disallowance of estimated bad debts by the 1986 Act, have tended to widen the gap between financial accounting and tax accounting. Overall, there has probably been a shift toward greater conformity.

IDENTIFYING THE TAXPAYER

There frequently is a question about which taxpayer should include items in gross income. Sometimes this results from a deliberate attempt of the taxpayer to *assign income*—that is, to have the income taxed to someone else, usually a family member with a lower income and, consequently, a lower tax rate than that of the taxpayer. In other cases the confusion over the taxpayer who should report income arises from the effects of state laws or uncertainty as to who owns the property that generates the income.

Income of Minor Children

The Regulations provide:

> Compensation for personal services of a child shall, regardless of the provisions of State law relating to who is entitled to the earnings of the child, and regardless of whether the income is in fact received by the child, be deemed to be the gross income of the child and not the gross income of the parent of the child. . . . The income of a minor child is not required to be included in the gross income of the parent for income tax purposes.[29]

The opportunity immediately obvious in this rule to shift income through transfers of income-earning property to the taxpayer's child, or to pay a child reasonable wages for services rendered in the parent's trade or business, will be discussed subsequently.

Income Assignment

In general, income derived from a service must be taxed to the person who rendered the service, and income from property must be taxed to the person who owns the property. Income earned by one entity cannot be assigned to another entity. For instance, if Mary, who is to receive interest income from a note receivable, directs the debtor to pay the interest to Mary's mother, the interest is nevertheless taxable to Mary.

In spite of the general rule that the income of one taxpayer cannot be assigned to another taxpayer, it is possible for one taxpayer to transfer to another *property* that generates the income, with the income earned after date of the property transfer being taxed to the transferee. Thus, if in the

---

[29]Reg. Sec. 1.73-1.

preceding example Mary had made a bona fide gift of the note, interest earned after the date of the gift would have been taxed to the mother.

The Uniform Gift to Minors Act permits an adult to give a minor child gifts of intangible property such as cash, savings accounts, certificates of deposits, bonds, and stocks. The Act permits the adult to be the custodian of the fund even though the income belongs to, and is taxed to, the child. As we have seen in Chapter 3, however, under the 1986 Tax Reform Act net unearned income of a child under 14 is taxed to the child as if it were the parent's income. The tax is calculated by determining what the parent's tax would have been if the child's net unearned income were added to the parent's taxable income.[30] However, since there is an exception provided for the first $500 of taxable unearned income and the child may offset up to $500 of the standard deduction against unearned income, effectively $1,000 of unearned income can still be shielded from the parent's higher rates.

Another important provision in the 1986 Act was added to curtail the ability of taxpayer to shield income by transferring income to children. Prior to that Act a taxpayer could effectively assign income by making a "temporary" gift of the property. This could be achieved if the property owner placed the property in a "Clifford trust" for the benefit of another person, provided the period of the trust was more than 10 years and provided the grantor of the trust (the transferor of property rights) divested himself or herself of control.[31] After the 10-year period, the property could revert back to the grantor without affecting the tax status of income distributed during the existence of the trust. The 1986 Act provided that income from transfers after March 1, 1986, that will revert to either the grantor or his spouse will be taxed at the grantor's tax rates if the reversionary interest exceeds 5% of the value of such trust.[32] Thus, the Clifford trust has ceased to be a viable income-shifting technique, although trusts created on or before March 1, 1986, are not affected by the new rules.

Allocation of Income and Deductions Among Taxpayers

Individuals are not the only entities who attempt to assign income and deductions in order to reduce the total tax liability of related parties. Corporations, partnerships, and other business entities often have the same goal in mind in arranging their financial and operating affairs. For example, if several corporations are owned by the same owner or owners and these corporations have dealings with one another, they might be able to reduce their total tax liability through such devices as altering "intercompany transfer prices," adjusting intercompany management fees, and changing

---

[30]Sec. 1(i).
[31]The name is derived from *Helvering v. Clifford*, 309 U.S. 331 (1940), which dealt with a short-term trust.
[32]Sec. 1(i).

overhead allocation methods. The potential for controlling tax liability is especially apparent when an American corporation has foreign affiliates or subsidiaries.

Section 482 of the Internal Revenue Code grants to the Internal Revenue Service broad and sweeping powers to control such legerdemain. Section 482 states:

> SEC. 482. Allocation of Income and Deductions Among Taxpayers.
> In any case of two or more organizations, trades, or businesses (whether or not incorporated, whether or not organized in the United States, and whether or not affiliated) owned or controlled directly or indirectly by the same interests, the Secretary may distribute, apportion, or allocate gross income, deductions, credits, or allowances between or among such organizations, trades, or businesses, if he determines that such distribution, apportionment, or allocation is necessary in order to prevent evasion of taxes or clearly to reflect the income of any of such organizations, trades, or businesses.

Income From Community Property

Eight states (Arizona, California, Idaho, Louisiana, Nevada, New Mexico, Texas, and Washington) have *community-property* laws affecting the property rights of married persons. The other 42 states are referred to as *separate-property* or common-law states. In community-property states, property that was acquired by a person before marriage may be deemed to be owned solely by that spouse as "separate property." Similarly, property received by a person through inheritance or gift after that person's marriage may be held as property owned solely by that spouse. All other property acquired by either of the spouses after marriage is deemed to be community property, owned one half by each spouse, unless that property can be shown to have been acquired using identifiably separate property of one spouse.

The federal income tax law follows state laws in determining to whom income earned by spouses is taxable. One half of income from personal services such as salaries and wages is deemed to belong to each spouse in community-property states. Similarly, each spouse is deemed to be taxable on one half of the income earned from community property. In some states (Idaho, Louisiana, and Texas) income earned on separately owned property is treated as *community income,* with one half being allocable to each spouse. In the other five community-property states, income from separate property is deemed to be the income of the spouse owning the property.

Since 1948, married couples in all states have been permitted to file joint returns, effectively permitting them to treat all gross income of the couple as belonging one half to each spouse. Joint returns are discussed in detail in Chapter 11.

To illustrate the treatment of income received after marriage from property considered as separate property, assume that Tom and Sue, who live in Texas, were married throughout the year and that during the year they received the following income: Tom's salary, $50,000; dividends on stock held by Sue as separate property, $1,200; and interest on bonds held as community property, $1,600. If the taxpayers file separate returns, each spouse will report income of $26,400. If, however, the taxpayers had lived in Arizona rather than in Texas, Tom would report $25,800 as gross income and Sue would report $27,000. (The taxpayers will probably file a joint return because that would yield a lower tax liability than filing separate returns.)

PROBLEMS

1. Under what conditions can each of the following taxpayers use a fiscal year ending June 30?
   a. An individual
   b. A C corporation
   c. A trust
   d. A partnership

2. An individual has used a fiscal year ending October 31 for tax purposes. In June 1988, the taxpayer decides to change to a calendar year. Assuming this is acceptable, explain how the taxpayer will make the change.

3. Assuming a taxpayer may properly use a fiscal-year basis of reporting, when may the fiscal year end?

4. The Metro Corporation was founded in June 1988. Under what conditions, if any, may it adopt the cash basis of accounting?

5. James T. operates a shoe repair shop. To accommodate his customers, he has a rack on which such items as shoestrings, shoe polish, and shoehorns are displayed for sale. During 19X8, total receipts from shoe repairs were $86,000, and sales of shoestrings and so on were $1,268. Can James T. use the cash-basis of accounting? Explain.

6. Wilson, an attorney, uses the cash basis of accounting and a calendar year. In December 19X1, Wilson received $18,000 in cash from clients; billed other clients for $6,000, for which she expects to be paid in 19X2; received from a client a note receivable with both a principal amount and fair value of $4,000 due in February 19X2; and received a $1,000 City of Chicago bond with a fair market value of $920 in settlement of services of $1,800 billed to the client in July 19X1. How do these items affect Wilson's 19X1 taxable income?

7. To what extent may a taxpayer using the accrual basis estimate and provide in advance for estimated expenses and losses such as bad debts, repairs, and warranties?

8. Malakoff reports his taxable income on the accrual basis of accounting. In 19X1, he had the following receipts:

Collections on accounts receivable from customers	$290,000
Sales on account to customers	314,000
Cash received on September 1, 19X1, for sublease of part of his office space covering period Sept. 1, 19X1, through Feb. 28, 19X2	6,000
Cash received in February 19X1 representing sublease of part of office space for December 19X0 and January 19X1	2,000

What is the amount Malakoff should include in gross income in 19X1 on account of the above?

9. Under what circumstances can a cash-basis taxpayer defer recognition of prepaid income beyond the year of receipt?

10. Under what circumstances can an accrual-basis taxpayer defer recognition of prepaid income beyond the year of receipt?

11. Explain the "claim-of-right" doctrine.

12. What is meant by the "hybrid basis" of accounting?

13. An individual is filing a tax return for the first time. Must the taxpayer obtain permission from the Internal Revenue Service to use the cash basis of accounting?

14. A taxpayer is filing a tax return for the first time. Must the taxpayer obtain permission from the Internal Revenue Service to use the accrual basis of accounting?

15. Carl Mays, an employee of Merit Corp., received a salary of $50,000 from Merit in 19X1. Also, in 19X1 Carl bought 100 shares of Share Corp. common stock from Merit for $30 a share, when the market value of the Share stock was $50 a share. Merit had paid $20 a share for the Share stock in 19X5. In addition, Carl owned a building that he leased to Boss Co. on January 1, 19X1, for a 5-year term at $500 a month. Boss paid Carl $8,000 in 19X1 to cover the following:

Rent for January to December 19X1	$6,000
Advance rent for January 19X2	500
Security deposit, to be applied against the final three months' rent in the fifth year of the lease.	1,500

How much gross income should Carl report in 19X1?

16. Dr. Wells, a physician, reports on the cash basis. The following items pertain to Dr. Wells's medical practice in 19X1:

Cash received from patients in 19X1	$200,000
Cash received in 19X1 from third-party reimbursers for services provided by Dr. Wells in 19X0	30,000
Salaries paid to employees in 19X1	20,000
Year-end 19X1 bonuses paid to employees in 19X2	1,000
Other expenses paid in 19X1	24,000

What is Dr. Wells's net income in 19X1 from his medical practice?

17. Sue Shine, a cash-basis taxpayer, earned an annual salary of $80,000 at Thrace Corp. in 19X1 but elected to take only $40,000. Thrace, which was financially able to pay Sue's full salary, credited the unpaid balance of $40,000 to Sue's account on the corporate books in 19X1 and actually paid this $40,000 to Sue on April 30, 19X2. How much of the salary is taxable to Sue in 19X1?

18. The following events affecting Miss Turner occured at the end of 19X5:
   (1) On December 31, National Corporation mailed Turner a dividend check of $600 from New York. The dividend was received by Turner, who lives in California, on January 6, 19X6.

(2) California Savings Company credited Turner's savings account with "dividends" of $120 on December 31.

How do these transactions affect Turner's gross income for 19X5?

19. Roscoe opens a "cash-and-carry" retail grocery store in 19X4. In addition, Roscoe works as an employee for an accounting firm and operates a part-time tax service. Roscoe wishes to use the cash basis of accounting for the retail store because he uses the cash basis for his other activities. Will this be possible? Assume, instead, that Roscoe wishes to use the accrual basis of accounting for his retail store. Will this be possible?

20. In November 19X3, Yuri received a check from a well-known medical insurance company for $325. The accompanying stub stated: "In payment of your claim No. 123456." Yuri had made no claim, but he nevertheless cashed the check. In June 19X4, Yuri received a letter from the insurance company telling him that the check sent him in the preceding year resulted from a computer error and asking him to repay the $325. Yuri repaid the amount in July 19X4.

How do these facts affect Yuri's taxable income in 19X3 and 19X4?

21. Surrey owns an apartment building. In addition to the rents applicable to the current year, Surrey receives the following:

   (1) Damage deposits from new tenants. These are refundable when tenants move if no damage is done.

   (2) Payments for the last month's rent on rental contracts. These are prepayments for the final month on each contract.

   How do these amounts affect Surrey's income for the year if Surrey uses the cash basis of accounting? If Surrey uses the accrual basis?

22. Jason operates a retail appliance store. He uses the cash basis of accounting except for items related to gross profit from sale of merchandise. Jason offers purchasers of appliances from his store a warranty contract under which Jason agrees to repair free of charge any appliance purchased from him (including parts and labor) for 36 months from date of sale. During 19X4 Jason received $24,000 from the sale of such contracts. An analysis shows that $13,000 relates to work to be performed in 19X5, 19X6, and 19X7.

   a. How much of the $24,000 must Jason include in gross income in 19X4?

   b. Assume the same facts as above, except that Jason uses the accrual basis of accounting. How much of the $24,000 must Jason include in gross income in 19X4?

23. Louise, a divorcée, was married to Henry in 19X4. Louise's 6-year-old daughter is a child model. During 19X4 the child's total income from modeling was $60,000. Of this amount, $20,000 was earned before Louise and Henry were married and $40,000 after that date. Louise had the modeling agency put the entire $60,000 into a trust fund for the child, and no part of it was withdrawn during 19X4. Louise and Henry live in a community-property state.

   How does the $60,000 affect the gross income of the various parties during 19X4?

24. Chris made a $10,000 loan, bearing interest at 12%, to a friend. Chris directed the friend to pay the interest to Chris's 15-year-old daughter. During the current year the daughter received $1,200 interest.

   How much income is reported, and by whom, during the current year?

25. Tex Corporation was formed in 1985 and properly elected to use the cash basis of accounting. Its gross receipts for the first five years of operations were:

1985	$2,200,000
1986	3,800,000
1987	5,900,000
1988	6,400,000
1989	8,200,000

Is the corporation allowed to use the cash basis in 1987? 1988? 1989? Explain your answers.

26. Mary and John both lived in Texas throughout 19X4. They were married on April 1, 19X4. Prior to their marriage, Mary had interest income of $600 and a salary of $3,000 in 19X4. During that period John earned a salary of $4,500 and received dividend income of $300. After marriage, Mary's salary was $9,000 for the remainder of 19X4, and John's salary was $14,000. After marriage Mary also received interest of $1,800 on interest-bearing securities owned at the time of marriage. John's dividends received after marriage on stocks owned before marriage were $1,000.

   If Mary and John file separate returns for 19X4, how much income will each report?

27. Assume the same facts as in problem 26, except that Mary and John live in California. How much gross income will they each report in 19X4?

28. Periodically Mrs. Sand makes deposits to a savings account at the Federal Savings and Loan Association. The account was opened by Mrs. Sand in the following name: Mrs. R. T. Sand, Trustee for William Sand. William Sand is her 6-year-old son. The trust was created under the Uniform Gift to Minors Act. It is Mrs. Sand's intent to continue such deposits until William becomes an adult, at which time he will have full control of the account. During the current year, Federal Savings and Loan Association credited the account with $430 of interest. To whom is the interest taxable?

29. A child, age 13, who is claimed by his parents as a dependent, had the following income in 1988:

Earnings from paper route	$ 900
Interest on savings account established by his grandfather	1,300
Interest on a savings account established by his parents	1,400

The parents' marginal tax rate is 28%. Explain how the $3,600 income will be taxed in 1988.

30. In 1983, Mason established a Clifford trust for his son. During 1988, $3,800 of income from the trust was paid to the son. How will the $3,800 be taxed in 1988?

31. Assume the same facts as in problem 30, except that the trust was created in 1987 rather than 1983. How will the $3,800 be taxed?

CHAPTER 6

Taxable Entities

> *In consequence of this perversion of the word Being, philosophers looking about for something to supply its place, laid their hands upon the word Entity, a piece of barbarous Latin, invented by the schoolmen to be used as an abstract name, in which class its grammatical form would seem to place it; but being seized by logicians in distress to stop a leak in their terminology, it has ever since been used as a concrete name.*
> *John Stuart Mill,* A System of Logic *(1843)*

This chapter addresses the important basic question: Who are the taxpayers? The income tax could be levied on many different entities. Innumerable legal, economic, natural, and cultural entities exist in our society. A list of some of the more important ones will illustrate the diversity: natural persons or individuals; family units, business proprietorships; partnerships, corporations, groups of corporations with related owners, religious groups, eleemosynary organizations of all types, trusts, estates, government units, and social organizations of an infinite variety. Theoretically, any of these could serve as a taxable entity, and the entity's periodic income could be used as the base for an income tax; but some of them can almost automatically be excluded from consideration. To use cities or other local governmental units, for example, would create the problem of reallocating the tax imposed to the entity's citizens, though it would minimize the number of taxpayers. Taxation of churches, legitimate charities, and social organizations would serve to discourage these activities and to transfer the cost of many of their functions to governmental units. Similar problems would be associated with the choice of most groups, organizations, or entities in society. From the earliest days of the income tax in the United States, the taxable entities have been individuals, corporations, and fiduciaries (estates and trusts.)[1] The choice of individuals deserves no comment. As explained in Chapter 3, corporations were subject to an "excise" tax on their incomes before passage of the income tax and have been subject to the income tax since. Fiduciaries are really only quasi taxpayers, owing a tax on their incomes only to the extent the income is not distributed to their beneficiaries.

While corporations and fiduciaries may *pay* the income tax, only individuals can *bear* a tax. Taxes are transfers from the private to the public sector, and such transfers are a "burden" because they decrease consumption and savings in the private sector. Only individuals can consume and save. The corporate income tax, then, is borne by the corporation's owners, its customers, its employees, or some other human being eventually, and thus the incidence problem explained in Chapter 2. The income tax levied on a fiduciary is presumably borne by its beneficiaries.

Even though these artificial, legal entities do not finally bear a tax, they do play an important role in determining the taxes paid by individuals. Some "artificial" entities that are not taxpayers are also important for the same reasons. Principal among these are partnerships and Subchapter S corporations, the latter being a corporation–partnership hybrid that exists only in the tax law. The role of these four entities—corporations, fiduciaries, partnerships, and Subchapter S corporations—in our income tax laws is the subject of this chapter.

Note that the above legal entities are appropriately described as artificial only for tax purposes. These forms obviously have important economic and financial functions. For example, corporations and partnerships permit the pooling of capital beyond the wherewithal of single individuals. Also, businesses, especially those organized as corporations, often have substantial reality due to their size and longevity. From a tax standpoint, however, these nonhuman entities are artificial since all taxes are finally borne by individuals. In addition, many of these entities owe their existence to the tax law; they are created and used because of the effects they have on the tax liability of the individuals involved. For example, an individual who operates a retail store as a proprietor may decide to incorporate that business solely because of the tax effects of such incorporation. Or an investor in raw land who has decided to subdivide the tract and retail lots may join in a partnership with others in order to change the tax impact of the dispositions of his land. Commonly, of course, both tax and nontax considerations (for example, legal and financial) are present in the use of an artificial entity. In this course, we will deal only with the tax considerations.

We are concerned, then, with how the use of artificial entities changes an individual taxpayer's relationships with real economic events, as portrayed in Figure 6-1. Note that the creation and use of the entity creates new relationships—those between the individual and the new entity. If, for example, two CPAs who have previously practiced on their own account

---

[1] In tax jargon, the word person does not mean a human being but instead any entity —individuals, trusts, estates, partnerships, associations, companies, and corporations [Sec. 7701(a)(1)].

FIGURE 6-1   Use of Artificial Entities

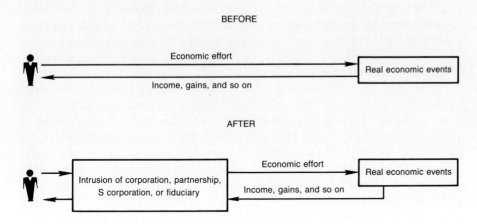

decide to form a partnership, the old economic relationships change from practitioner–client to accounting firm–client, and new relationships are created—partners–firm.

To understand how these artificial entities affect the individuals, four basic questions must be answered:

1. Are transfers of property to the entity by the owners with respect to their ownership interest taxable events? For example, does a proprietor who incorporates an operating business recognize gain or loss upon receipt of corporate stock for his assets?

2. Are transfers of property from the entity to the owners with respect to their ownership interest taxable events? When a partner takes cash or other property out of a partnership, does the partner recognize income?

3. How does the entity affect the tax character of items of income, deductions, and so on. For example, if a corporation receives tax-exempt interest on government bonds and later distributes that income to shareholders, is it still tax exempt?

4. Is an owner (shareholder, partner, and so on) who works in the business an *employee* of the entity? As an employee the owner might be entitled to exclude from income the value of fringe benefits.

As the entities are discussed below, we will explain the general concepts that govern the answers to these questions. First, a brief profile of the individual taxpayer.

THE INDIVIDUAL TAXPAYER

Section 1 of the Internal Revenue Code reads in part, ". . . there is hereby imposed on the taxable income of every individual . . . a tax. . . ." Note the selection of *every* individual and note that the term used is "individual," not "citizen" or some other term. This language makes the tax all-inclusive. Such factors as age and mental condition have no direct effect on the levying of the tax. For example, a minor who has income from property or who earns income must file a return and pay the tax just as an adult. In cases where a guardian has been appointed, the guardian files the return (and signs it) for the minor. The same applies to individuals who are legally incompetent because of insanity; the guardian only files for the incompetent person.

Note that Sec. 1 does not refer to U.S. citizens but to individuals. Naturally, the U.S. government cannot levy a tax on everyone in the world. According to Treasury Regulations, however, one need not be a citizen in order to be subject to the tax. All resident aliens in the United States are subject to the tax, and even nonresident aliens may be subject to an income tax to the extent that they receive income from U.S. sources. The statute defines a resident alien as an individual who has been lawfully admitted to the U.S. as a permanent resident, has met certain artibrary tests for substantial presence within the U.S., or has made a proper election to be treated as a resident. The tax is also levied on U.S. citizens who are residents of foreign countries. In the latter cases, however, the U.S. tax liability is reduced by a limited exclusion for income earned abroad and/or by a credit for taxes paid to foreign governments.

Every citizen and resident of the U.S. files an annual return if gross income exceeds certain threshold amounts explained in Chapter 11. The return is made on some version of Form 1040 as illustrated in Part IV below.

The Family as Taxpayer

While the choice of the individual as the principal taxpayer is practically dictated by our property laws, the family is the most important unit both socially and economically. While income and property may belong to individuals, families consume that income, and families fulfill many of the functions necessary in a civilized society—hygiene, child rearing, moral and ethical education, and so on. Any attempt to relate the tax burden to ability to pay must look beyond the individual to the family circumstances.

With this problem in mind, Congress has traditionally taken the family into account. Until the 1940s, Congress used the exemption deduction to take care of varied family responsibilities. Since that time, the tax rates applicable to individuals have depended, in part, on marital status and existence of dependents. Refer to Appendix A. Four different rate schedules apply to individuals:

1. Married individuals filing joint returns and certain widows and widowers with dependent children are entitled to the lowest rates.

2. Heads of households, certain unmarried individuals with responsibility for their children or other dependents, pay at the next lowest rates.

3. Single taxpayers, other than heads of households and surviving spouses, pay at the next to the highest rates.

4. The highest rates apply to married taxpayers who elect to file separate returns, an option rarely exercised.

The technical definitions of these classes are rather complex, involving the definition of dependents in two cases. These rules, and the historical development of the different rate schedules, are reserved for Chapter 11. For a statistical profile of individual taxpayers, see Chapter 8.

Proprietorships Not an Entity

Financial accounting rules usually require a separate accounting and reporting for businesses operated as proprietorships. Financial statements prepared for a proprietorship will not include the proprietor's nonbusiness income, expenditures, assets, and liabilities, thus providing a clearer picture of the business operations.

For tax purposes, a proprietorship has no standing as an entity, and the items of income, deductions, and so on of a proprietorship are reported on Schedule C (F for farming) of the proprietor's Form 1040. Note, however, that taxpayers engaged in the operation of more than one trade or business may use different acceptable accounting methods for each business. An attorney, for example, may use the cash method for his law practice, even though he is required to use the accrual method for the operation of a second business, say an office supply house, where inventory is a material income-producing factor.

CORPORATIONS

Our tax laws treat C corporations[2] as separate entities. This separation of C corporations from their owners is in accord with financial accounting practice and the legal realities. Under long-standing concepts, a corporation is a separate legal person that can own property, contract in its own name, and be sued for nonperformance. It is this separate status that gives corporations the sometimes desirable attributes of limited liability, unlimited life, and readily transferrable shares. Attendant with these financial and legal advantages of incorporation are the formal rules that must be observed in the formation and operation of the entity: for example, obtaining a charter, maintaining stock transfer records, holding necessary meetings of shareholders and directors, and recording the minutes of such meetings, to name only a few.

In a recent year (1983), almost three million corporations filed federal income tax returns reporting net income subject to the tax of about $210

---

[2]Henceforth, corporations that are treated as separate taxpayers will be designated as C corporations (rules for them are in Subchapter C of the Internal Revenue Code) to distinguish them from S corporations.

billion and a gross tax liability of approximately $92 billion.[3] The vast majority of these are closely held corporations; only 21,800 corporations reporting in 1983 held assets in excess of $25 million. An even smaller number were "public" corporations, that is, those subject to federal or state security regulations because of public trading. This large number of closely held corporations is due partly to the legal advantages of that form, and partly due to the several tax advantages of incorporation. As the following sections explain, the tax advantages of incorporation may be more than offset by disadvantages due to changes in the 1986 Act. You will see that our law is surprisingly consistent in treating the C corporation as a separate entity.

The Corporate Taxpayer

As a separate entity, a C corporation is a full-fledged taxpayer, reporting its income annually on Form 1120. With a few important exceptions explained later, the rules for calculation of a C corporation's taxable income are the same as those for individuals. The tax rates for C corporations have traditionally been quite different from those for individuals. The C corporation rates for years after June 30, 1987[4] are as follows:

If taxable income is		Tax is		
Over	But not over	Amount Plus	% of	Excess over
—	$ 50,000	0	15	—
$ 50,000	75,000	$ 7,500	25	50,000
75,000	100,000	13,750	34	75,000
100,000	335,000	22,250	39	100,000
335,000	—	113,900	34	335,000

A corporation with a taxable year that includes July 1, 1987, must "blend" the new rates with the old rates since the new rates are lower than the old rates, which went as high as 46%.

Note from the above schedule that the highest new rate is really only 34%. The 39% rate that applies from $100,000 to $335,000 includes a 5% surtax that eliminates the benefits of the rates below 34% for C corporations with taxable incomes above $335,000. The gross tax liability for a C corporation

---

[3]Internal Revenue Service, *Source Book, Statistics of Income, Corporate Income Returns* (Washington, DC: U.S. Government Printing Office, 1986), p. 7ff.
[4]For several years before July 1, 1987 the C corporation rates were:

First $25,000 (of taxable income)	15%
Next $25,000	18%
Next $25,000	30%
Next $25,000	40%
Taxable income over $100,000	46%

For 1985 and 1986, a 5% surtax on taxable income from $1,000,000 to $1,405,000 eliminated the advantages of the rates below 46%.

with taxable income in excess of $335,000 can be obtained by applying the flat 34% rate.

Throughout most of the history of our U.S. income tax until 1987, corporate rates have been lower than the top rates that applied to individuals. For several years before 1981, for example, the top individual rate was 70% compared to a top corporate rate of 46%. Thus a traditional benefit from incorporation was the lower rates. An individual with a thriving business owned as a proprietorship would incorporate that business and pay lower rates on the business income. The former proprietor, now a corporate officer would, of course, take a salary from the corporation. This salary would be a deduction to the C corporation and income to the officer–owner. This division of the business income between the owner–officer and the C corporation also saved taxes because both taxpayers enjoyed the low initial marginal rates on the schedules.

All of this changes with the post-1986 rate schedules. Chapter 7 contains a further comparison of rates for C corporations and individuals. The conclusion reached there is that the opportunities for savings through the use of C corporations to "shelter" income from individual rates are limited indeed.

Taxable Income of C Corporations

The tax formula for C corporations is the same as the general formula.

    Income broadly conceived
 − Exclusions

 = Gross Income
 − Deductions

 = Taxable income
 × Applicable tax rate

 = Gross tax liability
 − Tax credits and prepayments

 = Net tax payable

The statutory rules for income, exclusions, deductions, and credits generally apply to all taxpayers, individuals, C corporations, and fiduciaries. Some statutory provisions, by their nature, obviously apply to individuals only. Refer to the list of exclusions in Chapter 8. Death benefits (Sec. 101), compensation for injuries (Sec. 104), and meals and lodgings (Sec. 119) only apply to individuals, as is true for most of these exclusions. Others, income from discharge of indebtedness (Sec. 108), apply to all taxpayers. The deductions in Chapter 9 also generally apply to all taxpayers except for those obviously intended for individuals. When in doubt, the Code always clearly designates the taxpayers affected by a given provision. A few deductions uniquely apply to C corporations only, as explained in the following paragraphs.

DIVIDENDS-RECEIVED DEDUCTION   Distributions from a corporation to its shareholders out of the corporation's earnings and profits are usually taxable income to the shareholder. This *double* taxation of dividends has often been labeled unfair, obviously by people who own stock, despite the fact that this double taxation is consistent with the general concept that treats the corporation as a separate entity. (We discuss this further later in this chapter.) At present, our law contains one provision to relieve the presumed inequity of double taxation, the dividends-received deduction.

The problem of double taxation is particularly troublesome when the shareholder is a corporation. Without some special relief, a single corporate intermediary between the corporation earning the income and the individual taxpayers would have the effect of triple taxation: first, when the subsidiary corporation earned the income; next, when the income was distributed to the parent corporate shareholder, and third, when the income was distributed as a dividend to individual shareholders. To relieve this inequity, a corporate shareholder is allowed a deduction equal to 80% of the dividends received from taxable domestic corporations. The deduction is 100% if the dividend is from small business investment companies (as specifically defined in the law). The dividend deduction is also 100% between members of an affiliated group of corporations.

To illustrate, Corporation X owns shares in Y (not a substantial percentage) and receives a cash dividend from Y, say $10,000. This $10,000 is included in X's gross income, but X is entitled to a deduction of $8,000 (80% of $10,000). This deduction is generally limited to 80% of the corporation's taxable income before the dividends-received deduction, except where the full 80% of the dividend creates or increases a net operating loss.

OTHER SPECIAL CORPORATE DEDUCTIONS   Under financial accounting practices, corporate organizational expenses are typically capitalized and carried on the corporate books as assets until the corporation ceases to exist. For tax purposes, corporations may defer such costs until liquidation or amortize them over a 60-month period beginning with the month active business is begun. For this purpose, organization expenses are narrowly defined as capital expenditures directly connected with the creation of the corporation. Though the amounts are usually small, most corporations elect the 60-month amortization to avoid the indefinite deferral of these costs.

Corporations do not incur many of the personal expenses incurred by individuals—for example, medical expenses and alimony—but they do make contributions to charitable organizations. C corporations may deduct contributions, but these are subject to a special limit of 10% of the corporation's income before the contribution deduction. What constitutes a deductible contribution and the application of this 10% limit are explained in Chapter 20.

Over the years, most special deductions allowed corporations have been added to the statutes to encourage foreign trade. During the 1930s, our government's foreign policy was concerned with extending the political influence of the United States in China and the Western Hemisphere. As a result, special deductions were allowed companies engaged in trade in those two areas. Recognizing that these somewhat archaic policies should no longer be encouraged by reduced taxes, Congress provided for the elimination, or phaseout, of the special deductions for China Trade Corporations and Western Hemisphere Trade Corporations in the 1976 Tax Reform Act.

Controlled Groups of Corporations

Prior to 1970, a much-used tax-planning device was to divide a business or a group of businesses with common ownership into several separate C corporations. For example, in a chain of retail outlets, each outlet would be organized as a separate C corporation. Under this arrangement, each corporation enjoyed the lower rates on the first dollars of taxable income. For example, under the 1968 rate schedule, each corporation would have $50,000 taxed at only 15%, and $25,000 taxed at only 25%. Since 1969, this advantage has been restricted. Currently, the taxable incomes of corporations that are members of a controlled group must be combined for purposes of applying the marginal rates below 34%.

A controlled group of corporations is defined in Sec. 1563 to include parent–subsidiary, brother–sister, and combined groups. The parent–subsidiary form includes any one or more chains of corporations connected with common 80% corporate–parent ownership. Thus, for example, if Corporation C-1 owns 100% of Corporation C-2, and C-2 owns 80% of C-3, corporations C-1, C-2, and C-3 would constitute a parent–subsidiary form of controlled group, and they would have to share the benefits of the rates below 34%. A brother–sister group includes any two or more corporations (1) that are at least 80% owned by five or fewer persons (including individuals, estates, and trusts) and (2) in which those five or fewer persons own more than 50% of the value of all stock ". . . taking into account the stock ownership of each such person only to the extent such stock ownership is identical with respect to each such corporation" [Sec. 1563(a)(2)(B)]. Obviously, reasonable people might well disagree as to the meaning of the quoted portion of the Code! In general, however, this subparagraph suggests that you must add together the common ownership in each set of commonly owned corporations to determine the "identical ownership" considering only the least common ownership percentage existing between the five or fewer common stockholders. To illustrate, consider the following ownership of a group of three corporations:

Individual Stockholder	Percent of Corporations owned			Identical Ownership
	C-1	C-2	C-3	
1	40	30	20	20
2	40	40	20	20
3	20	30	60	20
Total ownership	100	100	100	
Identical ownership				60

This group of corporations (C-1, C-2, and C-3) would constitute a brother-sister form of controlled group and would be required to combine their incomes in the determination of their tax liabilities. However, assume we rearrange the ownership slightly, as follows:

Individual Stockholder	Percent of Corporations owned			Identical Ownership
	C-1	C-2	C-3	
1	70	10	20	10
2	20	70	10	10
3	10	20	70	10
Total ownership	100	100	100	
Identical ownership				30

Although the three common owners (1, 2, and 3) would still satisfy the 80% ownership test, the three corporations (C-1, C-2, and C-3) would *not* be considered a controlled group because the three owners do not satisfy the second (that is, the 50% identical ownership) test. Consequently, each of the three corporations could still determine its own income tax liability without regard for the other two corporations' taxable incomes.

If a controlled group exists, the taxable incomes of group members are combined for purposes of applying the rates below 34%. Each bracket subject to a tax rate lower than 34% must be allocated among the group members. The agreement among the members of the group may specify the allocation of each bracket separately, and the agreement may be changed each year to obtain maximum benefits.

For example, assume that Corporation C-1 earns a $60,000 taxable income; Corporation C-2, a $30,000 taxable income; and Corporation C-3, a $110,000 taxable income, for a combined total taxable income of $200,000. If the three corporations are members of a controlled group, their total income tax liability is $61,250 [$22,250 + 39%($100,000)]. Exactly how they allocate the total tax among themselves is subject to their own agreement. On the other hand, if the three corporations are not members of a controlled group, each determines its own income tax liability in an independent manner. Thus, C-1's gross tax liability would be $10,000; C-2's $4,500; and C-3's $26,150. The $40,650 combined liability is $20,600 less simply because the three are not members of a controlled group.

The existence of these rules illustrates an important point about the use of corporations and other artificial entities. Some corporations, indeed, have an existence apart from their owners, though that existence is often threatened by takeover bids and unprofitable operations leading to bankruptcy. Most C corporations are created to obtain an advantage for the owners, commonly a tax advantage. Most smaller, closely held C corporations are not *really* separate entities. Separate treatment of them in our tax law is unreal, and the fiction creates many problems.

Corporation–Shareholder Transactions

In the introduction of this chapter, we identified four questions about the effects of the use of artificial entities. For a C corporation, are the answers to these questions consistent with the separate-entity concept? Surprisingly, the answer is yes, and the important exceptions are few in number. A note of caution is appropriate here: some of our most complex tax rules deal with the relationships between the various artificial entities and their owners. Treat what follows as rough generalizations, important to your understanding, nevertheless.

PROPERTY TRANSFERS TO CORPORATIONS   Transfers of property from shareholders to corporations in exchange for corporate stock are taxable transactions. For example, if an individual transferred land with a tax basis of $15,000 and a fair market value of $25,000 for stock in a corporation, presumably having a value of $25,000 also, the individual would realize a gain of $10,000 that is generally recognized. (If the property transferred were cash, then obviously there would be no gain.) This transfer of property for stock must be distinguished from a contribution to the capital of a corporation by an existing shareholder. In the latter, there would be no *exchange* because no stock would be received and, therefore, there would be no realization of gains and losses.

An important statutory exception to the taxability of transfers of property for stock is included in the law at Sec. 351 (see explanation in Chapter 20). If shareholder or shareholders transferring property for stock own 80% of the corporation's stock immediately after the transfer, no gain or loss is recognized. Congress included this exception many years ago to facilitate the use of corporations for legitimate legal and financial reasons, for example, when a family business goes public.

Does the corporation that issues its stock for property recognize gain on the exchange? If so, what is the corporation's cost or basis in the stock newly issued? Treasury stock acquired in a market transaction would have a cost or basis, but not new stock. The tax law solves this dilemma by providing that the issuing corporation has no gain or loss, a rule that applies to treasury shares as well as new shares.

PROPERTY TRANSFERS TO SHAREHOLDERS   Property transfers from a corporation to its shareholders with respect to their stock fall into two categories: transfers in exchange for stock when the corporation redeems shares or distributes assets in liquidation; and distributions of dividends out of the corporation's earnings and profits (retained earnings).

All such transfers are taxable events to the shareholder receiving the property. If the shareholder surrenders stock in a redemption or liquidation, gain or loss is recognized equal to the difference between the fair market value of the property received and the basis of the stock. Amounts received as dividends are recognized as income, measured by the fair market value of the property received.

The corporation that transfers property to its shareholders must also recognize gain as a general rule. This results in both the distribution of dividends and transfers in exchange for its stock. (The corporation obviously has no gain when it distributes cash.) For historical reasons too complicated to detail here, the distributing corporation does not recognize losses on property transferred to the shareholders unless the distribution is a liquidating distribution.

To illustrate these rules, assume that Corporation X distributes land to its sole shareholder, Mr. Y, who has a $5,000 basis in the X stock. The land has a fair market value of $50,000 and a cost basis to X of $20,000. On this distribution, X must generally recognize a $30,000 gain, whether the distribution is a dividend or in exchange for X's stock in redemption or liquidation. If the property is depreciated in value below its basis, X will *not* recognize a loss unless the transfer is in complete liquidation. Until recently, corporations did not recognize gain on these transactions and some important exceptions to the rule still exist.

If the distribution by X to Mr. Y is a dividend, Mr. Y has income of $50,000, the fair market value of the land. If the land is distributed in liquidation of X, Mr. Y surrenders his stock and reports a gain or $45,000 ($50,000 fair market of land less $5,000 basis in the stock).

What happens if Corporation X, wholly owned by Mr. Y, receives an item of income that enjoys tax preference and immediately distributes the cash or other asset representing the income to Mr. Y as a dividend? Say, for example, that X receives some tax-exempt interest income or some other excluded income. Does the income received now by Mr. Y retain its tax character? If the corporation is a separate entity, then the determination of tax effect should be for X and the distribution treated as an independent event. This is precisely what the law provides. The dividend received by Mr. Y is taxable income without regard to its treatment to X.

The treatment of transfers to shareholders is the major limitation on the use of corporations in tax planning. The corporate income is taxed twice, once at the corporate level and again when distributed to shareholders. While "double taxation" is entirely consistent with the idea of the corporation as a separate entity, "double taxation" is commonly proposed as a weakness of our tax laws, usually by people who own corporate shares and would like to lower their own taxes. The controversy over double taxation is discussed in Chapter 20.

SHAREHOLDERS AS CORPORATE EMPLOYEES   Individual shareholders of a C corporation who work for the corporation can also be treated as employees for tax purposes, a result consistent with the separate-entity concept. This means that the corporation can obtain a deduction for fringe benefits paid for such employees but that the value of the benefits may be excluded from the income of the employee–shareholder. (See Chapters 8 and 12 for exclusions.) For example, a corporation contributes $5,000 to a "qualified" pension plan on behalf of its president, who also owns 90% of the corporate stock. If within limits specified by the law, the $5,000 is deductible to the corporation and is not included in the president's gross income. As noted in Chapter 12, some exclusions apply to highly compensated employees only if the same fringe benefit is available to employees generally.

Illustration of Corporate Formula

To illustrate the computation of a C corporation's taxable income and net tax payable, assume the following:

Revenues:
From sales of merchandise	$210,000
From (domestic) corporate dividends	10,000
From city bond obligations	5,000

Routine "expenses":
Cost of goods sold	$110,000
Wages and salaries	35,000
Other expenses	10,000
Prepayment of tax liability	9,000

Table 6-1 below displays the necessary calculations based on these facts.

TABLE 6-1

USING THE CORPORATE TAX FORMULA

Income broadly conceived	$115,000	[($210,000 − $110,000) + $10,000 + $5,000]
less		
Exclusions	(5,000)	(interest on the city bond)
equals		
Gross Income	$110,000	(Again, observe that the cost of goods sold has already been "deducted" for tax purposes.)
↓		
less		
↓		
Routine deductions	(45,000)	($35,000 + $10,000)
and		
Special deductions	(8,000)	(80% × $10,000)
equals		
↓		
Corporate taxable income times appropriate rate(s) 15% × $50,000 = $7,500 25% × 7,000 = 1,750	$57,000	
$9,250		
↓		
equals		
Gross tax	$9,250	
↓		
less		
↓		
Prepayments and credits	(9,000)	
equals		
↓		
Nex Tax Payable	$ 250	

PARTNERSHIPS

Conceptually, the tax treatment of partnerships is the opposite of that afforded C corporations. A partnership is merely an aggregation of the proprietary interests of partners in the underlying operations and assets. A partnership, therefore, is not a taxpayer but only a "reporting" unit whose income, gains, losses, deductions, credits, and other taxable items are allocated to and reported by the partners. Other implications of this "aggregate" concept are explained in the following sections. Here, as elsewhere, unfortunately, policy considerations dictate several important inconsistencies between the tax rules and the basic concept.

For tax purposes, "the term partnership includes a syndicate, group, pool, joint venture, or other unincorporated organization through or by means of which any business, financial operation, or venture is carried on, and which is not, within the meaning of this title, a corporation or a trust or estate."[5] Partnership must be distinguished from a mere joint tenancy or tenancy in common. While both legal forms involve joint ownership, a partnership results where there is joint proprietary operation of the property. At the other extreme, partnerships that have a sufficient number of corporate attributes may be "associations," a term that means the organization is a de facto corporation and taxed as such. The rules that follow, then, apply only to an organization that falls between these extremes—a partnership.

Partner–Partnership Transactions

Except when practical policy considerations take precedence, tax rules ignore the existence of the partnership and treat each partner as though he or she owned the underlying assets directly and operated them as a proprietor.

TRANSFERS OF PROPERTY TO AND FROM THE PARTNERSHIP   Assume that individuals A and B form a partnership for the purpose of subdividing land and selling residential lots. A contributes cash of $100,000, while B contributes land valued at $100,000 but with a basis to him of only $40,000. A and B agree to share capital and profits equally. From a legal standpoint, A and B have exchanged their assets for a new property, an interest in a partnership. For tax purposes, the exchanges are not taxable events. A clearly has no gain or loss, having exchanged cash, and under the aggregate concept the same result applies to B. The partnership also has no gain or loss.

To extend the above example, assume that after several years of successful operation, the AB Partnership distributes cash or other assets in equal shares to A and B. Generally, such distributions are not taxable events to either the partners or to the partnership, though a few exceptions beyond our scope apply here. Note, however, that A and B have reported their shares of the

[5]Section 761(a).

partnership income as it arose, as distinguished from the distribution to the partners of assets resulting from profitable operations. Note, also, that the results here are the same as those obtained for a proprietor who keeps separate records and a bank account for the proprietorship. He realizes no gain or loss when he "transfers" his own assets into the business, nor does he have income when he decides to consume assets arising from profitable operations of the business.

REPORTING PARTNERSHIP OPERATIONS   As explained in Chapter 5, a partnership must use a taxable year that is the same as that of its principal partners, usually December 31 where the partners are individuals. The partnership files an information return (on Form 1065) that shows the partnership's taxable items of income, gains, losses, deductions, credits, and so on. The return also shows each partner's "distributive share" of these items. The partners then report their distributive shares on their individual tax returns. Where the partnership's taxable year is different from that of a partner, the partner reports his distributive share for the partnership year that ends within the partner's year.

Distributive shares of taxable items are generally allocated based on each partner's interest in the partnership capital. However, items can be allocated between the partners in any manner that the partners agree on, provided the allocation has "substantial economic effect." This latter term means that the allocations are properly recorded in the capital accounts and that capital accounts are used to determine each partner's share of partnership properties at liquidation.

To illustrate these points, assume that partnership CD reports for the current year an ordinary loss (excess of ordinary deductions over ordinary income) of $12,000 and a capital gain of $8,000. If C and D are equal partners, each reports an ordinary loss of $6,000 and a capital gain of $4,000. If the partners agree, the entire ordinary loss could be allocated to C, for example, provided the loss is properly recorded in C's capital account and provided the capital accounts reflect C's interest for purposes of liquidation. An important point illustrated by the preceding example is that the tax character of an item does not change because of the partnership. The capital gain is still a capital gain to the reporting partner. The tax attributes of all items flow through the partnership to its partners.

The above illustration also raises a question: Is there any limit on the amount of partnership losses that can be reported by a partner? Recall that tax accounting, like general accounting rules, is based on historical cost. Thus, the losses reported by a partner could never exceed his cost basis in the partnership. Assume that individual E contributes cash of $10,000 and individual F contributes land with a fair market value of $10,000 and a basis of $1,000 to an equal partnership. After a year of operations, and assuming it still holds the land and has no liabilities, EF shows a loss of $5,000, obviously representing a loss of E's cash. If $2,500 of this loss is allocated to each partner, F can only deduct $1,000 (against other sources of income) because that is the extent of his investment in the partnership at cost. If EF has liabilities of $4,000 at year's end, F would be treated as owing one half of these liabilities, and the basis of his investment would be $3,000, the $1,000 basis from the contributed land plus one half of the debt. In this event, F could deduct his share of the loss, and his basis at the end of the year would become $500. Likewise, if EF had earned a profit, instead of a loss, F would have reported his share of the profit on his tax return, and his basis in EF would have increased. Note that if F's share of the loss had been greater than his basis, he could have increased his basis by making an additional contribution of assets to the partnership. Distributions of assets from the partnership to partners generally reduce basis.

The ability of a partner to increase basis by his or her share of partnership debt is an important reason why partnerships (and not corporations) have often been used as vehicles for tax shelters. If the partnership's major assets are largely financed by debt (real estate, for example) the partners will be able to absorb losses greater than their cash investment. This sharing of liabilities may not hold for limited partners in a limited partnership, nor is an increase in basis permitted when the partners are not "at risk" for the debt.

PARTNERS NOT EMPLOYEES   If a partnership is a mere aggregation of proprietors, partners cannot be employees for tax purposes, and the exclusions for fringe benefits are not available in the partnership setting. In partnership agreements partners commonly draw "salaries." These payments serve only as allocations of partnership income and do not make the partners employees.

OTHER RULES—SOME INCONSISTENCIES   The effective administration of the income tax, unfortunately, requires that partnerships be treated as separate entities for some purposes. With only minor exceptions, elections relative to accounting periods and methods must be made at the partnership level. If a partnership uses the accrual method, then each partner must use that method for reporting partnership items even though a particular partner might prefer the cash method. The partnership is a "reporting" unit for tax purposes, and use of a single method for partnership items is an administrative necessity.

Partnerships are also treated as separate entities for purposes of determining the character of partnership items. If property is held by a partnership as inventory, gain on the disposition is ordinary income, even if the inventory would be a capital asset if held directly by the partners.

Finally, a partnership usually has a continuing existence for tax purposes, even when some event occurs that terminates a partnership under local law. Admission of a new partner, retirement of an old partner, or sale of an existing partnership interest to a new partner (if less than 50% of partnership capital) does not terminate a partnership for tax purposes. The statute provides for continuation of a partnership unless it ceases to do business or unless control of the partnership changes hands by sale within a 12-month period.

S CORPORATIONS

An S corporation is a hybrid entity with some of the characteristics of both C corporations and partnerships. When added to the statute in 1958, the intent of Congress was to provide taxpayers with a vehicle they could use to obtain the financial benefits of a corporation (primarily limited liability for the shareholders) without the burden of double taxation. Under the rules adopted in 1958, the taxable income of an electing S corporation was taxed directly on the returns of its shareholders. Similarly, an S corporation's net operating losses were deductible by its shareholders, subject to certain limits. Except for the flow-through of taxable income and net operating losses, S corporations were subject to the usual separate-entity rules generally applicable to corporations. The rules adopted in 1958 were complex and often resulted in tax effects that reduced the benefits of the S corporation election.

In 1983, Subchapter S was substantially revised. Congress adopted rules for S corporations identical in many ways to those applicable to partnerships. For years after 1982, every taxable item—that is, income, gain, loss, deduction, and credit—of an S corporation flows through to its shareholders, just as taxable items flow through a partnership to the partners. The usual corporate rules, however, still apply to the formation of S corporations and to some corporate distributions. As explained below, the aggregate concept that gives the simple rules applicable to partnerships cannot be applied to S corporations because a corporation may change from C status to S status, or vice versa, during its life.

Election of Subchapter S Provisions

The Subchapter S provisions are elective and available only when the following conditions are met:

1. The corporation must be a domestic corporation with only one class of stock outstanding.
2. All stockholders must be individual citizens or residents, estates, or certain trusts.
3. There must be 35 or fewer stockholders.
4. The corporation must not be a member of an affiliated group.
5. Every stockholder must consent in writing to the original election.

Once made, the election applies to all subsequent years unless the shareholders agree to revoke the election. This power to revoke the election is essential to effective tax planning. For example, the election may be made for a new venture for which losses are expected for a few years then revoked after operation has turned the corner and begins to produce substantial amounts of income. Once revoked, a new S election cannot generally be made for a 5-year period. Revocation of an election requires the positive action of shareholders owning more than one half of the stock. The election is also terminated when the corporation ceases to meet the conditions listed above.

Reporting S Corporation Income

The basic tax accounting for an S corporation generally parallels that for a partnership. Each shareholder reports his or her share of the S corporation's taxable items for the S corporation's year that ends during the shareholder's taxable year. Taxable items are allocated pro rata to stock ownership. Recall that S corporations have only one class of stock, a requirement that facilitates this allocation. Taxable items of income, gains, losses, and deductions that are not subject to special tax rules are grouped together as the S corporation's "ordinary" taxable income (loss). All items subject to special rules are separately allocated among the shareholders. Recall that partners can agree to "special" allocations so long as the allocations have substantial economic effect. The law permits only pro-rata allocations for S corporations. S corporation losses reported by shareholders are limited to each shareholder's basis in his or her stock.

Calculation of basis in an S corporation generally parallels the calculation of basis for a partnership. In contrast to the partnership rules, only direct loans made by the shareholder to the corporation increase the shareholder's basis. Unlike partners, S shareholders are not treated as sharing the corporate liabilities (because they are not legally liable), and their bases are not increased by general debt of the corporation. Basis initially equals the investment in the corporation. It is increased when income of the corporation is taxed to shareholders and decreased when losses of the corporation flow through to shareholders. Asset distributions reduce basis, and additional contributions increase it.

Other examples of S corporation rules that parallel partnership rules are: (1) accounting elections are made at the S corporation level, not by each shareholder; (2) the tax character of items is determined at the corporate level; (3) shareholders of an S corporation who own directly or indirectly more than 2% of the corporate stock cannot be employees of the corporation for tax purposes; and S corporations must generally use December 31 as their taxable year.

Corporate–Shareholder Transactions

The tax law treats the S election as a temporary condition. S corporations are still corporations to which the separate entity concept applies. Transfers of property for corporate stock are taxable events unless Sec. 351 applies to the exchange (see Chapter 20). Distributions of assets from the S corporation to its shareholders, in liquidation or redemption, result in a gain or loss to the shareholder measured by the difference between the basis in the stock and the fair market value of the property received. An S corporation that makes a noncash distribution recognizes gain (but not loss) on the distributed property. (Note that gain on distributions along with other income is allocated to and reported by the shareholders.)

These corporate rules that result in double taxation cannot, of course, apply to "dividend-like" distributions from the S corporations to their shareholders. If the shareholders pay tax currently on corporate income, a distribution of assets representing such income must be tax-free to the shareholders, just as a distribution of assets is tax-free in the partnership setting. To accomplish this result, C corporations maintain an "accumulated adjustment account," (AAA), the rough equivalent of a retained earnings account for the years of the S election. Distributions of assets to shareholders out of this AAA account are tax-free to the shareholders. Separate-entity rules would still result in gain recognized to the S corporation if appreciated property is distributed.

An illustration will make these rules more concrete. Individual A owns all the stock of S and has a basis of $22,000 in the stock. S distributes property to A with a fair market value of $50,000 and a basis to S of $42,000. If this distribution is not in exchange for A's stock—that is, in liquidation—treatment of it depends on the balance of S's AAA account. Assuming that account has a balance of over $50,000, the distribution is tax-free to A. If this is a liquidating distribution, A has a gain of $28,000 ($50,000 − $22,000). In every event, S must recognize a gain of $8,000 ($50,000 − $42,000). A will include this gain on his individual return.

This hodgepodge of corporate and partnership rules is necessary because a corporation can change from C to S status and vice versa. Obviously the objective of simple tax laws would be better served if the election were made at the corporation's inception and if the election then remained in effect for the corporation's entire life. Then S corporations would be governed by partnership rules entirely, except for the treatment of corporate liabilities.

FIDUCIARIES

In both common parlance and the law generally, a fiduciary is simply any person to whom property has been entrusted for the benefit of another. For federal income tax purposes, when the adjective "fiduciary" is used to modify the noun "taxpayer," this everyday definition may not suffice. For these tax purposes, the term fiduciary includes only certain estates and trusts. Some of the more important details associated with the income taxation of fiduciaries are explained in the next section of this chapter.

An Estate

When an individual who owns property dies, an estate is created. Local law and the terms of the will (if any) determine whether title to the property passes first to the estate and later to the beneficiaries, or directly to the heirs or devisees of the decedent taxpayer. If title passes to the estate and the will directs the administrator of the estate to pay debts of the estate, any income earned on the property during a reasonable period of administration will ordinarily be taxed to the estate and paid from assets of the estate. If a will does not direct the adminstrator to pay the debts of the estate and title passes directly to the heirs or devisees, those individuals rather than the estate will usually pay any federal income tax attributable to whatever income is derived from the property during the period of adminstration.

The estates of wealthy individuals owning many properties may require several years to settle. In this instance, of course, the estate will typicallly continue to be recognized as a separate taxpayer until all administrative matters are resolved and all assets distributed. Should an executor try to unduly prolong the existence of an estate solely for income tax advantages, however, the estate may be terminated for tax purposes before it is terminated for other purposes.

A few of the terms commonly associated with an estate include the following words and phrases:

Decedent: the person who died.

Devisee: an individual specifically designated in a will as one to receive some part or all of the property of a decedent.

Executor (male) or executrix (female): the individual legally responsible for the administration of a decedent's estate.

Heir: an individual who may, by operation of local law and/or the terms of a will, receive part or all of a decedent's estate.

Intestate: dying without a will.

Law of descent and distribution: local law that determines, in absence of a will, how the property of a decedent must be distributed.

Subchapter J: the portion of the Code (Secs. 641–692) that contains much of the income tax law pertinent to estates, trusts, and decedents.

Testate: dying with a will.

Understanding these terms is often helpful in interpreting tax provisions pertinent to the taxation of estates.

A Trust

The word *trust* generally refers to a fiduciary relationship (or legal entity) in which a trustee temporarily holds title to property for the benefit of another. The property put into trust is often called the *corpus* (or body) of the trust. The person who puts the property in trust may be referred to as the *grantor* or *settlor* of the trust. The instructions given by the grantor to the trustee, which generally established both the powers of the trustee and the eventual disposition of any residual property remaining at the termination of the trust, are referred to as the trust *indenture.* Because a trust may exist for many years, it is common to name a corporate "person" (such as a bank, or a professional legal firm) as trustee simply to insure the trustee's living long enough to carry out all of the terms of the trust indenture. Persons designated

FIGURE **6-2**   Fundamentals of a Trust

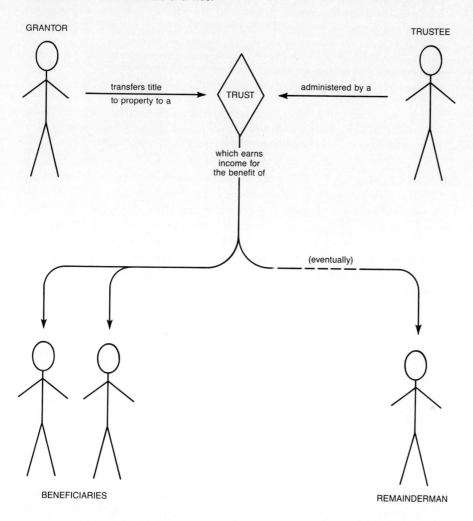

by the grantor as potential recipients of trust benefits are called *beneficiaries*. A *life beneficiary* is one who can benefit from a trust only so long as he or she lives; at death, a life beneficiary has no remaining interest in any of the trust assets. The person who will receive whatever property is left at the termination of a trust is called the *remainderman*. The fundamentals of a typical trust can be illustrated as in Figure 6-2.

In addition to the technical terms already used to describe the fundamental notion of a trust, there are many other words and phrases the definition of which can be very helpful (if not essential) to understanding the federal income tax treatment of trusts. A short list of such words and phrases follows:

Clifford trust: a trust (a) created for either (1) a period of more than 10 years or (2) the life of a beneficiary, and (b) providing for a return of the trust corpus to the grantor at the expiration of the trust term.

Complex trust: any trust that, by terms of the indenture, is not a simple trust.

Executory trust: an incomplete trust—that is, one requiring the execution of something further before it will have full effect.

Inter vivos trust: a trust created during the life of the grantor.

Power: the legal right or ability granted by one person to another enabling the latter person to do something for him.

Reversionary interest: any right in a property, that has been placed in trust, that may revert to the grantor.

Simple trust: a trust that, by requirements stated in the trust indenture, (1) must distribute all of its income currently *and* (2) has no charitable beneficiaries.

Testamentary trust: a trust created at the time of the grantor's death.

WHY CREATE TRUSTS?   The reasons that a person may have for creating a trust vary widely. In many instances these reasons have nothing to do with taxation. For example, parents may create a trust just to be certain that their mentally retarded child will have sufficient assets to pay for his or her needed care for life. A trust might also be created to allow an individual with little or no business acumen to benefit from the income generated by a business that would best be managed by someone else. Or a trust may be utilized simply to accumulate assets for the later benefit of a minor, quite possibly to pay for the minor's college expenses sometime in the future.

On the other hand, many trusts in the past were created primarily for tax reasons. The motivating tax law could have been either the income tax or the donative transfer tax. The income tax was a common explanation in the 50 or so years before 1987 when the marginal tax rates of individuals typically started at low levels but moved quite rapidly up to top marginal rates of 50%, 70%, or even more. The basic idea was very simple: if a taxpayer in a high marginal tax bracket could redirect the income, generated by a property that the taxpayer owned, away from himself or herself and to another person (usually another family member) who was in a lower marginal tax bracket, then the after-tax wealth of the family unit could be increased. For example, suppose that a woman in the 70% marginal tax bracket could, via a trust, redirect $1,000 in interest income (from a certificate of deposit) away from herself and to her daughter who was in a 15% marginal bracket. That simple legal rearrangement would save the mother-daughter pair $550 each year in federal income taxes. That is, instead of the mother paying a tax of $700 on the $1,000 interest income, the daughter could pay a tax of only $150 on that same $1,000 of interest.

THE TAXATION OF TRUSTS   Given the relative ease with which major tax savings could be achieved under these circumstances, it is not surprising to discover that many trusts are *not* recognized as a separate taxpayer for federal income tax purposes even though they are completely viable legal entites for all other purposes. Thus the most critical tax question is: Under what circumstances will a trust be recognized as a taxable entity separate and distinct from the taxpayer who created it? For purposes of this general introduction to the taxation of trusts, we can answer that question as follows:

1. For trusts created after March 1, 1986 (as well as trusts created before that date *if* any additional property is transferred to the trust after March 1, 1986) the trust will be recognized as a separate taxpayer *only if* the chance that any trust property may revert to the grantor (or the grantor's spouse) is 5% or less.

2. For trusts created on or before March 1, 1986 (and to which no additional property has been transferred since that date) the trust will be recognized as a separate taxpayer so long as any trust property can *not* revert to the grantor
   a. In 10 years or less, *or*
   b. Until the death of a designated life beneficiary.

Trusts that are *not* recognized as a separate taxable entity are called *grantor trusts*. This means, of course, that the federal income tax liability for any income earned by a grantor trust will be determined by adding that income to all other taxable income earned by the grantor *regardless of any actual distribution of the trust income by the trustee per the terms of the trust indenture*.

To illustrate, let us assume that individual (I) puts in trust a property that earns $20,000 each year. In addition, assume that I earns another $300,000 of taxable income each year. If the trust indenture provides that the trustee must retain the property for a minimum of 11 years, and gives the trustee the power to either distribute the income to C (C being I's child) or to accumulate it for later distribution to C, the question is: Who must pay the income tax on the $20,000 annual income earned by the trust? The answer, of course, generally depends on the date this trust was created. If it was created in, say, 1982, either the trust or C would report the $20,000 income and pay the income tax. (The taxpayer would be the trust, if and to the extent that the trustee retained the income; it would be C, if and to the extent that the trustee distributed the income to C.) On the other hand, if the trust were created in 1987, the entire $20,000 income would have to be reported on I's tax return *even if* the trust retained the income or distributed the income to C.

As a second illustration, assume that this same individual (I) created a trust giving the trustee only *limited* powers over the property put in trust. For example, the trust indenture could provide that the trustee must pay the entire $20,000 annual income earned by the trust to P, I's 94-year-old parent, for so long as P shall live, and that on P's death the property shall automatically revert to I. Furthermore, should I have need for the property before P's death, I retained the right to demand that the trustee return the property to I at any time. Under these modified circumstances, it would not make any difference when this trust was created. Because I retained the power to force the trustee to return the property to I at any time, this trust would automatically be a grantor trust and the $20,000 annual income would automatically be taxed to I, even if the trustee paid the $20,000 income to P each year for the next 6 years! If we modify this scenario slightly, and delete I's right to demand a return of the property before P's death, then the date of the trust once again becomes critical. If it were created in February 1986, the $20,000 would be taxed to P; if it were created in April 1986, it would be taxed to I. Incidentally, both the original illustration and the *revised* version of the second illustration, above, are classic examples of the Clifford trust that was so popular just a few years ago. Because of changes in the 1986 tax law, there will be relatively few Clifford trusts created today.

OTHER TAX DETAILS   For other than grantor trusts, a simple trust is authorized an exemption of $300 per year; a complex trust, one of $100. No standard deduction is allowed any trust. Finally the tax rates for trusts in 1988 and thereafter are as follows:

First $5,000	15%
$5,000 to $13,000	28
$13,000 to $26,000	33
Above $26,000	28

The reason for the 33% marginal rate for taxable incomes of between $13,000 and $26,000 is, of course, to phase-out the benefit of the lower rate on the first $5,000 of taxable income by way of the 5% surtax. This means, of course, that most trusts of any size will now pay a tax rate of 28%—the same rate generally applicable to individuals earning large amounts of income. For this reason, trusts will have lost much of their tax luster for well-heeled citizens. In Chapter 21, we will again consider trusts and how they can be used in tax planning.

USES OF ENTITIES IN TAX PLANNING

The tax environment explained in this chapter is complicated—no other description is truthful. From a planning prospective, these complications, along with the very diversity of the rules, are useful. Except where legal or financial factors dictate otherwise, we usually have a choice of the artificial entity used, if any, and the game is to select the one that gives the best tax results. Before turning to a summary of the uses that have been made of artificial entities, consider the following illustration:

Comprehensive Illustration

Assume that Mr. and Mrs. Buz Ness are actively engaged in several business ventures and that they own a substantial number of corporate stocks. During the current year their activities encompassed no less than five ventures:

1. Buz Cleaners—a chain of drive-in laundry and dry-cleaning establishments organized as a corporation. Mr. Ness receives a $20,000 annual salary from Buz Cleaners. After paying all of its expenses, including the owner–employee's salary, Buz Cleaners, Inc. reports a $22,000 taxable income. The corporation paid $1,200 in dividends to Mr. and Mrs. Ness, the sole owners of Buz Cleaners stock.

2. Goode-Ness Manufacturing Company—a new venture intended to produce commercial washing machines that will reduce waiting time by 50%. Goode-Ness is

owned equally by James Goode and Buz Ness, who are not related. During the current year, Goode-Ness reported a taxable loss of $16,000. The firm is organized as a corporation but has elected S corporation treatment for tax purposes. Neither Goode nor Ness receives any salary from the firm, and no other assets were distributed by Goode-Ness during the year.

3. B.R.E.D. Board—a retail pastry shop organized as a partnership. Mrs. Ness owns a one-fourth interest in the partnership assets and profits. As one of four partners, she draws a $6,000 annual salary. After paying partners' salaries and all other operating expenses, B.R.E.D. Board reports a net income of $8,000, which is reinvested in the business.

4. Loc-Ness Trust Fund—a collection of assets put into trust by Buz Ness's parents prior to their deaths several years ago. The trust agreement provides that the trustee can make distributions of trust income, at his discretion, to Mr. or Mrs. Ness or to any of their children. On the death of the last of Buz Ness's children, the remaining assets are to be distributed to their heirs. During the current year, the trust earned a total income of $60,000. Of this, the trustee distributed $10,000 to each of the four Ness children. He retained $20,000 of the income within the trust fund.

5. Ness Insurance—an insurance agency operated as a sole proprietorship. During this year, the agency earned an income of $30,000. Buz withdrew $1,000 a month from the agency for personal living expenses. The remaining $18,000 was reinvested in a new office building to house the insurance agency.

The Ness's five business ventures and the related cash flows between these ventures and the individual members of the Ness family are diagrammed in Figure 6-3. In terms of economic and physical realities, this arrangement obviously involves at least five distinct business operations and six people. In terms of taxable entities, however, there are one corporation (Buz Cleaners), one fiduciary (Loc-Ness), and six individuals (Mr. and Mrs. Ness and their four children). Two of the businesses (Goode-Ness and B.R.E.D. Board) must file information tax returns, but they are not liable for any tax as separate entities.

In terms of tax calculations, Mr. and Mrs. Ness probably file one joint tax return on which they report the following items of gross income:

From Buz Cleaners, Inc.:	
As salary	$20,000
As dividend	1,200
From Goode-Ness Manufacturing Co.:	
Half of the net operating loss	(8,000)
From Loc-Ness Trust Fund:	
Nothing	
From B.R.E.D. Board:	
As salary	6,000
As operating income (¼ interest)	2,000
From Ness Insurance:	
As operating income	30,000
Total from all sources	$51,200

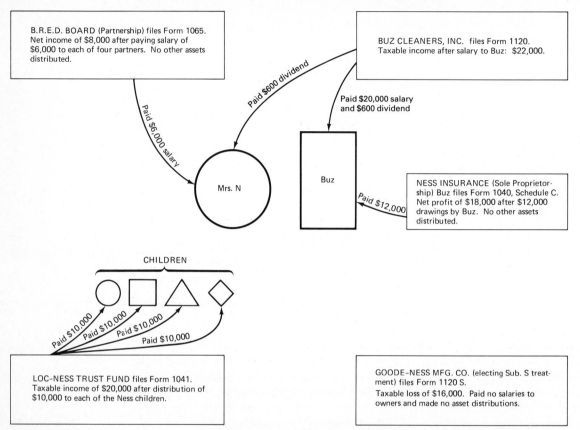

FIGURE **6-3**   Ness Family Business Interests and Cash Distributions

Observe that although the total cash received by Mr. and Mrs. Ness is only $39,200, they must report as gross income a total of $51,200 from their several business interests. Both Ness Insurance and B.R.E.D. Board contributed more to their gross income than to their cash flow; Goode-Ness Manufacturing Company, on the other hand, provided a tax deduction even though it did not require a cash contribution from either Mr. or Mrs. Ness.

On their joint tax return, Mr. and Mrs. Ness probably claim each of their four children as well as themselves as personal and dependent exemptions. Additionally, each of the children files his or her own tax return, as explained in Chapter 11.

Buz Cleaners, Inc., would file a tax return and pay tax on an income of $22,000. Observe that Buz Cleaners gets a tax deduction for the salary it paid to its owner–employee but that it does not get a deduction for the dividend it paid to Mr. and Mrs. Ness. Had Buz elected to do so, he may have been able to increase his salary to reduce or even eliminate any taxable income for Buz

Cleaners, Inc. This action would, of course, have increased their personal tax liability accordingly.

Unlike Buz Cleaners, Loc-Ness Trust is treated as a separate taxable entity only to the extent that it retains its income. Thus, by paying out $10,000 to each of the four Ness children, Loc-Ness Trust reduces its taxable income from $60,000 to $20,000. Note, however, that the trust agreement is a little too good to be true. For income taxes, the arrangement can effectively spread the income among Mr. and Mrs. Ness and their children. The original grantors of the trust were Buz Ness's parents. Prior to 1987, this type of trust would pass the trust corpus to the great-grandchildren of the creators (or grantors) and successfully avoid the federal estate tax on the two intervening generations. Under new rules, on the deaths of each succeeding generation that enjoys a life estate—a right to receive income for life—a wealth-transfer tax is levied on the trust corpus. This tax on generation-skipping transfers applies also to "direct skips"—gifts and testamentary transfers to heirs two or more generations younger than the transferor.

Matching Entity Attributes with Objectives

The important question left unanswered in the above illustration is: Why did Buz's tax advisor use the particular entities actually employed? Would other legal arrangements be preferable from a tax standpoint? The selection of the "best" entity is no mean task, and we cannot set out a simple set of rules that can be followed to solve the problem. Some general statements with examples, however, are helpful, with the proviso that generalization of a complex subject carries unavoidable risks.

Remember that the form used may be dictated by legal considerations. A multinational conglomerate with numerous owners requires the corporate form. Two oil companies that join together to drill a single oil or gas well will want the simplicity of a partnership. And the parent who wants to protect a spendthrift child from his or her own foolishness will use a trust. Here, we are concerned solely with the tax attributes of the entities and with choosing the one with the proper attributes for the circumstance.

The C corporation generally requires the active conduct of a trade or business, and the form can only be used when the problem of double taxation can be solved. After 1986, remember, the traditional rate advantage enjoyed by C corporations no longer exists, except in very limited circumstances illustrated in Chapter 7. The other major tax advantage of incorporation is the ability to use fringe benefits for officer–owners, an advantage that will not normally offset the disadvantages of double taxation.

The double tax on C corporations is usually avoided by not paying dividends and by reinvesting the after-tax earnings in the business. Such constant reinvestment of earnings delays the double tax until the corporation is liquidated. (If the corporate stock passes to a younger generation by inheritance, the gain to the shareholder is virtually eliminated but not the gain to the liquidating corporation; see Chapter 16.) If the eventual liquidation, and the resulting double tax, is far enough in the future, the present value (penalty) of the second tax is insignificant. The reinvestment of C corporation earnings, however, creates other tax problems. The law contains two special penalty taxes that are levied when earnings retained are not reinvested in an active business. The first of these is the tax on Personal Holding Companies (PHC). Originally added to the law to prohibit the incorporation of investment portfolios, the penalty tax applies when more than 60% of a corporation's income is from passive activities (technically, PHC income that includes income from personal service contracts in some cases). The second penalty applies when a corporation accumulates its earnings and profits beyond the foreseeable, reasonable needs of the business.

Just how useful C corporations will be after the rate changes made in the 1986 Reform Act is uncertain now. Tax practitioners are inventive, and new, advantageous uses of C corporations will no doubt emerge. One certain use explained in Chapter 21 is the use of C corporations to avoid the passive loss rules that generally do not apply to them.

The best and most common use of partnerships is for leveraged investments that produce current tax losses. Due in large part to tax rules, investment in oil and gas, farming, and real estate are the usual ones. The partnership form permits deduction of the losses by the partners, and the treatment of partnership debt as debt of the partners, thereby increasing the partner's basis in the interest, which serves as a limit on losses. Tax rules for partnerships also permit the special allocation of gains, losses, and so on. In real estate, for example, partner–investors have often been allocated all depreciation, which increases their losses now, with the expectation that capital gains will be allocated to them later to recoup the losses.

The importance of partnership was diminished by the passive loss rules in the 1986 Reform Act. Recall from Chapter 3 that rental real estate is by definition passive. Furthermore, a limited partner by definition has a passive role without regard to the partner's actual participation. On the other hand, many practitioners are only now gaining an appreciation of the use of special allocations as well as other partnership attributes beyond our scope here.

The 1986 Reform Act will, no doubt, spawn new uses for partnerships. For example, some profitable C corporations have liquidated and transferred their assets to limited partnerships. The partnership form permits a single tax on the income at the partner level. As an added advantage, this income received by a limited partner is passive income, not portfolio income, and it can be used to offset passive losses. Note that the limited partnership gives many of the legal advantages of incorporation, especially limited liability to all but the general partner.

The future role of S corporations is very uncertain. We can expect smaller C corporations to make S elections and avoid the double tax. If more than 35 investors are involved, however, a limited partnership is indicated. For new ventures with less than 35 investors, the partnership form will usually be preferable. While the taxable items of an S corporation are taxed only and to its shareholders, the double tax idea still applies when appreciated corporate assets are distributed to shareholders. Instances where S corporations offer a clear tax advantage over the partnership form are rare.

Tax motivations for the use of trusts were also reduced substantially by the 1986 Act. For trusts, the 15% rate applies only to the first $5,000 of income, and the advantage of the 15% rate is phased out entirely at $26,000. The advantages of the 15% rate might be expanded by creating several trusts for the same beneficiary. Congress, however, has declared war on multiple trusts, and the I.R.S. will not treat multiple trusts separately unless nontax reasons justify their existence. The trust still has limited usefulness to shelter a limited amount of income, especially of beneficiaries younger than 14 whose unearned income is taxed at their parents' marginal rates.

While the role of these artificial entities in tax planning is less certain now after the 1986 Act, their proper use is still the most important subject for the serious tax student. That most of the subject matter in graduate tax programs deals with the use of entities attests to this fact.

PROBLEMS

1. a. As two extreme alternatives to our current entity structure, (1) we could exclude corporations from the list of entities recognized for tax purposes on the grounds that all corporate income ultimately belongs to individuals and that, until such time as that income is distributed by the corporation, it ought not to be subject to tax; or (2) we could tax all corporations exactly as we tax single taxpaying individuals and then exclude from individuals' income any amounts distributed (as dividends) by the corporations. What practical consequences would follow from each of these extreme alternatives? Explain.

   b. As another alternative to our present corporate income tax, we could *currently* allocate all corporate incomes to the (ultimate) individual stockholders, whether or not the corporation distributed any income. We could then exclude corporations from any income tax. (In other words, we could treat corporations the way we treat partnerships for tax purposes.) What practical reasons preclude the general acceptance of this alternative?

   c. Finally, as another alternative to our current corporate income tax, we could recognize the corporation as a separate entity only to the extent that the corporation retained income. This could be accomplished simply by allowing the corporation a deduction for dividends paid. (In essence, this is the way we treat trusts for tax purposes.) Why do you suppose that this alternative has never been accepted by Congress?

2. Many foreign countries levy very high taxes on corporate earnings that are not distributed to stockholders as dividends. Compare this with the U.S. treatment of corporate income and explain the probable effects of each alternative on the source of corporate funds.

3. Prior to the 1986 Act, C corporations were often used to obtain lower tax rates on income. To what extend does this possibility still exist, if at all? What *tax* factors might justify the use of a C corporation after 1986?

4. ABC Corporation received the following items of income in the current year:

Revenue from sales of merchandise	$130,000
Dividends from domestic corporations	10,000
Interest from State of Kansas bonds	5,000

In addition, ABC Corporation incurred the following expenses:

Cost of merchandise sold	$80,000
Other operating expenses	12,000
Contributions	5,000

a. What is ABC's taxable income for the year?
b. What is ABC's gross tax for the year?
c. Calculate ABC's current earnings and profits for this year's operations.

5. DEF Corporation received the following items of income in the current year:

Revenue from sales of merchandise	$230,000
Interest from State of Florida bonds	50,000

DEF Corporation also incurred the following expenses:

Cost of merchandise sold	$120,000
Other operating expenses	20,000

Based on 1988 rates, what is DEF Corporation's:
a. marginal tax rate?
b. average tax rate?
c. "real" or "effective" tax rate?

6. Handford Dixon has decided to incorporate his retail sports shop. His lawyer obtained a new corporate charter from the state, and Handford transferred the following assets to the corporation:

	FMV	Adjusted Basis*
Accounts receivable	$ 60,000	$ 60,000
Inventory	110,000	50,000
Furniture and fixtures	40,000	15,000
	$210,000	$125,000

*Same as book value

Handford received 1,000 shares of the corporation's no-par stock.
a. Does Handford have to recognize the $85,000 gain ($210,000−$125,000) for tax purposes? Explain.
b. Does the corporation have gain when it issues stock for the assets? Explain.
c. Assume that Handford later sells his corporate stock for $300,000. How much gain will he have?
d. What is the corporation's cost basis in the inventory received from Handford?

7. Mohigan, Inc. has operated successfully for many years. All its stock is owned by Mrs. M, and her basis in the stock is $100,000. Mohigan has earnings and profits of $350,000. Listed below are distributions made by Mohigan to Mrs. M. For each give the tax effects (1) for Mrs. M and (2) for the corporation.
a. Cash of $100,000. No stock surrendered.
b. Land with a basis of $60,000 and a FMV of $100,000. No stock surrendered.

   c. All Mohigan assets, with a basis of $550,000 and a FMV of $800,000 in complete liquidation. Mrs. M surrenders all her stock.

8. Gummo, Inc. has the following items of income and deductions for the year:

Income:	
Gross income from sales of inventory	$200,000
Net capital gain	20,000
Dividends from domestic corporations	40,000
Deductions:	
Operating expenses	90,000
Loss on sale of machinery	6,000
Contributions	20,000

Gummo was formed two years ago and at that time incurred organizational costs of $5,000.
   a. Calculate Gummo's taxable income for the year.
   b. Calculate Gummo's gross tax for the year.

9. Contrast the tax treatment of corporations and partnerships in the United States. Why are these entities treated differently? In your answer, consider both historical accident and rational tax policy.

10. If Congress were suddenly to enact a change in our current tax laws that would treat sole proprietorships and partnerships as separate taxable entities, as they are treated in financial accounting, what would you expect to happen if
   a. these new taxable entities were subject to the same rates as unmarried individual taxpayers?
   b. these new taxable entities were subject to the corporate tax rates?
Under either part a or b, would the concept of "controlled corporations" have to be extended to proprietorships and partnerships as well? Explain.

11. M and N, two individuals who use the calendar year, formed a partnership in January of the current year. Each partner has a 50% interest in profits, losses, and capital. For his capital interest, M contributed property with a basis of $60,000 and a fair market value of $100,000. During the year, partnership MN had the following items:

Ordinary loss from operations	($30,000)
Short-term capital gain	$10,000

At December 31, MN owed creditors $25,000. In December, each partner withdrew cash of $7,500.
   a. Does M recognize gain on his contribution to MN? If so, what is its nature?
   b. How does the MN operation affect M's personal return?
   c. How does the $7,500 withdrawal affect M's personal return?
   d. Calculate M's basis in his partnership interest at the end of the year.

12. S and T, two individuals, form a partnership for purposes of building a small apartment house. Each contributes cash of $50,000, and the partnership ST then borrows $900,000. The $1 million is used by the partnership to buy land and construct an apartment house. Because of high interest charges and large depreciation, ST shows a loss of $70,000 for its first year of operations and $60,000 for its second year.
   a. If S and T share these losses equally, will they be allowed a deduction for the full amounts? Explain.

b. S and T agree that S will receive all losses from this venture. Will this agreement be recognized for tax purposes? Explain.

13. S corporations are often characterized as "tax corporations treated as partnerships." Is this true? If not, discuss some major differences between treatment of the two entities.

14. Jack Warden, who files a joint return, is a successful banker who owns a small country bank. His income and deductions for recent years have been constant and, as a result, his taxable income has been about $103,400 for the past several years. In January 19x1, Jack found an experienced and dependable manager and opened a seed and fertilizer store in the rural town in which his bank is located. The new venture was incorporated as the Community Seed and Fertilizer Company, Inc., of which Jack owns 100% of the stock. The operating results of the corporation were as follows:

	Gain (Loss)
19×1	($50,000)
19×2	(30,000)
19×3	5,000

a. Calculate the combined tax of the corporation and Warden for 19x1 through 19x3 (assuming that Warden's taxable income was $103,400 per year). Use 1984 tax rates. The corporate losses can be carried forward (but not back, because 19x1 was the first year of operation).

b. Calculate the total tax for Warden for 19x1 through 19x3, assuming that Warden made a proper S corporation election for the years involved. Use 1984 tax rates. Warden's cost of his stock exceeds the losses.

15. The statements below describe some major tax characteristics of one or more of the entities (other than individuals) discussed in this chapter—corporations, S corporations, trusts, partnerships. For each statement, which is the appropriate entity or entities?

a. A separate entity for all purposes under the tax law.

b. An entity that serves only as a conduit for income and deductions.

c. An entity that functions as a taxpayer only to the extent that its income is not distributed.

d. An entity that serves as a rate shelter because it is subject to lower tax rates.

e. An entity that serves as a rate shelter only because it increases the number of taxpayers.

CHAPTER 7

Tax Rates and Computations

The accumulation of tax exclusions and deductions over the years has substantially eroded the tax base, forcing higher rates of tax on income that is subject to tax. High marginal tax rates create disincentives for saving, investing, and working. These in turn constrict economic growth and productivity.
President's Tax Proposals to the Congress for Fairness, Growth and Simplicity May 29, 1985

As indicated in the general formula at the beginning of Chapter 3, a gross income tax liability can be determined by multiplying the applicable tax rate(s) by the taxpayer's taxable income for the year. In Chapters 3, 4, and 5 we examined the general concepts of income, deductions, and measurement of income. In this chapter, we examine the general concept of our income tax rates.

At the outset, observe that income tax rates are applied to the *annual* income of *each* taxable entity. The concept of income has meaning only for a period of time, and the annual period has a long tradition. Thus, income tax rates are generally applicable each year to each taxpayer without regard to the taxpayer's previous history. In addition, the gross tax liability of each entity is determined independently, and the applicable tax rate for any one taxpayer is ordinarily determined without regard to the tax burden of any other taxpayer. Although the two facts just stated may appear intuitively obvious, their importance to tax planning is easily overlooked. We explain later how major tax savings can often be achieved by the entirely legal shifting of income or deductions, or both, between (1) two or more tax years and (2) two or more taxable entities.

In the United States, three fundamental taxable entities are recognized: *every* individual, *every* corporation, and *every* fiduciary (that is, every estate or trust). Differences between the taxation of these entities were discussed in Chapter 6. For the moment, however, we ignore those differences to the maximum extent possible and focus on the more fundamental concepts related to tax rates.

FUNDAMENTAL CONCEPTS

The Code implicitly accepts three fundamental concepts regarding income tax rates. First, all income tax rate schedules are progressive. Second, the Code applies a single, or unitary tax rate schedule to the entire income realized by each taxpayer. Third, the tax rate schedule applicable to each taxable entity—that is to individuals, corporations, and fiduciaries—is unique. We shall soon discover, however, that the fundamental concepts are quite often more illusory than real.

Progressivity

The tax rates for individual taxpayers are stipulated in Sec. 1(a)–(d); those for corporate taxpayers, in Sec. 11; and those for fiduciaries, in Sec. 1(e). For reasons explained in Chapter 11, the Code actually provides not one but four different sets of tax rates for individual taxpayers. Ignoring these sometimes important differences for the moment, we may observe the general progressivity of the tax rate structure imposed on taxable income by the federal government by an examination of Table 7-1.

TABLE **7-1**

GENERAL PROGRESSIVITY OF U.S. TAX RATES

	Number of Tax Brackets			Range of Marginal Rates					
				Minimum			Maximum		
Taxpayer	1986	1987	1988	1986	1987	1988	1986	1987	1988
Individuals	14-15	5	2	11%	11%	15%	50%	38.5%	28%[a]
Corporations	5	3	3	15	15	15	46	34[b]	34[b]
Fiduciaries	14	5	2	11	11	15	50	38.5	28[a]

[a]Ignoring the 5% surtax phasing out the 15% tax bracket for high income individuals and fiduciaries.
[b]Ignoring the 5% surtax on corporate taxable income between $100,000 and $335,000.

FIGURE 7-1   A Hypothetical Progressive Tax Schedule

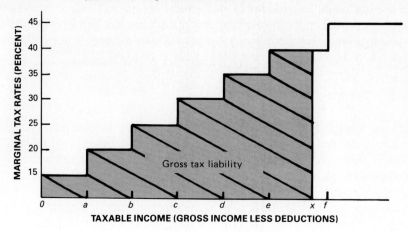

Note that while the nominal rate schedules for 1987 and 1988 remain progressive, they are much less so than in 1986 (prior to the Tax Reform Act of 1986). There are fewer brackets, and the range from the minimum to the maximum marginal rates is narrower. Further, special provisions in the law eliminate the benefit of the lowest bracket for high-income taxpayers.

Conceptually, when you think of the federal income tax rates, you should think of a rate schedule that looks something like the hypothetical one depicted in Figure 7-1, which has seven tax brackets ranging from 15 to 45%. The gross tax payable is represented by the area under the curve for any given amount of taxable income. For example, a taxable income of Ox dollars would be subject to a gross tax liability equal to the shaded area in Figure 7-1. To simplify the arithmetic, tax rate schedules are usually stated in the Code in columnar form. For example, if the distances *Oa, ab, bc,* and so on in Figure 7-1 were each equal to $2,000, the related but imaginary Code section might read as follows:

There is hereby imposed on the taxable income of every taxpayer a tax determined in accordance with the following table:

If taxable income is

Over	But Not Over	The Tax is	Plus	Marginal Rate	Times	Amount in Excess of
$ 0	$ 2,000	$ 0		15%		$ 0
2,000	4,000	300		20		2,000
4,000	6,000	700		25		4,000
6,000	8,000	1,200		30		6,000
8,000	10,000	1,800		35		8,000
10,000	12,000	2,500		40		10,000
12,000		3,300		45		12,000

This form of rate schedule facilitates the actual computation of the tax because it accumulates the tax in each preceding bracket and eliminates the need for repeated application of the rates in each bracket. For example, based on this hypothetical schedule, a taxpayer with an income of $10,200 would pay a tax of $2,580 [$2,500 + 0.40 ($10,200 − $10,000)].

Unitary System

That the United States purports to have a unitary income tax system is implicit in the fact that we have only one income tax base—that is, taxable income. Many other countries have a schedular income tax system. A schedular system is like a unitary system in that tax rates are applied to an annual tax base for each entity each year. A schedular system differs, however, in that each taxpayer may have different types of income subject to different rates each year. In other words, each taxpayer separates total income each year into predesignated types or kinds of income and applies the stipulated tax rate(s) to each type of income, beginning with the lowest marginal tax rate for that type (year by year and entity by entity). In some of these countries, the stipulated tax rates are proportional, rather than progressive, at least for certain types of income. In Mexico and Central and South America, the number of schedules varies from two to nine, depending on the country under consideration. A hypothetical South American schedular tax system might look something like that shown in Table 7-2.

Although a schedular income tax system at first appears to be fundamentally different from a unitary system, that disparity is often only a matter of degree. Neither system is really found in pure form. The schedular system overtly recognizes a social distinction in kinds of income, and it frequently provides different tax rates for the different kinds of income. The unitary system—either by law or by administrative caprice—usually makes similar distinctions, although they are more difficult to identify.

TABLE **7-2**

A HYPOTHETICAL SCHEDULAR TAX SYSTEM

Schedule	Income	Marginal Tax Rates Minimum	Maximum
A	Interest from government securities	3%	6%
B	Compensation as an employee	1	10
C	Income from agriculture	0	
D	Income from rents	5	20
E	Oil and mining profits	6	30
F	Lottery prizes and other chance winnings	0	10
G	Income from sources not reported under any other schedule	1	8

In the United States, we purport to have a unitary tax system. Nevertheless, as we have already learned, by law, no federal income tax is imposed on the interest paid to creditors of state and local governments. Considering only this one exclusion, therefore, we could accurately argue that the United States really has at least two tax rate schedules, one of them imposing a zero tax rate. In the remainder of this chapter, we explain several other recent and current federal tax provisions that have similar results and that often have made our law quite difficult to comprehend.

Entity Differences

Although the Code does not overtly recognize different tax rates for different kinds of income, it clearly stipulates different tax rates for the different taxable entities. As noted in Table 7-1, the 1988 marginal tax rates for individuals and fiduciaries begin at 15% and increase to 28%. The tax rates for corporations, on the other hand, begin at the same rate (at 15%) but increase to 34%.

In the past, the unique and explicit differences between the federal income tax rates applied to the taxable income realized by individuals and those realized by corporations caused the corporate entity to be a common form of tax shelter in the United States. The major tax rate reductions in 1981-1984 for individual taxpayers substantially reduced the value of the corporate tax rate shelter. Figure 7-2 illustrates the limited tax savings that were available to any married couple who could arrange to have their personal taxable income *realized and recognized* within a single corporate entity in 1984. In general, of course, this result was easily achieved by the mere act of incorporating any business that would otherwise have operated as a sole proprietorship or a partnership.

FIGURE **7-2** Corporate Versus Married Individuals' Tax Rates for 1984

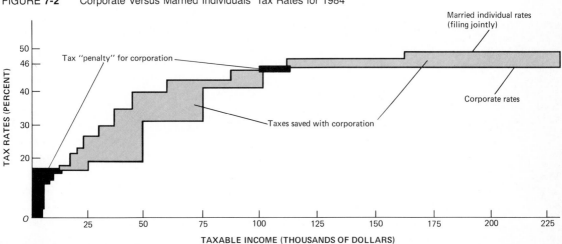

In contrast, compare Figure 7-2 with Figure 7-3, illustrating individual and corporate tax rate differences for 1988. Note that while savings can be achieved by incorporating when income is $75,000 or less, this advantage is quickly eliminated at higher income levels. These changes have led many commentators to predict much wider use of sole proprietorships, partnerships, and subchapter S corporations after 1986.

An illustration of the limited savings from incorporation will be helpful at this point. Assume that H and W file a joint return with two exemptions that shows taxable income of $180,000 and in which a net income of $120,000 from a proprietorship is included in the taxable income. If the taxable year is 1988, H and W owe a tax of $51,492 (28% of $180,000 + 28% of $3,900 value of the exemptions). See Appendix B for the 1988 rate schedule and Chapter 11 for further discussion of the individual tax calculation. If the business is incorporated, the $120,000 operating income can be split between H and W and the corporation by means of salaries and other payments deductible to the corporation. Assume that H and W take combined salaries of $50,000, leaving the corporation with taxable income of $70,000 ($120,000 − $50,000). H and W now have taxable income of $110,000 ($180,000 less the $70,000 taxed to the corporation). Total tax in 1988 is now:

On $70,000 taxed to corporation:		
$50,000 × 15%	$7,500	
20,000 × 25%	5,000	$12,500
On H and W's $110,000 using the joint		
schedule (Appendix B)		28,838
Total tax		$41,338

The savings is $10,154 ($51,492 − $41,338). This savings arises because the corporate taxable income is now taxed at rates below 28% and because H and W's income is taxed below 28% in part (and the value of the exemption deduction is not eliminated). Note that as the taxable incomes of the corporation and individuals increase, the rate becomes a flat 34% for the corporation and a flat 28% for the individuals, eliminating the possibility of savings.

The savings from incorporation illustrated carry with them several disadvantages. Ignoring tax law, the incorporation of the business means that the proprietors must now observe all legal rules that go along with the form—meetings of shareholders and directors, minutes, stock records, and so on. The corporate form is a lot of trouble. From a tax standpoint, the disadvantages are even greater. At some point, the law will extract a double tax. If dividends are paid, the savings become negative. Eventually, at liquidation, both the corporation and the shareholders must pay a tax on any gains that arise. Except for unusual circumstances, the incorporation of a business just to save taxes is a thing of the past.

Fiduciaries are also used to offset the individual tax rates, but not because the income tax rates applicable to fiduciaries are significantly different from those applicable to individuals. Indeed, the rates applicable to the taxable income of the two entities are approximately equal—beginning at 15% and

FIGURE **7-3**   Corporate Versus Married Individuals' Tax Rates for 1988*

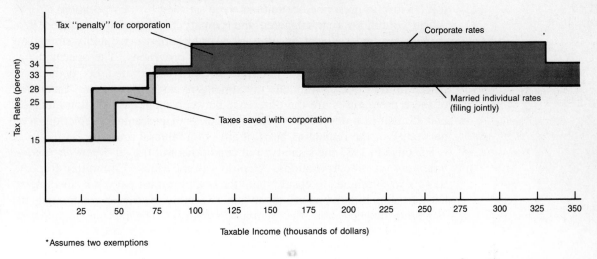

*Assumes two exemptions

rising to 28%. An individual who transfers income-producing property to a trust can effectively divide his or her income into two parts and then apply the lower rates on the schedules to each part each year, thereby reducing the total tax paid.

Unfortunately for the student, this is but the tip of the tax rate iceberg. The Code explicitly recognizes several exceptions to the general federal income tax rate schedules imposed in Secs. 1 and 11. Over the next several pages, we examine the general concepts of those major aberrations.

MAJOR ABERRATIONS FROM FUNDAMENTAL CONCEPTS

The Tax Reform Act of 1986 removed two of the major aberrations to a unitary system. The provisions affected were the treatment of capital gains and income averaging under Secs. 1301–1305. These two provisions will be briefly discussed along with several still-existing aberrations. As you consider these provisions, keep in mind that, fundamentally, we have a unitary system in which progressive rates are applied annually to each entity's taxable income. Our purpose here is to gain a general understanding of recent and present major exceptions to the fundamentals, leaving further details until later.

The Minimum Tax on Corporations

A major aberration from the otherwise unitary federal income tax rate schedule is known as the *minimum tax*. Prior to 1987, this tax was a penalty tax that had to be *added* to the gross income tax determined in the normal way, if certain prescribed conditions were satisfied by a corporation.

The conditions that triggered this penalty tax generally occurred if a corporation had reduced an otherwise sizable gross tax liability simply by taking advantage of various tax preference provisions. The specified tax preference provisions were in large measure accelerated tax deductions placed in the Code to stimulate investments in certain properties. Examples of these preferences are the difference between rapid depreciation methods and straight-line depreciation and the excess of percentage depletion over part or all of the remaining basis (if any) of a mineral property.

Effective in 1987 the same type of conditions will trigger a new *alternative minimum tax* on corporations. According to the House Committee Report, this tax was designed to ensure that "the taxpayer must pay a tax equalling at least [a minimum percent] of an amount more nearly approximating its economic income (above the exemption amount)." The alternative minimum tax for corporations is the amount by which 20% of *alternative minimum taxable income* (reduced by an exemption) exceeds the regular tax. Alternative minimum taxable income is taxable income modified by certain adjustments and preferences. The preferences are the same as under prior law with some modifications and additions. Perhaps the most controversial of these new preferences is one half of the amount by which the corporation's adjusted book income exceeds its alternative minimum taxable income. The Senate Committee Report states that "The committee does not intend otherwise to interfere with the choice of a reasonable accounting method by a taxpayer, to require that certain accounting principles be applied, or to establish the Secretary of the Treasury as an arbiter of acceptable accounting principles." Nonetheless, it seems likely that this provision will affect the choice of accounting methods for companies affected by the alternative minimum tax.

The Minimum Tax for Noncorporate Taxpayers

In certain circumstances, an *individual* (or a fiduciary) taxpayer does not pay the income tax determined in the normal way. Instead, he or she may have to pay an alternative minimum tax, calculated in a manner similar to that for corporations. This tax existed under prior law, but the 1986 Act raised the rate from 20 to 21% while at the same time lowering the top marginal regular rate from 50 to 28% starting in 1987. This narrowing of the difference between regular marginal rates and the minimum tax rate will cause many taxpayers to be affected by the new alternative minimum tax. The Act also significantly expanded the base for the tax. These changes in the base were specifically designed to increase the total tax liability for individuals who receive regular benefits from tax shelter investments.

Obviously both corporate and individual taxpayers will attempt to devise plans to mitigate the impact of the alternative minimum taxes. These strategies will be discussed later in Part Six.

Income Averaging

A second major aberration from our unitary tax rate structure is known as *income averaging*. Actually, two entirely different income-averaging provisions existed prior to 1987, and both were available only to *individual* taxpayers.

INCOME AVERAGING UNDER SEC. 402(e)   During their working years, many people participate in qualified pension and profit-sharing plans. In some instances, both the employer and employee make frequent contributions to the plan; in every instance, the amounts set aside are permitted to grow free of any income tax in the interim. When the time comes to withdraw the benefits, the individual typically is given a choice of how he or she wishes to receive the accumulated funds. Because the withdrawal of funds typically coincides with retirement, one option generally authorized is a lifetime annuity. In other instances, withdrawal may occur on the separation of an individual from a prior employment contract or at death. In these cases, a lump-sum payment is quite often the appropriate settlement option.

Because quite large sums of money may have accumulated in a qualified pension or profit-sharing plan, and because the income tax is normally imposed with a progressive tax rate schedule, any lump-sum settlement creates an inordinately large income tax liability if no special treatment is available for the previously untaxed benefits. Accordingly, the Code allows individual taxpayers to use a one-time five-year forward averaging with respect to a single lump-sum distribution received on or after the individual reaches age 59½. Until 1992, individuals may also elect to treat a portion of such distributions as capital gains, and certain individuals who attain age 50 by January 1, 1986, may use more favorable 10-year forward averaging rules.

Section 402(e) effectively breaks into five equal parts any lump sum received from a qualified pension or profit-sharing plan. The taxpayer must then determine the income tax on one fifth of the total as if that amount were his or her entire taxable income for one year. Finally, the tax liability just determined is multiplied by five, and the product is the optional income tax payable on the lump-sum settlement. Given the fact that most individuals will be subject to two tax brackets (15% and 28%) in 1988, this provision means that many lump-sum distributions will be taxed in their entirety at 15%. For a single individual, income up to $17,850 will be taxed in 1988 at 15%. Thus a distribution of five times $17,850 would effectively be taxed at a flat 15% rate. Larger distributions would be taxed at a rate combining the 15% and 28% brackets. In most cases, an individual receiving a lump-sum settlement also has other taxable income in the year he or she receives the settlement. Accordingly, this income-averaged tax is really added to the person's other income tax determined in the normal way.

INCOME AVERAGING UNDER SECS. 1301–1305   Prior to 1987, a second set of income-averaging rules were available to individuals who simply had unusually large taxable income in any one year. This aberration from the rate schedule was placed in the Code in explicit recognition of the fact that unusually large incomes realized in a single year may well be subject to an unduly heavy income tax burden solely because of our progressive rate structure. This provision was repealed as part of the Tax Reduction Act of 1986. The President's 1985 tax reform proposals had noted that with reduced tax rates and wider tax brackets, taxpayers could experience greater income fluctuations without becoming subject to higher progressive rates. Also, the proposal noted that many of the beneficiaries of income averaging were

> . . . taxpayers who experience sharp, sustained increases in income, such as young people who complete their studies and enter the work force for the first time. The availability of income averaging for such taxpayers is inconsistent with the principle of a progressive tax system.[1]

Capital Gains

Until December 31, 1986, the tax treatment of net capital gains represented the major aberration from the apparently unitary federal income tax rate structure. A net capital gain is generally the gain from the sale or exchange of capital assets held by the taxpayer for more than a prescribed time period. This concept is still important to the determination of taxable income and will be explained more fully in Part Five.

The Code, prior to the Tax Reform Act of 1986, provided special rules for the treatment of net capital gains of both corporate and noncorporate taxpayers, but the rules differed for each entity. Corporations were subject to an alternative marginal tax rate of 28% on net capital gains. Conceptually, a corporation's taxable income could be divided into two parts: one portion (Type I income) was income other than capital gains; the other portion (Type II) was the net capital gain. The Type II income was treated as the second tier of income and, thus, benefited from the alternative rate only if some portion of the corporate taxable income was subject to marginal rates in excess of 28%. The 1986 Act eliminated the alternative tax rate on net capital gains for corporations with tax years beginning after July 1, 1987 and provided a special transitional rule for corporations with tax years ending between January 1 and July 1, 1987.

Prior to January 1, 1987, all noncorporate taxpayers (individuals and fiduciaries) were allowed to claim a special deduction equal to 60% of the net capital gain realized in a year. Note that the Code did not modify the normal tax rate structure. To conclude that the net capital gains of individuals and fiduciaries were subject to normal tax rates would, however, be a gross error. Only 40% of net capital gains realized were included in the computation of their taxable income. A special deduction equal to 60% of the income realized is the equivalent of a 60% reduction in the normal tax rates. Thus, an

---

[1]*President's Tax Proposals to the Congress for Fairness, Growth, and Simplicity,* May 29, 1985, p. 111.

individual or fiduciary taxpayer whose 1986 income consisted solely of net capital gain enjoyed a *real*, or *effective*, tax rate not from the normal 1986 range of 11% to 50%, but from 4.4% (40% of 11%) to 20% (40% of 50%). The special 60% deduction for noncorporate taxpayers was repealed effective for tax years after 1986, but the highest tax rate that can be imposed on net capital gains is 28%.

Even without an examination of the details, it should be obvious that before 1987, capital gains represented a major tax advantage for anyone fortunate enough to realize a substantial part of his or her income in this form. For our wealthiest taxpayers, the name of the tax game in the United States was capital gains. And repeal for now (after 1987) of the advantages from capital gains does not mean that these provisions are dead. As explained in Chapter 4, the limits on capital losses still apply. Furthermore, the law still contains a "safety net" for the rich that provides for a maximum rate of 28% on net capital gains of individuals (34% maximum for corporations) should Congress raise rates in the future. Does this Congressional foresight in 1986 tell us that Congress expects that rates will be higher soon? Perhaps.

The Taxation of Nonresident Aliens

A final aberration from the unitary tax rate schedules is the tax rate applied to nonresident alien taxpayers, except to the extent that they earn income effectively connected with the conduct of a U.S. trade or business. As strange as it may seem, the United States theoretically taxes the income earned by *every* individual, *every* corporation, and *every* fiduciary worldwide! This income tax concept is known as a *global* tax. At first blush, the concept suggests that the United States taxes the income of all citizens and aliens in exactly the same manner. As you might suspect, however, that would be a difficult feat indeed, since the United States government certainly does not have the legal jurisdiction over most aliens.

In reality, the United States does attempt to tax the worldwide income of (1) all U.S. citizens (residents or nonresidents) and (2) all resident aliens, in essentially the same manner. Nonresident aliens, however, are subject to an income tax only on some parts of their income from U.S. sources. Prior to the 1984 Act, the tax rate imposed on passive income was a flat 30%, so long as that income was *not* effectively connected with the conduct of a U.S. trade or business; in other words, so long as it was passive income, such as interest or dividends. For certain debt obligations issued after the 1984 Act, nonresident aliens and foreign corporations are generally excused from paying any U.S. income taxes on interest they earn from these securities.

This change in the law was, in large measure, a reaction to a problem that had been increasing in complexity for several years. The tax treaties enacted between the United States and various foreign governments frequently included provisions that extended favorable tax rates to passive income earned by the citizens of one country in the other treaty country. To take advantage of these treaty provisions, foreign financing subsidiaries were frequently created in such exotic locations as the Antilles. The new tax rules effectively extend the most favorable possible treaty provisions (that is, the total exclusion of all passive income) to all nonresident aliens regardless of where they may live. This change was a severe economic blow to a few small island empires that have grown up solely for tax reasons. However, the same change may also have lessened the impact of our large federal deficit on the U.S. economy by attracting additional foreign capital to U.S. markets.

A few additional details of foreign taxation are discussed in Chapter 21. Observe that we have said nothing here about the taxation of either foreign corporations or foreign fiduciaries. Such advanced topics in taxation are best deferred for study at a later time, although brief mention will be made of them also in Chapter 21.

In summary, three general concepts concerning tax rates should be clearly understood. First, the U.S. income tax rates are generally progressive, but less so than at any time since World War II. Second, the precise degree of progressivity built into the tax rates varies from one class of taxpayers to another; that is, the prescribed rates for individuals, fiduciaries, and corporations have been differentiated deliberately. Third, subject to the several major aberrations described briefly in this chapter, a single set of tax rates applies to the entire taxable income reported by any one taxpayer in a given year. Among the major exceptions to the general rule just stated are the special tax provisions for:

1. An income-averaging option for individual taxpayers receiving lump-sum retirement benefits.
2. An alternative minimum tax for corporations.
3. An alternative minimum tax for individuals and fiduciary taxpayers.

TAX CREDITS

Effective tax rates are also affected by tax credits, which are direct reductions in taxes payable. While credits do not change the tax rate schedules, they do reduce the tax liabilities of taxpayers. To the extent that these credits attach to certain types of income or activities, they represent departures from the unitary system.

Credits Versus Deductions

An important distinction between a credit and a deduction should be obvious—although credits yield a dollar-for-dollar tax reduction, the tax decrease resulting from a $1 deduction depends on the marginal tax rate applied to net taxable income. To illustrate this important distinction, assume that an imaginary taxpayer's marginal (as well as average) tax rate is 20% and that his taxable income for the year is $10,000. Thus, the gross tax liability is $2,000 ($10,000 × 20%). Suppose that after computing taxable income and gross tax liability, as above, the taxpayer discovers that a $500 payment has been omitted from the computation. Suppose, too, that there is a legitimate question of whether the payment is properly to be considered a "deduction" or a "credit." The two tabulations below demonstrate the significant difference in impact on net tax payable resulting from this difference in classification.

	Payment Treated as Deduction	Payment Treated as Credit
Taxable income before considering payment	$10,000	$10,000
Payment treated as deduction	(500)	
Revised taxable income	$ 9,500	$10,000
Tax rate	× 0.20	× 0.20
Gross tax liability	$ 1,900	$ 2,000
Payment treated as credit		(500)
Net tax payable	$ 1,900	$ 1,500

Observe that if the payment is a credit, the entire $500 reduces the net tax payable from $2,000 to $1,500. If the payment is a deduction, however, the decrease in net tax payable is only $100—from $2,000 to $1,900. The important conclusion, stated earlier, is that the effect of a deduction on net tax payable depends wholly on the marginal tax rate. In the preceding example, if the taxpayer's marginal tax rate had been 50% rather than 20%, a $500 deduction would have resulted in a decrease of $250 in tax liability ($500 × 50%). Apparently, a given deduction can have widely varying effects on the dollar amount of tax liability of taxpayers at different marginal rate levels. On the other hand, a tax credit has the same dollar effect on the amount of net taxes payable, no matter what the taxpayer's rate level may be.

Uses of Tax Credits

Congress has shown a decided preference for credits in the last two decades, and most of the credit provisions in the law were added during that period. The popularity of credits may be due to their visibility. But as an economic or social incentive, credits have two other advantages over deductions. First, credits can serve to neutralize the effects of our progressive rate schedules. Second, credits do not involve a change in the definition of taxable income, and, as a result, their addition to the law does not involve numerous conforming amendments in other basic definitions. Thus, credit provisions can be neat, temporary adjustments of the tax burden.

This second factor was apparent in 1986 when several popular tax credits were either removed from the law or diminished in significance. Credits viewed as business incentives were especially affected. The investment credit was repealed while the rehabilitation credit, research and development credit, and the targeted jobs credit were all made less attractive than under prior law. A new credit designed to encourage investment in low income housing was added to the law. Several credits designed to address social and political problems were retained and in one case made more attractive to taxpayers. The value of the earned income credit, designed to benefit low income families with one or more children, was increased and the "phase-out" level of earned income was raised from $11,000 to $17,000. The credit for the elderly and the credit for child and dependent care were both retained in the law, but the credit for political contributions was repealed in the 1986 act. Most of the credits added during the "energy crisis" have been allowed to lapse or have been reduced in value, probably reflecting declining concern with the need to encourage energy conservation. The details of these credits will be discussed in later chapters as appropriate.

Despite all these exceptions, the U.S. income tax is essentially a unitary system, and one schedule of rates applies to the homogeneous taxable income of each taxpayer. With the elimination of the capital gains deduction, this fact affects most taxpayers, including those whose income is derived substantially from income-producing property rather than salaries and wages.

WHAT'S LEFT OF THE UNITARY SYSTEM?

Our tax law begins with the concept that income is homogeneous and that a single base, taxable income, should be subjected to a single rate. But we are far enough along to see that we do not really have a unitary system. Complex rules relating to type of income, to its geographic source, to the entrepreneurial participation of the taxpayer in the activity, to the form of legal organization used, and to the family status of the taxpayer affect the taxes actually paid on a given dollar of income. These sets of rules and the relationships between them are the very subject matter in taxation and cannot be generalized. Nevertheless, the following examples will give you some basic appreciation of how the rules fit together.

Interest Income

Amounts received as interest are generally taxable at ordinary rates. Interest earned on most state and local bonds is exempt—subject to a rate of zero. These rules apply equally to all entities.

The eventual treatment of taxable interest will depend on the classification of the activity with respect to which the interest arose. For a particular taxpayer, the interest income may be active business income, passive income, or portfolio income, and the classification will often affect the tax rate that applies to it. Interest arising in a passive activity will often be offset entirely by deductions and losses from such activities. If the interest income is portfolio income, the most common case, it will probably bear the full burden of the tax.

For purposes of active–passive classification, the type of entity makes a difference. The active–passive rules to not apply to C corporations, except for closely held C corporations and personal-service corporations. At the other extreme, interest income of a limited partnership becomes passive to the limited partners that report it.

Yet another classification can apply to interest income. If it is portfolio income, it increases the amount of investment interest expense that can be deducted. The preceding discussion ignores another complicating dimension: foreign sources versus domestic sources. Finally, we note that dividends, a type of income much like interest, are subject to numerous rules quite different from those for interest.

Operating Income of a Business

First, income that arises from sale of inventory must often be distinguished from service income, particularly from the personal services of specific individuals. Also, income from rental of property may be subject to different rules. The following assumes the business is a trading concern.

Again, as with interest, we start with the unitary notion that gains from inventory trading are fully taxable and losses fully deductible. Both the entity used and active–passive classification give different results. At the extremes, a C corporation (not a closely held corporation and not a personal service corporation) will combine operating profits with all other income; in a limited partnership, the same income is passive to the limited partner. For general partnerships and S corporations, the operating income is either active or passive to the partners and shareholders depending on the degree of their participation in the business. As explained in Chapter 3, the activity is passive to a particular taxpayer unless that taxpayer materially participates, which means participation that is regular, continuous, and substantial.

What about an individual taxpayer who operates a trading concern as a proprietorship? Does that automatically mean that the income is active? Evidently not, according to the committee reports for the 1986 Act. The activity will be passive with respect to the proprietor if he does not materially participate. Imagine the case of a proprietor with a profitable trading concern who also has substantial passive losses. Presumably the operating income is passive and can be used to offset the passive losses if the proprietor can show a lack of material participation. The I.R.S. will be skeptical in such cases, and rightly so.

Extend the preceding facts by the incorporation of the trading concern, and include in the corporation the properties that produce the passive losses. The former proprietor is the sole shareholder. Now, for reasons never explained by Congress, the trading income can be combined with the passive losses, even without material participation. Closely held C corporations can offset passive losses against active income (but not portfolio income.)

Our examples could include other dimensions with differing results. The relatively simple example carries the point: operating profits of a business are taxed at different rates, depending on many circumstances.

Rental of Real Estate

The tax treatment of income from the rental of real estate is unusually complicated because real estate investments were the most common tax shelter before the 1986 Act. The combination of rapid capital recovery under ACRS and large interest deductions on projects heavily financed with debt produced large current tax losses even for projects with positive cash flow. Current tax losses coupled with realization of income in the form of capital gains upon sale of a project after a few years made real estate a near ideal investment—so good, in fact, that many unsound projects were built because of the tax incentives. The 1986 Act included the passive loss rules, tightened the limits on investment interest, and made other changes to deal with the problem.

Rental real estate may constitute a trade or business or may be an investment (transaction for profit) depending on the type of investment. Large apartment houses are businesses and Sec. 162 applies. Unimproved land rented for agricultural uses is an investment to which Sec. 212 applies. The classification of real estate projects between these cases (for example, a duplex) is unclear.

The major factor affecting the tax burden on rental income is the entity used. Unlike operating profits, the degree of participation by the owners is of no consequence because the passive loss rules contain a presumption that all rental activities, whether real or personal, are passive (but hotel operations are more than rentals, and therefore not passive). C corporations, except for closely held and personal-service corporations, are not subject to the passive loss limits and can offset losses from rental real estate against either active income or portfolio income. Also, we explained earlier that closely held C corporations can offset passive losses against active income (but not against portfolio income). Taxpayers with leveraged real estate investments producing losses can still shelter income with these losses, but to do so they must realize the rental losses in a C corporation. That, of course, leads to double taxation.

As explained in Chapter 3, individual taxpayers can deduct up to $25,000 of passive losses from real estate rentals provided they actively participate. Remember, however, that this $25,000 limit is phased out as the taxpayer's A.G.I. rises from $100,000 to $150,000. This phase out means this measure is of little benefit to big investors. If the activity is organized as a partnership or S corporation, owners must meet the active participation test to enjoy the $25,000 loss limit. The use of a limited partnership forecloses active participation, just as it does material participation.

In summary, the examples show just how many different effective rate schedules can apply. The type of income, its geographic source, the legal entity used (or not used), the degree of participation, and, finally, the family status all affect the rates applicable to income. We will return to this problem under the heading of tax planning in Part Six.

Do the published rate schedules apply to any type or source of income without special provisions that, taken together, serve to reduce the rate? The answer is yes, almost. The salaries and wages of employees (but not self-employed individuals) bear the full burden of the rates except for the standard deduction, exemptions, and fringe benefits. That is the subject of Part Three.

PROBLEMS

1. Compare and contrast a unitary system with a schedular system.

2. Is the U.S. income tax system a schedular system or a unitary system:
   a. Technically?
   b. Practically?
   Explain.

3. What are the current highest and lowest marginal income tax rates for individual taxpayers in the United States? How do these rates compare with pre-1987 rates?

4. What are the current lowest and highest marginal tax rates for corporate taxpayers in the United States? How do these rates compare with pre-1987 rates?

5. In what sense may a corporate entity be described as a tax shelter? Discuss some disadvantages associated with incorporation.

6. If a taxpayer is nearing the end of a year with an unusually large taxable income, to the extent that it is legally possible and administratively convenient, what should the taxpayer try to do about the following:
   a. Additional items of gross income?
   b. Additional deductions?
   Explain briefly.

7. In general, how do the minimum tax provisions modify our otherwise unitary tax rates for
   a. Corporate taxpayers?
   b. Noncorporate taxpayers?

8. How do the income-averaging provisions modify our otherwise unitary tax rates for individual taxpayers who receive a lump-sum distribution from a qualified pension or profit-sharing plan?

9. One provision that Congress has often considered during deliberation of proposed tax legislation would allow taxpayers to take either a deduction of a specified amount or a credit of some other specified amount for each exemption. Assume that the choice is a credit of $250 or a deduction of $1,000 for each exemption. What option would be taken by a taxpayer with one exemption and whose marginal tax rate is
   a. 20%?
   b. 50%?

10. How would the proposed measure discussed in Problem 9 affect the relative tax burdens of taxpayers with high incomes and those with lower incomes, compared with the effect of a $1,000 deduction per exemption?

11. Some tax scholars believe that tax credits are popular because their visibility appeals to politicians. What do you think the word "visibility" means in this context?

12. Listed below are several sources of income realized by an individual. For each source, discuss the special provisions, if any, that might apply to the income. If no special provision applies, what could taxpayers do to reduce the rates on the income?

    a. Professional fees earned by a certified public accountant
    b. Gains or losses from the sale of inventory items
    c. Rental income from an apartment house
    d. Gain on the sale of corporate securities
    e. Royalty income received on a book that has been a best-seller for six months
    f. Bonus received by a college athlete on signing a professional contract
    g. Interest earned on corporate bonds
    h. A lump-sum distribution from a qualified retirement plan

13. What equity arguments might have been used to support the repeal of the 60% capital gains deduction for noncorporate taxpayers? (Refer to the discussion of horizontal and vertical equity in Chapter 1.)

14. A citizen and resident of Great Britain has interest and dividend income from several countries, including the United States. If that person is not a U.S. resident, is the U.S. income subject to our tax? If so, at what rate?

15. What general concepts or notions about taxation may be used to justify the income-averaging devices discussed in this chapter?

PART THREE

The Individual Taxpayer

Another example . . . took place within the lifetime of many of us; the revolution of the personal income tax. It has made impossible such displays of ostentatious magnificence as Hearst's Casa Grande in St. Simeon; it has stimulated the creation of foundations and nonprofit institutions; it has reduced the differences between the standards of living of the various socioeconomic classes; it has brought about a clear-cut distinction between wages and take-home pay. And no amount of wishful thinking will ever bring us back to pre-income-tax days.
J. Samuel Bois, The Art of Awareness
Wm. C. Brown Company, 1966

(1) Person—The term "person" shall be construed to mean and include an individual, a trust, estate, partnership, association, company and corporation.

Section 7701(a)(1) Internal Revenue Code of 1954

CHAPTER 8

The Individual Taxpayer: Income and Exclusions

Except as otherwise provided in this subtitle, gross income means all income. . . .
Section 61(a)

In Part Three, we are concerned with the tax problems that confront a typical individual taxpayer—determination of what is included in taxable income, of which expenditures are deductible and how they are classified, and computation of the tax liability. The section concludes with a discussion of tax incentives for individual savings.

From the earliest days of the U.S. income tax, the tax law has designated individuals, corporations, and fiduciaries (estates and trusts) as taxpayers. The primary purpose of this chapter is to consider in some detail what items must be included in an individual's taxable income. But first, it may be useful to learn more about the statistical profile of a "typical individual taxpayer."

WHO IS THE TYPICAL INDIVIDUAL TAXPAYER?

To begin with, an examination of income levels should help define a typical individual taxpayer. Table 8-1 shows percentages of taxpayers who in 1984 had adjusted gross incomes at various levels.

TABLE **8-1**

TAXPAYERS CLASSIFIED BY A.G.I. LEVEL AND
PERCENTAGE OF TOTAL TAXES PAID IN 1984

A.G.I.	Number of Returns as % of Total	Income Tax Paid as % of Total
< $10,000	33.8%	2.2%
$ 10 – 15,000	14.2	4.2
15 – 20,000	11.5	6.1
20 – 25,000	8.9	7.0
25 – 30,000	7.7	7.9
30 – 35,000	11.1	16.1
40 – 50,000	6.0	12.7
50 – 75,000	4.7	15.7
75 – 100,000	1.1	6.2
100 +	1.0	21.9

SOURCE: *Statistics of Income – 1984, Individual Income Tax Returns*

While the tax clients of professional accountants and attorneys are mostly drawn from individuals with A.G.I. of $50,000 or more, this group comprised less than 7% of taxpayers in 1984. The stakes for these taxpayers are high, however; they paid almost 44% of all federal income taxes in the same year.

Income sources provide another way of describing taxpayers. Table 8-2 reveals that wages and salaries are by far the most important income source, accounting for 84.5% of A.G.I. in 1984. "All other sources" includes a number of items such as alimony, partnership gains and losses, rental income and losses, and so on. Obviously, the distribution of these sources varies greatly by income level. For example, capital gains are far more significant an income source to high-income than low-income taxpayers.

A few other descriptive statistics will complete our profile of the typical individual taxpayer. In 1984, only 38.4% of all taxpayers itemized their deductions, and this number is expected to decrease because of some of the

TABLE **8-2**

INCOME SOURCES AS PERCENT OF A.G.I.–1984

Salaries and wages	84.5%
Interest received	8.2
Dividends in A.G.I.	2.3
Business net income and loss	3.3
Capital gains and losses	2.6
Pensions and annuities	3.8
All other sources	(4.7)

SOURCE: *Statistics of Income – 1984, Individual Income Tax Returns*

changes in the 1986 Tax Reform Act. Approximately 64% of all taxpayers filed Form 1040 (the so-called long form) tax returns, about 19% filed Form 1040-A, and the remainder filed form 1040-EZ. The last two are both short returns that do not permit itemizing. The average age of 1040 filers is estimated at 46.5; of 1040-A filers, 33.4; and 1040-EZ, filers 23.5.[1] Finally, it is estimated that 45% of all taxpayers used paid professional preparers to complete their tax returns in 1985.

Many of the issues discussed in this and the next four chapters are really not characteristic of "typical" taxpayers but are probably more characteristic of the 45% of taxpayers who hire tax professionals to help with their returns. Nonetheless, the profile provided here should help the new student of taxation to put some of the items discussed into perspective.

Now that we have examined the statistical profile of a "typical individual taxpayer," let us take a closer look at how the Code defines an individual taxpayer. Section 1 of the Internal Revenue Code reads in part, ". . . there is hereby imposed on the taxable income of every individual . . . a tax. . . ." Note the selection of *every* individual, and note that the term used is *individual,* not "citizen" or some other term. Use of the term "every individual" raises several important questions. Are minors "individuals"? What about citizens of foreign countries who earn income in the United States as residents or nonresidents? How are U.S. citizens who are permanent residents of a foreign country taxed?

Age

An individual's age is of no direct importance in determining the individual's standing as a taxpayer. The income tax is levied from the cradle to the grave, though the taxpayer's age may affect the amount paid in some instances. Generally, a legal minor cannot hold title to property directly. He or she can, however, hold title through a parent or other legal agent and thereby be liable for federal income tax. Thus, if a proud grandparent makes a gift of cash to a newborn descendent and that cash is placed in a savings account or otherwise invested to produce income, the newborn child is a taxpayer and a potential tax is due on the income.

Citizens and Residents of the United States

U.S. citizens are taxed on their worldwide income. A citizen who has established a permanent residence in a foreign country and never expects to return to the United States on a permanent basis remains a U.S. taxpayer until he or she officially renounces U.S. citizenship. Note that the foreign government may also levy a tax on that citizen's income, particularly on

[1]Bryan Musselman and Paul Grayson, "Individual Income Tax Returns, 1983: A Demographic Snapshot," *Statistics of Income Bulletin,* Summer 1986, pp. 57–62.

income derived from sources within the country of residence. A citizen's income may thus be taxed by two governments. In this situation, the U.S. tax law contains three major provisions aimed at reducing the impact of double taxation:

1. The foreign tax credit, briefly described in Chapter 11, may be applied against the U.S. tax.

2. A U.S. citizen who is a bona fide resident of a foreign country throughout a taxable year or is absent from the United States for a period of 330 days out of 12 consecutive months may exclude his or her foreign *earned* income up to a maximum limit of $70,000. An individual who qualifies for the foreign earned income may also receive tax benefits for "excess" housing costs incurred while living abroad.

3. Our government has entered into tax treaties with many foreign countries aimed at eliminating double taxation.

The same income tax levied on U.S. citizens is also levied on all resident aliens. The statute defines a resident alien as an individual who has been lawfully admitted to the U.S. as a permanent resident, has met certain arbitrary tests for substantial presence within the U.S., or has made a proper election to be treated as a resident.[2]

INCOME AND EXCLUSIONS

The formula used to calculate the tax liability for an individual was introduced in Chapter 3. Recall that the first two steps were determination of income broadly conceived and of exclusions permitted the taxpayer in order to calculate *gross income.* The intent of Sec. 61(a) is that a taxpayer must find authority to exclude an item from income broadly conceived. Chapter 3 contained a lengthy list of provisions outlined in the Code giving taxpayers authority to exclude specific items from taxable income. In the following pages, we have attempted to classify some of the major exclusions according to their apparent purpose. In many cases the classification must be a matter of personal opinion, either because there are multiple bases for the exclusion or because the purpose of a particular exclusion is not apparent. These examples by no means illustrate all exclusions authorized by the Code.

Before beginning this discussion, it should be noted that a number of exclusions are fringe benefits of employment. In order for many of these benefits to be considered tax free to all recipients, the Code requires that they be offered on a *nondiscriminatory* basis to employees. That is, the plans under which the benefits are offered must not discriminate in favor of highly compensated employees. A highly compensated employee is defined in

[2]Section 7701(b)(1)(A)

Sec. 414(q) as one who at any time during the year or the preceding year was a 5% owner of the employer, received compensation from the employer in excess of $75,000, received compensation from the employer in excess of $50,000 and was in the top-paid group of employees for the year (top 20%), or was at any time an officer and received compensation greater than 150% of the amount specified in the Code as the dollar limit for defined contribution plans (presently $30,000).

The 1986 Tax Reform Act provided comprehensive nondiscrimination rules for group term life insurance plans, accident or health plans, qualified group legal service plans, educational assistance plans, and dependent care assistance plans. The last three types of plans are included under the new rules only if the employer elects to treat them as statutory employee benefits. A complicated set of rules is designed to ensure that these plans do not discriminate in favor of highly compensated employees as described above. Basically, this is accomplished by requiring that gross income of highly compensated employees will include an amount equal to such employees' *excess benefit* under the plan (the excess over the benefit that would be permitted if the plan met all the nondiscrimination rules). Therefore, the exclusion of benefits is maintained for employees who are not highly compensated but may be limited for those who are.

Exclusions Related to Illness

Sections 104, 105, and 106 provide for a variety of exclusions related to accidents and illness. Section 104 excludes most amounts received for injuries or sickness; Section 105 excludes certain amounts received under an accident and health plan; and Section 106 excludes from income most amounts contributed by an employer to an accident and health plan that exists for the benefit of the employees. The number of exceptions to these general rules demands that we examine each rule with care. To do that, we proceed in reverse order because (1) the last general rule (that is, Sec. 106) is the simplest and (2) the other two general rules often involve payments that derive from (and may be influenced by) the plans described in Sec. 106.

SECTION 106   Section 106 excludes from the employee's taxable income the value of any contributions made by the employer on behalf of the employee to accident or health plans for compensation (through insurance or otherwise) for personal injuries or sickness of the taxpayer, spouse, or dependents. Note that Sec. 106 is *not* concerned with the amount *received* by an employee from an insurance company. Rather, it excludes from income either (1) the cost of the premiums paid by the employer to purchase insurance or (2) the employer's contributions to a fund that may later provide for payments to the employee.

For example, suppose that James Wilson's employer purchased a health and accident insurance policy that reimburses Wilson and other employees for expenses related to injury or illness. During the tax year, the employer paid a total of $1,200 of premiums on the policy covering Wilson and his family. This $1,200 is *not* taxable income to Wilson.

In 1979, both the U.S. General Accounting Office and the Congressional Budget Office issued reports critical of the exclusion of employer's contributions to health insurance programs for employees. These two groups claimed that the exclusion is inflationary because it encourages employees to acquire more health insurance coverage than they otherwise would, and this encourages more frequent use and more elaborate forms of medical care. This, in turn, drives up health-care costs. The reports also concluded that employees have opted for more tax-free benefits—such as improved medical insurance —instead of wage increases, which are taxed. The reports estimated that the exclusions resulted in $9.6 billion in lost revenues to the federal government in 1979. In that year, a controversial proposal was introduced in Congress to eliminate the tax-free status of employer contributions to health insurance policies. The proposal was rejected, but a less drastic proposal to include a limited amount of employer contributions in income surfaced in the President's 1985 tax reform proposal. The proposal argued that the exclusion from income of employer-provided health insurance is unfair to individuals who are not covered by such plans and must therefore pay for their plans with after-tax dollars. Congress did not adopt the proposal in the 1986 Tax Reform Act, but this question will certainly be debated in future sessions of Congress.

One change that Congress did make in 1986 was to prohibit nondiscrimination in favor of highly paid employees. Prior to this change, a closely held corporation could obtain coverage for its officers only, who were also shareholders, and the officers could exclude the value from income. Now, the nondiscrimination rules of Sec. 414(q) must be met.

SECTION 105   Section 105 excludes some, but not all, amounts received by an employee under an accident and health plan. The following receipts can be excluded:

1. Amounts that "constitute payment for the permanent loss or loss of use of a member or function of the body, or the permanent disfigurement of the taxpayer, his spouse, or a dependent" [Sec. 105(c)(1)]

2. Amounts that are "computed with reference to the nature of the injury without regard to the period the employee is absent from work" [Sec. 105(c)(2)]

3. Amounts paid "directly or indirectly to the taxpayer to reimburse the taxpayer for expenses incurred by him for the medical care (as defined in Sec. 213(d)) of the taxpayer, his wife, and dependents." [Sec. 105(b)]

This last exclusion does *not* apply, however, if the taxpayer receives the medical expense reimbursement in a year following a year in which he or she claimed a medical expense deduction for the item now being reimbursed, to the extent the taxpayer benefited from the earlier deduction. For example, suppose a taxpayer incurred and paid medical expenses of $10,000 in 19x1. If these expenses were also reimbursed in 19x1 under an accident and health plan, the taxpayer could exclude the $10,000 from gross income. Of course, the taxpayer would not claim a medical deduction. On the other hand, if the taxpayer did not receive the $10,000 medical reimbursement until 19x2, and if the taxpayer claimed a $6,000 medical expense deduction in 19x2 ($4,000 of the medical expense being disallowed by a "floor" that is explained in Chapter 11), then he or she must include $6,000 of the $10,000 received in 19x2 as part of gross income; the other $4,000 could still be excluded.

Any amounts received under an accident and health plan for reasons other than the three explicitly stated above cannot be excluded from gross income if (1) the premiums on the plan were paid by the employer and (2) those premiums were not taxed to the employee (by operation of Sec. 106, discussed above). To illustrate, suppose that a taxpayer received $9,000 in sick pay under an accident and health plan provided by the employer at no tax cost to the employee. The $9,000 payment could *not* be excluded from gross income by the employee because it is not one of the three items listed above.

For many years, closely held corporations used Sec. 105(b) to provide tax-free health and accident benefits for all family members of only a select few corporate owners and officers. Corporations achieved this result by having their boards of directors adopt, as corporate policy, a provision that allowed a direct reimbursement for any family medical costs incurred by designated employees. Typically, these arrangements did *not* provide for a general insurance policy carried through an external insurance company. The 1978 Revenue Act ended this ploy by providing in Sec. 105(h) [now Sec. 105(i)] that payments made under a *direct* health and accident reimbursement plan (that is, one not provided under an insurance policy) are tax free to the recipient only if the plan does not discriminate in favor of certain highly compensated officers and stockholders. If the plan does discriminate in favor or highly compensated individuals, the "excess reimbursement" to these individuals (discussed above) is included in their income.

SECTION 104   Section 104 excludes from gross income certain other payment received in compensation for injury or sickness. This list includes:

1. Payments "received under workmen's compensation acts as compensation for personal injury or sickness" [Sec. 104(a)(1)]

2. Payments for "damages received (whether by suit or by agreement and whether as lump sums or as periodic payments) on account of personal injury or sickness" [Sec. 104(a)(2)]

3. Payments "received through accident or health insurance for personal injuries or sickness" *unless*
   a. paid directly by the employer, or
   b. paid by an insurance company whose premiums were paid by the employer and excluded—under Sec. 106—from the gross income of the employee [Sec. 104(a)(3)]

4. Payments received as a pension or other allowance "for personal injuries or sickness resulting from active service in the armed forces" or certain other governmental service [Sec. 104(a)(4)]

5. Payments received by government employees for injuries received as a direct result of designated terrorist attacks outside the United States [Sec. 104(a)(5)]

Section 104(b) limits and defines the veterans' payments excluded in item 4. Although some overlap exists between Sec. 104(a)(3) and Sec. 105(b) (described earlier), the former provision can be important to many taxpayers. It allows a taxpayer to exclude from gross income payments received as compensation for injuries or sickness under an accident or health insurance plan purchased directly by the taxpayer. For example, a taxpayer could exclude from gross income a $15,000 payment received as sick pay, under an insurance plan, if the premiums for that plan had previously been paid by the taxpayer from his or her own after-tax income.

Exclusions Related to Death

Code Sec. 101 excludes from taxable income a number of income items related to an individual's death. The tax law of 1913 provided that amounts received under a life insurance contract paid because of the insured's death are, with minor exceptions, tax free; this rule continues today. It was presumably designed to encourage individuals to provide adequate insurance for their survivors. Presumably, too, Congress assumed that the recipient of insurance proceeds would typically face financial hardships meriting the exclusion.

Until 1987, a further exclusions of up to $1,000 of *interest* income per year was allowed to the surviving spouse of a decedent when life insurance proceeds (payable because of the death of the taxpayer's spouse) were left with the insurer, under an option or agreement in the insurance contract, to be paid in installments. Presumably this provision, which was repealed by Congress in the 1986 Act, was designed to protect beneficiaries by encouraging them to leave life insurance proceeds in the "safety" of the insurance company.

An exception to the exclusions of insurance proceeds paid on account of the insured's death is proceeds from a policy obtained "for a consideration." For example, supposed that Arner, the insured, owed a $4,000 debt to Milroy. In settlement of the debt, Arner assigned to Milroy an insurance policy on Arner's life. The policy provided for a death benefit of $14,000. After acquiring the policy, Milroy paid premiums of $2,000 on the policy. On Arner's death, Milroy was paid the full $14,000 amount. Milroy must report income of $8,000 ($14,000 − $4,000 − $2,000).

In addition to life insurance benefits, certain other proceeds to beneficiaries relating to death are nontaxable. Section 101(b) provides that beneficiaries of a decedent may exclude a total of $5,000 paid by the decedent's employer, or employers, if the payments are made solely on account of death. When the decedent has more than one beneficiary who receives payments, the exclusion is prorated among the beneficiaries in proportion to the amount that each receives. For example, suppose that Smith, a long-time employee dies. Because of his death, the employer makes payments of $8,000 to Smith's widow and $4,000 to each of his two children. The beneficiaries may exclude a total of $5,000, divided as follows:

$$\text{Wife: } \frac{\$8,000}{\$16,000} \times \$5,000 = \$2,500$$

$$\text{Each child: } \frac{\$4,000}{\$16,000} \times \$5,000 = \$1,250$$

Thus, the widow would include in her taxable income $5,500 of the amount received; each child would include $2,750.

This provision was first enacted in 1951 and was intended to "eliminate the 'hardship' resulting from the fact that the exclusion for death benefits under the then existing law was limited to life insurance."[3] In contrast, the President's 1985 tax reform proposal argued that the provision should be repealed because it is an alternative form of employee compensation that is unavailable to many taxpayers such as self-employed individuals. In spite of this recommendation, the provision remains in the law.

The exclusions related to death benefits from life insurance, like most other exclusions, have long been debated by tax scholars. As Richard Goode points out, if all life insurance proceeds payable because of death are tax free, "no distinction is drawn between the components of death benefits, which comprise pure insurance proceeds, the return of the insured person's savings, and the interest earned on savings."[4] The question may be raised whether the three elements of proceeds should be treated differently for tax purposes. Certainly, the insured's savings element should be returned tax free, but there is less unanimity of opinion concerning taxability of the other two elements.

Another exclusion related to life insurance is provided in Sec. 79, which encourages employers to establish life insurance programs for employees. Premiums paid by an employer for *group term life insurance*—up to $50,000 face amount of insurance for each employee—may be excluded from the employee's income, although premiums paid by the employer on whole-life insurance for either an individual or groups, as well as premiums paid on individual term policies, are taxable to the employee.

If an employee is covered by group term insurance with a face value greater than $50,000, the premium applicable to the excess is taxable. The amount includible is determined by referring to a table in Treasury Regulation 1.79-3. For example, the table provides that for a taxpayer 40 to 44 years of age, the premiums applicable to each $1,000 of face amount *over* $50,000 is $0.17 per month. Thus, if an employee who is 44 years old is covered throughout the year by a group term life insurance policy with a face amount of $80,000, and if the premiums paid by the employer are $336, the amount taxable is $61.20 (.17 × 12 × 30), and the amount excluded is $274.80. Obviously in this example, use of the I.R.S. table results in a greater amount being excluded than if the premium paid had been prorated between the $50,000 subject to exclusion and the $30,000 not subject to exclusion.

[3]Senate Report 781, 82d Congress, 1st Sess.
[4]Richard Goode, *The Individual Income Tax* (Washington, D.C.: The Brookings Institution, 1964), p. 130. Goode presents a very thorough and interesting discussion of this topic on pp. 130–139.

Exclusions Related to Age

Our tax laws have been freely amended to reflect a growing concern about the social and economic needs of the aged. Many provisions include special deductions, while other relate to the definition of income. For example, the taxpayer who is 65 or over is allowed an increased standard deduction.

Prior to 1983, Social Security benefits were exempt from taxation as a result of administrative decisions. However, the recipient must now include in gross income the lesser of

1. One half of Social Security benefits received during the year, or
2. One half of the amount by which the sum of one half of Social Security benefits received during the year plus the "modified adjusted gross income" exceeds the "base amount."

Modified gross income is (1) adjusted gross income before considering Social Security benefits and before the exclusion for U.S. citizens living abroad, plus (2) tax-exempt interest. (*Adjusted gross income* is defined in Chapter 10.)

The base amount is $32,000 for a married couple filing jointly; zero for a married person filing a separate return if the married person did not live apart from his or her spouse for the entire year; and $25,000 for a single person or married person filing a single return and who lived apart from the spouse for the entire year.

For example, suppose that during 19X1 Henry and Susan filed a joint return. During the year they received tax-exempt interest of $4,000 and had adjusted gross income of $26,500 from Susan's salary. Henry was unemployed and received Social Security benefits of $4,200. The amount of Social Security benefits taxable is $300.

1. One half of Social Security benefits ($\frac{1}{2} \times$ $4,200) $2,100
2. One half of sum of one half of Social Security benefits and modified A.G.I. over the base amount:

One half Social Security benefits	$ 2,100
A.G.I. from salary	26,500
Tax-exempt interest	4,000
Total	$32,600
Less base amount	32,000
Excess	$ 600
One half of excess	$ 300

In addition, two other special provisions merit attention. The first is the *credit for the elderly* (Sec. 37), which permits the taxpayer who is 65 or older to reduce his or her tax bill by an amount up to $375. This tax credit is discussed in detail in Chapter 12. The second is found in Sec. 121, which allows a person who is 55 or older to exclude from gross income up to

$125,000 of the gain realized on the sale of a personal residence. This provision is examined in detail in Chapter 18.

Exclusions and Intergovernmental Relations

A traditional aspect of the U.S. tax structure has been an immunity of governmental units from taxation by other units. As a result of this concept, Code Sec. 115(a) specifically excludes from the federal income tax:

(1) income derived from any public utility or the exercise of any essential governmental function and accruing to a State or Territory, or any political subdivision thereof, or the District of Columbia; or
(2) income accruing to the government of any possession of the United States, or any political subdivision thereof.

One of the most controversial provisions of the Code is Sec. 103, which provides that interest on "the obligations of a State, a Territory, or a possession of the United States, or any political subdivision" is excluded from gross income. This exclusion, which has been a part of our tax laws since 1913, has been supported on a number of different bases—most vigorously on the basis of an alleged constitutional relationship between governmental units. Under the 1894 income tax law, which was declared unconstitutional in the Pollock case (see Chapter 2), interest on state and local bonds was specifically included in income, and this inclusion was partially responsible for the Court's decision. The Court's logic was that taxing of income from the bonds was essentially taxing the bonds themselves and was, therefore, an encroachment on a sovereign power of the State.

Perhaps a more pertinent argument is that removing the exclusion would substantially increase the costs of state and local governments. The traditionally low interest rates on bonds issued by these governments exist because high-income purchasers are willing to accept a low tax-free income that in the past has had a high degree of security in preference to substantially higher income subject to the federal tax. In other words, the exclusion can be viewed as an indirect means for the federal government to grant financial assistance to state and local governments.

Critics of interest exclusion base their arguments on the equity concept that equal incomes should bear equal taxes and on the supposition that tax-free governmental securities are held primarily by corporations and by individuals with high incomes. Thus, they argue, the exclusion provides tax benefits where they are least needed, especially since these securities can be freely bought and sold with little risk or expense. Critics object not only to the inequitable distribution of tax benefits but to the diversion of high-income investors from risky private investments to government securities. This diversion of resources allegedly reduces risk taking and innovation. However, the difficulties encountered by some American cities in meeting their debt obligations in recent years has definitely increased the risk that an investor assumes in buying local government bonds. It should also be noted that a large increase in interest rates has accompanied the growth of uncertainty.

In recent years, another controversy has arisen over the tax-free status of interest on state and local securities. Many municipalities and other governmental units have issued tax-free bonds to procure funds, which are then loaned to either nonprofit or profit-seeking groups for certain purposes. In other cases, governmental units may acquire assets to lease or resell to these groups. Usually, the funds are intended to promote industrial growth of the municipality or other governmental body or to finance other specific purposes.

The President's 1985 tax reform proposal noted that "a total of $58 billion of such bonds was issued in 1983, accounting for 61 percent of all long-term tax-exempt bonds issued that year."[5] The proposal charged that these bonds have caused serious erosion in the federal income tax base, that the subsidy is inefficient because it is "filtered through high-income investors," that the bonds have had "anti-competitive and distortive" effects on the economy, and that the volume of the bonds has worked to the detriment of bonds issued to finance state and local governments by raising rates for all tax exempts. The 1986 Tax Reform Act put severe restrictions on the ability of state and local governments to issue "private activity bonds." New Code Sec. 135 provides that for interest on private activity bonds to be tax exempt, the bonds must fall within volume limits set for each state, satisfy a number of requirements spelled out in Sec. 147, and be issued for specified purposes (such as airports, sewage facilities, certain rehabilitation projects, and so on). The volume limits (starting in 1988, after a phasein period) will be the greater of $150 million or $50 per capita. The Sec. 147 requirements limit the maturity of certain tax-exempt private activity bonds to 120% of the economic life of the facilities financed by the issue, specify several unacceptable uses for the proceeds (such as gambling establishments), and place a number of restrictions on the issuance and use of the bonds.

One final aspect of the interrelationship between governmental units should be mentioned. Before 1941, interest on bonds issued by the United States was exempt as a part of the overall philosophy of government tax immunity; and before 1939, the salaries and wages of state and local employees were exempt from the federal income tax. The tremendous pressure for tax funds during those years was largely responsible for elimination of these two exclusions.

Exclusions Related to Double Taxation

Several provisions of the law stem from the idea that income should be taxed once and once only to the person earning it. Prior to 1987, for example, the double taxation of corporate dividends was partially mitigated by a small

---

[5] *President's Tax Proposals to the Congress for Fairness, Growth, and Simplicity* (May 29, 1985), p. 283.

exclusion allowed shareholders. The dividends-received deduction discussed in Chapter 4 is a current example of a double-taxation provision. In this section, we discuss gifts and inheritances, prizes and awards, and return of capital.

GIFTS AND INHERITANCES   Section 102 provides that "gross income does not include the value of property acquired by gift, bequest, devise or inheritance." These exclusions are usually supported on the theory that such transfers of property are a redistribution of a donor's or deceased taxpayer's income rather than the creation of a new income, especially in the case of transfers to close relatives. In addition, cumbersome administrative problems would arise if such items as small Christmas and birthday gifts were included in taxable income. On the other hand, the exclusion of gifts creates the administrative problem of separating donative transactions from nondonative ones—in many cases a difficult line to draw. The donee who renders any service to the donor will likely have a difficult time proving that what he or she received was in reality a tax-free gift rather than taxable compensation.

Some tax scholars favor including transfers by gift, bequest, or inheritance in gross income. Others do not support taxation of the total value of such transfers but suggest that unrealized gains on property transferred by gift or death should be taxed at the time of the transfer, arguing that current laws act as a deterrent to the transfer of assets because taxpayers are encouraged to retain assets that have increased in value. If these assets are sold, taxable gains would result. On the other hand, if they are retained until death, no income tax is paid on the gain. In addition, a degree of inequity is involved, because these provisions benefit primarily those who can arrange their affairs in such a way as to avoid realizing the gains prior to death. Transfer taxes are levied on gifts and estates by the federal government and also by most states, but they tend to be less than the income taxes that would result if unrealized gains were taxed at the time of transfer.

PRIZES AND AWARDS   Before 1987, certain prizes and awards received for literary, scientific, and charitable achievements, and so on granted by tax-exempt organizations were excluded from gross income, provided the taxpayer–recipient was not required to take action in order to receive the award and was not required to perform future services. For years after 1986, the exclusion outlined above applies only if the recipient assigns the award to a recognized charity. A taxpayer that receives a Pulitzer Prize, or the National Book Award, for example, has no gross income if he assigns the award to a charity. Naturally, he gets no charitable deduction—the income is never his (included) to give away. Except for prizes and awards that meet the conditions above and certain nominal value awards received by employees from employers, all other prizes and awards must be included in gross income at cash or fair market value.

The 1986 Act creates arbitrary, specific rules governing the treatment of employee awards that can be deducted by the employer and excluded from the gross income of the employee. First, to be excluded (and deducted), the employee achievement award must be based on length of service, or safety achievements, and must be a part of a meaningful presentation (a lot of hoopla). The dollar limit is $400 for any year for a single employee, unless the award is from a "qualified plan," in which case the limit is $1,600 for any year for an employee. A qualified plan is a written plan that does not discriminate in favor of highly paid employees and where the average award per year per employee does not exceed $400. Awards for a year in excess of these dollar limits are gross income to the recipient and cannot be deducted by the employer. Any "gifts" from an employer to an employee not covered by these rules are gross income to the employee.

RETURN OF CAPITAL   Several other provisions in the Code are indirectly related to the concept of double taxation. The most important of these are based on the *return-of-capital* concept, which permits a taxpayer to recover tax free an investment in an asset because the original investment represents a capital base that has already been taxed.

Suppose, for example, that a taxpayer worked for a salary and each payday invested a portion of her net pay in a simple annuity. During her working life, she invested a total of $10,000 in the annuity. She has reached 60 years of age and, under the contract, is now paid $2,000 a year for eight years. How are the $2,000 payments taxed? Obviously, a portion of each $2,000 represents a return of her original investment, and a portion represents income. To determine the part that is a tax-free return of investment, she simply divides the total investment of $10,000 by the number of years (eight) over which she receives payments and finds, in this way, that each year she may exclude $1,250 as a return of capital. The remaining $750 is taxable income.

As a practical matter, however, it is typically more difficult to determine what portion of a retirement annuity is income and what portion is a return of capital (see Chapter 12). Other applications of the return-of-capital idea are examined in detail in later chapters.

Exclusions Related to Education

One exclusion of special interest to students is that of scholarships and fellowships under Sec. 117. Generally, if a college student who is a candidate for a degree receives an award that does not require him or her to perform duties such as teaching classes or grading papers, the scholarship is not included in the student's gross income to the extent the scholarship is used for tuition and books, fees, supplies, and equipment required by the course of instruction. Prior to 1987, the exclusion covered the entire scholarship, including amounts for room, board, and other living costs. After 1986, fellowships received by a taxpayer who is not a candidate for a degree are gross income. Degree candidates can exclude scholarships from gross income to the extent explained above, even though the scholarship is paid by a corporation or individual not related to the educational institution, provided the payment is not compensation for past or future services.

Another exclusion related to education benefits received by employees under *educational assistance plans* merits attention. In recent years many employers have encouraged employees to receive additional education by paying tuition, purchasing books and supplies, and so on, for employees. Under Sec. 127, payments made by the employer on behalf of the employee for such costs as tuition and books during the years 1974–1987 were tax free to the employee if made under nondiscriminatory educational assistance programs. At the same time, no deduction was allowed the employee for expenses for which he or she was reimbursed under such tax-free plans. The maximum amount that can be excluded under such a plan is $5,250 per employee.

Exclusions for Fringe Benefits

All forms of compensation made by an employer to an employee are generally taxable. This includes such things as salaries and wages, bonuses, commissions, and all "gifts," unless such gifts are achievement awards or minimum fringe benefits to be discussed below. Also, amounts paid by an employer to someone else for the benefit of an employee (in other words, fringe benefits) are taxable to the employee. Preceding parts of this chapter have covered some exceptions to this last rule: health and accident insurance premiums, group term life insurance premiums, death benefits, and educational assistance programs. One important fringe benefit is discussed in Chapter 12—pension and profit-sharing plans. The following sections cover other common fringes that employees can exclude from income under specific conditions.

MEALS AND LODGINGS   Certain forms of compensation are tax free on the basis that they are "for the convenience of the employer." For example, Sec. 119 excludes the value of meals furnished by an employer to an employee for a "substantial noncompensatory" business reason unless the employee has an option to take cash instead. Under this rule, meals provided to food-service employees have generally been excluded, even though meals are consumed before or after duty hours. Cash allowances in lieu of meals are generally taxable. For example, in a decision involving New Jersey state troopers who were given a mid-shift meal allowance and were permitted to eat wherever they desired as long as they remained on call in their assigned duty area, the Supreme Court held that the meal allowances were compensation, in part at least, because the meals were not served on the employer's premises.[6] Similarly, the value of lodging provided the employee is excluded under Sec. 119 only if the employee must accept the lodging on the employer's premises to perform his or her duties properly.

If the exclusion for meals or lodgings does not apply, the employee must usually include the fair value of the service received in gross income. The 1986

---

[6]*Kowalski*, 434 U.S. 77 (1977).

Act, however, contains two exceptions to this rule. Section 119(d) generally limits the annual fair rental to 5% of appraised value for lodging furnished by educational institutions. Second, employees have no income from food facilities operated by an employer on or near the employer's premises so long as the revenues from the activity cover the costs.

INCENTIVE STOCK OPTIONS   Until 1976, a popular means used by corporations for compensating and retaining key officers and employees was the *qualified stock option.* Under certain conditions, an employee could be granted an option to purchase shares in the employer corporation and would pay no taxes on exercising the option, even though the purchase price was less than the stock's market value at date of exercise. When the employee subsequently disposed of the shares, the gain was taxed as a capital gain—at a very favorable rate if the stock had been held for a minimum period. In 1976, Congress repealed the Code provisions permitting qualified options and reestablished the general rule that property acquired at a discount from an employer is taxable.

To provide incentives for increasing productivity, Congress in 1981 essentially reinstated qualified stock options. Under the rules of Sec. 422A, an employee recognizes no income on exercise of an *incentive option.* (Conversely, the employer corporation must agree to take no deduction for employee compensation in connection with the option.) If the employee holds the shares for more than one year (and until a date at least two years after the option was granted), any gain qualifies for long-term capital gains treatment.

A number of conditions must be met for the option to qualify as an incentive option. These relate to the time during which the option must be exercised, require that the price of the option must be at least 100% of the stock's market value at the time of the grant, place restrictions on the transferability of the option, and limit the total value of shares on which options may be granted. The law permits certain options outstanding when the law was enacted to be given tax-free treatment. To illustrate an incentive option plan, let us assume that the president of a company is granted an option to purchase shares of the company at $100 per share, which is equal to or more than the market price of the shares on the date the option is granted. Two years after the option is granted the president exercises the option, paying $100 per share when the stock's fair market value is $125. The $25 bargain element is not income. If the president later sells the stock for $150 after holding the stock for more than a year, the gain of $50 per share is recognized as a capital gain. The incentive option thus permits the deferral of income and the conversion of compensation into capital gains.

The 1986 Act made several changes in the technical rules for incentive stock options; for example, one change clarifies the annual dollar limit on options for each employee. The elimination of the net capital gain deduction by the 1986 Act has an indirect effect on these options that is much more important. Now, the options merely serve to defer income (assuming the stock price rises). The more important earlier effect was the conversion of ordinary income (compensation) into capital gain.

OTHER FRINGE BENEFITS   Under Sec. 125, employer contributions for tax-free employee benefits (those that would not normally be included in the employee's gross income) made under a *cafeteria plan* (plans in which the employee may choose between tax-exempt benefits and taxable benefits, such as cash or property) remain tax free only if the cafeteria plan does not discriminate in favor of highly compensated participants.

Section 120 provides that amounts contributed by an employer to a qualified group legal services plan on behalf of an employee or the employee's dependents through 1987 are excludable from the employee's income. Similarly, if the legal services are performed by the employer, the value of such services are excludable.

Under Sec. 129, the value of child or dependent care provided by an employer under a written nondiscriminatory plan is generally not included in the employee's income. For an unmarried taxpayer, the exclusion cannot exceed the amount of the employee's earned income for the year. In the case of married employees, the limitation is based on the earned income of the spouse with the lower earned income. If the spouse is incapacitated or a student, earned income is imputed to that spouse at the rate of $200 per month if one qualifying person is involved or $400 per month if more than one qualifying individual is involved. The 1986 Act further limits the amount excluded to $5,000 per year for each employee.

And the beat goes on. Section 132 permits an exclusion of the value of services that have no cost to the employer—for example, free tickets for airline employees. That same section also excludes services that have a very small value and employee discounts on purchases that do not exceed prescribed limits. Details on these exclusions as well as others not mentioned can be found in any tax service.

Other Exclusions

Among the many other exclusions, four warrant a brief discussion.

IMPROVEMENTS CONSTRUCTED BY TENANT   The first exclusion stipulates that a property owner generally has no income either when a tenant constructs improvements on the lessor's property or when the property, including improvements, reverts to the lessor on termination of the lease. If the improvements are constructed *in lieu of rents,* however, the lessor must report as income the fair value of the improvements when they are placed on the property.

DISCHARGE OF INDEBTEDNESS   Taxpayers who settle debts for less than their "book" amount have an increase in net worth. However, if the taxpayer is insolvent both before and after the forgiveness, the income is excluded from taxation by Sec. 108. The amount of indebtedness eliminated in bankruptcy proceeds is also excluded from income. When creditors reach a "compromise" agreement, however, the forgiveness of all or part of the taxpayer's debt may result in taxable income, but not in excess of the amount by which the taxpayer is solvent after the compromise. For example, if the taxpayer has assets of $100,000 and liabilities of $120,000 before the compromise settlement and the creditors reduce the debt to $87,000, the taxpayer must report $13,000 of the forgiveness as income.

Prior to the 1986 Act, the forgiveness of debt incurred in a trade or business could be accounted for by a reduction of the basis of assets. This option is no longer available, and income results unless the taxpayer is bankrupt or insolvent.

INCOME EARNED ABROAD   To further the U.S. version of colonialism, earned income from sources outside the U.S. has enjoyed a sizable exclusion (about $20,000 in the late 1970s) for several years. This exclusion apparently was based on the premise that Americans living abroad do not benefit from services and facilities provided by the federal government within the United States and, therefore, should be excused from paying a part of the cost of these services. Another factor leading to the exclusion has been the emphasis on the value and benefits of international development and business and on the need and desirability of having Americans work abroad. The Foreign Earned Income Act of 1978 eliminated the exclusion but permitted U.S. citizens abroad to deduct a portion of their living costs in specified circumstances or, alternatively, to exclude from income $20,000 per year in limited cases.

After 1981, qualified taxpayers may exclude a limited amount of income. An individual who is a bona fide resident of a foreign country or who is present in a foreign country or countries for 330 days out of any 12-consecutive-months' period may elect the exclusion. The exclusion was $75,000 for tax years beginning in 1982 and $80,000 for the years 1983–1986. The 1986 Act reduces the amount to $70,000 for 1987 and later years.

Income earned from personal services abroad, other than as an employee of the U.S. government or its agencies, qualifies for the exclusion. Distributions of corporate earnings do not qualify for the exclusion, and a maximum of only 30% of the income derived from a trade or business in which both capital and personal services are material income-producing factors may be treated as earned income.

In addition, the taxpayer entitled to the foreign income exclusion may exclude a portion of amounts paid or provided by the employer for foreign housing costs. The calculation of the exclusion for housing is beyond our scope here.

PAYMENTS TO MEMBERS OF ARMED FORCES AND TO VETERANS   Although regular pay for members of the armed forces is taxable, certain benefits and allowances to service personnel and their dependents may be excluded. For example, the value of quarters provided a person in the service (or the cash payment made to him or her in lieu of quarters) is tax free, as is the basic allowance for quarters for his or her dependents. Similarly, the value of subsistence (or cash payment in lieu of subsistence) is not taxable. Uniform and equipment allowances are likewise excluded.

Former service personnel also receive certain tax breaks. The mustering-out pay on termination of service is tax exempt. Although pensions paid to military retirees who have retired because of length of service are taxable, pensions or other allowances based on personal injury or sickness resulting from active duty are exempt. Under Sec. 104, personnel entering service after September 24, 1975, may exclude disability pensions only if the benefits are based on a combat-related injury. Payments made for education and training allowances (the "GI Bill") are excluded, as are bonus payments received by veterans from state governments.

The brief survey of the rules governing gross income and exclusions has been from the perspective of the individual taxpayer. You will note that some of the exclusions, by their nature, apply to other entities as well. The exclusion for discharged indebtedness is an example. In the next chapter we turn to the deductions that apply to the individual taxpayer.

PROBLEMS

1. Jim and Mary Barlow are married and have one daughter, Kristin, who is one year old. During the current year, Jim worked for Ace Corporation and earned $18,000; Mary sold cosmetics part-time and earned $4,000. Kristin, an unusually beautiful one-year-old, modeled infants' clothing for the Best Department Store and earned $4,000. How many taxpayers are in the Barlow family? What minimum number of tax returns must the Barlow family file? How do you account for the discrepancy between the number of taxpayers and the number of returns that must be filed? Would you advise Jim and Mary to file separate returns? Explain each answer.

2. Several years ago, David Nipon became disenchanted with U.S. politics and moved to the Mediterranean coast of France. Although he has not returned to the United States, he draws income from extensive real estate holdings in Illinois and from various U.S. securities. Nipon also has substantial wealth invested in companies located throughout Europe. As a resident of France, he is subject to the French income tax, although he continues to hold a U.S. passport. Is Nipon subject to the U.S. income tax? If so, does the U.S. tax cover his foreign-source income? If he is taxed by both countries, what provisions in the U.S. tax mitigate the effects of double taxation?

3. How does the tax law define a "highly compensated employee"? Why is this distinction important?

4. What is the primary method employed by Congress to limit the use of private-activity tax exempt bonds?

5. In each of the following independent cases, indicate the amount that the taxpayer would report as "gross income" for the year:
   a. In 19x3, Y's employer paid premiums for a health and accident policy for each employee. During the current year, the employer paid $1,250 on behalf of Y.
   b. Mr. Y has two health and accident policies on which he pays all premiums. During 19x2, when he was hospitalized for hepatitis, his hospital and doctor bills amounted to $500. Y paid these bills, and, before the end of 19x2, collected $300 on one policy and $350 on the other policy.
   c. In 19x2 Mr. Y received reimbursement for $3,000 of medical expenses that he

had paid in 19x1. Mr. Y claimed a medical expense deduction in 19x1 for the entire $3,000.

d. Mr. Y's employer has a direct health and accident reimbursement plan under which it directly pays medical bills of its employees. The plan is offered on a nondiscriminatory basis to all employees. This year Mr. Y's employer paid $480 of medical bills for him.

6. What is the amount of "gross income" in each of the cases?

a. Taxpayer was involved in an accident and as a result received a $5,000 personal damage judgment plus $800 reimbursement for medical costs incurred.

b. Amos is injured on the job. As a result of his injury, he is paid $400 under workmen's compensation insurance and also receives $800 under health and accident insurance policies to reimburse him for medical costs. Additionally, he receives $500 under a disability income policy that he purchased and paid for himself.

c. Peter and his wife were injured in an automobile accident during the year. Because of the accident, Peter and his wife were paid $1,300 to reimburse them for medical costs and $8,900 for personal injury and suffering.

d. Mr. Y's car was struck in the rear by a speeder in September of last year. Mr. Y suffered from whiplash and had severe pains in his neck and upper back. He filed a claim for damages against the speeder and his insurance company. Y went to the doctor with the problem but was never hospitalized because the doctor could not diagnose the ailment. To avoid a costly court fight, the speeder's insurance company settled with Y in February of the current year for $1,000.

e. Z was ill throughout most of the current year. She received $300 per month for nine months from a wage-continuation policy. Z paid all the premiums on the policy.

7. In each of the following independent cases, indicate the amount that the taxpayer should report as "gross income" for the year:

a. Mary's husband died during the current year, leaving a life insurance policy with a face value of $50,000 payable to Mary. She received the $50,000 from the insurance company in November.

b. Assume the same facts as in part a, except that the $50,000 was not withdrawn from the insurance company at the time of the insured's death but was left with the company under an option provided in the policy, with five installments of $13,000 each to be paid to Mary. During the year, she received her first installment of $13,000.

c. Jones, who had been holding two jobs, died during the current year. Because of Jones's death, the first employer paid Mrs. Jones $8,000, and the second employer paid her $6,000.

d. Mrs. McDonald died during the current year. Her employer paid Mr. McDonald $8,000 and each of her two children $3,500. Payments were made solely on account of her death.

e. Rufus died during the current year. His wife was paid $10,000 under a group term life insurance policy that had been paid for by Rufus's employer. In addition, the employer paid Rufus's wife $4,000 on account of Rufus's death.

f. T. Cash surrendered his life insurance policy and received a lump sum of $8,000. He had paid total premiums of $7,200 on the policy in previous years.

g. Mr. Friendly loaned $5,000 to his neighbor Adams. Adams ran into financial difficulty, so he assigned a life insurance policy to Friendly, naming Friendly beneficiary. Face amount of the policy was $7,000. After receiving the policy,

Friendly paid premiums of $420. At that point, Adams died, and Friendly received a check for $7,000 from the insurance company.

8. In each of the following independent cases, indicate how much, if any, of the amounts involved must be reported as income by the recipient:
   a. Anthony's employer carries a substantial insurance program for his employees. During the current year, the employer paid premiums of $960 on health and hospital insurance policies for Anthony. In addition, the employer pays life insurance premiums of $400 under a group term life insurance program. This life insurance provides for a death benefit of $40,000 payable to Mrs. Anthony in the event of Anthony's death.
   b. Taxpayer's employer purchased an ordinary, whole-life insurance policy for every employee. During the current year, the employer paid premiums of $400 on the taxpayer's policy.

9. Herman and Elsie file a joint return. For the year, they had the following items of income:

Dividends on stock in domestic corporations	$14,000
Tax-exempt interest	20,000
Taxable interest	3,000
Social Security benefits	5,000

Compute their adjusted gross income for the year.

In Problems 10–17, give the dollar amount that should be included in the computation of the taxpayer's gross income.

10. a. Taxpayer inherited land from a deceased aunt. The land had a fair market value of $60,000 when inherited.
    b. Professor Graham was selected by the business students at State University as their "outstanding" teacher and was given a cash award of $1,000 by the student association.
    c. Sue was chosen Miss City. She won both the bathing suit and the talent contests. Many people speculate that she will ultimately become Miss America. As an award for being chosen Miss City, she was given cash and merchandise totaling $2,000.
    d. Professor Samples was awarded a Pulitzer Prize of $15,000 for writing a book on the history of the Apache Indians.
    e. Professor Goodman was awarded a Nobel Prize in recognition of his contribution to the field of medicine. He assigned the $190,000 award to a charitable organization established to carry on cancer research.
    f. Teresa inherited several State of Illinois bonds on the death of her uncle during the current year. The bonds had a fair value of $60,000 at his death. After receiving the bonds, Teresa was also paid $1,800 by the state, representing interest earned on the bonds after her uncle's death.
    g. Kamp, a rabid baseball fan, attended every home game of the city team. He was surprised one evening when his ticket stub contained the "lucky number," and he won an automobile with a fair value of $7,000 in the ticket drawing.
    h. Max received a $300 safety award this year from his employer at the annual recognition banquet. The award was given to all employees who had worked for 10 years without an accident.

11. Taxpayer received the following interest and dividends during the year:
    a. $3,500 dividends from domestic corporations

   b. $2,000 interest on general revenue bonds issued by the State of Texas
   c. $80 "dividends" from a credit union
   d. $4,200 interest on U.S. treasury bills

12. A salaried worker purchased an annuity policy from an insurance company when he was 35 years old. The policy required that the worker pay the company $500 per year for the next 30 years. At that time, when the worker was 65 years old, the insurance company would pay him either (1) a lump-sum payment of $20,000 or (2) annual payments of $1,300 for 20 years.
   a. Assume that the worker elected option 1.
   b. Assume all facts as before, except that this worker elected option 2. (Answer relative to one year's payment of $1,300.)

13. Roger invested $20,000 in an annuity. Beginning in 19x1 and continuing through the next nine years (a total of 10 years), he is to be paid $3,000 each year. How much, if any, of the $3,000 received in 19x1 must be included in gross income?

14. a. Alice, a university student working on her BBA degree, received a scholarship of $2,000 from the university. Alice's tuition is $2,500. The scholarship was based on grades, and she had no services to render.
   b. Assume the same facts as above in part a, except that the scholarship was awarded by an industrial firm.
   c. Assume the same facts as in part a, except that Alice is working on a PhD.
   d. Assume the same facts as in part a, except that Alice's tuition and course related supplies amounted to $1,500 during the period covered by the scholarship.
   e. Robert received his PhD in 19x1. Beginning in September 19x1 and continuing to December 19x4 he received a postdoctoral fellowship from a tax-free foundation to continue study and research. The fellowship paid him $500 per month.
   f. Margaret S. is working toward a PhD in chemistry. She receives a $5,000 "scholarship" from the university. Margaret's tuition is $6,000 per year. To get the scholarship, she must work 10 hours each week in the laboratory. This laboratory work is required of all students working toward the PhD in chemistry at that university.
   g. Joann, a graduate student at State University, received a $1,000 fellowship grant, $350 for grading accounting papers, and $2,000 from her father. She used the $3,350 to pay tuition ($1,000) and living expenses ($2,350).

15. a. Taxpayer is a university student. He works in the university cafeteria and receives as payment three meals each day. Total value of the meals consumed during the current year is $1,450.
   b. Taxpayer manages an apartment house throughout the year. He is required by his employer to live in one of the apartments, which is given to the taxpayer rent free. Similar apartments are rented to tenants for $3,600 per year. Taxpayer's salary as manager is $12,000 per year.
   c. Taxpayer manages an apartment house throughout the year, for which he makes a cash salary of $4,000. In addition, his employer offered to give him another $200 per month in cash or to let him live rent free in an apartment. Choosing the latter, taxpayer received an apartment that has a fair rental value of $4,000 per year.
   d. Maude is a waitress at a local cafe. Her income for the year consists of wages of $6,500 and tips of $3,200. In addition, she eats her noon meal while on duty at the cafe, free of charge. She estimates that the value of meals consumed during the year is $650.

e. Guardman lived rent free in a house owned by his employer on the employer's premises during the year. The rental value of the house was $1,800 for the year. Although Guardman lived in the house for the convenience of the employer, he was not required to live there and could have lived somewhere else.

f. Lynn works for an accounting firm. During "busy season" she often works until 10:00 P.M. On these occasions, her employer provides a $15 meal allowance. This year, she received $600 as meal allowances. She actually spent $400 for meals on evenings when she worked late.

16. a. Thompson served in the U.S. Army in Southeast Asia. As a result of combat injury in 1967, Thompson was retired from the military and awarded a pension. During the current year, he received total payments of $8,400 from the pension.

b. On January 1 of the current year, Careerman retired from the U.S. Air Force after 15 years of service. During the current tax year, he received retirement pension payments of $7,600.

17. a. Stewart is an airline steward for Great Fly Airlines. One of his fringe benefits is the right to fly free of charge on the airline, and Stewart takes advantage of this right. He estimates that during 19x1 the flights taken on short vacations would have cost him $1,200 if he had been required to pay for them.

b. Appleton, who is single and earns $38,000 per year, works for a company that provides dependent child care under a nondiscriminatory plan. Preschool-age children of employees are cared for in a daycare facility provided by the employer. The value of the daycare provided Appleton's daughter this year was $6,000.

c. Jackson's employer offers a nondiscriminatory cafeteria plan. Jackson can choose from such items as medical insurance, group term life insurance, legal assistance, and disability insurance. In lieu of these items Jackson chose $1,200 extra cash compensation this year.

18. In January of 19x1, Big Dome Corporation issued its president, H. Bellows, a qualified incentive stock option to purchase 2,000 shares of the corporation's stock at $20 per share. On the date of issue, the stock had a value of $19 per share. Bellows exercised the option on March 15, 19x2, when the stock had a market value of $22 per share. He sold the stock on April 1, 19x3, for $30 per share. How much income and what kind of income does Bellows have in 19x1, 19x2, and 19x3?

19. a. Art has been in business for many years. Because of his illness in the current year, Art's corporation suffered severe losses. On September 1, the corporation's assets totaled only $180,000, and its liabilities were $231,000. Because Art had been a valuable customer for many years, and because he had recovered from his illness and the outlook for future profits was good if Art could correct the immediate insolvency, the creditors agreed to reduce the corporation's debt. How much gross income does Art have

(1) if the debts were reduced to $200,000?

(2) if the debts were reduced to $171,000?

b. Salmonson owned a small plot of land in Midcity. In 1960, she leased the land to Acme Company, which built a small building on the property at a cost of $24,000. This amount was also considered to be the building's fair market value. When the lease expired in the current year, the building became the property of Salmonson. At that time, the building had a fair market value of $6,000.

(1) How much income did Salmonson have in 1960 as a result of the building's construction?

(2) How much income did she have in the current year when the lease expired?

20. Friedsam, single, lost his job in August of the current year. He could not secure another job; during August and September, he received unemployment benefits of $380. In October, he qualified for Social Security retirement benefits, and during the remainder of the year he received $980 of Social Security benefits. His only other income was a salary of $19,900 for January through August. What is the amount of Friedsam's gross income this year?

21. Acorn Corporation adopted a plan under which the corporation would pay the costs of tuition, books, and supplies for any corporate officer or for any operating department head who enrolled in not more than two courses at an accredited university. Zemat Turin, the corporation's controller, enrolled in a tax course at the university. The corporation reimbursed Turin $270 for tuition, $22 for books, and $6 for other supplies. What part, if any, of the reimbursement is taxable to Turin?

22. This year North lived and worked in France as an employee of a U.S. corporation for the entire year. She earned $90,000 salary. North also earned $2,000 interest on a bank account in France and $15,000 dividends and interest on investments in the U.S. How much is North's gross income?

SUPPLEMENTAL PROBLEMS

23. H. McGregor Malcolm is president and chairman of the board of Malcolm Industries. In preparing Malcolm's tax return for the year, you discover the following facts:

(1) The company provides Malcolm with an automobile for his business and personal use. Each year the automobile is traded in for a new one.

(2) The company also provides Malcolm's wife, who works on a part-time basis for the company, with an automobile for her exclusive use. Her car is replaced every third year.

(3) Malcolm Industries has 325 employees. It does not have a general hospitalization insurance plan for employees, but it has secured a medical insurance policy for Malcolm that covers all medical costs for Mr. and Mrs. Malcolm. During this year, premiums on the policy totaled $1,500.

(4) Malcolm attends many "marketing" and "trade association" meetings. His wife always accompanies him because he thinks she is very helpful in making business contacts and in securing sales orders. The corporation pays all expenses for both.

(5) The company has a dining room for officers, directors, and selected high-level managers. Meals are served at a price that is roughly one half the price charged for similar meals at public restaurants.

(6) The company frequently receives "premiums" from suppliers. These premiums are usually resold, but occasionally Malcolm and the other stockholder–employees take premiums for their personal use. During the current year, Malcolm took a color television set, a microwave oven, and a television computer game for his use.

(7) Malcolm Industries subscribes to many magazines for use in its reception area.

Malcolm regularly takes home several of these magazines. After the Malcolms have read them, the magazines are returned to the company's offices.

(8) During the year, as part of a promotional campaign, one of Malcolm Industries' suppliers offered its customers an all-expense-paid Mediterranean cruise for each $750,000 of merchandise purchased. Malcolm Industries purchased over $1,500,000 during the year and thus was eligible for two free trips. Mr. and Mrs. Malcolm took the cruise.

a. Comment on the effect of each of the foregoing items on Mr. and Mrs. Malcolm's gross income for the year.

b. Comment on the effect of each item on the gross income of Malcolm Industries for the year.

24. Davis was a candidate for mayor during the current year. She received contributions from friends totaling $13,200, and her expenses in the campaign were $11,800. Davis retained the additional $1,400 for use in subsequent campaigns. How much income, if any, must Davis include in gross income?

25. Herman Preachmore retired as a minister of the Big City Church on December 31, 19X1. For 19X1, his remuneration was

Salary	$30,000
Housing allowance	7,200
Home utilities allowance	4,800
Auto allowance	3,600

On December 31, the church congregation held a special meeting at which Preachmore received the following letter: "To show our appreciation for your devotion to this church, the trustees and congregation have voted to present you a gift, the sum of $1,000 per month as long as you may live, beginning January 15, 19X2." At this time, his life expectancy was 15 years.

a. What part of the $45,600 paid in 19X1 is taxable to Preachmore?

b. What is the proper tax treatment of the $1,000 per month beginning January 19X2?

CHAPTER 9

Classification of Deductions: Deductions Subject to 2% A.G.I. Floor

Each group plays a powerful, persuasive or pitiful case. When power, persuasion, and pity are all rolled into one—and then circumstances combine to make tax relief appear as the only practical solution—who can blame Congress for occasionally succumbing?
Walter Heller, 1959 Compendium

The general statutory rules for deductions were discussed earlier in Chapter 4. Recall that Sec. 162 provides broad authority for deduction of expenses related to conducting a trade or business and that Sec. 212 provides similar authority for deduction of expenses incurred for the production of income. In addition, Sec. 165 authorizes the deduction of certain losses, and a number of other provisions, the deduction of specific expenditures. In this chapter we first turn our attention to the importance of correctly *classifying* deductible expenditures on individuals' tax returns. Second, we examine more closely one of these classifications—itemized deductions that are deductible only to the extent they exceed two percent of A.G.I.

CLASSIFICATION OF DEDUCTIBLE EXPENDITURES

An expanded version of the formula presented earlier can be used to calculate the tax liability for an individual. Some key terms—such as income, exclusions, deductions, and credits—were discussed at length in earlier chapters, but the definitions of other new terms in this formula are critical to an understanding of the income tax law as it relates to individuals.

With the exception of the multiplication of the tax rates by taxable income to obtain the gross tax, note that every arithmetic operation in this formula is a subtraction. The order of these subtractions is very important. The intermediate remainders—gross income and adjusted gross income—must be correctly calculated before several critical decisions can be made about the amount of tax due the government.

> Income broadly conceived
> − Exclusions
> ―――――――――――――――――――――――
> = Gross income
> − Deductions for adjusted gross income (A.G.I.)
> ―――――――――――――――――――――――
> = Adjusted gross income
> − Deductions *from* adjusted gross income (the larger of a standard deduction or itemized deductions)
> − Personal and dependent exemptions
> ―――――――――――――――――――――――
> = Taxable income
> × Applicable tax rate(s)
> ―――――――――――――――――――――――
> = Gross tax
> − Tax credits and prepayments
> ―――――――――――――――――――――――
> = Net tax payable

Gross Income

As discussed in Chapters 3 and 8, gross income is income broadly conceived after subtracting all allowed exclusions (Sec. 61). The correct definition of gross income is important because this amount determines which individual taxpayers must file a return. The precise amounts of gross income an individual must have before he or she is required to file a return are detailed in Chapter 11.

To illustrate the importance of properly classifying exclusions and deductions, consider the following two situations: A wealthy widow has several million dollars in capital invested in tax exempt municipal bonds. She realizes an income of $100,000, all from tax exempt securities. Such interest is excluded, and her gross income is zero. She is *not* required to file a return. A second widow depends on rental property for her livelihood. She receives gross rents of $10,000 but incurs deductible expenses related to the rental property of $8,000. Her net income from the rental property is only $2,000, but her gross income is $10,000. She must file a return because the $10,000 of gross income exceeds the minimum amount of income explained later. Logic might tell us that the widow with the larger income is a more likely candidate for reporting to the government, but the law clearly nominates the widow with the very small *net* income as the one who must make an accounting to the Internal Revenue Service.

Adjusted Gross Income

An important yet troublesome calculation in the tax formula for individuals is that of adjusted gross income (commonly abbreviated A.G.I.). Note from the formula above that the deductions allowed individuals are divided into two classes—deductions *for* A.G.I. and deductions *from* A.G.I. The proper classification of deductions is important because, for many taxpayers, the actual amount of the deductions *from* A.G.I. is based in part on A.G.I. For example, medical expenses, which are deductions from A.G.I., can be deducted only to the extent they exceed 7½% of A.G.I.

ADJUSTED GROSS INCOME DEFINED   The term *adjusted gross income* is explicitly defined in Sec. 62, which is titled "Adjusted Gross Income Defined." This section is used for definitional purposes only. The determination of whether a given expenditure is deductible must be based on the sections discussed in Chapter 4. Section 62 simply tells the taxpayer whether a deductible item can be deducted as part of the determination of adjusted gross income. Twelve such deductions are listed in Sec. 62, reproduced below:

Sec. 62 Adjusted Gross Income Defined.
For purposes of this subtitle, the term "adjusted gross income" means, in the case of an individual, gross income minus the following deductions:
  (1) Trade and business deductions.—The deductions allowed by this chapter (other than by part VII of this subchapter) which are attributable to a trade or business carried on by the taxpayer, if such trade or business does not consist of the performance of services by the taxpayer as an employee.
  (2) Certain Trade and Business Deductions of Employees.—
    (A) Reimbursed Expenses of Employees.—The deductions allowed by part VI (sec. 161 and following) which consist of expenses paid or incurred by the taxpayer, in connection with the performance by him of services as an employee, under a reimbursement or other expense allowance arrangement with his employer.
    (B) Certain expenses of Performing Artists.—The deductions allowed by section 162 which consist of expenses paid or incurred by a qualified performing ʻartist in connection with the performances by him of services in the performing arts as an employee.
  (3) Losses from Sale or Exchange of Property.—The deductions allowed by part VI (sec. 161 and following) as losses from the sale or exchange of property.
  (4) Deductions Attributable to Rents and Royalties.—The deductions allowed by part VI (sec. 61 and following), by section 212 (relating to expenses for

production of income), and by section 611 (relating to depletion) which are attributable to property held for the production of rents and royalties.

(5) Certain Deductions of Life Tenants and Income Beneficiaries of Property. —In the case of a life tenant of property, or an income beneficiary of property held in trust, or an heir, legatee, or devisee of an estate, the deduction for depreciation allowed by section 167 and the deduction allowed by section 611.

(6) Pension, Profit-Sharing and Annuity Plans of Self-Employed Individuals. —In the case of an individual who is an employee within the meaning of section 401(c)(1), the deduction allowed by section 404.

(7) Retirement Savings. —The deduction allowed by section 219 (relating to deduction for certain retirement savings).

(8) Certain Portion of Lump-Sum Distributions from Pension Plans Taxed Under Section 402(e). —The deduction allowed by section 402(e).

(9) Penalties Forfeited Because of Premature Withdrawal of Funds from Time Savings Accounts or Deposits. — . . .

(10) Alimony. —The deduction allowed by section 215.

(11) Reforestation Expenses. —The deduction allowed by section 194.

(12) Certain Required Repayments of Supplemental Unemployment Compensation Benefits. — . . .

Thus, by omission, Sec. 62 also defines deductions *from* A.G.I., because any allowable deduction not listed in Sec. 62 cannot be deducted from gross income to determine A.G.I. It should be noted that the Tax Reform Act of 1986 removed a number of important deductions from Sec. 62. These include nonreimbursed *employee* travel and transportation expenses, moving expenses, the long-term capital gains deduction, and the deduction allowed two-earner married couples. The last two deductions were repealed, and the first two were reclassified as deductions *from* adjusted gross income.

Of the twelve deductions for adjusted gross income listed in Sec. 62, several deserve further attention because of the large number of affected taxpayers.

Deductions related to conduct of a trade or business.   The various tests applied to an activity to determine if that activity constitutes a trade or business were discussed in Chapter 4. Recall that new rules affecting tax years after 1986 limit the deductibility of losses from business activities in which the taxpayer does not materially participate (so called "passive activities"). Thus, the provision in Sec. 62(1) that expenses incurred in a trade or business are deductions *for* A.G.I. assumes that the expenses are deductible, either because the business is an active trade or business or because the passive activity rules permit deduction.

The trade or business expenses included in this category cannot consist of service as an employee. Only *reimbursed* expenses of an employee (unless a qualified performing artist) are allowed as deductions *for* A.G.I. A brief example clarifies this distinction. Assume the case of a CPA who is a sole practitioner with a small office staff. The CPA attends a seminar on recent tax developments and incurs the following expenses: registration fee $105 and transportation $75. As a sole proprietor, both of these items are deductions *for* A.G.I. because they are trade or business expenses of a self-employed individual. As an alternative, assume that the CPA is an employee of a large firm, incurs the same costs, and is reimbursed for the registration fee but not for the transportation costs. The registration fee is a deduction *for* A.G.I., whereas the transportation cost is a deduction *from* A.G.I. The reimbursement will be included in gross income.

The Tax Reform Act of 1986 added Sec. 162(m), which permits self-employed individuals to deduct 25% of medical insurance premiums paid for the taxpayer and family as deductions for A.G.I. The amount deducted cannot exceed the taxpayer's earned income from self-employment. Obviously, these amounts cannot also be counted as medical expenses for purposes of determining the taxpayer's deductions from A.G.I.

Losses from sale or exchange of property.   Section 62(4) refers to losses from the sale or exchange of property allowed by sections 161 and following. These sections include Sec. 165(c), which limits losses permitted individuals to those incurred in a trade or business, any transaction entered into for profit, or losses arising from theft or casualty. Since losses arising from a theft or casualty of personal use property are neither transactions entered into for a profit nor the result of a sale or exchange, they generally would not be treated as deductions for A.G.I. under Sec. 62(4). Personal casualty and theft losses may, however, be treated as deductions for A.G.I. as capital losses if *personal* casualty gains exceed *personal* casualty losses. In this situation, all such gains and losses are treated as gains and losses from the sale or exchange of capital assets. If personal casualty losses exceed personal casualty gains, then the transactions are deductions from A.G.I. and subject to special limits described in the next chapter.

Deductions related to transactions entered into for profit.   A confusing group of deductions are those related to transactions entered into for profit. These deductions are authorized primarily by Sec. 212 for the production of income and the maintenance of income-producing property. The most common transactions in this category involve investments in securities and in unimproved land held for speculation. The distinction between an activity that constitutes a trade or business as opposed to a transaction for profit is often a very thin line. Does the ownership and rental of a single dwelling unit constitute a business? Is a college professor who writes one or two books engaged in the business of writing textbooks? Or, alternatively, are these activities properly classified as transactions for profit? Fortunately, we do not have to reach a decision in these examples for purposes of classifying deductions. Section 62 provides that all (allowable) deductions related to the production of rents and royalties are deductions for A.G.I. With this exception, however, other deductions under Sec. 212 related to transactions for profit are deductions from A.G.I. Examples include the amounts paid for subscriptions to investment services and fees paid to tax consultants.

Alimony.   A taxpayer may deduct for A.G.I. amounts paid as alimony. This deduction has been supported on two grounds. First, alimony payments may be considered merely a means of dividing income between two taxpayers. Second, they may be considered in the nature of extraordinary, unavoidable expenses that significantly affect the taxpayer's ability to pay income taxes, similar to casualty losses and medical expenses. The major controversy surrounding alimony payments in the tax structure is the distinction between periodic payments, which represent a sharing of income between the parties, and property settlements, which are not deductible by the spouse making payments and are not taxable to the spouse receiving payment. Likewise, child support payments are neither deductible by the payer nor taxable to the recipient. Given these general rules, it is easy to understand why the definition of alimony has been a source of conflict between (1) the I.R.S. and taxpayers and (2) former spouses. Current rules are that, in general, alimony includes only cash payments that the divorce or separation agreement does not specify as being for something else (such as property settlements). Further, special "recapture" rules prevent "front loading" of property settlements disguised as alimony payments during the first three post-separation years. Calculation of recaptured alimony occurs in the third post-separation year. Any amounts determined to have been property settlements as a result of this calculation are added to the gross income of the person who paid them and are treated as deductions for A.G.I. of the recipient in the third year. Any payments that will (per the terms of the divorce or separation agreement) change in amount because of a contingency relating to a child are classified as child support payments. For example, if a divorce decree stipulates that a spouse's payment will decrease by $100 per month when a child reaches age 18, then $100 of each monthly payment will not be considered to be alimony.

Retirement plans.   Contributions to certain retirement plans, especially Individual Retirement Plans (IRAs) and to "Keogh" Plans for self-employed individuals are important deductions *for* A.G.I. and are discussed in Chapter 12.

Deductions from A.G.I.

After segregating and deducting expenditures allowed *for* A.G.I., individuals are allowed other deductions for various expenditures. These are deductions *from* A.G.I. and are generally referred to as "itemized deductions." (Technically, the deduction for personal and dependent exemptions is a deduction *from* A.G.I., but the deduction for exemptions is allowed without regard to actual expenditures and presents no classification problems.) A taxpayer "itemizes deductions" when he or she has actual deductions from A.G.I. in excess of the standard deduction amounts allowed. For 1987, these amounts are

Single individuals and head of household filers	$2,540
Married individuals and surviving spouses	3,760
Married individuals filing separately	1,880

Additionally, elderly or blind taxpayers are entitled to larger standard deduction amounts. For 1987 the basic amounts available to an individual who is age 65 or older *or* blind are

Single individuals	$3,000
Head of household filers	4,400
Married individuals and surviving spouses	5,000
Married individuals filing separately	2,500

After 1987 these same standard deduction amounts will apply to all individual taxpayers. Beginning in 1987 these amounts will be increased by $600 for a married individual or surviving spouse age 65 or older or blind ($1,200 if the individual is both blind and 65 or older) and by $750 for a single individual age 65 or older or blind ($1,500 if the individual is both blind and 65 or older). Thus, in 1987 a married couple filing jointly with one spouse over age 65 will be entitled to a $5,600 standard deduction, whereas the same couple would be entitled to a $6,200 standard deduction if both were age 65 or older. A single individual age 65 or over would be entitled to a standard deduction of $3,750. All of these amounts will be adjusted for inflation after 1988 with increases rounded down to multiples of $50.

Note that an individual who can establish actual itemized deductions in excess of these amounts is entitled to deduct the larger amount. Thus, a single taxpayer filing in 1988 who actually incurs $7,200 of itemized deductions is entitled to deduct this amount rather than the $3,000 standard deduction. However, a single individual who incurs only $2,300 of itemized deductions is entitled to the larger standard deduction.

In certain situations, the law provides that taxpayers are not entitled to take the full standard deduction. The most common situation encountered involves a taxpayer's dependent child who has income and must file a return. In such a case, the child's standard deduction may not exceed the greater of $500 or the amount of his or her earned income (up to the standard deduction allowed). For example, a child who is claimed by her parents as a dependent and has $1,200 of interest income is entitled to only a $500 standard deduction. If the same child has $300 of earned income, then she is still entitled to a $500 standard deduction. If she has $750 of earned income, then she is entitled to a $750 standard deduction. Note that these examples assume that the child has no actual deductions from A.G.I., which is usually true of minor children. If the taxpayer who is a dependent of another has deductions from A.G.I., the amount of such deductions is used if it exceeds the amount otherwise allowed.

In addition to the situation described above, if married individuals file separate tax returns and one spouse itemizes and the other does not, then the standard deduction for the nonitemizing spouse is zero. Nonresident aliens and certain other individuals who have exempt income from U.S. possessions are also denied a standard deduction.

Thus, the law provides that without regard to the actual amounts spent by a taxpayer for personal living expenses, no tax is levied unless the taxpayer's A.G.I. exceeds the exemption amount allowed plus the larger of the standard deduction or itemized deductions. The allowed itemized deductions include expenses incurred in transactions for profit under Sec. 212 and certain specific personal expenses such as medical expenses, contributions, interest, and taxes. These itemized deductions will be considered in more detail later in this chapter and in the next.

The proper classification of an individual's deductions between those *for* A.G.I. and *from* A.G.I is critical if the maximum deduction *from* A.G.I. is to be obtained. Note first that the standard deduction is not related to the taxpayer's actual expenditures. Thus, if deductions are incorrectly classified as from A.G.I., the taxpayer may elect to take the larger itemized deductions, whereas a correct classification might permit some items to be deducted for A.G.I. and still permit the use of the standard amount. To illustrate, assume that in 1988 a bachelor has gross income of $10,000 and allowable deductions of $3,400 consisting of $1,000 of reimbursed travel expenses plus $2,400 of personal taxes and contributions. If the deductions are all classified by him as from A.G.I., the taxpayer would itemize, giving him total itemized deductions of $3,200 ($2,400 + $1,000 − 2% of $10,000). If the $1,000 of reimbursed travel expenses were correctly classified as a deduction for A.G.I., however, the taxpayer's A.G.I. is $9,000 ($10,000 gross income − $1,000 deductions for A.G.I.). The taxpayer would still be entitled to the standard deduction of $3,000. The net effect is an increase in his total deductions to $4,000 ($1,000 for A.G.I. + the $3,000 standard deduction) and a decrease in taxable income of $800.

The correct classification of deductions can also be important for taxpayers whose itemized deductions are clearly greater than the standard amount. As explained later in this chapter, Sec. 212 deductions (other than those related to rents and royalties) as well as unreimbursed employee business deductions are deductible only to the extent they exceed 2% of adjusted gross income. Additionally, as we learn in the next chapter, both medical deductions and personal casualties are subject to thresholds that are percentages of A.G.I. Thus, the correct classification of a deduction that lowers A.G.I. automatically increases these deductions that must exceed a percentage of A.G.I.

ITEMIZED DEDUCTIONS SUBJECT TO 2% A.G.I. FLOOR

The 1986 Act imposed a new 2% of A.G.I. floor on certain itemized deductions. Sec. 67 states that "miscellaneous itemized deductions for any taxable year shall be allowed only to the extent that the aggregate of such deductions exceeds 2 percent of adjusted gross income." Further, "miscellaneous itemized deductions" are defined negatively as all itemized deductions except:

1. The deduction under Sec. 163 for interest
2. The deduction under Sec. 164 for taxes
3. The deduction under Sec. 165(a) for losses
4. The deduction under Sec. 170 for charitable contributions
5. The deduction under Sec. 213 for medical expenses
6. The deduction under Sec. 217 for moving expenses
7. Any deduction for impairment-related work expenses
8. The deduction under Sec. 691(c) for estate tax in case of income in respect of the decedent

9. Any deduction allowable in connection with personal property used in a short sale

10. The deduction under Sec. 1341 relating to computation of tax where the taxpayer restores a substantial amount held under claim of right

11. The deduction under Sec. 72(b)(3) relating to deduction where annuity payments cease before the investment is recovered

12. The deduction under Sec. 171 relating to deduction for amortizable bond premium

13. The deduction under Sec. 216 relating to deductions in connection with cooperative housing corporations

Essentially, any deductible item not on this list and not included in Sec. 62 as a deduction for A.G.I. will be subject to the 2% floor. The deductions subject to the floor are basically unreimbursed employee business expenses allowed under Sec. 162 and investment expenses (other than those associated with rents and royalties) allowed under Sec. 212. Each of these categories will be discussed below.

Unreimbursed Employee Business Expenses

Sec. 162 allows the deduction of a number of expenses related to employment. These include travel and transportation, entertainment expenses, education expenses, union dues, uniforms, and various professional expenses such as dues and subscriptions.

The 1986 Act imposed new limits on the deductibility of meals and entertainment expenses. For tax years after 1986, only 80% of allowable meals and entertainment costs are deductible. Earlier, the President's 1985 tax reform proposal had noted that:

> The liberality of the law in this area is in sharp contrast to the treatment of other kinds of expenses that provide both business and personal benefits. In some cases, such as work-related clothing, the presence of any personal benefit is deemed sufficient reason to disallow any deduction. In other cases, taxpayers are allowed to deduct only the portion of expenses allocated to business. In contrast, present law often allows full deductibility of entertainment expenses that entail substantial personal consumption.[1]

Similar arguments were made elsewhere in the proposal with regard to meals. The proposal noted that it is not possible to specify the precise percentage of personal benefit in situations that combine business and pleasure. Nonetheless, Congress decided that 20% was an appropriate approximation of the personal benefit embodied in business meals and entertainment. Note that if an employee is fully reimbursed for such expenses they are treated as deductions *for* A.G.I., and it is the employer who is disallowed 20% of the

---

[1] *President's Tax Proposals to the Congress for Fairness, Growth, and Simplicity,* May 29, 1985, p. 75.

deduction. On the other hand, if the employee is not reimbursed, then the expenses become deductions *from* A.G.I. subject first to the 20% disallowance and then to the 2% A.G.I. floor.

TRAVEL AND TRANSPORTATION EXPENSES   The Code prohibits the deduction of costs of commuting from the taxpayer's residence to his or her regular place of employment. If the taxpayer has more than one job, however, cost of going from the first job to the second one is deductible as transportation expense. Similarly, a taxpayer whose sole employment requires movement from one location to another during a single day (for example, a physician, a building contractor, or a plumber) may be entitled to a transportation deduction, excluding the cost of getting from home to the first work assignment and from the last assignment to home. Of course, any transportation cost incurred by the employee in connection with employment, while on the job, is deductible.

The employee deducts actual transportation costs incurred if public transportation facilities are used. If the employee uses a personal automobile, he or she may deduct either the actual costs incurred or a standard mileage allowance of 21 cents per mile for the first 15,000 business miles driven during the year and 11 cents per mile for each mile in excess of 15,000.

In recent years many court cases have involved the transportation costs of a commuting employee who at the same time transports job-required tools or equipment. According to the I.R.S., the taxpayer may deduct only the difference between the cost of transportation actually used and the cost of the same mode of transportation without the tools. Under the I.R.S. interpretation, therefore, the deductible cost often amounts to little or nothing. This may appear to be grossly unfair to the worker who would ordinarily ride a bus to work but, because he is carrying tools, must take an auto, thus increasing his transportation costs solely because of the tool problem.

The basic authority for deducting travel costs rests in Sec. 162(a)(2) of the Code, which provides for the deduction of all ordinary and necessary expenses paid or incurred during the year in carrying on a trade or business, including:

> (2) traveling expenses (including amounts expended for meals and lodging other than amounts which are lavish or extravagant under the circumstances) while away from home in the pursuit of a trade or business. . . .

Traveling expenses thus include transportation, meals, and lodging costs. Meals consumed while traveling are subject to the 20% reduction rule discussed above. One of the exceptions provides that prior to January 1, 1989, this reduction will not apply to meals at a "qualified meeting," which is defined as a convention, seminar, annual meeting, or similar business program with respect to which (1) an expense for food or beverages is not separately stated, (2) more than 50% of the participants are away from home, (3) at least 40 individuals attend, and (4) such food and beverages are part of a program that includes a speaker. This exception expires on December 31,

1989. Evidently Congress found the element of personal pleasure in such affairs to be impossible to estimate.

Although travel costs are deductible if they are incurred purely in connection with business "away from home," a fact question is often raised when the travel is for both business and personal purposes. For example, if the taxpayer, while on a business trip, takes time out for sightseeing or other pleasure activities, the question may arise whether all travel costs should be deductible as business expenses. The reverse situation may be found: the taxpayer may take a pleasure trip and, while traveling, take time out for certain business activities. The question in this case is whether any part of the costs are deductible as business expenses.

The basic factors that must be considered in determining whether or not travel costs are deductible include the ordinary, necessary, and reasonable criteria discussed in Chapter 4. The rule followed is logical; if the trip is primarily for business purposes, incidental sightseeing or other pleasure activities do not change the character of the trip, and, therefore, expenses incurred—except those directly related to the pleasure activity—are deductible. On the other hand, if the primary purpose of the trip is pleasure, incidental business activities do not change the nature of the trip, and only the expenses directly associated with the business activity are deductible.

In many cases it is difficult, if not impossible, to determine the taxpayer's true intent. The taxpayer may not know the real purpose of the trip. This is especially true of attendance at meetings or conventions of trade associations and professional organizations. Business conventions often are held in resort areas or other pleasant surroundings to encourage attendance by members. In some cases, the convention may be merely a sham, whereas other business conventions may be invaluable to the participants.

In recent years many taxpayers have found it "necessary" to make "business" trips to foreign countries and have taken the opportunity to combine a personal vacation with the business trip. Special rules apply to the taxpayer who travels on business or attends a convention or seminar in a foreign country. If the travel does not exceed one week or if the portion of the taxpayer's time outside the United States that is not attributable to trade or business activity is less than 25% of the total time on such travel, all the transportation costs may be deductible. If more than one week is spent abroad and 25% or more of the time is spent on nonbusiness activities, the transportation costs must be allocated on the basis of time spent, and the nonbusiness portion is not deductible. Of course, all expenses attributable to nonbusiness activities are nondeductible. Allowable deductions for transportation (including meals and entertainment) by "luxury water transportation" are limited to a daily amount equal to twice the per diem travel allowance for U.S. government executive branch employees away from home but within the United States ($126 as of July 1, 1986). Furthermore, if the purpose of foreign travel is to attend a convention or seminar, no deduction whatsoever is allowed unless it is as "reasonable" for that meeting to be held outside the North American area as within it.

The definition of the term "away from home" is also critical to the deduction for travel. A taxpayer's "tax home" is what the law refers to, and this may not coincide with the taxpayer's residence. Construction workers, executives who take temporary jobs with the government, and others may be away from their traditional homes for months or even years. The question becomes: Is the new job site merely temporary, or is it a new tax home? Congress has provided no arbitrary guidance on this point, and the case law is inconsistent. The question turns on the intent of the taxpayer (Is the new location temporary?) and on what actually happens later (Did the taxpayer return to the former location?).

Even though the various rules followed in determining if travel costs are deductible may be "logical," the application of the rules is often difficult, and the facts of each case must be studied carefully. Even then, skillful and rational people may disagree in their conclusions in a specific case.

ENTERTAINMENT EXPENSES   Entertainment expenses—that is, expenses for food, liquor, theater tickets, sporting events, and similar activities—are often more difficult to relate specifically to business purposes than are travel costs. Business entertainment costs are generally deductible; nonbusiness costs are personal expenditures and are therefore not deductible. As a general rule, to be classified as a business-related activity, the entertainment must be of customers or others with whom the taxpayer has, or may be expected to have, a business relationship.

Most of the criticisms of "expense account" spending as a means of tax avoidance have dealt with entertainment costs. The reasons are obvious, as the following example illustrates. Suppose the taxpayer enjoys the theater (or a nightclub or any other particular form of entertainment). An individual with whom he has some business connection is coming to town, so the taxpayer purchases theater tickets for himself, his wife, and the visiting businessperson. Is this expenditure really for business? Was the attendance of the taxpayer's wife reasonable and necessary? As a result of this entertainment and the goodwill generated, the taxpayer may very well achieve important business objectives even though the two do not directly discuss business during the evening. The inherent problems are obvious.

The question of whether entertainment costs are ordinary, necessary, and reasonable is largely a subjective one. For this reason, Sec. 274 of the Code contains unusually detailed rules for determining which costs should be allowed and which should not. Portions of this section are quoted below to indicate the nature of its restrictions:

[Sec. 274(a)] (1) In General.—No deduction otherwise allowable under this chapter shall be allowed for any item—
(A) With respect to an activity which is of a type generally considered to constitute entertainment, amusement, or recreation, unless the taxpayer establishes that the item was directly related to, or, in the case of an item directly preceding or following a substantial and bona fide business discussion (including business meetings at a convention or otherwise), that

such item was associated with, the active conduct of the taxpayer's trade or business, or

(B) Facility—With respect to a facility used in connection with an activity referred to in subparagraph (A).

[Sec. 274(a)] (2) Special Rules—For purposes of applying paragraph (1)—

(A) Dues or fees to any social, athletic, or sporting club or organization shall be treated as items with respect to facilities.

(B) An activity described in sec. 212 shall be treated as a trade or business.

(C) In the case of a club, paragraph (1)(B) shall apply unless the taxpayer establishes that the facility was used primarily for the furtherance of the taxpayer's trade or business and that the item was directly related to the active conduct of such trade or business.

[Sec. 274(b)] Gifts.—

(1) Limitation.—No deduction shall be allowed under sec. 162 or sec. 212 for any expense for gifts made directly or indirectly to any individual to the extent that such expense, when added to prior expenses of the taxpayer for gifts made to such individual during the same taxable year, exceeds $25. For purposes of this section, the term "gift" means any item excludable from gross income of the recipient under sec. 102 which is not excludable from his gross income under any other provisions of this chapter . . . .

[Sec. 274(d)] Substantiation Required.—No deduction shall be allowed—

(1) under sec. 162 or 212 for any traveling expenses (including meals and lodging while away from home),

(2) for any item with respect to an activity which is of a type generally considered to constitute entertainment, amusement, or recreation, or with respect to a facility used in connection with such an activity, or

(3) for any expense for gifts,

(4) with respect to any listed property (as defined by sec. 280F(d)(4), unless the taxpayer substantiates by adequate records or by sufficient evidence corroborating his own statement, (A) the amount of such expense or other item, (B) the time and place of the travel, entertainment, amusement, recreation or use of the facility, or the date and description of the gift, (C) the business purpose of the expense or other item, and (D) the business relationship to the taxpayer of persons entertained, using the facility or property, or receiving the gift. . . .

The committee reports associated with the 1986 Act indicate that Congress intended that deductions for meals should be subject to the same business-connection requirement as other entertainment expenses. Under prior law taxpayers could deduct the cost of entertainment such as a lunch with a potential client even though business was not actually discussed, so long as the atmosphere was considered conducive to business discussion (Reg. Sec. 1.274-2(f)(2)(i)). Under the new rules, such meals would not be deductible unless business is discussed during, or directly before or after, the meal. If the taxpayer is traveling away from home, a business discussion is not required unless the taxpayer dines with business associates. For example, it would be permissible for a traveling salesman to deduct the cost of a meal eaten alone or with nonbusiness associates so long as a deduction is claimed only for the taxpayer's meal.

After 1986, taxpayers will also be subject to special limitations on the deductibility of entertainment tickets and "skyboxes" at sports arenas. Like other entertainment costs, these expenditures are subject to the 20% reduction rule discussed above. Additionally, no more than face value can be deducted for entertainment tickets. Thus, a taxpayer who purchases two football tickets from a "scalper" at $100 each when the face value is $25 each can deduct only $40 (80% of $50), provided all other requirements for a deduction are met. After 1988, deductions for skybox seats leased for more than one event are limited to the face value of nonluxury box seat tickets. In 1987 one third of the difference in price is disallowed, and in 1988 two thirds of the difference is disallowed.

The regulations associated with travel and entertainment expenses are relatively precise in specifying the reporting and accounting requirements for these deductions. Because of the great amount of detail and because they are frequently changed, these reporting requirements are not detailed here. Basically, however, the employee who "accounts to his employer" need not report business expenses or reimbursements on his own return if reimbursement equals expenditures. If reimbursement exceeds expenditures, the employee must report the excess as income. If expenses exceed reimbursement and the employee claims a deduction for the excess, some of the details must be reported. An "accounting" includes either (1) a detailed record of expenses or (2) a reasonable per diem allowance and mileage allowance even though no detailed record is submitted by the employee. Per diem rates up to the maximum authorized to be paid by the federal government in the locality in which the travel was performed and mileage allowances up to 21 cents per mile are deemed to be "reasonable" by the I.R.S. Employees who do not account to their employers must report details of expenses and reimbursements on their returns. Deductions for travel and entertainment expenses are a source of frequent conflict between the taxpayer and the I.R.S.

EDUCATIONAL EXPENSES   In recent years the tax status of education expenses has received much attention because of the substantial increase in educational costs at all levels. Various proposals have been made to grant special tax benefits to taxpayers incurring such costs, especially when related to higher education. These proposals included recommendations that taxpayers with children in college either be permitted to deduct part of the expenses involved or be granted a credit against the tax. It has also been suggested that taxpayers be allowed to capitalize the costs of their college educations and to amortize these costs over their expected productive lives.[2]

[2]For an interesting discussion of the treatment of education expenses, see Richard Goode, "Educational Expenditures and the Income Tax," in Selma J. Mushken, ed., *Economics of Higher Education,* Bulletin No. 5 (Washington, DC: U.S. Department of Health, Education, and Welfare, Office of Education, 1962), pp. 281–304.

At the present time, however, there are stringent limitations on the deduction of education expenses. The basic provisions relating to educational expense deductions are explained in Treas. Reg. Sec. 1.162-5(b). A deduction may be taken for expenditures if the education

(1) Maintains or improves skills required by the individual in his employment or other trade or business, or
(2) Meets the express requirements of the individual's employer, or the requirements of applicable law or regulations, imposed as a condition to the retention by the individual of an established employment relationship, status, or rate of compensation.

This regulation permits deductions only for education expenses incurred purely for business purposes. This has been interpreted to mean that the costs of acquiring the basic education necessary for the taxpayer's *entrance* into his or her trade, business, or profession are *not* deductible, because they represent personal expenditures. After the taxpayer has attained the minimum educational requirements and is active in a job, however, he or she may deduct expenditures made to maintain or improve job skills. Costs of education undertaken *primarily* to obtain a promotion, an increase in pay, or a new job are nondeductible. It is extremely difficult in many cases to determine why education costs are incurred by the taxpayer. As a result, there have been frequent changes in the regulations and many conflicting court decisions over the deductibility of education costs. Not surprisingly, many tax advisors simply decide that if any doubt exists, they should attempt to take a deduction for educational costs.

One area of controversy between taxpayers and the I.R.S. has been over the deductibility of travel as an education-related expense. Treas. Reg. Sec. 1.162-5(d) states that such expenditures are deductible "only to the extent [they] are attributable to a period of travel that is directly related to the duties of the individual in his employment or other trade or business." The obvious problem with such travel is determining whether it is primarily personal or primarily to obtain education. Code Sec. 274(m)(2), added by the 1986 Act, overrides the regulation cited above and denies any deduction for travel that would be deductible only on the ground that the travel itself constitutes a form of education.

Expenses of transportation, travel (including meals and lodging while away from home overnight), tuition, books, and so on are examples of deductible education-related expenses. These costs are deductions for A.G.I. if they are reimbursed by the employee, deductions from A.G.I. if not. Of course, only 80% of unreimbursed meals can be deducted. Further, like all reimbursed expenses, the education costs must be otherwise deductible for the employee to include them in deductions for A.G.I.

Many valid arguments support a liberalization of the policy on deduction of education costs. It may be argued that the costs of obtaining basic education contribute to future earning capacity and, therefore, are similar to capital outlays for machinery and equipment. If so, these costs should be capitalized when incurred and then amortized over the productive life of the taxpayer. It is also argued that regulations governing educational expense deductions do not provide adequate incentives or rewards for the ambitious taxpayer wishing to acquire higher skills and educational levels.

Although it is impossible to determine the marginal effect that the deductibility of education expenses would have on the number of individuals pursuing higher education, or on the intensity with which they would pursue their education, the argument that a highly educated populace is desirable for social, economic, and cultural reasons has encouraged considerable support for the liberalization of the present rules. This topic will continue to be a subject of popular debate, if for no other reason than the political appeal it has to the large number of voters who would be affected by such action.

OTHER EMPLOYMENT-RELATED ITEMIZED DEDUCTIONS SUBJECT TO THE 2% FLOOR

A number of other employment-related deductions are allowed employees. These include union dues, professional fees and dues, work-related uniforms, and home-office costs to the extent deductible. This last deduction is allowed to employees only to the extent that a portion of the home is used exclusively for the convenience of the taxpayer's employer. It is not sufficient that use of an office at home would be appropriate or helpful. Thus, a schoolteacher who grades papers at home in the evening would not be permitted a deduction under this provision.

Investment Expenses Allowed Under Section 212

The second major category of expenses subject to the 2% of A.G.I. floor are those permitted by Sec. 212 for the production or collection of income; the management, conservation, or maintenance of property held for the production of income; or in connection with the determination, collection, or refund of any tax. Typical Sec. 212 expenses relate to portfolio income (interest, dividends, and royalties) as well as to property held for investment that is not a passive activity (for example, vacant land held for speculation). Recall that Sec. 62 permits deductible expenses associated with rents and royalties as deductions for A.G.I., but other expenses associated with investments are deductions from A.G.I. Some examples of items included in this category are fees paid for investment counsel, subscriptions to publications such as the *Wall Street Journal,* and the cost of safe-deposit boxes used to hold securities. For tax years after 1986, no deduction is allowed for attending a convention, seminar, or similar meeting if the deduction must be justified under Sec. 212 (that is, related to investments, financial planning, and so on). Thus, a taxpayer who wishes to learn more about investing in the stock market could not deduct the cost of attending a seminar on this subject unless his or her trade or business (as a stockbroker, for example) justifies the deduction. Sec. 212 also permits the deduction of expenses in connection with the determination, collection, or refund of any tax.

In the next chapter we will consider all the itemized deductions allowed to individual taxpayers and not subject to the 2% of A.G.I. floor. These include medical expenses, casualties, interest, taxes, charitable contributions, and a few miscellaneous deductions. The chapter will conclude with a comprehensive example.

PROBLEMS

1. The correct classification of the various subtractions in the individual tax formula is very important.
   a. Why is the accurate calculation of gross income important?
   b. Why is the accurate calculation of adjusted gross income important?

2. The Supreme Court recently (February 1987) held that a full-time gambler has a trade or business. Explain the significance of this decision for a taxpayer so classified.

3. Explain the difference between the tax treatment of reimbursed and nonreimbursed expenses of taxpayers who are employees.

4. Section 212 authorizes the deduction of expenditures related to transactions entered into for profit. How are these expenditures classified on an individual taxpayer's tax return?

5. Explain why the parties to a divorce are very interested in whether payments are classified as alimony, property settlements, or child support.

6. In the Tax Reform Act of 1986, the extra exemptions previously granted elderly and blind taxpayers were repealed. Explain what provisions were substituted.

7. Discuss two situations in which taxpayers are not entitled to take full advantage of the standard deduction.

8. Why did Congress decide to make 20% of expenditures for meals and entertainment nondeductible?

9. Explain why an employee who spends $1,000 per year on work-related travel and transportation might be willing to take a $1,200 cut in pay in exchange for having his or her employer reimburse him for these expenses.

10. List five itemized deductions that *are* subject to the 2% of A.G.I. floor. List five that are not.

11. Which of the following individuals will benefit from itemizing deductions? In each case, indicate the standard deduction to which the individual is entitled.
    a. Mary, a single individual, who has actual itemized deductions of $2,700.
    b. Mary, a head of household, who has actual itemized deductions of $3,800.
    c. Mary, a surviving spouse, who has actual itemized deductions of $3,800.
    d. Mary, who is married and files separately from her spouse, who itemizes his deductions. Mary has actual itemized deduction of $900.
    e. Mary, who is blind and age 72 and has actual itemized deductions of $4,000.
    f. Mary and Jack, who are married and file jointly, have actual itemized deductions of $7,300. They have four dependent children.
    g. Mary is a 10-year-old dependent child. This year her only income is $700 of interest. She has no actual itemized deductions.
    h. Mary is a 10-year-old dependent child. This year her income consists of $700 interest and $400 from babysitting. She has no actual itemized deductions.
    i. Same facts as in part h, except that Mary earns $750 from babysitting.

12. In each of the following independent cases, indicate whether the amount involved is (1) deductible *for* A.G.I., (2) deductible *from* A.G.I., or (3) not deductible at all. Put an asterisk next to items in category (2) that are subject to the 2% A.G.I. floor.

   a. Taxpayer paid $8 rent on a bank safety deposit box in which he kept the few shares of stock that he owned.
   b. Taxpayer paid expenses of $1,200 applicable to rental property that he owned.
   c. Taxpayer replaced the roof on rental property that he owned. The new roof cost $1,000.
   d. Taxpayer purchased a vacant lot for investment. During the year, she paid $50 to have it mowed and cleaned.
   e. Taxpayer, a nurse, is employed at a local hospital. She spent $105 for uniforms during the year and was not reimbursed.
   f. Millsaps, a public school teacher, spent $40 for magazine subscriptions and was not reimbursed. The magazines were used in his classroom activities.
   g. Herman, a department store "buyer," attended an out-of-town "market" at which he examined new merchandise. His total costs were $308 (meals $50, lodging $200, transportation $58). He was not reimbursed by his employer.
   h. Taxpayer paid $650 real estate taxes on property used in his business.
   i. Harry pays $500 per month in alimony and $200 per month in child support to his former wife Victoria.
   j. Bill and Jane Rollins were divorced during the current year. The divorce decree provided that Bill should pay Jane a $42,000 lump-sum property settlement, which he paid this year.

13. In each of the following independent cases, indicate whether the amount involved is (1) deductible *for* A.G.I., (2) deductible *from* A.G.I., or (3) not deductible at all. Put an asterisk next to items in category (2) that are subject to the 2% A.G.I. floor.

   a. Taxpayer, a carpenter working as an employee, spent $65 for small tools used on her job.
   b. Taxpayer, an employee working for a public accounting firm, lives in a suburban community and commutes to the city to work. During the year, commuting costs were $360.
   c. Taxpayer operates an antique shop on the first floor of a house and lives on the second floor. Fire insurance for the entire house was $600 for the year (which does not include insurance on the antique inventory or personal belongings). Floor space on each floor is approximately equal.
   d. Taxpayer is a corporate executive. Because of his high pay, he is not reimbursed for entertainment expenses, even though his position requires him to entertain the corporation's customers. During the year he spent $2,200 on legitimate entertainment.
   e. Taxpayer's employer provides uniforms, but she has to pay to have them dry-cleaned. This year she spent $130 having the uniforms cleaned.
   f. Taxpayer is a self-employed special duty nurse. He spent $120 for nursing uniforms.

14. Indicate how each of the following items will be treated on the individual's tax return. Your answer should include an indication of whether or not the item (or a portion of it) is subject to the 2% A.G.I. floor.

   a. Jake spent $1,200 this year on work-related education expenses, including $800 for tuition and $400 for transportation. Jake's employer reimbursed the $800 tuition.

b. George spent $800 entertaining prospective customers. George is a self-employed consultant.

c. Same facts as in part b, except that George is an employee of a consulting firm. He was not reimbursed for the entertainment.

d. Tillie is employed by an accounting firm. This year she traveled out of town on several audit engagements. She spent $1,500 on airfare, $600 on hotel costs, and $450 on meals. Tillie was reimbursed for all of these costs.

e. Same facts as in part d, except that Tillie is a self-employed accountant.

f. Donald attended an A.I.C.P.A. annual convention in Kansas City. As part of the convention, he paid $40 to attend a banquet (attended by 500 CPAs) at which a U.S. senator spoke about how auditors should perform their services.

g. Terry, an employee of a major defense contractor in St. Louis, was sent to Memphis to inspect a new plant. Terry had grown up in Memphis, so he took advantage of the trip to visit with several high school friends by going out to dinner with them. The cost of Terry's share of the dinners was $45. The second night that Terry was in Memphis he went to dinner with a business associate, a supplier of parts for the Memphis plant. They did not discuss business. Terry paid for both meals at a total cost of $70. Terry was not reimbursed for any of these meals.

h. Nick, an employee, spent $1,000 for transportation during the year. Of this amount, $600 was allocated to the cost of going from home to work sites and back, while $400 was spent on transportation between work sites during the day. None of these costs was reimbursed.

i. Linda, a self-employed physician, attended two professional conventions on the West Coast connected with her practice. The first convention was held on Monday, Tuesday, and Wednesday in Los Angeles. The second was held on Monday and Tuesday of the following week in San Francisco. Between the two conventions, Linda stayed at Carmel for a short vacation. The costs were air travel from her home to Los Angeles and from San Francisco to her home, $225; hotel for three days in Los Angeles, $210; meals for three days in Los Angeles, $150; auto rental for trip from Los Angeles to Carmel and from Carmel to San Francisco, $180 (Linda estimates that one third of this cost represents the cost of pleasure trips while in Carmel); hotel for two days in San Francisco, $180; meals for two days in San Francisco, $120.

j. Jim paid an accountant $200 to prepare his tax return this year.

15. In each of the following independent cases, indicate whether the taxpayer is entitled to deduct expenses (depreciation, utilities, insurance, and so on) applicable to an "office in the home":

a. Pete is an accounting professor at a state university. One room in his home has been converted into an office used by Pete solely for such tasks as grading papers, preparing exams, and reading journals.

b. Joe is a law professor in a state university. One room in his home has been converted into an office used solely by Joe for grading papers and other class-related activities and also for writing and revising textbooks from which Joe receives substantial royalties.

16. Indicate how much, if any, is deductible as educational expenses in each of the following independent cases. Briefly explain your answer, and indicate in each case whether the amount deductible is *for* A.G.I. or *from* A.G.I. Ignore the 2% A.G.I. floor.

a. Haskins is a senior in college majoring in accounting. His college expenses for the current year were:

Tuition	$1,200
Books and supplies	340
Room	540
Meals	1,680

b. Bernard was a practicing certified public accountant in the tax department of a national accounting firm. During July of this year, Bernard decided that he should secure a law degree to further his career, so he resigned from the accounting firm and entered law school. His expenses relating to law school this year were $950.

c. Raymond works for an accounting firm. During this year, he attended several professional development programs sponsored by the American Institute of Certified Public Accountants. These programs were two- or three-day seminars or workshops held in other cities (requiring overnight travel), dealing with areas of accounting in which Raymond is involved. His expenses in attending these programs totaled $800, and they were not reimbursed by his employer. The costs were as follows: registration fees, $200; transportation, $400; lodging, $110; and meals, $90.

d. Assume the same facts as in part c, except that Raymond is a self-employed accountant with his own public accounting firm.

e. Clifton, unmarried, is employed as a public school teacher. He possesses a BA degree, but the school board has stipulated that each teacher in the school system must return to college for additional course work at least each third summer. During this year, Clifton returned to the state university. His costs were as follow: tuition, $120; meals, $540; lodging, $285; transportation from his home town to the university and return, $23; and books, $40.

f. Dennis, who lives in Milwaukee, is a high school teacher. This January he traveled to Phoenix to attend a seminar entitled "How to Become a Millionaire by Investing in Real Estate." Dennis has not previously invested in real estate, but he is interested in doing so, especially if he can become wealthy. He paid $250 for airfare, $300 for lodging, $200 for food, and a $500 registration fee for the seminar.

g. Elsie, a high school French teacher, spent three weeks in France this summer for the purpose of improving her command of the French language and her understanding of French culture.

17. Assume that the first 10 seats in a commercial airliner flying from Los Angeles to New York City are filled with the following persons:

Seats 1 and 2: Farley and Emily Dickens, who are planning to attend a four-day insurance convention. Farley, an insurance salesman, is traveling at company expense; Emily (at two-thirds fare) is traveling at her own expense. While in New York, the insurance salespeople are kept in business sessions throughout each day; the spouses are free to do whatever they wish. The Dickenses plan to spend two additional days, following the convention, in personal sightseeing trips, attending the theater, and so on.

Seats 3 and 4: Chuck and Bettina Hardsell, who are going to the same insurance convention. Like Farley, Chuck is traveling at company expense. Bettina's ticket also is being paid by Chuck's employer because he sold more insurance than any of the other agents in his district during the first six months of this year.

Seats 5 and 6: Samuel and Sarah Johnson, who are moving to New York permanently so that Sarah may accept a new job with Dilly Corporation. The Johnsons sold their car before leaving California.

Seat 7: Ned Younger, a law student who is being interviewed by Ring, Rang, &

Rung, a noted law firm. The firm will reimburse Ned for all his travel expenses regardless of his job decision.

Seat 8: Larry Outer, a college student who plans to interview at five firms for a possible position. Because Larry will soon graduate in the lower quarter of his class, none of the firms is willing to pay his transportation expenses for an interview trip. However, Larry is convinced that a personal appearance will guarantee his getting a good job offer. (In solving this problem, assume that he did get such an offer but that no one reimbursed him for his travel expenses.)

Seat 9: Jane Doe, a veteran flight attendant for Tomorrow Airline. Jane is on vacation and is flying without charge, on an employee's pass, to London via New York. Every airborne employee with more than 10 years' service receives courtesy passes from connecting airlines to travel worldwide free of charge (except for meals, hotels, and other personal expenditures) for himself or herself and spouse (if married) or for himself or herself and parents (if single).

Seat 10: Mary Doe, mother of Jane Doe. Mrs. Doe is accompanying her daughter without charge on the pass described above.

a. Which of these persons may deduct their travel expenses for federal income tax purposes?

b. Must any of these persons report receipt of taxable income because of this trip? Explain your answers.

SUPPLEMENTAL PROBLEMS

18. In the current year, Mr. A. Big Shot, who operates an advertising agency, paid $1,600 for membership dues in a hunting lodge in Canada for the purpose of entertaining clients and prospective clients. In November, Shot took three clients to the lodge for hunting. He paid their transportation costs, totaling $620; their meals for the three-day period at the lodge, $460 for the guests and $181 for Shot; their room costs, $900 for the guests and $300 for himself; $220 for a hunting guide; $210 for guns and ammunition; and $120 for miscellaneous items such as phone calls and drinks. What part of the expenditures listed above is deductible by Shot?

19. Tom Medirent, a physician, is employed in a hospital 40 hours per week. He also owns and manages six rental properties. He lives in a two-bedroom condominium and uses one bedroom exclusively as an office for bookkeeping and other tasks associated with the property management activities.

a. Is the property management activity a "business"? Is the office a "principal place of business activity"?

b. Can the costs (depreciation, utilities, taxes, and interest) related to the office be deducted by the doctor?

c. Can the transportation expenses incurred in driving from the office to the rental properties be deducted by the doctor as business expenses?

20. Professor Jones, a bachelor, earns a salary of $35,000. Because Jones lives in a rented apartment, his itemized deductions typically are less than the standard deduction. On July 1, 19x1, Jones assumed duties (in addition to his university teaching appointment) as editor of a quarterly trade publication. As compensation, Jones is paid $3,000 annually by the association that publishes the journal. The first $3,000 payment will be made on June 30, 19X2.

To help complete his new editorial duties, Professor Jones immediately hired an assistant to do typing and clerical duties. The assistant earned $200 per month, which was paid from Jones's personal funds. At the end of 19X1, therefore, Jones had not received any payment for his services as editor, although he had incurred and paid expenses of $1,200 in connection with these duties. In preparing his tax return for 19X1, Jones asks you how he should report the $1,200 payment to his editorial assistant. If possible, Jones desires to claim the standard deduction. Using whatever materials are available in your school library, determine if the $1,200 payment should be a deduction for or a deduction from Professor Jones's A.G.I.

CHAPTER 10

Other Itemized Deductions

> *Taxpayers who benefit from special provisions commonly insist that these do not give them an advantage over the rest of the taxpaying public, but merely put them on a par with everyone else by recognizing that their situations are in fact somewhat different.*
> Walter Blum, *quoted in* Federal Tax Policy for Economic Growth and Stability *(1955)*

In the previous chapter we discussed the class of itemized deductions that must in the aggregate exceed 2% of adjusted gross income in order to be deductible. In this chapter we discuss the remaining itemized deductions that are available to individual taxpayers. These deductions can be divided into two major categories: (1) those intended to relieve economic hardships (the medical and casualty deductions) and (2) those providing subsidies to some taxpayers or groups (interest, taxes, and contributions). Finally, we consider some miscellaneous deductions also not subject to the 2% floor.

ITEMIZED DEDUCTION: LARGE, UNUSUAL EXPENSES AND LOSSES

The U.S. income tax is filled with special provisions and rules intended to promote the general welfare. The deductions for medical expenses and casualty losses are both designed to relieve the economic hardships of individuals whose medical expenses and/or casualty losses exceed certain threshold amounts.

Medical Expenses

GENERAL RULE   The basic authority for deduction of medical expenses is Sec. 213, which reads in part as follows:

> (a) Allowance of Deduction—There shall be allowed as a deduction the expenses paid during the taxable year, not compensated for by insurance or otherwise, for medical care of the taxpayer, his spouse, or a dependent (as defined in Section 152), to the extent that such expenses exceed 7½% of adjusted gross income.

Medical care is further defined in Sec. 213(d)(1) as follows:

> (1) The term "medical care" means amounts paid—
>   (A) for the diagnosis, care, mitigation, treatment, or prevention of disease, or for the purpose of affecting any structure or function of the body.
>   (B) for transportation primarily for and essential to medical care referred to in subparagraph (A), or
>   (C) for insurance . . . covering medical care referred to in subparagraphs (A) and (B).

Thus, medical costs include unreimbursed amounts paid for medical and dental care, such as physicians' charges, hospital rooms, nursing care, laboratory charges, dentures, optical care, glasses, insulin, prescription drugs and medicines, and premiums on health and hospitalization insurance policies.

Expenses for items such as vitamins and toothpaste—that is, items intended to improve or preserve the general health—are generally not deductible. Vitamins prescribed by a physician, however, are deductible. The cost of birth control pills, as well as the cost of a vasectomy or a legal abortion, is deductible as a medical expense.

Transportation costs "primarily for and essential to" medical care are considered medical costs, as are lodging costs on a trip essential to medical care if the care is provided in a hospital or medical care facility related to a hospital and there is "no significant element of personal pleasure, recreation, or vacation in the travel away from home" [Sec. 213(d)(2)(B)]. In no case can the lodging costs exceed $50 per night for each individual while that individual is an "outpatient." The taxpayer who uses his or her personal automobile for transportation to secure medical care may deduct either the actual expenses incurred or use the standard allowance of nine cents per mile, plus parking fees and toll charges.

Capital expenditures related specifically to an individual's illness may also be deductible. For example, the cost of a wheelchair would be deductible in full in the year purchased. However, capital expenditures that increase the value of property are not allowed as a deduction to the extent of the increase in the property's value. For example, the cost of a swimming pool installed in the home of an individual whose doctor recommends daily swimming as therapy is deductible only to the extent that its cost exceeds any increase in the value of the home. Additionally, the Conference Committee Report associated with the Tax Reform Act of 1986 makes it clear that the full cost of specified capital expenditures "incurred to accommodate a personal residence to the needs of a physically handicapped individual, such as construction of entrance ramps or widening of doorways to allow use of wheelchairs, constitute medical expenses . . ." can be deducted immediately. Evidently Congress believed that such expenditures would not increase the fair market value of a residence and should therefore be fully deductible.

The observant student quickly recognizes the familiar problem of distinguishing between expenses that are purely "personal" and those that are properly deductible. The problem has been particularly evident in cases in which pleasure activities are involved in the expenditure. For example, a physician may recommend that the taxpayer leave the cold weather of Michigan and go to the sunshine of Arizona for the winter. Under current rules, only the transportation costs involved would be in question. However, based on the simple facts given above, no hard and fast answer could be given to the question of whether even these costs are deductible. Presumably, if the change in climate is recommended for treatment of a specific or chronic ailment, the costs would be deductible. A change recommended for "general health" reasons would be disallowed.

Another common situation in which it is difficult to distinguish between a bona fide medical expense and simply a personal expenditure arises when a family member is placed in a nursing home or home for the aged. If the individual is placed in the institution because of his or her physical condition and the availability of medical care in the institution, all the costs incurred (including meals and lodging) would be considered medical costs. However, if the main reason for placing the individual in the institution is personal convenience or desire, only the costs actually spent for medical care would be deductible. Similarly, if an individual is hired to perform both nursing care and household work in the taxpayer's home, only that portion of the cost applicable to nursing care would be considered a medical cost. If an expense is allowed as the basis of a credit for child care under Sec. 21, it cannot be treated as a medical expense.

Note that the medical expense deduction is allowed only for amounts *paid* during the tax year. Thus, if the taxpayer incurs medical expenses in the current year, but does not make payment until next year, no deduction would be allowed until next year. However, if payment is made by credit card, the deduction must be taken in the year charged to the account, regardless of when that account is actually paid. In general, no deduction can be taken for prepaid medical expenditures even though insurance premiums are deductible. A possible exception to this rule applies in the case of lump-sum payments to nursing homes and in the case of certain insurance premiums paid by a taxpayer before he or she reaches the age of 65.

COMPUTING THE DEDUCTION FOR MEDICAL EXPENSES   The taxpayer may take a deduction only for medical expenses paid during the taxable year for himself or herself, a spouse, or dependent[1]—and only to the extent that they are not reimbursed by insurance or otherwise. As previously pointed out, medical expenses are deductible only to the extent they exceed 7½% of the taxpayer's adjusted gross income.

To illustrate the medical expense deduction, let us assume that a taxpayer and spouse with an A.G.I. of $20,000 paid the following medical expenses during the tax year for themselves and dependents:

Hospital insurance premium	$1,210
Prescription medicine and drugs	620
Doctor bills	420
Dental care	170
Optical care	150
	$2,570

The taxpayers would be entitled to include $1,070 in itemized deductions:

Medical expenses incurred	$2,570
Less 7 1/2% of A.G.I.	1,500
Medical expense deduction	$1,070

Reimbursement of medical expenses subsequent to year of deduction. When insurance or other reimbursement for medical expenses is received in a year after that in which the expenses were actually paid, the reimbursement is treated as income only to the extent that it represents repayment of expenditures that resulted in a tax benefit in a prior year. For example, suppose that last year a taxpayer had A.G.I. of $10,000 and had excess deductions. The taxpayer paid medical costs of $780 and therefore deducted medical expenses of $30 that year. This year the taxpayer receives insurance proceeds of $200 as reimbursement for part of the $780 spent last year. If the taxpayer had received the insurance payment last year, he or she would have had no medical expense deduction. Thus, of the $200 received, $30 is reported as gross income this year because it represents repayment of an amount deducted last year; the other $170 is not considered gross income because it does not represent a tax benefit in prior year. Of course, if the taxpayer did not have sufficient itemized deductions to benefit from itemizing, no part of the reimbursement would be considered income.

HISTORY AND FUNCTION OF THE MEDICAL DEDUCTION   Deductions for medical and dental expenses were first permitted in 1942. As stated by the Senate Finance Committee at that time, this provision was recommended "in

---

[1]Note that for this purpose a person need satisfy only three of the usual five criteria applicable to the determination of dependency status. They are the "support," the "relationship," and the citizen or resident criteria.

consideration of the heavy tax burden that must be borne by individuals during the existing emergency and the desirability of maintaining the present high level of public health and morale."[2]

The original legislation relating to medical expenses was proposed by the Treasury and was intended to give more equitable treatment to taxpayers with extraordinary expenses.[3] In the initial Act of 1942, and until the 1954 law was passed, medical expenses in excess of 5% of A.G.I. were deductible. Beginning in 1954, medical expenses in excess of 3% of A.G.I. were deductible. The 1954 Code also provided, however, that only those medicine and drug costs in excess of 1% of A.G.I. were considered medical expenses. Between 1951 and 1967, a taxpayer 65 years of age or older (or having a spouse 65 or older) was permitted to deduct all medical expenses, without regard to the percentage exclusion. The 1964 Act exempted the elderly from even the 1% exclusion on medicines and drugs. This favorable treatment for the elderly was eliminated in 1967 because of their new privileges under Medicare. For tax years 1983 through 1986 we returned to the rules of the 1942 Act, with deduction of all medical expenses, including prescription medicines, in excess of 5% of A.G.I. Finally, in the Tax Reform Act of 1986, Congress increased the percentage to 7½% of A.G.I. for tax years after 1986.

Much of the public discussion relating to the medical expense deduction has stemmed from its rationale. The basic concept has been that only extraordinary expenses should be deductible, because extraordinary expenses reduce the taxpayer's disposable income and, therefore, his or her ability to pay taxes relative to other taxpayers with the same income. Obviously, however, what is considered "ordinary" and "extraordinary" is a matter of personal opinion. Congress apparently believed from 1942–1953 that "extraordinary" meant something in excess of 5% of A.G.I. Beginning in 1954, "extraordinary" meant something in excess of 3% of A.G.I. (or 4%, if we include the 1% exclusion of medicines and drugs). From 1951–1966, all medical expenses were "extraordinary" for the elderly. Today, the tax laws reflect the belief that the taxpayer should be able to bear medical expenses up to 7½% of his or her A.G.I. without any tax relief.

Many individuals feel that a prime concern of the community should be for the health and physical welfare of the individual and that the community has a responsibility for ensuring that everyone receives adequate medical care. By making all medical costs deductible, the government would be furthering this goal by cutting the cost of medical care and, at the same time, leaving the allocation of funds in the hands of individuals. Following this line of reasoning, it may be argued that the 7½% floor on medical costs should be abolished.

---

[2]Senate Report No. 1631, Senate Finance Committee, 77th Congress, 2nd Session (Washington, DC: U.S. Government Printing Office, 1942), p. 6.
[3]Statement of Randolph E. Paul, hearings before House Ways and Means Committee, "Revenue Revision of 1942," 77th Congress, 2nd Session (Washington, DC: U.S. Government Printing Office, 1942), pp. 1612–13.

Casualty and Theft Losses

The second type of deduction related to a taxpayer's economic hardship is the deduction for casualty or theft losses of the taxpayer's property. In this section, we examine the general provisions controlling casualty and theft loss deductions and explore some common detailed definitional and computational problems.

GENERAL PROVISIONS FOR DEDUCTION OF CASUALTY AND THEFT LOSSES   As you learned in Chapter 4, the general provisions of Sec. 165 permit the deduction of losses sustained during the year to the extent of any amount "not compensated for by insurance or otherwise" if the loss is incurred in a trade or business or in a transaction entered into for profit. In addition, a deduction for losses of property not related to trade or business resulting from fire, storm, or shipwreck has been allowed since the original tax law of 1913. In 1916, the deduction was extended to include losses from "other casualties, or from theft." Today, for individual taxpayers, Sec. 165(c)(3) provides for the deduction of unreimbursed losses, as follows:

> (c) Limitation on Losses of Individuals—. In the case of an individual, the deduction under subsection (a) shall be limited to—
>
> (1) losses incurred in a trade or business;
>
> (2) losses incurred in any transaction entered into for profit, though not connected with a trade or business; and
>
> (3) except as provided in subsection (h), losses of property not connected with a trade or business, if such losses arise from fire, storm, shipwreck, or other casualty, or from theft.

Subsection 165(h) contains the specific rules relating to casualty and theft losses:

> (h) Treatment of Casualty Gains and Losses—.
> (1) $100 limitation per casualty.—Any loss of an individual described in subsection c(3) shall be allowed only to the extent that the amount of the loss to such individual arising from each casualty, or from each theft, exceeds $100.
>
> (2) Net casualty loss allowed only to the extent it exceeds 10 percent of adjusted gross income. —
> (A) In general.—If the personal casualty losses for any taxable year exceed the personal casualty gains for such taxable year, such losses shall be allowed for the taxable year only to the extent of the sum of—
> (i) the amount of the personal casualty gains for the taxable year, plus
> (ii) so much of such excess as exceed 10 percent of the adjusted gross income of the individual.

    (B) Special rule where personal casualty gains exceed personal casualty losses.—If the personal casualty gains for any taxable year exceed the personal casualty losses for such taxable year—

      (i) all such gains shall be treated as gains from sales or exchanges of capital assets, and

      (ii) all such losses shall be treated as losses from sales or exchanges of capital assets.

Generally, property held by a corporation is automatically deemed to be either used in a trade or business or acquired as the result of a transaction entered into for a profit, so that for a corporation, losses on such property come under the general rule calling for recognition of losses.

The deduction for losses of nonbusiness property, like that for medical expenses, is intended to provide tax relief to taxpayers suffering unusual, involuntary losses large enough "to have a significant effect upon an individual's ability to pay Federal income taxes."[4]

Prior to 1964, the full amount of each casualty loss was deductible; since that year, casualty and theft losses on property used in trade or business have been deductible in full, but the deduction for such losses on nonbusiness property has been limited.

DEFINING *CASUALTY* AND *THEFT*   Subsection 165(c) specifically includes "fire, storm, or shipwreck" in the definition of casualties, and it provides for the general inclusion of "other casualties." However, "other casualties" are not identified, and it is often difficult to determine if loss of property resulting from a particular event constitutes a casualty for tax purposes. In general, the law requires a sudden, unexpected, or unusual event as well as an external force before a given event can be considered a casualty. Thus, losses caused by vandalism, car and boat accidents, earth slides, hurricanes, and sonic booms have been deductible. No deduction is allowed for breakage of china, glassware, furniture, and similar items under normal conditions, and tax deductions have been disallowed for damage due to rust, corrosion, termites (although some courts have allowed deductions for termite damage), insects, disease, and other slow-acting destructive forces. Because of the imprecision of the general criteria pertinent to the determination of a deductible casualty loss, litigation of specific facts is commonplace.

The definition of a theft loss is somewhat clearer, but whether a theft has occurred is still a matter of factual determination. The term *theft* is deemed to include, but is not limited to, larceny, embezzlement, and robbery. No deduction is allowed for property the taxpayer simply lost or misplaced. The reasons for the stringent rules are apparent if you consider the multiple opportunities for tax evasion that would arise under more lenient rules.

A deduction is allowed for loss to the taxpayer's own property only; no deduction is allowed for damage caused by the taxpayer to the property or

---

[4]House Report No. 749, House Ways and Means Committee, 88th Congress, 1st Session (Washington, DC: U.S. Government Printing Office, 1963), p. 52.

body of another. The regulations under Sec. 165 state clearly that a loss to the taxpayer's property may be deductible even though the taxpayer is at fault, but not if the loss is due to the willful act or willful negligence of the taxpayer.

DETERMINING THE BASIC AMOUNT OF LOSS   The amount of loss for physical damage to the taxpayer's property is basically the decrease in value of the property resulting from the casualty (but the deduction cannot be in excess of the "adjusted basis" of the property). For example, if a taxpayer's property had a fair market value of $6,000 just before a casualty and a fair market value of $2,000 just after the casualty, the basic measure of loss sustained would be $4,000. In some cases, the cost of repairs to the property damaged is acceptable as evidence of the loss of value if (1) the repairs are necessary to restore the property to its condition immediately before the casualty, (2) the amount spent for such repairs is not excessive, (3) the repairs do not improve the property beyond the damage suffered, and (4) the value of the property after the repairs does not exceed the value immediately before the casualty.

No provision is made for deduction of premiums paid for insurance against casualty losses (except, of course, under the general provisions concerning deductions related to trade, business, and income-producing activities). Tax scholars often charge that the nondeductibility of insurance premiums discriminates against the insured taxpayer, especially because any insurance proceeds received as a result of the loss reduce the amount otherwise deductible and actually result in gain to the extent that the proceeds exceed the adjusted basis of the property.

DETERMINING THE AMOUNT DEDUCTIBLE   The amount of loss deductible from casualty or theft of the taxpayer's property depends on a number of factors: the decrease in value; whether the property is used in trade or business, for income production, or for purely personal purposes; whether the property is completely destroyed or only partially destroyed; and the amount of insurance or other reimbursement.

Business property completely destroyed.   If property used in a trade or business or held for income production is completely destroyed, the adjusted basis of the property, less any amount of reimbursement, is deductible. For example, assume that a property with an adjusted basis of $20,000 and a fair market value of only $15,000 that is used in the taxpayer's business is completely destroyed by fire. The taxpayer collects insurance proceeds of $12,000 for the loss. The amount of deductible loss is $8,000—the $20,000 adjusted basis less the insurance received.

Business property partially destroyed.   When property is only partially destroyed, the amount of loss is the adjusted basis of the property or its decrease in fair market value, whichever is less, reduced by insurance proceeds or other reimbursements. For example, assume that a property used in the taxpayer's trade or business is damaged by fire. The property's fair market value before the fire was $8,000; after the fire, it was appraised at $2,500. Insurance proceeds of $3,000 were received, and the adjusted basis of the property was $5,000. The amount deductible is $2,000 as shown.

Value before fire	$8,000
Value after fire	2,500
Decline in value	$5,500
Basis of property	$5,000
Lesser of basis or value decline	$5,000
Less insurance proceeds	3,000
Deductible loss	$2,000

Nonbusiness property. For property not used in a trade or business or held for income production, the initial measure of the loss is always the smaller of the property's adjusted basis or the decline in value resulting from the casualty. This is true whether the property is completely destroyed or only partially destroyed. Effective as of 1987, individuals who are insured for personal losses must file a timely insurance claim to the extent they are insured with respect to such losses in order to deduct them. In addition, only the excess of each nonbusiness property loss over $100 can be treated as a casualty loss. Finally, only to the extent that the total of such excesses exceeds 10% of the taxpayer A.G.I. can losses be deducted.

To illustrate this "floor," assume that a taxpayer whose A.G.I. was $30,000 suffered the following two casualty losses to personal use properties during the year:

1. A fire destroyed the taxpayer's home. The adjusted basis of the home was $70,000, and its fair market value before the fire was $90,000. She received insurance proceeds of $60,000.
2. The taxpayer had an accident in her pleasure boat. The boat's basis was $14,000; its fair market value before the accident was $9,000. After the accident, the boat's fair market value was $4,000. Reimbursement of $2,000 was received from an insurance company.

The amount deductible as a result of these two casualties is $9,800, as computed below.

	Home		Boat
Decline in value	$90,000		$ 5,000
Adjusted basis	$70,000		$14,000
Lesser of above	$70,000		$ 5,000
Less reimbursement	60,000		2,000
Balance	$10,000		$ 3,000
Less $100 floor	100		100
Loss considered	$ 9,900		$ 2,900
Total loss considered		$12,800	
Less 10% of A.G.I.		3,000	
Loss deductible		$ 9,800	

Obviously, the 10% of A.G.I. floor introduced in 1983 eliminates almost all deductions for personal casualty losses.

If insurance proceeds or other reimbursement exceeds the basis of the property, the taxpayer has a taxable gain (unless the gain is reinvested in replacement property, as discussed in Chapter 18). For example, assume that a taxpayer owned jewelry costing $30,000 and that just before it was stolen it had a fair market value of $75,000. Insurance proceeds of $45,000 were received. Even though the taxpayer suffered a loss in terms of market value, a gain of $15,000 has resulted from this transaction. If a taxpayer has both personal casualty gains and losses, then the losses (after the $100 floor) and the gains must be netted together. If the losses exceed the gains, then the net loss must exceed 10% of A.G.I. in order to be deductible. If the gains exceed the losses, then all the gains and losses are treated as capital gains and losses. The treatment of capital gains and losses will be discussed in Chapter 15.

OTHER CONSIDERATIONS   A number of other factors may complicate the property tax treatment of casualty and theft losses. A few of the more common of these are briefly summarized in the following paragraphs.

Generally, a corporation's casualty and theft *losses* are combined with its *gains* from casualty and theft. If a net loss exists, the loss is treated as an ordinary deduction from gross income. For individual taxpayers, however, only a casualty or theft loss associated with property used in trade or business or with property used for the production of rents or royalties is treated as a deduction *for* adjusted gross income. Casualty and theft losses associated with other assets held for investment or income production by individuals, as well as property held for purely personal use, are generally treated as itemized deductions *from* adjusted gross income.

Another complication arises in the case of married taxpayers. Spouses who file a joint return are subject to a single $100 floor for each casualty. If they file separate returns, however, each one is subject to the $100 floor for each casualty. Thus, if a thief in a single theft stole items belonging to both husband and wife, they would have a floor of $100 each for their personal casualty loss if they filed separate returns. If they filed a joint return, a single floor of $100 would be imposed.

One final complication in measuring the amount of loss should be mentioned. In measuring the loss from casualty or theft related to business property, each single identifiable item damaged or destroyed is treated separately in measuring the decrease in value. For example, if a storm damages a building used in trade or business and also damages or destroys ornamental shrubs on the premises, the decrease in value of the building is computed separately from the decrease in value of the shrubs. However, for property not used in a trade or business, the real property and any improvements must be considered an integral part of one property. Thus, if a storm damaged the building and shrubs on the premises, the decline in value would not be computed for each item, but a single figure for the total decline in overall value of the property would be determined.

A number of complications arise regarding the year in which a casualty or theft loss should be deducted. In general, a loss is allowed as a deduction only for the year in which the loss is sustained. A loss arising from theft, however, is sustained in the year the theft is discovered, rather than in the year the actual theft took place. If there exists a claim for reimbursement and there is a reasonable prospect of recovery, no portion of the loss with respect to which reimbursement may be received is deductible until it can be determined with reasonable certainty whether reimbursement will be received. Any portion of the loss not covered by a claim for reimbursement is deductible, however, in the year the casualty occurred or the theft was discovered.

In some cases, if a loss results from a disaster in an area that the president of the United States subsequently declares to be a "disaster area" warranting federal assistance, the taxpayer may deduct the loss in the year the loss occurs or may deduct the loss on the tax return for the year preceding the year in which the loss actually occurred. Thus, for example, if a taxpayer's home were destroyed by flood in February 19x2, and the area was declared a "disaster area," then the taxpayer could claim the loss on his or her 19x1 tax return.

If a taxpayer deducts a loss in one year and in a subsequent tax year receives reimbursement, he does not recompute the tax for the taxable year in which the deduction was taken, but includes the reimbursement in income in the year it is received, to the extent that the reimbursement represents recovery of an amount that gave rise to a tax benefit when the deduction was taken.

Another provision relating to insurance received in connection with casualties permits a taxpayer to exclude from gross income all or a portion of insurance proceeds received as reimbursement for living expenses during the period that the taxpayer must temporarily live in another residence while his or her home is being repaired. The exclusion is limited to the amount by which actual living expenses of the taxpayer's household exceed the living expenses it would normally have incurred during that period, and includes amounts spent for such items as rent, transportation, food, utilities, and so on.

ITEMIZED DEDUCTIONS REPRESENTING SUBSIDIES

Because the deductions for taxes, contributions, and interest normally represent personal expenditures not related to the production of income, the granting of a tax deduction for each of them has frequently been criticized as an unjustified subsidy to a particular group in society. For example, the deductibility of the interest and property taxes incurred on an owner-occupied home has been said to constitute an inequitable subsidy to home-owners because no comparable deductions are available to taxpayers who rent a home.

State and Local Taxes

Certain taxes paid to state and local governmental units are deductible even though they are not incurred in connection with a trade or business or other income-producing activity. Section 164(a) provides:

(a) General Rule.—Except as otherwise provided in this section, the following taxes shall be allowed as a deduction for the taxable year within which paid or accrued:

(1) State and local, and foreign, real property taxes

(2) State and local, personal property taxes

(3) State and local, and foreign, income, war profits, and excess profits taxes

(4) The windfall profit tax imposed by section 4986

(5) The GST (generation skipping transfer) tax imposed on income distributions.

In addition, there shall be allowed as a deduction State and local, and foreign, taxes not described in the preceding sentence which are paid or accrued within the taxable year in carrying on a trade or business or an activity described in section 212 (relating to expenses for production of income). Notwithstanding the previous sentence, any tax (not described in the first sentence of this subsection) which is paid or accrued by the taxpayer in connection with an acquisition or disposition of property shall be treated as part of the cost of the acquired property or, in the case of a disposition, as a reduction in the amount realized on the disposition.

Taxes have been specifically mentioned as a deduction in every federal income tax law, including the 1861 Act, although the 1865 Act was the first to include specifically taxes not associated with income production. The 1865 law permitted the deduction of all national, state, county, and municipal taxes paid within the year. Similarly, the income tax law of 1913 specifically allowed deductions for all "national, state, county, school, and municipal taxes paid during the year," including the federal income tax itself. Gradually, however, the number of deductible taxes has been reduced. The deduction for the federal income tax itself was eliminated in 1917; the federal excise tax deduction was ended in 1943; the deduction for many state and local taxes (on tobacco, alcoholic beverages, automobiles licenses, drivers' licenses, and others) was removed in 1961;[5] and the deduction for state taxes on gasoline was eliminated for taxable years beginning after 1978. The President's 1985 tax reform proposal argued that no deduction should be allowed for state and local taxes unless related to a trade or business or the production of income.[6] Arguments were made that the deduction disproportionately benefits high-income taxpayers residing in high-tax states, that it seriously erodes the tax base, and that it is an inefficient subsidy to state and local governments. The 1986 Act did not go quite this far, however. Only the deduction for state and local general sales taxes was removed from the list of deductible taxes.

[5]Even though the specific provisions authorizing the deduction of automobile licenses was repealed in 1964, the citizens of some states can still claim them as a deduction under Sec. 162(a)(2). If the auto license fee is based on value (an *ad valorem* basis), it can be considered a property tax and, as such, is deductible.

[6]*President's Tax Proposals to the Congress for Fairness, Growth, and Simplicity*, May 29, 1985, pp. 62–64.

TABLE **10-1**

ITEMIZED DEDUCTIONS BY CLASSES—1984

Type	Amount (in billions)	Percentage of Total
Interest	155.2	43.6%
Taxes	115.9	32.5
Contributions	42.4	11.9
Medical expenses	21.3	6.0
Others	21.5	6.0

SOURCE: *Statistics of Income Bulletin,* Spring 1986.

IMPORTANCE OF THE DEDUCTION FOR TAXES   Although many taxes are no longer deductible, this item continues to be large on returns itemizing deductions. Table 10-1 shows that taxes have been the second most important itemized deduction, making up about 32.5% of the total in 1984. The amount of taxes deducted has also consistently increased, as shown in Table 10-2, as a result of the rapid growth of state and local property, sales, and income taxes.

RATIONALE FOR DEDUCTING TAXES   Several arguments have been advanced to support the deduction of state and local taxes. Perhaps the most important is that the deduction facilitates the smooth functioning of the federal system, providing a greater flexibility to local governmental units in their own taxing activities. In effect, the deduction represents a federal subsidy to state and local governments because it reduces the net cost of state and local taxes to those taxpayers who itemize deductions on their federal tax returns. Presumably, this permits local governmental units to increases taxes with less

TABLE **10-2**

DEDUCTION FOR TAXES ON RETURNS ITEMIZING DEDUCTIONS FROM A.G.I.

Year	Amount of Taxes Deducted (in billions)
1954	$ 4.08
1960	10.53
1964	14.07
1970	32.02
1975	44.11
1977	51.8
1979	60.6
1981	77.7
1983	100.2

SOURCE: *Statistics of Income,* various years, and *Statistics of Income Bulletin,* Winter 1984–85.

opposition from taxpayers. Furthermore, because it tends to reduce intercity and interstate tax differentials, permitting state and local taxes to be deducted reduces the fear, common to many local governmental bodies, that high tax rates will cause business and population to move to areas with lower tax rates.

Before the 1965 reduction of the maximum federal tax rate for individuals to 70% (from a previous high of 91%) it was often suggested that unless some provision were included in the federal tax structure for deduction of taxes paid to state and local governments—especially state and local income taxes—the marginal rate might be more than 100%. Although this extreme is not likely to occur, some degree of coordination between taxing activities of the national and local governmental units is desirable, and the deduction for state and local taxes on the federal tax return gives some relief from multiple taxation and provides limited control of the total tax burden. (Incidentally, state income taxes usually allow a deduction for the federal income tax paid.)

Finally, some persons argue that the taxpayer should not have to pay "a tax on a tax." Essentially, this concept considers taxes in much the same light as medical costs and casualty losses—unavoidable, involuntary payments that reduce the taxpayer's wherewithal to pay the federal income tax.

ARGUMENTS AGAINST THE DEDUCTION FOR TAXES   Most tax scholars favor the abolition of the deduction for taxes, with the exception, perhaps, of state and local income taxes. They refute most of the arguments supporting the deduction.

First, they point out that taxes paid state and local governments are actually for such services as police protection, schools, streets, and similar services and are very much like payments for services from the private sector of the economy. This argument is sometimes deemed especially pertinent in the case of taxes earmarked for specific direct benefit or services. Most of these taxes (for example, auto licenses and drivers' licenses) have been made nondeductible in recent years. The logic may easily be extended to taxes not earmarked for specific purposes.

Most tax experts also point out that making state and local taxes deductible tends to reduce the progressivity that has been deliberately built into the tax structure. This is true because a deduction for state and local taxes generally results in a greater income tax saving for individuals in higher income tax brackets. Moreover, the deduction for state and local property taxes often discriminates between taxpayers with equal incomes and tax-paying ability. For example, it permits the homeowner to deduct taxes but allows no similar deduction to the tenant whose monthly rental surely includes an element for property taxes.

Even the most logical reason for permitting the deduction of state and local taxes—to make it easier for local governmental units to levy taxes—is subject to criticism. Not only is this a helter-skelter and inefficient means of providing a subsidy, but it provides assistance to the wrong communities. Presumably, a greater need for federal aid exists in poor communities, where both income and wealth (property) are relatively low. However, the aid provided by deduction of state and local taxes is of greatest benefit to communities whose taxpayers are in higher income tax brackets and are wealthier.

Charitable Contributions

Both individual and corporate taxpayers may deduct charitable contributions made to qualifying recipients. Most questions regarding contribution deductions involve either the determination of the eligibility of a particular gift to qualify for a deduction or the determination of the amount that may be deducted. Although many provisions applicable to contribution deductions apply equally to the individual and the corporate donor, enough differences do exist to justify their separate consideration.

PROVISIONS RELATING TO CONTRIBUTIONS BY INDIVIDUALS   Contributions made by individuals are deductible within limits, if they are made to (or "for the use of") one of the types of organizations listed in Sec. 170(c), which reads as follows:

(1) A State, a possession of the United States, or any political subdivision of any of the foregoing, or the United States or the District of Columbia, but only if the contribution or gift is made for exclusively public purposes.

(2) A corporation, trust, or community chest, fund, or foundation—

   (A) created or organized in the United States or in any possession thereof, or under the law of the United States, any State, the District of Columbia, or any possession of the United States;

   (B) organized and operated exclusively for religious, charitable, scientific, literary, or educational purposes, or to foster national or international amateur sports competition . . . or for the prevention of cruelty to children or animals;

   (C) no part of the net earnings of which inures to the benefit of any private shareholder or individual; and

   (D) which is not disqualified for tax exemption under section 501(c)(3) by reason of attempting to influence legislation, and which does not participate in, or intervene in (including the publishing or distributing of statements), any political campaign on behalf of any candidate for public office.

   A contribution or gift by a corporation to a trust, chest, fund, or foundation shall be deductible by reason of this paragraph only if it is to be used within the United States or any of its possessions exclusively for purposes specified in subparagraph (B). . . .

(3) A post or organization of war veterans, or an auxiliary unit or society of, or trust or foundation for, any such post or organization—

   (A) organized in the United States or any of its possessions, and

   (B) no part of the net earnings of which inures to the benefit of any private shareholder or individual.

(4) In the case of a contribution or gift by an individual, a domestic fraternal society, order, or association, operating under the lodge system, but only if

such contribution or gift is to be used exclusively for religious, charitable, scientific, literary, or educational purposes, or for the prevention of cruelty to children or animals.

(5) A cemetery company owned and operated exclusively for the benefit of its members, or any corporation chartered solely for burial purposes as a cemetery corporation and not permitted by its charter to engage in any business not necessarily incident to that purpose, if such company or corporation is not operated for profit and no part of the net earnings of such company or corporation inures to the benefit of any private shareholder or individual.

Note that to be deductible, charitable contributions must be made to a qualifying organization that fits into one of the classes listed in Sec. 170(c). Contributions to individuals, no matter how needy, are not tax deductible.

A contribution made to a qualifying organization is just what the words imply—a direct gift to the organization. A contribution made "for the use of" an organization is an indirect gift. For example, an individual might make a gift to a trust and, in turn, direct the trustee to contribute that gift (and, possibly, any income that it produces) to a qualifying charity. Alternatively, an individual might pay a liability originally incurred by a charitable organization. In either of the latter two cases, the gift is "for the use of" the recipient organization and is subject to special rules for tax purposes.

Measuring the amount contributed.   To be deductible, a charitable contribution must be in money or property; the taxpayer cannot deduct the value of services donated to an organization. Contribution of tangible, personal property must be of "present interest"—that is, a taxpayer cannot get a deduction now for a transfer that takes place at his or her death if the property involved is tangible, personal property. Contributions of "future interest" in real property are, however, possible under certain circumstances.

In some instances, it is difficult to determine if a particular contribution consists of a property or a service; for example, the donation of blood has been held to be a service, not property. Similarly, the law denies a taxpayer the value of "lost rents" as a deduction when the taxpayer permits a charity to occupy rental property free of cost. A taxpayer who uses a personal automobile on behalf of a charitable organization is entitled to deduct only the out-of-pocket costs (gasoline, oil, and so on) or a flat 12 cents per mile. However, the 1986 Act provided that a charitable deduction for travel away from home would not be permitted "unless there is no significant element of personal pleasure, recreation, or vacation in such travel."

When the taxpayer contributes cash, the amount of the contribution cannot be questioned. If the taxpayer contributes other property, the amount deemed to have been contributed depends on both the nature of the property and, in some cases, the nature of the donee organization.

Ordinary income property.   If the sale of contributed property would have resulted in ordinary income (that is, not capital gain), the taxpayer may deduct only the fair market value of the property reduced by the amount of ordinary income that would be recognized if the property were sold. This rule generally results in a deduction equal to the cost or adjusted basis of the property. For example, if an individual who is a sole proprietor contributes routine inventory items that cost $2,000 but had a normal retail sales price of $3,000, the amount of the contribution would be $2,000. This restriction is applied regardless of the nature of the donee organization.

Several other types of property, in addition to inventory, are ordinary income property. For example, the term includes the following:

1. Capital assets (such as shares of stock and land held for investment) if held for six months or less (one year after 1987)
2. Art objects, literary works, and so on, produced by the taxpayer
3. Property used in a business or held for investment to the extent that its sale would result in ordinary income (usually through depreciation recapture) (See Chapter 16.)
4. Inventories of consumable supplies that would be charged to expense when used in the business
5. Letters and memoranda by or to the taxpayer

Consequently, the donation of any of these properties to a qualifying organization usually creates a deduction that is less than the fair market value of the property.

Prior to 1970, a taxpayer was entitled to deduct the fair market value of *any* noncash property contributed to a charity. As a result, it was possible to have a greater positive cash flow from making a contribution than from selling. For example, if a taxpayer in the 70% rate bracket in 1969 contributed to a qualified organization merchandise inventory that cost $1,000 but had a fair market value of $2,000, he or she would deduct $2,000 as a contribution, resulting in an income tax saving of $1,400. Thus, the tax saving would exceed the cost of the item contributed by $400. Had the taxpayer sold the same inventory, the $1,000 ordinary income would have been subject to a $700 tax, thus leaving only $300 in excess of the cost after taxes.

Capital gain property. If the sale of contributed property would have resulted in *long-term* capital gain, the fair market value of the property is deemed to be the amount contributed. Capital gain property is property that would result in long term capital gain if sold. Examples are shares of stock, land, buildings, and purchased works of art held for more than six months (one year after 1987). (See Chapter 15 for a further definition of capital gain property.) There are two exceptions to the rule that donations of capital gain property are equal to the fair market value of the property:

1. Tangible *personalty* (not realty), unrelated to the donee organization's exempt function (for example, an object of art that will be resold by the donee charity)
2. Any capital gain property contributed to a nonoperating *private* foundation that does not meet certain technical requirements (Because this exemption is rarely encountered, we will not discuss it further.)

In the case of property that fits into the two exceptions above, the amount deemed to have been contributed is the property's fair market value reduced by the amount that would have been capital gain had the property been sold. For example, if a taxpayer paid $1,000 for a painting four years ago and this year, when its fair market value was $4,000, contributed the painting to a university, the amount deductible would depend on the university's expected use of the painting, which is a capital asset to the taxpayer. If it were hung in the university's art gallery, the amount deductible would be the fair market value of $4,000. On the other hand, if it were resold by the university, the amount deductible would be only $1,000.

The maximum amount deductible.   The deduction for contributions by an individual cannot exceed 50% of the taxpayer's adjusted gross income, depending on the nature of the property given and the type of donee to which the contribution is made. As a practical matter, these limits are rarely applicable.

Contributions to 50% limit organizations.   The deduction for contributions made directly to public charities generally is limited to 50% of A.G.I. Public charities include church groups, educational institutions, institutions and organizations for medical care, governmental units or other organizations that get a substantial portion of their support from the public or from a governmental unit, and a relatively small number of "private foundations" that meet specific requirements.

The deduction for contributions to public charities of appreciated capital gain properties is, however, subject to a special limit of 30% of A.G.I. For example, assume that in the current year, Mason, whose A.G.I., is $9,000, contributes a work of art (that cost him $2,000 ten years ago and had a fair market value of $8,000 at the date of gift) to the city art museum to be used as part of its permanent exhibition. The deduction of this contribution would be limited to 30% of Mason's A.G.I., or $2,700.

When applying the overall 50% limit, contributions of 30% limit property are the last to be considered. For example, if a taxpayer with A.G.I. of $10,000 gives $2,600 to public charities and a capital gain property with a fair market value of $4,000 to a public museum, he or she can deduct only $5,000, or 50% of A.G.I. this year. The deduction consists of the $2,600 cash contribution and $2,400 of the value of the capital gain property. (The $1,600 excess of capital gain property contributed over the 50% limit can be carried forward to future years, as discussed later in this chapter).

Maximum contributions to certain organizations.   The deduction for contributions to *private* foundations that do not meet specified requirements is limited to 30% of the taxpayer's A.G.I.[7] If contributions are made to both public charities and private foundations, the contributions to public charities must be deducted first. Since the rules are extremely unlikely to affect the "typical individual taxpayer" described at the beginning of Chapter 8, contributions to private foundations will not be considered further.

---

[7]Before 1984, this limit was 20%; the new 30% limit does not apply to capital gains property, 20% still applies. The same limit also applies to contributions made *for the use of,* rather than *directly to,* public charities.

Time of deduction.   Under most circumstances an individual taxpayer may deduct contributions only in the year in which he or she actually transfers the cash or other property to the qualified recipient. Pledges of contributions are not deductible until paid. This restriction applies equally to accrual-basis taxpayers and to cash-basis taxpayers. Payments by credit card, however, are treated like cash payments in the year the credit slip is signed.

Any contributions to public charities in excess of 50% of the taxpayer's A.G.I. can be carried over to the following year and treated as having been paid in that year. If the sum of the carryover and the actual contributions made to public charities in the second year again exceeds 50% of the taxpayer's A.G.I., the excess may be carried over to the following year. This procedure can be repeated for up to five years. If because of the percentage limitation a contribution cannot be fully deducted during the five-year carryover period, an unused amount is simply lost as a deduction. In each year, the contributions actually paid during that year must be deducted before any of the contribution carryover is used. If excess contributions are carried over from more than one tax year, the carryovers are used in order of occurrence (a FIFO basis).

The relation between the contribution carryover and the contributions actually made during a year can be illustrated in a simple tabulation. Assume that a taxpayer's only contributions were made in cash to public charities in the amounts shown in the tabulation below. Also, assume that the taxpayer had A.G.I. of $60,000 each year. This taxpayer must exhaust the 19x6 contribution carryover by December 31, 19x9, because it comes from the 19x4 excess contributions.

Year	Amount Contributed (All to Public Charities)	Amount Deductible in Current Year	Contributions Carryover
19x1	$50,000	$30,000	$20,000
19x2	40,000	30,000	30,000
19x3	20,000	30,000	20,000
19x4	32,000	30,000	22,000
19x5	20,000	30,000	12,000
19x6	20,000	30,000	2,000

Contributions of appreciated capital gains property that exceed the 30% limit may be carried over to future years and added to the capital gain contributions of the future years, subject to a five-year carryover limit. A taxpayer can avoid the 30% limit by electing to reduce the deduction for capital gain property by the amount of the unrealized appreciation. For example, assume a taxpayer gave capital gain property with a fair market value of $10,000 and an adjusted basis of $8,000 at a time when his A.G.I. was only $20,000. If the taxpayer wishes to deduct the fair market value of the property, he must carry over $4,000 to the succeeding year. On the other hand, he could elect to deduct the adjusted basis ($8,000) all in the current year since this amount is less than 50% of A.G.I. Of course, there would be no carryover if this election were made.

PRESENT PROVISIONS RELATING TO CONTRIBUTIONS BY CORPORATIONS   Corporations may deduct charitable contributions made to the same organizations previously listed for individual taxpayers. A special provision permits corporations using the *accrual* method of accounting to deduct an accrued contribution as long as it is paid on or before the due date of the corporation's federal tax return. This exception is available only if the gift was authorized by the directors of the corporation prior to the close of the tax year.

Deductions for charitable contributions by a corporation are limited to 10% of taxable income computed before deductions for (1) the contributions themselves, (2) any net operating loss carryback to the taxable year, and (3) certain special deductions allowed corporations, the most important of which is the deduction for dividends received. Contributions in excess of the 10% limit may be carried over for five consecutive years and added to contributions made in the years to which they are carried, in the same manner as the carryover of contributions by individuals.

As previously noted, since 1969, the deduction for a contribution of "ordinary income" property has been limited to the fair market value of the property reduced by the amount that would have been reported as ordinary income if the property had been sold at its fair market value. Enactment of the 1969 provision effectively eliminated the abuses previously mentioned and also resulted in reduced contributions of those types of property to charitable organizations. Charitable organizations that provide food, clothing, medical equipment, supplies, and so on to the needy and disaster victims found that contributions of such items were reduced. As a result, corporations (other than S corporations) may take a deduction for up to one-half the appreciation on certain types of ordinary income property contributed to a public charity (except governmental units) or to a private foundation. The donee's use of the property must be related to its exempt purpose and solely for the care of the ill, the needy, or infants. Certain other requirements must also be met. The amount of the deduction is generally the sum of (1) the taxpayer's basis in the property and (2) one-half the unrealized appreciation. No deduction is allowed for an amount that exceeds twice the basis of the property or for any part of the appreciation that would have been ordinary income (if the property had been sold) because of the application of various "recapture" provisions such as Sec. 1245.

In addition, to encourage scientific research, the amount deductible is increased for the contribution of newly manufactured scientific equipment or apparatus to a college or university or to a tax exempt organization operated primarily to conduct scientific research if the property is used by the donee in research or experimentation in physical or biological sciences. The amount deductible is the basis of the property plus one-half the property's appreciation. However, the deduction may not exceed 200% of the corporation's basis in the donated property.

IMPORTANCE OF THE CONTRIBUTIONS DEDUCTION BY INDIVIDUALS   Contributions have been the third most important group of itemized deductions (following interest and taxes) made by individuals. As shown in Table 10-1, during 1984, deductions for contributions on individual returns totaled $42.4 billion, or 11.9% of the tital of all itemized deductions on such returns.

It is normally assumed that persons subject to high tax rates are more influenced in their giving by tax considerations than those in lower brackets. Studies by the I.R.S. have shown that contributions are relatively more important in the two highest tax brackets ($500,000 to $1,000,000 and over $1,000,000 A.G.I.) but that a substantial portion of contributions are made by taxpayers with incomes below $10,000. These studies also show a distinct difference in the pattern of giving by large and small contributors. Large contributors give substantial support to educational institutions, hospitals, welfare agenices, and private foundations; low-income taxpayers make most of their contributions to religious groups. For tax years 1982–1986, limited charitable contributions by persons who did not itemize deductions were permitted, but Congress did not renew this provision in the 1986 Act.

Until 1970, wealthy taxpayers were able to use private foundations to achieve some personal financial or other objectives. Today, deductibility of any contributions to private foundations depends on the foundation's compliance with Treasury Department requirements. If a foundation is found to be no longer exempt, a steep penalty tax is imposed unless the foundation's assets are used for charitable purposes. Additionally, excise taxes are levied on certain transactions in which the foundation seeks to achieve such aims as exerting political influence, providing operating capital for donor corporations, and other objectives not compatible with its tax-exempt status.

THE CONTRIBUTION DEDUCTION AND SOCIAL WELFARE   Deductions for contributions to philanthrophic organizations were first allowed in 1917 because of the fear that high wartime tax rates would cause a decline in contributions. A deduction allowance for contributions is usually justified as an encouragement to a socially desirable activity. Presumably, contributions provide highly desirable activities with finances that are not adequately provided by other sources and would have to be provided by the state if they were not supplied by voluntary contributions. Many people would describe the charitable deduction as simply a subsidy to charitable causes.

Many tax scholars question the effectiveness of the charitable deduction as an incentive for giving, pointing out that little is known about the actual value of gifts to philanthropies. Professor Harry Kahn has presented evidence to indicate that the relation between contributions and income has been rather stable over the years, regardless of the contribution provisions of the income tax laws in existence.[8] Various other studies have arrived at conflicting conclusions about the impact of deductibility on charitable giving.

---

[8]C. Harry Kahn, "Personal Deductions in the Individual Income Tax," *1959 Compendium*, pp. 392–95.

A possible alternative to the contribution provision might be to eliminate the deduction and, instead, allow the government to match contributions, at a given rate, by a refund of the contributor's tax directly to the philanthropy to which the taxpayer made the gift. This would overcome the almost impossible task the I.R.S. now has in auditing contribution deductions, because it would then deal with several thousand philanthropic organizations rather than millions of taxpayers. Also, with this scheme Congress could delineate more clearly the activities it wishes to subsidize.

An important question is whether it is proper for the taxpayer, by making a deductible contribution, to force "the government in effect to make a partial matching grant for a purpose of his own choosing and to an organization whose operations are not subject to government review or control. Sectarian, provincial, eccentric, or frivolous uses of money may be aided along with the most worthy."[9] However, the lack of government control may be a positive advantage because it allows many educational, scientific, and cultural activities to maintain diversity and independence they would not have if Congress scrutinized each deduction. The appropriations process is not well suited to the nourishment of new and unpopular ideas, and the usual procedures for handling public funds to finance many activities of philanthropic organizations would be cumbersome and unsatisfactory.

Of course, freedom from control is not completely achieved under the current system of contribution deductions. Professor Melvin White observed this limitation of the current system in the following words:

> The policies and administration of recipient institutions can scarcely be expected to remain independent of the viewpoint of major suppliers of their funds. There are the limitations on the size of deductible contributions, probably rarely reached, and the Government itself sets eligibility requirements for recipient institutions. But . . . the Government's program is biased to expand the influence of the rich as compared to the moderate- and low-income giver.[10]

Interest Expense

Perhaps the most controversial itemized deduction is that for interest, which in 1984 was the single most important itemized deduction, accounting for $155.2 billion, or 43.6% of all itemized deductions. The extremely rapid growth in the itemized interest deduction is indicated in Table 10-3.

Essentially, since the beginning of the modern income tax law in 1913, nearly all interest expense has been deductible. Although it is almost unanimously agreed that interest incurred in trade or business, or in

[9]Richard Goode, *The Individual Income Tax* (Washington, DC: The Brookings Institution, 1964), p. 169.
[10]Melvin I. White, "Proper Income Tax Treatment of Deductions for Personal Expense," *1959 Compendium*, p. 371.

TABLE **10-3**

DEDUCTIONS FOR INTEREST ON RETURNS ITEMIZING DEDUCTIONS FROM A.G.I.
(IN BILLIONS)

Year	Itemized Interest Deduction
1954	$ 3.20
1960	8.41
1964	12.45
1970	23.93
1973	31.94
1975	38.62
1977	47.14
1979	73.62
1981	108.72
1983	132.47

SOURCE: *Statistics of Income,* various years, and *Statistics of Income Bulletin,* Winter 1984–85.

connection with the production of any other taxable income, should be treated in the same manner as other deductible expenses, there has been far less agreement over the propriety of a deduction for interest paid on funds to finance the purchase of personal consumer goods and services. The 1986 Act significantly reduced the amount of such interest that individuals could deduct.

The general provision authorizing the deduction of interest is contained in Sec. 163, which reads as follows:

(a) General Rule.—There shall be allowed as a deduction all interest paid or accrued within the taxable year on indebtedness.

This all-inclusive rule is significantly modified and limited by several other sections disallowing certain types of interest. One of these provisions prohibits the deduction of interest on funds borrowed to earn tax-exempt income and on those used to purchase a single-premium life insurance or endowment policy. Other limiting provisions require that the indebtedness be the taxpayer's if a deduction is to be allowed. Another important restriction, discussed later in some detail, limits the amount of deductible "investment interest." Also, certain "construction period" interest and taxes must be capitalized. Finally, the 1986 Act disallows the deduction for personal interest (except "qualified residence interest") for tax years after 1990 with a phased-in limitation for years between 1986 and 1991. Each of these limitations will be discussed later in more detail.

CONTROVERSIES OVER THE INTEREST DEDUCTION   Presumably, the broad deductibility of interest resulted from the difficulty encountered in trying to distinguish clearly between borrowed funds used for income-producing activities and those used for personal activities. It is extremely difficult to trace the relationship between debts owed by the taxpayer and specific assets or services acquired. In many cases, funds borrowed ostensibly for business purposes are used for personal purchases, and funds acquired for consumption purposes are used in a business venture. In addition, prudent manipulation of the taxpayer's finances could ensure that borrowed funds would be used first in business and that equity capital would be used first for personal expenditures if interest on the former, but not the latter, were deductible.

Proponents of this deduction agree that interest expense represents a reduction of the taxpayer's economic income, regardless of why the expense was incurred and, thus, should be deductible in recognition of this difference in wherewithal to pay tax. On the other hand, interest expenses may be considered part of the purchase price of commodities or services acquired—a premium for obtaining the goods and services now rather than waiting until later. This element of price, so the argument goes, should be treated in the same manner as the other portions—that is, interest related to personal expenditures should be nondeductible.

The most difficult aspect of the interest deduction, and the most controversial, has related to interest paid by taxpayers on funds obtained to purchase a home or durable consumer goods. A definite inequity exists between the homeowner and the tenant, which can be easily seen by assuming that one taxpayer makes monthly rental payments of $400 on his residence, whereas a second taxpayer makes mortgage payments of $400 per month, including an average of $300 per month in interest. The former taxpayer can take no deduction on his tax return, but the latter may deduct all of the interest paid; in addition, the homeowner also may deduct property taxes paid. Because the second taxpayer is not required to include in income the imputed rental value of his owner-occupied home, he or she obviously has a distinct tax advantage over the tenant, even though the two of them may have essentially the same economic income.

This inequity has been recognized throughout the history of the modern income tax. For example, in the debate over the initial act in 1913, it was pointed out that

> here is a man . . . who has purchased a home. He has given a mortgage upon it . . . and is paying . . . $1,000 interest. Under this bill that would be deducted from his net income. But if his neighbor has rented a house, and instead of virtually paying what the first-named man does in the form of interest, he pays directly $1,000 rent. He gets no deduction whatever, and yet the situation of the two is to all intents and purposes precisely the same.[11]

Many tax scholars argue that the only real solution to this inequity is to require that the homeowner include in his or her taxable income the imputed rental value of his or her home. Then the interest paid on a home mortgage

---

[11]50 *Congressional Record* 3848 (1913) quoted in Samuel H. Hellenbrand, "Itemized Deductions for Personal Expenses and Standard Deductions in the Income Tax Law," 1959 *Compendium*, p. 378.

would be deductible as a cost of earning income. The practical difficulties of this solution are obvious. Additionally, home ownership is highly valued by American taxpayers, many of whom evidently believe that the deductibility of home mortgage interest makes home ownership possible. At any rate, when Congress decided in 1986 to repeal the deductibility of personal interest, there was no serious consideration of also removing the deductibility of home mortgage interest.

DEDUCTIONS FOR PERSONAL INTEREST   Beginning in 1987, the amount of personal interest that can be deducted will be limited to "qualified residence interest" with a "phaseout" of the deductibility of other personal interest. Personal interest is defined in Sec. 163(h)(2) as any interest allowed as a deduction other than:

(A) interest paid or accrued on indebtedness incurred or continued in connection with the conduct of a trade or business (other than the trade or business of performing services as an employee),
(B) any investment interest (within the meaning of subsection (d))
(C) any interest which is taken into account under section 469 in computing income or loss from a passive activity of the taxpayer
(D) any qualified residence interest . . .
(E) any interest payable under section 6601 on any unpaid portion of the tax imposed by section 2001 . . . [the estate tax]

This definition in effect instructs the taxpayer that if interest cannot be classified into one of these five categories, then it cannot be deducted (except for the limited deductibility of personal interest through 1990). Note that special limitations, discussed below, apply to interest related to investment or passive activities and to qualified residence interest. What is disallowed, of course, is interest on consumer debt, such as personal credit card purchases and automobile loans. Interest on unpaid tax liabilities is also disallowed unless it is interest on estate taxes deferred under Secs. 6163 or 6166.

Rather than completely eliminating such deduction, Congress provided a phasein of the disallowance. The percentage of personal interest deductible through 1991 is as follows:

1987	65%
1988	40
1989	20
1990	10
1991	0

Therefore, a taxpayer who in 1988 has $600 interest on a personal automobile loan will be allowed to deduct $240 of the interest.

QUALIFIED RESIDENCE INTEREST   Recall that the phaseout of the deduction for personal interest does not include "qualified residence" interest expense. A qualified residence is the taxpayer's principal residence and one second residence, such as a vacation home. A second residence can qualify only if the taxpayer's personal use exceeds the greater of 14 days or 10% of the number of days of rental use. Otherwise, the property will probably be treated under the passive activity rules described later.

Outstanding qualified debt on a qualified residence cannot exceed the lesser of the fair market value or the original purchase price plus improvements unless the excess debt is incurred for certain educational or medical expenses.[12] Thus, the maximum amount of qualified debt on a house with an original cost plus improvements of $100,000 and a fair market value of $130,000 is $100,000. If the taxpayer incurred $110,000 of debt on the house, the interest on the $10,000 excess debt would not be deductible unless it was for educational or medical expenses. The amount of disqualified interest is determined at the rate charged on the latest portion of the debt.

Note that these rules permit a taxpayer to circumvent the repeal of the deductibility of personal interest by making home equity loans for such purposes as purchase of a new automobile. Obviously, not all taxpayers can take advantage of this "loophole," either because they do not own homes or if they do, they have insufficient equity to borrow any more money against the value of the home.

INTEREST RELATED TO PASSIVE ACTIVITIES   As described earlier in Chapter 3, the 1986 Act included new rules limiting the deductibility of losses from "passive activities," that is, activities such as ownership of rental property or limited partnership interests that are not considered a trade or business or in which the taxpayer does not materially participate. Losses from passive activities are allowed only to the extent of gains from similar activities. Disallowed losses can be carried forward to offset income from passive activities in later years. These rules, of course, limit the deductibility of interest associated with passive activities. As with the consumer interest rules, a five-year phasein period is provided. For passive activities held by the taxpayer on the date the law was passed, 65% of net losses are allowed in 1987, 40% in 1988, 20% in 1989, and 10% in 1990. Losses from passive activities are examined in greater detail in Chapter 21.

EXCESS INVESTMENT INTEREST   The rules that permitted deduction of all interest expense permitted taxpayers to voluntarily incur substantial interest expenses on funds borrowed to acquire or carry investment assets. Often these funds were used to purchase stocks that had growth potential but returned small dividends currently. This gave rise to an immediate deduction and permitted the taxpayer to report gain on sale of the appreciated securities as long-term capital gain. To curtail excessive abuse of this tax break, tax laws limit the amount of interest deductible on funds borrowed by noncorporate taxpayers to purchase investment property. The limit for deductibility of investment interest is the amount of net investment income for the year.

Investment interest is defined as the sum of gross income from property

---

[12]A "transition rule" provides that if the excess debt was incurred on or before August 16, 1986, it remains deductible.

held for investments ("portfolio income" as described in Chapter 3) plus any net gain attributable to the disposition of investment property, regardless of holding period. Investment income does not include income from passive activities such as limited partnership interests. Expenses (other than interest) related to investment properties are deducted from investment income to compute net investment income.

Prior to 1987, taxpayers could deduct investment interest to the extent of net investment income *plus* $10,000. The new rule, limiting the deduction to no more than net investment income, is being phased in, with 65% of the amount disallowed because of repeal of the $10,000 allowance allowed in 1987, 40% in 1988, 20% in 1989, and 10% in 1990.

To illustrate, assume the following facts. A taxpayer paid interest of $45,000 on funds borrowed to purchase investment property. During the year, he received investment income consisting of interest and dividends totaling $5,000 and incurred investment expenses of $2,000. His investment deduction, assuming the year was 1986, would be limited to $13,000, computed as follows:

Basic amount deducted without restriction	$10,000
Excess investment income over investment expenses ($5,000 − $2,000)	3,000
Amount of investment interest deductible in 1986	$13,000

Given the same facts in 1987 rather than 1986, the allowable deduction for investment interest would be $9,500 ($3,000 net investment income plus 65% of $10,000 disallowed under new rules). The remaining investment interest paid by the taxpayer would be carried forward and treated as interest paid on accrued in the succeeding tax year. Thus, in effect, an unlimited carryover exists.

CAPITALIZATION OF INTEREST (AND TAXES) DURING CONSTRUCTION PERIOD
Prior to 1976, amounts paid or accrued for interest, as well as for property taxes, attributable to the construction of real property were allowed as current deductions unless the taxpayer elected to capitalize those items as carrying costs (Sec. 266). As a result, individual taxpayers in high marginal income tax brackets, especially those involved in real estate "shelters," could avoid payment of income taxes on a substantial portion of their economic income by expensing such costs as they were paid or accrued.

Sec. 189, added to the Code as part of the 1976 tax reform act, provided that construction period interest and real estate taxes were to be capitalized and then amortized over a fixed period (ten years in 1986). The Tax Reform Act of 1986 repealed Sec. 189 and added new uniform capitalization rules (Sec. 263A). These rules require that interest costs be capitalized if the debt is paid or incurred to construct, build, install, manufacture, develop, or improve real or tangible personal property that is produced by the taxpayer and that has (1) a long useful life, (2) an estimated production period exceeding two years, or (3) an estimated production period of less than one year and cost exceeding $1,000,000. An asset is deemed to have a long useful life if it is real estate or it is property with a class life of 20 years or more. These capitalized costs become part of the basis of the asset for purposes of depreciation or determining gain on sale.

MISCELLANEOUS DEDUCTIONS NOT SUBJECT TO 2% FLOOR

Recall from the previous chapter that a number of "miscellaneous" expenses are deductible only to the extent that they exceed 2% of A.G.I. Code Sec. 67 lists itemized deductions not subject to the 2% floor. The list includes interest, taxes, medical expenses, contributions, casualty and theft losses, and a number of less significant items. Here we consider several of these miscellaneous deductions not subject to the 2% floor.

MOVING EXPENSES   Section 217 of the Code permits the taxpayer to deduct the expenses of moving either on beginning employment as a new employee or on changing job location in his or her present employment. The moving expense deduction is now available to both employees and self-employed persons. The major requirements for eligibility are as follows:

1. The move must be to a new principal *job site* that is at least 35 miles further from the old residence than was the old *job site;* or at least 35 miles from the taxpayer's former residence if he or she had no former principal place of work.
2. An *employee* must be a full-time employee at the new job location for at least 39 weeks during the 12-month period immediately following arrival at the new job location. A *self-employed* person must perform services on a full-time basis in the new location for at least 78 weeks in the following 24-month period.

Death, involuntary separation, and other job transfers for the convenience of the employer remove the time limitations.

The deductible moving costs fit into two broad groups:

1. Direct costs, deductible without limit. The two main elements of direct costs are (a) transportation of household goods and personal effects and (b) travel costs of the taxpayer and family en route from the former to the new residence. If the taxpayer uses a personal automobile in the move, he or she may deduct the actual out-of-pocket costs incurred (gasoline, oil, and so on) or use an allowance of nine cents per mile.
2. Indirect costs, limited to a total deduction of $3,000. The three main elements of indirect costs are as follows:
   a. Pre-move house-hunting costs at new location after new employment has been obtained
   b. Temporary living costs for taxpayer and family at new principal job location (up to 30 days)
   c. Costs related to selling old residence, terminating old lease, and obtaining new residence or living quarters

Meals are not subject to the 80% limitation. Furthermore, the amount deductible for house-hunting costs and temporary living quarters [items 2(a) and (b)] is limited to a total of $1,500.

Military personnel who must make service-connected moves are not required to meet either the 35-mile test or the 39-week test.

If the new place of employment is outside the United States, the period during which temporary living costs may be deducted is 90 days rather than 30 days. Similarly, the overall limit on indirect costs that may be deducted is $6,000 rather than $3,000; the limit on the amount deductible for house-hunting costs and temporary living costs is $4,500 instead of $1,500.

BUSINESS EXPENSES OF HANDICAPPED INDIVIDUALS   Beginning in 1987, handicapped individuals are allowed to deduct payments for impairment-related work expenses including attendant care services at the individual's place of employment and other expenses necessary for the individual to be able to work.

GAMBLING LOSSES   Gambling winnings are includable in gross income. Losses from gambling are permitted as deductions, but only to the extent of gains from gambling. Therefore, a taxpayer who won $100 in a state lottery could deduct the cost of losing lottery tickets purchased in the same year up to $100. However, gambling losses are deductible only as itemized deductions unless gambling is the taxpayer's trade or business.

Comprehensive Example

Assume that Ron and Nancy Anderson, both accountants employed by "Big Eight" accounting firms, had adjusted gross income in 1987 of $60,000, including net investment income of $2,000. Additionally, they incurred the following expenses:

Medical expenses	$1,000
Charitable contributions	3,000
Home mortgage interest	6,000
Interest on auto loan	800
Investment interest	2,500
Casualty loss from auto accident	1,200
Property taxes on home	2,000
General sales tax	600
State income tax	4,000
Unreimbursed professional dues	500
Educational expenses related to Ron's job (all tuition)	1,500
Professional entertainment expense	300
Cost of attending AICPA annual meeting (includes $200 for meals)	1,000
Moving expenses (from St. Louis to Milwaukee)	1,400

The Andersons' total allowed itemized deductions amount to $21,245, calculated as follows:

Medical expenses	$1,000		
Less 7 1/2% A.G.I.	(4,500)	$ 0	
Taxes			
State income tax	$4,000		
Property tax on home	2,000		
General sales tax	0	6,000	
Interest			
Home mortgage	$6,000		
Auto loan (65% x 800)	520		
Investment interest	$2,000		
Net investment income + 65% × $500 excess	325	2,325	8,845
Charitable contributions			3,000
Casualty loss	$1,200		
Less $100 floor	(100)		
	$1,100		
Less 10% A.G.I.	(6,000)	0	
Miscellaneous deductions			
Moving expenses	$1,400		
Subject to 2% floor			
Professional dues	$ 500		
Educational expense	1,500		
Entertainment (300 − 20%)	240		
Annual meeting [1000 − 20%(200)]	960		
	$3,200		
Less 2% A.G.I.	1,200	2,000	3,400
Total itemized deductions			$21,245

Since this amount is well in excess of the standard deduction for a married couple filing jointly in 1987 ($3,760), the Andersons will obviously choose to deduct the total itemized amount of $21,245.

PROBLEMS

1. What common justification is given for permitting the deduction of both medical expenses and casualty losses?

2. How does the tax treatment of insurance premiums for health and hospitalization insurance compare with the tax treatment of insurance premiums for fire, theft, and other casualty insurance on nonincome producing assets (for example, a home)? Comment.

3. Under what circumstances, if any, would amounts paid by a taxpayer for costs of living in a retirement home or nursing home be deductible?

4. Two types of "floors" for determining the amount of involuntary costs (medical expenses and casualty losses, for example) deemed to be extraordinary or unusual

are discussed in this chapter. Compare the two, discussing their relative effects on taxpayers of different income levels.

5. What differences, if any, are found in measuring the deductible amount of a casualty loss on property held for personal use and property used in a trade or business?

6. Under what circumstances, if any, may the taxpayer treat the amount of a repair bill as a measure of loss from a casualty?

7. To what extent, if any, does the quality of medical care or its luxuriousness determine the extent to which it is deductible? For example, are different rules applied in determining deductibility of a bed in a hospital ward compared with one in a private room in an exclusive hospital? for contact lenses versus ordinary glasses?

8. What arguments can be given for removing the 7½% floor on medical costs?

9. What reasons may be given to justify the deduction of taxes on nonincome producing property (for example, on the taxpayer's home)?

10. Explain how the deduction for contributions may be considered a subsidy.

11. No interest deduction is allowed on loans made to carry an investment if the income from the investment is tax exempt, or on loans made to obtain a single-premium policy. Assume that this tax rule did not exist. Devise two schemes, one related to state or municipal bonds and one related to life insurance contracts, that would result in a financial windfall from the assumed loophole.

12. Once a taxpayer has purchased a home, he or she almost always has excess itemized deductions. Explain why this statement generally is accurate.

13. What was the purpose of the provision requiring capitalization of construction period interest and taxes? What change in these rules did the Tax Reform Act of 1986 make?

14. In 19x1, taxpayer deducted medical expenses of $1,400. In 19x2, she received a $1,200 reimbursement of the expenses incurred in 19x1. If the reimbursement had been received in 19x1, the taxpayer's deduction for medical expenses that year would have been $200. What part of the reimbursement in 19x2, if any, is treated as gross income to the taxpayer?

15. Which of the following items are deductible as medicine or medical costs?
    a. Aspirin
    b. Cost of dental plate
    c. Contact lenses
    d. Artificial limb
    e. Vitamins prescribed by doctor
    f. Transportation to and from doctor's office
    g. Health food purchased by vegetarian
    h. Bill for having teeth cleaned by dentist
    i. Annual trip to Arizona to give the sinuses a rest
    j. A legal abortion
    k. A wheelchair
    l. Repairs to the wheelchair
    m. Nonprescription antihistamines taken to combat allergies

16. Erv Single took out a medical insurance policy at a cost of $60 per month. Fortunately for Erv, he was not sick once during 19x1 and therefore incurred no medical expenses. What is his medical expense deduction for 19X1 if he earned $10,000 A.G.I.?

17. Marcus and Tania reported A.G.I. of $20,000 in a year in which they incurred the following medical expenses:

Dentist's charges	$ 450
Physician's charges	900
Hospital costs	1,800
Prescription drugs	180
Medical insurance premiums	700
Remodeling home to accommodate Tania's wheelchair	5,000

The insurance company reimbursed Marcus and Tania for $1,700 of their hospital bill and $800 of their physicians charges. What is their medical expense deduction for the year?

18. Ted Granger retired from Chicago to Miami, Florida, after 50 years of service with Bidwell Corporation. Each June, Ted flies back to Chicago for an annual physical examination by Dr. Knowbetter, a heart specialist who treated Ted 10 years ago. This annual physical requires approximately one week to complete. Between trips to the physician's office, Ted visits family and friends. The trip costs him $500 for transportation, $300 for a hotel ($50 per day), $140 for food, $200 for medical expenses, and $100 for incidentals. Which of these costs, if any, might Ted deduct? Explain your answer.

19. Mary, a college student, has for several years been concerned about her overbite and its impact on her personal appearance. She visited a local orthodontist, who suggested that she have her teeth realigned and straightened. Total cost of the work is expected to be $3,000. During the current year, Mary paid $1,400 to the orthodontist. What amount, if any, is treated as medical expense for this year? Explain.

20. Marie, unmarried, had a legal abortion at a cost of $1,500, which was paid directly to the doctor by John, who caused the pregnancy. What amount can Marie treat as medical costs? John?

21. John Beal, age 65, and wife, Miriam, age 39, filed a joint return for the current tax year showing an A.G.I. of $45,000. Mrs. Beal's son by a former marriage is now a full-time university student and is fully dependent on the Beals. The Beals also provide over 50% of the support of Mr. Beal's mother, who is 85 and bedridden. Grandmother Beal receives a $2,100 annual payment from a trust fund. Medical expenses in excess of reimbursements were paid by John and Miriam in the amounts stated below:

	John	Miriam	Son	Mother
Hospital insurance premium	$1,240	$ 0	$ 0	$ 0
Prescription drugs	150	350	10	400
Medical expenses	200	300	100	300
Nurse	0	0	0	5,200

Show your computation for the medical expense deduction that can be taken on Mr. and Mrs. Beal's joint tax return.

22. Last summer, Korioth, a local professor, suffered severe pains in his neck. His local physician advised Korioth that he needed a most serious and delicate operation, which only a few surgeons in the United States could perform. The recommended surgeon was at the Mayo Clinic in Rochester, Minnesota. Korioth flew to Minnesota for consultation with the surgeon. He spent $140 for transporta-

tion, $55 for hotel bills (one night), and $12 for food. The surgeon recommended that the operation be performed as quickly as possible, which was two weeks later because the surgeon was leaving the country on vacation. He further advised Korioth that Korioth's wife should accompany him to Minnesota to be there during the surgery, to care for Korioth in a hotel for two weeks after surgery, and to return with him on his trip home. Korioth and his wife dutifully followed the doctor's instructions. The round-trip plane fare was $340 for the two of them. The hotel room cost a total of $600. This bill included $40 per day for the two of them during the period before surgery (two days), $120 for Mrs. Korioth during the four days that Korioth was in the hospital, and $400 for the two of them for ten days after his dismissal from the hospital. Korioth's food costs outside the hospital were $150; Mrs. Korioth's food costs were $140. She spent $51 for taxi fares going to and from the hospital twice each day. Additionally, after Korioth's release, he spent $16 for taxi fares going to the hospital. What amount is deductible?

23. In each of the following cases, indicate the amount of casualty loss deductible and indicate how the loss would be handled on the income tax return. Assume there are no other casualties or thefts and that the taxpayer's A.G.I. is $14,000 in each case.

   a. Taxpayer was vacationing in Miami. While taxpayer was swimming, a thief stole his wristwatch (cost $220, with a fair market value of $180) and his billfold. The billfold contained $120 cash, which was not recovered. The billfold itself, with a value of $5, cost $10. Taxpayer was not insured.

   b. Berry owned a lake cabin with an adjusted basis of $16,000. On January 18, the cabin had a fair value of $14,000. On the next day, a tornado completely demolished the cabin, which was not insured. The cabin was held solely for personal use.

   c. Corona owned a frame building with an adjusted basis of $20,000. In July of this year, the building caught fire and was partially destroyed. The value just before the fire was $21,000 and just after the fire was $4,000. The building, which was not insured, was Corona's personal residence.

   d. Assume the same facts as is part c, except that insurance proceeds of $12,000 were received.

   e. Ishmael backed his car out of his garage into a neighbor's automobile. Ishmael's automobile suffered $600 damage. (Its basis was $3,500.) Damage suffered by the neighbor's automobile was $520, which Ishmael paid out of his own pocket because he carried no insurance of any kind.

   f. Maranto fell asleep at the wheel of her new BMW and drove off the road, causing extensive damage to the car. Repairs cost $5,500. As this was Maranto's third accident in five years, she chose not to make a claim against her insurance policy for fear of cancellation of the policy. Presumably, she could have collected all but the $100 deductible on the policy.

   g. Jackson's home was burglarized. The thief took Mrs. Jackson's jewelry, which had a fair market value of $1,800 and a basis of $1,200. He also took Jackson's watch, which had a fair value of $150 and a basis of $300. Jackson and his wife, who filed a joint return, were not insured.

   h. Assume the same facts as in part f, except that the Jacksons filed separate returns. Jackson's A.G.I. was $10,000; his wife's A.G.I. was $4,000.

   i. Karl owns an automobile used half for business and half for pleasure. The automobile had cost $8,800, and Karl had taken depreciation of $1,200 on the business portion. In August of this year he had an accident. At that time, the fair value of the auto was $4,400. Just after the accident the auto had a value of $3,000. Insurance proceeds of $1,240 were recovered.

    j. In the current year, Becker was in an auto accident. As a result he was sued by another individual in the accident and was required to pay "damages" of $16,000 to the other party.

24. Marcus owned a home. In his front yard he had a number of trees that he had set out 15 years ago. This year a high wind demolished all the trees. A man from the local tree service estimated the trees were worth $1,200, although Marcus had paid only $120 for them. Just before the wind, his home had an appraised value of $32,000 (cost, including trees, $20,200). Just after the wind, his home had an estimated value of $31,500. Marcus paid $160 to have the debris cleaned up. What is the amount of his casualty loss deduction, ignoring the 10% of A.G.I. "floor"?

25. A taxpayer was involved in a traffic accident and suffered substantial damage to his personal automobile (cost $4,000) and to himself. Because the accident was the taxpayer's fault, he ended up paying $500 for damages to the other party's automobile, $800 for medical expenses of the other party, and $200 to avoid a lawsuit. In addition, he paid $150 in medical bills for himself. His automobile had an estimated value before the accident of $2,700; after the accident it was valued at $2,000. The taxpayer received a $200 reimbursement for damage to his own automobile; all other costs were paid from his personal funds. What is this taxpayers deductible "casualty loss," assuming his A.G.I. is $5,000?

26. Which of the following taxes are deductible for federal income tax purposes?
    a. Gift tax
    b. FICA tax on business employees
    c. State gasoline (excise) tax on gasoline used in family auto
    d. Federal gasoline tax on gasoline used in family auto
    e. State income tax
    f. Property tax on family residence
    g. State excise tax on cigarettes for personal consumption
    h. State excise tax on liquor consumed while entertaining business clients
    i. State excise tax on liquor for private consumption
    j. Automobile license (your state) for family auto
    k. State general sales tax on goods purchased for private consumption

27. In each of the following independent cases, indicate the amount that the taxpayer may deduct as "taxes" on his or her federal income tax return. Indicate whether any amount deductible is *for* A.G.I. or *from* A.G.I.
    a. In July of this year, Atkins inherited some property from a deceased aunt. He paid a state inheritance tax of $1,200 on the inheritance.
    b. During the year, Bartholomew purchased various bottles of alcoholic beverages for personal use. The amount he paid for these beverages included $118 federal excise taxes, $32 state excise taxes, and $8 state retail sales tax.
    c. During the year, Irma paid the following real estate taxes on her home: state, $69; county, $64; city, $345; school district, $360. In addition, the city made a special assessment for paving the street and installing a curb and gutter in front of her home, $280.
    d. Farmer had the following expenditures for taxes during 19x2: payment of 19x1 state income tax, $84; quarterly estimates of his 19x2 federal income tax, $4,600; final payment of net amount due on 19x1 federal income tax return, $310.
    e. Goodman purchased real estate on May 1 of this year for $18,000. The estimated taxes for the year were prorated and the cash payment to the seller

was reduced by $80, the estimated taxes through April 30. In December, Goodman paid the real estate taxes due for the year, $272.

f. Homer operates a business. During the year, he remitted to the federal government $19,000 of income taxes withheld from employees' earnings. He also remitted $9,000 in FICA taxes, representing $4,500 deducted from employees' paychecks and Homer's matching contributions. Also, he paid $170 federal unemployment compensation taxes and $920 state unemployment compensation taxes on his employee's earnings.

g. Ironman operates a business. During the year, he imported jewelry for resale in the business, paying an import tariff of $980. In addition, he imported some furs for his wife's personal use, paying an import tariff of $230.

h. Stella operates a retail gift shop. During 19x1 she paid $720 of "self-employment" taxes on her net earnings for the previous year, 19x0. (Answer for 19x1.)

i. Collins purchased a $10,000 computer for use in his business. He paid state sales tax of $600 on the purchase of the computer.

28. In each of the following independent cases, indicate the amount that may be deducted as charitable contributions:

a. Adamson had A.G.I. of $22,000. During the year, he made the following cash contributions:

Boy Scouts	$3,000
Local church	6,000
Local university	4,200

b. Bartholomew had A.G.I. of $16,500. During the year, he made the following cash contributions:

Boy Scouts	$5,000
Democratic party	2,000
Needy family in neighborhood	400
London School of Economics (England)	800
Local Catholic hospital	1,000

c. Converse owns 1,000 shares of X Corporation stock for which she paid $10,000 in 1962. During the current year, she contributed 600 shares of this stock to the First Church of Centertown. On the date of the contribution, the shares had a market price of $25 per share. Converse's A.G.I. this year was $25,000.

d. Farley operates a retail furniture store as a sole proprietorship. In July of this year, he contributed to the local hospital a number of items of furniture from his merchandise inventory (tables, chairs, and sofas). These items had cost him $3,800 but had a normal retail value of $7,400. Farley's A.G.I. is $40,000.

e. Inglewood is active in the Boy Scouts. During the past year, he served as a scoutmaster. At year-end, he calculated that he had spent $80 for various scout activities such as fund-raising drives. In addition, he had driven his automobile an estimated 300 miles in connection with scout work. He also had lost 38 working hours from his job, with a loss in pay of $190.

f. Robb and three other adults traveled with a youth group from her church for a four-day ski trip in Colorado. Robb spent $150 for airfare; the church paid for her food and lodging while in Colorado.

29. Burns contributed to the local art museum a painting that she had purchased several years ago for her private collection at a cost of $1,500. At the time of the

gift, the painting was appraised at a value of $5,000. She also made cash gifts this year of $6,000 to various charities. Her A.G.I. for the year is $80,000, and she itemizes deductions. Determine her total charitable contributions deduction for the year under the following two assumptions:

a. The museum intends to hang the painting in its permanent collection.

b. The museum intends to sell the painting.

30. What amount may the taxpayer deduct as "contributions" in each of the following cases?

a. Jacques purchased five tickets from the Boy Scouts. These tickets were to a local benefit performance of the city symphony, with all proceeds going to the Scouts. Normal cost of these tickets would have been $2.50 each, but because they were for a benefit, they cost $5 each. Jacques and his family attended the performance, using all five tickets.

b. Assume the same facts as in part a, except that Jacques purchased the tickets as a purely charitable gesture with the intent of throwing them away—and he did so.

31. Alpha Corporation earned $30,000 taxable income, excluding its contribution deduction, its dividends-received deduction, and any net operating loss carry-backs. What is the maximum charitable contributions deduction that Alpha Corporation can claim in the current year?

32. a. In 19x1, a severe tornado struck Midtown. Martha, the sole proprietor of a retail drugstore, answered the call for help by contributing medicines, drugs, bandages, and other items to the local Red Cross to be used in treating the sick and wounded. The items cost Martha $800 and had a fair value of $1,400. What is the amount of Martha's "contribution"?

b. Assume the same facts as in part a, except that the taxpayer was a corporation instead of Martha. What is the amount of the "contribution"?

33. In 19x1, the Saver family decided to dispose of unused clothing in a garage sale. To their surprise, the Savers found they had apparently discarded almost none of their old clothes through the years. They found dresses, pants, shirts, coats, and other items quickly outgrown by their children, relatively unused clothing of Ms. Saver, made obsolete by style changes, and many usable suits discarded by Mr. Saver because of the dress requirements of his job as attorney. Proceeds from the two-day sale were $180, but over half the clothes were unsold. In fact, the price tags on the unsold clothes totaled $210, which represented about 15% of the original cost. The Savers contributed the unsold items to the Salvation Army. Mr. Saver is obviously interested in the possibility of a tax deduction for the contribution. Advise him.

34. Giver contributed to two "funds" during the year, giving $100 to the City United Fund Drive and $20 to the Office Remembrance Fund where she is employed. The Remembrance Fund is used to buy flowers for employees who are ill, die, or get married. It is also used to buy Christmas presents for custodial workers and for similar purposes. What part, if any, of these contributions can Giver deduct on her tax return for the year?

35. In each of the following independent cases, indicate the amount that the taxpayer may deduct as interest on his or her federal income tax return:

a. Alexander paid interest of $2,100 on a loan secured to purchase City of Midville bonds on which he received interest of $2,800.

b. Elmot made the following interest payments during the year: $60 on a loan obtained to buy his wife some jewelry on their 25th wedding anniversary; $670 on his home mortgage; $45 on a loan obtained at the bank by his dependent 23-year-old son (Elmot also paid the loan principal to protect the family name even though he had no legal liability for the note or interest); $48 to the life insurance company on the loan value of his policy withdrawn to pay for his daughter's high school graduation present; and $92 on amounts owed on gambling debts.

c. Eileen is a majority stockholder in Town Corporation. In 19x1, Town suffered a financial reverse. To protect the corporation's good name, Eileen paid $6,000 of interest owed by the corporation to a local bank.

d. Cox paid $50,000 for his home ten years ago. Today, it is worth $100,000, and the balance due on his original mortgage is only $30,000. Cox recently borrowed $25,000 on a "home equity mortgage," using the proceeds to buy a new car and travel to Europe. This year, interest payments on the original mortgage were $2,400, while interest payments on the home equity mortgage were $2,500.

e. Assume the same facts as in d, except that Cox used the $25,000 to help pay tuition for his twin daughters, both of whom are in medical school.

36. In the current year, Lemon and his wife filed a joint return showing adjusted gross income of $80,000. Included in their tax information were the following items:

Interest paid on funds borrowed last year to purchase stock and bonds	$48,000
Investment income	12,000
Investment-related expenses	800
Interest paid on home mortgage	6,200
Interest on personal loans	3,500

Compute the Lemons's interest deduction for the year.

37. Arno Grey has lived in New Orleans for five years working in an electrical manufacturing plant. In August of last year, he moved to St. Louis to take a new job and was still employed there at year-end. A review of Grey's records revealed the following facts related to his move and new job.

In June, Grey decided that he was tired of the hot weather in New Orleans, so he read the classified ads in the local newspaper and found a help-wanted ad by the St. Louis employer. He wrote the St. Louis company and was told that all applicants must appear in person at the company's home office, but that the company could not pay his travel costs for an interview. Grey went to St. Louis in early July for the interview. Cost of the plane ticket was $260, and he paid $20 for limousine service to and from airports. He arrived in St. Louis on Sunday evening, spent the night, and visited the company on Monday morning. He was immediately hired and planned to return to New Orleans on Monday evening. However, the employer suggested that Grey find a place to live. He therefore spent Tuesday and Wednesday looking at apartments and houses, spending $30 for taxi fares and telephone calls. Finding no suitable apartment, he purchased a house for $104,000. Grey's hotel room was $68 per night, and he spent $28 each day for food (Monday, Tuesday, and Wednesday). He returned to New Orleans on Wednesday evening.

Grey sold his home in New Orleans for $48,000 (it had cost him $19,000) but had to pay a real estate commission of $2,880 on the sale. Other selling costs included an abstract fee of $120 and legal fees of $105.

Grey shipped most of his furniture by truck, at a cost of $1,820, but he also rented a trailer for $98 and moved some himself. He and his family drove to St.

Louis, spending $52 for meals and $64 for one night in a motel. He spent $84 for gasoline and $1.20 for oil on the trip. On arriving in St. Louis, Grey was shocked to find that the former owner of his house had not moved out, so Grey and his family had to live in a hotel for 18 days. Their costs while living there totaled $900 for room and $808 for meals. In addition, Grey paid $96 to have his furniture stored, and another $157 to have it delivered when he got possession of the house. Determine Grey's moving expense deduction.

38. This year David and Susan Martin had adjusted gross income of $50,000. They also incurred the following unreimbursed expenses:

Medical expenses	$ 900
Interest on home mortgage	7,200
Interest on auto loan	150
Uninsured theft loss from burglary	3,000
Charitable contributions	900
State sales tax	300
Property tax on home	1,700
Moving expenses (Houston to Omaha)	2,000
Cost of attending professional meeting (including $100 for meals)	300
Tax return preparation fee	100
Union dues	150
Education costs related to Susan's job (tuition and transportation)	800

Determine the Martin's itemized deductions.

SUPPLEMENTAL PROBLEMS

39. If a taxpayer builds an indoor swimming pool at a cost of $194,660 "to prevent paralysis from . . . a spinal injury," what part of that cost do you think that taxpayer might deduct as a medical expense? After you have made a guess, read and prepare a short report on *Ferris* v. *Commissioner,* 582 F.2d 1112 (CA-7, 1979) *rem'dg* TC Memo 1977-186.

40. Taxpayer provided $600 per month during 19x1 toward the cost of maintaining his mother in the Sunshine Nursing Home. The Home was chosen primarily because it had a physician and nurse on duty at all times. Taxpayer's mother had a series of heart attacks in recent years, and although her situation was not critical and she was not confined to her bed, the taxpayer felt it necessary to have immediately available medical care for her. In addition to the $7,200 provided by taxpayer, the mother also received $3,600 from Social Security benefits and $2,000 from a fully taxable pension during 19x1, all of which was used for the mother's living costs. What part, if any, of the $7,200 will the taxpayer be allowed to treat as medical expenses on his 19x1 tax return?

41. In 19x1, Jones had A.G.I. of $30,000. He made the following contributions during the year:
    (1) Cash of $5,000 to his church.
    (2) Shares of stock that cost him $10,000 in 1960 to Stanford University. Fair market value at date of gift was $12,000.
    (3) A painting that cost him $3,000 in 1950 to a local hospital. Fair value at the date of the gift was $7,000. The hospital immediately sold the painting.

    a. What amount may Jones deduct as a contribution in 19x1?

    b. What amount, if any, does Jones carry forward to 19x2?

42. The following data are given for Mayday Corporation:

Gross profit on sales	$200,000
Dividend income from nonaffiliated domestic corporations	5,000
Operating loss carryover from prior years	1,000
Operating expenses (exclusive of charitable contributions)	102,000
Charitable contributions	12,250

What is Mayday's taxable income?

CHAPTER 11

The Individual Tax Computation

The art of taxation consists in so plucking the goose as to obtain the largest amount of feathers with the least amount of hissing.
Jean Baptist Colbert, French Financial Minister under King Louis XIV (1638–1715)

The previous chapters in Part Three explain the individual's tax formula except for the exemption deduction, the actual calculation of the tax, tax credits, and prepayments. The current chapter treats these topics, beginning with the exemption deduction. The chapter concludes with rules covering payment of the tax.

DEDUCTION FOR PERSONAL EXEMPTIONS

The deduction for personal exemptions is the product of the number of exemptions allowed on a return times the exemption amount. The amount is an arbitrary figure decided on by Congress. It was $1,000 (adjusted for inflation) for many years prior to 1987. Under the 1986 Act, the exemption amount is: 1987, $1,900; 1988, $1,950; 1989 and later years, $2,000. After 1989 the $2,000 amount will again be adjusted for inflation. Determining the number of exemptions allowed on a return is the complicated part.

Exemptions for Taxpayers

One exemption is allowed for the taxpayer on each return. With one exception, then, each return has one exemption deduction equal to the correct exemption amount. The exception occurs when a taxpayer on one return is claimed as a dependent on another return. In such a case, no exemption deduction is allowed. Instead, the dependent is entitled to a standard deduction of at least $500, as explained in Chater 9. The usual instance is a child (under 19 or a full-time student) claimed as an exemption by the parents.

As explained later, a married couple usually files a joint return. When a joint return is used, both spouses are considered to be "taxpayers," and each is entitled to one exemption. Thus, there is always a minimum of two personal exemptions on the joint return. If only one spouse files a return, that spouse may claim an exemption for the other spouse only if the latter has no gross income and is not claimed as a dependent of another taxpayer. Obviously, if spouses file separate returns, neither may take an exemption for the other.

Prior to the 1986 Act, the law allowed extra exemptions for blind taxpayers and taxpayers 65 and older. This long-standing relief measure for such taxpayers was scrapped by Congress to raise a few additional dollars of revenue in the "Grand Reform." Now, the standard deduction for these taxpayers has been increased (see Chapter 9).

In addition to one exemption for the taxpayer and one exemption for the taxpayer's spouse, in some cases the taxpayer is entitled to one exemption for each individual who qualifies as the taxpayer's dependent.

Exemptions for Dependents

The rules governing exemption deductions for dependents are much more complex and difficult to interpret and apply than those relating to exemptions for the taxpayer and spouse. As a result, there have been many controversies on this point between taxpayers and the I.R.S., and numerous court decisions involving dependency exemptions have been reported. Although subject to many exceptions and special interpretations, five basic requirements must be satisfied for the taxpayer to claim an exemption for a "dependent":

1. The dependent must *not* be a nonresident alien.
2. The dependent, if married, must not file a joint return with his or her spouse. (However, if the dependent and spouse are not required to file a return, but do so merely to get a refund of taxes withheld, a joint return is allowed.)
3. A specified "relationship" must exist between the taxpayer and the dependent.
4. The taxpayer must provide over one half of the dependent's support for the year.
5. The dependent must have gross income of less than the amount of an exemption for the year.

The first two requirements need no interpretation. The last three, however, require further explanation and elaboration.

THE RELATIONSHIP TEST   The Internal Revenue Code generally provides that the dependent must be a *relative* of the taxpayer and delimits the necessary relationship as follows:

(1) A son or daughter of the taxpayer, or a descendant of either,
(2) A stepson or stepdaughter of the taxpayer,
(3) A brother, sister, stepbrother, or stepsister of the taxpayer,
(4) The father or mother of the taxpayer, or an ancestor of either,
(5) A stepfather or stepmother of the taxpayer,
(6) A son or daughter of a brother or sister of the taxpayer,
(7) A brother or sister of the father or mother of the taxpayer,
(8) A son-in-law, daughter-in-law, father-in-law, mother-in-law, brother-in-law, or sister-in-law of the taxpayer.[1]

When a joint return is filed, the relationship test is met if the person claimed as a dependent is a qualified relative of either spouse. Even after termination of a marriage, a relationship established by the marriage is continued for tax purposes. Finally, an adopted child is treated as a natural child for dependency purposes.

The law also provides for the taxpayer to claim an exemption for an individual who *resides* in the taxpayer's home throughout a tax year, even though not a relative as specified above.

(9) An individual (other than an individual who at any time during the taxable year was the spouse, determined without regard to section 153, of the taxpayer) who, for the taxable year of the taxpayer, has as his principal place of abode the home of the taxpayer and is a member of the taxpayer's household. . . .[2]

This provision of the law permits dependency exemptions for persons—such as foster children not legally adopted or foster parents—who do not meet the relationship test in (1) through (8). Foster children who pass the residence test are treated in all respects as though they are blood relatives of the taxpayer.

This provision does not apply if the relationship with the taxpayer is contrary to local law. For example, if state law prohibits common-law marriage, no exemption can be claimed for the taxpayer's consort. Children born into such an arrangement, however, can be dependents.

THE SUPPORT TEST   The taxpayer must provide over one-half the dollar value of the dependent's support during the calendar year (or that part of the year that the dependent was alive). Support includes all expenditures for such items as food, clothing, shelter, medical care, education, and child care. A scholarship received by a student who is the taxpayer's child is not counted as part of the total support in determining whether the taxpayer provided more than half the student's support. Recall from Chapter 8 that the 1986 Act limits the exclusion for scholarships to the amount spent for tuition, books, and

[1]Sec. 152(a)(1)–(8).
[2]Sec. 152(a)(9).

incidentals, making scholarships that cover room and board subject to the tax. For purposes of the support test, however, the entire amount of the grant is excluded from the calculation of support.

The major exception to the support test occurs when two or more persons furnish a dependent's support but no one taxpayer provides over half the support. In this event, any one of the taxpayers who provides over 10% of the dependent's support and who satisfies the relationship test may claim the exemption if every person who provides more than 10% of the dependent's support during the year, and who satisfies the relationship test, signs a multiple support statement agreeing *not* to claim an exemption for the dependent. For example, if each of four brothers provides 25% of his father's support, any one of the four may claim the father as a dependent for the year provided the other three sign a multiple support agreement.

If both divorced parents contribute support for their child or children, the parent who has custody for the major part of the calendar year is generally presumed to have provided more than 50% of the support. These rules may also apply to parents who simply live apart for the last six months of the year. The parent without custody can take the exemption deduction if the custodial parent signs an agreement that such parent will not take the exemption.

THE GROSS INCOME TEST   Section 151(c) provides that generally the dependent's gross income must be less than the amount of an exemption allowance for that year ($2,000 after 1988) for the taxpayer to claim an exemption for him or her. This rule does not apply to a taxpayer's child, or qualified foster child, who is either a full-time student or under age 19 at year-end. Generally, a student is defined as one who during each of any five months of the calendar year was in full-time attendance at an educational institution or took a full-time, on-farm training course during any five months of the year. The taxpayer's child who is either a student or under 19 and has sufficient gross income must, of course, file a tax return.

This exception to the gross income test usually means that the parent is entitled to a dependency exemption if the parent meets the support test. If the parent claims an exemption for the child, you will remember, the child is not entitled to an exemption deduction.

The exemption for the taxpayer, plus one for the spouse—where appropriate—plus one for each dependent, *times* the exemption amount gives the exemption deduction. Itemized deductions (or the standard deduction, if larger) are subtracted from adjusted gross income, along with the exemption deduction amount, to obtain taxable income. The tax rates, based on the individual's family status, are applied to the taxable income to determine the gross tax liability.

THE INDIVIDUAL RATE SCHEDULES

The original selection of the individual as a basic taxpaying entity was virtually dictated by the property laws in this country. Excepting corporations, most property is owned by individuals, and the income from property benefits individuals. Similarly, only individuals are employed and earn income. Most personal income, however, is not used or consumed solely by the individual with the legal right to it. Instead, it goes into the family "coffers" and is used by the family. From 1913 to the present, Congress has made an effort to give consideration to the family situation in levying the tax.

When Congress wrote the first law, its concept of the taxpayer was a mature male adult, the head of a family and its principal wage earner. The original law provided for a basic family exemption that would leave "untouched" income sufficient to "rear and support" a family according to "a proper standard of living."[3] The original exemption was very high relative to the average family income of the period, and most personal income was therefore not subject to tax prior to World War II. At that time, however, Congress lowered the exemptions, ostensibly to finance the war but primarily in fact to control inflation. Exemptions remained at the lower levels after the war for the same purpose. As a result, the income tax that affected only 4% of the population in the boom year 1929 affected 70% of the population in the middle 1950s.

Between World War II and 1969, Congress resisted all efforts to increase exemptions. Beginning with the Tax Reform Act of 1969, as well as in later amendments, the exemptions were increased, as was the standard deduction. These changes reaffirm the original policy of taxing the family as the basic taxable unit.

In the period immediately following World War II, changes in rates were made to reduce the tax on family units and to recognize the special circumstances of widows, widowers, and other unmarried individuals who maintain homes for relatives. In dealing with the problem of rates, Congress settled on a "normal" progression of events for most citizens. First, single individuals with no direct family responsibilities use Rate Schedule X, which results in the highest tax.[4] Next comes marriage and a family, and the husband and wife file jointly and generally enjoy the lowest rates on Schedule Y—Joint. If one spouse dies before the children are fully grown, the surviving spouse still enjoys low joint return rates for a two-year period. After the two-year period, the surviving spouse who still maintains a residence for his or her children is a head of household and enjoys approximately 50% of the benefits available from the joint return rates by using Schedule Z. Finally, after all family responsibilities are met, and assuming no remarriage, the taxpayer is again "single" and subject to the highest rates.

This simple scheme of things is, of course, subject to many exceptions. In addition, Congress did not develop the scheme and then enact the law as it now exists. As is often true, Congress rather wandered into the current framework over a period of years. Indeed, the first step, the joint return provisions, was passed to avoid a problem arising from state property laws.

---

[3]Everett M. Kassalow, "To Restore Balance and Equity in Family Income Taxation," *1959 Compendium*, p. 515, deals with the development of this doctrine.

[4]Actually, the rates on Schedule Y—Separate result in the highest tax. However, this is a historical accident.

Joint Returns and Surviving Spouses

Prior to 1948, the law contained only one rate schedule for all individuals. Married individuals residing in the eight states with community-property laws (Arizona, California, Idaho, Louisiana, Nevada, New Mexico, Texas, and Washington) enjoyed a definite advantage as a result. They could combine their incomes and split them equally on two returns. Because of the progressive rates, the tax on one half of the family income paid twice on two returns was substantially less than the tax levied on that same amount of income on a single return, usually the husband's, in a common-law state. Splitting the income in community-property states, in other words, lowered the marginal rates applicable to the income. After World War II, other states began to adopt community-property rules to obtain the same advantage for their citizens, and, as a result, Congress adopted a "joint" return rule in 1948 giving the "split" income advantage to citizens in common-law states.

As originally conceived, a joint return resulted in the same tax as would result by combining the income of the husband and wife, dividing it in half, computing a tax on that half using the basic rate schedule, and then doubling that amount. Over the years, as Congress added other rate schedules, this basic objective is no longer evident, though the taxes obtained from using Schedule Y—Joint are still lower than the other schedules. (Refer to Appendix A.) For years after 1987, the rate rises to 28% at $29,750 on joint returns, compared to $17,850 for single individuals and $23,900 for heads of households.[5]

The statute provides criteria that must be met before a taxpayer may use the joint return. Two taxpayers may file a joint return if

1. They are married (not divorced or legally separated) on the last day of their taxable year or they were married at the date of death of one spouse during the taxable year
2. Neither spouse is a nonresident alien at any time during the year unless an irrevocable election is made to include the worldwide income of both husband and wife on the return

Note that a joint return is permitted for the tax year within which one spouse dies, provided the survivor does not remarry before year-end.

In 1954, Congress recognized that the death of a spouse often causes economic hardship, especially if children are in the home, and extended the benefits of income splitting by permitting the surviving spouse to use Schedule Y—Joint in the two years following the tax year in which the spouse dies, provided the surviving spouse has a dependent child or stepchild who lives with the taxpayer in the home. Of course, an exemption for the deceased spouse is not available on the surviving spouse's return during those two years. The special status of surviving spouse automatically terminates after

---

[5]Rates applicable to 1987 only appear in Appendix B. These schedules resemble the schedules in effect for 1986 and later years and are not discussed here. See Chapters 3 and 7 for comparisons.

the two-year period, by remarriage during the period, or by the loss of the dependency status of the child or stepchild.

For example, suppose that in 19x1 taxpayer's wife died, leaving a 14-year-old child who qualifies as the survivor's dependent. In the year of death, the survivor is entitled to file a joint return and claim three exemptions (one each for taxpayer, deceased spouse, and dependent child). If the child continues to live in the taxpayer's home and to qualify as a dependent, the taxpayer may use Schedule Y—Joint in 19x2 and 19x3, as well, but is entitled to only two exemptions (one for the taxpayer and one for the dependent child) in those two years.

Head of Household

By extending the joint return privilege to married taxpayers only, Congress ignored widows and widowers, as well as other individuals who are responsible for rearing children or maintaining a home for dependents. The increase in tax rates (above even the levels of World War II) occasioned by the Korean conflict and the attendant inflationary pressures magnified the conflict in Congress over income splitting. In 1951, Congress was asked to extend the benefits of income splitting to all family units, and their compromise was the creation of Rate Schedule Z for taxpayers who meet the statutory tests for head of household. This schedule gives the qualified taxpayers approximately 50% of the tax savings available from income splitting.

The major requirements for using the head-of-household rate schedule are:

1. At the end of the tax year, the taxpayer cannot be classified as a married taxpayer or as a surviving spouse. (However, as discussed later in this section, certain married persons living apart may use the head-of-household rate schedule. In addition, in certain circumstances a taxpayer married to a nonresident alien may qualify.)
2. The taxpayer must maintain a home that, for more than one half of the year, is the principal place of abode of a dependent of the taxpayer. If the taxpayer maintains a home for a child or other direct descendent, such person need not be a dependent if the descendent is unmarried. If the descendent is married he or she must qualify as a dependent. "Child" includes stepchild and adopted child for this purpose (but not foster child). If the taxpayer supports his parents and maintains the parents' home, the taxpayer need not live in the same residence.
3. The taxpayer must pay more than 50% of the cost of maintaining the home.
4. The taxpayer must be a U.S. citizen or resident alien.

As mentioned previously, the head-of-household rates may also be used by a married person who meets certain special tests. These requirements are:

1. The taxpayer must file a separate return.
2. The taxpayer must maintain a home that for one half of the taxable year is the principal place of abode of a dependent child or stepchild for whom the taxpayer is entitled to a dependency exemption.

3. The taxpayer must furnish more than half the cost of maintaining the home.

4. The taxpayer's spouse must not live in the household during the last half of the taxable year.

This provision is apparently designed to provide a tax break for "abandoned" spouses but is broad enough to include other married persons who simply choose to live apart but for some reason do not wish to file a joint return.

To illustrate application of the head-of-household requirement, let us return to the facts previously given in which taxpayer's spouse died in 19x1, leaving a dependent child who resides in the taxpayer's home. In 19x1 the taxpayer files a joint return with the decedent, and in 19x2 and 19x3 taxpayer filed as a surviving spouse but was not entitled to an exemption for the deceased spouse. In 19x4 and later years, the taxpayer may use the head-of-household rate schedule if the child continues to reside in the household and taxpayer provides more than one half of the cost of maintaining the household. Even though the child may not qualify as taxpayer's dependent, taxpayer may still file as head of household unless the child is married.

The Single Individual

Married taxpayers enjoy the benefits of income splitting in all situations. The privilege is not affected by the level of income or by the number of family members. For this reason some unmarried taxpayers have claimed that the joint return rates are inequitable. In the upper-middle and upper income brackets, only a minimal sacrifice is required to raise a family of average size. Certainly it can be argued that a married man with no children who earns a salary of $100,000 a year is just as *able* to pay the income tax as a bachelor with the same income. We might argue that the bachelor's expenses are perhaps higher than the incremental amount spent by a married man as a result of being married.

The happily *unmarried* group finally got the ear of Congress in 1969, possibly because their numbers have increased in recent years but probably because of an organized lobby. For years after 1970, single individuals who are not heads of households use Rate Schedule X (shown in Appendix A). Note that taxes obtained from Schedule X are still lower than those from Schedule Y—Separate, the schedule that gives the highest tax. Note that the rate rises to 28% at $27,850 on Schedule X, as compared to $14,875 on Schedule Y—Separate. This slight difference is all that is left of the singles' lobbying efforts for lower taxes.

Because of the differences just noted, however, two single individuals with approximately equal incomes pay a lower tax than a married couple in comparable circumstances. To illustrate, assume that for 1988 M and F, two individuals, each have taxable income of $30,000. Each would pay a tax of:

On $17,850 at 15%	$2,677.50
On excess ($30,000 − $17,850) at 28%	3,402.00
	$6,079.50

Combined, M and F would pay a tax of $12,159 on their combined taxable income of $60,000. If M and F were married and filed a joint return, their tax for 1988 would be (assuming the taxable income on the joint return were $60,000):

On $29,750 at 15%	$4,462.50
On Excess ($60,000 − $29,750) at 28%	8,470.00
	$12,932.50[6]

M and F's taxes would increase by $774 ($12,933 − $12,159) as a result of marriage. Is this penalty enough to discourage the regularization of cohabitation through marriage? For a few really greedy people, perhaps. The penalty will not apply, and, instead, a benefit will result from the use of Schedule Y—Joint if the income belongs primarily to one of the partners.

Married Individuals Filing Separately

The law provides that married individuals may file separate returns. Only under most unusual circumstances do separate returns result in a lower tax, because Congress has taken great pains to close possible loopholes. Note that on separate returns the standard deduction is half the amount for joint returns. In a similar manner, most other possible advantages are eliminated by the statute. For the most part, married individuals filing separate returns do so because of marital or financial disagreements that have not yet reached the point of divorce or legal separation. On a joint return, both spouses are jointly and severally liable for the *combined* tax, a legal obligation that one spouse may be unwilling to assume even if it results in a lower tax on his or her own income.

Unearned Income of Minor Children

For years after 1986, a special rate schedule exists for children under 14 years of age who have net unearned income. The law now taxes such net unearned income of these young people using the highest marginal rate of the child's parents (of the custodial parent in the case of divorce or separation). Congress adopted this rule to curtail the shifting of income to family members to obtain lower marginal rates (15% after 1987). Wealthy parents have traditionally transferred income-producing properties—such as stocks, bonds, savings accounts—to children and grandchildren to reduce total family taxes.

Net unearned income is the child's gross unearned income—for example, interest, dividends, and so on—less $1,000. (The $1,000 is increased in the unlikely event that the child's itemized deductions directly connected with the production of the *unearned* income exceed $500.) The net unearned income cannot, of course, exceed the child's taxable income, and any taxable income

---

[6]The same tax would result if M and F filed separate returns and used the required Rate Schedule Y—Separate.

that the child has in excess of net unearned income is taxed at the child's rate—15% up to $17,850.

To illustrate, assume that a 12-year-old has interest income of $4,000 and $1,500 of income earned by delivering a paper route. He is supported entirely by his parents who claim him as an exemption. The parents file a joint return, with taxable income of $40,000. The child's taxable income is as follows:

Gross income (and A.G.I.) ($1,500 + $4,000)	$5,500
Less: standard deduction (limited to earned income)	1,500
Taxable income	$4,000

(Note that no exemption deduction is allowed in these circumstances.) Net unearned income is:

Unearned income	$4,000
Less arbitrary deduction allowed	1,000
Net unearned income (taxed at parents' rate)	3,000

Tax is:

Parent's rate (28% × $3,000)	$840
Child's rate on remainder [$4,000 − $3,000) × 15%]	150
Total tax	$990

Without this special schedule, this child would owe a tax of only $600 ($4,000 × 15%). Computation of the tax is more complicated when more than one child of a parent has unearned income and more than one marginal rate applies to the net unearned income.

This new schedule is effective after 1986 and can have a retroactive effect. Unearned income arising from gifts made to the child before 1987 is subject to the rule just as income from gifts after 1986.

Phaseout of 15% Rate and Exemptions

Refer to the rate schedules in Appendix B showing the individual rates applicable to 1988 and later years. The next-to-last bracket has a variable upper limit depending on the number of exemptions. We explained in Chapter 8 that the benefit of the exemption deductions are phased out as taxable income increases. Figure 11-1 is a 1988 rate schedule for a single individual that shows these phaseouts.

For single individuals, the benefit of the 15% rate is phased out at a 5% rate as taxable income rises from $43,150 to $89,560. Note that the area from 28% to 33% over that range of income is $2,320.50, which is same as the area from 15% to 28% over taxable income of $17,850.

In 1988, the exemption amount is $1,950, and, at a rate of 28%, each exemption in 1988 has a benefit of $546. This benefit is also phased out at 5%

FIGURE 11-1   1988 Rate Schedule for Single Individual with One Exemption

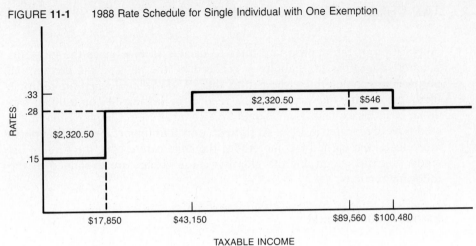

SOURCE: Internal Revenue Code of 1986, Sec. 1(c) and (g).

over taxable income of $10,920 ($546 ÷ 5%). In Figure 11-1, the distance from $89,560 to $100,480 is $10,920, and a 5% surtax (from 28% to 33%) on that distance gives a tax of $546. (In 1989, the exemption amount is $2,000, and $11,200 will be added to the rate schedules for each exemption.) For a single individual with one exemption, the rate returns to 28% at $100,480.

After the schedules in Appendix A are adjusted for the number of exemptions, the tax computation is simple. For a single individual with one exemption and taxable income of $95,000 in 1988, the tax is:

On $43,150	$ 9,761.40
On ($95,000 − $43,150) × .33	17,110.50
Tax on $95,000	$26,871.00

For a single taxpayer whose taxable income in 1988 is at least $100,480, the tax can be obtained from the schedule or by applying a flat rate of 28%. If the flat 28% is used you must first add back to taxable income the exemption deduction. For a single taxpayer with one exemption in 1988 and taxable income of $110,000, the tax is 28% of $111,950, or $31,346.

Before leaving this discussion of the rate schedules, note that for years after 1987 when the new rates become effective the difference between the schedules will be much less than in the past. Under the new format, everyone with sufficiently high income eventually pays a 28% marginal and average rate (excluding exemptions). On the pre-1988 schedules, the tax savings from using a favorable schedule—for example, Schedule Y—Joint—were substantial and were not phased out at higher incomes. The differences now between the schedules are the thresholds for going to the 28% and the 33% rates. Perhaps Congress should simplify this part of the law now by dropping these distinctions and by returning to one schedule that applies to all individuals.

TAX CREDITS FOR INDIVIDUALS

Application of the appropriate rates to taxable income gives the gross tax liability. The gross tax liability is reduced by the allowed tax credits and prepayments to determine the net tax that should be paid when the return is filed. Tax credits, like prepayments, reduce the tax liability on a dollar-for-dollar basis, as explained in Chapter 7. Also recall from Chapter 7 that many credits were repealed in 1986. At present, only four important credits apply to individuals: the earned income credit, the child-care credit, the foreign tax credit, and the credit for the elderly. These credits are explained in the following sections.

Earned Income Credit

Added to the tax law in 1975, the earned income credit contains many characteristics of a negative income tax. Congress had several objectives in mind when adding the credit, and they are reflected in the technical aspects of this provision (Sec. 32). To qualify for the earned income credit, a taxpayer must maintain a household in the United States that is the principal place of abode of the taxpayer and the taxpayer's dependent child. The credit is only available to married taxpayers and to taxpayers qualified to file either as a surviving spouse or a head of household. If the taxpayer is a head of household, an unmarried child living with the taxpayer does not have to qualify as the taxpayer's dependent, although a married child does have to qualify as the taxpayer's dependent. The credit is based on earned income, defined as salaries, wages, other employee compensation, and earnings from self-employment. Unlike the other personal credits, the earned income credit is refundable. If this credit (plus any prepayments) exceeds the gross tax liability, the taxpayer gets a refund.

For years after 1986, the basic credit is 14% of the qualified individual's earned income up to $5,714, giving a maximum credit of $800 ($5,714 × .14). To accomplish the limited objective of providing relief for low-income families that work, the credit is phased out at the rate of 10% of adjusted gross income, or earned income if greater, above $9,000. Thus, a taxpayer with A.G.I. or earned income of $17,000 or more has no credit. (For the year 1987, the phaseout is from $6,500 to $14,500.) Since the phaseout is based on the larger of earned income or A.G.I., the credit is reduced or even eliminated by unearned income such as dividends, interest, and gains. To illustrate, imagine a qualified taxpayer in 1988 with salary income of $10,000, interest income of $1,000, and no deductions for A.G.I. The basic credit is $800, 14% of $5,714. This credit is reduced by 10% of the $2,000 excess of the $11,000 A.G.I. over $9,000, giving a credit of $600. The actual amount of the credit must be determined from a table provided by the I.R.S. (The table for 1987 was not available at publication date.)

Obviously, the earned income credit is designed to benefit low-income taxpayers. It was passed specifically to offset partially the rapidly growing impact of Social Security taxes. As noted previously, the real significance of this credit is that it provided, for the first time in this country, a form of "negative income tax." It differs from a true negative income tax in that the credit increases as the taxpayer's earned income increases, and the taxpayer with no earned income would receive no credit. Most proposals for a negative income tax provide a larger "subsidy" as income decreases. However, one intent of the earned income credit is to encourage individuals to obtain employment. Presumably, Congress felt that the credit would effectively increase the wage rate for low-income taxpayers, thus providing added incentive to work.

Credit for Child-Care Expenses

A taxpayer who seeks gainful employment outside the home must often incur substantial expenses for the care of children and other dependents incapable of self-care. Such expenses are especially common when young parents both work outside the home. Congress included in the law the credit for child care to mitigate the hardship. The credit also works as an incentive to encourage the proper care of children during the working day.

While the credit commonly applies to working parents of children under 15, the credit is also available for a spouse or a dependent who is physically or mentally incapable of self-care, without regard to age. The important provisions of the current law are as follows:

1. The credit is allowed on certain employment-related expenses paid during the taxable year to enable the taxpayer to work either full- or part-time as an employee or as a self-employed individual.

2. The credit is 30% of qualified expenses up to $2,400 for one qualifying individual, or $4,800 for two or more qualifying individuals. Thus, the maximum credit is $720 when there is one qualifying individual or $1,440 when there are two or more qualifying individuals. However, the basic 30% rate decreases by 1 percentage point for each $2,000 increment (or part thereof) of adjusted gross income in excess of $10,000. The rate is never reduced below 20%. To illustrate, let us assume that taxpayers A, B, and C pay $3,000 each for child-care expenses, and each has one qualifying dependent. A's adjusted gross income is $9,000; A is therefore entitled to a credit of $720 (30% of $2,400). B's adjusted gross income is $17,000; B's credit is $624 (26% of $2,400). C's adjusted gross income is $35,000; C's credit is $480 (20% of $2,400).

3. The expenses on which a credit may be based are those for care of, or housekeeping related to, a member of the taxpayer's household who (1) is a dependent under 15 years of age, (2) is a person physically or mentally incapable of self-care, and for whom the taxpayer is entitled to claim a dependency exemption (or would be entitled to claim a dependency exemption except that the person has gross income of $1,950 or more in 1988), or (3) is the taxpayer's spouse who is physically or mentally incapable of self-care.

4. Qualified expenses can be for care outside the taxpayer's residence if the qualifying dependent is (1) under age 15 or (2) another qualifying individual

who regularly spends at least eight hours each day in the taxpayer's household. (The taxpayer would still have to maintain a residence for the qualifying individual.) Payments for food, clothing, and education do not qualify. However, if the care provided includes expenses that cannot be separated, the full amount paid is considered for the qualifying individual's care. Thus, the full amount paid to a nursery school is considered for the care of the child even though the school also furnishes a lunch. Educational expenses for a child in the first or higher grade level are not considered expenses for the child's care.

5. Generally, the expenses considered cannot exceed the earned income of the taxpayer. For single individuals, this rule means that earned income must at least equal the base for the credit. Special rules apply to married individuals. First, married couples must file joint returns. Second, the amount used as the base is the lesser of the husband's or wife's earned income. For purposes of this last test, in which (1) one spouse is a full-time student (five months out of any calendar year) or (2) one spouse is incapable of self-care, some earned income is imputed to that spouse. If one qualifying individual lives in the household, the earned income imputed to the unemployed spouse is $200 per month (or $2,400 per year). If there are two or more qualifying individuals, the earned income imputed to the unemployed spouse is $400 monthly (or $4,800 per year). Imputing earned income to the unemployed spouse means that the full base is allowed if the earned income of the working spouse is equal to or greater than the base.

6. If a married taxpayer is legally separated from his or her spouse, the taxpayer is considered unmarried for purposes of this credit. The law contains a special rule for married individuals who are not legally separated but who live apart. These rules are similar to the abandoned spouse rule used for heads of households. A married individual is considered unmarried if he or she (1) maintains a household that is the principal place of abode for a qualifying individual for more than one half of the tax year, (2) furnishes over 50% of the cost of maintaining the household for the taxable year, and (3) if the individual's spouse is not a member of the household during the last six months of the taxable year.

7. A special rule applies for divorced parents who have children under 15 or children incapable of self-care. If both or either parent, without regard to which parent has custody, provides over 50% of the child's support for a taxable year, and if the child is in the custody of one or both parents for more than six months of such year, then the child is treated as a qualifying individual with respect to the parent who has custody for the longest period of time. This rule waives the strict dependency test under the circumstances outlined; that is, the taxpayer may have a "qualifying" child who is not that taxpayer's dependent.

8. Child-care costs qualify even though paid to a relative of the taxpayer (relative being defined in the same manner as for the dependency test) and even though the relative lives in the taxpayer's household, *provided* the relative is not a "dependent" of the taxpayer or the taxpayer's spouse. (An

exception to this last prohibition applies if the dependent rendering the child-care service is a child of the taxpayer who is 19 years of age, or older, at the end of the taxable year.)

9. If payment for child care is made in a year subsequent to the year the service was rendered, the credit may be taken in the year of actual payment.

Prior to the introduction of the child-care credit in 1976, the law permitted some workers to treat child-care payments as deductions from A.G.I. The availability of that child-care deduction was severely restricted by its classification as an itemized deduction and by its complexity. The treatment of child-care expenditures as itemized deductions denied any beneficial tax recognition of such expenses to taxpayers who did not itemize deductions. This was especially typical of low-income taxpayers, who are in greatest need of a tax benefit from such payments. Although changing the deduction provision to a system of credits may provide greater relief for low-income groups, it can be argued that the law still discriminates in favor of those with higher incomes because those in low-income groups cannot afford such services as child care or household work. These persons must perform the work themselves at night or on weekends, and their children may be left unattended. Undoubtedly, some discrimination does exist in favor of high-income persons employing baby-sitters.

Taxpayers' deductions for child-care expenses have steadily increased. The importance of the child-care provision is not the amounts involved, however, but the fact that it established a major precedent that "unavoidable" work-related personal expenditures may be deductible or give rise to a credit. Similar treatment of other personal expenses—such as clothing, transportation to work, and even food consumed during working hours—may just as logically be justified on the basis of necessity, even though the law currently contains no provisions for such deductions.

Credit for the Elderly and Disabled

The statute provides a limited credit for taxpayers who are 65 years old before the end of the year, or who are retired on a disability that is diagnosed as permanent. Because of a restrictive income phaseout explained later, the credit offers tax relief for only those with very low incomes.

Although this provision is technically a "credit" (a direct reduction of the tax bill), its practical effect is that of an exclusion. The taxpayer computes gross tax in the usual way but reduces the tax by an amount equal to 15% of the amount subject to the credit. The base for the credit is what the statute calls an "initial amount," which is as follows: (1) $5,000 for a single person or for a married couple filing jointly when only one spouse is 65 or older and (2) $7,500 for a married couple filing jointly when both are 65 or older (only $3,750 on separate returns). The initial amount is reduced by the following items to arrive at the base for the credit: (1) Social Security retirement benefits; (2) railroad retirement benefits; and (3) veterans' pensions and certain payments from U.S. government life insurance. In addition, the initial amount is reduced by one half of the adjusted gross income on the return in excess of $7,500 for a single individual and $10,000 for married individuals ($5,000 if separate returns are filed).

The initial amounts described above apply to taxpayers 65 or older. For a disabled taxpayer who has not attained the age of 65, the initial amount is limited to the taxpayer's disability income. Disability income is income from disability retirement pay or amounts received under an employer's health and accident plan that represent payments in lieu of wages. Special rules apply to the determination of the initial amount for married taxpayers where one is 65 and the other is disabled.

To illustrate a simple computation of the credit for the elderly, assume an unmarried taxpayer, age 68, has the following income during 1988.

Interest	$1,510
Wages	7,800
Social Security	400
Total	$9,710

Because the Social Security benefits may be excluded, the taxpayer has adjusted gross income of $9,310. A retirement income credit of $554.25, computed below, may be subtracted from his tax liability:

Initial amount of income for computation of credit		$5,000.00
Deduct: Social Security benefits	$400.00	
Excess AGI*	905.00	1,305.00
Balance subject to credit		$3,695.00
Tentative credit: 15%×$3,695		$ 554.25

$$*\frac{9,310-\$7,500}{2}=\$905$$

The credit is limited to the taxpayer's gross tax, of course. Note from this example that substantial Social Security benefits will eliminate the credit, as will substantial amounts of any income.

Prior to 1976, this credit existed in a different form as the "retirement income credit" and applied only to selected types of retirement income. The main purpose of the credit originally was to equalize the tax burden between those who received retirement income from Social Security and railroad retirement plans (both of which were tax free) and those who received retirement income from interest and other taxable income sources. In addition, the system imposed severe limits on the amounts of "earned income" that could be received without reducing the credit. The 1976 Tax Reform Act increased the coverage by making the credit applicable to gross income from any source and drastically increased the amount of earnings that a retired person could receive without affecting the amount of the credit.

Foreign Tax Credit

Citizens and residents of the U.S. must generally pay the U.S. tax on their worldwide income. Exceptions to this rule include the exclusion for foreign-earned income and income excluded from double taxation by treaty. With these exceptions, a citizen or resident is often subject to the U.S. tax and a tax by the host country for foreign-source income. The U.S. law therefore provides a credit against the U.S. tax for income taxes paid to foreign countries.

All foreign taxes, including income taxes, are often deductible by taxpayers as trade or business expenses under Sec. 162 or as taxes under Sec. 164. Taxpayers, therefore, can elect to take a credit or to deduct foreign income taxes. The credit, with rare exceptions, results in the greatest reduction in the U.S. tax liability.

The foreign tax credit is limited by several provisions beyond the scope of this text. In no event can the credit claimed for foreign taxes exceed the taxes assessed by the U.S. on the foreign-source income. The general upward limit is calculated as follows:

$$\text{Limit} = \frac{\text{Foreign-source income}}{\text{Worldwide taxable income}} \times \text{U.S. tax before credits}$$

For example, imagine a single taxpayer (with one exemption) who has taxable income of $120,000 for 1988. The U.S. tax on that would be $34,146 ($121,950 × .28). The taxpayer derived $50,000 of this income from a foreign country to which he paid an income tax of $12,000. The limit for the foreign tax credit is computed as follows:

$$\frac{\$50,000}{\$120,000} \times \$34,146 = \$14,228$$

The taxpayer can claim a $12,000 credit, the taxes actually paid.

We should note at this point that the law specifies an order for the subtraction of credits. Proper ordering is important because the earned income credit is refundable, and some business credits are carried back or forward if not fully used currently. The order of subtraction is specified on Form 1040 and need not be repeated here.

Use of Tax Tables

The statute provides that the I.R.S. must provide tax tables to make the tax computation simpler. Appendix D shows the tax tables used to file for 1986. At the time of publication, the I.R.S. had not released the tables for 1987.

For 1986, taxpayers with taxable incomes of $50,000 or less were required to use the tax tables. Presumably, the I.R.S. will prepare similar tables for 1987, which will work the same as those for 1986 but with fewer brackets. Just what the I.R.S. will do for 1988 and later years is anyone's guess.

SOME MISCELLANEOUS PROCEDURES

The final section of this chapter covers some miscellaneous procedural rules related to individual tax returns. It begins with the rules outlining who must file returns, then explains the use of tax tables, and finally discusses the requirements for payment of the tax.

Who Must File

As mentioned earlier in Chapter 9, an individual whose *gross income* is below a specified amount is not required to file a return. Given the rules for exemptions and the standard deductions, certain taxpayers would obviously never have a gross tax liability, if their gross incomes were as shown:

	1987	1988
Single, under 65 years of age	$ 4,440	$ 4,950
Single, 65 years or older	5,650	5,700
Qualified surviving spouse under 65	5,660	6,950
Qualified surviving spouse over 64	7,650	7,700
Married couple filing jointly, both under 65	7,560	8,900
Married couple filing jointly, one spouse over 64	9,400	9,500
Married couple filing jointly, both over 64	10,000	10,100

As explained above, a single individual who is a dependent of another and has unearned income (dividends, interest, and so on) must file a return if gross income exceeds $500. The law provides that only $500 of the standard deduction can be used to offset earned income. In addition, a taxpayer who has a net income of $400 or more from self-employment must file.

Individuals whose gross incomes are below these amounts may, of course, file a return to obtain a refund of amounts withheld from wages or to take advantage of the earned income credit. Remember, the test of who must file is based on gross income, not on adjusted gross income or taxable income.

Payment of the Tax

The law contains a "pay-as-you-go" system for individuals. Employers withhold the FIT for the salaries and wages of employees. Taxpayers with income not subject to withholding pay estimated quarterly taxes. Finally, the net tax liability due when the return is filed can be reduced by excess FICA taxes paid and by taxes paid on fuel used off the highways.

WITHHOLDINGS   Every employer must withhold from an employee's wages an amount of income tax based on the employee's marital status, number of exemptions claimed, and earnings and remit the withholding to a depository of the federal government within specified time periods. Essentially, the withholding provision is designed to put the employee on a pay-as-you-go basis as far as his or her income tax is concerned. *Wages* include all remuneration for services performed by an employee for an employer, including the cash value of all remuneration paid in any medium other than cash. Each January the employer must give the employee two copies of Form W-2, showing the total amount of remuneration subject to income tax paid the employee during the year, the amount of income tax withheld, the amount of earnings subject to Social Security taxes, and the amount of Social Security tax withheld. The employee attaches one copy of this form to his or her income tax return sent to the Internal Revenue Service. The amount withheld for income taxes is, of course, a prepayment that is subtracted from the gross tax payable, after tax credits, to arrive at the net tax payable (or refundable).

Estimated Taxes

Individuals who have income from sources not subject to withholdings are required to declare and pay their estimated income taxes during the tax year. The *estimated tax* is the excess of a taxpayer's gross tax over his or her credits and withholdings. A taxpayer must make quarterly payments of his or her estimated tax if such amount exceeds $500. Prior to 1983, taxpayers were required to file a declaration of estimated tax under certain specified conditions, even when no estimated tax payment was due. There was no penalty for failure to file the declaration; the penalty came from failure to pay the estimated tax on a timely basis. While the declaration is no longer required, the penalty is still in effect for underpayment of the estimated tax.

For calendar year taxpayers, quarterly payments of the estimated tax are due on April 15, June 15, and September 15 of the taxable year, and January 15 of the following year. The penalty is assessed on underpayments of the estimated quarterly amount. An underpayment is the excess, if any, of the quarterly installment required by law over the actual amount paid for the quarter. The required quarterly installment is generally 22.5% of the actual taxes shown on the return for the year. Use of 22.5% to determine the required installment means that no penalty is due if the estimated tax paid in equal quarterly installments equals 90% of the tax shown on the return. The penalty is computed using the short-term interest rate charged by the government for late payments of the tax applied from the time of the underpayment until such time as the tax is due, compounded daily. The penalty is treated as an additional tax, not as deductible interest.

The statute contains two exceptions to the application of the underpayment penalty. First, no penalty applies if each of the quarterly installments equals 25% of the tax shown on the return for the preceding year. A zero tax liability for the preceding year can be used only if the preceding year was a 12-month year and if the taxpayer filed a return for such year. Second, no penalty is assessed if the quarterly payment equals 22.5% of the annualized tax for the year, based on the actual transactions of the taxpayer for the months of the year preceding the due date of the installment. This provision protects taxpayers whose taxable incomes unexpectedly increase after the payments of earlier installments.

Numerous other exceptions and special rules related to the calculation of the estimated tax and the underpayment penalty exist but are beyond the scope of this introduction.

REFUND FOR NONHIGHWAY USES OF FUELS   When a consumer purchases gasoline or lubricating oil, the purchase price includes a federal excise tax imposed on users of highways to provide funds for construction and maintenance of roads. When the gasoline or oil is purchased for nonhighway uses, such as farming or operating a motorboat, the taxpayer must pay the tax on purchase but may file a refund claim for the amounts paid. Section 34 allows the taxpayer to take a credit against his or her federal income tax for the amount of excise taxes paid on gasoline and oil bought for nonhighway use, thus providing a simple refund procedure. In essence, these amounts are treated as prepayments of income taxes.

EXCESS FICA TAXES   Employees pay a FICA tax (Social Security) on their wages. Currently (1987), the rate is 7.15% on wages up to $43,800. (Employers also pay this same tax for each employee.) Employees who work for more than one employer during the year and have combined earnings greater than the $43,800 threshold overpay the FICA tax. Such overpayments are treated as payments of the income tax.

In this chapter, we have learned to apply the proper rates to taxable income to obtain the gross tax. From the gross tax we subtract the credits allowed and the prepayments to determine the net tax (or refund) due when the return is filed. We will return to the problems that arise after filing when returns are audited by the I.R.S. and additional taxes are assessed.

PROBLEMS

1. In each of the independent cases below, calculate the number of exemptions for the taxpayer, assuming the current tax year is 1988.
   a. Taxpayer, age 67, and wife, age 63, file a joint return.
   b. Taxpayer, age 68, and wife, who became 65 on January 1 on the year following the tax year, are both blind and file a joint return.
   c. Taxpayer and husband, both 48, spent $3,000 toward living expenses of their son who is 25 and in college. The son also earned $2,500 during the summer, received a scholarship of $400, and received $450 under the GI Bill. The son used all of these funds for his living costs.
   d. Taxpayer received her divorce decree on January 8 and has not remarried. The divorce decree requires her ex-husband to pay $3,000 a year for the support of their child, who is 5 years old and lives with the mother. They have not discussed who is to claim an exemption for the child.
   e. Assume the same facts as in part d, except that the divorced couple have agreed that the father is to claim an exemption for the child. The taxpayer is the mother.

f. Taxpayer is 67 years old. He pays $350 per month to keep his mother, age 88, in a rest home. The mother also receives an old-age pension of $450 during the year and gross rental income of $2,500 (rental expenses consume $1,800 of this.) She uses all the available funds for routine living costs.

g. Taxpayer is 64, his wife is 53. They provide over one half of the support for their 35-year-old son who became disenchanted with his occupation two years ago and since that time has been a full-time college student working on a degree in accounting. The son earned $2,100 during the year and also received a scholarship of $500, both of which were used to pay his living costs.

h. Smith and his wife have great compassion for orphaned children. Currently, they have living in their home and are completely supporting five children, all of whom are in school. The five foster children have been living in Smith's home all year, but none of these has been adopted. None of the children has any income.

i. Williford and his wife have a foster child living in their home for the entire year for whom they provide major support. The foster child, age 15, has gross income of $2,500 for the year.

j. An unmarried taxpayer supports his 17-year-old brother, who does not live with the taxpayer. The brother earned $2,500 during the year.

2. For each of the following independent situations, determine the proper number of exemptions to be taken, assuming the current tax year.

   a. Taxpayer, age 66, and his spouse, age 62, file a joint return. Both have good vision. They have one son, age 22, who is a student at State University. The son earned $2,100 in a summer job and received a $1,000 scholarship from State University. During the year, the son's total support cost $5,300, of which $2,200 was paid by the father.

   b. Taxpayer and spouse, both under 65, file a joint return. They provided more than 50% of the support of two unmarried children, both under 19. One child earned $2,100 from part-time work. Taxpayer also provided most of the support for his blind mother, who is over 65. The mother received $2,200 in Social Security payments.

   c. Taxpayer, unmarried, under 65 and with good vision, provides more than 50% of the support for his brother and sister-in-law, who attend State University. The brother earned $2,200 in a part-time job. The sister-in-law had no income. The brother filed a separate return, claiming one exemption.

   d. Taxpayer, unmarried, under 65, provides more than 50% of the support for his nephew and the nephew's wife, who attend State University. The nephew earned $2,200 on a summer job. The nephew filed a separate return in order to receive a refund of tax withheld. He did not claim an exemption.

3. Determine the correct number of exemptions for each situation described below.

   a. John Smith, a 66-year-old bachelor, maintains a home in which his deceased friend's 24-year-old son has lived for the past 14 years. The young man is a full-time college student who earned $2,500 during the year. John can prove that he furnishes 65% of the young man's support.

   b. Jacques, a widower for four years, age 63, maintains a home that is the principal abode for himself, his married daughter Joan, and his grandchild Zed. Jacques's son-in-law is a wandering bum. Jacques provides more than 50% of the support of all those who live with him. Joan and her husband file a joint return, but they do not claim Zed as their dependent because their joint earnings are only $7,800.

   c. Alan Standard contributes more than one half the support of both his mother and father, who live with him. Alan is 38 and single; his father is 66, his mother, 64. Alan's father earned $2,100 during the year and filed a separate return claiming himself as an exemption.

d. Jack and Jill, who file a joint return, have two children. Andrea, who is 5 years old, models clothes for a local department store. Because Andrea earned $2,100 during the year, she had to file a tax return. Their son Don, who is 2 years old, was born blind. Jack and Jill have also been raising (without adopting) 6-year-old Ted, who was orphaned by an automobile accident. The total expenditures for Ted amounted to $2,500 during the year. Of the $2,500, Jack and Jill paid $1,500 from their personal funds; the remainder was provided by a county welfare program.

4. The Whiten family consists of Herman, Joann, husband and wife, and their 4-year-old son, Junior. Herman earns $35,000 as a warehouse foreman. Joann earned $15,000 as a Tupware representative. Junior has interest income of $8,000 from money given to him by his grandmother.

   a. How many taxpayers are there in this family?
   b. What minimum number of returns must the family file?
   c. Should Herman and Joann file separate returns?
   Explain all answers.

5. For each of the following independent situations, can John and Marsha file a joint return for 19x1? Explain your answers.

   a. John and Marsha married on December 20, 19x1, after a whirlwind courtship. Following a violent argument on December 28, 19x1, Marsha went home to mother, vowing never to return. No legal action was taken during 19x1.
   b. After years of marriage, John and Marsha were legally separated on December 30, 19x1.
   c. While on temporary assignment in England for a large corporation, John married Marsha, a citizen of Great Britain. They were still in London at the end of 19x1, but they returned to the United States in January 19x2. They made no election for 19x1 to include Marsha's worldwide income on a U.S. return.
   d. John died on January 2, 19x1, after years of happy marriage to Marsha.

6. Indicate in each of the following cases whether taxpayers may file a joint return. If they are not allowed to do so, indicate the reason.

   a. Jones, a widower, and his mother live in the same house. Jones has gross income of $8,000; mother has income of $6,000.
   b. Kuehn, an American citizen, married Greta while he was stationed in Germany. Kuehn and his wife now live in New York. Greta is not yet an American citizen, but at the end of the tax year she was taking steps to become an American citizen.
   c. Smith's wife died in the preceding year, and he has not remarried. Smith's 3-year-old daughter lives with him.
   d. Bellmon's wife died on January 2 of the current year. He has not remarried.
   e. Ratliff and his wife were divorced on December 18 of the current tax year.
   f. Whitlaw and his wife are both U.S. citizens. Whitlaw's wife's parents live in England and are seriously ill. His wife spent the entire tax year in England with her parents.

7. In the following situations, can Mac use Rate Schedule Z (head of household) for the year involved?

   a. Mac, a widower, maintains a home, and his unmarried grandson lives with him. The grandson is 23 years old, has a good job, and therefore does not qualify as Mac's dependent.

b. Mac maintains a home for his two dependent children. Mac's wife died last year.

c. Mac's parents live in an apartment at a resort center in Florida. They have no income, so Mac, who is a bachelor and lives and works in New York, supports them.

d. Mac is a widower living in New York. His wife died five years ago. Mac pays all the living costs of his 18-year-old unmarried duaghter, who has no income and lives in Miami, Florida.

8. Indicate in each of the following independent cases whether the taxpayer may file a surviving-spouse return.

a. Taxpayer's husband died in the preceding tax year. Taxpayer maintains a home in which resides her unmarried 20-year-old daughter, a college student, who qualifies as taxpayer's dependent.

b. Taxpayer's husband died in the preceding tax year. Taxpayer maintains a home in which resides her unmarried 20-year-old sister, a college student, who qualifies as taxpayer's dependent.

c. Taxpayer's wife died during this tax year. Taxpayer maintains a home in which resides his unmarried 18-year-old daughter, who qualifies as taxpayer's dependent.

d. Taxpayer's husband died during the preceding year. Taxpayer maintains a home in which reside her married 17-year-old daughter and the daughter's 18-year-old husband. Taxpayer supports both her daughter and son-in-law and properly claims both of them as her dependents.

e. Taxpayer's wife died four years ago. Taxpayer has not remarried and maintains a home in which reside his two stepchildren, ages 7 and 8. Taxpayer properly claims both stepchildren as dependents.

9. Which rate schedule (X, Y—Joint, Y—Separate, or Z) *should* each of the following taxpayers use?

a. Sue's husband died last year. She maintains a home in which her married son and his wife live. Both of them qualify as Sue's dependents.

b. Mary's husband died last year. She maintains a home in which her married son and his wife live. Mary supports both of them, but the son and daughter-in-law file a joint return.

c. Herman and Victoria were married on December 31 of the current tax year. Herman earned $18,000 during the year, and Victoria earned $7,200. Victoria is a resident alien and has income in several countries.

d. Wilma's husband died four years ago. Wilma maintains a home in which reside her 6-year-old daughter, her 21-year-old son, and her 20-year-old daughter-in-law. The son and daughter-in-law file a joint return. Wilma provides all the support for everyone in the household.

e. Jones, whose wife died earlier in the current tax year, has not remarried. He has no children or other dependents.

f. Joe, a bachelor, maintains a home in which resides his nephew. The nephew is not a dependent.

g. Thomas was divorced from his wife in November of the current tax year. Thomas's unmarried dependent daughter lives with him.

10. Hank, a lawyer, expects to have gross income of $40,000 for the year. Debbie works for an advertising agency and her gross income will be $30,000. Neither has dependents nor deductions for A.G.I. After an extended courtship, the two plan to marry before the year-end.

    a. Calculate their combined tax liability if they decide to forgo marriage.

    b. What amount of additional tax results from the marriage?

11. Mary and John are married residents of New York and have two small children. They depend on John's salary of $50,000 per annum for their livelihood. In January 19x2, Mary learned that John was in hock to his bookie to the tune of $200,000 and that the bookie was getting impatient. New York is not a community-property state. Mary has no current income, but her family is quite wealthy and she expects to inherit substantial amounts in the near future. What would you advise Mary about filing status for 19x1?

12. Hermie is 12 years old and a dependent of his parents. During the year (after 1987) he received interest income of $6,000, his only source of income. Hermie's parents file a joint return showing taxable income of $110,000.

    a. What is Hermie's tax liability?

    b. Answer part a assuming that Hermie earns $1,200 during the year on a paper route in addition to the interest income.

13. One provision that Congress has often considered is the substitution of a $400 credit instead of a $2,000 exemption deduction.

    a. Would taxpayers with a marginal rate of 15% prefer the credit or the deduction? taxpayers with a 28% marginal rate?

    b. How would adoption of the credit affect the relative tax burdens of low-income taxpayers relative to high-income taxpayers?

14. H and W are married and file a joint return showing adjusted gross income of $35,000. During the year H and W spent $6,000 to care for their two dependent children, ages 4 and 6, in a "qualified" child-care center. What is the amount of the dependent-care credit if H is employed as an accountant but:

    a. W is not gainfully employed during the year?

    b. W has a part-time job and earns $2,000 during the year?

    c. W is a full-time student?

    d. W is physically incapable of self-care, and the $6,000 includes amounts spent for her care?

    e. W earns $10,000 as a model?

15. In each of the following independent cases, compute the earned income credit for 1988.

    a. Taxpayer and spouse file a joint return. They have no dependents. Their income consists of salaries of $6,800 and interest of $600. Gross tax liability is $240.

    b. Taxpayer and spouse file a joint return. They maintain in the U.S. a household for their dependent 14-year-old child. Their combined adjusted gross income is $7,400, all from wages. Gross tax liability is zero.

    c. Same facts as in part b, except that their total adjusted gross income of $10,400 is made up of $8,800 wages and $1,600 interest. Gross tax liability is $240.

    d. Same facts as in part b, except that their adjusted gross income is $3,600 consisting solely of wages. Gross tax liability is zero.

    e. Same facts as in part b, except that their adjusted gross income is $3,800, consisting solely of taxpayer's net profit from a small motor repair shop. Gross tax liability is zero.

16. In each of the following independent cases, determine the amount, if any, of the taxpayer's credit for child-care expenses. Assume that payment is made to enable taxpayer to be gainfully employed unless otherwise stated.

a. Taxpayer is a widow employed as a corporate controller. She earns $88,000 during the current year. In order to be gainfully employed, she pays her cousin $150 per month to take care of her 6-year-old child in the cousin's home.

b. Taxpayer is unmarried, earns $17,000 per year, and supports her two younger brothers, ages 8 and 17. During the year she paid a baby-sitter $250 per month to care for the 8-year-old.

c. Sue is divorced. She earned $8,200 during the current year, but had to pay a housekeeper $200 per month to care for her two children, ages 4 and 5, while she worked. The housekeeper also cleaned the house and prepared all the meals. It is estimated that the housekeeper spends one half of her time caring for the children and the other one half doing housework.

d. Margaret is unmarried. She has two dependent children, ages 8 and 14. Both children attend school, but she paid the 14-year-old $480 during the year to take care of the younger child after school until 5:30 P.M. each day. Margaret earned $8,000 during the year.

e. John is a bachelor and supports his aged parents who live with him. John pays a neighbor $300 per month during the year to take care of his parents, both of whom are bedridden, while John works. John's income was $18,000 for the year.

17. Matte Harmon, a widow, age 67, had adjusted gross income of $8,000 during the current year. Matte also received $1,800 during the year from Social Security.
   a. What is Matte's credit for the elderly?
   b. What is her credit if her Social Security benefits amount to $5,500?

18. Dave, a bachelor, suffered a severe heart attack last year at the age of 60. His employer retired Dave on a disability pension. Dave has no income except for his pension and Social Security payments. He also uses the zero-bracket amount. Calculate the amount of Dave's disability credit for this year if:
   a. the disability pension is $4,500 and Dave receives $3,600 from Social Security.
   b. the disability pension is $7,000 and Dave receives $3,600 from Social Security.
   c. the disability pension is $7,000 and Dave receives $6,000 from Social Security.

19. In each of the following independent cases, compute the taxpayer's credit for dependent-care expenses. Assume the payments are necessary for gainful employment unless otherwise stated.
   a. Macomb and his wife have five small children, ranging in age from 2 to 9. During the current year Macomb earned $7,400; his wife earned $8,200. They paid a baby-sitter $200 per month to care for the children while they both worked. They filed a joint return.
   b. Assume the same facts as in part a, except that they paid the sitter $410 per month for caring for the children.
   c. Ann, a widow, was employed throughout the year, earning $10,200. She paid a baby-sitter $70 per month throughout the year to care for her two children. The younger is 9, the other became 15 on August 1 of this year.
   d. The taxpayer, a widow, works as an interior decorator and has income of $50,000. During the year she paid $400 per month for maid service including care of her two dependent children, ages 10 and 12. The amount allocated to child care was $1,500.
   e. The taxpayer, a widow with A.G.I. of $12,000, paid her mother $100 per month during the year to care for her 5-year-old dependent child. The mother is not a dependent of the taxpayer.
   f. John and Sue are married and file a joint return. John is a full-time student but earned $1,000 from part-time jobs during 19X1. Sue is employed and earned

$9,400 during the year. In order for Sue to work and John to attend classes, they paid a baby-sitter $900 ($75 per month) to take care of their 2-year-old child.

g. Ray and Ellen are married and file a joint return. Ray is employed and earned $20,000 during 19X1. Ellen is not gainfully employed but paid a college student $600 during the year to take care of her small child while Ellen did her shopping, attended meetings, and so on.

20. T's taxable income for the current year is $80,000, and his gross tax for 1988 as a single individual is $27,146. T had dividend income of $5,000 from a Canadian corporation that withheld $750 of the dividend under Canadian income tax law.
   a. Should T claim the $750 as a deduction (and reduce his taxable income to $79,250), or should he claim a foreign tax credit?
   b. If he claims the credit, what amount is allowed?

21. Herman's tax liability after credits last year was $8,000, the tax due on Herman's income from the operation (as a sole proprietor) of a pool hall. Because of police harassment, Herman's business was slow. Based on his business through March annualized for the year, Herman paid a quarterly estimate of $1,000 on April 15. Using the same procedure, he paid $1,000 on June 15. Due to a new police chief, business began to improve in the summer and continued at unprecedented levels for the remainder of the year, resulting in a tax liability of $15,000. For the last two installments on September 15 and January 15, Herman paid $3,000 per installment.
   a. Calculate Herman's underpayment for each quarter.
   b. Is Herman subject to the underpayment penalty? Explain.

22. Consider the following taxpayers and determine which one must file a return:
   a. Mrs. X, a widow, who has income of $150,000, all interest on tax-exempt state bonds
   b. Mrs. Y, a widow, with rental income of $18,000, deductible expenses related to the rental property of $16,500, and Social Security benefits of $5,000
   c. Z, a 15-year-old with taxable interest income of $1,500, who is claimed as a dependent by his parents

CHAPTER 12

Incentives for Savings: Pension Plans

> *The treatment of pension and other employee benefit plans under the income tax laws is a vitally important aspect of the American tax structure. It affects, directly or indirectly, the great majority of taxpayers.*
> *John K. Dyer Jr. 1959* Compendium

A long-term concern of some economists and policy makers has been the effects of the income tax on individual savings. In Keynse's model of how economies work, savings are finally translated into new investment, the motor force behind economic growth and overall health. High individual income tax rates, many believe, have decreased the propensity to save, with the possible long-run problem of inadequate growth.

Our tax policy since World War II has generally dealt with the problem of economic growth by trying to encourage investment in new plant and equipment. For example, the law has contained provisions for accelerated depreciation and the 10% investment tax credit intended to stimulate new investments. As explained later in Chapter 15, provisions like accelerated depreciation and the investment credit increase the profitability of investments and thus serve as incentives to acquire assets. The incentive for savings is indirectly increased by these investment incentives because of increased demand for needed funds. Still, the incentives for investment were not concerned with savings except in this indirect way.

The 1986 Act is a clear departure from the past. The recurring theme throughout the Reagan years has been that substantially lower tax rates will permit the savings necessary to ensure a high level of new investments. Many proponents of lower rates would go even further and change the income tax to a tax on consumption by giving taxpayers a deduction for income saved and invested.[1] The 1986 Act thus repealed the investment credit, extended the periods for cost recovery, and decreased other investment incentives. Since the tax reductions under the 1986 Act are nominal for middle- and lower-income groups, particularly when combined with the social security tax, the Reagan administration clearly expects the new savings to occur among the wealthy, with the benefits from their investments "trickling down" to the lower classes.

We have discussed this major new incentive for savings, i.e., lower rates, at numerous places already, and nothing more need to said here. In this chapter we cover the other tax provisions that serve directly as incentives for savings. Qualified pension and profit-sharing plans are far and away the most important, so most of the chapter is devoted to these. Before we consider these qualified plans, something must be said about life insurance and annuity contracts and about various public retirement plans, especially Social Security. The last part of the chapter explains how some traditional tax shelters, to the extent they survived the 1986 Act, are savings incentives.

LIFE INSURANCE AND ANNUITY CONTRACTS

We have not traditionally thought of life insurance and commercial annuity contracts as tax shelters. Prior to 1987, many other investments were superior to such contracts for tax purposes, as explained in the following paragraphs.

Life Insurance Contracts

An ordinary life insurance[2] contract works as follows: The owner of the policy pays premiums, usually for a stated period of years or for the life of the insured, to the insurance company. The insurer contracts to pay a fixed sum upon death of the insured, usually the owner. In lieu of the death payment, the owner may borrow against the policy, cash it in for its cash surrender value, or elect to draw down the cash value over a period of years as an annuity.

Premium payments by the owner are not deductible for tax purposes. If the insurance proceeds are paid at the death of the insured, the proceeds are

---

[1] See Michael Boskin, "Saving incentives: The Role of Tax Policy," *New Directions in Federal Tax Polity for the 1980's* (Cambridge: Ballinger Publishing Company, 1986), p. 93–110.
[2] This term does not include term life insurance that provides insurance against death only, that is, has no investment element.

excluded from gross income of the beneficiary, as explained in Chapter 8. If the owner borrows against the policy, the loan itself, as opposed to interest paid on it, has no tax effect because it does not change the borrower's net worth. If the owner takes the cash value, as a lump sum or as an annuity, gross income includes the amount received in excess of total premiums paid.

We ignore here the exclusion of the death benefit as a saving incentive, though it can be a powerful incentive where the owner is also the beneficiary. The tax benefit that accrues to the owner, even though he later pays tax on the gain when the policy is cashed in, is the deferral of tax on the income earned over the life of the policy. The policy owner pays premiums, and these premiums are invested by the insurance company. Over the years, the policy value increases, but no income is reported until the policy is surrendered. In contrast, if the policy owner buys term insurance and makes separate investments in stocks and bonds, the interest and dividends on these investments are taxed currently and only the *after-tax* earnings are available for reinvestment.

Compared to the typical pre-1986 tax shelter, life insurance did not come out well even where the insurance company guaranteed high returns. In the competing typical shelter, income was deferred to later years, and income was eventually realized as a capital gain. The life insurance contract gives this deferral but produces ordinary income, a fact of no concern after 1987. As a result, such contracts will undoubtedly receive more attention in the future.

Annuity Contracts

An annuity is simply a contract calling for a series of monetary payments at stated intervals for either a fixed or a contingent time period. For example, an individual might purchase from an insurance company the right to receive $100 per month for a period of 10 years beginning on January 1, 1988, with the last payment made on December 1, 1997. If the purchaser paid for this contract with a single lump-sum payment on July 1, 1986, it might be diagramed with a time line as in Figure 12-1.

TYPES OF ANNUITIES   There are several types of annuities. For example, the annuity illustrated in Figure 12-1 is commonly known as a *simple annuity,* or a *term annuity;* that is, an annuity that is payable for a fixed time period (in

FIGURE **12-1**

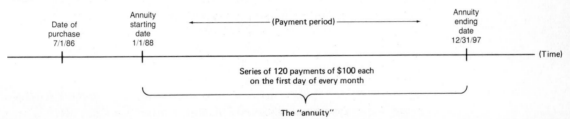

this case, for 10 years). Because most individuals use annuities as a source of retirement income, they are not interested in simple annuities; instead, they typically desire life annuities. A *life annuity* is payable for "so long as the annuitant (the person designated to receive the payment) shall live." Married persons usually want retirement income for so long as either spouse shall live, so they arrange for a joint-and-survivor annuity. Obviously, a *joint-and-survivor annuity* provides for a series of payments for so long as either the annuitant or his or her spouse shall live. The amount of the payments may vary, depending on whether only one or both spouses are living. For example, a joint-and-survivor annuity might provide for $800 a month for so long as both spouses live and for a lesser amount—$500—for so long as either spouse survives.

No one knows, of course, exactly how long any individual may live. An insurance company's actuaries know, however, how long an "average" person will live; that knowledge is necessary to their writing life annuity contracts with literally thousands of individuals. The fundamental idea behind a life annuity is shared risk—some annuitants will die shortly after their payments begin; others will live for many years. Because of this risk for a short life following the starting date of any annuity, some individuals desire a guarantee that they or their heirs will receive at least a minimum amount in return. For example, if an individual has $75,000 invested in an annuity, he or she might insist on a contract that will return (either to the annuitant or heirs) the $75,000 cost, even if the annuitant dies shortly after the annuity starting date. To satisfy these demands, *refund annuities* have been created. Thus, the adjectives that modify the word annuity describe its contractual details. Consider, for example, the meaning of a *joint-and-survivor refund annuity*.

In Figure 12-1 we assumed that an annuitant purchased an annuity with a single payment. Most individuals do not acquire their retirement annuity in that manner. Indeed, nearly all private annuities are accumulated from a series of payments made during an individual's working years. In some cases, only the annuitant's employer contributes to the fund that eventually pays the retirement annuity; this annuity agreement is a *noncontributory* plan. If the annuitant makes some or all of the contributions to the fund that eventually pays the annuity, the plan is a *contributory* one. In addition to the payments received from an annuitant and/or the annuitant's employer, any private retirement fund should have an accumulation of compound earnings derived from the investment of the payments received.

Figure 12-2 conceptualizes a typical contributory annuity plan where both the employer and employee contribute. Note that the income earned on the contributions is not a set amount (a straight line), because the earnings of the plan will vary depending on the success of the plan managers. In the typical commercial annuity, as opposed to an employee annuity plan, the insurance company guarantees a set rate of return.

TAXATION OF ANNUITY CONTRACTS   First, the income earned on the taxpayer's premiums or purchase cost is sheltered from taxation, that is, the taxpayer does not report the increase in value as income. With the exception

FIGURE **12-2**

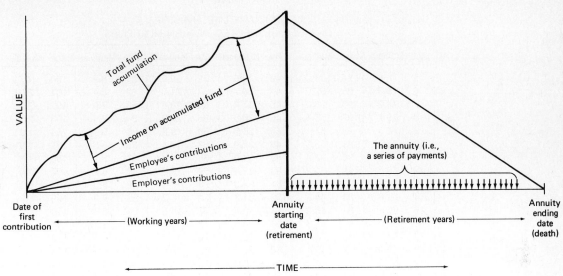

Total fund accumulation

Income on accumulated fund

Employee's contributions

Employer's contributions

VALUE

The annuity (i.e., a series of payments)

Date of first contribution

(Working years)

Annuity starting date (retirement)

(Retirement years)

Annuity ending date (death)

TIME

of the employer's contributions to "qualified" plans, the taxpayer is acquiring the annuity contract with *after-tax* dollars. In other words, neither premiums paid for a commercial annuity nor employee contributions to a plan are deductible for tax purposes. Thus the taxpayer is entitled to recover his cost basis in the contract as he collects the benefits.

From the inception of the income tax in 1913 to 1934, taxpayers were allowed to apply the first returns from an annuity to recovery of capital. No income was recognized until the returns exceeded the annuity's total premiums or cost. This treatment of annuities had a major drawback in that it often created taxable income for the oldest taxpayers when inflation had already reduced the adequacy of their annuity. Beginning in 1934, the 3% rule was placed in the law. Under this procedure, 3% of the annuity's total cost was included in income each year. The portion of the annual return in excess of 3% of the cost was treated as a return of capital. After total capital was recovered, however, the entire amount received was treated as income. The rule was unfavorable to taxpayers, because the 3% was actually higher than the interest paid by insurance companies at that time and because it still taxed the oldest taxpayers at the most inopportune time.

Since 1954, consistent with the 3% rule, proceeds from an annuity are assumed to consist partly of a return of investment and partly of interest income on the investment. The taxpayer may exclude the portion of the proceeds that represents return of investment. The portion excluded is the ratio that the investment in the contract bears to total expected return from the contract.

The I.R.S. provides actuarial tables to be used in computing the expected return under annuity contracts involving life expectancy. These tables indicate a "multiple" to be applied to the annual payments received by taxpayers

TABLE 12-1
ORDINARY LIFE ANNUITIES
ONE LIFE—EXPECTED RETURN MULTIPLIES

Age	Multiple	Age	Multiple	Age	Multiple	Age	Multiple	Age	Multiple	Age	Multiple
5	76.6	24	58.0	43	39.6	62	22.5	81	8.9	100	2.7
6	75.6	25	57.0	44	38.7	63	21.6	82	8.4	101	2.5
7	74.7	26	56.0	45	37.7	64	20.8	83	7.9	102	2.3
8	73.7	27	55.1	46	36.8	65	20.0	84	7.4	103	2.1
9	72.7	28	54.1	47	35.9	66	19.2	85	6.9	104	1.9
10	71.7	29	53.1	48	34.9	67	18.4	86	6.5	105	1.8
11	70.7	30	52.2	49	34.0	68	17.6	87	6.1	106	1.6
12	69.7	31	51.2	50	33.1	69	16.8	88	5.7	107	1.4
13	68.8	32	50.2	51	32.2	70	16.0	89	5.3	108	1.3
14	67.8	33	49.3	52	31.3	71	15.3	90	5.0	109	1.1
15	66.8	34	48.3	53	30.4	72	14.6	91	4.7	110	1.0
16	65.8	35	47.3	54	29.5	73	13.9	92	4.4	111	.9
17	64.8	36	46.4	55	28.6	74	13.2	93	4.1	112	.8
18	63.9	37	45.4	56	27.7	75	12.5	94	3.9	113	.7
19	62.9	38	44.4	57	26.8	76	11.9	95	3.7	114	.6
20	61.9	39	43.5	58	25.9	77	11.2	96	3.4	115	.5
21	60.9	40	42.5	59	25.0	78	10.6	97	3.2		
22	59.9	41	41.5	60	24.2	79	10.0	98	3.0		
23	59.0	42	40.6	61	23.3	80	9.5	99	2.8		

of various ages at the annuity's starting date. Table 12-1 gives the life multiple for a single life annuity. Note that the table, which applies to annuities beginning after July 31, 1986, is a unisex table and does not distinguish between males and females as earlier tables did. The Revenue Service has also published tables for joint-lives and joint-survivor annuities. The life multiples from the tables must be adjusted by yet another table when the annuity contains a guaranteed feature.

To illustrate the current rules, let us assume that an employee of a state government contributed a total of $27,000 to the state retirement program during his working years. Assume further that this program provides for a retirement annuity of $200 per month, beginning at age 65, for so long as the annuitant shall live. With these additional assumed facts, we can determine the correct tax treatment of this taxpayer's retirement annuity.

Table 12-1 shows that for an annuitant, age 65 at the annuity starting date, the appropriate multiple is 20.0. Thus, the total expected return under the contract is $48,000 ($2,400 × 20.0). The exclusion ratio is

$$\frac{\text{Investment in contract}}{\text{Total expected return}} = \frac{\$27,000}{\$48,000} = 56.25\%$$

Each year the taxpayer excludes $1,350, 56.25% of the $2,400 received. The remaining $1,050 is included in taxable income. Prior to 1987, once the exclusion ratio was set it applied to all amounts received under the contract, whether the taxpayer recovered more or less than his actual cost. After 1986, the exclusion ratio is used only until all costs are recovered. Afterward, the total received is included in income. If the annuitant dies before the costs are recovered, the unrecovered amount is a deduction on the final return.

The rules for annuities, like life insurance, permit the deferral of taxes on the earnings of the contract over its life. This advantage applies to both commercial annuity contracts and annuities from retirement plans.

PUBLIC RETIREMENT PROGRAMS

Undoubtedly the most important public pension and retirement plan in the United States today is that provided under the Old Age, Survivors, and Disability Insurance Act (OASI) of the federal government, providing for old-age retirement benefits, disability benefits, benefits for survivors of the insured, and hospital insurance benefits. This program, generally referred to as *Social Security,* is a more important social and economic force each year as a larger portion of the citizenry becomes subject to its provisions, as both the number and percentage of the population actually receiving benefits increase and as the payroll taxes levied to finance the plan increase. The tremendous growth in the Social Security program through 1979, the last year for which data are available, is reflected in Table 12-2.

Many taxpayers do not think of the Social Security program as a tax-induced saving program, probably because the benefits are not closely tied to

TABLE **12-2**

FEDERAL RECEIPTS AND PAYMENTS OF BENEFITS FROM SOCIAL SECURITY AND RAILROAD RETIREMENT PLANS
(IN MILLIONS OF DOLLARS)[a]

	1940	1950	1960	1969	1972	1976	1980	1984
Benefits paid								
Old-age retirement benefits	$100	$ 838	$ 8,790	$18,467	$28,756	$62,140[b]	$123,300[c]	$186,600[c]
Disability benefits	31	77	715	2,499	4,762	9,222	—	—
Survivorship benefits	7	321	2,517	6,777	9,932			
Total	$138	$1,236	$12,022	$27,743	$43,450	$71,362	$123,300	$186,600
Receipts	$725	$2,656	$10,818	$33,219	$43,200	$74,000	$121,800	$189,500

SOURCES: U.S. Bureau of the Census, *Statistical Abstracts of the United States,* various years (Washington, D.C.: U.S. Government Printing Office), and Joint Economic committee, *The Federal Tax System: Facts and Problems,* 1964 (Washington, D.C.: U.S. Government Printing Office), p. 293.

[a]Figures do not include the hospital insurance program nor the supplementary medical program. During 1972, receipts from these two programs totaled $8.8 billion, and expenditures for benefits were $8.8 billion. In 1984, receipts were $68.3 billion, and expenditures were $62.7 billion.
[b]Old-age retirement benefits and survivorship benefits are combined for 1976 and later years.
[c]All benefits grouped together after 1979.

total contributions. Social Security is still relatively new, particularly the expensive medical provisions. Many citizens have received benefits in excess of their contributions, introducing an element of welfare into the program. For many citizens, the Social Security program represents the only significant savings for old age and medical disaster.

Social Security Contributions

The Social Security program for employees is financed by charges levied against the employee and the employer based on the employee's earnings during the year. Both the tax rates and the maximum amount of yearly earnings subject to the tax have increased over the years and are certain to increase still further in future years. The combined rate for old-age, survivors, and disability insurance and hospitalization insurance in 1987 is 7.15 on the employee and on the employer. These rates are applied to the first $43,800 paid to the employee during the year, and the employer and employee each contribute that amount. Thus, the total contribution in 1987 is 14.3% of the first $43,800 paid each employee during the year.

Self-employed persons are also included in the program. A self-employed person must contribute 12.3% of the first $43,800 earned during 1987.

The contribution of an employee or a self-employed person is not deductible in computing the federal income tax, but an employer may deduct Social Security taxes paid on the wages of an employee as an expense of conducting a trade or business. Social Security taxes paid on wages of domestic servants and others rendering services of a purely personal nature are not deductible by the employer.

Social Security Benefits

For years before 1984, all benefits received under the Social Security program were tax exempt under a provision of an administrative decision made in 1941.[3] Since 1984, taxable income has included a limited amount of these benefits as calculated by the formula explained in Chapter 8 (p. 8-8). This change affects taxpayers in the upper-middle and upper income brackets; for most citizens, the benefits are still excluded from gross income. This general exclusion of Social Security benefits differs from the treatment accorded benefits from private plans where the taxpayer can only exclude his or her cost or investment in the plan. Because of inflation and other factors, Social Security benefits substantially exceed the contributions made by current recipients. The exclusion of these benefits can be viewed as a tax preference compared with the benefits from private plans. The 1984 change may be the first step toward the elimination of this preference.

---

[3]IT 3447, 1941-1 C.B. 191. (See also Rev. Rul. 70.217, 1970-1 C.B. 12.)

Treatment of Social Security benefits in a manner comparable to the treatment of private plans would be difficult to implement, however. Proceeds from private retirement plans are treated in much the same way as proceeds from simple annuities. Such treatment requires an estimation of expected return under the contract. However, measurement of the expected benefits under Social Security is virtually impossible; benefit formulas can be changed at will by Congress and may fluctuate as amounts earned by the taxpayer from other sources change.

Applying the same tax rules to Social Security benefits as to other retirement plans might conflict with the social and economic objectives of the law. For example, poorly paid workers with many dependents contribute a substantially lower portion of their expected benefits than do higher paid workers with no dependents, and this disparity is increasing as the base subject to the tax increases. This benefit formula is intentional, making the plan provide benefits where they are most needed (even though the Social Security program is not technically a "welfare" program). If the exclusion of benefits should be based on contributions made, the greatest tax benefit would be received by persons with the least need.

Other Public Retirement Programs

At the federal level, the Railroad Retirement program applies to railway employees and parallels the Social Security program. The civil service, the military, the foreign service, and many state and local governments also provide retirement plans for their employees. Nearly all of these public plans are qualified plans; therefore, the employer's contributions have never been taxed to the employee. If the plan is a noncontributory plan—the military retirement program is an example—then any benefits are fully taxable when received. [An exception applies under Sec. 103(a)(4) for certain military disability pensions started before 1976 or due to a combat injury.]

In many other public retirement programs, the employee must contribute to the retirement plan, and, in most cases, these employee contributions are *not* tax sheltered. In other words, the employee must include in gross income throughout his or her working years the entire wage or salary earned, including the dollars that he or she must contribute to a public retirement plan. In these instances, therefore, the employee has a capital investment that he or she is entitled to recover under the annuity rules described above.

PRIVATE RETIREMENT PLANS

Perhaps no aspect of American economic life has had more far-reaching social implications than the tremendous growth in formal private retirement plans during the past 30 years. This growth is reflected in Table 12-3. The total reserves of these plans in 1984 amounted to $948.2 billion, a significant

TABLE **12-3**

PRIVATE PENSION AND DEFERRED PROFIT-SHARING PLANS[a] 1950–1975
(ESTIMATED IN MILLIONS)

Year	Coverage,[b] End of Year	Employer Contributions	Employee Contributions	Number of Beneficiaries, End of Year	Amount of Benefit[c] Payments	Reserves, End of Year (in billions)
1940	4.1	$ 180	$ 130	0.2	$ 140	$ 2.4
1950	9.8	1,750	330	0.45	370	12.1
1955	14.2	3,280	560	0.98	850	27.5
1960	18.7	4,710	780	1.78	1,720	52.0
1965	21.8	7,370	990	2.75	3,520	86.5
1970	26.3	12,580	1,420	4.74	7,360	137.1
1975	30.3	27,560	2,290	7.05	14,810	212.6
1980	N.A.	N.A.	N.A.	N.A.	N.A.	584.6
1984	N.A.	N.A.	N.A.	N.A.	N.A.	948.2

SOURCE: Data for 1940 from Daniel M. Holland, "Some Characteristics of Private Pension Plans," *1959 Compendium,* p. 1305. Data for 1950 and subsequent years from *Statistical Abstract of the United States.* 1986.

[a]Includes pay-as-you-go, multiemployer, and union-administered plans, those of nonprofit organizations, and railroad plans supplementing the federal railroad retirement program. Insured plans, are, in general, funded through trustees.
[b]Excludes annuitants.
[c]Includes refunds to employees and their survivors and lump sums paid under deferred profit-sharing plans.

portion of the total wealth invested in securities. Many factors account for the growth of pension plans since 1940. Some of these factors reflect general social and demographic changes in our society; others are the direct result of tax laws.

First, during and immediately following World War II, there were direct governmental controls over wages. As a result, workers became more interested in various fringe benefits, including pensions. Employers were eager to hold trained employees and considered pensions and other fringe benefits a relatively cheap method of doing so, especially because such costs were deductible in computing taxable income, which was subject to very high tax rates. In recent years, organized labor groups have placed far greater emphasis on fringe benefits, especially pension and profit-sharing arrangements. On the other hand, business managers have realized that favorable retirement plans may be a powerful incentive to workers, resulting in greater efficiency and a reduction in employee turnover.

The much-publicized increase in life expectancy, coupled with earlier retirement ages, has led not only to a much larger population in older age groups but also to a great increase in the average number of years spent in retirement—a time when some source of income is essential to replace the loss of wages. A growth in the general awareness and concern for economic security has been both a result and a cause of the widespread use of formal retirement plans. Another important factor has been the decline in the portion of the population engaged in agriculture and the increase of those living in urban areas and requiring more complete and complex arrangements for financing the living costs of retirement.

Unfortunately, many of the private pension and profit-sharing plans developed after World War II proved to exist almost solely on paper. A congressional committee investigation in 1974 disclosed that, frequently, pension plans were not adequately funded, that vesting schedules made it almost impossible for many participants ever to receive the full benefits they anticipated, and, in general, that requirements of plans made it difficult and costly for employees to change jobs. The result of this investigation was widespread public and congressional demand for reform of the entire private pension system, leading to passage of ERISA, the 1974 Pension Reform Act.

ERISA established detailed and complex rules governing such pension plan provisions as the maximum waiting period before an employee is covered, schedules for vesting of benefits from employee and employer contributions, financial reporting and disclosure of pension trust funds, and minimum funding requirements. It also established a program for providing insurance for pension funds and developed many other rules designed to safeguard employee benefits and rights.

Qualified Plans—General Rules

One major factor in the growth of retirement plans is the income tax law. A plan that qualifies—that is, meets the tests discussed later—provides the following tax advantages:

1. The right of an employer to claim an *immediate deduction* for any amount contributed.
2. The right to *invest* (and reinvest) the contributed funds throughout the annuitant's working years *without* any payment of *income tax* on the income earned.
3. The right of the annuitant to *defer any* payment of *income tax* on some or all of the contributions to the fund *until the annuity starting date* (usually the date of retirement or death).
4. The right of the annuitant to *make certain elections* as to the method of payment at the annuity starting date. (For example, an annuitant might elect a lump-sum payment in lieu of a life annuity.) Retirement benefits under a qualified plan must begin no later than the taxable year of retirement, and all benefits remaining at the participant's death must be distributed within five years.

With these potential rewards, Congress has had a difficult time fashioning rules that give the desired economic and social effects without wholesale abuse. ERISA, passed in 1974, was a comprehensive overhaul, but the rules have been changed often since. Recent changes, including the 1986 Act, have generally restricted the benefits for highly paid employees and have provided for wider required participation. Without covering specific rules, which are clearly beyond our scope here, current rules require that a qualified corporate retirement plan have the following attrtibutes:

1. *Be Nondiscriminatory.* This means that the qualified plan generally cannot treat certain corporate officers, stockholders, business owners, highly paid executives, and so on in a way that is preferential to that given the rank-and-file employee. (Note, however, that this does *not* require equal treatment. For example, contributions equal to 6 or 8% of every employee's salary would be nondiscriminatory even though some employees earn much larger salaries than others.)

2. *Satisfy Vesting Requirements.* This means that an annuitant's rights to receive benefits under the qualified plan must become nonforfeitable—even if the annuitant should change jobs before retirement—within a reasonably short time period. This requirement is satisfied by any one of four different vesting provisions found in ERISA. (Note, however, that vesting does *not* mean that an annuitant is necessarily entitled to withdraw his or her accumulated benefits prior to retirement or death. It simply means that some benefits are guaranteed either at that time or at an earlier date.)

3. *Satisfy Coverage Requirements.* This means that nearly all the full-time employees of any trade or business must be included in the plan before it can become a qualified plan.

4. *Provide Immediate Funding.* This means that cash must be put aside currently to cover the payment of promised future benefits; the "full-faith-and-credit promise" of an employer is not adequate.

5. *Account and Report to Designated Persons.* This means that any qualified plan must keep written records of all details associated with the plan and make periodic reports to both the beneficiaries of that plan and to the government (specifically, the I.R.S. and the Department of Labor).

The most important qualified plans are those of corporations, particularly the large corporate units in our economy. Other types of qualified plans include self-employment plans, individual retirement accounts, and simplified employee plans. The rules for "qualification" of these other types vary somewhat from corporate plans, as explained below.

Corporate Qualified Plans

While our primary concern is with pension plans, other types of corporate plans exist, including profit-sharing and stock-bonus plans. As its name suggests, a retirement plan is intended to provide an income for an individual during his or her retirement years. The basic concept of a qualified retirement plan includes other employee-oriented sharing arrangements. A profit-sharing plan is also just what its name suggests—a plan by which an employer shares profits with its employees. The same ERISA requirements that apply to qualified retirement plans also cover qualified profit-sharing plans, except for the funding provisions. A contribution to a qualified retirement plan is mandatory whether or not the employer makes a profit; a contribution to a profit-sharing plan is dependent on profit and typically varies with the amount of profit earned by the employer. Since no contribution is guaranteed in a profit-sharing plan, it really cannot be considered a retirement plan, but the two are given generally comparable tax treatment.

The essence of stock-bonus plans is that payments are made in the employing company's stock. This is the least popular of the three types of programs. In recent years, however, a great deal of publicity has been given to employee stock ownership plans (ESOPs) and to employee stock owner-ship trusts (ESOTs). Under an ESOT, the employer corporation may contribute its stock to a tax-exempt employees' trust, deducting the value of the stock. Under another form of ESOT, a trust is established that borrows money from a lending institution to purchase stock of the employer company. The loan, usually guaranteed by the employer corporation, is repaid by cash contributions made by the employer to the trust. ESOT plans have been allowed since 1954 but have not proved popular. Because the value of an ESOP or ESOT is wholly dependent on the value of the employer corporation's stock at the time of an employee's retirement, these plans are generally not considered to be true retirement plans although they receive generally equivalent tax treatment.

Finally, qualified corporate plans fall into two distinct groups, *defined-contribution plans* and *defined-benefit plans*. The former calls for a fixed dollar payment into a fund during the annuitant's working years but says absolutely nothing about what the annuitant will receive at retirement. The monthly retirement payment may vary, for example, with the value of the funds accumulated in the annuitant's account on a year-by-year basis. A defined-benefit plan, on the other hand, contractually specifies exactly what the annuitant must receive during his or her retirement years. Depending on general economic conditions, therefore, the amount contributed by an employer to a defined-benefit plan may vary significantly from year to year. The actuary has the difficult responsibility of predicting exactly how much contribution must be made now in order to deliver the promised benefits to a large group of individuals at some future date. With this introduction to qualified corporate plans, we can now turn to tax rules that apply to the corporate employer, the employees, and the trusts.

THE CORPORATE EMPLOYER   The employer may deduct contributions as they are made to qualified retirement programs. The maximum amount deductible depends on whether the plan is a pension, profit-sharing, or stock-bonus plan. The general thrust of these rules, far too complicated to cover in detail here, is the limitation of the amounts set aside for highly paid employees.

For pension plans that are defined-benefit plans, the allowed deduction is basically the current contribution, actuarily determined, needed to fund the eventual benefits. The maximum annual benefits for an employee is $90,000, and this limit must be reduced if the employee retires before the age of 65. For defined-contribution plans such as profit-sharing plans, the deduction is generally limited to 15% of the aggregate annual compensation of an employee. For qualified plans that are combinations of pension and profit sharing, the deduction cannot exceed 25% of the employee's compensation. The 1986 Act placed a maximum limit of $200,000 on compensation that qualifies.

The deduction limits just discussed must be distinguished from the limits on the amounts employers can contribute to the plan (and thereby shelter income on the contribution). Under the 1986 Act prohibitive excise taxes apply to excessive contributions.

THE EMPLOYEE   An employer's contributions made on behalf of an employee to a qualified retirement plan are not included in the employee's income when the contribution is made. Neither is income earned by the trust included in the employee's income for the year. Only when benefits are distributed to the employee does he or she have taxable income. Most employee contributions to a plan (if any) are treated as personal expenditures and are not deductible; in other words, generally the employee's payments are made with after-tax dollars.

If benefits from a qualified plan are received by the employee in the form of an annuity, the excluded portion is determined in the same manner as for annuities received by government employees (see page 12-7). The employee's investment in the annuity is the amount he or she contributes to the plan; these contributions represent a recoverable investment because they were made from after-tax income. The employer's contributions, on the other hand, were not previously taxed to the employee and, therefore, do not constitute recoverable investment. If the employee has made no after-tax contributions to the plan, all benefits are included in gross income.

To illustrate, assume that Cecil Rust worked for the National Company from 1948 through 1987. During this period National Company contributed $20,000 to a qualified pension fund for Rust's benefit. Rust also contributed $20,000 to the fund. Because the fund was qualified, the contributions made by National were not taxable to Rust when they were made; but Rust's cost, which he is entitled to recover tax free, is the $20,000 that he has contributed. Rust began drawing benefits of $4,000 per year in 1987 when he was 65 years old. Reference to the proper annuity table shows that the appropriate multiple is 20.0 (essentially meaning that Rust's life expectancy is 20 years). Thus, Rust would exclude $1,000 from income each year.

$$\frac{\$20,000 \text{ cost}}{\$80,000 \text{ expected return } (\$4,000 \times 20)} \times \$4,000 = \$1,000$$

The remaining $3,000 would be taxable to Rust. If Rust has made no contributions to the fund, the entire amount received would be taxable to him because he would have no "cost."

A more important and more controversial exception is made when the employee or beneficiary receives a lump-sum distribution of the accumulated benefits under a qualified plan. The taxable portion of a lump-sum distribution in a year beginning on or after January 1, 1974, is deemed to be the total amount of the distribution less the amounts contributed to the plan by the employee and less any unrealized appreciation of employer securities. (The unrealized appreciation of employer securities is taxed when the employee sells the securities.) The cost basis of the employer's securities contributed to the plan by the employer and distributed to the employee is included in the taxable portion of the distribution.

For distributions made after 1986, the taxable portion of a lump-sum distribution is generally taxed using a 5-year forward averaging rule. This new 5-year rule, which is illustrated below, replaces a more favorable 10-year averaging rule effective before 1987 and a rule that permitted some part of the distribution to be treated as capital gain. The new 5-year rule can only be used once by a taxpayer during his or her lifetime and only for distributions received after reaching the age of 59½. (A special transition rule applies to taxpayers that were at least 50 years old on January 1, 1988.) Other lump-sum distributions are taxed as ordinary income.

The 5-year averaging rule works as follows: First, the taxpayer computes the tax using regular rates on taxable income *excluding* the lump-sum distribution. To this is added the tax on the distribution. The taxable distribution is first reduced by the *minimum distribution* allowance, an arbitrary amount concocted by Congress to reduce the tax on smaller distributions. The deduction is 50% of the first $20,000 of the taxable distribution but is phased out at the rate of 20% as the distribution rises from $20,000 to $70,000. After subtracting the minimum distribution deduction, the remaining distribution is divided by 5 (5-year averaging!), a partial tax is computed on this one fifth using Rate Schedule X—single, and this tax is multiplied by 5 to obtain the total tax on the distribution.

To illustrate, assume that in 1988 a married taxpayer has taxable income of $55,000 before considering a lump-sum distribution of $100,000. This $100,000 is also the taxable distribution because the taxpayer did not contribute to the plan and the plan held no securities of the employer. The tax for 1988 is as follows:

Taxable distribution		$100,000
Less: Minimum distribution deduction		
−one half of $20,000	$10,000	
Less .20 ($100,000−$20,000)	10,000	–0–
(limit $10,000)		$100,000
Net distribution		$ 20,000
One fifth of above		$ 3,280
Tax on above (Schedule X—Single)		× 5
Multiply by 5		$ 16,400
		11,533
plus tax on $55,000 (Schedule Y—Joint)		$ 27,933
Total tax for 1988		

Without this special averaging rule, the tax on $155,000 using Schedule Y—Joint would be $43,688. The savings is due to the fact that the 15% rate applied to most of the lump-sum distribution.

The law contains strict rules that govern the timing of distributions. Distributions from a plan cannot begin before the employee reaches the age of 59½ (with exceptions for death and separation from service), and they must begin no later than April 1 after the year in which the employee becomes 70½. Excise taxes, generally at a 10% rate, apply to improper distributions.

THE TRUST   Income earned on the assets of a funded retirement plan is not taxable to the trust if the plan is qualified. The importance of the tax-exempt status for the trust fund of a retirement plan cannot be overemphasized. The benefits of tax-free status can be dramatically illustrated by a simple example. Assume that an employee works for 35 years for an employer with a pension plan and that the employer contributes $2,000 per year to the fund on behalf of the employee. Assume further that the average earnings of the pension plan are 6% before taxes, and that the trust would, if taxable, pay income taxes at a marginal rate of 50%. Thus, if the trust were taxable, its after-tax rate of earnings would be only 3%. Reference to a table showing the "amount of a $1 annuity at the end of each period" shows that a contribution of $2,000 per year for 35 years would accumulate to approximately $223,000 at the employee's retirement if the rate of earnings is 6%. On the other hand, if the rate of earnings is only 3%, the contributions of $2,000 per year for 35 years accumulate to approximately $121,000. If we further assume that the employee draws benefits for 15 years after retirement and that the same pretax earnings rate of 6% applies to the trust, the annual pension would be approximately $22,900 from a tax-exempt trust, whereas the annual pension from a taxable trust would be only about $10,000, considerably *less than half* that received from a tax-free trust. With current interest rates in excess of 6%, the tax-exempt status is even more important than it appears in this illustration.

Self-Employment Retirement Plans

For many years, critics have complained that the tax laws permitting employees to benefit from retirement programs were unfair to self-employed individuals. In 1962, after much controversy and conflict, Congress passed a law (P.L. 87-792) that permits self-employed persons to establish retirement plans for their own benefit and to deduct all or a part of the contributions made to such plans. These plans are popularly known as either *Keogh plans* or as *H.R. 10 plans.*

Prior to 1984, Keogh plans were subject to numerous restrictions and limitations that did not apply to qualified corporate plans. The restrictions generally reflected Congress's reluctance to provide qualified plans for self-employed individuals. Under old rules, for example, a self-employed person could only deduct contributions to the plan up to 15% of earned income, limited to $15,000 per year. Changes made by the Tax Equity and Fiscal Responsibility Act of 1982 (TEFRA) provide for parity generally between Keogh plans and corporate plans. For years after 1982, deduction and contribution limits are the same as for corporate plans.

To replace the restrictions on Keogh plans, the 1982 Act introduced a new safeguard against the abuses of qualified plans that stack the benefits in favor of key employees and owners. This new safeguard, which affects *all* plans, requires "top-heavy" plans to meet many restrictions on vesting and benefits that formerly applied only to Keogh plans.

To provide some benefit to individuals with low earned income, the law provides that a deductible contribution of up to $750 can be made without regard to the 15% limit, as long as the amount contributed does not exceed the individual's earned income.

Funds contributed to such plans may be put in a trust or custodial account (usually administered by a bank or savings and loan association), invested directly in individual annuity contracts issued by an insurance company, or invested in special retirement bonds issued by the federal government. Contributions for a taxable year must be made by the due date for filing the taxpayer's federal tax return for that year, not including extensions.

Distributions to self-employed persons are taxed in general in the same way as distributions from employee trusts. However, payments must not begin before the taxpayer reaches the age of 59½, unless he or she is permanently disabled. The 5-year averaging rules also apply here, subject to the once-in-a-lifetime rule.

Shareholder–employees of S corporations have traditionally been treated as self-employed individuals for purposes of qualified plans. Before 1984, the restrictions on contributions and deductions for Keogh plans applied also to employees of S corporations who owned more than 5% of the corporate stock. Because of the general parity between corporate plans and Keogh plans after 1983, shareholder–employees are treated like other employees. Plans for small S corporations are subject to the new restrictions on top-heavy plans.

Individual Retirement Accounts

Section 408 permits an individual to establish his or her own individual retirement plan and to deduct limited amounts of compensation (or earned income in the case of a self-employed person) for contributions to the plan. Prior to 1982, IRA plans were limited to individuals who were not covered by a qualified private or governmental retirement plan, but the Economic Recovery Tax Act of 1981 extended coverage to individuals who are already covered by some other qualified plan. The deduction for A.G.I. is limited to the lesser of $2,000 or 100% of the individual's compensation or earned income. As a result of changes made in 1986, explained below, the deduction allowed is scaled down or eliminated if the taxpayer is covered by an employer's plan and if adjusted gross income exceeds certain specific amounts. IRAs are, therefore, "qualified" plans in that they result in the deferral of taxes even though they do not meet the general test for corporate qualified plans.

For years after 1986, the maximum limit on contributions by taxpayers covered by an employer's plan is reduced when adjusted gross income exceeds $25,000 for single taxpayers and $40,000 for married taxpayers. The IRA limit of $2,000, and therefore the deduction, is phased out over a $10,000 range above these arbitrary amounts. For example, a married individual with A.G.I. of $45,000 is subject to a $1,000 limit ($5,000 excess divided by $10,000 equals the percentage disallowed). A single individual with A.G.I. of $31,000 would be limited to a deduction of $800 ($6,000 excess over $25,000, divided by $10,000 equals 60%, the disallowed percentage). Married couples with A.G.I. of $50,000 or more and single individuals with A.G.I. of $35,000 are entitled to no deduction. Remember that this new limit applies only to taxpayers already covered by an employer's plan, including plans of the U.S., state, and local governments.

The benefits of an IRA have also been extended to certain nonworking spouses, in recognition of the fact that a spouse not working outside the home but performing valuable household work should have the privilege of a tax-sheltered retirement program. A working spouse may (in lieu of a traditional IRA) establish an account for the benefit of the nonworking spouse. A contribution to a spousal IRA is deductible only if a joint return is filed. The working spouse may establish an IRA in joint names or, instead, establish separate account for the two spouses. If a joint account is opened, the maximum deductible contribution is the lesser of 100% of compensation or $2,250. If separate accounts are opened, the maximum deduction of $2,250 can be used so long as not more than $2,000 is contributed to the account of either spouse. The limits discussed above based on adjusted gross income also apply to spousal accounts. A married couple with A.G.I. of $45,000 that has a spousal account can deduct a maximum of $1,125 (50% of $2,250).

Under the law, the retirement funds can be invested in a custodial or a trust account in a bank or savings association or similar organization; can be invested directly in an individual annuity contract issued by an insurance company; or can be invested in special retirement bonds issued by the federal government. The retirement fund must not be withdrawn until the individual reaches age 59½ except in the case of death or disability, and the individual must start drawing it upon reaching age 70½. Any distribution from an IRA before the taxpayer reaches age 59½ is subject to a 10% penalty tax unless the taxpayer has been disabled. When the funds are received during retirement, the entire amount is taxed as ordinary income.

One important, though incidental, use of IRA accounts is the avoidance of the current taxation of lump-sum distributions when an employee leaves a covered employment and must withdraw his or her interest in the plan. The distribution is not taxed if it is "rolled over" into an IRA account. If the same employee later takes a job with a new employer, he or she may be able to again "roll over" the earlier distribution into a qualified plan of the new employer if the plan so permits. If, between the two jobs, the employee is not covered by a qualified plan, he or she can open an individual IRA account.

For years after 1986, taxpayers can make nondeductible contributions to an IRA account. The benefit from the nondeductible contributions is the exemption of earnings on the account from taxation until the account is distributed. The limit on such contributions is also earned income of $2,000 ($2,250 with spousal accounts), and these nondeductible contributions can be made by otherwise covered employees even when their A.G.I. exceeds $25,000 (if single) or $40,000 (if married). The nondeductible amounts must be kept in separate accounts from deductible contributions to ensure proper accounting upon distribution. Contributions to an IRA in excess of the deductible plus the nondeductible limits are subject to a 6% excise tax.

Distributions from an IRA are not subject to the special 5-year averaging rules. If the taxpayer has deducted all contributions, there is no cost basis, and the entire distribution is ordinary taxable income when withdrawn. If nondeductible contributions have been made, the taxpayer has a cost, having used after-tax dollars. In this case, when the account is drawn down in installments, the annuity rules discussed earlier in this chapter apply.

SEP-IRAs

To simplify some of the rules surrounding qualified retirement plans, the Revenue Act of 1978 greatly liberalized provisions permitting employers to deduct contributions to an employee's individual retirement account in what is commonly known as a SEP-IRA, or simplified employee plan. The amount deductible by the employer is limited to $30,000. The employee must include in gross income the employer's contributions to the IRA but may deduct the amount of the employer's contributions limited to $30,000. If the employer contributes less than the maximum amount permitted as a deduction by the employee under a regular IRA plan (100% of compensation, or $2,000, whichever is less), the employee may contribute and deduct the difference.

The rules governing simplified employee plans contain strict nondiscrimination provisions. The plan must not discriminate in favor of officers, shareholders, self-employed individuals, or highly compensated individuals. In addition, employer contributions must be based on a written, specific allocation formula and must bear a uniform relationship to the total compensation of each employee maintaining a simplified plan. Contributions must be made to the plan for each employee who has (1) attained age 21, (2) performed services for the employer in at least three of the preceding five calendar years, and (3) received compensation of at least $300 per year. In addition, withdrawals from the IRA by the employee must not be prohibited, the employee's rights to employer contributions must be 100% vested, and employer contributions must not be conditional on the retention in the IRA of any amount contributed by the employee. If the employer makes contributions that are discriminatory on behalf of employees, the $2,000 limit applies.

Congress has made SEP-IRAs even more flexible for years after 1986 by providing that employees can either elect to receive cash or have the employer make deductible contributions to the accounts. Details of these new rules as well as the rules for other elective type plans under Sec. 401(k) are beyond the scope of this discussion.

Nonqualified Corporate Plans

Although the tax rules for nonqualified plans are much simpler than those for qualified plans, we consider them in detail for each of the three possible major parties to the nonqualified corporate plan—the employer corporation, the employee, and (possibly) the trust.

THE EMPLOYER   The contribution made by the employer to plans that are not qualified may be deducted if the employee's rights in the plan are nonforfeitable. If the employee's rights are not vested when the employer makes the contributions, a deduction can be taken at a later time when the rights become nonforfeitable.

THE EMPLOYEE   For a nonqualified retirement plan, the employee must report as income the employer's contribution when it is made if the employee's rights are vested at that time. If the employee's rights do not vest when the employer's contribution is made, but do become vested at a later date, the employee must report such contributions as income at the time of vesting.

If benefits from a nonqualified plan are paid to the employee as an annuity, the annuity proceeds are generally treated in the same way as annuity proceeds from a qualified plan. However, if the employee was required to report the employer's contributions as income when they were vested to the employee, then the employee's "investment" in the contracts increased by the amount of employer's contributions previously included in the employee's income. The special rules that apply to cost recovery in the first three years of benefit payments from an annuity under a qualified plan do not apply to a nonqualified plan. The entire excess of a lump-sum distribution from a nonqualified plan over the employee's investment is treated in full as ordinary income in the year of distribution, and the special averaging rules do not apply.

THE TRUST   A nonqualified employees' trust must pay tax on its income in the same manner as any other taxable trust (see Chapter 6).

Controversies Over Treatment of Qualified Plans

The tax rules for qualified plans are a strong incentive for savings. The employer gets a deduction now, the trust funds escape taxation, and the employee usually pays a tax after retirement, often at favorable rates. These incentives are so powerful that Congress has been forced to pass restrictive rules, particularly to curb abuses for smaller corporate units with owners also functioning as key employees. The rapid growth of these plans raise some intriguing and troublesome social and economic questions, especially the effects on savings and investment and on the mobility of capital.[4]

EFFECTS ON SAVINGS   Table 12-3 shows that at the end of 1984 the accumulated reserves of private retirement funds totaled $948.2 billion. Evidence is inadequate to show clearly how these accumulated reserves have affected the total volume of personal savings, and there is probably no accurate way to determine whether retirement fund reserves represent, in whole, in part, or not at all, savings that would have been accumulated some other way in the absence of such plans.

To the extent that taxpayers have in mind a definite amount of total savings, presumably the retirement fund would be considered merely a means of achieving these savings. On the other hand, if individuals have a given propensity to save a certain portion of their current cash income, the retirement fund probably represents additional savings, at least in part. The degree of conscious rational consideration given to retirement funds by individuals in reaching decisions about the magnitude of their personal savings is a relatively unknown factor. It has been suggested that self-employment retirement funds, as well as deferred compensation contracts negotiated between an individual employee and the employer, are important in the individual's decision on how much to save, whereas group retirement plans are less important. There seems to be little correlation between the percentage of wages contributed by employers to retirement plans and the relationship between personal savings and personal income.

On balance, it would seem that retirement funds do add substantially to the total volume of savings. Some economists fear that continued increases in the number and size of retirement funds may result in too rapid a growth of savings, with the consequence that there will be an oversupply of investment funds and underconsumption that may cause severe economic imbalance.

EFFECTS ON INVESTMENT   Proponents of tax laws that encourage retirement funds often base their arguments on the notion that these plans increase the supply of available funds for investment in industry. This theory is the basis of the Reagan administration's saving incentive programs of 1981. Statistical evidence showing an increase in the percentage and amount of retirement funds invested in corporate stock supports this conclusion. Obviously, however, the mere investment of retirement funds in corporate stock does not necessarily indicate an inflow of capital into corporations, but it may represent the purchase of outstanding corporate shares, whose prices are pushed upward by the existence of large quantities of investment funds. A

[4]For an interesting discussion of these questions, see *The Federal Tax System*, Joint Economic Committee, 1964, pp. 125–28.

special problem of "inflation" in market value of high-grade stocks may exist at times. Because of the legal, contractual, and financially prudent restrictions placed on the types of investments made by retirement funds, such stocks are in great demand, which limits the supply of these shares to other investors. An associated problem is that many funds acquire high-quality securities for long-term investment and then retire from the market, which freezes investment capital. Undoubtedly, the existence of retirement funds does tend to make it easier for an existing corporation to market new shares of stock.

Many financial experts argue that retirement funds exert a stabilizing influence in the economy because they are sensitive to short-run economic fluctuations. For example, in periods of high economic activity, retirement fund savings rise, exerting a dampening influence by removing capital otherwise available for consumption expenditures. On the other hand, in recessionary periods, savings of this type decrease, leaving a greater percentage of personal income for consumption expenditures and thus exerting a countercyclical influence. It is doubtful, however, whether the "automatic stabilizer" effect of retirement funds is really of major importance.

One further comment on the effects of such large capital accumulations should be made. Many economists have expressed grave fears over the actual or potential economic power given to a relatively few trustees and other administrators responsible for the management of trust funds.[5] The potential import of this problem is undoubtedly very great.

MOBILITY OF LABOR   Reduction of employee turnover is one major advantage sought by employers in establishing retirement plans. This is also one of the chief criticisms levied against such plans—the adverse effects on labor mobility.

Most employee plans provide full vesting of the employee's rights only after several years of participation in the plan. The employee who changes jobs after only a few years of coverage may lose all or part of his or her rights under the plan. Because it is impossible to transfer rights from one plan to another, labor mobility may be severely restricted. Unfortunately, the 1974 Pension Reform Act did not solve this problem, even though it did require minimum vesting schedules that in general provide improved vesting of benefits. In addition, mobility is increased because of the opportunity to avoid current taxation on a lump-sum distribution by placing it in an IRA account. Obviously, the existing law still does not resolve the conflict between the social goals of providing pension income for retired persons and freedom of the individual to change jobs. Studies have estimated that prior to the 1974 Act, fewer than one-half the employees covered by a plan would ever receive benefits from it.

---

[5]For example, see A. A. Berle, *Power Without Property* (New York: Harcourt Brace Jovanovich, 1959), p. 43 ff., one of the earliest books warning of this danger. Another interesting discussion of this problem is found in Rifkin and Barber, *The North Will Rise Again: Pensions, Politics, and Power in the 1980's* (Washington, D.C.: The People's Business Commission, 1978).

Retirement plans may also create a bias against the hiring of older employees. Qualified plans must not discriminate against workers on account of age, but the hiring of an older worker may necessitate higher employer contributions, causing some resistance to his or her employment.

Even with individually negotiated plans, labor mobility is curtailed. Key employees with deferred compensation contracts may forgo higher current salaries to obtain the contract, especially when income tax advantages are significant. A change in employment may result in the employee giving up rights under the deferred payment contract or in unfavorable tax consequences. In addition, the high cost to a new employer of matching the employee's income given up under an old employment contract may be prohibitive.

OTHER SAVINGS INCENTIVES

As we said in the introduction to this chapter, the treatment for retirement plans is the major saving incentive in the tax law. There are other incentives for saving not covered above that deserve some mention.

Deferred Compensation

One procedure commonly used by executives, athletes, entertainers, and other highly paid employees is a deferred pay arrangement. For example, for a fixed number of years the employer and employee enter into an employment contract that provides for a specified amount of current compensation and an additional amount of nonforfeitable deferred compensation. The deferred compensation is credited to a reserve account on the employer's books and is paid in a specified number of installments after the employee's retirement.

Revenue Ruling 60-31 describes in detail various types of arrangements, such as that above, that the I.R.S. considers eligible for tax deferral. In general, the employee may not have the right to receive the compensation immediately, and the plan must be unfunded. As long as these two requirements are met, the employee is not deemed to have "constructive receipt," and, therefore, no tax is payable until the money is received. We should note that the deferred compensation would usually mean deferred consumption, and these plans result in "savings" in that sense. The deferred amounts are atypical savings in that they are not available for allocation for new investment through the usual institutions.

Traditional Tax Shelters

Many tax-shelter vehicles have traditionally been an incentive to save as well as a method of saving taxes. Shelter investments commonly involve initial investments by the taxpayer and then subsequent contributions of capital to cover operating losses and/or debt amortization. Note that these subsequent enforced contributions did not necessarily result in a stored value, since in many cases the losses were very real.

The congressional judgment in the 1986 Act holds that these shelters were not effective incentives. The tax benefits for real estate shelters before 1986 were so valuable that promoters of uneconomical projects were able to attract capital, particularly in the Sunbelt. The elaborate passive loss rules effective after 1986 is the congressional answer. Under these rules, passive losses from shelter-type activities in which the taxpayer does not materially participate may only be deducted against passive income, and not against active or portfolio income as was true in the past.

Working interests in oil and gas wells are exempt from these passive loss rules. Also, real estate rental properties are subjected to special rules where passive losses up to $25,000 per year are sometimes allowed (See Chapter 4). Undoubtedly, the passive loss rules have some (intended?) loopholes. In short, we will still have shelter activity under the new law; we just can't predict the extent of it.

Part Three of the text has covered the basic income tax rules for individuals, beginning with gross income rules in Chapter 8, then individual deductions in Chapters 9 and 10, and the tax computation in Chapter 11. This final chapter of Part Three covers saving incentives, the most important of which are qualified pension plans. In Part Four we turn to the tax rules for business income and deductions.

PROBLEMS

1. Thirty years ago, Tom began payments to a 30-year endowment policy. This policy provides $50,000 life insurance coverage plus various options for conversion during life. Tom paid total premiums of $19,000. In the current year (after 1986), Tom surrenders the policy and receives its cash value of $36,000.
   a. How must he treat the receipt of the $36,000 for tax purposes?
   b. In what way, if any, has this policy "sheltered" Tom's income from taxation?
   c. Is a shelter such as this more useful now than in earlier years? Explain.

2. What is an annuity? What unusual income tax problems does a typical employee's retirement annuity present?

3. How are retirement benefits received under the federal Social Security program taxed? Why are they not taxed like other employee annuities?

4. Why is the rapid growth in retirement plans receiving so much critical attention from scholars? What tax aspects of retirement plans are open to question? What nontax aspects of retirement plans are of major importance?

5. For a qualified plan, explain how the following are treated for tax purposes:
   a. Employer contributions
   b. Trust income
   c. Annuity-type distributions

6. Many political and economic writers deplore the concentration of economic power in the hands of a relatively few people who manage the assets of huge retirement funds. Explain how the tax laws have contributed to the growth of these funds.

7. a. A taxpayer and his employer each contributed $25,000 to a retirement annuity, which pays the taxpayer $5,000 during each of his retirement years. The employer's contributions were *not* treated as taxable income of the employee at the time they were deposited in a tax-free employee trust fund. At retirement, the appropriate "multiple" to be used in computing expected return was 18.0. How much of his annual $5,000 retirement income must the employee report as taxable income?

   b. B. D. Evers retired from employment on December 31, 19X0. Beginning on January 10, 19X1, Evers received monthly payments of $320 from his employer's qualified profit-sharing and pension plan. In recent years, the employer had made all contributions to the fund. Several years ago, however, the plan provided for optional contributions by the employee, and during that time Evers contributed $8,000 to the plan. At the date of retirement, Evers was 65 years old. Compute the amount Evers will include in income in 19X1.

   c. Roger invested $20,000 in an annuity. Beginning in 19X1 and continuing through 19Y0, a total of 10 years, he is to be paid $3,000 each year. How much, if any, of the $3,000 received in 19X1 must be included in gross income?

8. Refer to part a of problem 7 above:
   a. What happens if the taxpayer lives more than 18 years? Assume he collects $5,000 in the nineteenth year.
   b. What happens if the taxpayer dies after receiving benefits for 15 years?

9. In 19X1, Willford Manufacturing Company established a pension program for its employees. Mr. Willford, the president, was especially interested in this program, and the final proposed plan largely reflected his desires. The plan's basic feature was a trust fund to which annual contributions would be made. Each employee with more than five years of service would be eligible to participate. A contribution equal to 5% of the employee's compensation would be made for each employee with earnings in excess of $25,000; contributions of 4% of compensation would be made for each employee with earnings in excess of $15,000 but less than $25,000; and contributions of 3% of compensation would be made for employees with earnings of $15,000 per year or less. Is this likely to be a "qualified" plan? Explain.

10. City Manufacturing Company has established a nonqualified pension trust. Contributions are made each year for each employee who has been employed by the company for more than one year. These contributions are forfeitable by the employee if he or she leaves the company at any time before five full years of employment. Howard McVey began work for the company in June 19x0. In 19x1, 19x2, 19x3, and 19x4, the company contributed $200 each year (in December) to the fund on behalf of McVey. On June 12, 19x5, McVey's rights in the plan became nonforfeitable.
    a. How much income, if any, did McVey report in 19x1, 19x2, 19x3, and 19x4?
    b. How much income, if any, did McVey report in 19x5?

11. Tom Executive began employment with Grosso Corporation on July 5, 1956, and retired from the company on June 30, 1988. He was covered by his employer's qualified retirement plan. While Tom was employed, he contributed $18,000 to the plan, and his employer contributed $62,000. On September 1, 1988, Tom

withdrew his cash benefits of $124,000 in a lump-sum distribution and invested the proceeds in a new business venture.

Tom and his wife file a joint return. During 1988 he has other net taxable income of $60,000. Compute his tax liability for 1988, assuming he elects income averaging on the entire distribution.

12. Determine the maximum deduction in an IRA account for each of following independent cases:

a. Howard, a bachelor, has earned income of $30,000 and has an adjusted gross income of $32,000. Howard is not covered by an employer's plan.

b. Same as in part a, except that Howard is covered by an employer's plan.

c. Same as in part a, except that Howard is married, but his wife has no earned income.

d. Same as in part b, except that Howard is married, but his wife has no earned income.

e. Helen works and earns $44,000. Her husband has no earned income. The A.G.I. on their joint return is $44,000 also. Helen is covered by an employer's plan.

f. John, a bachelor, lives mainly on interest but earned $1,500 during the year. His A.G.I. is $20,000.

13. David retired in the current year; he is 60 years old. He had contributed $21,000 to his IRA account, all deductible. The balance of the IRA account is $38,000.

a. How is David taxed if he draws this down in a lump sum?

b. How is he taxed if he draws the balance down as an annuity of $4,000 a year?

c. Are your answers to parts a and b the same if David retires at the age of 55 and immediately draws down the balance?

14. In 1988 Harris received a $60,000 lump-sum distribution from a noncontributory plan. Harris is married, and his taxable income, excepting the distribution, is $50,000.

a. Assume that Harris is 65 years old at the time of the distribution. Compute his tax for the year.

b. How is Harris taxed on the distribution if he is only 56 years old? What are his alternatives?

FOUR

Deductions for Trades or Businesses

As the world economies become increasingly competitive, it is more important that investment in our capital stock be determined by market forces rather than by tax considerations.
Tax Reform Act of 1986

CHAPTER 13

Business Deductions for the Individual Taxpayer

> . . . home office deductions should be disallowed in the absence of specified circumstances indicating a compelling reason for business use of the home.
> Tax Reform Act of 1986

Business deductions can be defined as those items that are subtracted from business gross income in computing business taxable income. Typically, most items that are considered to be business deductions for federal tax purposes are also classified as business expenses by financial accountants. A student with a sound financial accounting background can thus rely heavily on his or her financial accounting knowledge when determining if an expenditure qualifies as a business deduction.

This chapter will examine several of the expenditures that qualify as trade or business deductions. They will be examined from the viewpoint of the individual taxpayer who is operating a sole proprietorship. These deductions will be reportable by such taxpayer on a Schedule C. The net income calculated on the Schedule C is a direct addition to the individual taxpayer's adjusted gross income.

GENERAL PROVISIONS

Most of the general provisions that must be considered in determining the deductibility of a business expense have already been discussed in Chapter 4. The following summary of the general provisions provides only a brief review of some of the material discussed in that chapter. Section 162 provides that there shall be allowed a deduction for all ordinary and necessary expenses paid or incurred during the taxable year in carrying on any trade or business. Section 165 permits the deduction of losses incurred in a trade or business. A "trade or business" generally is created when the taxpayer devotes significant personal effort of an entrepreneurial nature to a venture that is intended to make a profit and, if it fails to be profitable, the venture is not classified as a "hobby." An expenditure is considered to be "ordinary" if it is commonplace among taxpayers who find themselves in similar circumstances, even though those circumstances may be very unusual. "Necessary" means that the expenditure must appear to be capable of making a contribution to the profitability of the trade or business at the time it is incurred. Finally, a deduction must be "reasonable in amount." The latter criterion is invoked primarily when related taxpayers are involved.

Even though an expenditure may satisfy the above requirements, it still will not be deductible if it fails one or more of the negative criteria discussed in Chapter 4. These criteria indicate that a deduction cannot be a capital expenditure, a personal expenditure, an expenditure related to the production of tax-exempt income, or an expenditure that is contrary to public policy.

Many trade or business deductions of an individual, partnership, or corporation have already been discussed in detail in Chapter 4. Trade or business deductions incurred by an employee were the focus of Chapter 9. Depreciation and cost recovery deductions will be discussed in Chapter 14. No attempt will be made in this chapter to examine any specific provisions that are discussed in those chapters. Instead, this chapter is devoted to examining certain other deductions that may be claimed by a sole proprietor.

EXPENDITURES FOR AN OFFICE

An individual taxpayer can obtain a deduction under Sec. 162 for the ordinary, necessary, and reasonable amounts he or she pays for the rental of a business office. Rent is deductible during the taxable year that the taxpayer uses the rented space for business purposes. Thus, advance payments of rent are not deductible at the time of payment but must be allocated to the taxable year when the property is used by the taxpayer.

Office rental deductions are relatively easy deductions to understand and handle properly if the office is being rented from a third party. Many individual taxpayers, however, maintain an office in their personal residence. They may do this for a variety of reasons. The home office may be created because a portion of the home was being underutilized by the taxpayer. An extra bedroom that was occupied by Aunt Fran when she came to visit for one week each Christmas might be an excellent room to use as a home office. If the taxpayer has a full-time job, the home office might be used for "moon-lighting" work. Finally, the home office may eliminate the need for the taxpayer to commute to work. In many of our larger cities, this clearly can be a major motivation for taxpayers to establish an office in the home.

An individual taxpayer may have difficulty justifying a deduction for some or all of the expenditures incurred in operating a home office. Section 280A, which contains the statutory tests for deducting home office expenses, creates tests that are often difficult to satisfy. In addition to being ordinary, necessary, and reasonable, home office expenses are only deductible if the portion of the home used as a home office is used "exclusively" and "on a regular basis" for one of the following business purposes:

1. It is the principal place of business for any business operated by the taxpayer.
2. It is a place that is used to meet with clients, customers, or patients that the taxpayer sees as part of a business.
3. It is a separate structure that is used in connection with the taxpayer's trade or business.

Exclusive use does not mean that the office must be a separate room. However, the room or portion of the room used for business purposes must be used only for such purposes. A home office that is used not only for operating the taxpayer's business but also is used to handle bookkeeping requirements for the taxpayer's personal finances will not qualify for a home office deduction.

Regular use of the home office is not related by the statute to any specific time periods. A taxpayer, for example, does not have to use the office for business use during eight hours each day to qualify the office for regular use. It is necessary, however, that the taxpayer make more than occasional use of the home for business purposes.

The home office will satisfy the principal place of business test if it is the office in which the taxpayer conducts one or more of his or her businesses. A taxpayer can operate more than one trade or business at the same time. For example, John could operate one trade or business in a deductible home office and also operate a separate trade or business in a rented location many miles away from home. Even an employee's job is considered a separate trade or business. However, it is almost impossible for an employee to obtain a home office deduction in connection with his or her employment because of additional tests that must be satisfied. These tests are not discussed in this chapter.

A home office that is not the taxpayer's principal place for conducting a trade or business may still be deductible if it is a place to meet with clients, customers, or patients. Occasional meetings with such people in the home office will not qualify—the meetings must be on a regular basis. A recent court decision stated that the physical presence of a client is necessary to satisfy this standard. Thus, the mere phoning of clients from the home office is apparently not sufficient to satisfy this requirement.

If the home office is a separate structure, it is only necessary that the structure be used exclusively and regularly in one of the taxpayer's businesses. This is the least restrictive of the three tests.

Finally, if the office is used for storing inventory or for day-care services, more lenient rules usually allow a deduction for expenditures incurred relative to such use of the taxpayer's home.

When a home office deduction is permitted, the taxpayer allocates a portion of the household expenditures to the home office. The calculation preferred by the I.R.S. and the courts is an allocation based on relative square footage. For example, if the home office consists of 400 square feet and the home contains 2,000 square feet, one fifth (400/2,000) of the utility costs, repairs, property taxes, insurance expenditures, and certain other costs incurred in maintaining the home may be allocated to the home office. However, merely allocating the costs to the home office does not mean the expenditures are automatically deductible. The statute provides that only an amount that does not exceed the gross income from the business, less the allocated expenditures that would be deductible anyway (such as mortgage interest and taxes), can be deducted as home office expenditures. For example, if Maggie operates a business out of her home office and incurs postage and secretarial expenses of $1,200 in the business, these expenses will be deductible whether or not she has a home office deduction. If Maggie earns gross income of $3,000 from the business, only $1,800 ($3,000 − $1,200) of the gross income will be available to cover the other expenditures that are not automatically deductible, such as mortgage interest and taxes. Accordingly, if she incurs $3,200 of properly allocated expenses for depreciation, insurance, and utilities, only $1,800 of such expenses will be deductible.

Historical Perspective

Prior to 1976, a deduction for a home office was relatively easy to obtain. The regulations simply provided that when a part of the home was used as a place of business, a portion of the household costs were deductible as a business expense. Because an employee is considered as being in a trade or business, it was even possible for an employee to deduct expenses of a home office if he or she could demonstrate that the expenditures for the home office were ordinary and necessary. The courts usually considered expenditures to be necessary if they were appropriate and helpful in the performance of the employee's job. In some court decisions, a deduction was permitted for a home office that somewhat duplicated the office provided the employee by the employer.

The I.R.S. became concerned that many taxpayers were obtaining unwarranted home office deductions. They were particularly concerned about those taxpayers who were deducting a home office maintained largely for their own convenience. In 1976, as part of the Tax Reform Act of 1986, the I.R.S.

persuaded Congress to pass legislation that largely mirrors the statute that exists today. As a result of this legislation, the availability of the home office deduction has been severely limited.

NET OPERATING LOSSES

An individual taxpayer is allowed to obtain a tax benefit for a net operating loss incurred in any given year. Although the details of the provision—Sec. 172—are as complex as any in the Code, the essential feature can be grasped quickly. If a taxpayer has greater deductions than recognizable gross income in any taxable year, he or she ordinarily is granted a "net operating loss deduction." This deduction can be carried back and forward to other profitable taxable years of the taxpayer. The deduction of the allowable net operating loss in each applicable year reduces or eliminates the taxable income for each year. The difference between the tax liability on this reduced taxable income and the tax liability originally paid by the taxpayer results in a refund to the taxpayer.

The underlying premises for permitting the net operating loss deduction are the annual reporting requirement for taxpayers and the wherewithal-to-pay concept. As we already know, if a taxpayer's business earns a profit in any given taxable year, the taxpayer generally must pay income taxes on that profit. The existence of the profitable year, however, does not mean that the business itself has been a profitable venture for the taxpayer. For example, assume a taxpayer's business reported the following net taxable incomes (or losses) for the three years the business has been operating:

19x1	$20,000
19x2	6,000
19x3	(30,000)

Although the business has been profitable in two of the three years it has been in existence, the business as a whole has incurred a net loss of $4,000 over the three years. Fairness would appear to dictate that the loss in 19x3 should be allowed to offset any taxable income in the other two years so as to eliminate any net tax payments by the taxpayer in 19x1 and 19x2. This is essentially what the net operating loss does, although the method used to compute the net operating loss of an individual is much more complicated than the simple netting of profits and losses.

The wherewithal-to-pay concept also helps justify the net operating loss deduction. When the business incurs a taxable loss of $30,000 in 19x3, the taxpayer will probably incur a significant reduction in his or her cash flow. Unless the taxpayer is given some tax relief, he or she may spiral into insolvency. By permitting the taxpayer to obtain a refund of taxes paid in 19x1 and 19x2, the Code not only recognizes the taxpayer's current inability to pay taxes but also recognizes the taxpayer's need for additional cash to help fund continuing operations.

Calculating the Net Operating Loss

Calculating the net operating loss is not a simple task. While a net taxable loss on the individual taxpayer's current tax return may provide a clue that the taxpayer may have a net operating loss, a net taxable loss does not always result in the creation of a net operating loss deduction. Congress believes that the net operating loss should be an "operating" loss, and, therefore, deductions that are related to nonbusiness operations should be permitted only to the extent that the taxpayer has nonbusiness income. Accordingly, excess nonbusiness deductions (including excess nonbusiness capital losses) are eliminated from the calculation of a net operating loss. Congress also believes that items that would ordinarily be deductible but do not require the disposition of funds should generally not be permitted to increase a net operating loss. Therefore, these deductions are also eliminated in calculating a net operating loss. The obvious effect of eliminating these deductions is to equate the loss recognized more closely with the real dollar loss sustained. In short, the taxpayer's wherewithal to pay is deemed to be reduced by the real dollar loss sustained. It is this amount that should be carried back and forward to profitable years to create a tax refund for the taxpayer and not the taxpayer's unadjusted net taxable loss.

Because "nonbusiness deductions" can increase a net operating loss deduction only if the taxpayer has "nonbusiness income," it is imperative that the meaning of these two terms be understood. Nonbusiness income is any income earned by the taxpayer that is not earned in the taxpayer's trade or business. Examples of nonbusiness income are dividends received, investment interest, alimony income, and annuity income. Nonbusiness deductions are those deductions that relate to the earning of the nonbusiness income. Stated differently, they are deductions that do not relate to the earning of business income by the taxpayer or to the earning of the taxpayer's salary. Examples of nonbusiness deductions are medical expenses, property taxes and interest on the taxpayer's personal residence, charitable contributions, and alimony payments. Strangely, deductible contributions to IRAs and self-employment retirement plans are considered nonbusiness deductions, even though the contributions are based on the amount of salary and self-employment income earned by the taxpayer.

In computing the net operating loss, the taxpayer first deducts nonbusiness deductions only to the extent he or she has nonbusiness income. If the taxpayer has nonbusiness deductions left over after this step, he or she may deduct the excess to the extent the taxpayer has net nonbusiness capital gains. A taxpayer determines the amount of his or her net nonbusiness capital gains by first subtracting the total of all nonbusiness capital losses for the year from the total of all nonbusiness capital gains incurred in the year. If the net amount is a net capital loss, this loss cannot increase the taxpayer's net operating loss and is eliminated from the calculation of the net operating loss. If the net amount is a net capital gain, the taxpayer's excess nonbusiness deductions can be deducted to the extent of the net capital gain. Any nonbusiness deductions that cannot be offset by nonbusiness income or the net nonbusiness capital gains are eliminated from the calculation of the net operating loss.

All business income and deductions are allowed in computing the net operating loss deduction. Business income is income from the taxpayer's trade or business or income from the taxpayer's employment. Business deductions include all typical business expenses such as rent, insurance, repairs, advertising, and postage expenses. In addition, the Code provides that moving expenses, most employee business expenses, and personal casualty and theft losses are business deductions.

Business capital losses are deductible to the extent of business capital gains incurred by the venture. If business capital losses exceed business capital gains, the excess capital losses may be deducted to the extent that nonbusiness capital gains exceed the sum of nonbusiness capital losses and excess nonbusiness deductions (see discussion above). Any excess business capital losses that cannot be offset are eliminated from the calculation of the net operating loss.

Finally, the Code requires that certain additional mechanical adjustments be made when computing the net operating loss. Any net operating loss that is carried back or forward from another taxable year is not allowed to increase the current year's net operating loss. In addition, the net operating loss cannot be increased by the taxpayer's personal and dependent exemptions.

The mechanical application of these very complicated rules can be better understood through an example. The following illustrates the calculations needed to compute both the taxable loss and the net operating loss for a single individual taxpayer:

	Taxable Loss Computation	*Net Operating Loss Computation*
Income:		
Salary	$20,000	$20,000
Business income	10,000	10,000
Dividend income	3,000	3,000
Interest income	2,000	2,000
Long-term capital gain (nonbusiness)	6,000	6,000
	$41,000	$41,000
Deductions:		
Personal casualty loss	($ 4,000)	($ 4,000)
Charitable contributions	(3,000)	
Property tax on residence	(2,000)	
Contribution to IRA	(2,000)	(5,000)
Interest on residential mortgage	(7,000)	
Personal exemption	(1,900)	
Loss on rental property	(25,000)	(25,000)
Long-term capital loss (nonbusiness)	(9,000)	(6,000)
Business expenses	(9,000)	(9,000)
	($62,900)	($49,000)
Taxable loss	($21,900)	
Net operating loss		($ 8,000)

The difference between the taxable loss of $21,900 and the net operating loss of $8,000 is attributable to three different modifications that must be made to the taxable loss when computing the net operating loss deduction. First, no deduction is permitted for personal exemptions when computing a net operating loss deduction. Next, the net operating loss calculation permits a deduction for nonbusiness capital losses only to the extent the taxpayer incurs nonbusiness capital gains. Because the nonbusiness capital losses ($9,000) exceed the nonbusiness capital gains ($6,000), the $3,000 difference cannot be deducted in computing the net operating loss.

Finally, the net operating loss calculation limits the deduction for certain nonbusiness deductions to the amount of the taxpayer's nonbusiness income. These itemized deductions·include the charitable contributions ($3,000), property tax on residence ($2,000), contribution to IRA ($2,000), real property taxes ($2,000) and interest on mortgage ($7,000). Because the nonbusiness income for our taxpayer totals only $5,000 ($3,000 dividend income + $2,000 interest income), the taxpayer is only permitted to deduct $5,000 of these nonbusiness deductions in computing the net operating loss deduction.

The calculation of the net operating loss can also be explained in a slightly different fashion. Rather than directly calculating the net operating loss as was done above, the taxpayer may wish to use the net taxable loss as the starting point for the calculation and then "add back" to this amount the items that are not permitted to increase a net operating loss deduction. This approach would result in the following calculation:

Net taxable loss		($21,900)
Add back:		
Personal exemption	$1,900	
Excess capital loss	3,000	
Excess nonbusiness deductions	9,000	13,900
Net operating loss deductions		($ 8,000)

The Benefit of the Net Operating Loss Deduction

Since the taxpayer has both a taxable loss and a net operating loss in the example above, the taxpayer clearly will have no income tax liability during that year. However, the lack of current tax liability could have been determined simply by noting that the taxpayer had a taxable loss for the year. The real benefit the taxpayer receives from the net operating loss deduction is the ability to carry the net operating loss deduction back to the earliest of 3 years and then forward 15 years from the year in which the net operating loss was incurred. Generally, the net operating loss must be carried back and forward in chronological order—that is, the loss must be used to the extent possible in the earliest available year before it can be carried forward to the next year. The taxpayer is permitted, however, to forgo the entire carryback period and only carry the net operating loss deduction forward. An advantage of carrying the loss back is that an "immediate" refund is made; on the other hand, if the loss is carried forward the taxpayer receives only a future benefit.

The taxpayer receives a refund of some or all of the taxes paid in a carryback year by recalculating the tax for that year. The refund is the difference between the tax originally paid and the lower tax computed after deducting the net operating loss deduction available in that year. Any net operating loss used in a carry-forward year simply reduces the amount of the tax liability that would otherwise be paid in that year.

After a net operating loss deduction has been carried to and used in a given taxable year, the amount of the net operating loss deduction that may be carried to the next taxable year depends on the amount of the loss that is deducted in the prior year. Thus, an amount can be carried to the next taxable year only if the net operating loss deduction is greater than the adjusted taxable income in the prior year. Net operating loss deductions are carried forward chronologically until used up in this same manner or until the carry-forward period expires. Thus, if a taxpayer has a net operating loss of $20,000 that she uses to obtain a refund of taxes that she paid three years before when she had a taxable income of $70,000, none of the net operating loss deduction will be available to carry forward since it has been used completely in the third prior year.

SPECIAL DEDUCTIONS FOR FARMERS

The agricultural segment of our economy poses a dilemma for tax policy. On one hand, we know that trace elements, humus, and natural plant nutrients are being depleted from the soil at an alarming place in many areas. The erosion of topsoil also continues despite a fairly vigorous federal program that has been in existence for over four decades.

On the other hand, agricultural production is high, and an oversupply of many basic commodities exists, particularly cereal grains. Hybrid strains of grains, processed fertilizers, chemical weed control, and labor-saving machines have made the American farmer the most efficient in the world. This efficiency on the farm is reflected in a decrease in the absolute number of farmers and a rapid decrease in farmers as a percentage of the total population. American consumers spend around 20% of their disposable income for food compared with from 40 to 60% in European countries and virtually 100% in some primitive economies.

The population explosion further complicates the equation. Will new technology enable the agricultural sector to keep pace with population growth without increases in food prices relative to other prices? Are ecologists right when they predict that misuse of the soil, combined with population growth, will result in a severe shortage of food? The policy makers in Washington have responded to the problem in two ways. They have written into the law some incentives that increase food production and, at the same time, have placed restrictions on deductions of agricultural activities that may reduce the flow of capital into the agricultural segment.

Incentives for Farmers

Beginning with the 1954 Code revision, Congress has added to the law several sections aimed at encouraging good land use by farmers. Certain practices are encouraged by allowing the farmer to deduct immediately costs that would otherwise be added to capital accounts. Expenditures for the following purposes may be deducted in the year paid or incurred, subject to some rather severe maximum limits:

1. Soil and water conservation, including the cost of moving earth for leveling, grading and terracing, contour furrowing, construction of diversion channels, and similar projects. No deduction is permitted unless the expenditure is consistent with a plan approved by certain governmental agencies (Sec. 175).
2. Fertilizer, lime, ground limestone, marl, or other materials to enrich, neutralize, or condition land (Sec. 180).

In every case, the taxpayer claiming a deduction for these expenditures must be engaged in the business of farming. In addition, the land must be used in farming. These requirements are intended to prevent the use of these provisions by speculators and developers to charge off costs that would otherwise be added to the basis of the land and be recovered at the point of sale. Recovery at point of sale would merely decrease the capital gain, whereas the immediate deduction might offset ordinary income in full.

The provisions governing soil and water conservation expenditures were added to the law in 1954. Section 180 was enacted in the early 1960s. The hearings before the House Ways and Means Committee on soil and water conservation were combined with the hearings on R&D, and all witnesses appearing before the committee as well as all communications read into the record supported the measure. Arguments made for current deduction were similar to those made for the immediate deduction of R&D—with some special twists. Some witnesses noted the need to preserve our natural heritage, citing decreases in cultivable land due to wind and water erosion. Others cited as inequitable the fact that farmers who received government grants for conservation projects had to include the grant in income but could not deduct the costs until the land was eventually sold. (Capital expenditures would be added to the basis of the land.) Still other witnesses suggested that government subsidies for agricultural projects might eventually be reduced by encouraging investments by individual farmers. One candid witness recommended the provision because it would make the farmers honest; most farmers, according to this witness, were going to deduct these expenditures in any event.[1]

---

[1] For testimony on this provision, see *Hearings on Internal Revenue Revision,* House Ways and Means Committee, 83rd Congress, 1st Session, Topic 21 (Washington, DC: U.S. Government Printing Office, 1953), p. 946.

The taxpayer engaged in the business of farming may elect to treat both types of expenditure as current deductions or as capital expenditures. Current deduction is an obvious choice, particularly for the large number of part-time farmers who are, by definition, engaged in the business of farming but who nevertheless have a speculative interest in land values. To these "gentlemen farmers," conservation and soil improvement not only make sense agriculturally but also increase the rate of appreciation in land values. Of course, farming losses incurred by these part-time farmers may be deducted from income from other sources.

The facts just cited account for the rather strict limitations imposed by Congress on soil and water conservation expenditures. The deduction for any year is limited to 25% of the *gross income derived from farming*. When these expenditures exceed 25% of gross income derived from farming, the amounts not deducted are carried over to later years [Sec. 175(b)]. The deduction for fertilizer and the like is not limited.

OTHER TRADE OR BUSINESS EXPENSES

An individual taxpayer may generally deduct the amount he or she pays to attorneys, accountants, and other professionals that provide services to the individual's trade or business. The amounts paid must be reasonable, and the service provided must be of a deductible nature. A payment of $500 to a CPA for compiling the annual balance sheet and income statement for the business will be deductible. The payment to an architect for designing the office building the taxpayer uses in his trade or business must be capitalized in the cost of the building.

Rental payments made for property used in the taxpayer's trade or business generally may be deducted by the taxpayer. For example, amounts paid to a company for rental of a large computer will usually be a deductible expenditure. Special rules apply to leased automobiles. When a lease is actually a disguised purchase of the property, the taxpayer must recast the transaction as a purchase and treat the rental payments as consisting of amounts paid to purchase the property and as payments of interest.

Prepaid rental payments are deductible only when the property is used by the taxpayer. This applies, regardless of whether the taxpayer is on the cash or accrual basis of accounting.

Amounts expended to repair the taxpayer's business property can be deducted as a business expense provided the expenditure is not required to be capitalized. Differentiating between deductible repair expenses and capitalized repair costs is not an easy task since the distinction between the two is not well defined. In general, a repair does not appreciably increase the asset's value or significantly increase its useful life. A repair just keeps the asset in normal operating condition. Capital expenditures, on the other hand, usually significantly prolong the assets life, materially increase the asset's value, or make the asset available for a different use in the business. A routine replacement of a part in a machine that produces ceramic tiles would be a repair. The cost of a major modification designed to make the machine capable of producing pottery would be a capitalized cost.

Insurance premiums paid to cover casualty and theft losses on business property are deductible. Also deductible are premiums paid for insurance to reimburse the taxpayer for overhead expenses incurred during the time the taxpayer is disabled. Generally, premiums paid for worker's compensation insurance and for indemnity bonds are also deductible. Life insurance paid by the taxpayer on his or her own life is not deductible.

Selling expenses, such as commissions and advertising costs, are generally deductible by the taxpayer. Also deductible are amounts paid for postage, freight, telephone services, and supplies used in the taxpayer's trade or business.

BAD DEBTS

An individual taxpayer can incur a bad debt in a variety of ways. The individual can invest in a corporate bond that the corporation is unable to repay upon maturity. A loan to a family member may not be repaid because the family member's business was unsuccessful or because one or both parties believed the loan to be more in the nature of a gift. A loan to a business associate may not be able to be repaid when the associate files for bankruptcy. While all of these bad debts result in economic losses to the taxpayer, each will be treated differently for tax purposes. Before a taxpayer can determine the proper treatment of a bad debt, he or she must determine if (1) a valid debt exists, (2) the debt is a business or a nonbusiness debt, (3) the debt has any basis, and (4) the debt became wholly or partially worthless during this taxable year.

Business Bad Debt Deductions

When an amount owed to a taxpayer is uncollectible, the taxpayer must first determine if the amount was ever really collectible at all. The Code permits a deduction for a bad debt only if a bona fide debt was owed to the taxpayer. Loans to family members may actually be disguised gifts that never were intended to be repaid. Failure to repay such "gifts" are not deductible by the lender as a bad debt.

Once it is determined that a bona fide debt exists, the taxpayer must then decide if the debt is a business or nonbusiness bad debt. A nonbusiness debt is a debt that was created or acquired outside the taxpayer's trade or business. Thus, a business debt will be one that is created or acquired in connection with the taxpayer's trade or business. The critical distinction between these two types of debt is discussed in Chapter 4. If a debt is determined to be a nonbusiness bad debt, it will be deductible as a short-term capital loss. Business bad debts, on the other hand, are deductible as ordinary deductions. Worthless stocks and bonds are placed in a separate category and are treated as capital assets sold on the last day of the taxable year during which they become worthless. Thus, investors in stocks and bonds will typically receive long-term capital loss treatment on the worthlessness of such investments. It will be assumed in the remaining paragraphs that the taxpayer's debt qualifies as a business bad debt eligible for treatment as an ordinary deduction.

The taxpayer is permitted a deduction for a business bad debt only if the taxpayer has a basis for the debt. A cash-basis taxpayer may not have a basis for a receivable, because the income and receivable are not recognized on the books until the receivable is collected. Since the receivable is never formally booked, no loss can be recognized when it is determined to be uncollectible. Accrual-basis taxpayers, however, create a basis for their receivables at the time of sale. The uncollectibility of such receivables will result in the recognition of a bad debt.

When a debt becomes worthless must be determined on a case-by-case basis. No magic formula exists to help make this decision. Factors that must be examined include the debtor's history of not paying debts, the debtor's bankruptcy, and the debtor's insolvency when the debtor dies or becomes severly ill. No legal action is necessary if it can be reasonably determined that the debtor would not be able to pay in the event of a judgment against the debtor. A deduction is also permitted for partial worthlessness of a business bad debt if it can be determined that the debt is only partially collectible. In each case, the deduction is permitted in the year that the debt is determined to be wholly or partially worthless.

Direct Charge-off Method

Prior to the passage of the Tax Reform Act of 1986, business bad debts could be deducted under either the reserve method or the direct charge-off method. The reserve method allowed the taxpayer to make a reasonable addition annually to a reserve for bad debts. The mechanical application of this method mirrors the method used in financial accounting. The taxpayer determined a reasonable reserve based on a percentage of annual sales or a portion of accounts receivable on hand at the end of the year. The amount that was considered reasonable usually needed to be tested under the Black Motor Car formula, which required the taxpayer to track his or her bad debt experience over a six year period. The addition to the reserve was booked by debiting bad debt expense for the amount of the addition and crediting a contra-asset account entitled "Allowance for Bad Debts." When a debt was determined to be wholly or partially worthless, the allowance account was debited and the receivable account was credited.

The Tax Reform Act of 1986 eliminates the reserve method for all taxpayers except financial institutions. For taxable years beginning after December 31, 1986, the only method available to individuals for deducting business bad debts will be the direct charge-off method. This method permits a bad debt deduction in the year when the debt becomes wholly or partially worthless. The bad debt is accounted for as a debit to bad debt expense and a credit to the receivable.

PROBLEMS

1. The Tax Reform Act of 1976 made it virtually impossible for an employee to deduct any maintenance costs, operating expenses (other than taxes and interest), and depreciation on that portion of his or her home used as an office in connection with employment. In your opinion, why were these tough rules adopted?

2. How do you reconcile the apparent liberalization of tax laws relating to some expenses (such as the credit for child care and deduction for moving costs) with a simultaneous tightening of laws in other cases (such as curtailment of deductions relating to an office in the home and business travel)?

3. John is a self-employed writer who has had some success in writing and publishing novels. While he has not become wealthy from his writing efforts, he has managed to produce a profit each year from his writing. In 19x7, John received royalty payments of $45,000 from his publishers. Among the expenses he incurred in writing his novels was a office in his home that he used exclusively and regularly in his trade or business as a writer. The office was a room that comprised one sixth of the total square footage of the home. During 19x7, John incurred the following expenses related to his home. How much of each of these expenses will be deductible?

Utilities for the home	$2,100
Supplies used in the office	500
Secretarial costs for typing manuscripts	7,500
Maid service for cleaning entire home	1,200
ACRS deduction that would be permitted if entire home were used as an office	3,000

4. Dr. Smith owns a two-story home. He resides on the second floor and operates his medical practice from the first floor. Both stories are exactly the same size. One fourth of the first floor consists of an office in which Dr. Smith reviews patients files and reads the latest medical journals. He maintains no office on the second floor. During 19x7, Dr. Smith incurred the following costs in maintaining the office. How much of each of these costs will be deductible? Assume the medical practice earns considerable profit each year.

ACRS deduction for entire first floor	$4,000
Supplies for patient's files	700
Janitorial service for cleaning the first floor each evening	2,000
Cost of medical journals	1,000

5. Logan is an architect who operates her practice in a small building in her backyard, which was originally a guest house. The building is not attached to her home. During 19x7, Logan incurred the following costs in maintaining her office:

Utilities	$2,100
ACRS deduction on the guest house	3,000
Janitorial service for cleaning guest house	1,500
Supplies used in office	6,000

How much can Logan deduct for her home office?

6. In each of the following independent cases, indicate whether the taxpayer is entitled to deduct expenses (depreciation, utilities, insurance, and so on) applicable to an "office in the home."

   a. Pete is an accounting professor at a state university. One room in his home has been converted into an office used by Pete solely for such tasks as grading papers, preparing exams, and reading journals.

   b. Joe is a law professor at a state university. One room in his home has been converted into an office used solely by Joe for grading papers and other class-related activities and also for writing and revising textbooks from which Joe receives substantial royalties.

   c. Marilyn, married, operates a part-time typing service in her home. In her bedroom, she has an "office" with desk, typewriter, file cabinet, and so on. She uses the office approximately 15 hours per week in her typing service.

   d. Jane is a sales representative for several companies. She uses a room in her home solely as an office in which she takes orders, makes telephone calls, prepares reports, and so on.

7. The net operating loss deduction is based on the annual reporting concept and the wherewithal-to-pay concept. Explain.

8. Derek Smit is a self-employed businessman during the current year. His business has gross income of $25,000 and incurs $26,000 of business expenses. Smit earns $1,000 of dividend income from an investment in a mutual fund and contributes $2,000 to his undergraduate college and $500 to the Red Cross. Smit is a single taxpayer. What is his net operating loss for the current year?

9. Rhonda Rail was an employee of XYZ Corporation who has decided to use her expertise in her own sole proprietorship. She worked for XYZ from January 1 to July 31 and earned a salary of $17,000 during that time. During the remainder of the taxable year she earned gross income of $15,000 from her sole proprietorship and incurred business expenses of $31,000. Rhonda has a rental property that produced a $15,000 tax loss during the year. She earned $1,500 of dividend income but incurred a long-term capital loss of $10,000 when she sold the stock that produced the dividend. She also made charitable contributions of $700 and paid $4,000 interest on her home mortgage. She is a single taxpayer. What is her net operating loss for the current year?

10. Jerry Walker operates a retail store during the week and works occasionally as a clothing salesman at a local department store. During 19x7, Jerry had the following income and deductions on his federal income tax return:

Income:		
Gross income from sole proprietorship	$60,000	
Commissions earned from salesman job	2,500	
Interest income	600	
Dividend income	400	
Long-term capital gain on sale of personal investments	7,000	$70,500

Expenses:

Business deductions from sole proprietorship	($75,000)	
Personal casualty loss (after limitations)	(2,000)	
Long-term capital loss on sale of personal investments	(1,000)	
Interest paid on home mortgage	(7,000)	
Charitable contributions	(1,000)	
Personal exemption	(1,900)	(87,900)
		($17,400)

Compute Walker's 1987 net operating loss.

11. Embryo, Inc., suffered a net operating loss of $10,000 in 19x4. The loss was attributable to circumstances that management does not expect to recur. Embryo, Inc., has reported taxable income since its inception in 19x1 as follows:

Year	Taxable Income
19x1	$ 5,000
19x2	30,000
19x3	90,000
19x4	(10,000)

Management projects Embryo's taxable income to be $150,000 in 19x5. Using current corporate tax rates in all years (19x1 through 19x5), explain the potential value of the 19x4 corporate net operating loss by completing the following blanks: Management has a choice; it may elect to receive a refund of $_____ immediately or hope for a deduction worth as much as $_____ next year.

12. John Atwood, a successful attorney, earned a net profit of $80,000 from his practice in 19x1. John is also a "gentleman farmer," and the results of his farming operations for 19x1 were as follows:

Sales of livestock and commodities	$12,000
General operating expenses	14,000
Soil conservation expenditures	4,000
Fertilizer and soil improvements	3,000

John had deductions from A.G.I. of $4,800 and deductions for exemptions of $3,000. Compute his taxable income.

13. Lois Howell, a corporate executive with a large salary, has decided to purchase a 500 acre farm. She intends to spend a considerable amount of money over the next few years on building new fences, constructing ponds, leveling out erosion ditches, and planting high-yield permanent grasses. Her aim is to run an efficient cattle operation eventually, but she expects to have sizable losses for several years.
   a. What election should Howell make relative to her accounting method? for other specific anticipated expenditures?
   b. Explain how Howell can make money on this scheme because of our tax laws even though she just breaks even economically.
   c. What can Howell do to avoid the "hobby loss" rules?

14. In June 19x1, Jenkins purchased an undeveloped farm for $80,000, paying $23,000 cash and signing a note for the balance. During 19x1, he had the following expenditures relating to the farm:
   (a.) Erection of dirt dams for tanks, $1,800. Of this amount, the U.S. government paid $500 under a water conservation program.

(b.) Cost of setting out grass "sprigs" and planting grass seed, $680.

(c.) Cost of removing undergrowth, leveling land, and filling ditches (on land to be used for pasture), $1,200.

(d.) Cost of fertilizer for grass, $150.

(e.) Construction of new fences on property, $450.

(f.) Eradication of underbrush and scrub trees on area to be left for timber production, $300. Eradication was undertaken so that existing trees could grow.

(g.) Costs of driving from home in city, where Jenkins practiced law, to farm for overseeing and helping in work (total 15 trips), $100.

(h.) Real estate taxes on property for period owned by Jenkins, $140.

(i.) Interest paid on loan, $3,200.

(j.) Cost of drilling well for water supply for cattle, $800.

(k.) Equipment for water well in (10), $250.

(l.) Cost of cattle for breeding purposes, $4,000.

Jenkin's only income from the property was from the sale of three calves for $240. Show the amount of each expenditure that Jenkins may deduct currently, assuming that he wishes to deduct the maximum.

15. Joan Creek operates a cash-basis comedy club. The club is a sole proprietorship that incurs the following expenditures in 19x7. Which of these expenditures will be deductible in 19x7?

a. $600 paid to attorneys for drafting contracts between the club and the guests performing at the club.

b. $4,500 ($300 per month) paid for rental of the club. The rent covers the period from January 1, 19x7, through March 31, 19x8.

c. $500 paid for repairing some broken furniture at the club.

d. $1,000 paid for a whole-life insurance policy on Joan's life.

e. $2,000 paid for advertising the club during 19x7 on a local radio station. It is expected the advertising will benefit the club in both 19x7 and 19x8.

f. $1,000 premiums paid for worker's compensation insurance. The insurance covers employees of the club.

16. Roger Goodheart has loaned money to many companies and individuals during the past several years. During 19x7, some of these loans were determined to be worthless. Determine the proper tax treatment for each of these worthless loans on Roger's 19x7 tax return.

a. $2,000 loaned to Betty Badfaith, a former friend who Roger had met at a local health club.

b. $1,000 loaned to his nephew, Bill Bigeyes, who was starting a business and needed the loan to buy advertising time on the radio. Roger thought that Bill's business would be a good customer for products that Roger produced in his sole proprietorship.

c. $3,000 loaned to his daughter to help her buy a used car. No note was signed, and Bill did not really expect her to repay any principal or interest on the loan.

d. $5,000 loaned to XYZ Corporation, a valued customer for the products sold by Goodheart's sole proprietorship. XYZ Corporation had what it hoped was a temporary cash flow problem.

e. A $600 receivable, which was to be paid to Goodheart by Joe Blough. The receivable was generated by services performed by Goodheart in helping Blough start a business.

17. Pat Parsons loaned $10,000 to a business associate in 19x4. The loan terms provided that the associate would pay Pat $2,000 of principal and interest at 14%

on the unpaid principal starting February 1, 19x5, and on each February 1 through 19x9. The associate paid principal and interest on the loan until the associate declared bankruptcy two days before making the February 1, 19x7, payment. Pat settled for $1,500 in full payment of the remaining debt with the bankruptcy court on September 1, 19x7. How much is Pat's bad debt deduction in 19x7 and what is its character?

SUPPLEMENTAL PROBLEM

18. Karen is a professor at the local university. She has an office at the university but finds that she can often work more efficiently in an office she maintains at her home. The home office is used regularly and exclusively by Karen for grading papers, preparing classroom lectures, and writing research papers that the university requires her to write. Can Karen obtain any deduction for the costs incurred in maintaining her home office? Why or why not?

CHAPTER 14

Depreciation and Cost Recovery

A word is not a crystal, transparent and unchanged; it is the skin of a living thought and may vary greatly in color and content according to the circumstances and the time in which it is used.
Justice O. W. Holmes, Towne v. Eisner, 245 U.S. 418 (1918)

DEPRECIATION AND COST RECOVERY

Several of the more important provisions of the federal tax law are based primarily on the goals of full employment, industrial efficiency, and national defense. A direct method of increasing the efficiency of a capital investment is to provide for a rapid recovery of capital. The timing of the recovery of capital has been a constant problem for legislators, administrators, and the courts. Current income tax law provides four methods of cost recovery.[1]

1. Immediate deduction of the total cost when paid or incurred.—This method is currently used for research and development, for intangible development costs of natural resources, and for other payments whose benefits are intangible, such as an advertising campaign. Taxpayers may expense a limited amount of the cost of tangible personal property used in a business, as explained later in this chapter. The

---

[1]For a discussion of the different economic effects of these four methods, see Joel Dean, "Capital Wastage Allowances," *1959 Compendium*, pp. 813–26.

usual result is a deduction of the expenditure prior to recognition of the income that arises from it.

2. Deferral of cost until property is sold or otherwise disposed of.—Investments in land and securities are now treated in this manner, on the assumption that these properties do not waste away or necessarily depreciate in value over their lives. For years, railroads used this method (sometimes called the retirement method) for some properties. It provides no deduction for the use of property over its life but allows a sizable deduction on retirement if the property has in fact decreased in value.

3. A deduction based on a percentage of income from the property over its life.—This method is now used to compute the deduction for depletion of most natural resources.

4. "Timetable" deductions—With the exceptions mentioned above, the cost of property is deducted over a period of years (or sometimes over the number of units to be produced), beginning at the date the property is placed in use, based on a more or less arbitrary timetable. This method of spreading cost is known as depreciation.

In this chapter we consider the various rules for "timetable" deductions, or depreciation. Because of the time value of money, which includes a business's payment of its income tax bill, any provision that permits the immediate deduction of a capital investment is obviously superior to one that requires the recovery of capital over a period of years.

How Accelerated Capital Recovery Increases the Return on Capital Investments

A prudent businessperson considering an investment in plant and equipment ignores all past costs and expenses and looks only at future cash transactions. In addition, future cash receipts are not worth as much as today's cash receipts. Depreciation methods can have an important effect on the present value of future cash receipts.

To illustrate, let us imagine that a businessman is considering a $500,000 investment in a new plant. He estimates that the new plant will produce a net cash return before taxes of $90,000 a year for 20 years, ignoring for now the effects of depreciation. We assume his tax rate is 40%. Thus, his after-tax return will be $54,000 per year, still ignoring depreciation. He might begin with the following comparisons:

Outlay in cash now	$ 500,000
Expected cash return net of taxes (20 years at $54,000)	1,080,000

A conclusion based on this simple analysis would be incorrect. The $500,000 cost is paid now, but the return is spread over 20 years. If we assume that the businessman uses 10% as an expected rate of return, the present value of the expected future returns would be only $459,756 ($54,000 annual net return after taxes times 8.514, the factor used to determine the present value of a series of 20 equal annual payments at 10%). If this $459,756 amount is compared with the $500,000 cost of the investment, the investment appears to be unprofitable. This simple comparison is also deficient because it does not consider depreciation or amortization of investment cost.

Because of the time value of money, the sooner the tax law permits recovery of capital (by deducting it from gross income), the more attractive a given investment will be to an investor. Using the same facts as in the above illustration, assume that the tax law permits an immediate deduction of $500,000 invested. Assume further that the taxpayer has enough income to use the entire deduction. If the taxpayer's marginal tax rate is 40%, the $500,000 deduction immediately produces a $200,000 decrease in tax payments, and the net cost of the investment is only $300,000. The $459,756 present value of the expected returns from the investment now includes a handsome profit.

As a comparison, assume that the law required the depreciation of the $500,000 investment on a straight-line basis over a 20-year period. Calculation of the present value of the capital recovery would be:

Depreciation per year ($500,000/20 years)	$25,000
Times tax rate	40%
Tax savings per year	$10,000
Present value of 20 annual payments of $10,000, each at 10%	$85,140

With this extended depreciation schedule, the net cost of the investment is $414,986; that is, the $500,000 paid out reduced by the $85,140 present value of the future depreciation. Given the $459,756 present value of the expected return, the investment might still be made, but its potential profitability is significantly reduced by the deferral of the deduction.

As a final illustration, let us now assume that this particular investment qualifies for depreciation or amortization over a 5-year period. Tax savings will be $40,000 per year; that is, the $100,000 annual depreciation times the 40% tax rate. The present value of the savings, again using a 10% rate, is $151,640. This more rapid recovery reduces the net cost of the project to $348,360, and the investment's prospects are enhanced significantly compared with the 20-year recovery period.

EARLY HISTORY OF DEPRECIATION

When drafting the original income tax law, Congress could not foresee the many problems that would arise in administering it. As originally conceived, expenditures would be either revenue charges (current expense deductions) or capital charges (related to acquisition of property). Assets were divided on a commonsense basis between those properties that did not wear out or waste away and those that did. The cost of nondepreciable property could only be matched against the eventual sales price to determine gain or loss. For the other group of assets, the Revenue Act of 1913 provided "a reasonable allowance for depreciation by use, wear and tear of property, if any." Later acts used substantially identical language but included "obsolescence."[2]

The Straight-Line Concept

Prior to passage of the first income tax law, accountants had recognized the need for systematically spreading or allocating the cost of a wasting asset over the accounting periods benefited. At the turn of the century, accounting textbooks and manuals usually recommended the following procedure for determination of the periodic charge against revenue:

$$\frac{\text{Cost to be allocated}}{\text{Estimated life}} = \text{Depreciation}$$

An alternate expression is:

$$\text{Cost to be allocated} \times \frac{1}{\text{Estimated life}} = \text{Depreciation}$$

(The fraction in the latter expression is the rate of depreciation.) This procedure provides for a constant charge for each period during which the asset is used. Prior to the influence of the tax law, however, most businesses did not use this systematic method but charged off varying amounts of depreciation from year to year. In good years, when income was high, a large amount of depreciation might be charged off, looking forward to the bad years when income would be insufficient to absorb depreciation.[3]

In the period from 1913 to 1933, the efforts of the Bureau of Internal Revenue were directed toward establishing systematic depreciation on a straight-line basis as outlined above. The Bureau allowed taxpayers maximum freedom in selecting the rate of depreciation, or estimated life. The attitude of the Bureau was summarized in the publication of Bulletin F in 1920:

> It is considered impracticable to prescribe fixed, definite rates of depreciation which would be allowable for all property of a given class or character. . . . The taxpayer should in all cases determine as accurately as possible according to his judgment and experience the rate at which his property depreciates.[4]

When the taxpayer used a rate systematically, the taxpayer's deductions were allowed unless the Bureau could produce clear and convincing evidence to show that the deduction was unreasonable. Needless to say, clear and convincing evidence was available only in extreme cases.

[2]Eugene L. Grant and Paul T. Norton, Jr., *Depreciation* (New York: Ronald Press, 1955), p. 209. This book has a good discussion of the early history of depreciation.

[3]See Dorothy A. Litherland, "Fixed Asset Replacement a Half Century Ago," *The Accounting Review,* 26 (October 1951), p. 475.

[4]Grant and Norton, *op. cit.,* p. 216.

Prescribed Rates

In 1933, the Roosevelt administration sought new sources of revenue to finance its ambitious programs. A subcommittee of the House Committee on Ways and Means proposed a reduction in the depreciation deductions of all taxpayers by one fourth for a three-year period. As a more equitable solution, the Bureau proposed to decrease the deduction by exercising more control in the following three ways: (1) by requiring taxpayers to furnish detailed depreciation schedules with their returns; (2) by shifting to the taxpayer the burden of proving the reasonableness of the rates used; and (3) by issuing a revision of Bulletin F that would specify "reasonable" depreciation rates for numerous assets. The rates in Bulletin F would be used except when the taxpayer could prove that the specified rate was inappropriate.

With the adoption of these proposals, which remained unchanged until the early days of the Eisenhower administration in 1953, the depreciation deduction became a constant source of controversy between taxpayers and the Bureau. Taxpayers claimed that the asset lives in Bulletin F were unrealistically long, that the use of these long lives did not allow them to recover their investments rapidly enough, and that, as a result, investment in new plant assets was reduced. However, the Treasury Department remained firm, claiming that the rates in Bulletin F were based on empirical evidence and that, after all, the taxpayers could use shorter lives when individual circumstances warranted them (provided the taxpayer could prove that Bulletin F was inappropriate).

The adoption of the Internal Revenue Code of 1954 ushered in the era of "accelerated" depreciation. After 1953, taxpayers could use the declining-balance method, which had rates up to twice the straight-line method, or the sum-of-the-years'-digits method. In addition, the IRS adopted a policy of not challenging the rates used by taxpayers unless "clear and convincing" evidence existed that such rates were unreasonable.[5]

In the years after 1954, other changes liberalized the rules related to an asset's estimated useful life, providing for shorter lives and therefore higher rates. In 1962, Depreciation Guidelines replaced the asset lives in Bulletin F, and in 1971, Congress adopted the Class Life System, which outlined a limited number of "classes" for business properties. All properties in a class were assigned the same life, so estimating a useful life for each asset was avoided.

In 1981, Congress adopted the Accelerated Cost Recovery System (ACRS). This new system shortens the estimated lives for most properties, divides the properties covered by the system into a number of classes, and specifies the rates applicable for each class. The new system generally results in more rapid capital recovery than prior law. In 1986, modifications were made in the ACRS system, resulting in one set of ACRS rules applying to assets placed into service after 1980 and before 1987 and another, more

---

[5]Joint Economic Committee, *The Federal Tax System: Facts and Problems* (Washington, D.C.: U.S. Government Printing Office, 1964).

restrictive set of rules applying to assets placed into service in 1987 and later years.

Although the adoption of ACRS is a boon to the business community, it creates a headache for the tax student. Currently, three different sets of rules govern the depreciation allowed most taxpayers. The remainder of this chapter is divided between these three sets of rules, beginning with the pre-1981 rules.

DEPRECIATION OF PROPERTY ACQUIRED BEFORE 1981

The general rule for depreciation (but not the accepted method) was virtually the same from 1913 through 1980. Today, Sec. 167(a) of the Code reads in part as follows:

> (a) General Rule.—There shall be allowed as a depreciation deduction a reasonable allowance for the exhaustion, wear and tear (including a reasonable allowance for obsolescence)—
> (1) of property used in a trade or busines, or
> (2) of property held for the production of income. In the case of recovery property (within the meaning of section 168), the deduction allowable under section 168 shall be deemed to constitute the reasonable allowance provided by this section. . . .

The last sentence above was added by the Economic Recovery Tax Act of 1981 specifying that the Accelerated Cost Recovery System in new Sec. 168 applies to recovery property acquired after 1980.

The general rule in the first sentence of Sec. 167(a) applies to all properties, both tangible and intangible, but only if the property is used in a trade or business or held for the production of income. Properties held for personal use—such as a personal automobile or a residence—are not subject to depreciation. Notice also that the section only applies to property subject to wear, tear, or obsolescence. Examples of property not qualifying are corporate securities, land, and goodwill. This general rule has a long history in the law; other subsections added to Sec. 167 have been aimed at removing some restriction imposed under the general rule. The most important provision is the subsection dealing with allowable methods.

Depreciation Methods

In 1954, Sec. 167(b) was added to the law. It reads as follows:

> (b) Use of Certain Methods and Rates.—For taxable years ending after December 31, 1953, the term "reasonable allowance" as used in subsection (a) shall include (but shall not be limited to) an allowance computed in accordance with regulations prescribed by the Secretary under any of the following methods:

(1) the straight line method,

(2) the declining balance method, using a rate not exceeding twice the rate which would have been used had the annual allowance been computed under the method described in paragraph (1),

(3) the sum-of-the-years'-digits method, and

(4) any other consistent method productive of an annual allowance which, when added to all allowances for the period commencing with the taxpayer's use of the property and including the taxable year, does not, during the first two-thirds of the useful life of the property, exceed the total of such allowances which would have been used had such allowances been computed under the method described in paragraph (2).

Nothing in this subsection shall be construed to limit or reduce an allowance otherwise allowable under subsection (a).

Although this subsection specifies the use of the straight-line, declining-balance, and sum-of-the-years'-digits methods, it also provides for the use of "any other consistent method." The only restriction on the use of these other methods is that they must not produce a total allowance greater than the declining-balance method over the first two thirds of the property's useful life. Congress has placed certain restrictions, discussed below, on the use of methods other than the straight-line method. Finally the depreciable basis of property is the basis that would be used to determine gain on disposition.

STRAIGHT-LINE METHOD   Under the straight-line method, the original cost of the property (including commissions, fees, and other incidental acquisition costs), less the salvage value, is allocated in equal amounts to each year of the property's estimated useful life. This method has been in general use since 1913 and corresponds to the accounting concept of straight-line depreciation.

For depreciable personal property acquired after October 10, 1962, and before 1981, with the exception of livestock, salvage value used was reduced by an amount up to 10% of the property's basis (cost). The provision was elective and available only when the property had an estimated useful life of three years or more. Note that the rule applied only to personal property; real property, such as buildings, typically had no salvage value. Instead, salvage of depreciable real property often resulted in expenditures greater than scrap value. The rule was intended to reduce the number of controversies over salvage value when salvage was an insignificant amount relative to cost. In many cases, salvage value was ignored completely for the specified property. The rule applied to all depreciation methods.

DECLINING-BALANCE METHOD   Under the declining-balance method, a constant rate is applied to the undepreciated basis of the property. The maximum rate allowed was twice the straight-line rate, and most taxpayers who elected this method to accelerate their depreciation chose the maximum rate. This 200% declining-balance method (sometimes referred to as the double declining-balance method) gave the maximum deduction in the early years of an asset's life. The following example illustrates several problems connected with the use of this method.

TABLE **14-1**

AN EXAMPLE OF 200% DECLINING-BALANCE DEPRECIATION

Year	Undepreciated Balance	Rate (percent)	Depreciation Deduction
1	$20,000	40	$ 8,000
2	12,000	40	4,800
3	7,200	40	2,880
4	4,320	—	2,160
5	2,160	—	2,160
		Total depreciation	$20,000

A taxpayer acquires a new machine on January 2, 19x1, at a cost of $20,000. The estimated life is 5 years, and salvage value after 5 years is $1,500. The straight-line rate is 20% (1/5 years), so the maximum rate permitted under declining balance is 40%. Depreciation allowed each year would be as shown in Table 14-1.

Two things should be noted in this example. First, because salvage value is less than 10% of the original cost, the calculation of depreciation ignores salvage value, and the total depreciation over the life of the property is $20,000. However, even if the taxpayer had not elected to ignore salvage value, or to the extent salvage had exceeded 10% of the cost, the undepreciated basis would still not be reduced by salvage value. In the declining-balance method, the rate is always applied to cost before the reduction for salvage value. When salvage value is used with this method, depreciation deducted in the later years may never reduce the undepreciated cost below salvage value.

The second point to note in our example is that the 40% rate is not applied to the undepreciated balance in years 4 and 5. If this rate had been used, the depreciation would have been only $1,728 in year 4 and only approximately $1,041 in year 5. In this case, the entire $20,000 cost would not have been spread over the 5-year period. To overcome this inherent weakness in the declining-balance method, the law provides that taxpayers who use this method may change at any time to the straight-line method. Thus, in year 4, the taxpayer in the example changes to the straight-line method and spreads the remaining $4,320 equally over years 4 and 5. The change from declining balance to straight line is made in the year when the straight-line rate exceeds the declining-balance rate. Thus, at the beginning of year 4, the asset has a remaining life of 2 years and the straight-line rate is 50%. The change to straight line can be made without the consent of the Commissioner of Internal Revenue.

The above example uses the maximum rate of twice the straight-line rate. Because of restrictions imposed by Congress, taxpayers commonly were required to use the declining-balance method with a lower rate. The rate for used personal property, for example, was restricted to 150% of the straight-

TABLE **14-2**

AN EXAMPLE OF SUM-OF-THE-YEARS'-DIGITS DEPRECIATION

Year	Depreciable Basis	Rate	Depreciation Deduction
1	$20,000	5/15	$ 6,667
2	20,000	4/15	5,333
3	20,000	3/15	4,000
4	20,000	2/15	2,667
5	20,000	1/15	1,333
15		Total depreciation	$20,000

line rate. Applied to the above illustration, this restriction would result in a declining-balance rate of 30% (1/5 × 1.5).

SUM-OF-THE-YEARS'-DIGITS METHOD   The third method applies a declining rate to the depreciable cost, reduced by salvage value, if any. For the first year of the property's life, the rate, or fraction, is composed of a numerator equal to the estimated remaining life at the start of the year and a denominator equal to the sum of the numbers representing the successive years in the asset's estimated life. For the second year, the numerator of the fraction is reduced by one, but the denominator remains unchanged. Applying this method to the preceding example yields depreciation as shown in Table 14-2.

Salvage value, when applicable, must be subtracted from the cost basis to obtain the depreciable basis before applying the rate. The denominator, 15, is the sum of $5 + 4 + 3 + 2 + 1$, an amount that can be obtained by using the formula for an arithmetic progression $[n \times (n + 1)/2]$. The IRS has constructed rate tables that may be applied to the original basis minus prior depreciation (a declining basis) to obtain the sum-of-the-years'-digits depreciation. For example, the tables show a 33⅓ rate during the first year for assets with a remaining life of five years. With the sum-of-the-years'-digits method, there is no reason to change to the straight-line method in later years; the entire depreciable basis is allocated to the 5-year period because the sum of the five fractions is one.

The accelerated methods just described were not available for all properties. First, they applied only to tangible properties; the costs of intangibles were amortized on the straight-line basis (discussed in more detail below). Second, declining-balance rates were restricted for used properties, for nonresidential real property, and for certain other properties. Election of the maximum rate and method allowed by law was a problem that arose at acquisition. Rates and methods for acquisitions after 1980 are specified by ACRS. For pre-1981 properties, remaining allowances are generally computed under methods and rates already established.

CHANGES IN DEPRECIATION METHOD   The law does not allow taxpayers to change from one depreciation method to another without the consent of the

Commissioner. There are two important exceptions to this general rule. First, as noted above, taxpayers can change from the declining-balance method to straight line. Second, taxpayers can also change from the sum-of-the-years'-digits method to straight line for properties subject to special recapture rules explained in Chapter 16 on the text. In 1974, the IRS announced that consent would be given on a liberal basis to other changes in method. The pronouncement specified the following changes; from straight-line to an accelerated method; from sum-of-the-years'-digits to declining-balance and vice versa; and from one declining-balance percentage to another percentage. The taxpayer who wishes to change must file an application with the Commissioner within the first 180 days of the year when the new method is to be used.

ACCOUNTING PROBLEMS   Future sales or other dispositions of properties acquired before 1981 will not usually occur on the last day of a taxable year. How much depreciation is allowed in the year of disposition for property acquired before 1981? Normally, depreciation is computed to the nearest month when the taxpayer's property accounts are kept on an item-by-item basis. When composite or group accounts are maintained, and the taxpayer observed some averaging convention to account for depreciation in the year of acquisition, the same convention applies to the year of the disposition.

Another common complication in calculating depreciation under the pre-1981 rules is a change in the asset's estimated life. Rules provide that, at the end of any taxable year, the undepreciated cost of an asset (reduced by salvage value) is depreciated over the estimated remaining life of the property. Estimated life is estimated when the property is acquired. This original estimate, however, should be changed whenever the actual life of the property is clearly more or less than the original estimate. In some cases, taxpayers have a written agreement with the IRS concerning the estimated life of a property. When such an agreement is in effect, changes in estimated life are prohibited.

To illustrate the effect of a change in estimated life, we can assume that a machine that cost $20,000 was originally estimated to last 20 years and that a $2,000 salvage has been used to calculate straight-line depreciation. After 10 full years, depreciation deductions would amount to $9,000, or

$$\frac{\$20,000 \times \$2,000}{20 \text{ years}} \times 10 \text{ years}$$

and the undepreciated cost would be $11,000 (that is, $20,000 − $9,000). Assume, finally, that unusual wear and tear has reduced the remaining life to just 5 more years, with the same salvage value of $2,000. Depreciation in the eleventh year would be $1,800 [($11,000 − $2,000)/5].

Similar procedures are followed when the accelerated methods are used. For the 200% declining-balance method, the straight-line rate is computed based on the new estimate. The new rate is doubled and then applied to the undepreciated cost. With the sum-of-the-years'-digits method, change in life is effected very easily by using IRS generated tables based on the remaining life of the property.

Amortization of Intangibles

The general provisions of Sec. 167(a) apply to all properties acquired before 1981, both tangible and intangible, that have a limited life, but intangibles can be amortized only on a straight-line basis. The life of some intangibles is limited by law (patents, 17 years; copyrights, the life of the author plus 50 years), and this legal life normally is a basis for amortization. The lives of some intangibles—such as trademarks and franchises—are sometimes limited by agreements. In still other situations, economic conditions may limit the life of an intangible. In any event, the period used by the taxpayer for amortization of the costs should be the economic life of the asset.

As explained below, ACRS applies only to tangible properties. For intangible properties acquired after 1980, the rules under Sec. 167 apply, and straight-line amortization is still the rule.

ACCELERATED COST RECOVERY SYSTEM PLACED IN SERVICE FOR PROPERTY BETWEEN 1981 AND 1986

The accelerated cost recovery system actually consists of two separate sets of rules. The first set applies to property acquired from 1981 through 1986. The second applies to assets acquired after 1986.

The first set of rules was designed to provide for economic expansion and full employment. The focus of these rules was to provide for a quick recovery of the cost of acquiring property. The goal of the system was to reduce the present value-after-tax cost of recovery assets, thus encouraging business to invest in more of these assets. With more assets being acquired, Congress reasoned that business should be willing to employ more people. Eventually, if all goes as planned, the goals of economic expansion and full employment are better achieved.

The second set of ACRS rules were passed as part of the Tax Reform Act of 1986. The focus of this Act was to reduce individual and corporate tax rates without decreasing total tax collections. Since these two goals are not complementary, Congress needed to finance the reduction in tax rates by increasing the taxable income taxpayers' report. Recovery deductions were an inviting target for modification since a relatively small change in the accelerated cost recovery system can create a large effect in taxable incomes. The change created in the accelerated cost recovery system by the Act results in the cost of most assets being recovered more slowly. This increases taxable incomes in the short run and helps reduce the negative effect on revenues created by the decline in rates.

The original ACRS rules will be discussed now. These rules continue to apply to all ACRS property placed in service before 1987. The ACRS rules applicable to post-1986 property will be discussed in the next section of this chapter.

Rules for the ACRS are located in Sec. 168.[6] As noted earlier, the deduction under ACRS is always a "reasonable allowance" under the general depreciation rules. The operating rules of ACRS for assets placed into service between 1981 and 1986 are in Sec. 168(b), which reads in part as follows:

> (b) Amount of Deduction.—
>> (1) In general.— . . . the amount of the deduction allowable (by this section) for any taxable year shall be the aggregate amount determined by applying to the unadjusted basis of recovery property the applicable percentage determined in accordance with the following tables. . . .

ACRS substitutes a fairly precise formula for the traditional idea of a "reasonable allowance." The rule quoted above contains the following elements:

1. Recovery property—The properties subject to ACRS are tangible properties placed in service after 1980, but the law contains numerous exclusions from the definition of recovery property.
2. Applicable percentage—Recovery properties are divided into four basic classes, and the statute provides a recovery percentage for each year of a property's life.
3. Unadjusted basis—Generally the original cost of the property, the concept of unadjusted basis is defined so that many accounting problems are eliminated.
4. Aggregate amount—Using the unadjusted basis and the applicable percentage, an allowance is obtained for each property. The deduction for the taxable year is the total of these amounts.

The above terms are further defined and illustrated in the following paragraphs. Note that under ACRS estimated useful life and salvage value do not enter into the calculation. ACRS is a system of cost recovery, but it makes no pretense of matching the costs of properties against the revenues produced from their use.

Recovery Property

Section 168 defines recovery property as property that meets the following four tests: (1) tangible (as opposed to intangible); (2) either used in a trade or business, or held for the production of income; (3) subject to wear, tear, or obsolescence; and (4) placed in service after 1980. Except for the restrictions to post-1980 acquisitions and to tangible properties, this definition is the same as that under traditional depreciation rules. Note that recovery property includes both new and used property.

---

[6]There are currently two versions of ACRS. The first version, which applies to assets placed in service between 1981 and 1986, is discussed in this portion of the chapter.

Property that might otherwise qualify is excluded from ACRS under three circumstances. First, but not of interest to most taxpayers, public utilities can use ACRS only if the utilities use a "normalization" method of accounting, that is, if they compute their tax expense for rate-making purposes based on the depreciation expense used for rate purposes. Second, taxpayers may exclude properties from ACRS if they use units-of-production depreciation or some other method not expressed in terms of years for such properties. This election is available on a property-by-property basis. Because ACRS generally provides for a mroe rapid recovery than under the possible alternatives, this election should not be used often. Third, Congress included rules to control "churning," that is, the movement of properties between entities owned by the same taxpayers or between related taxpayers to avoid the post-1980 restriction. For example, individual A acquires property before 1981 and then, after 1980, transfers the property in a nontaxable transaction to a corporation controlled by A. The property is not recovery property under ACRS to A's controlled corporation.

Applicable Percentage under ACRS

The second step in the calculation of the deduction under ACRS for properties placed into service from 1980 through 1986 is the determination of the applicable percentage from the tables. The basic tables in the statute apply to most personal property and to some real property. A different table applies to most real property. The following explanation is divided along those lines.

BASIC RATE TABLES   Table 14-3 shows the rates for property placed in service after December 31, 1980 and before January 1, 1987. Use of the tables requires the assignment of all property into the following classes:

1. Three-year class—automobiles, light trucks, tangible personal property used in research and development activities, and other tangible personal property with a useful life of 4 years or less.
2. Five-year class—all machinery and equipment not included in the 3- or 10-year classes, single-purpose agricultural structures, storage facilities used in petroleum distribution, and public utility property with a class life of more than 4 but less than 18 years.
3. Ten-year class—railroad tank cars, recreational facilities and theme-park structures, qualified coal conversion facilities of public utilities, manufactured homes, public utility property with a class life of more than 18 but less than 25 years, and depreciable real property with a class life of 12½ years or less.
4. Fifteen-year public utility class—public utility property with a class life greater than 25 years.

Perusal of the above classification scheme reveals that for most businesses all depreciable tangible personal property is either 3-year or 5-year property. The 10-year class includes various special-purpose properties (theme-park

TABLE **14-3**

ACRS BASIC RECOVERY PERCENTAGES FOR 1981–1986

Recovery Year	Property Class			
	3-year	5-year	10-year	15-year Public Utility
1	25%	15%	8%	5%
2	38	22	14	10
3	37	21	12	9
4		21	10	8
5		21	10	7
6			10	7
7			9	6
8			9	6
9			9	6
10			9	6
11				6
12				6
13				6
14				6
15				6

structures) and properties used in specific industries. The 15-year class is of interest only to public utilities.

The percentages for each class in Table 14-3 provide for depreciation equal to that obtained using the 150% declining-balance method with a half-year convention for the first year and a change to the straight-line method at the optimum point. Congress originally planned for further acceleration of the recovery rates in 1985 and in 1986, but the changes were repealed in 1982.

With the preceding definitional problems solved, the computation of the allowance is simple. To illustrate, we assume that in 1984 taxpayer A acquires a lathe for use in his metal fabricating business at a total cost of $20,000. The Class Life System assigned a life of 15 years to this property. The property thus belongs to the 5-year ACRS class because the class life is greater than 4 years and the property is not listed in the 10-year class. In 1984, the first recovery year, the allowance for this property is $3,000 ($20,000 × 15%). In 1985, the recovery allowance is $4,400 ($20,000 × 22%). If the property is sold, retired from service, or otherwise disposed of before the end of the recovery period, no recovery allowance is allowed in the year of disposition. The law accomplishes this result by providing that the unadjusted basis of a property disposed of during the year is zero for purposes of computing the allowance. If A disposes of the $20,000 machine in 1988, the fifth year, the allowance for that year is zero.

RECOVERY PERCENTAGES FOR 19-YEAR REAL ESTATE   Table 14-4 shows the recovery percentages for real estate that is not low-income housing. This table applies to real estate placed in service after May 8, 1985, and before January 1, 1987. Other tables, not reproduced here, apply to buildings placed in service after 1980 and before May 9, 1985, and to low-income housing.

TABLE **14-4**

ACRS RECOVERY PERCENTAGES FOR 19-YEAR
REAL ESTATE (OTHER THAN LOW INCOME HOUSING)

Realty Placed in Service After May 8, 1985

Recovery Year	Month Property is Placed in Service											
	1	2	3	4	5	6	7	8	9	10	11	12
1	8.8	8.1	7.3	6.5	5.8	5.0	4.2	3.5	2.7	1.9	1.1	.4
2	8.4	8.5	8.5	8.6	8.7	8.8	8.8	8.9	9.0	9.0	9.1	9.2
3	7.6	7.7	7.7	7.8	7.9	7.9	8.0	8.1	8.1	8.2	8.3	8.3
4	6.9	7.0	7.0	7.1	7.1	7.2	7.3	7.3	7.4	7.4	7.5	7.6
5	6.3	6.3	6.4	6.4	6.5	6.5	6.6	6.6	6.7	6.8	6.8	6.9
6	5.7	5.7	5.8	5.9	5.9	5.9	6.0	6.0	6.1	6.1	6.2	6.2
7	5.2	5.2	5.3	5.3	5.3	5.4	5.4	5.5	5.5	5.6	5.6	5.6
8	4.7	4.7	4.8	4.8	4.8	4.9	4.9	5.0	5.0	5.1	5.1	5.1
9	4.2	4.3	4.3	4.4	4.4	4.5	4.5	4.5	4.5	4.6	4.6	4.7
10	4.2	4.2	4.2	4.2	4.2	4.2	4.2	4.2	4.2	4.2	4.2	4.2
11	4.2	4.2	4.2	4.2	4.2	4.2	4.2	4.2	4.2	4.2	4.2	4.2
12	4.2	4.2	4.2	4.2	4.2	4.2	4.2	4.2	4.2	4.2	4.2	4.2
13	4.2	4.2	4.2	4.2	4.2	4.2	4.2	4.2	4.2	4.2	4.2	4.2
14	4.2	4.2	4.2	4.2	4.2	4.2	4.2	4.2	4.2	4.2	4.2	4.2
15	4.2	4.2	4.2	4.2	4.2	4.2	4.2	4.2	4.2	4.2	4.2	4.2
16	4.2	4.2	4.2	4.2	4.2	4.2	4.2	4.2	4.2	4.2	4.2	4.2
17	4.2	4.2	4.2	4.2	4.2	4.2	4.2	4.2	4.2	4.2	4.2	4.2
18	4.2	4.2	4.2	4.2	4.2	4.2	4.2	4.2	4.2	4.2	4.2	4.2
19	4.2	4.2	4.2	4.2	4.2	4.2	4.2	4.2	4.2	4.2	4.2	4.2
20	0.2	0.5	0.9	1.2	1.6	1.9	2.3	2.6	3.0	3.3	3.7	4.0

To illustrate, assume taxpayer A began the use of a new apartment building on May 14, 1985, the fifth month. The building cost $300,000, and is not low-income housing. For 1985, the recovery rate was 5.8% and the allowance $17,400 ($300,000 × 5.8%). The column of percentages in Table 14-4 under the fifth month shows the rates for all recovery years for 19-year properties. The recovery percentage for 1986 is 8.7%, 7.9%, and so on. When real property is sold, the allowance is based on the months held in the year of disposition (unlike other classes in which there is no allowance in the year of disposition). Assume that taxpayer A disposes of the apartments in late September 1988, the fourth year, when the recovery rate is 7.1%. The allowance for 1988 is $15,975 ($300,000 × 7.1% × 9/12).

ELECTIVE STRAIGHT-LINE RATES   As an alternative to the accelerated rates above, taxpayers could elect a rate based on the straight-line method. The election was available each year but had to be made for all assets within a given ACRS class placed in service during the year, except for real property, for which the election was available on a property-by-property basis.

Under this election, the rates were based on the basic class life or certain permitted "extended class lives," as follows:

Property Class	Extended Class Life
3-year class	Either 5 or 12 years
5-year class	Either 12 or 25 years
10-year class	Either 25 or 35 years
15-year class (public utility)	Either 35 or 45 years
15-year real estate	Either 35 or 45 years
18-year real estate	Either 35 or 45 years
19-year real estate	Either 35 or 45 years

Thus, for property in the 3-year class, permissible straight-line rates were 33⅓% (3-year basic life), 20% (5-year extended life), or 8⅓% (12-year extended life). A single rate had to be elected for all properties within a class placed in service within the year. Taxpayers who elected the straight-line rate for properties in a given class for a year could not change the rate during the properties' lives.

Note that the election affected only the applicable rate. Other rules—such as the half-year convention in the year of acquisition or the actual months of service for real estate—were unchanged by the election.

Unadjusted Basis

The base used to compute the recovery allowance throughout a property's life is its unadjusted basis. This is the property's cost less the portion of the basis treated as an expense in the year of acquisition, a provision discussed later in this chapter. The unadjusted basis is initially taken into account for computation of the allowance in the year the property is placed in service, which may be later than the year of acquisition.

As previously explained, the unadjusted basis for a property is zero in the year of disposition or retirement from service. Chapter 15 of this text covers the rules for recognition of gain or loss on disposition, and the rules under ACRS do not generally affect the results explained there. However, a taxpayer who maintains a "mass" account for recovery property can elect to include as income the total proceeds from dispositions without reduction of the unadjusted basis for purposes of the allowance. Note that a "mass" account is restricted to properties within an ACRS class for a given year; otherwise, the annual allowances over the recovery period cannot be computed.

For real property, the unadjusted basis is the total cost of the entire property. Division of the costs into components—for example, central air-conditioning and heating units—to obtain shorter lives is not allowed. However, a substantial improvement to real property is treated as a separate property for purposes of computing the allowance. A substantial improvement is one completed within a 24-month period whose cost exceeds 25% of the adjusted basis of the structure. Special transitional rules may apply to any building already under construction, but not yet placed in service, on the various effective dates of the major changes in the depreciation provision.

Aggregate Amount of Allowances

The deduction allowed for depreciation for any year under ACRS is the sum of the allowances for all recovery property. This amount is deemed to be a "reasonable allowance" for wear, tear, and obsolescence under Sec. 167. All intangibles are still amortized under the old rules over their estimated useful life. Most taxpayers will continue to calculate the deduction for pre-1981 property under the old rules discussed earlier in this chapter.

ACCELERATED COST RECOVERY SYSTEM FOR PROPERTY PLACED INTO SERVICE AFTER 1986

As noted before, the Tax Reform Act of 1986 was designed to minimize the effect on total tax collections. If individual and corporate tax rates were to be decreased, certain deductions, such as those under ACRS, needed to be modified. The net effect of the 1986 changes in ACRS is to slow down the rate of recovery deductions, thereby increasing current taxable income and current tax liabilities.

Because adjustments in the cost recovery system do not affect all industries equally, the 1986 changes in ACRS will shift tax burdens from service industries to capital intensive industries. Figure 14-1 illustrates the expected effect of the 1986 changes in ACRS and the elimination of the investment tax credit. Note that the industries that are most affected by the change are those industries that require large amounts of capital expenditures. These industries generally have not competed well in international markets in recent years, and the modifications in ACRS should only reduce their competitiveness.

The 1986 changes to ACRS will be discussed in the same topical order as the previous discussion of the original ACRS provisions. Because the Tax Reform Act of 1986 leaves the basic ACRS structure intact, the majority of the following discussion will examine the modifications to the basic system created by the Act. ACRS provisions that were not changed by the Act will be discussed only briefly.

Property that is subject to the modified ACRS rules is identical to the property that was subject to the original rules. A new antichurning rule provides that property being recovered under the original rules cannot be recovered under the modified rules if it is transferred after 1986 to the same or related taxpayer. For example, if a taxpayer is recovering the cost of property under the original ACRS rules and transfers the property to a related taxpayer, the related taxpayer must use the original ACRS rules. It is not possible for the related party to use the new modified ACRS rules for recovering the cost of the property.

All items of property will be assigned to one of eight classes. All property other than nonresidential real property and residential rental property is assigned to one of the following six classes.

FIGURE **14-1**   Comparison of Cost Recovery Under Prior and New Law

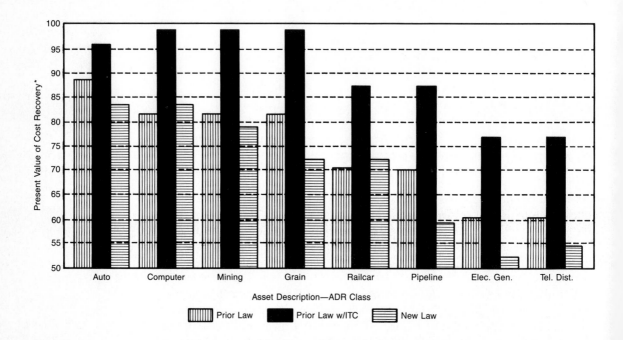

*Computations assume an inflation rate of 4% and a 4% real rate of return.

1. Three-year class—in general, all items in the original ACRS 3-year class will be included in this class except for cars and light-duty trucks, which are switched to the 5-year class.

2. Five-year class—includes most items in the original ACRS 5-year class except for office furniture, fixtures and equipment, and single-purpose agricultural structures, which are switched to the 7-year class.

3. Seven-year class—includes property with a class life of at least 10 and less than 16 years and property that has no class life and is not specifically assigned by the law to another class.

4. Ten-year class—includes property with a class life of at least 16 and less than 20 years. Examples are assets used in the manufacture of some food and tobacco products.

5. Fifteen-year class—includes property with a class life of at least 20 and less than 25 years. Examples are telephone-distribution and sewage-treatment plants.

6. Twenty-year property—includes property with a class life of 25 years or more. The most common example of this type of property is a municipal sewer.

Residential rental property is placed in a 27.5-year class. A 31.5-year class is established for nonresidential real property.

Most tangible personal assets used in a trade or business will be included in the 5- or 7-year classes. Because the original ACRS rules usually placed such assets into 3- and 5-year classes, the modifications to ACRS will generally result in lengthening the recovery period for most business assets.

The modified ACRS system does not use depreciation tables or percentages. Instead, the modified system prescribes the recovery method to use. Property in the 3-, 5-, 7-, and 10-year classes will be depreciated under the 200% declining-balance method with a switch permitted to straight-line depreciation when it optimizes the deduction. Property in the 15- and 20-year classes will use 150% declining-balance with a permitted switch to straight-line depreciation to optimize the deduction. Assets assigned to the two real property classes must use straight-line depreciation.

In general, a half-year convention will apply to all personal property and a mid-month convention will apply to real property. The half-year convention allows the taxpayer a half-year depreciation in the year the asset is placed into service and a half-year depreciation in the year the asset is sold. Under the original ACRS rules, no depreciation was permitted in the year the asset was sold. The mid-month convention considers real property to have been placed into service at the middle of the month regardless of when it was actually placed into service during that month.

An example may help clarify these concepts. Assume that a light-duty business truck is acquired for $10,000 on January 13, 1987, by a calendar year taxpayer. The truck will be assigned to the 5-year class (it was a 3-year asset under the original ACRS rules) and will be depreciated using 200% declining balance. The truck will be deemed to have been placed into service in mid-1987, thereby considerably reducing the depreciation available in 1987. Table 14-5 illustrates the amounts that may be recovered under both the original and modified ACRS systems. Note that the modified system both lengthens the write-off period and reduces the amount of write-offs in the first 3 years of the asset's ACRS life.

Congress was concerned that some taxpayers were placing large amounts of assets into service during the last part of a taxable year and claiming a half-year depreciation on the assets under the half-year convention. Therefore, under the modified ACRS rules, a mid-quarter convention will be required if the aggregate bases of nonrealty placed into service within the last 3 months of the taxable year exceed 40% of the aggregate bases of all nonrealty placed into service during the taxable year. The mid-quarter convention requires the taxpayer to compute depreciation as if all assets bought within a quarter were purchased in the middle of quarter. Thus, assets placed into service in the first quarter of the taxable year will get 10½ months of recovery deduction while assets placed into service in the last quarter can only claim 1½ months of recovery deductions.

An alternative depreciation system is also available for assets placed into service after December 31, 1986. In general, this alternative system provides for even slower write-offs. The alternative system must be used for purposes of computing depreciation under the alternative minimum tax (Chapter 22) and for certain types of property that are not commonly encountered.

TABLE **14-5**

EXAMPLE OF ACRS RECOVERY AMOUNTS

Year	Modified ACRS	Original ACRS
1987	$2,000	$2,500
1988	3,200	3,800
1989	1,920	3,700
1990	1,152*	
1991	1,152	
1992	576	

*Switch to straight-line

Because this system is discussed in Chapter 22, it will not be examined further in this chapter.

After reading this chapter, it should be clear that depreciation computations are not the relatively simple procedure they were before 1981. It is very likely that the accountant will need to deal with three basic sets of recovery rules and several specific exceptions to these rules. For example, a taxpayer who has placed buildings into service in 1980, 1984, and 1987 must contend with all three methods of recovery write-offs. The need to know all three sets of rules (and their exceptions) will continue into the immediate future.

Election to Expense Cost of Depreciable Assets

For 1958–1980, the law contained a provision for additional first-year (or bonus) depreciation for tangible personal property with a life of at least six years. The "bonus" allowance was 20% of the cost of qualified properties up to $10,000 ($20,000 on a joint return). This first-year allowance was permitted with regard to the asset's life and without regard to the timing during the year of the acquisition.

The Economic Recovery Tax Act of 1981 enlarged this bonus write-off of property for years after 1981 and before 1987. This elective provision allowed a taxpayer to charge to expense in any tax year up to $5,000 of qualifying property.

The Tax Reform Act of 1986 modified this provision for assets placed into service after 1986. The expensing deduction for such property is now $10,000 per year. However, additional restrictions may make this increased limit appear better than it really is. If more than $200,000 of qualifying property is placed into service in any taxable year, the deduction is reduced dollar for dollar by the amount of qualifying property in excess of $200,000. Accordingly, a business with $210,000 of qualifying property would not get any benefit from this provision.

Other restrictions apply. Married couples filing separate returns are limited to a single $10,000 limit between them. If the amount expensed exceeds the taxable income from the trade or business in which the asset is used, the expensing deduction is limited to the trade or business income. Any amount not deductible currently because of this limitation is carried forward to the next year. Finally, if the expensed property is converted from trade or business to personal use at any time before the asset's ACRS life, income is recognized in an amount equal to the excess of the amount expensed over the amount of ACRS deductions that would have been allowed if automatic expensing had not been elected.

Properties qualifying for the write-off are the same as those qualifying for the investment tax credit under pre-1986 law. Generally, qualifying property is depreciable, tangible, personal property. However, depreciable real estate other than buildings qualifies under some circumstances. The qualified property must be acquired by purchase (as opposed to an exchange) from an unrelated party. Property placed into service after 1986 must be used in an active trade or business.

The law treats the amount expensed under the election as depreciation. Thus, the adjusted basis of a property for purposes of computing gain or loss is its cost less the amount expensed plus subsequent depreciation. For example, if a taxpayer pays $20,000 for a qualified property in 1987 and elects to expense the maximum of $10,000, the remaining $10,000 is subject to depreciation. The $10,000 expensed is treated as depreciation for purposes of subsequent gain or loss calculations.

Special Limits on Certain Properties

Special limits on depreciation deductions apply to certain properties placed in service after June 18, 1984. These properties include (1) luxury automobiles, (2) entertainment and recreation type assets, and (3) computers and peripheral equipment. The depreciation on luxury automobiles placed into service after December 31, 1986, for example, cannot exceed $2,560 in the first year or $4,100 in any subsequent year. Additional details on these new special limits—which generally apply only to those properties that are commonly used for both business and personal reasons—are not discussed further in this edition.

PROBLEMS

1. The depreciation deduction for tax purposes often exceeds depreciation expense reported for financial accounting purposes. Cite three Code provisions that help to explain these differences. What reasons can be given in support of the different treatments for tax and accounting purposes?

2. On which of the following properties could a taxpayer claim a depreciation deduction?

a. Personal residence
b. A building used in business
c. The land on which the business building is located
d. A former residence, which the taxpayer now rents to another individual
e. A car used 25% of the time for personal reasons and 75% for business purposes
f. A building leased from another taxpayer (This building is used in a business.)

3. Explain what makes the accelerated depreciation methods advantageous to most taxpayers. Under what conditions might accelerated depreciation be a distinct disadvantage?

4. Three different methods by which we might account for the cost of an asset that benefits more than one accounting period are listed below. Give an example of each that illustrates the use of this alternative in federal income taxation. If financial and tax accounting treat a particular item differently, explain a possible reason for the different treatments.
a. Deduct entire cost when incurred.
b. Deduct nothing until asset is disposed of; then calculate gain or loss.
c. Select an arbitrary percentage of income produced by the property as a measure of the property "consumed" during that period.

5. Thomas acquired a machine for use in his business. The asset was purchased on January 3, 1980, at a cost of $24,000. Estimated life is six years, and estimated salvage value is $900. Prepare a depreciation schedule for the six years of the asset's life, assuming that Thomas wishes to accelerate the depreciation as much as possible. Thomas is married and files a joint return with his wife, and this is the only asset purchased during the year.

6. International Machines, Inc., is considering the investment of $1,000,000 in two alternative projects. The cost of Project A can be recovered in five years using double declining-balance depreciation. The cost of Project B must be amortized over 10 years on a straight-line basis. Both projects are expected to yield the same amount of net cash flow before depreciation, the present value of which is $940,000 using a 12% internal rate of return. The corporation's marginal tax rate is 40%. Compute the amount of the economic advantage arising from the rapid capital recovery of Project A as contrasted with Project B.

7. In January 1980, Jed Klampet acquired a new machine for use in his business at a cost of $20,000. The asset's estimate life is five years, and its estimated salvage value is $3,000. The depreciation schedule of this asset for 1980 and 1981 is as follows:

Year	Undepreciated Cost	Rate	Depreciation
1980	$20,000	40%	$8,000
1981	12,000	40	4,800

Complete the above schedule for the remainder of the asset's life.

8. Under depreciation methods in effect before 1981, estimated useful life was the critical variable in determining the amount of depreciation. Under ACRS, estimated useful life does not enter directly into the calculation. At what point under ACRS does estimated life come into play?

9. Whoopie Corporation, a soft drink bottler, acquired and placed in service the following assets in 1984:

Description	Estimated Life (years)	Cost
Automobile	3	$ 10,000
Tractor and trailer	5	40,000
Office copying machine	10	8,000
Forklift truck	8	16,000
Bottling machine	15	120,000

The estimated lives are taken from the Class Life System.
  a. If Whoopie elects to expense the maximum amount of the acquired assets, how much can be expensed in 1984? Which asset's cost should the corporation elect to expense?
  b. If the costs are not expensed under the election, what is the maximum ACRS allowance for 1984?

10. Bert Jones began construction of a new apartment house in 1983. Total cost of the building when completed in 1984 was $2,500,000. Rental of units began in May 1984. What is the maximum ACRS allowance for 1984? What alternative rates could Bert use for the apartments?

11. Under ACRS, taxpayers may elect to use a rate based on the straight-line method over the basis life or specified extended lives for each ACRS class. Under what circumstances would you expect taxpayers to use this straight-line election?

12. In July 1987, Zachary Corporation purchases and places into service the following assets:

Description	Cost
5 trucks	$40,000
10 desks	2,000
25 chairs	2,500

These are the only assets placed into service by the corporation in 1987.
  a. What is the maximum ACRS allowance for 1987?
  b. If it is assumed that Zachary Corporation placed the assets into service in December 1987, what is the maximum ACRS allowance for 1987?

13. Robert acquires and places into service a new apartment complex in March 1987. The price of the complex is $3,000,000. What is Robert's maximum ACRS allowance for 1987?

14. Tempe Corporation is considering the addition of a new wing to its manufacturing plant. The old building has been in use since 1965 and has an adjusted basis of $5,000,000. The new wing will cost $3,000,000. Assuming the new wing is completed in 1987, how will its cost be recovered?

SUPPLEMENTAL PROBLEMS

15. The two basic methods of stimulating the economy are a decrease in taxes, which increases aggregate demand, and acceleration of capital recovery (or the investment credit), which increases the marginal efficiency of capital. Using materials in your library, determine, if possible, which approach is more effective as a short-run stimulant. In your research, consider the period beginning in 1960.

16. Taxpayer is an orthodontist with an annual net profit from the practice of $200,000. He has complained to you about his high tax bill and has asked your advice about how he might lower it. In talking with some colleagues, he discovered that a number of them had invested in office buildings during the 1960s. Advise him on a plan to save taxes.

Property Transactions

That which flows from capital, like interest, rent and other items of income, is separate and distinct from the capital which produces it as gathered fruit is separate from the tree that bore it. While income may be transformed by accumulation into capital, like fruit, the seed of which produces another tree, the growth itself of neither capital nor the tree is income.
Godfrey N. Nelson, "The Question of Taxing Capital Gains" (1940)

The root of the problem is that the capital gains concept itself is clear and consistent neither in practice nor in principle.
Peter Miller, "Capital Gains on Personal Efforts" (1954)

CHAPTER 15

The Capital Gains Controversy

> The term "capital assets" includes all classes of property not specifically excluded by section 1221. Reg. Sec. 1.1221-1(a)

Tax experts and legislators have, for many years, deliberated the correct tax treatment of the gains and losses that may be realized when a property other than inventory is sold or exchanged. The two initial questions are:

1. Should the gains and losses deriving from property transactions be included within the notion of income?
2. If so, should they be given special treatment for income tax purposes?

If the answers to both of the first two questions are yes, two additional questions must then be answered. The two follow-up questions are:

3. Precisely which property transactions should be eligible for special tax treatment?
4. Exactly what special tax treatment should be extended to these gains and losses?

Collectively these four questions have, at least in the United States, become embodied in what can best be described as the capital gains controversy. As will be explained later, the U.S. has moved from one extreme position to the other over the past 100 years. That is, during the years of the Civil War income taxes, the U.S. wholly excluded certain property gains from income taxation; today the U.S. taxes those same gains like any other form of income. Between 1922 and 1987, however, certain property gains were taxed, but only at preferential rates. The detailed answers to questions 3 and 4, above, changed frequently during this 65-year interim period. In general, gains were treated very favorably; losses, quite unfavorably. The latter conclusion remains true today; that is, even though most property gains are now taxed as ordinary income, the deduction of a loss realized on the sale or exchange of property may be subject to stringent limitations in the computation of taxable income.

Incidentally, even though Congress eliminated the special treatment for capital gains in the 1986 Act, it retained nearly all of the complex capital gain and loss provisions within the Internal Revenue Code. Most tax experts believe that Congress did this so that it can reinstate a preferential treatment for capital gains easily if the marginal tax rates on ordinary income should once again be increased to reduce the current, large, federal deficits. A few of those provisions are also necessary, of course, because of the remaining limitations on capital loss deductions.

In the first part of Chapter 15 we will review the basic capital gain concept; thereafter we will discuss the most important general rules that determine the correct tax treatment of those gains and losses. Chapter 16 is a brief introduction to a few of the complexities which sometimes expand, and at other times contract, the more general capital gain and loss provisions that are introduced in this chapter. Because of their limited importance today, some instructors may elect to skip Chapter 16.

THE CAPITAL GAIN CONCEPT

The American concepts of ordinary income and capital gain evolved in large measure from the essential features of the economies prominent in the temperate zones of Europe during the eighteenth and nineteenth centuries.[1] In such economies, dependent primarily on agriculture, income was the value of an annual harvest, and capital was the land on which the annual harvest was nurtured. Under these conditions, both income and capital could be specifically identified, at least conceptually, as separate physical phenomenon.

The early American economy was not entirely comparable with this European setting. It, too, was initially an agricultural economy, but in America the growth of the frontier provided a major source of financial opportunity. Our country was long characterized by cheap, plentiful land, and land ownership carried limited social prestige. Some of the first American fortunes were made from transactions in land, whereas stable incomes from

---

[1]For an interesting development of this theme see Lawrence H. Seltzer, *The Nature and Tax Treatment of Capital Gains and Losses* (New York: National Bureau of Economic Research, Inc., 1951).

rents and interest were relatively rare. Population was both growing and mobile. These conditions were conducive to an increase in the market value of business enterprise and real estate, and entrepreneurs often realized substantial gains by selling their "basic" assets and reinvesting the proceeds in other ventures and in other locations. In short, the concept of capital prevalent in this country placed a greater emphasis on value and lesser emphasis on things than did the concept prevalent in Europe.

Judicial Concept of a Capital Gain

In spite of the diversity between the European and the early American economies, the first American courts to struggle with problems of income taxation and capital gains applied English common law and concluded that any gain realized on the sale of a capital investment was not income. In fact, little or no attention was given to the pecuniary measurement of capital investments. This English legal concept prevailed in the 1872 case of *Gray* v. *Darlington,* in which Justice Field said:

> The mere fact that property has advanced in value between the date of its acquisition and sale does not authorize the imposition of the tax on the amount of the advance. Mere advance in value in no sense constitutes the gains, profits, or income specified by the statute. It constitutes and can be treated merely as increase in capital.[2]

By 1918, however, the U.S. Supreme Court modified its earlier position and held that under the 1913 income tax act the sale of an investment or capital asset resulted in a taxable gain or loss to the extent of the difference between the proceeds and the cost (or adjusted basis). The most widely quoted judicial statement of this revised position is found in *Eisner* v. *Macomber,* in which the Court, adopting the definition used in two earlier cases, said: "'Income may be defined as the gain derived from capital and from labor, or from both combined,' provided it be understood to include profit gained through a sale or conversion of capital assets. . . ."[3] As a consequence, between 1913 and 1922 the gain or loss realized on the sale or exchange of a capital asset was subject to income taxation in precisely the same manner as were more ordinary forms of income. The Revenue Act of 1921, which became effective on January 1, 1922, provided the first special treatment for capital gain. Some distinction between ordinary income and capital gain has been retained from 1921 to 1987.

[2]15 Wall. 63 (1872), p. 66.
[3]252 U.S. 189 (1920), p. 207. Quoted in the decision are words used earlier in Stratton's *Independence* v. *Howbert,* 231 U.S. 399 (1913) and *Doyle* v. *Mitchell Bros. Co.,* 247 U.S. 179, 185 (1918).

Professor Lawrence Seltzer summarized the essentials of the judicial concept of a capital gain in the following words:

> In both law and common speech, capital gains are generally regarded as the profits realized from increases in the market value of any assets that are not part of the owner's stock in trade or that he does not regularly offer for sale, and capital losses, as the losses realized from declines in the market value of such assets.[4]

This definition of a capital gain emphasizes the nature of the asset owner's trade or business or, more basically, the owner's intended use or disposition of a specific property. If the owner intends to hold a particular asset only until he or she can sell it at a price that returns a satisfactory profit, then, according to the legal concept, any gain realized on sale or other disposition constitutes ordinary income. Alternatively, if the owner holds the asset either for the production of recurring income or as a long-range investment, with little or no intention of offering the basic asset for resale in the short run (even if the asset were to increase in value), the asset would constitute a capital asset, and the gain realized on its sale would constitute a capital gain.

When applied to taxation, this legal definition of a capital gain creates the obvious difficulty of having a third party determine objectively a taxpayer's intentions regarding each asset owned. Moreover, it would be necessary to determine his or her intention at a particular moment in time, because an asset owner may alter his or her intentions over time. An asset owner may discover that an item originally held solely for long-range investment purposes is now so valuable that it must be reclassified as one held primarily for resale. Of course, when the asset is actually sold and the gain is realized, the question arises of which date and which classification should prevail.

A second difficulty inherent in the legal definition of the capital gain is the requirement that the asset be offered regularly for sale before it is classified a noncapital asset. Are three, four, or five sales necessary (and over what time period) to categorize an item as one that is regularly offered for sale? Problems such as these force tax authorities to resort to common denominator tax classifications to expedite administration of a law that is less than perfect and that must be applied to a variety of slightly differing fact situations.[5]

It should be reemphasized that the legal concept of the capital gain depends on the relationship that exists between a taxpayer and each asset he or she owns. Even if we accept the premise that a capital asset can be specifically identified, however, we cannot necessarily conclude that gains or losses on

---

[4]Lawrence H. Seltzer, *The Nature of Tax Treatment of Capital Gains and Losses* (New York: National Bureau of Economic Research, 1961), p. 3.

[5]Consider, for example, Sec. 1237, which provides that any gain from the sale of more than five lots or parcels of real estate from a single tract shall be considered ordinary income rather than capital gain. In this section, as elsewhere in the law, the arbitrary classifications involve numerous "qualifications."

the disposition of such assets should be treated in any particular manner for tax purposes. If the pecuniary, or value, aspects of a transaction are the dominant feature, it can be forcibly argued that undue emphasis should not be placed on the res, or thing, involved in that transaction. On the other hand, if the res concept is deemed of primary importance, the value aspects may be subordinate.

The law generally emphasizes the res concept. This conclusion is particularly clear in the case of trust law. That law ordinarily provides that the trustee clearly distinguish between the corpus and the income of the trust. Gains and losses realized on the sale or exchange of the corpus typically are recognized as part of the corpus and are not distributable to the income beneficiary. Similarly, depreciation deductions are used to reduce distributable income and to retain corpus. In short, the corpus of a trust is viewed as a distinct res, or thing, and changes in its value are not deemed to be income. For purposes of taxation, these gains are included in taxable income, but they are given special treatment. The important point is to understand that the law clearly emphasizes the res concept.

Economic Concept of a Capital Gain

In the classical economists' model of free enterprise, capital gain and loss are nonexistent. Such assumed parameters as perfect competition, perfect knowledge, conditions of certainty, and freedom of entry ensure the rapid and perfect adjustment of costs and price throughout the market to eliminate pure economic profit. In the real world, of course, the assumed parameters do not exist. Economists concerned with divergences of the real world from the model sometimes define, often indirectly, the capital gain (or loss) as the gain attributable to one or more imperfect conditions.

WINDFALL GAINS AND LOSSES   Unanticipated gains and losses, especially if nonrecurring, are often described as "windfall" gains and losses and, as such, are distinguished from ordinary income. In practice, a recurrence criterion is somewhat easier to apply than an unanticipated criterion, because the latter requires knowledge of expectations. Even such economically advanced countries as England have, until recently, excluded from income taxation any windfall gains (determined primarily by a nonrecurrence criterion) on the grounds that these gains were not income. Theoretically, the unanticipated characteristic of such a gain is more important than its nonrecurrence.

In the classical economic model, the reallocation of scarce resources is attributable to the temporary existence of a pure economic profit (that is, a greater-than-normal return). Producers and suppliers allegedly migrate toward the pure-profit industry in the anticipation of making a greater-than-normal profit in the short run. In the long run, of course, the reallocation process drives down the price (and/or drives up the cost) until the pure profit has been eliminated. In this model, unanticipated gain and loss cannot assist in the reallocation process except in an ex post way; that is, the first appearance of an unanticipated gain causes others to migrate to an industry. In this model, the unanticipated gain or loss is distinguished from the anticipated one, and the former gain may, by default, be characterized as a capital gain or loss.

This economic concept of a capital gain leaves a great deal to be desired when it is applied to taxation. Observe that this concept, like the legal res concept, places a premium on a personal factor; expectations are as difficult for courts and tax administrators to determine as are intentions. Moreover, businesspersons normally have no specific expectation of gain on each asset they own. They hope, of course, that their operations as a whole will result in greater revenues than expenses, but they cannot identify with any precision the gain anticipated on each asset owned. If a precise measurement were possible, then part of the gain on the sale of ordinary inventory—that is, any excess of actual profit over anticipated profit—might be an economic capital gain. Finally, this concept of a capital gain—like the res concept—presents a time specification that creates difficulties for tax assessment. If a taxpayer modifies expectations over time, which moment's expectation should control for tax purposes?

NONPRODUCTIVE GAIN AND LOSS   The branch of economics known as national income analysis produces yet another concept of capital gain. Once again, capital gain is distinguished from national income, and once again the reason is conceptual. National income is a measure of a country's current economic productive activity. Capital gain in this model is realized by the exchange of assets "produced" in another accounting period. If, for example, a person sells his or her personal residence at a gain, that "capital gain" is not reflected in the current year's national income account because the home was constructed in another period. The value of newly discovered natural resources is similarly excluded from current national income measures, even if the property on which the resources are discovered changes hands and the old owner realizes a significant gain on the sale. For national income purposes, the income associated with natural resources is reported in the period(s) of production, that is, when the resources are actually "tapped."

The economists' measures of national income are compiled, for reasons of convenience, largely on the basis of completed market transactions. Such a concept of income and capital gain apparently constitutes a desirable basis for income taxation. But that conclusion is not justified, because the final measure of national income excludes a number of market transactions —including the illegal activities and transfer payments as well as capital gains—and includes an imputed value for such selected nonmarket activities as owner-occupied dwellings and employee perquisites. Moreover, the arbitrary exclusion of "nonproductive" gain from income taxation would provide undue economic incentive to purely speculative transactions in existing assets and would place an economic disincentive on productive activities. The exclusion of illegal activities from income taxation would provide economic incentives for precisely the activities society desires to discourage. Both exclusions would create significant inequities among taxpayers who seem to be equally situated. Finally, the imputation of nonmarket transactions into a tax base is administratively cumbersome because of the subjectivity of the imputation process, particularly at the individual level. In short, neither the nonproductive gain concept of the capital gain nor the national income concept of income is useful for purposes of income taxation.

REAL INCOME AND CAPITAL GAIN   Many economists stress the fact that monetary incomes cannot be equated to real incomes. These persons sometimes argue that capital gain is simply the illusory gain created by changes in the price level. To illustrate, assume that a taxpayer purchased an asset 20 years ago for $10,000 and sold it this year for $15,000. If during the 20-year interval the general price level increased by 50%, then in terms of that taxpayer's command over the world's want-satisfying goods and services, the $5,000 "gain" realized on the sale is truly illusory. Today, it would cost the full $15,000 to repurchase goods and services equivalent to those that could have been purchased 20 years ago for $10,000. Obviously, if a tax were imposed on the illusory gain, the taxpayer would be worse off after the sale because the after-tax proceeds would be insufficient to repurchase goods or services equivalent in value to those sold. Any tax imposed would constitute a tax on capital rather than a tax on income.

The problem is clear enough in principle, but critics who use it as an objection to the taxation of capital gain generally fail to observe that the effects of a change in the price level are not restricted to any particular asset form. The retailer who discovers that the cost of replacing stock is increasing is faced with the identical problem: paper profits exceed real income. The manufacturer with large investments in plant and equipment is in a comparable position: charges for depreciation are inadequate for replacement, and, therefore, income is overstated and "overtaxed." Even the wage earner who receives a cost-of-living adjustment discovers that the larger paycheck is wholly illusory and that real after-tax income is decreased by a progressive tax system that fails to adjust for changes in the price level. If we argue against taxation of capital gain on the basis of changing price levels, we must argue that all gain (income) be similarly deflated (or inflated).

INTEREST RATES AND CAPITAL GAIN   Changes in the interest rate cause problems in income measurement analogous to the questions raised by changes in the price level. Ordinarily, the fair market value of an interest-bearing obligation varies inversely with changes in the interest rate. If an investor purchases at par a $10,000 bond bearing 10% interest (assume for the sake of simplicity that the bond has no due date), then the investor has guaranteed himself or herself a $1,000 annual return as long as the obligor remains solvent. If the "normal" interest rate (that is, the "price" of money) for investments of this type should fall from 10% to 5%, then this investor would discover that the market value of the bond had risen to approximately $20,000, since other investors could now obtain a $1,000 annual return only by investing that larger sum elsewhere. Those objecting to the taxation of capital gain contend that the gain on the sale of bonds under these circumstances ought not to be taxed, because the investor could not purchase an income stream equivalent to that held before sale if required to surrender any portion of the sale proceeds in the form of income taxes.

Once again, the conceptual problem noted is a very real one, and there is a serious question of the wisdom of taxing such illusory gains (or of permitting the deduction of such illusory losses). It must be understood, however, that once again the problem is not endemic to a limited form of investment. Although conventionally the average businessperson, for accounting purposes, is not assumed to receive a specified rate of interest on a basic investment (including investment in inventory), the criticism leveled above applies equally to all investments and, therefore, to some parts of ordinary income.

An Accounting Concept of a Capital Gain

To the accountant, capital gain or loss is perhaps best described as that gain or loss that occurs only at irregular intervals and is attributable to imperfect knowledge and, hence, imperfect measurement of income in earlier periods. Oscar S. Nelson, a former professor of accounting at the University of Pennsylvania, expressed such an accounting concept in the following words:

> The question of the distinction between operating income and capital gains was raised at the recent meetings of the American Accounting Association. In theory there is no distinction, since both result from business effort, i.e., the employment of capital, labor and management by an enterprise with profit as the motive. Capital gains or losses are a manifestation of imperfect income measurement and result because of the requirement of modern business for periodic computation of net profit or loss. Capital gains or losses are composites of imperfect estimates of depreciation, imperfect allocations of costs, imperfect separation of capital and revenue expenditures, disregard or of imperfect adjustment for price level changes, etc.[6]

This accounting concept of capital gain is comparable to the economic concept in denying, in theory, the existence of a distinct thing that can be meaningfully labeled as a capital gain. Like the economist, the accountant observes certain phenomena that do not fit into the ideal model—the accountant recognizes the imperfections of the real world and defines capital gain and loss loosely as those income items that are attributable to real-world imperfections.

Except when acting as a tax advisor, the accountant is concerned with presenting financial information fairly to third parties. Although the accountant considers it necessary to distinguish between routine income items and

[6]Oscar S. Nelson, "Capital Gains from Price Level Increases," *The Accounting Review*, 26 (January 1951), p. 31.

other "material amounts" of "nonrecurring" gains and losses, he or she sometimes may characterize such gains and losses as "capital" ones only because this terminology may have meaning to financial statement readers. Thus, in presenting financial data, the accountant accepts the age-old notion that recurrence is a necessary condition of operating income, and nonrecurrence, a necessary condition of capital gain.

Beyond this, little can be said to clarify the accounting concept of capital gain. To admit that certain gains or losses occur because of imperfect knowledge and imperfect income measurement does not provide a sound basis for deciding whether they ought to be excluded from income taxation, taxed at preferential rates, taxed at equal rates, or taxed at penalty rates.

Unfortunately, the most desirable tax treatment of a capital gain is not determined any more easily than is the concept of a capital gain. Once we accept the notion that a given transaction deserves special tax treatment, we must define the transaction so that it may be recognized among the many transactions subject to the income tax. Ideally, this definition would be subject to objective tests, render equitable results, and contribute to administrative simplicity. These are obviously conflicting objectives—however desirable they might be individually.

The frequency and severity of change in the capital gain and loss tax provisions, and the lack of a sound theoretical framework for these changes, implies that, at least for tax purposes, it is best to accept the notion that capital gain and loss are what the Code says they are—and nothing more pretentious. Concepts of capital gain differ in other disciplines; the greatest danger in comparing these concepts lies in failing to realize that what constitutes a sound concept for one purpose is wholly inadequate for another purpose. A major disadvantage of separating ordinary income from capital gain for tax purposes is that this separation adds more complexity to our Code. By retaining the pre-1987 capital gain and loss provisions, Congress missed a golden opportunity to vastly simplify our tax law.

THE CURRENT PROVISIONS

The statutory provisions which govern the tax consequences of the gain or loss realized on the sale or exchange of a capital asset can be divided into two general categories, namely: (1) a "pure case", and (2) numerous modifications to the pure case. This somewhat unusual categorization is suggested by the way Subchapter P—the portion of the Code that deals with capital gains and losses—is organized. Parts I, II, and III of Subchapter P (Sections 1201 through 1223) provide some reasonably straight-forward rules for a pure case; thereafter, Parts IV, V, and VI (Sections 1231 through 1297) provide a lengthy series of often complex exceptions to (and extensions of) the basic concept. In the remaining pages of this chapter we will summarize and illustrate only the general rules found in Parts I through III of Subchapter P.

In Chapter 16 we will examine a few of the more common modifications to the pure case; i.e., to some of the more frequently encountered sections found in Parts IV through VI. As suggested in the introductory remarks to this chapter, some instructors may very well opt to skip Chapter 16 simply because the capital gains rules are of only limited importance to the vast majority of all taxpayers today.

Finally, before looking at any specific provisions of Subchapter P, we must introduce a few other Code provisions that apply to property transactions generally—regardless of whether the property involved is a capital asset or an ordinary asset. These general sections tell the taxpayer how to measure (or quantify) the gain or loss realized whenever a property is sold or exchanged. After we have learned how to quantify the gain or loss realized, we will learn to separate the capital transactions from the ordinary ones. Finally, in the last pages of this chapter, we will learn how to determine the correct tax treatment of those gains and losses that are properly classified as capital gains and losses.

Gain and Loss Measured

Briefly, the amount of any gain or loss realized on the sale or exchange of a property is the difference between the amount realized and the adjusted basis of the asset that has been sold or exchanged. The phrases "amount realized" and "adjusted basis" obviously are technical terms that must be studied with care.

AMOUNT REALIZED   The Sec. 1001 definition of "amount realized" is as follows:

> (b) Amount Realized.—The amount realized from the sale or other disposition of property shall be the sum of any money received plus the fair market value of the property (other than money) received. In determining the amount realized—
> (1) there shall not be taken into account any amount received as reimbursement for real property taxes which are treated under section 164(d) as imposed on the purchaser, and
> (2) there shall be taken into account amounts representing real property taxes which are treated under section 164(d) as imposed on the taxpayer if such taxes are to be paid by the purchaser.

(For our purposes, subparagraphs (1) and (2) add little to the general definition, but they demonstrate a basic quality of the Code—extensive cross-referencing—that is often frustrating to the tax student.) In addition, the student of taxation must be aware that case law—law decided by judges—often constitutes an important adjunct to understanding the statutory law. In determining the amount realized, the courts have held that the assumption of a seller's mortgage by a buyer constitutes a positive element in the calculation of amount realized just as much as do money and fair market value of property received.[7] For example, suppose that the buyer of a home gave the seller $10,000 cash and a second-hand car with a fair market value of $1,500 and that the buyer assumed the seller's mortgage on the home in the amount of $48,000. The amount realized by this seller would be $59,500 ($10,000 + $1,500 + $48,000).

One of the most administratively difficult aspects of this definition is establishing the fair market value of property received, and the practical importance and complexity of establishing such valuations in the real world should not be underestimated. The phrase "fair market value" assumes a willing buyer and a willing seller acting with full knowledge and without obligation in an arm's-length transaction. The value is, therefore, ultimately a question of fact that frequently must be determined by a court. Fortunately for the student, fair market values are almost always explicitly stated in the textbook, and, thus, a major problem in actual tax administration has been circumvented.

ADJUSTED BASIS   The phrase "adjusted basis" is much more difficult to define than is the phrase "amount realized." The applicable Code section is deceptively brief:

> Sec. 1011. Adjusted Basis for Determining Gain or Loss.
> (a) General Rules.—The adjusted basis for determining the gain or loss from the sale or other disposition of property, whenever acquired, shall be the basis [determined under section 1012 or other applicable sections of this subchapter and subchapters C (relating to corporate distributions and adjustments), K (relating to partners and partnerships), and P (relating to capital gains and losses)], adjusted as provided in section 1016.

The necessarily elementary discussion of adjusted basis that follows considers, in turn, purchased property, inherited property, and property acquired by gift, because the method of acquisition is usually the critical factor in determining a particular property's adjusted basis. (The cost basis of property acquired in a nontaxable or partially taxable exchange can be sufficiently difficult to determine, and, as such, its discussion requires separate consideration in Chapter 17.)

Property Acquired by Purchase   The determination of the tax basis of purchased property generally coincides closely with the determination of book value in accounting. Under most circumstances, the adjusted basis is the sum of the historical cost of the original property and the cost of any capital improvements made to that property subsequent to acquisition, less the depreciation or ACRS deduction claimed (for tax purposes) on the same

---

[7]See *Crane v. Commissioner*, 331 U.S. 1 1935).

property and improvements since acquisition. To illustrate, let us assume that a building was purchased in 1960 for $100,000 and that an addition costing $25,000 was constructed in 1965. If the tax deductions allowed on the building and the addition total $50,000 through last year, then the adjusted basis for tax purposes on January 1 of this year would be $75,000 ($100,000 + $25,0000 − $50,000).

Obviously, in implementing this kind of basis definition, the tax accountant shares many of the financial accountant's problems. For example, in determining historical cost at acquisition, the following problems are typical: separating a single purchase price into costs of component assets (for which the financial accountant and the tax accountant use a common solution — allocation of purchase price on the basis of relative fair market values of the component assets); determining fair market values of noncash acquisitions; and allocating overhead and other indirect costs to assets constructed by the taxpayer for his or her own use. Another common problem, although greater for tax accounting than for financial accounting, is the strong pressure to charge to expense (and hence to obtain an immediate tax deduction) what is actually a capital expenditure that should be charged to an asset account. Controversy in this area of income taxation is commonplace.

One major tax modification to the definition of basis for purchased property should be noted, even though its significance is decreasing. Because income was not subject to taxation in the United States in the four decades immediately preceding 1913, property that was purchased prior to that date and that had increased in value by March 1, 1913, takes a "substituted basis" for tax purposes. The rule, stated in Sec. 1053, is that, for tax purposes, property acquired prior to March 1, 1913, takes as its basis on that date the higher of its cost or its fair market value. Notice that this leaves the taxpayer in a "heads-I-win, tails-you-lose" position. If market values decreased between the date of purchase and March 1, 1913, the taxpayer retains his or her higher cost basis in the determination of gain or loss — that is, the taxpayer pays tax on a smaller gain. On the other hand, if market values increased between the purchase date and March 1, 1913, the taxpayer may use the higher fair market value as basis and thereby again minimize the taxable gain.

Property Acquired by Inheritance   The basis of property received from a decedent generally is the fair market value of the property on the date of the decedent's death. An exception to this general rule applies if the executor or executrix of the estate elects the alternate valuation date; in that event, the basis is generally the fair market value six months after the decedent's death. To illustrate these rules, assume that Tom Tucket purchased stock A for $10,000 on February 5, 1970, and stock B for $20,000 on September 5, 1974. Tom died on October 16, 1987, when the fair market value of both stock A and stock B were $15,000. Any beneficiary of Tom's estate who received those shares would take as his or her basis the $15,000 fair market value on Tom's death, assuming that Tom's executor or executrix made no election to value properties on the alternate valuation date. This means, of course, that the $5,000 unrealized or "paper" gain implicit in stock A would forever go unrecognized for income tax purposes, and the $5,000 unrealized or "paper" loss implicit in stock B would also forever go unrecognized for income tax purposes.

If an executor or executrix elects the alternate valuation date and also distributes some property prior to that date, then—for the property distributed before the valuation date—the basis is the fair market value of the property on the date it was distributed.

Property Acquired by Gift   A third common method by which an individual taxpayer acquires property is by gift. January 1, 1921, marked a major change in the rules of determining the basis of property received by gift. A taxpayer's basis for property acquired by gift and disposed of after December 31, 1920, is generally the donor's adjusted basis. A major exception to this general rule applies if the fair market value of the property given is less than the donor's basis on the date of the gift. In that event, the donee's basis for loss (only) is the fair market value on the date of the gift. This means, of course, that a donee may have two different tax bases for properties—one basis for gain and another for loss.

To understand the idea behind the law, we need only observe the possibilities for tax avoidance in the absence of such wording. If the law provided simply that in all cases the donee would take the donor's cost basis (as it did prior to 1921), then a donor in a low tax bracket could give a property with a substantial "paper loss" to a family member, friend, or acquaintance in a higher tax bracket, and the two individuals combined could achieve a significantly greater tax benefit from the one economic or paper loss than the donor alone could have received. On the other hand, suppose the law provided simply that the donee had to take the lesser of the fair market value of the property on the date of the gift or the donor's cost basis. In that case, if the donor's cost basis was higher than fair market value at date of gift, and if the donee eventually sold the property for more than that cost basis, an unrealistically large gain (in a consolidated sense) would have to be reported. Hence the law is written as it is—trying concurrently to close a loophole and yet not to create an unduly harsh tax credit.

The provisions that relate to gift taxes further complicate the rules used to determine the cost basis of property acquired by gift. For gifts acquired after September 2, 1958, and before January 1, 1977, if the donor paid a federal gift tax on the transfer of the property, the donee can increase the donor's basis by the total amount of the gift tax as long as the sum of the two (donor's cost and gift tax) does not exceed the fair market value on the date of the gift. If the sum of these two amounts does exceed the fair market value, then the donee's basis is the fair market value on the date of the gift. Note that if the donor's cost exceeds the fair market value on the date of the gift, none of the gift tax paid can be added to the donee's basis, even if the property is eventually sold for more than the donor's cost. To illustrate the basis rules applicable to gifts made before January 1, 1977, consider the following three examples:

Example 1   Taxpayer A purchased stock for $15,000. On the date of the gift, June 1, 1976, the stock had a fair market value of $20,000. Gift taxes of $1,000 were paid. In this case, the donee's basis for gain and loss is $16,000 ($15,000 cost + $1,000 gift taxes).

Example 2   Taxpayer B purchased stock for $15,000. On the date of the gift, June 1, 1976, the stock had a fair market value of $10,000. Gift taxes of $1,000 were paid. In this case, the donee's basis for gain is $15,000; the donee's basis for loss is $10,000. If the stock is sold by the donee for any amount greater than $10,000 and less than $15,000, he or she reports neither gain nor loss.

Example 3   Taxpayer C purchased stock for $15,000. On the date of the gift, December 28, 1976, the stock had a fair market value of $15,500. Gift taxes of $1,000 were paid. In this case, the donee's basis for gain and for loss is $15,500 (the sum of the donor's basis plus the gift tax paid, but not in excess of the fair market value of the property on the date of the gift).

The Tax Reform Act of 1976 changed the rules for property acquired by gift after December 31, 1976, insofar as the step-up in basis for gift taxes is concerned. The 1976 Act provides that the gift tax added to appreciated property is calculated as follows:

$$\text{Addition to basis} = \text{Gift tax paid} \times \frac{\text{Net appreciation in gift property}}{\text{Total value of gift property}}$$

The "net appreciation" equals the excess of the gift's fair market value on the date of the gift over the donor's basis at that time.

To illustrate the step-up basis for gift taxes paid on gifts made after December 31, 1976, consider the following three examples:

Example 1   Taxpayer X purchased securities at a cost of $20,000 in 1970. This year, he gave these securities to a donee when their fair market value was $50,000. Total gift tax paid on the transfer was $10,000. The donee's basis for gain and loss is $26,000, computed as follows:

Donor's basis	$20,000
Gift tax adjustment:	
$10,000 \times \dfrac{\$50,000 - \$20,000}{\$50,000}$	6,000
Total	$26,000

Under the rules in effect prior to January 1, 1977, the donee's basis would have been $30,000 ($20,000 cost + $10,000 taxes).

Example 2   Taxpayer Y purchased securities at a cost of $20,000 in 1970. This year, he gave these securities to a donee when their fair market value was $15,000. Total gift tax paid on the transfer was $1,000. No portion of the gift tax can ever be added to the donee's basis, because the fair market value on the date of the gift was less than the donor's cost. Thus, the donee's basis for gain is $20,000; the basis for loss is $15,000.

Example 3   Taxpayer Z purchased securities at a cost of $48,000 in 1970. This year, she gave these securities to a donee when their fair market value was $50,000. Total gift tax paid on the transfer was $10,000. The donee's basis for gain and loss is $48,400, calculated as follows:

Donor's basis	$48,000
Gift tax adjustment:	
$10,000 \times \dfrac{\$50,000 - \$48,000}{\$50,000}$	400
Total	$48,400

For gifts prior to January 1, 1977, the donee's basis for gain and loss would have been $50,000 (the $48,000 cost + $2,000 gift taxes).

Transfers Shortly Before Death   What happens if a donor taxpayer dies shortly after giving property to another? Will the recipient determine the basis according to the gift rules or according to the inherited property rules? The answers to these questions have been changed several times during the past few years. At the moment, gifts made to a person shortly before his or her death are generally treated as any other gifts. Inherited property, regardless of how the decedent acquired the property, is generally treated as any other inherited property. One major exception to this rule exists, however, for property given to a decedent within one year of his or her death if that same property is subsequently inherited back by the donor or the donor's spouse. In that event, the "heir" must carry over the donor's basis in spite of the fact that he or she technically inherited the property from the deceased donee. Although the reason for the new rule may not be obvious, suffice it to observe that it eliminates some tax benefits previously associated with deathbed giving.

Summary   In summary, the amount of gain or loss is the difference between the amount realized on the sale or exchange of a property and the adjusted basis of that property on the date it is sold or exchanged. The amount realized is

1. Money received, *plus*
2. Fair market value of other property received, *plus*
3. Amount of debt transferred from the seller to the buyer.

The adjusted basis of property acquired by purchase generally is

1. Cost of the property surrendered, *plus*
2. Cost of capital improvements to that property, *less*
3. Depreciation or ACRS deductions claimed on the property.

The adjusted basis of property acquired by inheritance or by gift is determined according to special rules.

Gains and Losses Realized but Not Recognized

Primary among these special statutory provisions are the sections that, under specified circumstances, provide that the gain or loss realized on a particular transaction may not be recognized for tax purposes in the year it is first realized. Even though these sections are not restricted to capital gain and loss transactions, they are often of importance to them. Because the nonrecognition sections are discussed in much greater detail in Chapters 16 and 17 of this text, the following discussion is very brief.

Four important nonrecognition provisions are contained in Sec. 1031 (the exchange of property held for productive use or investment); Sec. 1033 (the possible gain on the involuntary conversion of a taxpayer's property); Sec. 1034 (the sale or exchange of a personal residence); and Sec. 1091 (the loss on the sale of securities—commonly dubbed "wash sales"). The rationale of three of these sections was explained briefly in connection with the wherewithal-to-pay tenet. The fourth section (Sec. 1091) is a "loophole closer," without which taxpayers could sell securities solely to obtain a tax deduction and, at the same time, retain their real economic position by an immediate repurchase of the securities sold. Section 1091 denies a taxpayer an immediate loss deduction for any security sold if, within 30 days before or after that sale, he or she purchases substantially identical securities. The loss denied is then added to the "new" basis of the securities purchased so that the tax consequence on final disposition gives recognition to the loss deduction denied earlier.

Whatever the reasons for the various provisions, the important conclusion for our purposes is that if certain conditions prevail, a gain or loss realized from a consummated transaction may not be immediately recognized for tax purposes. Suppose, for example, that a taxpayer exchanges his GMC stock, which has a fair market value of $100,000 but which cost him $70,000 several years ago, for shares of an equivalent fair market value in the Ford Motor Company. Because no provision exists in the Code that modifies the general rule in this case, the $30,000 gain realized in this transaction (the exchange) must be recognized for tax purposes. On the other hand, suppose that the same taxpayer also exchanged a warehouse having a fair market value of $100,000 (but having an adjusted tax basis of only $70,000) for a vacant lot with a fair market value of $100,000. Section 1031 would require the taxpayer to defer recognition of this $30,000 gain, even though the gain was realized in the same sense that it was in the GMC–Ford Exchange.

Capital Gain and Loss Defined

The Internal Revenue Code does not define capital gains and losses per se; rather, it defines a capital asset and then states that a capital gain or loss is simply the gain or loss from the sale or exchange of a capital asset. In addition, the Code defines capital asset negatively—that is, it states that all property except that specifically exempted by the Code is a capital asset. The complete statutory definition of a pure capital asset is as follows:

Sec. 1221. Capital Asset Defined.

For purposes of this subtitle, the term "capital asset" means property held by the taxpayer (whether or not connected with his trade or business), but does not include—

(1) stock in trade of the taxpayer or other property of a kind which would properly be included in the inventory of the taxpayer if on hand at the close of the taxable year, or property held by the taxpayer primarily for sale to customers in the ordinary course of his trade or business;

(2) property, used in his trade or business, of a character which is subject to the allowance for depreciation provided in section 167, or real property used in his trade or business;

(3) a copyright, a literary, musical, or artistic composition, a letter or memorandum, or similar property, held by—

   (A) a taxpayer whose personal efforts created such property,

   (B) in the case of a letter, memorandum, or similar property, a taxpayer for whom such property was prepared or produced, or

   (C) a taxpayer in whose hands the basis of such property is determined, for the purpose of determining gain from a sale or exchange, in whole or in part by reference to the basis of such property in the hands of a taxpayer described in subparagraph (A) or (B);

(4) accounts or notes receivable acquired in the ordinary course of trade or business for services rendered or from the sale of property described in paragraph (1); or

(5) a publication of the United States Government (including the Congressional Record) which is received from the United States Government or any agency thereof, other than by purchase at the price at which it is offered for sale to the public, and which is held by—

   (A) a taxpayer who so received such publication, or

   (B) a taxpayer in whose hands the basis of such publication is determined, for purposes of determining gain from a sale or exchange, in whole or in part by reference to the basis of such publication in the hands of a taxpayer described in subparagraph (A).

Numerous interesting questions are apparent on even the most superficial examination of this definition. Such phrases as "stock in trade," "primarily for sale," and "trade or business" contain enough ambiguities to guarantee ample controversy between taxpayers and the government. For example, suppose a taxpayer inherited some jewelry that he or she had no intention of keeping and, in fact, promptly disposed of through another party. Would those jewels be "property held by the taxpayer primarily for sale to customers?" If so, the gain on their sale would be ordinary income; if not, the gain would be capital gain.[8]

An interesting corollary issue is the definition of a taxpayer's "trade or business." Many challenging tax problems arise because of this phrase. For instance, can a taxpayer have more than one trade or business concurrently?[9]

[8]For a decision of the First Circuit Court of Appeals on this fact case, see *R. Foster Reynolds* v. *Commissioner*, 155 F.2d 620 (1946).

[9]Apparently so. See John H. Saunders, *Trade or Business—Its Meaning Under the Internal Revenue Code*, 12th Annual Institute on Federal Taxes, University of Southern California, 1960, p. 693.

Assume that a salaried employee also owns, and rents to another, a single dwelling unit. Does this rental activity constitute a second and separate trade or business for the taxpayer? If it does, the dwelling is depreciable property used in the trade or business and, therefore, is not a capital asset. If the rental activity is not a trade or business, then the property is a capital asset.[10]

Perhaps the most illogical part of the capital asset definition is the exclusion [in Sec. 1221 (2)] of depreciable and real property used in the trade or business. If asked to give an example of a capital asset, most business-oriented persons uninitiated in federal taxation would quickly respond with such examples as plant, equipment, and business realty. Yet these items are clearly eliminated from the capital asset definition in the Code. During the depression years of the late 1930s, Congress decided that the limitation on the deduction of capital losses was unduly restricting the sale of plant and equipment purchased in the roaring twenties. Hence, Congress enacted this definitional exclusion, which effectively transformed the losses on the sale of such assets into ordinary losses and, therefore, into losses not subject to capital loss limitations. At the same time, of course, the definitional exclusions also transformed the gains into ordinary gains, which are taxed in a less advantageous way. By 1942 this factor was so important, because tax liability was sizable on such gains, and pressures for change had so built up, that Congress modified the Code (Sec. 1231).[11] The modification allows certain gains to be treated as capital gains (when the gains exceed the losses on the sales and exchanges of certain properties during a given tax period), although, by definition, several of the assets included are still not capital assets. To complicate matters further, this definitional riddle has been modified again so that today some portion or all of the gain that could be treated as capital gain under Sec. 1231 must now be treated as ordinary income because of Secs. 1245, 1250, or related sections, which deal with the recapture of depreciation charges for tax purposes. (These and other matters are discussed in Chapter 16 and are mentioned here only to forewarn you.)

The exclusion in Sec. 1221(3) is an interesting example of a conceptual problem inherent in capital gain taxation. The only way that most persons can earn a living is by "selling" a service that involves a physical or mental process or both. For example, a person might dig a ditch, diagnose an illness and prescribe a medication, or repair an automobile. A few persons, however, create a property that when sold provides an income. For example, artists create art objects; authors and composers create copyrighted works; and inventors create patentable ideas. If all property were capital assets, then

---

[10]The Tax Court has maintained, at least until recently, that the mere ownership of improved rental property constituted a trade or business. See, for example, *Hazard*, 7 TC 372 (1946). However, other courts have required continuous, systematic, and substantial taxpayer activity with the property—in addition to mere ownership—before there could be a trade or business. See, for example, *Union National Bank of Troy, Exec.* 195 F.Supp.382 (DC NY, 1961). In a recent decision involving a home-office deduction related to rental property, the Tax Court seems to have modified its original position as stated in *Hazard*. See Edwin R. Curphey, 73 TC 424 (1979).

[11]Originally Sec. 117(j) of the 1939 Code. See Chapter 16 for additional details.

persons whose efforts resulted in a property would reap the benefits of the capital gains tax, whereas all other persons would be subject to the less favorable ordinary tax rates. To preclude this result, Sec. 1221(3) was inserted into the Code. Observe, however, that the current statute does not exclude patents and that the exclusion extends only to the individual whose efforts created the property and to those who assume the creator's tax basis. (The basis concept is clarified earlier in this chapter.)

The exclusion contained in Sec. 1221(3)(B) was added to the Code in 1969 to end the large tax deductions previously available to former presidents of the United States. Under prior law whenever an ex-president contributed his papers and other memorabilia to a specially created library named in his honor, a major charitable deduction was created. After lengthy debate, Congress decided that Lyndon Johnson was to be the last of the presidents to be so privileged. Because "ordinary income property" creates a charitable deduction equal only to the taxpayer's basis in the property and since a president's basis in his papers is generally zero, Sec. 1221(3)(B) ensures that presidents no longer receive major personal tax benefits from their public service. Richard Nixon's attempt to claim a charitable contribution deduction for the alleged donation of his vice presidential papers before the effective date of this change in the tax law was widely reported in the daily press.

One final observation relative to the definition of capital assets demonstrates the care that must be exercised in dealing with this portion of the Code. Suppose a local accountant sells his entire practice to another accountant for a fixed sum, payable immediately. Is all or any part of the sale proceeds to be allocated to the sale of a capital asset? More specifically, if the proceeds exceed the fair market value of the tangible assets and uncollected receivables, does the excess represent the sale of goodwill, and, if so, is this intangible asset a capital asset? As a general rule it is; however, a slight difference in facts may modify this conclusion. If, for example, the covenant of sale includes an agreement not to compete, all or a part of the excess may be ordinary income. Careful tax planning by an expert is absolutely essential to guarantee the tax rights of both the purchaser and seller in these and other similar arrangements.[12]

For tax purposes, the most numerically important group of capital assets is stocks and bonds. Except when held for resale by dealers, these assets generally are capital assets, and, therefore, the gain or loss on their sale or exchange is a capital gain or loss. Personal assets such as residences, family automobiles, and pleasure boats are also common forms of capital asset. Observe that a single asset may be both capital and noncapital—for example, a car that is used 50% of the time in a trade or business and 50% of the time for family driving is treated for tax purposes as two assets, one capital, the other not.

To determine that a particular gain or loss is a capital gain or loss, however, is not always the most important tax fact. Even though the loss on the sale of a personal residence may correctly be categorized as a capital loss, the most

---

[12]As an illustration of this conclusion, read the decision in *Dairy Service*, TC Memo 1966-113.

significant tax factor in this instance is that this loss is never deductible. The reason for this result stems from a fundamental rule that nothing is deductible unless authorized by the Code or Regulations. Losses on purely personal property are deductible only if they arise from a casualty or theft. Hence, the loss realized on the sale of a personal automobile would not be deductible even though a gain on that same automobile would be taxed like any routine capital gain. In other instances, nonrecognition of gains and losses stems from other special statutory provisions.

Short and Long-term Distinctions

Prior to 1987, the distinction between a short- and a long-term capital gain or loss was very important. That distinction still has some importance for a few individual taxpayers today; after December 31, 1987, it will have no importance for any taxpayers. Because of their limited importance, we will review the rules relative to the short-term and long-term distinctions only very briefly.

Sec. 1222 divides capital gains and losses into four categories based solely on a six-month holding period. The four categories are (1) short-term capital gains, (2) short-term capital losses, (3) long-term capital gains, and (4) long-term capital losses. In general, short-term capital gains are gains from the sale or exchange of capital assets held for equal to or less than six months; short-term capital losses, losses from the sale or exchange of capital assets held for equal to or less than the six months. Long-term capital gains are gains from the sale or exchange of capital assets held for more than six months; long-term capital losses, losses from the sale or exchange of capital assets held for more than six months.

To determine tax results for some individual taxpayers in 1987 it will be necessary to separately consolidate all short-term capital gains and losses and also to consolidate long-term capital gains and losses and, thus, to determine both the *net* short-term capital gain or loss and the *net* long-term capital gain or loss for the year. For example, suppose that in 1987 a taxpayer had three transactions that were categorized correctly as short-term capital transactions: One resulted in a $600 gain, a second resulted in a $100 loss, and a third resulted in a $200 loss. This taxpayer would have a *net* short-term capital gain of $300 (i.e., $600-$100-$200). Suppose that instead of the $200 loss assumed above, the third transaction had resulted in a $1,000 loss; then the taxpayer would have had a *net* short-term capital loss of $500 (i.e., $600-$100-$1,000). In 1987 an individual taxpayer would also have to combine all long-term capital gains and losses to determine *net* long-term capital gain or loss in the same manner.

Obviously, it is possible for a taxpayer to combine net short-term and net long-term capital gains and losses into a single net capital gain or loss, an amount that the Code refers to as "capital gain net income." This final combination, however, is meaningful only in certain select cases, as detailed below. More frequently, an individual will have to determine an amount the Code refers to as *net capital gain*.

Obviously it would be possible for a taxpayer to combine the net short-term and the net long-term capital gains and losses into a single net amount. In general, however, that is not required. In lieu thereof, the Code requires taxpayers to determine if their *net long-term capital gain* (NLTCG) exceeds their *net short-term capital loss* (NSTCL). Only this one unique combination of the two net amounts yields a figure which the Code calls a "net capital gain" (NCG). (See Sec. 1222(11).) In other words:

$$NLTCG + NSTCG \neq NCG$$

and

$$NSTCG - NLTCL \neq NCG$$
$$(\text{even if NSTCG} > \text{NLTCL}).$$

Those and other possible combinations are termed "capital gain net income." (See Sec. 1222(9).) Any combination of the two net capital amounts in which the losses exceed the gains is properly referred to as a "net capital loss" (NCL). (See Sec. 1222(10).) Thus,

$$NLTCL - NSTCG = NCL$$
$$(\text{if NLTCL} > \text{NSTCG}) \text{ and}$$
$$NSTCL - NLTCG \text{ also} = NCL$$
$$(\text{if NSTCL} > \text{NLTCG}).$$

The tax treatment of these various possible combinations may, as noted before, still have some significance for the year 1987.

Tax Consequences of Net Capital Gains and Losses

After all of a taxpayer's capital gains and losses for 1987 have been correctly identified, quantified, and classified as long or short term, the taxpayer must determine the correct tax treatment. The most pertinent Code provisions are Secs. 1 and 1201, which may permit taxpayers to apply a special tax rate to some or all of the capital gains realized in 1987, and Secs. 1211 and 1212, which prescribe the tax treatment of net capital losses (in all years). The specific provisions applicable to capital gains differ significantly from the rules applicable to capital losses.

TAX CONSEQUENCES OF A NET CAPITAL GAIN   A noncorporate taxpayer's net capital gain in 1987 will be taxed at 15% if the taxpayer is in a 15% marginal tax bracket and at 28% if the taxpayer's marginal tax bracket is 28%. However, if a noncorporate taxpayer is in a marginal tax bracket in excess of 28%, any amount of net capital gain (only) will in 1987 not be taxed at any rate above 28% per Sec. 1(j). (Remember that the term net capital gain refers *only* to NLTCG-NSTCL.) In effect, this subsection creates an alternative tax rate for some NCGs realized by noncorporate taxpayers in 1987.

Corporate taxpayers were subject, for taxable years beginning after December 31, 1986, and before July 1, 1987, to a maximum tax rate of 34% on their net capital gains per Sec. 1201. For all corporate capital gains realized after June 30, 1987, there is no further distinction between capital gain and ordinary income.

TAX CONSEQUENCE OF A NET CAPITAL LOSS   Tax detriments often result from transactions involving capital assets. First, many capital losses simply are not deductible for tax purposes. As noted earlier, the capital loss sustained on the sale of a personal automobile is not deductible, even though the gain on the sale of the identical asset would be taxable, simply because losses on the sale or exchange of purely personal assets are not deductible per Sec. 165(c). Because casualty losses are deductible under Sec. 165(c)(3), however, the destruction (total or partial) by fire, flood, or wind of a personal automobile may result in a tax deduction. The precise treatment of deductible casualty losses is discussed in Chapter 16. At this juncture, it is necessary only to realize that many capital losses simply are not tax deductible at all or, if deductible, only to some limited extent.

A second possible tax detriment in transactions involving capital assets occurs because net capital losses that are deductible are subject to a maximum limitation. For noncorporate taxpayers, net capital losses incurred in any given year are deductible (if deductible at all) only to the lesser of (1) $3,000 or (2) taxable income determined without subtracting personal exemptions. (The maximum for a married taxpayer filing a separate return is $1,500.) If the deductible net capital loss in any particular year exceeds this maximum, for all noncorporate taxpayers the excess is carried forward to all subsequent tax years until exhausted or until the taxpayer dies.

Corporate taxpayers cannot offset any of the net capital loss against their ordinary incomes. Notice that the rule just stated is concerned with net capital losses; in other words, capital losses can be offset against capital gains without limit. Even though a corporation is not permitted to offset any capital losses against ordinary income, all corporate net capital losses can be carried back three years and forward five years and offset against capital gains realized in those years. If the corporation is unable to generate sufficient capital gains to offset capital loss carryforwards by the end of the five-year carryforward period, then the capital losses are lost forever for tax purposes. If a corporation has capital losses in two or more successive years, the losses are offset in the order in which they were incurred; in other words, they are applied on a first-in, first-out basis.

Under prior law there were important distinctions between the way short- and long-term capital losses were treated, both for corporate and noncorporate taxpayers. Except in the case of capital loss carrybacks for corporations to years before 1987, however, those distinctions are no longer of much importance. We will, therefore, not discuss those differences in this introductory text.

Planning Implications

Because of limitations on the deduction of capital losses from ordinary income, taxpayers will generally be tempted to classify any "questionable losses" as ordinary losses rather than as capital losses. For example, suppose that an individual realizes a $50,000 loss on the sale of a depreciable real property in 1988. Depending on the facts—i.e., the reasons the taxpayer originally had for acquiring the property and the way in which it was used after its acquisition—that property may or may not be a capital asset. (If this uncertainty is confusing, review once more the definition of capital assets found in Sec. 1221, giving particular attention to Secs. 1221(1) and 1221(2). See also the discussion on page 15-18, supra.) If the individual can reasonably claim either (1) that the property sold *was* held primarily for resale or (2) that it *was* used in a "trade or business," then the $50,000 loss realized can be immediately offset against the taxpayer's ordinary income from other sources, such as salary, professional fees, and/or business income. One risk in making this choice, however, is the fact that the tax laws could be revised, in the not too distant future, in such a way as to once again give capital gains preferential treatment. If that should happen, one can not help but wonder if the hasty action to classify questionable losses in 1987 and 1988 could come home to haunt the taxpayer in later years. In other words, would the admission that certain properties were *not* held as investments in 1987 or 1988 taint other similar properties that might be sold in 1989 and beyond?

Because capital gains are now generally taxed as ordinary income, taxpayers after 1987 will not ordinarily care whether properties sold or exchanged are classified as capital assets or as ordinary assets. However, if a taxpayer has a large capital loss carryforward in 1988 or thereafter, it may still be beneficial to categorize questionable cases as producing capital gains rather than ordinary income. This option would, of course, allow the taxpayer to utilize the capital loss carryforward at the earliest possible time.

PROBLEMS

1. Courts and tax commentators have for years compared capital to a tree, and income to the fruit of that tree; that is, income is viewed as something that can be separated from capital, leaving the productive base "unscathed." Discuss the possible weaknesses of this metaphor.

2. Assume that 10 years ago a high school teacher earned an annual salary of $12,000 and that today her annual salary had risen to $18,000. If we can establish that the general price level increased 50% in the interim, what increase in real income did she have, in terms of the (original) "base" salary, in the 10-year interval? What portion of the $6,000 increase would be treated as a capital gain for tax purposes?

3. Many less economically developed nations of the world have begun to institute an income tax during the past 20 years. Generally, these countries exclude "capital gain" from the income tax base. What good reasons might they have for such an exclusion? What undesirable consequence, in terms of economic development, could follow from this exclusion?

4. Based on your own intuition, how would you describe a capital gain? (In responding to this question, ignore this textbook and base your answer on any general notions you might have gathered from your other studies thus far in college.) As a part of your class discussion, be prepared to explain why basic differences in concepts exist.

5. Some authorities have proposed the elimination of all taxes on capital gains. They argue that such a change would eliminate many complexities from the law. Do you agree? Why or why not?

6. In 1965, Betty paid $10,000 for Property A, and Bob earned $10,000 for his services. In 1987, Betty sold Property A for $20,000, and Bob was paid $20,000 for his services. If the consumer price index (CPI) increased from 100 in 1965 to 200 in 1987:
   a. How much real income has Betty realized on Property A in 1987?
   b. How much of an increase in real wages has Bob realized after 20 years' work?
   c. Do you believe that Betty should pay an income tax on the sale of the property in 1987? Explain briefly. (Note: This question asks for personal opinion; not the answer per the Code.)
   d. On what amount of income do you believe Bob should pay an income tax in 1987? Explain briefly. (Note: State your personal opinion.)
   e. Based on our current tax law (the Internal Revenue Code of 1986, as amended), will either Betty or Bob automatically get a tax break? If so, which one? What will this "tax break" be called?

7. Country N imposes no tax on capital gains; Country O treats capital gains just like ordinary income; Country P taxes capital gains as income but at preferential rates. If (1) the tax rates on ordinary income are substantial but identical in Countries N, O, and P, and (2) the definition of capital assets is identical in Countries N, O, and P;
   a. Would you expect to find a difference in the investments commonly made by the taxpayers in each of the three countries? Explain briefly.
   b. Which country would be the most industrial (other things being equal)?

8. Harry Fox operates a retail hardware store and owns the property listed below. Indicate whether each property is, for federal tax purposes, a capital asset or a noncapital asset in Fox's hands.
   a. A sailboat used solely for pleasure
   b. The building that houses his retail store
   c. A warehouse in which he stores his hardware
   d. The hardware items in the store
   e. The hardware items in the warehouse
   f. His personal residence
   g. His automobile, used 25% of the time for business, 75% for pleasure
   h. One hundred shares of Alpha Corporation stock
   i. A valuable painting, inherited from a favorite aunt
   j. Land on which the warehouse is located
   k. "Goodwill" purchased by fox when he acquired the business from its previous owner

9. The *Washington Dispatch,* a Delaware corporation, sold the following assets during the current year. Which of the sales by the *Washington Dispatch* corporation involved capital assets?
   a. A letter it received a year earlier from a well-known politician
   b. A letter from a former U.S. president to a New York attorney, which the *Washington Dispatch* purchased (from the attorney) in conjunction with a story it published this year
   c. A set of 25 photographs, taken by a staff photographer, which graphically depict the terror associated with a recent skyjacking
   d. Above normal sales (say, 100,000 extra copies) of a special edition of the *Dispatch*

e. A set of classified government documents given to the *Dispatch* by an anonymous person

f. All the common stock of a subsidiary corporation that publishes another newspaper in another city

g. A three-year-old printing press deemed obsolete

h. Illinois State bonds, which the *Dispatch* treasurer purchased as a temporary investment for excess corporate cash

10. Helen and Maria, two University of Hartford students, have almost covered the walls of their apartment with oil paintings. Helen's favorite painting is not a capital asset; Maria's favorite is a capital asset. Explain how this could be true.

11. In the six cases that follow, a donee has received property as a gift and subsequently disposed of it through sale. For each case, compute the donee's gain on the subsequent sale if:

a. The gifts were made in 1976.

b. The gifts were made in 1977 or a later year.

Case	Donor's Adjusted Basis	Fair Market Value at Date of Gift	Gift Tax Paid	Amount Realized
1	$10,000	$20,000	$1,000	$21,000
2	10,000	15,000	1,000	15,000
3	10,000	15,000	1,000	9,000
4	10,000	8,000	500	11,000
5	10,000	8,000	500	7,500
6	10,000	8,000	500	9,000

12. Taxpayer Y sold a building to taxpayer Z. Z paid Y $10,000 cash and assumed the $52,000 mortgage on the property. In addition, Z agreed to pay property taxes of $320 accrued to the date of the sale. What is the amount realized by Y? What is Z's adjusted basis at the time of purchase?

13. On August 10, Linn Berg, an airline pilot, sold 100 shares of Trimotor Aircraft Corporation stock (a listed security) for $1,000. Determine the gross amount of capital gain or loss that Linn should report if:

a. He purchased the shares on February 15 for $800.

b. He received the shares as a gift from his Uncle Jim on July 2 when their fair market value was $900. Assume that Jim purchased the shares for $300 in 1962 and that he paid a gift tax of $60 on this transfer.

c. All facts in part b apply, except that Jim purchased the shares for $1,020 rather than for $300.

d. He inherited the shares from his father, Charles, who died July 8 last year. Charles had purchased the shares for $300 in 1962. The fair market value of the shares on July 8 was $1,200. The executrix of Charles's estate elected to value all estate assets six months after Charles's death. On December 31, the shares had a fair market value of $900. On January 8 (this year), the shares had a fair market value of $880. The shares were distributed by the executrix to Linn on June 21, when they had a fair market value of $1,100.

14. Assume that on February 14 a donee sold, under the alternative conditions detailed below, an investment property she had received as a gift on January 8. Assume further that the donor had purchased the property on October 26, 1974. State the amount and class (short-term/long-term) of capital gain or loss realized.

Donor's Adjusted Basis	Gift Tax Paid By Donor	Value on Date of Gift	Amount Realized on Sale
a. $11,000	$ 600	$12,000	$13,000
b. 11,000	1,200	12,000	13,000
c. 11,000	500	10,000	9,000
d. 11,000	500	10,000	12,000
e. 11,000	1,500	10,000	10,500

15. Taxpayer, a surgeon, realized the following gains and losses during the current year:
   (1) Personal car sold at $1,600 loss
   (2) Business car sold at $200 gain
   (3) Personal home sold at $2,000 loss
   (4) Rental property sold at $3,000 gain
   (5) Purchased oil painting from personal art collection, sold at $100 gain
   (6) Bronze statue, cast by taxpayer in spare-time hobby, sold at $20 loss
   (7) Bronze statue, cast by taxpayer in spare-time hobby, stolen from uninsured private collection; cost, $180
      a. Which of the above gains and losses can be classified as capital gains and losses? Explain any troublesome classifications.
      b. Which of the above gains and losses would not be recognized for tax purposes in the current year?

16. Jim inherited four properties from his Aunt Zelda, who died on September 30. The executrix of Zelda's estate valued all properties on the date of death for estate tax purposes. Using the information below, determine Jim's tax basis in each property.

Property	Date Purchased by Zelda	Cost to Zelda	FMV on Sept. 30
Stock A	3/8/62	$10,000	$20,000
Bond B	6/22/68	20,000	10,000
Land	9/1/75	30,000	50,000
Oil painting	11/14/78	2,000	2,500

17. Determine the adjusted basis of the three assets detailed below:
   a. A building purchased for $100,000 16 years ago. Taxpayer paid $20,000 down and signed an $80,000 12% note payable. To date, only $35,000 in principal has been paid on this $80,000 note. After acquiring the building, taxpayer incurred $10,000 in repairs (which were expensed) and made $25,000 worth of capital improvements. Taxpayer has claimed depreciation of $50,000 on the building since acquisition.
   b. Taxpayer received a gift of 100 shares of ABC stock from his girlfriend. She purchased the stock in 1975 for $500. On the date of the gift, the shares were worth $11,500. A gift tax of $180 was paid.
   c. Taxpayer received stock two years ago as a gift from her grandmother. On the date of the gift, the stock was valued at $10,000; no gift tax was paid. Grandmother had purchased the stock in 1929 for $500. Grandmother died this year when the stock was valued at $11,000. Taxpayer, who was executrix of her grandmother's estate, did not elect the alternate valuation date. Six months after her grandmother's death, the same shares were valued at $12,000.

18. Arnold Roger sold the following securities:

Security	Date Acquired	Date Sold	Cost	Sales Price
ABC	9/21 two years ago	10/4	$2,000	$1,800
DEF	10/29 last year	3/10	6,000	6,600
GHI	1/15 last year	8/16	1,700	1,400
JKL	1/20 last year	3/10	3,000	4,500
MNO	5/8 last year	12/31	5,000	4,700
PQR	5/8 last year	12/31	5,000	5,300

Assuming that Roger is a cash-basis taxpayer and that the above transactions constitute all of his capital asset transactions for this year, calculate:

a. His net short-term capital gain or loss.

b. His net long-term capital gain or loss.

c. His capital loss carryforward to next year.

19. Assume that Harold Vine, a married taxpayer who files a joint return, had the following components of taxable income this year:

Salary	$53,200
Interest, rents, and so on (after exclusions)	30,000
Net short-term capital gain	10,000
Net long-term capital gain	75,000
Deductions from A.G.I. (including exemptions)	(20,000)

a. What is Vine's taxable income for the year?

b. What is his "net capital gain?"

c. Calculate Vine's minimum income tax liability. Use the current tax rates.

CHAPTER 16

Capital Gains: Modifications to the Pure Concept

Mr. Gross: . . . Why ask the farmers to hold their breeding stock for 12 months, whereas in any other matter it is a 6 months' proposition; why should there be a differential?
Mr. Mills: Of course there should not be a differential between the farmer and anyone else in the treatment afforded tax-wise; the gentleman is right about that. But I had understood that the livestock people were very well satisfied with this provision.
Congressional Record *(1951)*

Chapter 15 introduced the most important general rules that ordinarily determine the tax consequences of the gain or loss realized on a sale or exchange of a pure capital asset, as defined in Sec. 1221. In fact, the Code contains numerous other sections that modify that definition. In some instances, the modifying sections exclude a definitionally "pure" capital asset from capital gain and loss treatment. At other times, they provide capital gain treatment for assets that do not satisfy the puristic definition.

Part IV of Subchapter P (the subchapter of the Code concerned with capital gain and loss) contains many of the special rules to be applied in particular

16-1

fact circumstances. The following list of the sections contained in Part IV suggests the breadth of these special rules:

Sec. 1231.   Property used in the trade or business and involuntary conversions.
Sec. 1233.   Gains and losses from short sales.
Sec. 1234.   Options to buy or sell.
Sec. 1234A. Gains or losses from certain terminations.
Sec. 1235.   Sale or exchange of patents.
Sec. 1236.   Dealers in securities.
Sec. 1237.   Real property subdivided for sale.
Sec. 1238.   Amortization in excess of depreciation.
Sec. 1239.   Gain from sale of depreciable property between certain related taxpayers.
Sec. 1241.   Cancellation of lease or distributor's agreement.
Sec. 1242.   Losses on small business investment company stock.
Sec. 1243.   Loss of small business investment company.
Sec. 1244.   Losses on small business stock.
Sec. 1245.   Gain from dispositions of certain depreciable property.
Sec. 1246.   Gain on foreign investment company stock.
Sec. 1247.   Election by foreign investment companies to distribute income currently.
Sec. 1248.   Gain from certain sales or exchanges of stock in certain foreign corporations.
Sec. 1249.   Gain from certain sales or exchanges of patents, etc., to foreign corporations.
Sec. 1250.   Gain from disposition of certain depreciable realty.
Sec. 1252.   Gain from disposition of farm land.
Sec. 1253.   Transfers of franchises, trademarks, and trade names.
Sec. 1254.   Gain from disposition of interest in oil or gas property.
Sec. 1255.   Gain from disposition of section 126 property.
Sec. 1256.   Regulated futures contracts marked to market.
Sec. 1257.   Disposition of converted wetlands or highly erodible croplands.

Other scattered Code sections make still further modifications to the capital gain and loss complex. A partial list of those sections includes:

Sec. 165(g).   Worthless securities.
Sec. 166(d).   Nonbusiness bad debts.
Sec. 302.   Distributions in redemption of stock.
Sec. 303.   Distributions in redemption of stock to pay death taxes.
Sec. 304.   Redemption through use of related corporations.
Sec. 306.   Dispositions of certain stock.
Sec. 341.   Collapsible corporations.
Sec. 631.   Gain or loss in the case of timber, coal or domestic iron ore.

The objective of this chapter is to explain several of the more important modifications to the pure case of capital gain and loss taxation. Sections 1231, 1245, and 1250 receive our major attention because they are so commonly encountered. Collectively, these three sections deal with depreciable and real properties used in trade or business—"chameleon assets" that are not capital assets by Code definition but assets from the disposition of which gains may or may not be eligible for capital gain treatment. Although commonplace, these complex rules are of very limited significance in years after 1987.

DEPRECIABLE AND REAL PROPERTIES USED IN TRADE OR BUSINESS

Although excluded by the Code from the definition of a capital asset, depreciable and real properties used in trade or business effectively may result in a capital gain when sold or exchanged. The conditions that must be satisfied to obtain this result are delineated in Sec. 1231.

Section 1231

Section 1231 must be studied carefully to be understood. Three distinct complications may be confusing: First, the group of transactions that collectively constitute the whole of Sec. 1231 are at best mysterious; second, the import of Sec. 1231 cannot be determined until a tax period has closed and the net position of all Sec. 1231 transactions is known with certainty; and third, the apparent consequences of Sec. 1231 are often overridden by other sections that deal with the "recapture" of ordinary deductions. In the following pages, we discuss these three complications, in the order stated, in some detail.

Section 1231 encompasses two major classes of transactions:

1. Gains and losses from the sale or exchange of property used in the trade or business, but gains are included only to the extent not subject to such "recapture" sections as 1245 and 1250
2. Gains and losses from the involuntary conversion of both (a) property used in a trade or business and (b) capital assets held for more than six months, but only if the gains from such involuntary conversions, which are casualties, exceed the losses from casualties

To make matters even more complex, Sec. 1231(b) defines property used in a trade or business to include:

1. Real and depreciable properties used in a trade or business if held for more than six months
2. Timber, coal, and domestic iron ore (with respect to which Sec. 631 applies)
3. Livestock, but
   a. if cattle and horses held for draft, breeding, dairy, or sporting purposes, only if held for more than 24 months

    b. if other livestock (that is, other than cattle or horses) held for draft, breeding, dairy, or sporting purposes, only if held for more than 12 months

    c. never to include poultry

4. Unharvested crops, but only if the crop and the land are sold, exchanged, or involuntarily converted at the same time and to the same person

The reason for treating such a diverse collection of assets in a unique manner wholly escapes logic. The only good explanation of this definition is a historical one. Section 1231 originated in the turmoil between the Great Depression and World War II. Initially, it was intended to provide taxpayers with the rare opportunity of treating only the net gains on the sale of real and depreciable properties used in a trade or business as if they were capital gains and of treating net losses on the sale or exchange of those same properties as if they were ordinary (or noncapital) losses. This, of course, was the best of both possible tax worlds, and it is not surprising that special interest groups sought to be included with the purview of this provision. As suggested by the headnote to this chapter—part of a conversation between two members of Congress—logic often gave way to whatever satisfied those special interest groups.

In addition to the diverse collection of assets included within the definition of "property used in a trade or business," observe that Sec. 1231 applies to different kinds of assets under different conditions: it applies to sales and exchanges of properties used in a trade or business and to the involuntary conversion of a still larger set of assets. In the latter category, pure capital assets held for the prescribed time, as well as property used in a trade or business, are combined in a unique manner. Recognized gains and losses from involuntary conversion due to condemnations or the threat thereof are always included in the Sec. 1231 category. If the involuntary conversion is a casualty, however, gains and losses are first brought together to determine whether casualty gains exceed casualty losses. If a net gain results, the casualty gains and losses are included in the Sec. 1231 melting pot. If a loss results, all gains and losses from casualties are treated as ordinary gains and losses.

Observe that Sec. 1231 does not provide statutory authority for the deduction of losses incurred in an involuntary conversion. That authority stems from Sec. 165. Section 1231 simply tells the taxpayer how to treat certain gains and losses—that is, whether to treat a select group of transactions as ordinary transactions or as transactions involving long-term capital assets. The property tax treatment of casualty losses can be summarized usefully as in Table 16-1.

The concept of a gain associated with a casualty or theft loss may seem strange. The answer to the apparent conundrum is, of course, that the casualty or theft may trigger a retribution payment—most frequently in the form of an insurance claim—that is greater than the adjusted basis of the property that was destroyed or stolen. Thus, a gain has been realized even though there was no voluntary sale or exchange. If the retribution payment is

TABLE 16–1

SECTION 1231 AND RELATED CASUALTY LOSS PROVISIONS

Kind of Property Involved in the Casualty or Theft	Holding Period		
	Equal to or Less Than 6 Months or 1 Year*	More Than 6 Months	
		If Casualty and Theft Losses Exceed Gains	If Casualty and Theft Gains Exceed Losses
Real or depreciable property used in a trade or business	Ordinary deduction *for* A.G.I.	Ordinary deduction *for* A.G.I.	Sec. 1231
Income-producing capital asset (e.g., a single rental unit not deemed to be a "trade or business")	Ordinary deducation *from* A.G.I. unless associ-ated with production of rents or royalties, then *for* A.G.I.	Ordinary deduction *from* A.G.I. unless associ-ated with production of rents or royalties, then *for* A.G.I.	Sec. 1231
Non-income-producing capital asset (e.g., the family automobile)	Ordinary deduction *from* A.G.I.	Ordinary deduction *from* A.G.I.	Sec. 1231
Inventory	Ordinary deduction *for* A.G.I.	Ordinary deduction *for* A.G.I.	Ordinary income

*NOTE: For corporate taxpayers, no for–from A.G.I. distinction exists; therefore, the Sec. 1231 classification of corporate casualty loss deductions is simply a matter of ordinary versus Sec. 1231 treatment. Additionally, corporate assets generally are presumed to be either inventory or trade-business related.

less than the adjusted basis of the property destroyed or stolen, the amount deductible as a casualty loss depends in part on the classification of the property involved. The general rules needed to quantify casualty and theft losses are as follows:

1. For total destruction of business or investment property, the deduction equals the adjusted basis of the property destroyed less any insurance, salvage value, or other proceeds on disposition.

2. For partial deduction of business or investment property, the deduction equals the lesser of
   a. the difference between the fair market value of the property before and after the casualty, less insurance, salvage, or other proceeds; or
   b. the adjusted basis of the property destroyed less insurance, salvage, or other proceeds.

3. For the total or partial destruction of personal-use property, the same rules apply as in 2 above, less $100 per casualty; in addition, no deduction is allowed unless (and to the extent that) the total of all such losses (after applying the $100 per casualty "floor") exceeds 10% of the taxpayer's adjusted gross income.

To illustrate the application of Sec. 1231, assume that in a given year a sole proprietor incurred the following two unusual gains and losses:

1. A gain of $10,000 on the sale of a store building purchased 20 years earlier and depreciated on a straight-line basis
2. A loss of $3,800 on an 18-month-old business automobile demolished in a collision

Both of these events apparently fall within the purview of Sec. 1231. However, because the taxpayer incurred a net loss on casualty events, the $3,800 deductible casualty loss would be treated as a direct deduction for adjusted gross income and not be combined with the taxpayer's sole Sec. 1231 gain—the $10,000 attributable to the store building.

If we were to modify the facts in the preceding paragraph and attribute the $10,000 gain on the building to the difference between the insurance collected after the store was destroyed by fire and the adjusted basis of the building, the net of the two casualty events would be a gain, and both the automobile loss and the building gain would be part of Sec. 1231. The eventual disposition of the two transactions would then depend, in turn, on the net balance of the taxpayer's Sec. 1231 transactions for the year and, possibly, up to five prior years.

If the aggregate of all Sec. 1231 transactions is a net gain, each of the transactions included therein is treated for tax purposes as if it involved the sale or exchange of a capital asset held for more than six months. On the other hand, if the aggregate of all Sec. 1231 transactions for a year is a net loss, each of the transactions included therein is treated for a year as if it involved a noncapital asset. For years after 1984, a net Sec. 1231 gain must first be treated as ordinary income to the extent of nonrecaptured Sec. 1231 losses.

To illustrate, let us return to our sole proprietor and assume that he sustained the following three unusual events in 1987: the $3,800 loss in the auto collision; the $10,000 gain from the destruction of the store by fire; and the sale of the land on which the store building had stood at a $5,000 gain. As explained earlier, if the net of the two casualty events is a gain, both casualty transactions are part of the Sec. 1231 melting pot. Because the only additional Sec. 1231 transaction in this 1987 example also involves a gain, the net Sec. 1231 position is also a net gain and, therefore, all three of these transactions are treated as if they were long-term capital gains. In terms of the pure definition contained in Sec. 1221, none of the three assets involved is a capital asset. The store building, automobile, and land are all excluded from the pure definition by Sec. 1221(2). Nevertheless, they all are effectively reinstated to capital asset status by operation of Sec. 1231.

As a final illustration, assume that in 1987 a corporate taxpayer incurred a $20,000 loss on the sale of a warehouse and a $5,000 loss on the theft of a pure capital asset. In these circumstances, the $5,000 deductible theft loss is not part of Sec. 1231, because the net of the corporation's casualty and theft transactions for the year resulted in a loss. As indicated in Table 16-1, that $5,000 loss would be an ordinary deduction for the corporation. The $20,000 loss on the sale of the warehouse would automatically become part of the corporation's Sec. 1231 transactions. Because we assumed that that was the corporation's only Sec. 1231 transaction for 1987, and because that involved a loss, that loss also would be treated as an ordinary loss. Obviously, the net effect in this instance is the conversion of a $5,000 pure capital loss into an ordinary loss by operation of Sec. 1231.

As a final illustration, assume that in 1987 a corporate taxpayer incurred a $20,000 loss on the sale of a warehouse and a $5,000 loss on the theft of a pure capital asset. In these circumstances, the $5,000 deductible theft loss is not part of Sec. 1231, because the net of the corporation's casualty and theft transactions for the year resulted in a loss. As indicated in Table 16-1, that $5,000 loss would be an ordinary deduction for the corporation. The $20,000 loss on the sale of the warehouse would automatically become part of the corporation's Sec. 1231 transactions. Because we assumed that that was the corporation's only Sec. 1231 transaction in 1987, and because that involved a loss, that loss, also, would be treated as an ordinary loss. Obviously, the net effect in this instance is the conversion of a $5,000 pure capital loss into an ordinary loss by operation of Sec. 1231.

The primary importance of Sec. 1231 should now be obvious. Generally, it permits taxpayers to deduct losses on the sale or exchange of properties used in the trade or business, as well as casualty losses of these or of capital assets, without the restrictions imposed by the dollar limitations on the deductibility of net capital losses. On the other hand, it permits the taxpayer to tax as long-term capital gains the gain on the sale of properties used in the trade or business as long as these gains exceed the losses from the transactions described in Sec. 1231(a).

In concert with other Code provisions, Sec. 1231 was for many years a basic method for tax minimization. After Code permitted accelerated depreciation, it was not unusual for property used in the trade or business to be depreciated at an unrealistically rapid pace and then sold at a substantial gain. The large depreciation deductions obviously reduced taxable income—and therefore the ordinary income tax liability—by substantial amounts, whereas the gain realized on the sale of the asset could often be treated as a tax-favored capital gain. In short, ordinary income could be converted into capital gain through the combined use of rapid depreciation deductions and Sec. 1231 gains.

Various limits have been placed on this opportunity from time to time. In 1939, Congress stopped those who achieved this goal via sales to related parties. In 1962, it introduced the recapture concept for depreciable equipment generally, and in 1964 it extended that same concept to selected real estate. In 1984, it extended recapture to Sec. 1231 itself. That is, for years after 1984, Sec. 1231 will *not* result in long-term capital gains until all "nonrecaptured net Sec. 1231 losses" have been exhausted. The latter losses are defined as the aggregate net Sec. 1231 losses for the most recent five years since 1981. This provision is, however, of less general applicability than Sec. 1245, the original depreciation recapture provision.

Section 1245

The general effect of Sec. 1245 is to provide that any gain recognized on the disposition of "certain assets" should be reported as ordinary income to the extent of either the depreciation deduction claimed since 1961 or the ACRS deduction claimed since 1980, Sec. 1231 notwithstanding. Although the general effect of Sec. 1245 may be clear enough, exactly which assets are subject to which parts of this provision?

Prior to 1981, Sec. 1245 was solely concerned with the disposition of depreciable personal property—that is, with property other than buildings and building components. In general, this property was also eligible for the investment credit. As of January 1, 1981, however, ERTA amended the original Sec. 1245 to include both depreciable personal property and most buildings and building components. The former group of assets are technically known as Sec. 1245 property; the latter, as Sec. 1245 recovery property. The latter assets are included in Sec. 1245, however, only if they (1) were acquired after 1980, (2) were depreciated using an ACRS table method, and (3) are other than:

1. Residential rental properties
2. Properties used predominantly outside the United States
3. Certain low-income housing

Any gain or loss on real properties, the cost of which has been recovered utilizing a straight-line recovery method (in lieu of the ACRS methods illustrated and explained in Chapter 14), is Sec. 1231 gain or loss. A special exception to this general rule applies only to corporate taxpayers. The exception is explained under Sec. 1250, below.

In other words, today the technical definition of Sec. 1245 extends to both (1) any depreciable personal property that gave rise to either (a) some amount of depreciation deducted since 1961 or (b) an ACRS deduction claimed after 1980 and (2) most depreciable real property acquired after 1980 and before 1987—other than residential rental property and low-income housing—if the cost of that real property was being recovered using the ACRS method.

The rules of Sec. 1245 can be readily illustrated using two simple graphs (Figures 16-1 and 16-2). In both graphs, let the distance OA represent the cost of a Sec. 1245 property purchased at the date t_o, and let the curve represent the adjusted basis of this asset between t_o and t_1, the date that asset was sold or exchanged.

Figure 16-1 represents the combined rules of Secs. 1231 and 1245 for any depreciable personal property acquired after December 31, 1961, that was depreciated on a straight-line basis. (Special rules that are not explained in this text apply to depreciable personal properties acquired before 1962.) The linear function in Figure 16-1 implies that this property is depreciated on a straight-line basis. Note that if this asset were sold on date t_1 for any amount less than that represented by distance OB (the adjusted basis of the property on the date of sale), the resulting loss would be a Sec. 1231 loss. If that same asset were sold on t_1 for any amount greater that that represented by distance OA, then the portion of the gain equal to distance BA would be "recaptured" as ordinary income (by operation of Sec. 1245), and the remainder of the gain (that is, that in excess of OA) would be Sec. 1231 gain.

FIGURE **16-1** Sections 1231 and 1245: Combined Rules for Personal Property Acquired After 1961 if Straight-Line Depreciation Was Utilized

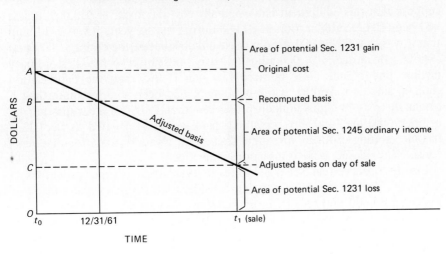

Figure 16-2 is similar to Figure 16-1. In Figure 16-2, however, the property is depreciated using a rapid method, as suggested by the nonlinear function. That rapid method could be either (1) the sum-of-the-years'-digits method or a declining-balance method for personal property or selected real properties acquired after 1980. Figures 16-1 and 16-2 collectively emphasize an important aspect of Sec. 1245: the recapture section applies to gains from the disposition of personal (nonreal) properties regardless of the depreciation method used, but it applies to selected real properties only if the ACRS tables are used to determine the cost recovery allowance.

FIGURE **16-2** Sections 1231 and 1245: Combined Rules for Personal Property Acquired After 1961 and for Selected Real Property Acquired After 1980 if ACRS Table Was Utilized

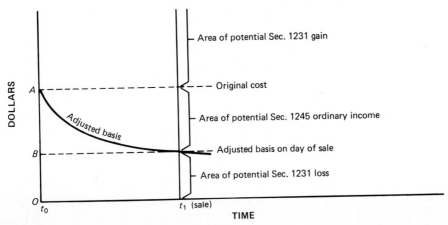

For example, let us assume that early this year a taxpayer sold some depreciable business equipment used during the preceding six years. Further suppose that this equipment had originally cost the taxpayer $10,000, that it had been depreciated a total of $9,000 during the six years it was used, and that it was sold for $4,000. Under these circumstances, the entire $3,000 gain ($4,000 sales price − $1,000 adjusted basis) must be recognized as ordinary income under Sec. 1245, because the gain is less than the depreciation claimed since acquisition. If the equipment had been sold for more than it originally cost—a highly unlikely prospect—then $9,000 of the gain would be ordinary income, and any remaining gain would be treated as Sec. 1231 income, getting ordinary or capital treatment, as appropriate for that year, considering all Sec. 1231 transactions collectively.

Finally, observe that Sec. 1245 tends to override most other provisions of the Code. To illustrate this last point, consider a situation in which a taxpayer realized a $5,000 gain because insurance proceeds exceeded the adjusted basis of business equipment destroyed by fire. If the taxpayer elected to recognize the gain (that is, did not elect to apply the nonrecognition provision contained in Sec. 1033), he or she might reasonably wonder if the entire gain could be mixed with other casualty transactions—thus possibly ending up with Sec. 1231 gains—or if only that portion of the gain not subject to depreciation recapture under Sec. 1245 could even be eligible for the casualty treatment. The taxpayer would discover that, unfortunately, Sec. 1245 takes precedence and only the gain in excess of the Sec. 1245 gain could even be considered along with his or her remaining casualty transactions. The few exceptions and limitations to Sec. 1245 that do exist are found in Sec. 1245(b). They include (1) disposition by gift (2) transfers made at death, and (3) certain completely tax-free transfers, some of which are explained in Chapters 17 and 18.

Section 1250

The ultimate effect of Sec. 1250 is to provide that only part of the gain recognized on the disposition of "certain real properties" should be reported as ordinary income. Although the general effect of Sec. 1250 is once again simple enough, the following two questions remain: (1) Exactly which real properties are subject to Sec. 1250? and (2) Exactly how much ordinary income must be recognized on their disposition?

When originally enacted in 1964, Sec. 1250 applied to virtually all real properties, and it provided for the recapture of only a portion of any "excess depreciation" (defined as the difference between the actual amount of rapid depreciation claimed and a lesser amount of straight-line depreciation that could have been claimed). Thus, under the original law, no recapture was necessary if a building was depreciated on a straight-line basis. Furthermore, the portion of this excess depreciation that had to be recaptured as ordinary income decreased with the passage of time. The longer the taxpayer held the property, the less the amount of ordinary income that had to be recognized. Unfortunately, Congress modified the original rules in 1969, 1976, 1981, and 1982. On each occasion, the new rules were not made retroactive; consequently, a single building purchased before 1964 and sold this year can actually be subject to five different sets of rules simultaneously! In trying to determine the amount of the gain that should be treated as ordinary income by operation of Sec. 1250, rather than as Sec. 1231 income, the taxpayer must determine which sets of rules apply and make the calculations accordingly. Although it is tempting to go into some of the details of these provisions—to demonstrate how ridiculous the tax law can actually be—we have elected instead to include only those rules applicable to two cases of general importance to most taxpayers today and one case of interest to corporate taxpayers only.

The two general and one special case of Sec. 1250 to be explained here apply to:

1. Any nonresidential building acquired after December 31, 1969, and before January 1, 1981, if the taxpayer elected to depreciate that building using a rapid depreciation method

2. Any residential building acquired after December 31, 1975, that was depreciated using a rapid method, including the ACRS table method of cost recovery for any residential rental property acquired after December 31, 1980

3. Real estate sold or exchanged by a corporate taxpayer after 1982

Individuals interested in other possibilities must simply consult a current tax service for additional details. Alternatively, they can try to follow the instructions of Form 4797. The rules applicable to the two general cases detailed above are illustrated on the simple graph in Figure 16-3. It must be emphasized again that this figure cannot be used for (1) residential rental property acquired before 1976; (2) nonresidential real property acquired before 1970 or after 1980; or (3) real properties depreciated on a straight-line basis.

In Figure 16-3, distance OC represents the initial cost of a depreciable building. The line represents the adjusted basis of the building based on straight-line depreciation; the curve represents the actual adjusted basis of the building based on the rapid depreciation method elected. The vertical difference between the line and the curve at any time represents the cumulative excess depreciation claimed. Thus, at t_1, the date of sale, the excess depreciation would be represented by the distance AB. If the building were sold at t_1 for something more than that represented by the distance OA but for less than that represented by the distance OB, the entire gain would be ordinary income by operation of Sec. 1250. Finally, if the building were sold at t_1 for something more than that represented by the distance OB, part of the gain—that represented by the distance AB—would be ordinary income via Sec. 1250, and the remainder would be classified as Sec. 1231 gain. Incidentally, for residential rental property acquired after 1980 and subject to the ACRS table deduction, the straight-line rate in Figure 16-3 is based on a 15- or 18-year life.

As a detailed investigation of Figure 16-3 would prove, the effect of Sec. 1250 is not as all-encompassing as the effect of Sec. 1245. The smaller impact

FIGURE 16-3   Sections 1250 and 1231: Combined Rules for Nonresidential Buildings Purchased After December 31, 1969, And before January 1, 1981, and for Residential Buildings Purchased After December 31, 1975, if a Rapid Cost Recovery Method Was Utilized

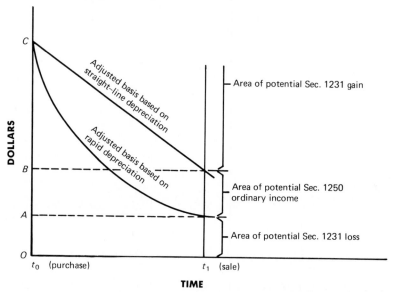

is attributable to the fact that Sec. 1250 does not apply at all unless a rapid depreciation method has been utilized, and, even if such a method has been used, the longer the asset is held the smaller the amount of excess depreciation. Note also that Sec. 1250 applies only to the gain attributable to the building; the gain on the sale of the land is always Sec. 1231 income. Thus, the allocation of the sales price between the land and the building can be very important.

The recapture rules of Secs. 1245 and 1250 were made even more complex for corporate taxpayers selling real estate after 1982 by the addition of Sec. 291. Stated briefly, Sec. 291(a)(1) requires a corporation to calculate the following two amounts whenever it sells or exchanges Sec. 1250 property:

1. The amount of ordinary income, if any, that must be "recaptured" by operation of the rules described above for sales of real estate in general

2. The amount of ordinary income, if any, that would have to be "recaptured" if the sale were one of personal property rather than (Sec. 1250) real property

If the second calculation results in more ordinary income than the first, the corporation must report 20% of this excess as additional ordinary income! The following examples should clarify this ridiculous new tax provision.

Example 1   In 1987, XYZ Corporation sold a building for $500,000 that it had acquired in 1977 for $600,000. XYZ claimed a total of $200,000 in straight-line depreciation on this building between 1977 and 1987. Because

XYZ claimed straight-line depreciation on this building, the entire $100,000 gain (that is, $500,000 amount realized − $400,000 adjusted basis) would generally be treated as Sec. 1231 gain. Because it is a corporation, however, XYZ must report $20,000 (that is, 20% × $100,000) as ordinary income by operation of Sec. 291(a)(1); the remaining $80,000 is still Sec. 1231 gain. Had XYZ Corporation sold personal property, with the same assumed amounts, the entire $100,000 gain would have been ordinary income by operation of Sec. 1245.

Example 2   Assume the facts in Example 1, but increase the sales price from $500,000 to $700,000. Had the sale been one of personal property rather than real property, $200,000 of the $300,000 gain would have been ordinary income by operation of Sec. 1245. The remaining $100,000 would have been Sec. 1231 gain. Therefore, XYZ Corporation must report $40,000 (that is, 20% × $200,000) as ordinary income by operation of Sec. 291 and $260,000 (that is, $300,000 − $40,000) as Sec. 1231 gain.

This 20% "cutback" in potential Sec. 1231 gain, via Sec. 291, applies only to the sale or exchange of real estate by corporate taxpayers. The rules previously explained in the text apply to sales of real estate by individual and fiduciary taxpayers.

The tax student who wants to understand the I.R.S. tax forms must understand the interaction of the capital gain and loss provisions and Secs. 1231, 1245, and 1250. In summary, depreciable properties used in the trade or business are excluded from capital gain and loss treatment by the definition of a capital asset in Sec. 1221. Nevertheless, part or all of the gain on the sale of these same properties can, under certain circumstances, be treated as long-term capital gain by operation of Sec. 1231. The amount of the gain eligible for Sec. 1231 treatment has been significantly reduced in the recent past by the depreciation recapture provisions contained in Secs. 1245 and 1250. (With laws so complex as these, is it any wonder Albert Einstein needed a tax consultant?)

The concept of recaptured depreciation, as first embodied in Secs. 1245 and 1250, was extended to include the potential recapture of farm losses in circumstances in which farm losses have been used to offset nonfarm income (in Sec. 1251) and to the gain from the disposition of farmland (in Sec. 1252). The former provision was repealed in the 1986 Act.

LOOPHOLE-CLOSING SECTIONS

The largest subset of statutory modifications to the usual rules probably is the collection of sections generally enacted to interdict any unintended tax benefits. Historically, these provisions frequently represent a final chapter in one branch of the ongoing saga of humanity's search for lower taxes. The story often begins with an isolated discovery; that is, an isolated taxpayer (or tax advisor) discovers a unique combination of facts and tax rules that leads to an unexpected tax windfall. The idea spreads—or is "rediscovered" by others—until the I.R.S. discovers the ploy and initiates administrative action to curb what it views as an abuse of the law. Typically, the I.R.S. is challenged by one or more taxpayers, and our judicial system must settle the dispute. Judicial solutions to conflicting interpretations of tax statutes are almost always slow and frequently unsatisfactory to all parties. A court can only address the precise situation presented to it; slightly different circumstances may call for, or at least may receive, different answers. Consequently, major differences of opinion are often best settled by remedial legislation.

The Recapture Provisions

A good example of the evolutionary process just described can be found in the Code sections that provide for the recapture of depreciation. As explained earlier, prior to the enactment of Secs. 1245 and 1250, taxpayers could convert large amounts of ordinary income into capital gain via the parlay of large (ordinary) depreciation deductions followed by profitable dispositions under Sec. 1231 (usually capital gain). Once the current depreciation recapture sections were operative, the only remaining major benefit of rapid depreciation was that derived from the present value of money.

The idea of "recapturing," from what otherwise would be capital gain, some part or all of any previous deductions against ordinary income was extended in Secs. 1251 and 1252 to certain gains on the disposition of farm properties. Wealthy taxpayers who are gentlemen farmers have for years converted ordinary income into capital gains through farming activity, particularly ranches and citrus groves. In the past, the costs of developing farming properties could be deducted currently, usually creating an operating loss that could be offset against ordinary income from other sources. The agricultural business would elect the cash basis, and all costs would be deducted currently. Ranchers would raise herds over several years. Farmers developed citrus groves that produced no income at all until the trees reached maturity. Usually the expenditures that produced the losses increased the value of Sec. 1231 property used in the farming business—such as breeding herds, citrus groves, and land. At disposition of the improved property, a sizable gain could be recognized as a Sec. 1231 gain and thereby would usually receive capital gain treatment.

The 1969 Tax Reform Act expanded the recapture rules in three ways in an effort to close the "farm loss" loophole:

1. Purchased livestock held for breeding, draft, or dairy purposes are now subject to the recapture rules of Sec. 1245 to the extent of depreciation deducted after December 31, 1969.

2. Under Sec. 1251, prior to 1987 gain from the sale of farm properties resulted in ordinary income to the extent of the "excess-deduction account." The farm properties included were depreciable personal property and land (including unharvested crops) held for over one year and livestock held for over two years. Buildings were not included. The excess-deduction account was generally an accumulation of net farm losses incurred after 1969 and before 1976. Losses were included in the excess-deduction account only to the extent that they exceeded

$25,000 per year, and only when the taxpayer had an adjusted gross income from nonfarming activities of $50,000 or more. The excess-deduction account was reduced by the amount of gain recaptured. This section was repealed as part of the 1986 Tax Reform Act; thus it has little or no remaining significance.

3. Under Sec. 1252, land development expenditures that are deductible against ordinary income may still be recaptured on the sale of land. Deductions claimed after 1969 for expenditures on soil and water conservation and for land-clearing costs are subject to partial recapture unless the land is held for more than 10 years. The percentage of such expenditures recaptured as ordinary income on disposition of the property at a gain is shown in the schedule below:

Holding Period	Percentage Recovered
5 years or less	100
6 years	80
7 years	60
8 years	40
9 years	20
10 years	0

The percentage is applied to either the deductible expenditures or the actual gain, whichever is less.

The Anti-Corporate-Manipulation Provisions

We have observed that the corporate entity is frequently an essential ingredient in tax planning. The closely held corporation is particularly susceptible to favorable manipulation, because it lacks the implicit diverse interests commonly found in large numbers of stockholders. Consequently, Congress has been forced to enact several complicated Code sections to modify rules that would otherwise yield unreasonably favorable tax results. Several of these prohibiting sections involve the distinction between capital and ordinary gains and losses, a distinction that was very important before 1987.

SECTION 302   Any time a corporation distributes corporate assets to its shareholders in their role as shareholders, the distribution is likely to be labeled a dividend and taxed accordingly. Technically, this conclusion is generally correct to the extent that the distributing corporation has either current or accumulated earnings and profits.[1] The fundamental elements of a dividend are portrayed in Figure 16-4. To understand the illustration, assume that the size of the rectangle represents the value of the net assets owned by the corporate entity. Thus, an ordinary dividend necessarily reduces the size of the rectangle—that is, it results in a diminution of the corporation's

---

[1]This rule is found in Secs. 301(c) and 316. Nowhere in this Code, however, is there a definition of "earnings and profits." Although the two are close relatives, the retained earnings concept of accounting is not wholly comparable.

FIGURE **16-4**   The Dividend Concept

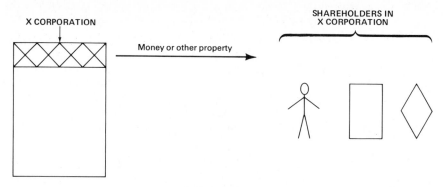

assets—in a "one-sided" transaction. Observe that the shareholders (individual, corporate, or fiduciary, as depicted by the stickperson, the rectangle, and the diamond, respectively) give nothing to the distributing corporation in exchange for the assets received. We know from prior chapters that such dividend distributions usually create ordinary income for the recipient shareholder.

In a closely held corporation, the shareholders could readily agree to give up some stock in the distributing corporation if it would benefit them to do so. In financial parlance, this would convert the "dividend" into a "stock redemption." The essential elements of a stock redemption are obvious in Figure 16-5. But what is the tax impact of a stock redemption?

Generally, a taxpayer must recognize a gross income the difference between any value received and any basis surrendered in a sale or exchange of property. Further, the character of that gross income is generally determined by the nature of the property surrendered. Applying these general rules to the stock redemption transaction suggests that the shareholder should recognize capital gain or loss because common stock is generally a capital asset. The possibilities this created for the closely held corporation were, under prior law, astounding. If not constrained in some way, closely held

FIGURE **16-5**   The Stock Redemption Concept

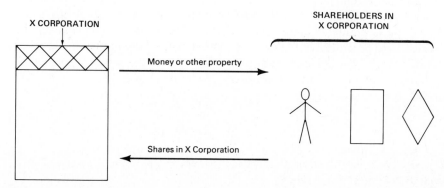

corporations could convert what otherwise would be an ordinary dividend into a capital loss! Each shareholder could surrender a pro rata share of ownership interest sufficient to cause the basis surrendered to be greater than the value received and thereby recognize a capital loss for tax purposes at no real economic cost.

As you might suspect, this was just too good to be true. Section 302 provides a relatively complex set of rules to determine whether a stock redemption should be treated as ordinary income or as capital gain. The result, in the situation described above, would be ordinary income. Hence, another exception to the general capital gain and loss complex was created by necessity. The general tax rules apply only if a stock redemption is "substantially disproportionate"; results in the complete termination of a shareholder's interest; or is a distribution in partial liquidation (made to a noncorporate shareholder) [Secs. 302(b)(2), 302(b)(4), respectively]. As tempting as it is to delve into the definition of the critical terms just suggested, we must leave their study to advanced income taxation volumes.

SECTION 304   Another variant of essentially the same tax scheme involved the use of two or more closely held corporations. This plan also took the legal form of an apparent sale. To illustrate the basic idea, suppose that taxpayer A owned either (1) 100% of Corporations X and Y or (2) 100% of X, which, in turn, owned 100% of Y[2]. For tax purposes, how should A report the sale to Y Corporation of some portion of his or her shares in X Corporation? The essential elements of this arrangement can be depicted as in Figure 16-6.

Both before and after the transaction, taxpayer A effectively, although not "legally," owns 100% of both corporations. Afterward, Y legally is the owner of some shares in X. The important fact, however, is that taxpayer A has more money (or other property) after the transaction, and this money came from Y Corporation. Should the transaction be treated as the sale of a capital asset, as it appears on the surface, or should it be treated as a dividend?

---

[2]The first ownership arrangement is commonly known as a brother–sister group, the second as a parent–subsidiary group. Although the difference has some legal significance, the economic reality of the arrangement is obvious.

FIGURE 16-6   Redemption Through Related Corporation

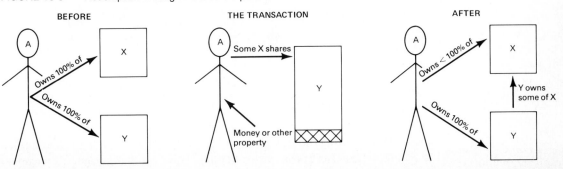

Without Sec. 304, the tax result would be a capital gain or loss. As you probably suspect, Sec. 304 is the stationary provision that converts the entire amount received by A into an ordinary dividend if the "seller" owns (directly or indirectly) 50% or more of the two corporations involved in this transaction. Indirect ownership in both corporations may be imputed to A using the constructive ownership rules found in Sec. 318(a).

These are but a few of the many sections that were put into the Code to stop the manipulation of corporate transactions that would otherwise yield capital gain rather than ordinary income. The preferred stock bailout (Sec. 306) and the collapsible corporation (Sec. 341) provisions involved even more complex plans and, therefore, more complex rules to preclude similar results. Today, of course, all of these complications are of very little importance since most capital gains are taxed exactly like ordinary income.

Section 1232

Investments in corporate stocks and bonds are ordinarily treated as capital assets. Furthermore, the amount received by a creditor on the retirement of any bond or (or other evidence of indebtedness) is generally treated as the amount received in exchange for the bond. Given only the two facts just stated, a taxpayer might assume that any discount feature of a corporate bond (or other evidence of indebtedness) would give rise to a capital gain when the bond is sold, exchanged, or retired. In other words, the amount realized (usually equal to the face value of the bond at maturity) would be greater than the taxpayer's cost basis in the bond by the amount of any discount existing when the bond was acquired. Section 1232 is the statutory provision that generally requires a creditor to amortize any original issue discount. In other words, Sec. 1232 requires the creditor to recognize part of any original issue discount as ordinary (interest) income each year from the date of acquisition to the date of retirement (or other disposition).

Because the creditor must report the amortized discount as ordinary income each year, he or she also receives an equivalent increase in the basis of the bond each year. Accordingly, if the bond is held to maturity, the adjusted basis of the bond normally equals the face value of the debt, and no amount of capital gain remains to be recognized.

ADMINISTRATIVE CONVENIENCE SECTIONS

Some of the apparently complicating provisions in the capital gain and loss complex are intended to simplify rather than to complicate procedures. We would include in this category such provisions as Sec. 1247 and Subsection 165(g). To understand these provisions, it may be necessary to refresh your memory concerning the statutorily pure definition of a capital asset contained in Sec. 1221(1). There, you may recall, the Code says that all assets are capital assets except those held "primarily for sale to customers." But how do we determine whether or not certain assets are held primarily for resale?

Section 1237

It is frequently difficult to distinguish between land held by the developer as a genuine personal investment and land held as a part of ordinary inventory. Section 1237 is intended to distinguish between the two by providing certain arbitrary tests that must be reported on the disposition of real property subdivided for sale.

In general, Sec. 1237 provides that an individual taxpayer who is not a real estate dealer should report a capital gain on the sale of subdivided real estate only if

1. The tract sold, or any part thereof, had not previously been held by the taxpayer as one primarily for resale;
2. In the year sold, the seller does not hold any other tract, or part thereof, as one primarily for resale;
3. The taxpayer directly or indirectly made no "substantial improvements" to increase the value of the lots sold during period of ownership; and
4. The land was owned for five years prior to sale, unless it was inherited.

Furthermore, even if all the above conditions are satisfied, only the gains on the sale of the first five lots from such a tract are entirely capital gain. Profits from the sale of the sixth and subsequent lots produce ordinary income equal to 5% of the selling price (unless a period of five years or longer has lapsed with with no sales); only the remainder is capital gain. Selling expense can, however, be offset against the ordinary income portion, rather than the capital gain, once the sixth and subsequent sales are made.

Although the enactment of Sec. 1237 does simplify a tax conclusion in a few circumstances, it is at best a quixotic solution to a much larger problem. Anyone interested in the continuing problem should study the several decisions in *Malat* v. *Riddell,* in which one taxpayer fought his case all the way to the Supreme Court only to discover that the word "primarily" means "of first importance" or "principally."[3] The continuation of similar cases in the post-*Malat* era suggests that even this startling discovery by our Supreme Court did not end the controversy. The taxing of capital gains as ordinary income will, however, complete the process.

Subsection 165(g)

An entirely different kind of problem was resolved by Subsection 165(g). Only the most meticulous study of Subchapter P of the Code would reveal the critical importance of a few words contained in Sec. 1222. There, capital gain

[3]383 U.S. 569 (1966).

(or loss) is defined as the gain (or loss) "from the sale or exchange of a capital asset." Given this choice of words, what happens taxwise when a taxpayer experiences a loss because a security has become wholly worthless? Obviously, if it is truly worth nothing, the taxpayer can neither sell it nor exchange it for anything else of value. Does this fact deny the taxpayer the right to deduct any loss? Much to their surprise, many years ago several taxpayers found this to be the conclusion of both the I.R.S. and the courts. Subsequently, taxpayers have usually found someone who would give them a dollar or two for what was, in reality, worth nothing.

To correct this obvious misinterpretation of the law, Congress passed the predecessor of Subsection 165(g) to create an artificial sale or exchange in the event of worthlessness. It reads as follows:

> If any security which is a capital asset becomes worthless during the taxable year, the loss resulting therefrom shall, for purposes of this subtitle, be treated as the loss from the sale or exchange, on the last day of the taxable year, of a capital asset.

Observe that this subsection does more than create the artificial sale or exchange; it also determines the end of the holding period. Unfortunately, however, it cannot, and does not, solve the problem of determining when a security finally becomes "worthless." Therefore, taxpayers and I.R.S. agents continue to disagree frequently over the exact year in which a taxpayer should claim a loss deduction on worthless securities.

ECONOMIC INCENTIVE SECTIONS

Other complications to the capital gain and loss complex must be attributed to a congressional desire to intervene in the marketplace of supply and demand. Other things being equal, the demand for any property could, prior to 1988, be increased if (1) the income from that property could be reclassified as capital gain, rather than as ordinary income or (2) any loss realized in relation to the property could be reclassified as an ordinary loss, rather than as a capital loss.

Section 1244

Small corporations often find it very difficult to raise sufficient capital to underwrite the costs commonly associated with new ventures. Congress has enacted several laws intended to assist these firms. Two of the tax provisions that help to reduce the risk of an investment in a small new corporation are the S corporation provisions and Sec. 1244. As we noted earlier, the general tax effect of making an S corporation election is to convert an otherwise separate taxable entity (the corporation) into a mere tax conduit for its owners. This election is especially useful to the new firm experiencing net operating losses in its first few years of operation. The election allows high-marginal bracket investors to offset "corporate" operating losses against their individual incomes from other sources. This opportunity causes many investors to assume risks they might otherwise be unwilling to consider. An investor in a 38.5% marginal tax bracket, for example, can make a $200,000 capital investment, with a real economic risk equivalent to only $123,000, if he or she can be assured that any loss sustained can be recognized for tax purposes as an ordinary loss. The S corporation election guarantees that tax result to the extent of the investor's pro rata share of the new corporation's net operating losses.

Section 1244 expands on the same fundamental economic incentive by providing an investor with the right to claim an ordinary loss deduction for up to $50,000 per year ($100,000 for married taxpayers filing a joint return) from any loss on the sale or exchange of stock in a "small business corporation." The Code goes on, of course, to define small business corporations in detail. In general, that term applies to the stock of any corporation with less than $1 million in equity capital. To qualify, however, the corporation must offer not more than $1 million as stock that qualifies under Sec. 1244. Thus, by combining the S corporation election with Sec. 1244 stock, the venture capital corporation can often market securities that otherwise would have a very limited reception. Observe that if the new corporation becomes a financially successful enterprise, the investor will have been allowed to convert ordinary loss deductions (via the early years, S corporation losses) into long-term capital gain (on the subsequent sale of the shares at a market price that reflects the entity's later financial success). In the interim, the investor was partially insured against further downside market values for the stock by Sec. 1244 protection.

Section 1253

By reclassifying a usually profitable ordinary asset as a noncapital asset, Congress was able (prior to 1988) to create an economic disincentive. The gain typically realized on the transfer of a franchise or a trade name was effectively removed from capital gain treatment by the enactment of Sec. 1253. That section reads in part as follows:

> (a) General Rule.—A transfer of a franchise, trademark, or trade name shall not be treated as a sale or exchange of a capital asset if the transfer retains any significant power, right, or continuing interest with respect to the subject matter of the franchise, trademark, or trade name.

It was hoped that this transformation of capital gain into ordinary income would dampen the almost uncontrolled growth of the franchising business. Concurrently it might also have reduced the monotony of the traditional buildings that house franchised restaurants, ice cream parlors, automotive brake and transmission shops, and even tax-return preparation businesses. Although the growth of these businesses was never harmful, the frequency of financial disaster associated with these operations suggested the need for some restraint. In all too many instances, only the party selling "the deal" benefited from the franchise.

OTHER MISCELLANEOUS MODIFICATIONS

Although this discussion of some modifications to the "pure case" of capital gain and loss can by no means be considered complete, a few of the modifications not discussed thus far may, for one reason or another, justify brief comment here.

Section 166(d)

Section 166 authorizes the deduction of bad debts in the computation of taxable income. Subsections (a) and (b) are concerned with business bad debts; subsection 166(d) reads as follows:

(1) General Rule.—In the case of a taxpayer other than a corporation—
    (A) subsections (a) and (c) shall not apply to any nonbusiness debt; and
    (B) where any nonbusiness debt becomes worthless within the taxable year, the loss resulting therefrom shall be considered a loss from the sale or exchange, during the taxable year, of a capital asset held for not more than one year.
(2) Nonbusiness debt defined.—For purposes of paragraph (1), the term "nonbusiness debt" means a debt other than—
    (A) a debt created or acquired (as the case may be) in connection with a trade or business of the taxpayer; or
    (B) a debt the loss from the worthlessness of which is incurred in the taxpayer's trade or business.

At least three aspects of this subsection are important. First, note that subparagraph (1)(B) makes a deduction possible by considering a bad debt as a loss from a "sale or exchange." Second, observe that this provision authorizes what, in its absence, would not be deductible because of its personal character. Recall that a personal capital loss, such as that incurred on the sale of a family car or residence, is not generally deductible in the computation of taxable income. Third, note that the Code specifies that nonbusiness bad debts must be treated as short-term capital losses, regardless of the time period they were owed to the taxpayer prior to worthlessness.

This provision allows a taxpayer to deduct as a short-term capital loss an amount loaned to a personal friend many years ago if the taxpayer can prove both the debt's existence and the fact that it is now worthless. The most surprising part of this subsection's interpretation, however, usually involves the closely held corporation. It is not unusual for the owner of a small, incorporated business to loan the business additional funds from personal assets to pay employees, utility bills, rent, and other general corporate creditors. Unfortunately, it is also not unusual for these small corporations to become worthless (that is, to go bankrupt). In that event, how should the loans made by the stockholder to his or her own corporation be treated for tax purposes; that is, are they business or nonbusiness bad debts?

Paragraph 166(d)(2) defines a nonbusiness debt as one not "created or acquired . . . in connection with a trade or business of the taxpayer." Most small business owners believe that they made those loans in connection with their trade or business. The I.R.S. agent usually contends, however, that the trade or business belongs to the corporation, not to the individual who may own and operate that entity. Consequently, these personal loans are generally found to be nonbusiness debts, and their worthlessness is treated as a short-term capital loss, not as an ordinary loss deduction. The courts have generally sustained the I.R.S. position, unless the taxpayer can prove that he or she (individually) is in the business of making loans or of creating venture corporations for resale. In the vast majority of the litigated cases, taxpayers have lost their attempts to claim the ordinary deduction.

Section 303

The modifications of the "pure case" found in Sec. 303 are of a different variety. As explained earlier in this chapter, a corporation's redemption of stock from its shareholders in the absence of complete or partial liquidation of the corporation may be treated either as a sale by the shareholder or as a dividend. Many redemptions in closely held corporations are treated as dividend distributions and are taxed to the recipient as ordinary income.

Section 303 extends the capital gain treatment to the proceeds when stocks are redeemed to pay death taxes, as long as the conditions of Sec. 303 are satisfied. Among these conditions are the following:

1. The stock being redeemed must have been included in the decedent's gross estate for federal estate tax purposes.
2. The redemption must occur after a stockholder's death and within a time period specified by the Code.
3. The value of the decedent's ownership in the corporation(s) concerned must have been more than 35% of the value of the adjusted gross estate.
4. The amount distributed under this special provision cannot exceed the amount by which the redeemed shareholder's interest in the estate has been reduced by death taxes and funeral and administrative expenses.

The importance of this Code provision to many taxpayers is that it permits a limited amount of what might otherwise be dividend income to be recognized tax free because the heirs, from whom this stock is redeemed, typically have a basis in their stock equal to its fair market value; thus no gains need be recognized if the transaction is treated as a sale rather than as a dividend.

PROBLEMS

NOTE: If no year is stated, assume that the transaction took place in the current tax year.

1. On January 10, Ed Burns sold some of his business equipment, which he had purchased for $3,750 seven years ago and on which he had properly claimed

straight-line depreciation of $500 per year since acquisition. The tax consequences of this sale depend on the selling price of the equipment. Indicate, for each of the selling prices listed below, whether the result would be taxable as ordinary income under Sec. 1245 or a Sec. 1231 gain or loss:

a. $1,400   b. $2,600   c. $3,800   d. $5,000

2. "The probability of a taxpayer's being able to recognize a capital gain on the sale of depreciable personal property (nonrealty) used in a trade or business has diminished to the point where, today, it is practically zero." True or false? Explain.

3. On January 8, Tom Lock sold a light construction warehouse that he had used in his business since building it exactly ten years ago. The warehouse cost Tom $40,000; he depreciated it on a 150% declining-balance method. The estimated life of the building was 20 years (thus, Tom used a 7.5% depreciation rate).

   a. If Tom sold the warehouse for $22,500, what amount of his gain is ordinary income (Sec. 1250), and what amount is Sec. 1231 income?

   b. If Tom had claimed straight-line depreciation on this warehouse, what amount of his gain would have been ordinary income?

4. Classify each of the following gains and losses as to whether it (1) has no tax consequence, (2) is ordinary income (or loss), (3) is capital gain (or loss), or (4) is a Sec. 1231 item. In each case, indicate the correct dollar amount that would be so classified. Treat each item individually; for example, in part c, assume it is the taxpayer's only casualty loss for the year. Each item has been held for at least 6 months.

   a. Sold personal oil painting at a $500 gain. (Taxpayer was not the artist or an art dealer.)

   b. Sold pleasure sailboat at a $500 loss.

   c. Collision damage to family car repaired at cost of $350. The car was 2 years old. Taxpayer's A.G.I. is $20,000.

   d. Sold business car at a $300 gain. Depreciation claimed since 1961 was $3,000.

   e. Sold business building at a $4,000 gain. Building had been used for previous 15 years. Straight-line depreciation of $7,500 had been claimed.

   f. Wind damage to rental property (assume the rental property does not constitute a trade or business) restored at cost of $6,000. Property had been owned for 6 years; insurance reimbursed $4,000. Adjusted basis at time of damage was $5,000.

5. Baldwell, a calendar-year taxpayer, operates a small manufacturing plant as a sole proprietor. He files a joint return with his wife; both are under 65 and have good vision. They have no dependents. During the year Baldwell disposed of the following property:

   a. January 23   Sold the family automobile for $2,000; acquired on January 16 two years ago for $4,500.

   b. January 28   Sold a machine for $4,500; acquired 5 years earlier for $10,000. It had an estimated life of 10 years. Baldwell used the ACRS tables applicable to 1980–1986 acquisitions.

   c. April 3   Sold 100 shares of ABC, Inc. for $4,000; purchased 16 months ago for $3,400.

   d. July 16   Sold a truck for $2,800; purchased 2 years ago for $8,000. Truck had an estimated life of 4 years. Baldwell used the ACRS tables applicable to 1980–1986 acquisitions.

All property sold was used in Baldwell's business except for the automobile and the ABC shares. In addition, Baldwell had net income of $22,000 and deductions for adjusted gross income of $2,160. Compute Baldwell's gross tax liability for the current year. Pay attention to the organization of your answer; label all amounts.

6. In years 1, 2, and 3 a taxpayer incurred the gains and losses shown below:

Item of Income or Loss	1986	1987	1988
Routine taxable income, excluding all transactions detailed below	$10,200	$28,200	$37,200
Capital asset transactions:			
Net short-term gain (or loss)*	800	200	1,000
Net long-term gain (or loss)*	(3,000)	4,600	3,000
Recapture of depreciation, under Sec. 1245 and/or 1250	1,000	1,100	3,000
Net gain (or loss) subject to Sec. 1231	(2,000)	3,000	2,000

*Excluding both capital loss carryforwards and Sec. 1231 transactions, detailed below.

   a. If the taxpayer in this problem is a corporation:
   (1) What amount of taxable income should it report in 1986?
   (2) Would its capital loss carryback be short- or long-term capital loss?
   (3) What amount would be eligible for the 28% long-term capital gains tax in 1987?
   b. If the taxpayer in this problem is an individual:
   (1) What would his or her taxable income be for 1986?
   (2) Would his or her capital loss carryforward to 1987 be short- or long-term loss?

7. Listed below are various assets and their uses. In each case, indicate whether the asset is Sec. 1245 property, Sec. 1250 property, or neither.
   a. Family automobile
   b. Machine used in a trade or business
   c. Family home
   d. Warehouse of manufacturing concern acquired in 1978 and depreciated on a 150% declining-balance method
   e. Electric transmission lines of utility
   f. Apartment house subject to ACRS cost recovery deduction

8. On July 4 this year, while the Kerns were enjoying a family picnic, someone broke into Jerry Kern's home and stole a valuable painting. This painting was purchased at an art auction in 1880 by Jerry's grandfather for $100. Jerry's father inherited the painting from his father in 1938 when it was valued for estate tax purposes at $800. Jerry received the painting from his father as a Christmas gift in 1968. Before giving it as a Christmas gift, Jerry's father had the painting cleaned by a competent art dealer who estimated its value at $1,500. Nothing happened to the painting between 1968 and July 4, this year, and therefore Jerry believes that it was worth at least $1,500. What is the amount of Jerry Kern's tax deduction for this theft loss before consideration of the 10% A.G.I. floor?

9. Assume the following facts:

| | Taxpayers | | |
	A	B	C
Taxable income excluding			
all transactions below	$43,200	$43,200	$43,200
Short-term capital gains	3,000	4,000	10,000
Short-term capital losses	(7,000)		
Long-term capital gains	30,000	3,000	22,000
Long-term capital losses		(13,000)	
Secs. 1245 and 1250 income	5,000		10,000
Sec. 1231 gains	2,000	5,000	3,000
Sec. 1231 losses	(12,000)		(5,000)
Casualty gains			14,000
Casualty losses		(1,000)	(4,000)

a. If the taxpayers in this question are married individuals, filing a joint return, determine
   (1) The taxable income of each taxpayer.
   (2) The amount and type (short- or long-term) of capital loss carryforward, if any. (Use current year's rules.)
b. If the taxpayers in this question are corporations, determine
   (1) The taxable income of each taxpayer.
   (2) The amount and type (short- or long-term) of capital loss carryback, if any.

10. U.S. courts do not agree on whether or not an individual taxpayer who rents only one piece of real property is engaged in a "trade or business." (The Tax Court says he or she is; see *Hazard*, 7 TC 372. The Second Circuit Court of Appeals says he or she is not; see *Grier* v. *U.S.*, 218 F.2d 603.) If a taxpayer sells his or her only rental property at a profit, does it make any difference which court opinion the taxpayer assumes is controlling if that property has been depreciated on
   a. A straight-line method?
   b. A rapid depreciation method? Explain briefly.

11. To determine the final import of property transactions on a taxpayer's taxable income, we must first classify the property gains and losses in one of several ways and then correctly combine those amounts. Assume that all classifications given for cases 1–4 below are correct. Demonstrate your knowledge of how the several amounts would combine to form taxable income in each case. Solve this problem for a noncorporate taxpayer.

	Case 1	Case 2	Case 3	Case 4
Property transactions:				
Net LT gain (loss)	$10,000	$ 5,000	$(4,000)	$(2,000)
Net ST gain (loss)	(2,000)	1,000	1,000	(2,000)
Net Sec. 1231 gain (loss)	(3,000)	3,000	3,000	(2,000)
Net casualty gain (loss)	1,000	(4,000)	3,000	(2,000)
All other (net) ordinary gain (loss)	30,000	40,000	50,000	60,000
Taxable income	$	$	$	$

12. The tax treatment of property transactions depends on their proper classification in one of the following five categories:

A—Ordinary gain or loss
B—Sec. 1231 gain or loss
C—Casualty gain or loss (really a subset of Sec. 1231)
D—Long-term capital gain or loss
E—Short-term capital gain or loss

By using the identifying letter indicated above, classify each of the following independent transactions in the way it should be treated initially.
a. Gain from sale or raised livestock held 3 years for breeding purposes.
b. Fire loss on inventory held 4 months.
c. Gain from sale of antique auto held 10 months by "classic" car dealer.
d. Gain on sale of pleasure boat owned for 14 months.
e. Loss on sale of customers' receivables held 14 months (Assume an accrual-basis taxpayer.)
f. Loss on condemnation of taxpayer's business parking lot.

13. Joe Schmoo purchased a small apartment house as an investment on January 1, 1986. Joe paid $50,000 for the land and $200,000 for the apartment house. If Joe were to sell this property on January 1, 1988, the tax consequences of the sale would depend to a great extent on both the selling price and the allocation of that price between land and buildings. Indicate the amount that must be treated as ordinary income (per Sec. 1250) and the amount that must be treated as Sec. 1231 gain or loss if the total sales price were $240,000, of which $60,000 is allocated to the land and $180,000 to the apartment house. (To compute ACRS depreciation, use Table 14-4; assume straight-line depreciation to total $21,052.)

14. Barton Spring and Dayton Fall each organized a new corporate business venture in year 1. Both men invested $100,000 cash in their wholly owned corporation, and both corporations experienced $20,000 operating losses in years 1, 2, and 3. Barton qualified his corporation under Subchapter S, whereas Dayton elected to have his corporation taxed in the normal way. In year 4, each man sold his corporation's stock for $40,000. Because of the S corporation election, Barton offset his corporation's annual $20,000 loss against his income from other sources, at the "cost" of reducing his basis in corporate stock. Dayton, on the other hand, got no current deductions for the losses experienced by his corporation in years 1 through 3, but neither did he have to reduce the basis of his stock. Therefore, on the sale of their corporate stock in year 4, Barton recognized no additional gain or loss, whereas Dayton recognized a $60,000 long-term capital loss.
a. Assuming that each man is independently wealth and that each typically reports a substantial ordinary income as well as capital gain, who made the better choice? Explain.
b. Would it have been beneficial for either taxpayer if their stock qualified as Sec. 1244 stock? Explain briefly.

15. Jan Drew made several stops on her way to the bank where she planned to make a deposit of $500 cash. Unfortunately, somewhere along the way Jan left the cash unattended, and, when she retraced her steps, she simply could not locate the money. She concluded that someone had stolen the $500.
a. Assuming that Jan is the cashier for Bout Corporation, would Bout claim a tax deduction for the loss? Explain, and cite your statutory authority for a deduction, if any.

b. Assuming that Jan was depositing her own cash, could she claim a tax deduction for the loss? Explain, and cite your statutory authority for a deduction, if any.

16. While you were a student at Ohio University 10 years ago, you loaned $300 cash to Barry Doubtful. This year you learned that Barry died penniless from an overdose of drugs. How should you report your $300 bad debt loss in the current year for tax purposes?

17. Philomena Leaky owned 38% of the outstanding stock of Leaky Corporation; her husband, Jack, owned another 10%; and her son, Joey, owned 5%. Philomena also owned 60% of Sneaky Corporation. On April 1, Philomena sold 500 shares of her Leaky stock to Sneaky Corporation for $25,000. Philomena's tax basis in the shares sold was $5,000. Assuming that Philomena had owned the Leaky shares for 12 years prior to this sale, what amount and kind of income should she report this year because of the sale?

18. On March 3 of this year, Walter Caringounce, a real estate dealer, sold a 12-acre tract of land for $120,000. Although Walter had purchased the property for $40,000 as an investment 6 years ago, he made minor improvements to the land during the past 18 months, and he actively advertised the property for sale for a year before closing the deal this year. How should Walter report his $80,000 gain this year?

19. Laura Engles owns 100% of Missouri Corporation, which in turn owns 100% of Ozark Corporation. On April 1, Laura sold 5,000 shares of Missouri common (which had a tax basis of $50,000) to Ozark Corporation for $150,000. (Assume that both Missouri and Ozark had substantial amounts of earnings and profits.)
a. What apparent tax advantage is Laura trying to obtain? Explain briefly.
b. Do you think that this tax plan will work? (If not, cite any Code section that you think might interdict the intended results.)

20. "Big" Fish owns all outstanding stock of three corporations, namely, Little Corporation, Pond Corporation, and Dud Corporation. The first two corporations (Little and Pond) have been highly successful financial ventures. However, Dud was a financial failure. During this year, Fish engaged in the three transactions detailed below. In each transaction, determine the amount and kind of income that Fish must report for federal income tax purposes.
a. On November 19, Fish sold 50 of his 500 shares of common stock in Little Corporation to Pond Corporation for $500,000 cash. His adjusted basis in the 50 shares sold was $10,000. The date basis of these shares was April 1, 1960.
b. On December 1, Fish sold all his stock in Dud Corporation to Evan Moore Stupid for $1,000 cash. His basis in the Dud shares sold was $45,000. The shares had a date basis of July 1, 1975. The Dud stock was Sec. 1244 stock.
c. On December 31, Fish was notified that Dud Corporation had been declared bankrupt and that no assets were available to distribute to any creditors. Accordingly, Fish knew that his $10,000 loan to Dud Corporation on September 1, 1978, would never be repaid.

21. Archie Goodwin and Peter Whimsey own all the outstanding shares of Lotus Corporation, a successful venture that they incorporated 15 years ago to take advantage of the lower corporate tax rates. Earnings have been retained in the business for expansion, but in recent years cash has begun to accumulate beyond corporate needs. Both Archie and Peter currently have high personal incomes, including salaries of $100,000 each from Lotus. To get cash out of the corporation,

they have decided that each will "sell" 25% of his shares to Lotus. They hope to avoid ordinary dividend treatment in this manner. Evaluate this plan.

22. Jay Gonzales has operated a restaurant for years in his hometown, and his name has become associated in the region with fine Mexican food. Rather than open additional locations, he has decided to franchise his name and recipes. Under the proposed agreement, Jay would reserve the right to specify the quality of ingredients and to inspect the franchised operations. For each location, he receives a $50,000 "sales price" when the agreement is signed, plus 5% of gross sales. How will the payments be taxed to Jay when received?

SUPPLEMENTAL PROBLEMS

23. Grand Corporation experienced two serious casualty losses this year. In May, Plant A burned to the ground; in September, Plant B was totally destroyed by a hurricane. Grand's adjusted basis in Plant A was $550,000; fire insurance proceeds amounted to only $350,000. Plant B was a much older operation, and therefore it had an adjusted basis of only $80,000 when it was destroyed. Because Plant B was still in good repair, however, Grand's management had insured the plant for $250,000. By the end of the year, the management of Grand Corporation had settled with the insurance company on the Plant A claim and was about to settle with another insurance company on the Plant B disaster when the controller suggested that any settlement on the latter be deferred until next year. Explain the apparent tax reason that could have prompted the controller to make this suggestion and try to determine whether or not his tax plan would be likely to succeed. Demonstrate his apparent objective with calculations based on the assumptions that Grand Corporation is an accrual-basis taxpayer and that it realized a $400,000 ordinary taxable income and a $60,000 excess of net long-term capital gain over net short-term capital loss this year. (These amounts exclude both of the casualty events. Ignore the effect of Sec. 291 in your solution.)

24. In 1970, Al Alred incorporated his automotive repair business as AA Motors, Inc. Because of failing health, Al decided to sell his business to Andy Algreen, AA's best mechanic. Andy told Al that it was immaterial to him whether he purchased (1) Al's stock in AA Motors, Inc. or (2) the individual assets that AA Motors owns—that is, the customer lists, accounts receivable, tools and equipment, building, and so on. At the time of the sale, Al owned 100% of the outstanding shares of AA Motors, Inc.

   a. If Andy purchases the shares of stock, who is the selling taxpayer—Al or AA Motors, Inc.?
   b. If Andy purchases the individual assets, who is the selling taxpayer—Al or AA Motors, Inc.?
   c. If Andy purchases the AA stock, does the seller report ordinary income, capital gain, or both?
   d. If Andy purchases the individual assets, does the seller report ordinary income, capital gain, or both?
   e. If Andy purchases the AA stock, what will the basis of the various assets be?
   f. If Andy purchases the individual assets, what will the basis of the various assets be?

25. Does it make any difference taxwise to the selling taxpayer whether part of the sales price involved in the sale of a business is allocated to a "covenant not to compete" rather than to "goodwill"? Explain.

26. Does it make any difference taxwise to the purchasing taxpayer whether part of the purchase price involved in the purchase of a business is allocated to a "covenant not to compete" rather than to "goodwill"? Explain.

27. Chapter 16 includes a discussion of three of the more important statutory exceptions to the pure capital asset definition of Sec. 1221. The courts have added yet other judicial exceptions not explained in this text. Perhaps the benchmark case is *Corn Products Refining Company* v. *Commissioner,* 350 U.S. 46 (1955). A recent restatement of this same judicial doctrine is found in *W. W. Windle Company,* 65 TC 694 (1976). Locate these two judicial decisions in your school library (you may have to go to the law library, and you may need some help in finding the correct volumes), read them, and then summarize briefly the judicial modifications to Sec. 1221 as detailed in the two cases.

28. Jones and Smith each own 2,500 of the 500 outstanding shares of JS Corporation stock. Each man has a tax basis of $10 per share of stock that he owns. For years, the two owners have allowed JS Corporation to accumulate most of the corporate profits for business expansion. In the current year, however, the owners see no further need for additional accumulation.
    a. If the JS Corporation declares a $60,000 dividend, how will Jones and Smith report the $30,000 that they each receive?
    b. If Jones and Smith were each to surrender back to JS Corporation 500 of the 2,500 shares of stock they each own, thereby technically creating a stock redemption rather than a simple dividend, how would Jones and Smith report the $30,000 that they each receive?
    c. Suppose that Jones was looking forward to an early retirement, whereas Smith anticipated a long future with JS Corporation. Under these circumstances, the two men may agree to distribute the entire $60,000 to Jones in exchange for 1,000 of his 2,500 shares of stock. How will Jones report the $60,000 he receives?
    d. If, at the time of incorporating their business, both Jones and Smith loaned JS Corporation $50,000 in long-term debt in addition to the capital investment they made, how would each man report the receipt of $30,000 in the current year if the corporate records clearly supported the contention that the distribution of cash was a reduction of this long-term debt?
    e. What does this problem suggest about the form of the capital structure of any new corporation?

29. On November 14 of the current year the authorities suspended all trading in Equity Funny Corporation stocks. Radcliff had purchased 1,000 shares of Equity Funny on February 13 last year for $32,500. The closing quotation for these shares on November 13 this year was $5 per share. The trading suspension was still in effect on December 31, so Radcliff could not sell his 1,000 shares although he desperately wanted to do so. What amount of capital loss can Radcliff deduct in the current year as far as his Equity Funny stock is concerned? Explain briefly.

30. Ted Engles, who is independently wealthy and earns a large income each year, also owns 3,000 shares of Onnex Corporation stock. Ted's basis in these shares is $30,000; their current fair market value is $330,000. Ted fears that the value of Onnex common may drop significantly in the near future, and, therefore, he would like to sell about one half of the shares. He does not, however, want to pay

a big capital gains tax immediately. Suppose that Ted sells half of his Onnex shares to his wife, Laura, for $165,000 in an installment sale calling for payment of $35,000 for each of the next five years. Suppose also that Laura almost immediately resells the same shares to an independent third party for $165,000 cash.

a. What apparent tax advantage is Ted trying to obtain? Explain briefly.

b. What are the tax consequences to Laura when she sells all the shares she recently purchased? Explain briefly.

c. Do you think that this tax plan will work? (If not, cite any Code section that you think might interdict the intended results.)

CHAPTER 17

General Concept of the Wherewithal to Pay and Tax Deferrals

This result gives me much puzzlement. Without the receipt of any money or of any property equaling the petitioner's investment in the mortgage notes, the petitioner is held liable to income tax upon a large amount of accrued interest which he did not receive. In the words of Nicodemus, "How can these things be?"
J. Smith, dissenting Nichols v. Commissioner 1 TC 328 (1942)

Where the taxpayer does not receive payment of income in money or property realization may occur when the last step is taken by which he obtains the fruition of the economic gain which has already accrued to him.
Helvering v. Horst 311 U.S. 112 (1940)

THE REALIZATION CRITERION

The words *realization, recognition,* and *transaction* are scattered throughout the literature of law, economics, and accounting. In introductory literature, especially, these words are typically used without specific definition. Authors of this literature presume that the reader can apply a generally accepted definition to each word and thereby reach a reasonably accurate conclusion about the thought the author is trying to convey. To understand the significance of these words to income taxation, a more detailed analysis of each word is required.

This chapter and the following chapter attempt to demonstrate that a wherewithal-to-pay concept is at least as important to understanding the income tax as the realization concept, which is more frequently cited. In other words, the authors believe that Congress, the I.R.S., and the judiciary rely as often on a wherewithal-to-pay concept as on a realization concept in settling specific income measurement problems for tax purposes.

This chapter begins with a discussion of the general wherewithal-to-pay concept and concludes with a discussion of like-kind exchanges and involuntary conversions. Chapter 18 covers other common nontaxable transactions including several nontaxable transactions that occur between corporations and their shareholders. We begin, then, with the general realization criterion and proceed to a rather extensive list of situations in which income recognition is postponed because the taxpayers involved do not have the wherewithal to pay the tax.

FUNDAMENTAL CONCEPTS

The income-generating cycle begins with an idea and ends with consumption. Intermediate steps may be numerous and complex or few and simple; the process may be concluded in a brief time span, or it may extend over many years. The more numerous, complex, and time consuming the intermediate steps, the greater are the problems of income measurement.

As noted in Chapter 3, the income concept common to taxation is more like the accounting concept than like the economic concept. For both tax and accounting purposes, income under most circumstances must be "realized" before it is "recognized." What does it mean to say that income is "realized"?

The Realization Criterion in Accounting

The verb realize has several possible meanings. Perhaps the three most common are: (1) to make real; (2) to convert into cash (money); and (3) to understand clearly.[1] Obviously, the second of these three meanings is the one pertinent to this discussion. When the realization concept is first introduced into a freshman or sophomore accounting course, the text—and often the instructor—hastens to illustrate the concept with a little story that usually goes something like this: "On August 10, Jones purchased 100 shares of ABC common stock for $600. On December 31, these shares had a fair market

---

[1]*The Random House Dictionary of the English Language,* unabridged edition (New York: Random House, 1973), p. 1196, lists eight different meanings.

value of $700. What is Jones's income for the year from this investment?" The student is expected, of course, to reply that Jones has no income because his $100 gain has not yet been "realized."

Applying the second definition to the problem about Jones, a student would be correct in assuming that until the shares are sold for cash (or money), no income is "realized." An accountant would probably not be as demanding as this definition. He or she likely would be willing to admit that income is realized as soon as the shares are converted into another property that has a high degree of liquidity and measurability. *A Dictionary for Accountants* defines realize as follows:

> To convert into cash or a receivable (through sale) or services (through use); to exchange for property which at the time of its receipt may be classified as, or immediately converted into, a current asset.[2]

This broad interpretation of the realization criterion is consistent with the position taken by American Accounting Association committees in 1957 and 1964. The 1957 committee statement suggests that "the essential meaning of realization is that a change in an asset or liability has become sufficiently definite and objective to warrant recognition in the account."[3] The 1964 committee added: "It is difficult to be precise about what is the current prevailing practice, but it appears that presently accepted tests for realization require receipt of a current (or liquid) asset capable of objective measurement in a market transaction for services rendered."[4]

The last pronouncement of the American Institute of Certified Public Accountants on the matter of realization comes reasonably close to the tax position. In its Statement No. 4, the Accounting Principles Board assigned the concept of realization the position of a pervasive measurement principle and then described it as follows:

> Revenue is generally recognized when both of the following conditions are met: (1) the earning process is complete or virtually complete, and (2) an exchange has taken place.[5]

This statement seems to differ from those offered earlier, with less emphasis placed on the liquidity of the asset received and more emphasis on the completion of the earning process.

---

[2]Eric L. Kohler, *A Dictionary for Accountants,* 2nd ed. (Englewood Cliffs, NJ: Prentice-Hall, 1957), p. 407.
[3]American Accounting Association, *Accounting and Reporting Standards for Corporate Financial Statements* (Menasha, WI: George Banta Company, Inc., 1957), p. 3.
[4]1964 Concepts and Standards Research Study Committee, "The Realization Concept," *The Accounting Review* (April 1965), p. 314.
[5]APB Statement No. 4, "Basic Concepts and Accounting Principles Underlying Financial Statements of Business Enterprise" (New York: American Institute of Certified Public Accountants, 1970), p. 59.

Although much more could be written about the realization concept in accounting, the most important facts are already apparent. At least until 1970, accountants generally held that income (revenue) was not realized until a transaction had been consummated and a measurable, liquid asset received. The latter requirement is consistent with the accountants' objectivity principle; for external financial reporting purposes, the accountant generally minimizes the need to establish fair market values in the absence of an arm's-length transaction.

The Realization Criterion in Income Taxation

The realization concept in income taxation is similar but not identical to the accounting concept just reviewed. Most of the differences between them are best explained by practical constraints—that is, by the accountant's legal liability for accurate statements on the one hand and by the objectives and administrative considerations common to income taxation on the other.

The realization criterion of income taxation is an interesting blend of statutory, administrative, and judicial law. In Sec. 61, which contains the general definition of gross income, the word realization does not appear. The Code provides only that "gross income means all income from whatever source *derived.*"[6] The Treasury Department's interpretation of this statute introduces the realization concept. It reads as follows:

> (a) General definition. Gross income means all income from whatever source derived, unless excluded by law. Gross income includes income *realized* in any form, whether in money, property, or services. Income may be *realized,* therefore, in the form of services, meals, accommodations, stock, or other property, as well as in cash.[7]

Observe that this administrative interpretation of the Code suggests that realization requires the receipt of some new service, property, or property right but does not specify anything relative to either the liquidity or the measurability of that item. This broad interpretation of realization is a practical necessity. In its absence, taxpayers would seek out obscure ways of avoiding income taxation by earning their income through barter transactions of infinite variety. Interestingly, Sec. 1001, which is titled "Determination of Amount of and Recognition of Gain or Loss," refers to amount realized.

The realization criterion has received judicial support from the beginning. The most celebrated statement is contained in a 1920 U.S. Supreme Court decision, which reads as follows:

> Here we have the essential matter: not a gain accruing to capital, not a growth or increment of value in the investment; but a gain, a profit,

---

[6]Section 61(a) (emphasis added).
[7]Treasury Regulation Sec. 1.61-1(a) (emphasis added).

something of exchangeable value proceeding from the property, severed from the capital however invested or employed, and coming in, being "derived," that is, received or drawn by the recipient (the taxpayer) for his separate use, benefit and disposal;—that is income derived from property. Nothing else answers the description.[8]

The words of the Supreme Court, like those of the regulation, seem to require a transaction or some significant event in addition to appreciation. These authorities make it amply clear that a mere appreciation in value, without realization, will not be taxed as income. The important question remains, however: Exactly what is required before income is "realized"?

For purposes of income taxation, assume that the singular requirement pertinent to the realization concept is the consummation of an "external transaction." The fact that nothing more is required is amply demonstrated in *United States* v. *Davis*. In that case, the Supreme Court found that a husband who transferred an appreciated property to his wife "in full settlement and satisfaction of any and all claims and rights against the husband"[9] realized gain equal to the difference between the fair market value of the rights received and the adjusted basis of the property transferred. Because the "rights received" were unique and certainly not liquid or easily measured— that is, they could be "purchased" only by this one man—the Court found that the value of the rights could be presumed equal to the (estimated) value of the property surrendered in order to measure gain. Although the specific conclusion of the *Davis* decision is effectively overruled by a provision in the 1984 Act, it still suggests that, in income taxation, the realization concept does not require the receipt of a measurable, liquid asset.

Interestingly, the wife in the *Davis* case apparently did not realize taxable income by surrendering her rights against her ex-husband for a property. One possible reason for the different treatment of these two taxpayers is that her settlement can be viewed as restitution; that is, her receipt of the property simply restores her to the financial position she had prior to her release of rights. The new anti-*Davis* rule can be found in Sec. 1041. It provides that no gain or loss shall be recognized on the transfer of a property either between spouses or between former spouses if transfer is incident to a divorce or separation.

Transaction Defined

As illustrated by the *Davis* decision, the word transaction must be defined broadly and positively for income tax purposes. In addition, the transaction concept must be separated clearly from the realization concept. Whenever these two concepts are not clearly distinguished, it is all too commonplace to find circular definitions: such as (1) income is recognized in the books of account only if it has been realized; (2) the realization of income (revenue)

---

[8]*Eisner* v. *Macomber*, 252 U.S. 189 (1920), p. 207.
[9]370 U.S. 65 (1962), p. 67.

requires a transaction with specified characteristics; and (3) a transaction is any event or condition that gives rise to an accounting entry.

As an alternative to such circular definitions, we can define a transaction as any significant change in the form or the substance of any property or property right. Internal transactions involve only one entity; external transactions necessarily involve more than one entity.

As stated earlier, the realization of taxable income generally requires the consummation of an external transaction. This transaction could be a sale, an exchange, an abandonment, or almost any other modification in a property or a property right. The transfer of raw materials into goods in process and eventually into finished inventory would not give rise to taxable income as long as the transfer does not extend beyond a single taxable entity. Such a transfer would constitute an internal transaction because it represents a significant change in the form of property. As such, it would be the occasion for an entry in the accounting records even though it would not be sufficient to trigger the realization of taxable income.

The discovery of oil in land owned by a taxpayer would not give rise to taxable income because it neither creates a new property or property right nor changes the form of an existing one. Rather, the discovery simply makes the land-owning taxpayer aware of a new dimension of the property rights that he or she has owned all along. The discovery of buried treasure, on the other hand, would give rise to taxable income because of the existence of possible adverse interests in such property by another entity and because treasure trove is not deemed to be part of the basic collection of rights that collectively constitute land ownership.

An interesting exception to the general rule we have just stated occurs when a taxpayer mortgages a property that he or she already owns. The placing of a mortgage against an appreciated property certainly could be classified as a significant change in that property owner's rights. For example, suppose that a taxpayer borrowed $10,000 against a property with an adjusted basis of $2,000 and a fair market value of $14,000. In an important sense, this taxpayer has realized at least part of his or her appreciation gain. Yet, the borrowing transaction, even when executed between external parties, neither constitutes realization nor, alternatively, does it give rise to income, because there is no net increase in the taxpayer's net worth. When the taxpayer borrows, liabilities increase by the same amount as assets, and, therefore, the taxpayer is deemed to have no taxable income. This exception to the usual rule that gain must be realized on the consummation of an external transaction is, in turn, subject to at least two notable exceptions. First, if a taxpayer transfers property with a related debt in excess of its adjusted basis in a transaction that would otherwise permit the temporary deferral of gain, the gain must be realized. Second, if an individual embezzles assets, he or she is treated as having realized an equivalent amount of income notwithstanding the fact that he or she, at least technically, owes a debt equal in amount to that taken illegally.

Another interesting aspect of the realization transaction criterion of income taxation can be observed in the transfer of property between business entities. Recall that entities recognized for tax purposes are not necessarily entities recognized for accounting purposes. For example, the transfer of a building from a personal account to a sole proprietorship would most likely give rise to an accounting entry and possibly even to accounting income. It would not, however, give rise to taxable income because the sole proprietorship is not viewed for tax purposes as an entity distinct from the individual owner. On the other hand, the transfer of the same building from the taxpayer to his or her wholly owned corporation could give rise to taxable income, as well as to an accounting entry, because the corporation is deemed to be a separate taxable entity.

The word "could" in the preceding sentence, is particularly important. Realization, as defined here, is a necessary but not a sufficient condition for recognition of taxable income.

Recognition

The adjective recognized, when used to modify income, means simply that the income item is to be admitted or acknowledged for the purpose at hand. For example, income recognized for accounting purposes is simply income that is included in the appropriate financial statement(s) prepared for that accounting period. Similarly, income recognized for tax purposes is simply income that must be included in the tax base reported for a given time period.

For financial accounting purposes, it frequently is argued that income should be recognized (under specified fact circumstances) prior to realization.[10] In general, these arguments are made to bring accounting income closer to the concept of economic income. The fact circumstances typically cited as justifying a prerealization recognition of income in financial statements are those involving a minimum of judgment in establishing fair market value. For example, if natural gas has been extracted by a U.S. producer but has not been sold or exchanged, a strong case can be made for the "early" recognition of this income, because the price of domestic natural gas is relatively stable and easily determined. Accountants hold widely varying opinions about (1) the degree of price predictability and (2) the state of completion required before unrealized income should be recognized in financial statements. The accountant only rarely argues that income recognition should be delayed until sometime after realization. In those few cases when this is done, the accountant usually does so because of an inability to estimate accurately some material postrealization expense. For example, if collection and foreclosure costs are estimated as material in amount, and if they are not subject to reasonably accurate estimation, then the accountant may argue for a cash collection basis of revenue recognition rather than a realization basis.

For tax purposes, income generally must be recognized in the same accounting period that it is realized. However, a number of exceptions to this

---

[10]For example, see Charles T. Horngren, "How Should we Interpret the Realization Concept?" *The Accounting Review,* XL (April 1965), pp. 323–33.

general rule exist. For tax purposes, income recognition only rarely precedes realization, but it quite often follows realization. This significant difference in income measurement techniques between accounting and taxation can be explained by the tax tenet called **wherewithal to pay.** The tenet suggests that under many circumstances "the income tax shall impinge at whatever time the taxpayer has the funds with which to pay the tax." In numerous situations, wherewithal to pay seems to outrank in importance more sophisticated refinements of income measurement that would cause income to be recognized at a time other than when the funds are readily available. Perhaps the outstanding example is the taxation of certain unearned revenues at the time of receipt.

In summary, the realization criterion of income taxation is like the accounting criterion in its insistence on a transaction. Unlike its accounting counterpart, however, the income tax criterion does not always depend on the receipt of a measurable, liquid asset. Furthermore, and also in contrast with accounting, income recognition almost never precedes realization for tax purposes but is often postponed until long after realization.

NONTAXABLE TRANSACTIONS

Income that has been realized by a taxpayer may (1) be recognized immediately, (2) be permanently excluded from gross income by definition or by act of Congress, or (3) have recognition partially or wholly deferred temporarily by Code provision. The third type of transaction is often referred to as a **nontaxable transaction.** In other words, the phrase "nontaxable transaction" is often a misnomer; as often as not, a nontaxable transaction is at least partially taxable.

Let us review briefly what we said earlier about taxability. All realized income is deemed taxable unless the taxpayer can find specific authority for excluding the income item from the tax base. The list of permanent exclusions is relatively brief. It includes gifts; inheritances; insurance proceeds paid on the death of the insured (unless the recipient has a purchased interest in the policy); most interest paid on state and local government bonds; scholarships and fellowships (under specified conditions); property settlements in lieu of alimony; on-premise food and lodging (conditions specified); the value of group term life (to $50,000 face), health, and accident insurance premiums (paid by the employer for the employees); some Social Security and railroad retirement benefits; and a few other miscellaneous items. The most important definitional exclusion is the "return of capital" concept, which is aptly demonstrated by the calculation of taxable gain on the sale of a security. A more complex illustration of the return of capital concept is embodied in the calculation of taxable gain on the receipt of a purchased annuity payment.

In addition, many routine transactions in which income is realized are not considered of immediate tax consequence because of the accounting method selected for reporting purposes by the taxpayer. For example, if a taxpayer can properly elect to report income on a cash basis, the only revenue transaction that is important for all routine business transactions is the collection of cash. Note, however, that even a cash-basis taxpayer must resort to other rules to determine the tax consequences of any nonroutine transaction in which he or she may be involved. In the latter group of transactions, the nontaxable transactions are especially important.

The General Rule

As a general rule, it is most accurate to presume that income must be recognized for tax purposes when it is realized unless a taxpayer can find good authority for a contrary treatment. As we have said, three levels of contrary authority are pertinent:

1. The realized income may constitute one of the income items permanently excluded from the income tax base.
2. The realized income may derive from a routine business transaction that is reported to the government for tax purposes on some alternative but acceptable accounting method.
3. The Code may provide for deferral of the recognition of gain realized for this specific kind of property or for this particular form of disposition.

In general, the rationale for the last two groups of exceptions is that the income tax should be deferred until such time as the taxpayer has the funds with which to pay the tax.

Exception by Accounting Method

The installment method of income recognition, a common exception to the general recognition rules, permits taxpayers to defer recognition of income until cash is collected and they have the wherewithal to pay the tax. The detailed requirements pertinent to the installment method are contained in Secs. 453, 453A, 453B, and 453C. The use of the installment method depends on whether the sale is by a dealer in personal property or the sale is of real estate or a casual sale of personal property.

Dealers in personal property normally report profits on sales of merchandise when the sale is made. Dealers who dispose of personal property under a contract providing for one or more deferred payments generally may elect to use the installment method of reporting such sales.

For most installment sales of real estate or of personal property by nondealers after October 19, 1980, the installment method of reporting gain applies automatically unless the taxpayer elects to report the entire gain in the year of sale. In other words, the installment method is the "normal" accounting method for most real estate sales and for casual sales of personal property by persons who are not dealers in those properties. Payments in the year of sale can be any percentage of the sales price, and the method applies even when only one payment is made in a later taxable year.

Assuming the installment method applies to a sale, the method of reporting taxable income under the installment method depends upon when the sale was made. If the sale is made after March 31, 1986, the more difficult rules created in the Tax Reform Act of 1986 apply to calculations for 1987 and later years. For installment sales made after 1980 but before April 1, 1986, the taxpayer reports as taxable income in any year only a fraction of the cash collections received from the installment sale. The appropriate fraction is called the **gross profit ratio,** the ratio of the gross profit realized on the sale to the "total contract price."[11] Total contract price means the amount of cash the seller eventually receives under the sale contract, excluding interest.

To illustrate the effect of the installment sale rules, assume the following facts. In 19x1, Ben, not an art dealer, made a casual sale of a painting for $2,000. He had purchased this painting for his personal enjoyment five years earlier, at which time he paid $1,200. The 19x1 sale contract called for five annual payments of $400, plus 12% interest on the unpaid balance; the first payment was due on delivery of the painting. Ben receives payment as follows:

November 10, 19x1	$400
November 10, 19x2	592
November 10, 19x3	544
November 10, 19x4	496
November 10, 19x5	448

Even if Ben is ordinarily a cash-basis taxpayer, he reports the gain on the sale of his painting on an installment basis. We summarize the tax consequences of the transaction in Table 17-1.

This example is important for at least two reasons. First, it demonstrates that a taxpayer may defer recognition of taxable income until such time as he or she has the wherewithal to pay simply by application of an appropriate accounting method. Had this method not been available, Ben might have had to recognize the entire $800 long-term capital gain in the year it was realized (19x1), even though he was a cash-basis taxpayer for routine business purposes. Second, the sale contract illustrated above explicitly provides for interest on the unpaid debt. An installment sales contract that does not provide explicitly for interest at a minimum rate will be presumed to include implicit interest at a rate prescribed by law. The reason for this presumption is apparent from the illustration. Without the rule, a seller would be able to convert ordinary (interest) income into a tax-favored long-term capital gain by increasing a contract price and reducing (or eliminating) interest. Although this conversion of ordinary income into capital gain is limited, the cash-collection basis of accounting for the interest still makes it possible to defer recognition of the interest portion of the sale until the taxpayer has the

---

[11]Regulation Sec. 1.453-1(b)(1): "Gross profit, in the case of a sale of real estate by a person other than a dealer and a casual sale of personal property, is reduced by commissions and other selling expenses." In other words, in these cases, gross profit usually equals the gain realized.

TABLE 17–1

INSTALLMENT BASIS REPORTING

Year	Cash Collected	Ordinary Taxable Income Reported (interest)[a]	Long-term Capital Gain Reported[b]
19x1	$400	$ 0	$160
19x2	592	192	160
19x3	544	144	160
19x4	496	96	160
19x5	448	48	160

[a]Reported on a cash basis.
[b]The gross profit ratio on this sale was 40%—that is, ($2,000 − 1,200)/$2,000. Hence, 40% of every noninterest dollar collected after the sale must be reported as taxable income in the year of receipt.

funds with which to pay the tax. Sometimes, the difference between the imputed or statutory rate and the current market interest rate still allows for limited conversion of ordinary income in some installment contracts.

An exception to the above rules applies for depreciable property sold in an installment sale after June 6, 1984. This exception requires that the ordinary income created by depreciation recapture must be recognized fully in the year of sale. For example, assume Mr. Tweed bought a machine used in his trade or business for $50,000; claimed $30,000 of depreciation on the machine; and sold the machine in 1982 for $45,000. The terms of the sale provided that no money would be received by Tweed until 1988. All $25,000 of the gain would be ordinary income under Sec. 1245 and would be recognized in 1987 at the time of the sale. This rule eliminates the benefit of the installment sales method for most current sales of property subject to Sec. 1245 recapture.

While the traditional method of taxing installment sales is logical and understandable when viewed within the context of the wherewithal-to-pay concept, it can permit, on occasion, a postponement of taxation until well after the proceeds are received. This result occurs when a taxpayer sells the property on an installment sale and then borrows money using the installment receivable as collateral. The seller thus receives cash from the sale immediately but traditionally has not been required to recognize income until the underlying receivable is collected.

Congress decided in the Tax Reform Act of 1986 to reduce the attractiveness of this type of transaction by creating the proportionate disallowance rule discussed below. This rule applies as of January 1, 1987, to certain installment sales made on or after March 1, 1986. The installment sales covered by these rules, termed "applicable installment obligations," are installment sales of property that are stock in trade to the seller, real property used in the seller's trade or business, or real property held for rental purposes. In the last two cases, the sales price must be greater than $150,000, and the seller or an affiliated party must hold the installment receivable. Excluded from the definition are certain personal use property and certain farm property.

The proportionate disallowance rule limits the effectiveness of the installment sales method by partially disallowing the benefits of using the method.

The rule requires the seller to treat certain amounts as received in the year of sale. The amount that is treated as received is the taxpayer's "allocable installment indebtedness" which is determined as follows:

$$AII = \frac{f}{fa + b} (avg) - AII (p)$$

Aii = Allocable installment indebtedness

f = The face amount of all outstanding "applicable installment obligations" at year-end

fa = The face amount of all outstanding installment obligations at year-end

b = The total adjusted bases of all other assets held by the taxpayer at year-end

avg = The average quarterly outstanding debt of the taxpayer

$AII(p)$ = The AII from all previous years' "allocable installment obligations"

For example, assume the calendar-year XYZ Corporation begins business in 1987. It sells a property for $500,000 (gross profit of $200,000) and receives no payments until 1988. The corporation's assets (excluding the receivable from the property sale) have an aggregate adjusted basis of $2,000,000 on December 31, 1987. The average quarterly debt for the corporation during 1987 is $400,000. The AII for the corporation for 1987 is $80,000 computed as follows:

$$\frac{\$500,000}{\$500,000 + \$2,000,000} (\$400,000) = \$80,000$$

XYZ Corporation is deemed to have received $80,000 cash from the sale, even though the corporation received nothing in 1987. The gross profit recognized by XYZ Corporation in 1987 is $32,000 ($200,000/$500,000 × $80,000).

In addition to treating the allocable installment indebtedness as a payment received, the Tax Reform Act of 1986 also eliminates the use of the installment method for revolving credit plan sales and certain other less common sales that previously could be taxed under the installment method.

Other special rules are provided in the Code for early dispositions of installment sale obligations and for foreclosures on installment sales contracts. The student interested in these and other possible complications is urged to consult a current and authoritative tax service for details.

Exceptions for Specific Transactions

Accounting methods generally apply to all qualifying transactions without regard for the nature of the property involved. Infrequently, however, the Code specifies a special method of reporting income from sales of selected forms of property or from properties disposed of in a certain manner. These unusual or irregular provisions are often best understood in light of a wherewithal-to-pay concept.

THE EXCHANGE OF PRODUCTIVE USE OR INVESTMENT PROPERTIES

When an old truck used in a trade or business is "traded in" on a new truck, the business owner will likely realize a gain on the transfer of the old truck. For example, if the old truck has an adjusted basis of $1,000 and a fair market value of $5,000, the realized gain will be $4,000. In addition, the business owner will probably pay an additional sum of cash to acquire the new truck. For tax purposes, there are at least three good reasons to postpone the recognition of taxable income in this situation. First, postponement avoids the administrative disputes that frequently accompany arbitrary determinations of fair market value. Second, arbitrary "list price" valuations are avoided, which, if accepted, often allow the taxpayer golden opportunities for tax avoidance.[12] Third, postponing the liability for any income tax that might attach to the exchange until such time as the taxpayer has the wherewithal to pay the tax is much fairer to the taxpayer.

Statutory Requirements

The exchange of productive use or investment properties is governed by Sec. 1031 which begins as follows:

> (a) Nonrecognition of Gain or Loss from Exchanges Solely in Kind.—No gain or loss shall be recognized on the exchange of property held for productive use in a trade or business or for investment if such property is exchanged solely for property of a like kind which is held either for productive use in a trade or business or for investment.[13]

Several aspects of Sec. 1031 cannot be overemphasized. First, observe that this section is mandatory, but it is applied only to direct exchanges. A taxpayer who exchanges one qualifying property for another has no option to recognize gain or loss if he or she wants to do so. Furthermore, if a taxpayer sells property and subsequently uses the proceeds of the sale to purchase similar or even identical property, such a transaction is not within the confines of Sec. 1031(a).

Second, Sec. 1031(b) excludes specified properties from the effects of Sec. 1031(a) even though those properties are held for trade, business, or investment purposes. Gains realized on the exchange of inventories (or other property held primarily for resale), stocks, bonds, receivables, interest partnerships, and a few other properties are specifically excluded from any special treatment by Sec. 1031(b).

---

[12]A major potential loophole was reduced significantly by the enactment of Sec. 1245. As explained on page 16-7, the big advantage of a high list price would have been to get large deductions for depreciation (which reduce ordinary income) at the cost of realizing a tax-favored long-term capital gain on disposition of the asset (via operation of Sec. 1231).

[13]Section 1031(a).

Third, observe that the exchange must involve "property of a like kind" before the gain or loss realized is not recognized by operation of Sec. 1031. The general "like kind" requirement is explained in the Treasury Regulations as follows:

> As used in section 1031(a), the words "like kind" have reference to the nature or character of the property and not to its grade or quality. One kind or class of property may not, under that section, be exchanged for property of a different kind or class. The fact that any real estate involved is improved or unimproved is not material, for that fact relates only to the grade or quality of the property and not to its kind or class. Unproductive real estate held by one other than a dealer for future use or future realization of the increment in value is held for investment and not primarily for sale.[14]

It is apparent from this regulation and from related judicial decisions that realty cannot be exchanged for personalty and still qualify for nonrecognition of gain under Sec. 1031. Beyond that general statement, however, it is difficult to determine the precise limits of the "like-kind" requirement. Suffice it to note that the courts have been reasonably liberal in their interpretation of this provision. Incidentally, Sec. 1031(e) explicitly removes livestock of different sexes from like-kind property. This exclusion is intended to reduce a taxpayer's opportunity to convert ordinary income into capital gain through livestock breeding and feeding operations.

The Role of "Boot"

It is unusual to find two taxpayers who want to enter into an exchange of like-kind property and whose properties just happen to be equal in value. Disparity in values, however, need not preclude the possibility of entering into a "tax-free" exchange. As with the exchange of delivery trucks, an additional "side payment" of cash constitutes the usual adjustment mechanism for the difference in the fair market values of the two properties. Giving boot (which is defined as the cash or other non-like-kind property involved in the exchange) may or may not result in the recognition of gain; receiving boot literally guarantees the recognition of some gain.

Giving boot causes the recognition of gain only in the event that the boot given constitutes property (other than cash) that (1) cannot be part of a nontaxable exchange—for example, an item of inventory, a stock, bond, or a property of non-like-kind—and (2) has a fair market value greater than its tax basis. To illustrate this possibility, let's return to the earlier example of the delivery trucks and assume that the taxpayer who traded the old truck gave the other party in the exchange a stock with a fair market value of $5,500 (rather than paying $5,500 cash). In that event, the difference between the

---

[14]Regulation Sec. 1.1031(a)-1(b).

taxpayer's basis in the stock and its fair market value would have to be recognized as taxable gain (or loss) at the time of the exchange. That is, if the taxpayer had paid $2,000 for the stock, he or she would have to recognize a $3,500 gain when it was transferred to the truck dealer (even though he or she had no real wherewithal to pay).

Receiving boot necessitates the recognition of taxable gain equal to the lesser of the gain realized or the boot received. This provision is, however, consistent with the wherewithal-to-pay concept. Because the boot received represents "surplus" tax-paying ability, it determines the amount of gain that must be recognized, subject, of course, to the fact that a taxpayer never need recognize more gain than he or she realized on the exchange. This conclusion can be demonstrated simply in the following tabulation for a taxpayer who receives boot in an exchange of like-kind properties:

	Boot Received	Gain Realized	Gain Recognized
Case A	$500	$1,000	$500
Case B	500	200	200

The exchange of a mortgaged property ordinarily is treated as an exchange involving boot. The taxpayer who is relieved of the mortgage (which may be accomplished by the other party's either assuming the mortgage or taking the property subject to the mortgage) is treated as having received cash in an amount equal to the face value of the mortgage. Obviously, the assumption that release from a mortgage constitutes tax-paying ability equal to the receipt of a comparable amount of cash is subject to challenge in many circumstances. This conclusion is virtually necessary, however, to close what could otherwise be a major loophole in the nontaxable exchange provisions. To illustrate the potential loophole, assume that taxpayer A owned outright a piece of investment property that cost $1,000 but had a fair market value of $5,000. If A could find a satisfactory property of like kind that he or she preferred to own, A might first mortgage the present property and acquire, say, $3,000 cash. Then, having mortgaged the old property, A would enter into a nontaxable exchange and acquire a new property worth $2,000. If the transfer of the $3,000 mortgage to the former owner of the new property were not considered to be boot, taxpayer A would be able to avoid taxes even though he or she obviously had at least $3,000 in wherewithal to pay. In short, even though treating the transfer of a mortgage as equivalent to receiving cash of an equal amount may sometimes necessitate the recognition of taxable income when no tax-paying ability exists, the alternative assumption could lead to an equally unsatisfactory conclusion, at least as far as the I.R.S. is concerned.

If both properties involved in a nontaxable exchange are mortgaged properties, then only the difference between the face amounts of the two mortgages is treated as boot. The taxpayer who is relieved of the larger mortgage will be assumed to have received boot equal to the difference between the mortgage transferred to the other party and the mortgage assumed.

Finally, note that Sec. 1031 may cause a realized loss to remain unrecognized. If a taxpayer exchanges a productive use or investment property with an inherent or "paper" loss for another property of like kind, the loss realized on the exchange cannot be recognized for tax purposes. If the taxpayer desires to recognize such a tax loss, he or she must first sell the old property and then use the sales proceeds to purchase the second property in a separate transaction. On the other hand, losses are recognized on any boot property included in an otherwise nontaxable exchange. If a taxpayer who owned a bond with a basis of $1,300 and a fair market value of $1,000 decided to exchange that bond and an old delivery truck for a new delivery truck, the $300 loss realized on the exchange of the bond would be recognized because a bond cannot generally be part of a "common nontaxable exchange."

Basis Adjustment

The realized gain or loss that may be deferred in an exchange of like-kind properties is ordinarily a temporary deferment. Recoupment of the gain or loss under normal circumstances is guaranteed by the reduction of basis in the property received. The basis of property acquired in a nontaxable exchange may be calculated in one of two ways:

> *Method I:*
> Basis of old property (property given up in the exchange)
> + Boot given (basis)
> + Gain recognized
> − Boot received (fair market value)
> − Loss recognized (on boot property given)
> = Basis of new property (like-kind property received)
>
> *Method II:*
> Fair market value of property received (like-kind property only)
> + Loss not recognized on the exchange
> − Gain not recognized on the exchange
> = Basis of new property (like-kind property only)

The successful application of these formulas to specific fact situations requires a fair degree of imagination and understanding. Consequently, at the outset, you should attempt to solve every application using both formulas. If the results agree, the calculations are probably correct; if the results disagree, the facts should be investigated for alternative interpretations under the circumstances. To assist you, a comprehensive illustration of the nontaxable exchange provisions applicable to like-kind properties is included in the following section.

Before proceeding to that illustration, however, one additional note on basis seems pertinent. It is sometimes necessary for a taxpayer to determine a "date basis" as well as a "cost basis" for selected properties. Properties that acquire a substituted basis—that is, properties that take as a basis some amount other than cost, by operation of one of the nontaxable exchange provisions—are typically considered to be a mere extension of the original property for purposes of determining the holding period. As a consequence, the holding period of the two assets is assumed to "tack"; that is, it includes the period of time the "old" asset was held as well as the period of time the "new" asset was held prior to disposition. For example, assume that a taxpayer owned a particular capital asset for two years, after which he or she exchanged the asset for a like-kind asset in a nontaxable exchange. Then, two months later, this taxpayer disposed of the new asset in a taxable transaction. Would the capital gain or loss be classified as long or short term? The correct answer generally is long term; the taxpayer's holding period is presumed to run from the date he or she acquired the original asset, not from the date of the exchange. (An early disposition may, however, be viewed as evidence that the taxpayer did not intend to hold the new property as "productive use" or as "investment" property and thus disqualify the exchange for Sec. 1031 treatment.)

Comprehensive Illustration

Assume that taxpayer R (a rancher) exchanged some ranch land for an apartment complex (land and buildings) and some bonds, which had been owned by taxpayer D (a dentist). Facts pertinent to the exchange are shown in Table 17-2.

The important tax questions that attach to this exchange may be summarized as follows:

1. What taxable income, if any, must R recognize on the exchange?
2. What taxable income, if any, must D recognize on the exchange?
3. What is the basis of (a) the apartment house, (b) the land, and (c) the bonds in R's hands after the exchange has been completed?
4. What is the basis of the ranch land in D's hands after the exchange has been completed?

To determine the answers to these questions, we must make several calculations. The first calculation should determine the gain realized. Let us begin with taxpayer R. (See equation at top of p. 17-18.)

TABLE **17-2**

DATA ON A NONTAXABLE EXCHANGE

Facts Relative to the Ranch Land		Facts Relative to the Land, Apartment House, and Bonds	
FMV of land	$230,000	FMV of the apartment complex	$160,000
Tax basis (in R's hands)	50,000	Tax basis (in D's hands)	100,000
Mortgage on property	30,000	FMV of bonds	40,000
(to be assumed by D)		Tax basis (in D's hands)	50,000

$230,000 *Amount realized ($160,000 FMV of apartment complex +*
          $40,000 FMV of bonds + $30,000 mortgage transferred to D)
−   50,000 *Basis given up (R's basis in ranch land)*
= $180,000 *Gain realized*

Of the $180,000 gain realized, how much gain must R recognize? Remember that in an exchange of like-kind productive use or investment property, a taxpayer who receives boot must recognize gain equal to the lesser of (1) the gain realized or (2) the boot received. In this instance, R received $70,000 in boot − $40,000 (FMV) in bonds and $30,000 by transfer of a mortgage. Hence, R must recognize $70,000 in taxable income; $110,000 of the realized gain remains untaxed (or unrecognized at the present time) by operation of Sec. 1031.

Determining the basis of the apartment complex and the bonds in R's hands, after the exchange, is not so simple. Because any non-like-kind property is not within the protection of Sec. 1031, it is fully taxable and takes as a basis its cost (or fair market value) at the date of the exchange. Therefore, we can begin by stating that the bonds must have a basis in R's hands of $40,000. In other words, the receipt of any property that cannot be part of the nontaxable exchange is automatically given a basis equivalent to what it would have received in any routine business transaction. The basis of the apartment complex is best determined by substituting pertinent data in the formula suggested earlier:

    $50,000 *R's basis in ranch land given up*
+   0 *Boot given*
+   70,000 *Gain recognized*
−   70,000 *Boot received ($40,000 bonds + $30,000 mortgage transferred)*
−   0 *Loss recognized*
= $50,000 *Basis of apartment complex in R's hands*

Using the alternative formula, we can confirm the above calculation:

    $160,000 *FMV of apartment complex*
+   0 *Loss not recognized on the exchange*
−   110,000 *Gain not recognized on the exchange ($180,000 realized − $70,000 recognize*
= $ 50,000 *Basis of apartment complex in R's hands*

Because the apartment complex includes both land (a nondepreciable asset) and buildings (a depreciable asset), it is further necessary to divide the $50,000 basis between the two assets. This is done on a relative fair market value apportionment. If we assume the land is estimated to be worth $32,000 and the buildings $128,000, then one fifth ($32,000/$160,000) of the $50,000 basis, or $10,000, must be allocated to land. The remaining four fifths, or $40,000, must be allocated to the buildings.

The tax questions applicable to taxpayer D can be answered in a similar manner. First, determine the amount of gain realized by D as follows:

$230,000 *Amount realized (FMV of ranch land)*
− 180,000 *Basis given up ($100,000 basis in apartment complex +*
$50,000 basis in bonds + $30,000 in mortgage assumed)
= $ 50,000 *Gain realized (net)*

Observe that the $50,000 gain realized is composed of two parts—a $60,000 gain realized on the apartment complex ($160,000 fair market value less $100,000 in basis) and a $10,000 loss realized on the bonds ($40,000 fair market value less $50,000 basis). Because the bonds cannot be part of a nontaxable exchange, the $10,000 loss is recognized. Because D did not receive any boot, he need not recognize any gain; hence, his $60,000 realized gain on the apartment complex remains unrecognized at this time.
D's basis in the ranch land may be computed as follows:

$150,000 *D's old basis in the apartment and bonds ($100,000 + $50,000)*
+ 30,000 *Boot given (mortgage assumed)*
+ 0 *Gain recognized*
− 0 *Boot received*
− 10,000 *Loss recognized*
= $170,000 *Basis of ranch land in D's hands*

Using the alternative formula, we can again confirm this calculation:

$230,000 *FMV of ranch land*
+ 0 *Loss not recognized on the exchange*
− 60,000 *Gain not recognized on the exchange*
= $170,000 *Basis of ranch land in D's hands*

Note that in the first calculation the bonds were included with the basis of the property given, not with the boot given. They cannot be included in both places without double counting. They are included in the property basis because a later line in the formula takes recognition of the fact that a loss was recognized on this portion of the exchange. In other words, the bonds could have been included with "boot given" (rather than with the basis of old property); however, if that had been done, the bonds would have to be entered at their after-loss recognition value ($40,000), and no further entry under loss recognized would be appropriate because the $10,000 recognized loss is implicitly included with the $40,000 valuation of the bonds.
It should be emphasized that Sec. 1031 harbors significant opportunities for tax-saving ideas. Corporations, businesspeople, and taxpayers of substantial means often find it advantageous to exchange productive use and investment properties rather than to dispose of them in some other manner because of the tax consequences that attach to each disposition. By minimizing the tax cost of the transaction, the taxpayer can maximize the capital value that remains "at work" producing further income. Under some circumstances, of course, the taxpayer may prefer to recognize the entire gain on a disposition in order to get a stepped-up basis on the property received. This is especially

true of depreciable properties that are used by a taxpayer in a high tax bracket.

These provisions, relating to the tax treatment of gain that may be realized on the exchange of productive use or investment property, are simply illustrative of several statutory modifications to the realization concept. They illustrate that realization is a necessary but not a sufficient condition to the recognition of income for tax purposes. They also illustrate how Congress tries, in certain circumstances, to postpone the recognition of income until the taxpayer is most able to pay an income tax.

INVOLUNTARY CONVERSION

Gains realized by a taxpayer because of an involuntary conversion of one or more properties generally are not recognized for tax purposes if the taxpayer replaces the property and elects the deferred treatment. This option to defer the recognition of a realized gain is contained in Sec. 1033.

Statutory Requirements

Section 1033 in its entirety is a relatively long and complex provision. It includes seven subsections, which deal with such special cases as "property sold pursuant to reclamation laws" [Sec. 1033(c)] and "livestock destroyed by disease" [Sec. 1033(d)]. Therefore, it is important for the taxpayer and his or her tax advisor to double-check the Code for special cases whenever they are dealing with an actual involuntary conversion. For purposes of general education, only selected portions of this section need be studied. The following portions are most important:

(a) General Rule. — If property (as a result of its destruction in whole or in part, theft, seizure, or requisition or condemnation or threat or imminence thereof) is compulsorily or involuntarily converted. —
(1) Conversion into similar property. — Into property similar or related in service or use to the property so converted, no gain shall be recognized.
(2) Conversion into money. — Into money or into property not similar or related in service or use to the converted property, the gain (if any) shall be recognized except to the extent hereinafter provided in this paragraph:
(A) Nonrecognition of gain. — If the taxpayer during the period specified in subparagraph (B), for the purpose of replacing the property so converted, purchases other property similar or related in service or use to the property so converted, or purchases stock in the acquisition of control of a corporation owning such other property, at the election of the taxpayer the gain shall be recognized only to the extent that the amount realized upon such conversion (regardless of whether such amount is received in one or more taxable years) exceeds the cost of such other property or such stock. Such election shall be made at such time and in such manner as the Secretary or

his delegate may by regulations prescribe. For purposes of this paragraph—

(i) no property or stock acquired before the disposition of the converted property shall be considered to have been acquired for the purpose of replacing such converted property unless held by the taxpayer on the date of such disposition; and

(ii) the taxpayer shall be considered to have purchased property or stock only if, but for the provisions of subsection (b) of this section, the unadjusted basis of such property or stock would be its cost within the meaning of section 1012.[15]

In common language, the recognition of a gain realized on the involuntary conversion of a taxpayer's property generally can be deferred by operation of Sec. 1033 if the taxpayer converts directly or indirectly (within prescribed time periods) into another property that is "similar or related in service or use" to the property involuntarily converted. These rules apply when property is converted due to a condemnation or to a casualty. If the taxpayer invests less in this replacement property than he or she realized on the involuntary conversion, the excess funds retained represent a wherewithal to pay, and the taxpayer is taxed accordingly. If the proceeds received in the involuntary conversion are less than the taxpayer's basis in the property destroyed, the realized loss is recognized for tax purposes unless the property is held for personal use. (In the latter case, a loss can be recognized only if it results from a casualty or theft.) One especially interesting aspect of this provision is that it permits the taxpayer to acquire "similar or related" property indirectly by acquiring an 80% voting interest in a corporation that owns such property. In the routine involuntary conversion, the taxpayer receives an indemnification payment from an insurance company (or a government unit that is condemning the property) and then reinvests this payment in comparable property.

"Similar or Related in Service or Use"

One of the more perplexing phrases in Sec. 1033 is that which requires the replacement property to be "similar or related in service or use" to the property involuntarily converted. Although this requirement may appear to be equivalent to the like-kind requirement of Sec. 1031, the two have been interpreted quite differently. The criterion of "similar or related in service or use" for most involuntary conversions has been interpreted by the I.R.S. and the courts to mean functionally related. For example, a delivery truck must be replaced with another delivery truck, an apartment complex must be replaced with another apartment complex, and so on. In the case of *McCaffrey* v. *Commissioner,* the court found that replacement of a rented parking lot with a rented warehouse was not within the meaning of this phrase.[16] The courts

[15]Section 1033(a).
[16]275 F.2d 27 (1960).

have permitted the replacement of used property with new property as long as the two were functionally related.

Subsection 1033(g) provides a special exception to the "similar or related in service or use" test for condemned real property held for productive use in a trade or business or for investment purposes. That special exception says that "property of a like kind . . . shall be treated as property similar or related in service or use to the property so converted." In other words, Subsection 1033(g) effectively substitutes the like-kind test of Sec. 1031 for the "similar or related in service or use" test of Sec. 1033 in the case of condemned real property. This provision was enacted when acquisitions for the interstate highway system were being made. The purpose of the change was to reduce disputes over the qualification of the replacement property.

Time Requirements

If the taxpayer replaces involuntarily converted property indirectly—that is, if the taxpayer goes from property to cash to similar property—he or she must acquire the replacement property within prescribed time periods if the taxpayer wishes to defer the recognition of gain. These requirements are stipulated in Sec. 1033(a)(2)(B) as follows:

> (B) Period within which property must be replaced.—The period referred to in subparagraph (A) shall be the period beginning with the date of the disposition of the converted property, or the earliest date of the threat or imminence of requisition or condemnation of the converted property, whichever is the earlier, and ending—
> (i) two years after the close of the first taxable year in which any part of the gain upon the conversion is realized, or
> (ii) subject to such terms and conditions as may be specified by the Secretary or his delegate, at the close of such later date as the Secretary or his delegate may designate on application by the taxpayer. Such application shall be made at such time and in such manner as the Secretary or his delegate may by regulations prescribe.

In other words, the taxpayer must make the replacement sometime during a period beginning with the earlier of (1) the date of disposition of the converted property or (2) "the date of the beginning of the threat or imminence of requisition or condemnation,"[17] and ending (a) two years after the close of the taxable year in which any part of the gain was first realized or (b) at a later date if such an agreement has been reached between the taxpayer and the I.R.S. A special rule applies to the involuntary conversion of real property used in a trade or business or held for investment. For condemned real property (only), the replacement period is three years, not the two-year period applicable to all other properties. Generally, the I.R.S. is

---

[17]Regulation Sec. 1.1033(a)-2(c)(3).

lenient in granting extensions beyond the periods allowed by the law, especially when taxpayers can show that they have made a bona fide effort to acquire replacement property.

The few practical problems that arise in relation to timely replacements of involuntarily converted property typically arise in conjunction with condemnation proceedings. It is sometimes difficult to know exactly what event should be deemed the first threat or imminence of requisition or condemnation. Rumors may precede actual condemnation action by a governmental body by several years. Obviously, if a taxpayer makes a direct replacement with similar property, time requirements cannot be a problem.

An Illustration

The following assumed facts illustrate the most important aspects of Sec. 1033. Taxpayer F's warehouse was completely destroyed by fire on the morning of March 1, 19x1. This warehouse had a basis in F's hands of $200,000; it had been insured for its estimated fair market value of $250,000. On October 1, 19x1, the insurance company settled the claim by paying taxpayer F $240,000. Although Taxpayer F realized a $40,000 gain on this involuntary conversion in 19x1, it is not necessary to recognize that gain if (1) sometime before December 31, 19x3, F replaces the destroyed warehouse with another warehouse costing $240,000 or more or (2) during the same time period F acquires for $240,000 or more an 80% voting control of a corporation that owns such a warehouse.

If taxpayer F replaces the warehouse with another costing less than $240,000, some part or all of the realized gain must be recognized. The following table suggests the importance of the wherewithal-to-pay concept in determining the amount of gain to be recognized in this situation:

Insurance Proceeds	Gain Realized	Amount Reinvested	Gain Recognized
$240,000	$40,000	$210,000	$30,000
240,000	40,000	150,000	40,000
240,000	40,000	260,000	0

In short, the recognized gain is always the lesser of the gain realized or the portion of the insurance proceeds not reinvested in replacement property.

If we modify the above illustration and assume that the insurance company paid taxpayer F only $170,000 (because of a coinsurance clause or some other requirement), it is immaterial whether F replaces the property or not. Under any assumption, F would recognize the $30,000 loss realized.

Basis Adjustment

If a taxpayer properly elects to defer the recognition of a gain realized on an involuntary conversion, the replacement property takes a substituted basis. Because boot ordinarily is not a problem in the involuntary conversion cases, the basis of the replacement property is readily computed using the following formula:

| Cost of replacement property | − | Gain not recognized on the involuntary conversion | = | Substituted basis of replacement property |

This formula is essentially equivalent to the Method II formula on page 17-16, excluding the possibility of nonrecognition of losses. As seen in the basis adjustment process, the intention of Sec. 1033 is to permit only a temporary deferment of gain.

PROBLEMS

1. Which of the following events would increase a taxpayer's "taxable income?" Explain each answer.
   a. Finding a $100 bill on the sidewalk.
   b. "Scalping" four 50-yard-line seats at a big football game for $100 each. The tickets cost $6 each. (Scalping tickets is illegal in the state in which they were sold and the was game played.)
   c. Having a $100 debt forgiven by a business creditor. (The creditor hoped, in this manner, to encourage you to do more business with him in the future.)
   d. Embezzling $100 from your employer's check-cashing fund.
   e. Having a $100 personal debt gratuitously forgiven by your brother.
   f. Selling a fishing boat for $100. (The boat originally cost you $200.)

2. Distinguish between realized income and recognized income for tax purposes.

3. What is the major difference between realized income for tax purposes and realized income in financial accounting?

4. Several years ago, John March, a calendar-year taxpayer, purchased a tract of land at a cost of $100,000. The unimproved realty was held as an investment. The land appreciated in value, and on December 19, 1985, John sold it for $400,000. The purchaser paid John $100,000 cash on December 29, 1985, and, in accordance with the sales contract, a second installment of $300,000, plus interest for the two-month period, was paid on February 27, 1986. How is John's income taxed?

5. Tom Richards sold a delivery truck for $8,000 on July 1, 1987, to a buyer on an installment sale. The truck originally cost Tom $15,000 and was fully depreciated on the date of sale. The terms of the sale provide that Tom will receive $4,000 as a down payment on July 1, 1987, and $2,000 plus interest on both July 1, 1988, and July 1, 1989.
   a. How much gain does Tom recognize from the sale in 1982?
   b. How much gain does Tom recognize from the sale in 1988? 1989?

6. Candy Corporation started business in 1987 and elected a calendar taxable year. On March 1, 1987, it sells real property used in its trade or business for $500,000. Candy Corporation received no money down and will receive five equal annual payments of $100,000 (plus interest) beginning in 1988. The adjusted basis for Candy Corporation's assets (excluding the installment obligation) on December 31, 1987, is $1,000,000. The corporation's average quarterly debt is $600,000. Candy Corporation's adjusted basis for the realty is $200,000. Assume this is the

only installment sale the corporation has made.

a. What is Candy Corporation's allocable installment indebtedness for 1987?

b. What is Candy Corporation's recognized gain in 1987 as a result of the sale?

7. An investor is considering the sale of 1,000 shares of IBM stock in September of the current year. The sales price will be $80,000. The taxpayer acquired the shares several years ago for $30,000. Two possible methods of payment have been proposed: (1) a payment of $20,000 in September when the sale is completed, and the remainder, plus interest at 12%, due in one year, and (2) no payment in the current year, and the $80,000, plus 12% interest, due in September of next year. How would the income be recognized under each alternative according to the general rules of the Code? What alternatives exist for recognition of the income?

8. In January of the current year, Maude Hughes sold 100 acres of unimproved real estate for $1,200 per acre (net of all selling costs). She acquired the property ten years ago for $500 per acre. Three years ago, she mortgaged the property, and at the time of the sale the mortgage balance was $30,000. The purchaser agreed to pay $15,000 cash at the closing, assume the mortgage, and pay the remainder in five $15,000 installments (plus interest at 10%) annually on the closing date.

a. What is Maude's realized gain on this disposition?

b. How will the gain be recognized?

c. Does Maude have any alternatives to the treatment in part b?

9. Dusty Rhodes, a road contractor, owned a light airplane used in his business. This plane had an adjusted basis of $8,000 when he exchanged it for a smaller plane with a fair market value of $10,000. Dusty received $3,000 cash when he made this trade. Straight-line depreciation claimed on the old plane since acquisition totaled $10,000.

a. How much gain was realized on this exchange?

b. What minimum gain must be recognized on this exchange?

c. Is the recognized gain a capital gain, ordinary income, or part of Sec. 1231? Explain.

d. What is Dusty's tax basis in the new plane?

10. Assume the following facts apply to a like-kind exchange of productive use or investment property and complete the schedule:

Adjusted Basis of Property Surrendered	Cash Given (or Received)	FMV of Property Received	Recognized Gain (or Loss)	Basis of New Property
a. $19,000	$5,000	$30,000	$_____	$_____
b. 8,000	(4,000)	20,000	_____	_____
c. 17,000	0	25,000	_____	_____
d. 17,000	0	15,000	_____	_____

11. Tora Corporation owned a machine, used in its business, that had cost $6,000 and on which depreciation of $2,200 had been taken up to January 2 this year. On that date, Tora exchanged the old machine for a new one to serve the same purpose. Using these facts, in each of the following cases compute (1) the recognized gain or loss on the exchange and (2) the tax basis of the new machine:

a. Value of new asset, $4,000; no boot given or received

b. Value of new asset, $3,000; boot received, $400

c. Value of new asset, $3,000; boot given, $300

d. Value of new asset, $4,000; boot received, $300

      e. Value of new asset, $4,000; boot given, $300

      f. Value of new asset, $3,700; boot received, $300

12. On October 10, 1946, Rancher Alpha purchased 500 acres of land on the Colorado River for $40,000. He used this land to graze cattle until November 1, this year, when he traded the ranch for a small complex of land and buildings that had just been completed in Nearby City. This complex was intended to constitute a neighborhood shopping center. At the tie of the trade, the estimated fair market value of the ranch was $250,000; that of the shopping center, $300,000. To equate the exchange, Rancher Alpha gave the builder 1,000 shares of Tractor stock, which had cost him $20,000 in 1965; they were worth $50,000 at the time of the exchange.

    Builder Beta, the contractor who constructed the shopping center complex, works independently with a small group of people. She makes her living by building homes and office buildings and selling them to interested parties. Her construction cost in this particular complex was $270,000; she started construction on February 4, last year.

   a. Relative to Rancher Alpha:

     (1) What amount of gain (or loss) did he realize on the exchange of the ranch and Tractor shares for the shopping center?

     (2) What minimal amount of gain (or loss) must he recognize on this same exchange?

     (3) What is the tax basis in the shopping center after the exchange has been completed, assuming he elects to pay a minimum tax now?

     (4) What is his date basis in the shopping center?

     (5) Is the shopping center a capital asset in Rancher Alpha's hands after the exchange? Explain.

     (6) Can you see any reason why Rancher Alpha may prefer to make this a taxable (rather than a nontaxable) event? Explain.

   b. Relative to Builder Beta:

     (1) What amount of gain (or loss) did she realize on the exchange of the shopping center for the ranch and Tractor stock?

     (2) What amount of gain (or loss) must she recognize on the exchange?

     (3) What is her tax basis in the ranch after the exchange has been completed?

     (4) What is her tax basis in the Tractor shares after exchange?

     (5) What is her date basis in the ranch and the shares?

     (6) Is the ranch a capital asset to Beta? Explain.

     (7) Are the Tractor shares a capital asset to Beta? Explain.

13. Sam Jones has operated a dairy farm on the outskirts of a large city for a number of years. He owns 200 acres of land for which he originally paid $150 per acre. The land is adjacent to a railway track, and a freeway through the area (but not on Sam's place) was recently completed. The Boyce Corporation has approached Sam about buying his place to use as the site for a large manufacturing plant. They offered Sam $1,000 per acre. Sam intends to continue in the dairy business but does not want to sell his land because he will get less than its value after paying the tax. Devise a plan that allows Boyce to obtain Sam's land and leaves Sam without diminution of the value of his investment in land.

14. Bracket Corporation's board of directors voted to close Plant 12 located in a congested area of New Jersey and to open the same operation in a semirural setting somewhere in the southwestern region of the United States. After making this decision, Bracket sent its secretary and treasurer on a search for the new plant site. The two corporate officers eventually selected an ideal 80-acre tract that was

for sale for $75,000. Instead of arranging an outright purchase of the new site, the men contracted with a New York broker, who agreed to acquire the 80 acres and to exchange it plus $5,000 cash for Bracket's old Plant 12. The parties agreed that the approximate fair market value of Plant 12 was $85,000 — $52,000 for the building and $32,000 for the land. Bracket's adjusted basis in the old building was $24,000; in the old land, $30,000. The broker acquired the new 80-acre tract for $72,000.

a. What amount of taxable gain must Bracket Corporation report in the year it completed this exchange?

b. What kind of gain—ordinary income, capital gain, or Sec. 1231 gain—does Bracket Corporation report because of this transaction?

c. What is Bracket's tax basis in the (new) 80-acre tract?

d. Why might Bracket Corporation have preferred to purchase the new site directly from the owner had it included a building as well as land? Explain.

e. What amount of taxable income must the New York broker report because of his role in this exchange?

f. Would the broker's income be ordinary income or capital gain? Why?

15. For each of the independent situations below, determine (1) the amount of gain or loss realized; (2) the amount of gain or loss recognized; and (3) the tax basis of the new land. Assume that during the current year the taxpayer exchanged one parcel of farm land for another; further assume that the taxpayer had held the original land for six years and that it had an adjusted tax basis of $50,000 at the time of the exchange.

a. Taxpayer received only the new land, which had a fair market value of $60,000.

b. Taxpayer received the new land, with a fair market value of $60,000, and $15,000 cash.

c. Taxpayer gave the other party to the exchange $5,000 cash in addition to the land and received in return land worth $45,000.

d. Taxpayer received only the new land, which had a fair market value of $60,000, and the other party to the exchange assumed taxpayer's $20,000 mortgage on the old land.

e. Taxpayer took the new land and assumed a $10,000 mortgage against that land. The other party to the exchange also assumed taxpayer's $6,000 mortgage on the old land. The new land has an estimated value of $60,000.

16. On July 22, this year, taxpayer exchanged 170 shares of Otis common stock for 300 shares of Lifter. Taxpayer's basis in the Otis shares was $850. Lifter shares were selling for $7 per share on the day of the exchange. Neither corporation was involved in any kind of reorganization.

a. What gain or loss must taxpayer recognize in this year?

b. What is taxpayer's basis in the 300 shares of Lifter stock?

17. Items a–h are eight suggested property exchanges. Which of the eight would not wholly qualify as a (tax-free) like-kind exchange? Explain any of the exchanges that would partially qualify. Assume that none of the property is an inventory item.

a. Gold jewelry for Dodge van. (Both for personal use.)

b. Ranch land for fully equipped restaurant (land, building, and equipment).

c. Stallion for a gelding. (Both used in business.)

d. Sailboat for a racehorse. (Both held as investment properties.)

e. Corporate stock for corporate bond.

f. Personal residence for a rental property.

g. Business truck for gold bullion. (Gold held for investment.)

h. Apartment house for bulldozer. (Apartment is investment; bulldozer is productive-use property.)

18. UAS Corporation exchanged land it owned near Tempe, Arizona, for other land near Provo, Utah. UAS's basis in the Arizona land was $800,000; it had a $750,000 mortgage outstanding against this property. The other party to the exchange, YUB Corporation, assumed the $750,000 mortgage. To complete the exchange, UAS Corporation paid YUB Corporation $300,000 cash (boot). The Utah land was valued at $850,000 and was clear of debt; the Arizona land was valued at $1,300,000. Assuming that both properties were held by UAS Corporation as an investment, what taxable gain, if any, must UAS recognize?

19. Assume the following facts apply to an involuntary conversion of business property and complete the schedule:

Adjusted Basis of Property Destroyed	Insurance Proceeds	Amount Expended for Immediate Replacement of Property	Recognized Gain (or Loss)	Basis of New Property
a. $26,000	$16,000	$24,000	$_____	$_____
b. 17,000	21,000	20,000	$_____	$_____
c. 20,000	25,000	27,000	$_____	$_____

20. Investo Corporation purchased several acres of land in 1936 for $400. This year, the state government took the land for highway right of way, and the taxpayer was awarded $21,000 for the land. Investo first received notification of the perspective conversion on January 4 and received full payment for the land on November 30. In each of the following cases, compute (1) the recognized gain or loss on the conversion under Sec. 1033 and (2) the tax basis of the replacement property in those cases when the property was replaced:
a. The land was not replaced.
b. New land was purchased on June 1 for $16,000.
c. New land was purchased on December 1 for $22,000.
d. New land was purchased on December 1 for $10,200.
e. New land was purchased on December 1 of the following year for $24,000.
f. New land was purchased on June 10 of the second following year for $30,000.

21. Categorize each of the following as (1) a like-kind exchange, (2) a replacement of similar property, or (3) neither:
a. Inventory of a trade or business is exchanged for an automobile to be used in a trade or business.
b. Land and a building used in a trade or business are exchanged for unimproved land that will be held for investment.
c. Common stock held by an individual is traded for land that will be held as an investment.
d. Manufacturing machinery that produces metal tanks is destroyed by fire; proceeds are used to acquire machines that produce combat boots.
e. An office building held as rental property is condemned by the city for a new park. Proceeds are used to acquire farmland, which is rented immediately following acquisition.
f. A dump truck used by a dirt contractor is exchanged for a family car.
g. Machinery that produces farm equipment is exchanged for office furniture that will be placed in rental property.

    h. Unimproved land is exchanged for machinery to be used in a trade or business.

    i. Four bulls are exchanged for 12 heifers by a rancher.

22. State whether each of the following statements is true or false. If false, explain why.

    a. The "like-kind" requirement of Sec. 1031 is generally interpreted more narrowly than the "similar or related in service or use" requirement of Sec. 1033.

    b. Any item of inventory must be considered as boot in an exchange that otherwise qualifies under Sec. 1031.

    c. An exchange of realty for personalty may sometimes qualify as a "like-kind" exchange under Sec. 1031.

    d. Loss may not be recognized following an involuntary conversion if the taxpayer reinvests all proceeds in similar property within the time period specified in Sec. 1033.

    e. Giving boot in a like-kind exchange does not necessitate the recognition of gain by the taxpayer giving the boot.

23. On April 18, Tom's Cleaners, Inc., lost one of its delivery vans in an auto accident. The van had an adjusted basis of $3,200 at the time of the accident. Straight-line depreciation of $4,000 had been claimed on the van before the accident. Insurance proceeds of $5,000 were received on May 1. On April 20, Tom's Cleaners, Inc., purchased a new delivery van for $8,000.

    a. What amount of gain did Tom's Cleaners, Inc., realize because of the accident?

    b. What minimum amount of gain must Tom's Cleaners, Inc., recognize because of the accident?

    c. If Tom's Cleaners, Inc., recognizes only the minimum amount of gain, what is the tax basis in the van purchased on April 20?

    d. What maximum amount of gain may Tom's Cleaners, Inc., recognize because of the accident? What kind of gain is this?

    e. If Tom's Cleaners, Inc., recognizes the amount of gain, what is its tax basis in the van purchased on April 20?

SUPPLEMENTAL PROBLEMS

24. Art Stahls, a cash-basis taxpayer, began his career as a professional writer in 19x1. He spent most of his first year writing a short but exciting novel, which he attempted to sell to a publisher during November and December. Although several publishers expressed an interest in this novel, only one made Art a firm offer of $3,000 for the manuscript. In March 19x2, he received a second offer, which gave him the option of receiving $5,000 ($3,000 immediately and $2,000 in November 19x3) or a 15% royalty based on actual sales. Art accepted the fixed-price option and received both payments as agreed.

Year	Economics	Accounting	Taxation
19x1			
19x2			
19x3			
Total			

    a. Draw up a table like the one above to indicate, as best you can, how each discipline—economics, accounting, and tax law—would likely "recognize" Art's income for 19x1–19x3.

b. Explain the differences in the annual incomes recognized by each discipline, as detailed above.

c. In what year (or years) did Art "realize" his $5,000 income?

d. What changes in the schedule you made for item "a" would be appropriate had Art elected the 15% royalty rather than the fixed fee? (Explain possible reasons for such changes.)

25. In April, Lucky was notified that he had won a preliminary round of a sweepstakes contest and that his $2 (cost) ticket had already won $8,000. By winning the preliminary round, he became eligible for the Grand Prize. Before the final selection was made, Lucky gave his winning ticket to his two children, making clear that they could have as a gift any amounts paid on the ticket. Lucky's ticket was selected as the sweepstakes winner, and the children were paid the $75,000 Grand Prize.

a. When was the $75,000 income realized? How much, if any, of the $75,000 that the children received was a gift and thus not subject to the income tax?

b. What amount of income, if any, must Lucky report?

c. What amount of income, if any, must Lucky's children report?

d. Would the taxable income be ordinary income or capital gain?

26. Emma Reynard owned acreage on the outskirts of Modest City, California, which she decided to sell. Her basis in this property was only $50,000, although the property had an estimated fair market value of $150,000. After trying to sell the property for three or four months, Reynard was approached by a realtor who suggested that she exchange her acreage (property A) for another property (B), which was also valued at approximately $150,000. The realtor made this sugges-tion because he had good reason to believe that he could quickly sell property B for Reynard and thus earn a substantial commission. Reynard made the exchange, and two weeks later the realtor sold property B for $160,000, of which the buyer paid $25,000 down.

Reynard reported the exchange of property A for property B as a Sec. 1031 (nontaxable) exchange and the sale of property B as an installment sale (under the provisions of Sec. 453). Is this a correct tax accounting for the facts indicated? If not, how should these events be reported, and what are the tax consequences of the alternative reporting? Support your conclusion with a citation to a case that involved facts similar to those recounted above.

27. Which of the following eight transactions constitute a realization event that ordinarily triggers the recognition of gain by a cash-basis taxpayer? To understand the question better, assume that the property involved is the taxpayer's private residence with a fair market value of $100,000 and a tax basis of $60,000.

a. Sold for $100,000 cash.

b. Sold for $40,000 cash and $60,000 promissory notes.

c. Exchanged for speculative land worth $100,000.

d. Mortgaged home for $75,000 cash. (Invested cash in stock market.)

e. Gave home to daughter and her husband.

f. Left home to church (a charitable organization) by will, at death.

g. Converted personal residence to a rental property.

h. Exchanged for corporate stocks valued at $100,000.

28. In each of the following independent transactions, (1) state the amount of gain or loss the taxpayer must recognize this year; (2) if gain or loss must be recognized,

indicate whether that gain or loss is an element of ordinary income, Sec. 1231 gain or loss, or a capital gain or loss; and (3) determine the tax basis of the newly acquired property.

a. Tractor used in taxpayer's business was totally wrecked on May 16. Insurance proceeds were $7,400. Adjusted basis of tractor at time of the accident was $5,900 ($2,500 straight-line depreciation had been claimed in prior years). Taxpayer invested $8,300 in new tractor 11 days after the accident.

b. Taxpayer's warehouse was destroyed by fire on September 4. Insurance proceeds amounted to $34,000. Taxpayer's adjusted basis in warehouse was $40,000; $10,000 straight-line depreciation had been claimed in 5 prior years. New warehouse, purchased within 30 days of the fire, cost $39,000.

c. Taxpayer exchanged 1,000 acres of Arizona ranch land for a duplex in Tempe. Taxpayer had inherited the land from her father's estate in 1971 when the land was valued at $30 an acre. The duplex had an estimated value of $46,000. Taxpayer, recently divorced, planned to live in half the duplex and to rent the other half. What amount of gain or loss, if any, must taxpayer recognize in this year because of this exchange? What is taxpayer's basis in the half of the duplex in which she lives? in the half that she rents?

CHAPTER 18

Other Nontaxable Exchanges

> Congress has found it desirable to provide a large number of special rules having to do with the timing of income and deductions which, for the most part, make no specific reference to "the method of accounting on the basis of which the taxpayer regularly computes his income in keeping his books."
> Leslie Mills, 1959 Compendium

RECOGNITION POSTPONED: OTHER COMMON NONTAXABLE EXCHANGES

As noted in Chapter 17, the wherewithal-to-pay concept provides the underlying support for many of the important provisions of the Internal Revenue Code. The consequence of each section is to establish unequivocally that a specified transaction, which might otherwise trigger the realization and recognition of a taxable gain or a deductible loss, is treated as a wholly or partially nontaxable event. Sections 1031 and 1033 are particularly good illustrations of the wherewithal-to-pay concept. In this chapter, we will discuss other statutory provisions that provide for postponement of a realized gain.

In addition to this orderly collection of special rules that may defer the recognition of realized taxable income (or loss), the Code contains other sections that reach a similar result but are scattered throughout the Code. Two such sections (1091 and 267) are examined briefly in this chapter to illustrate how the wherewithal-to-pay concept has also been used to deny the recognition of a realized loss for tax purposes.

REPLACING A PRINCIPAL RESIDENCE

Section 1034 provides a mandatory, special rule that defers any gain a taxpayer realizes on the sale or exchange of his or her principal residence. As usual in tax matters, certain conditions must be satisfied before this special rule applies.

Statutory Requirements

This Code section is a relatively long and complex provision. The most important and common restricting conditions, however, are stated in Subsection 1034(a), which reads as follows:

> (a) Nonrecognition of Gain. — If property (in this section called "old residence") used by the taxpayer as his principal residence is sold by him, and within a period beginning 2 years before the date of such sale and ending 2 years after such date, property (in this section called "new residence") is purchased and used by the taxpayer as his principal residence, gain (if any) from such sale shall be recognized only to the extent that the taxpayer's adjusted sales price (as defined in subsection (b)) of the old residence exceeds the taxpayer's cost of purchasing the new residence.

The remaining subsections deal with many special cases including the tenant–stockholder in a cooperative housing corporation [1034(f)]; members of the armed forces [1034(h)]; and condemnation of homes [1034(i)]. Thus, a tax advisor must always determine if any special rule might apply to a particular situation. The general rules, however, are adequately covered in Subsection 1034(a).

The important consequence of that subsection is its provision that under specified circumstances a (pure) capital gain that has been realized need not be recognized for tax purposes in the year it is first realized. The important conditions for this result include occupancy of the old residence as a principal residence prior to sale; acquisition of a new principal residence within 24 months (generally) from the date of sale of the old residence; and an investment in the new residence in an amount equal to or greater than the "adjusted sales price" of the old residence.

These general rules, as broadly stated above, are replete with exceptions and definitional distinctions not apparent to the uninitiated. For example, a taxpayer who owns more than one home can receive the special treatment only on the home that constitutes his or her "principal residence." The period of time a taxpayer has to acquire a new home is extended to four years if the taxpayer is a U.S. citizen working overseas or the taxpayer serves on extended active duty with the U.S. military services in the interim. The term principal residence includes condominiums and cooperative apartments, as well as mobile homes and houseboats. Finally, the meanings of "adjusted sales price" and "selling expenses" are specifically detailed in the Code and the related Regulations.

An Illustration

Although the special exceptions and restricted definitions noted above can be most important in particular fact cases, a thorough understanding of each of these is not necessary for an appreciation of the general application of Sec. 1034. The important general concept can be demonstrated simply, as in Figure 18-1.

Suppose that a taxpayer purchased a home 10 years ago for $48,000 and sold this same home this year for $64,500 cash. Without Sec. 1034, the taxpayer would have to recognize a taxable gain of $16,500. Because of Sec. 1034, however, he or she may not have to recognize part or all of the gain if a new home is purchased within 24 months. Let us assume, in fact, that the taxpayer paid a $3,000 realtor's commission on the sale of the old home; that fixing-up expenses of $1,500 were incurred preparing the old home for sale; and $70,000 was invested in a new home 5 months later. Given these additional facts, and substituting a pertinent data in the diagram, we can conclude that this taxpayer need not recognize any of the gain this year and that the tax basis of the new home is $56,500. The calculation is shown in Figure 18-2.

The relation of Sec. 1034 to the wherewithal-to-pay concept is demonstrated even more vividly if we assume, in our example, that the taxpayer invested only $58,500 in the new home. In that event, the taxpayer would be forced to recognize a gain of $1,500 ($60,000 adjusted sales price less $58,500 cost of new home). In a very important sense, this $1,500 of recognized taxable

FIGURE **18-1**   Diagram of Section 1034

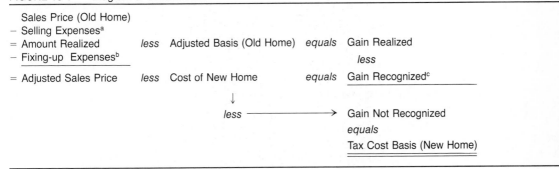

[a]Perhaps the most important "selling expense" is the broker's commission. See Reg. Sec. 1.1034-1(b)(4).
[b]"Fixing-up expenses" are defined rather narrowly in Reg. Sec. 1.1034-1(b)(6). The phrase refers to expenses incurred to help sell a property and includes such things as painting and papering a home. To qualify, however, these expenses must be incurred and paid within specified time periods. See a tax service for further details.
[c]Only if > 0; also, "gain recognized" can never be > "gain realized."

FIGURE **18-2**   Applying Section 1034

$64,500 Sales Price (Old Home)		
− 3,000 Selling Expenses		

= $61,500 Amount Realized	− $48,000 Adjusted Basis (Old Home)	= $13,500 Gain Realized
− 1,500 Fixing-up Expenses		*less*
= $60,000 Adjusted Sales Price	− $70,000 Cost of New Home	= 0 Gain Recognized

less

$13,500 Gain Not Recognized
equals
$56,500 Tax Basis of New Home

income equals this person's wherewithal to pay. The calculation process accounts for the fact that the taxpayer had selling expenses and that he or she purchased another home. Even after considering all of these facts, however, this taxpayer had $1,500 "left over," which therefore must be recognized as taxable income.

Notice also that the effect of Sec. 1034 (alone) does not permanently excuse the taxpayer from paying income taxes on this realized gain. The technique used to defer the gain temporarily is the basis adjustment. Although the taxpayer in the original example paid $70,000 for the new home, the tax basis in the new property is reduced by the amount of gain not recognized on the sale of the old home. Thus, if and when the taxpayer decides to sell the "new" home, and if at that time the taxpayer does not purchase another residence that costs at least as much as the adjusted sales price of the home sold, then the taxpayer must recognize the gain previously deferred. To illustrate, assume all facts as originally stated and further assume that 2 years later this taxpayer sold the new home for $71,000 without incurring any additional brokerage fees or fixing-up expenses. If the taxpayer decides to reside in a rented apartment for the next few years, then he or she must recognize at that time a $14,500 gain on the sale of the home. This recognized gain would consist of the $13,500 gain deferred on the original sale and the additional $1,000 gain attributable to the last home ($71,000 sales price less $70,000 cost). Because the taxpayer elected not to reinvest in a new home, he or she supposedly has the wherewithal to pay taxes on the entire gain at the later date.

Special Rule for Older Taxpayers

Section 121 provides an exclusion for part or all of the gain realized on the sale of a residence by a taxpayer 55 years of age or older if the property has been the taxpayer's principal residence for three out of the past five years. Although this special provision is really an exceptiion to the wherewithal-to pay concept of this chapter, it must be part of any discussion relative to the gain from the sale of a personal residence.

If a taxpayer is 55 years of age or older when his or her residence is sold; if that sale (or exchange) was made after July 26, 1981; and if the taxpayer at the time of the sale has resided in the house for at least three of the five years prior to sale, then up to $125,000 of the gain realized may be permanently excluded. To illustrate, let us assume that a 56-year-old taxpayer sold the home in Figure 18-2 and that he or she qualified for and elected to apply Sec. 121 privileges. The entire $13,500 gain realized could be permanently excluded from income even if the taxpayer did not purchase another home. This is, however, a once-in-a-lifetime election. If the realized gain exceeds $125,000, only that amount can be excluded from gross income.

The special $125,000 exclusion for older taxpayers is intended to help avoid the taxation of the only savings available for retirement for many low-income taxpayers. The often illusory (monetary) gain realized on the sale of a home owned for many years may thus be doubly protected—by the "rollover" provisions of Sec. 1034 and by the exclusion of Sec. 121.

A Comparison

The observant student will have noted many similarities between the Code provisions for the deferral of gain on the sale of a residence (Sec. 1034), the deferral of gain on the exchange of productive use or investment properties (Sec. 1031), and the deferral of gain on an involuntary conversion (Sec. 1033). The most important similarity is that in each instance the gain that may be recognized is determined in large measure by the taxpayer's wherewithal to pay following a given transaction or series of transactions. Table 18-1 depicts the major similarities and differences between these Code sections.

OTHER LESS COMMON NONTAXABLE EXCHANGES

We have now discussed three of the common nontaxable exchanges, which are of general interest to most taxpayers; the following provisions are of limited interest.

Section 1032 provides that a corporate taxpayer need not recognize any taxable gain when it receives money or other property in exchange for its own stock. Since 1954, this conclusion has been equally valid if the shares issued are treasury or original issue.

By operation of Sec. 1036, a stockholder need not recognize any taxable gain on the exchange of stock for essentially identical stock of the same corporation. Thus, a taxpayer may avoid any recognition of gain realized on the exchange of common shares for common shares in the same corporation or preferred shares for preferred shares in the same corporation. One important conclusion of this provision is that gains that might be considered realized by the declaration of a stock split are not recognized for tax purposes.

Section 1035 provides for nonrecognition of gain or loss realized on the exchange of certain life insurance policies. The nontaxable exchanges possible under this provision include those of contracts of life insurance for other contracts of life insurance, for endowment insurance, or for an annuity

TABLE **18-1**

COMPARISON OF SECTIONS 1031, 1033, and 1034

Comparison	Sec. 1031: Exchange of Productive-use or Investment Property	Sec. 1033: Involuntary Conversions	Sec. 1034: Sale of a Residence
1. Gain recognized, if any, is the lesser of the gain realized or . . .	Boot received	Proceeds not reinvested in similar property	Proceeds not reinvested in another residence
2. Indirect as well as direct conversion permitted?	No (but short delay is possible)	Yes	Yes
3. Time allowed for replacement?	None; must be a more or less direct exchange	Generally two years after end of year gain was first realized	Generally two years
4. Is provision mandatory or elective?	Mandatory	Elective	Mandatory with gains
5. Can loss be recognized if realized?	No; but basis carryover is permitted	Yes, always	Never; home is a purely personal asset

contract; endowment insurance for other endowment insurance, as long as payments under the new contract begin no later than they would have under the old contract; endowment insurance for an annuity contract; and annuity contracts for other annuity contracts.

Section 1037 permits the tax-free exchange of certain U.S. obligations. Special rules apply to the exchange of U.S. obligations issued at a discount.

Section 1039 authorizes the nonrecognition of gain realized on the sale of a low-income housing unit to its tenants or occupants or to a nonprofit organization formed solely for the benefit of such persons. Before nonrecognition privileges are granted, the sale must be approved by the Secretary of Housing and Urban Development. The seller has one year after the end of the year in which the sale was made to reinvest in another qualified housing project. Failure to reinvest in a qualified project within the prescribed time period, or failure to reinvest the entire proceeds of the sale, causes the recognition of all or part of the gain realized. Following the usual rules, the cost basis of the new property is its cost less any gain not recognized on the related sale. The holding periods of the two properties generally tack. However, if the investment in the new property exceeds the amount realized on the sale of the old property, the additional investment is treated as a separate property with a new holding period for purposes of depreciation recapture under Sec. 1250.

A relatively new common nontaxable exchange, Sec. 1040, allows an executor to satisfy a pecuniary bequest with an appreciated carryover basis property without triggering the recognition of gain in the estate. This special treatment does not apply, however, to any gain occurring after the property is valued for estate purposes and before the date it is distributed.

Anyone interested in the many specific details applicable to Secs. 1032, 1035, 1036, 1037, 1038, 1039, or 1040 should consult a current and authoritative tax service. Only the highlights of these provisions have been noted here.

LOSSES AND WHEREWITHAL TO PAY

The wherewithal-to-pay concept seems to have pertinence also to the nonrecognition of losses in certain circumstances. The loss realized on a "wash sale" is not recognized for tax purposes even though it would be recognized for accounting purposes. A wash sale occurs if a taxpayer elects to repurchase (within 30 days before or after a sale) securities "substantially identical" to those just sold at a loss; it is generally apparent that the taxpayer has not suffered a real economic loss. His or her early repurchase of substantially identical securities suggests that this taxpayer was quite willing to retain a basic investment in a particular security and that the apparent reason for selling the security was solely to realize a loss that might reduce reported taxable income. Under these circumstances, the Code provides in Sec. 1091 that the realized loss will not be recognized. This treatment can be justified because the taxpayer did not suffer an actual reduction in wherewithal to pay by going through the formalities of a sale and almost immediate repurchase of identical securities. If the taxpayer is willing to switch the investment to shares of another firm in the same industry, then he or she can recognize the loss, because these shares are not considered "substantially identical" to those sold. Gains on wash sales are recognized.

For essentially the same reasons, Sec. 267 denies a taxpayer the right to deduct a loss realized on the sale of property to a "related taxpayer." Among the relationships specified are family members and corporations in which the seller owns an interest of 50% or more. In the interest of equity, the related purchaser can add any disallowed loss to the tax basis of the acquired property, but only for purposes of determining gain.

A third possible illustration of the importance of wherewithal to pay and the recognition of losses is implicit in the statutory provisions for a net operating loss. The details of this provision are discussed in Chapter 13.

RECOGNITION POSTPONED: CORPORATE-SHAREHOLDER TRANSACTIONS

Recognition of a gain or loss that technically has been realized is frequently postponed in a second group of transactions—those between a corporation and its shareholders. The Code provisions establishing the tax treatment of these transactions are contained largely in Subchapter C but, unlike the common nontaxable exchanges discussed in the preceding chapter, are not collected neatly in a single subdivision. In this chapter, we consider a few of the nonrecognition provisions applicable to corporate–shareholder transactions, selected both because they illustrate well the importance of wherewithal to pay and because they are of almost universal interest in any economically developed nation. The following sections are discussed:

Sec. 305. Distribution of stock and stock rights.
Sec. 351. Transfer to corporation controlled by transferrer.
Sec. 354. Exchanges of stock and securities in certain reorganizations.
Sec. 361. Nonrecognition of gain or loss to corporations.
Sec. 368. Definitions relating to corporate reorganizations.

It must be clearly understood that the discussion in this chapter only scratches the surface of the complex sections listed above. No portion of the Internal Revenue Code is more complex than Subchapter C. Students who are interested in learning more about the fascinating tax problems of corporate–shareholder relations are urged to read an authoritative text devoted solely to these provisions.[1]

One reason for the unusual complexity of these provisions is the fact that corporate–shareholder transactions typically present nonroutine tax problems for both parties to the transaction. In most of the nonrecognition transactions mentioned thus far, the transaction was routine for at least one of the parties involved. For example, the payment of an insurance claim by an insurance company is a routine transaction and presents "unusual tax problems" only for the recipient of the payment; similarly, the sale of a residence ordinarily creates special tax problems only for the seller. If one party is a dealer in the assets exchanged, an exchange of productive use or investment property for property of a like kind also creates interesting tax problems only for the nondealer.

A second reason for the unusual complexity in corporate–shareholder transactions is the fact that distributions by a corporation to its shareholders may be treated as (1) dividends, which are taxed as ordinary income; (2) partial liquidations or stock redemptions, which may be taxed either as ordinary income, as capital gains, or as part gain and part return of capital; or (3) complete liquidations, which typically involve a return of capital as well as capital gain or loss.

A final complexity is added to corporate–shareholder transactions because the shareholder may be an individual, another corporation, or a fiduciary. Even though each of these separate taxable entities is subject to the same income tax provisions generally, enough differences in specific tax provisions do exist to make an already complex tax problem even more difficult.

---

[1]In particular, we recommend Boris I. Bittker and James S. Eustice, *Federal Income Taxation of Corporations and Shareholders,* 5th ed. (Boston: Warren, Gorham, & Lamont, Inc., 1984).

TAX ASPECTS OF FORMING A CORPORATION

Among the transactions common to the formation of a corporate entity are those involving an exchange of cash, other property, or services for stock or securities in the corporate entity. The exchange of cash for stock or securities presents few tax problems to either party. As noted previously, Sec. 1032 provides that the corporation need not recognize gain when it issues its own stock or securities for money or other property; the stockholder who pays cash for corporate stock has, in most circumstances, simply purchased another asset and established a cost basis in the shares acquired. In short, the cash-for-stock transaction generally does not create taxable gain (or loss) for either party.

At the other extreme, the exchange of personal services for stock in a corporation necessarily causes the realization and recognition of taxable income for the taxpayer who renders the service and receives the shares. Neither the Code nor the Regulations provide an exception to the general rules of income recognition in this situation; therefore, taxable income equal to the fair market value of the shares transferred must be recognized. The most difficult practical problem in this transaction, generally, is agreeing on fair market value; the smaller, more risky, and more closely held the corporation, the greater the difficulty in establishing value. If, at approximately the same time, other taxpayers have paid cash or transferred property with readily determinable values for substantially identical shares, the value of the shares exchanged for services may be imputed from these other exchanges.

Tax problems also are created by the exchange of noncash property for corporate stock or securities. The critical question in the transaction is whether the gain or loss realized on the exchange should be recognized for tax purposes. For example, if a taxpayer exchanges a building with a basis of $50,000 for corporate shares valued at $75,000, must the taxpayer recognize the $25,000 income realized? Under ordinary circumstances, the taxpayer would have to, for corporate stocks are treated as boot in an otherwise nontaxable exchange, and (except for Sec. 351, which is discussed below) no other provision would seem to justify the failure to recognize this gain.

Section 351(a)

Prior to 1921, the transaction described in the preceding paragraph would have been treated as a taxable event. In that year, however, Congress decided to make an exception in certain circumstances to facilitate business readjustments. The "certain circumstances" that would preclude the recognition of gain realized by the transfer of noncash property to a corporation in exchange for that corporation's stock are specified in Sec. 351(a), which reads, in part, as follows:

(a) General Rule. — No gain or loss shall be recognized if property is transferred to a corporation by one or more persons solely in exchange for stock or securities in such corporation and immediately after the exchange such person or persons are in control (as defined in section 368(c)) of the corporation. For purposes of this section, stock or securities issued for services shall not be considered as issued in return for property.

Incidentally, Sec. 368(c) defines control as ownership of "at least 80 percent of the total combined voting power of all classes of stock entitled to vote and at least 80 percent of the total number of shares of all other classes of stock of the corporation." Section 351(a) has, in its turn, created a number of new problems and has required considerable interpretation.[2]

Section 351(b)

The primary reason for not recognizing the gain realized by the transfer of property to a controlled corporation in exchange for its stock or securities is undoubtedly a desire to facilitate business readjustments. Without such a provision, the tax cost of forming a corporation might be prohibitive. Certainly the best economic interests of a nation are served whenever businesspeople are not unduly hampered by tax considerations in selecting and effecting the form of business organization most appropriate to their needs and circumstances.

However, the importance of wherewithal to pay is also of major interest. This consideration was noted in the case of *Portland Oil Co.* v. *Commissioner,* when the Court said:

It is the purpose of 112(b)(5) [Sec. 351 in the 1954 Code] to save the taxpayer from an immediate recognition of a gain, or to intermit the claim of a loss, in certain transactions where gain or loss may have accrued in a constitutional sense, but where in a popular and economic sense there has been a mere change in the form of ownership and *the taxpayer has not really cashed in on the theoretical gain.* . . .[3]

The same conclusion is further demonstrated by the requirements of Sec. 351(b). That subsection provides that the receipt (by the shareholder) of any property other than stock or securities is treated essentially like boot in the nontaxable exchange. Section 351(b) reads as follows:

[2]To illustrate just a few of the possible problems of interpretation that might arise under this Code provision, consider the following questions. Can shares issued for cash be included with those transferred for property in determining whether or not control has been obtained? Is there any limit to the number of persons constituting the group having control? If several taxpayers are transferring property concurrently and as part of a single plan, what time span will be allowed to complete these transfers and still satisfy the "immediately after the exchange" requirement? If momentary control is achieved, but the taxpayers quickly dispose of some of their interest so that the 80% control requirement is no longer satisfied, could the exchange remain unrecognized anyway? As noted earlier, these and similar questions constitute a fascinating aspect of the corporate–shareholder transaction arena.
[3]109 F.2d 479 (1940) at p. 488 (emphasis added).

(b) Receipt of Property.—If subsection (a) would apply to an exchange but for the fact that there is received, in addition to the stock or securities permitted to be received under subsection (a), other property or money, then

(1) gain (if any) to such recipient shall be recognized, but not in excess of—

    (A) the amount of money received, plus

    (B) the fair market value of such other property received; and

(2) no loss to such recipient shall be recognized.[4]

Basis Adjustment

The nonrecognition of gain in a transfer of property to a controlled corporation is like most other temporary nonrecognition provisions in that it demands an adjustment in the basis of the property received. If no gain is recognized on the exchange, the transferrer simply takes as his or her basis in the stocks or securities whatever basis he or she had in the property transferred to the controlled corporation. In those rare instances when gain must be recognized because the shareholder received other property, the determination of basis in the shares follows the usual nontaxable exchange pattern. In this case, the basis of the stocks or securities would be determined as follows:

    Basis of property transferred to the controlled corporation
 − Cash or FMV of other property received from the corporation
 + Gain recognized on the exchange
 ───
 = Basis of shares or securities received

This conclusion and a provision for relative fair market value allocations if more than one class of share or security is received are contained in Sec. 358.

The corporation's basis in the property it receives is also determined, in most circumstances, by the shareholder's former basis in the property. If the shareholder was forced to recognize gain (because he or she received property other than stocks or securities), the corporation may increase its basis in the property received by the amount of gain the shareholder recognized.

CORPORATE–SHAREHOLDER TRANSACTIONS SUBSEQUENT TO ORGANIZATION

The tax problems associated with corporate–shareholder transactions are more complex after the organizational period. The possible range of these transactions is infinite. The more important postorganization transactions include those in which the corporation distributes assets to its shareholders. These may include routine cash dividends, common stock dividends, pre-

---

[4]Section 351(b).

ferred stock dividends, property dividends, partial liquidations, divisive reorganizations, nondivisive reorganizations, and complete liquidations. A complete liquidation may be permanent, or it may be followed momentarily by a subsequent organization that makes the procedure tantamount to reorganization. The tax consequences and complexity of each suggested transaction are enormous. In this chapter, we can only note some of the more important transactions that defer the recognition of a realized gain or loss.

Stock Dividends

Corporations frequently distribute their own shares to stockholders in what is known as a stock dividend. In several ways, this is a most unfortunate phrase to describe what has taken place; witness the fact that the corporation is not distributing a corporate asset (the corporation's own shares can never constitute an asset to that entity), which is requisite to any true "dividend." As long as the distribution of stock is pro rata among all shareholders, the shareholders effectively have received nothing. Admittedly they have received additional pieces of paper, but collectively their ownership rights after the stock dividend are exactly equal to the rights they possessed prior to the dividend. If the distribution of stock is not pro rata, however, a significant change in ownership rights may be achieved.

Prior to 1969, stock dividends generally were not taxable as long as they were made in the same class of stock unless (1) any shareholder of that class had an option to receive cash or other property or (2) the stock dividend was in discharge of a preference dividend for the current or the preceding year. By carefully delineating the rights of various classes of stock, corporate managements could effectively accommodate the desires of some shareholders to receive cash and of others to accumulate their income rights for greater capital gain. Alternatively, by carefully timing disproportionate stock redemptions, dividends could effectively be paid at the cost of a capital gain tax. To discourage this managerial intrigue, Congress amended Sec. 305 to make taxable a number of previously untaxable stock dividends. Under current law, it is sometimes difficult to discern whether a particular distribution should be treated as a taxable or a nontaxable event. To complicate matters further, certain distributions made prior to January 1, 1991, are exempted from the 1969 changes. Unfortunately, the revised Sec. 305 is too complex to justify a thorough discussion in an introductory text. Suffice it to observe that if a stock dividend changes the proportionate interest of one or more groups of shareholders, the result is very likely a taxable transaction. When a single class of common stock is distributed pro rata on the outstanding common stock, the distribution does not shift ownership interests and is nontaxable.

Ignoring the more difficult question of determining whether a particular stock dividend is a taxable or a nontaxable event, we can summarize the result once the prior issue has been resolved. If a stock dividend is a taxable distribution, the shareholder recognizes ordinary (dividend) income equal to the fair market value of the shares received. The new shares take this value as their tax basis, and the date of the distribution is the beginning of the holding period for the newly acquired shares.

On receipt of a nontaxable stock dividend, the taxpayer must allocate his or her cost basis among the new, larger number of shares. If the shares received are identical to the shares already owned, the taxpayer simply divides the old basis by the new, larger number of shares to determine the adjusted basis per share. If the shares received are not identical to the shares owned, the taxpayer must allocate the original basis on the relative fair market value of each class of stock he or she now possesses. To illustrate, assume that taxpayer C owned 100 shares of ABC common, purchased for $2,200 several years earlier. If C received an additional 10 shares of ABC common as a nontaxable stock dividend, C's basis would be readjusted from $22 per share ($2,200/100) to $20 per share ($2,200/110). The date basis of the 10 dividend shares would be the same as that of the original 100 shares. Therefore, if taxpayer C sold the 10 dividend shares two days after receiving them, he or she would recognize a long-term capital gain or loss equal to the difference between the amount realized and the $20 basis per share surrendered in the transaction. (This assumes, of course, that the shares were a capital asset in taxpayer C's hands.)

If these 10 shares had been received in a taxable stock dividend, no allocations would have been made, and the taxpayer would have recorded as dividend income their fair market value of the date distributed. Any gain or loss on the sale two days later would have been short-term capital gain or loss.

If taxpayer C had received 10 shares of preferred stock, rather than 10 shares of common stock, as a nontaxable stock dividend, C would have allocated the old $2,200 basis between the two classes of stock based on their relative fair market values. If we assume that when the dividend was distributed the 10 preferred shares had a fair market value of $600 and the 100 common shares a fair market value of $2,400, then the basis of the 10 preferred shares would be $440 [$2,200 × ($600/$3,000)] and the basis of the 100 common shares would be $1,760 [$2,200 × ($2,400/$3,000)]. Although the date basis would still "tack," the taxpayer may have to recognize ordinary income on disposition of the preferred shares. The reason for this conclusion is not evident, and an adequate investigation of the problem leads us to Sec. 306 and the subject of preferred stock bailouts. Because time and space constraints prohibit such an investigation, suffice it to note that because the receipt of a stock dividend may not necessitate the recognition of income, and because the sale of corporate shares ordinarily results in capital gain rather than ordinary income, the distribution of a preferred stock dividend could— in the absence of Sec. 306—be abused to disguise a dividend payment (ordinary income) as a stock redemption (capital gain). In short, retained profits could be "bailed out" as capital gains rather than as ordinary dividend income.

Stock Rights

The distribution of stock rights, rather than actual shares, presents tax problems similar to those of the stock dividend. The general rules can be summarized briefly. First, the taxability of the stock right is determined in the same manner as the taxability of the stock dividend. Second, if the distribution is nontaxable, the recipient must allocate basis only if on the distribution date the fair market value of the rights is equal to or greater than 15% of the fair market value of the shares; if the rights have a value of less than 15% of the shares, allocation is optional for each recipient taxpayer. Third, if the taxpayer sells the rights, the date basis is presumed to "tack"—that is, the date basis of the rights is the same as the date basis of the old shares. However, if the taxpayer exercises the rights and acquires new shares, the new shares take a new date basis on the date they were purchased. The determination of a cost basis (and, therefore, of the gain or loss on the sale of the rights or of newly acquired shares) depends on whether or not the taxpayer voluntarily allocated part of the basis of the old shares to the rights.

To illustrate, assume that taxpayer F acquired 100 shares of DEF common on May 1, 19x1, for $1,600. On June 10, 19x4, she received 100 stock rights, which permitted her to buy additional shares at a bargain price. The agreement provided that one new share could be purchased for five rights and $20. If we assume that DEF common at that time was selling at approximately $30 per share, the rights obviously would be selling at approximately $2 per right. Because the value of the 100 rights ($200) is less than 15% of the value of the 100 shares ($3,000), taxpayer F would not be required to allocate any basis to the rights. If she elected to allocate, she would do so on a fair market value basis—that is, she could elect to allocate $100 [$1,600 × ($200/$3,200)] to the rights. If she makes this election, the basis in the 100 shares is, of course, reduced from $1,600 to $1,500. After receiving these stock rights, taxpayer F has two intelligent options: she might elect to sell the rights, or she might exercise them if she desires to acquire an additional interest in DEF. If she sells the rights for $200, she must recognize long-term capital gain equal to the difference between the $200 realized and the basis of the rights ($0 or $100, the latter amount if she elects to allocate basis). If she exercises the rights and acquires 20 new shares for her 100 rights and $400, the 20 new shares take a new date basis (the date they were acquired) and a new cost basis of $400 or $500 (the latter amount if taxpayer F elects to allocate). Taxpayer F also has one unintelligent option—to let the option lapse. If she does so, no loss is recognized.

In summary, the receipt of a stock dividend or a stock right in the distributing corporation's own shares may or may not trigger the recognition of a gain or loss that might be considered realized. If the taxpayer receives a property other than stock or rights in the distributing corporation, or if the relative rights of various owners are modified by the distribution, the shareholder is deemed to have the wherewithal to pay a tax, and income, usually in the form of a dividend, must be recognized. The distributing corporation typically does not recognize gain or loss when it distributes property to its shareholders in their role as shareholders.

Reorganizations

Corporate reorganizations may be divided into two broad groups—divisive and nondivisive. A divisive reorganization usually combines two or more corporate entities into one. In each instance, the "old" entity may remain or disappear after the reorganization. In the divisive reorganization, for example, existing corporation A may be divided into corporations A and B or into new corporations B and C. In the nondivisive reorganization, existing corporations A and B may be "merged" into continuing corporation B, or existing corporations A and B may be "consolidated" into new corporation C.

Regardless of such details, reorganizations necessitate numerous transactions. For example, a reorganization may involve the transfer of properties between corporate entities, as well as the exchange of corporate stocks and securities by shareholders. Because any transaction may be deemed adequate to cause the realization of taxable income or loss, the recognition question is paramount. As noted earlier, the reorganization provisions are inordinately complex and cannot be discussed even in a summary fashion. Consequently, at this juncture, we must paint only the broadest of pictures and warn constantly that no attempt should be made to "utilize" this picture in any factual situation.

In general, Sec. 354 provides that "no gain or loss shall be recognized if stock or securities in a corporation that is a party to a reorganization are, in pursuance of the plan of reorganization, exchanged solely for stock or securities in such corporation or in another corporation a party to the reorganization."[5] Obviously, this section is important because it sometimes permits a taxpayer to exchange stocks and securities in different corporate entities and to avoid the recognition of any gain or loss realized by this exchange transaction. The critical requirement, of course, is that the exchanged shares be in corporations that are parties to a reorganization. Whether or not a corporation is a party to a reorganization is determined by Sec. 368.

Section 368 is exclusively a definitional provision. Paragraph (1) of Subsection 368(a) describes seven transactions that constitute a reorganization for tax purposes. Reorganizations not falling within one of these prescribed transactions are ordinarily subject to no special tax treatment. It is, therefore, of utmost importance in most corporate reorganizations to determine well in advance whether a proposed transaction fits within a Sec. 368 definition. Even the most sophisticated tax advisor will typically insist on an advance ruling from the I.R.S. on a given set of fact circumstances before deeming it safe to proceed with a proposed corporate change.[6] In some instances, the parties could not proceed with the reorganization if it were to be a taxable transaction.

Section 361, like Sec. 354, depends on the definitional distinctions of Sec. 368 to determine its importance. In general, Sec. 361 permits one corporate party to a reorganization to exchange its property for stock or securities in another corporate party to the reorganization and to avoid the recognition of gain realized by this exchange.

---

[5]Section 354(a).
[6]An advance ruling is an administrative procedure by which a taxpayer may get a generally binding agreement with the I.R.S. on the tax consequences of a proposed transaction. This ruling is not binding on other parties in similar circumstances.

In many respects, the importance of wherewithal to pay in the corporate reorganization is exhibited in Secs. 356, 357, 358, and 362. Stated very crudely, the first two provisions determine the consequences of receiving boot (including the transfer of a liability) in a corporate reorganization. The other two provisions require a basis adjustment intended to guarantee that a nonrecognized gain or loss will be recognized for tax purposes at a later date. Although innumerable special rules apply in many situations, the general conclusion is the same as that derived in the preceding chapter. Realized gain must be recognized in most situations to the extent of the lesser of boot received or gain realized. Any gain not recognized reduces the basis of the "new" property from its cost or fair market value to a lower figure. Unrealized loss, on the other hand, may increase basis above cost.

In short, the theory behind the nonrecognition of gain in a corporate reorganization is comparable to that of other nontaxable exchanges: the taxpayer is deemed to have only a new "form" for an old investment. In a popular sense, this taxpayer has no funds with which to pay an income tax, and so no tax is assessed until he or she disposes of the new property in a taxable transaction. At that time, it is presumed, the deferred gain will be recouped. If the taxpayer does acquire, as part of the reorganization, a limited amount of property that cannot be treated as a mere continuation of the old investment, gain must, to that extent, be recognized immediately; the remainder of the realized gain may go unrecognized.

Even this very brief introduction to the corporate reorganization tax provisions should suggest their major impact on American business. The closely held corporation is often used as a temporary tax-rate shelter by individuals. By merging the closely held corporate entity, with large amounts of accumulated earnings and profits, into a conglomerate entity, the owner of the closely held firm can effectively "cash in" on previously sheltered corporate earnings with no immediate tax cost. The taxpayer can exchange the shares in his or her closely held corporation for shares in the merger-minded conglomerate giant without the imposition of an income tax if the transaction can be arranged as a qualifying corporate reorganization. In this manner, a business owner can free himself or herself of the day-to-day responsibilities of corporate management and obtain the economic diversification (and supposedly the minimization of risk) represented by the stock in the acquiring corporation. In many cases, the former owner of the acquired corporation is given a choice between receiving low-dividend, high-growth potential stocks; high-dividend, low-growth stocks; or some combination of the two. In this way, he or she can try to ensure that his or her retirement years include both a sufficient income flow and a strong capital base to make life as comfortable as possible. If an income tax had been imposed before the taxpayer could make such a change, the capital base and, therefore, the income flow would have been materially reduced. Finally, with the step-up in basis of inherited property, what started out as a temporary deferral of the income tax often becomes a permanent exclusion from the income tax when the shares pass through an estate.

Although the almost rampant merger movement of the decade 1962–1972 was largely halted by the stock market decline in 1973 and 1974, the momentum provided by the nontaxable reorganization provisions suggests that the movement will likely recur whenever the market value of the acquiring corporations' shares is favorable. We can only hope that future conglomerate giants will emerge and grow with more caution than many of their predecessors. The failure to investigate fully, and the failure to provide knowledgeable management in diverse industries, all too often resulted in economic chaos rather than the comfortable retirement liquidity sought by the stockholder of the acquired corporation.

PROBLEMS

1. In 1960, Tom Fahr purchased an $18,000 frame house for his family. Eventually this house was too small for Tom's growing family, so in April of this year, he sold the frame house for $62,000. The broker's fee on the sale was $3,700; Tom incurred $600 in fixing-up expenses prior to completing the sale. On June 1, the Fahr family moved into their new brick house. What gross income must the Fahrs report this year because of the sale of their frame house if
   a. the new residence cost them $80,000?
   b. the new residence cost them $60,000?
   c. the new residence cost them $56,000?
   What is the tax basis for the Fahr's brick house in each of the above situations?

2. A taxpayer purchased a residence in 1950 for $10,000. This year he sold the home for $21,000. He incurred and paid "fixing-up" costs of $300 in the month before sale. He also paid a real estate agent a commission of $1,260. Seven months after the sale of the old residence, the taxpayer purchased a new mobile home for $26,000. (It is a primary residence.)
   a. What amount of gain is recognized by the taxpayer under Sec. 1034?
   b. What would be the tax basis of the new home under Sec. 1034?

3. Assume the same facts as in problem 5, except that the new mobile home cost $15,400.
   a. Under Sec. 1034, what would be the recognized gain on the sale?
   b. What would be the tax basis of the new mobile home?

4. This year Mr. Elder (age 64) sold his residence for $140,000. He and Mrs. Elder had lived in this home since 1940. They originally paid $18,000 for the home, but they immediately remodeled it at a cost of $3,000. Since then only routine upkeep was required. The Elders paid a realtor $8,400 commission for selling the house; they also incurred fixing-up expenses of $500 one month prior to the sale. One month after selling their home, the Elders purchased a small cottage on a nearby lake for $48,000. They intend to make this lake cottage their home whenever they are not traveling.
   a. What minimum amount of gain must the Elders include on their tax return this year because of the sale of their old home?
   b. Would this be a capital gain or ordinary income?

    c. If Mr. Elder had been 54, rather than 64, when he sold this home, what minimum amount of gain would he have been required to report as taxable income?

5. Discuss briefly the rationale behind
   a. the "wash sale" provisions.
   b. net operating loss provisions.

6. Jetstream Airlines, a Delaware corporation, reported the following taxable income during years 1 through 5:

Year	Taxable Income
1	$ 82,500
2	23,000
3	190,000
4	230,000
5	(250,000)

   The large loss in year 5 was attributable to a general strike that lasted for over four months and increased labor costs after settlement by 14%. Explain, in general, how Jetstream will handle this net operating loss.

7. Taxpayer, age 57, sold her former home for $132,500. Broker's commission on this sale was $8,000, and fixing-up expenses totaled $350. Taxpayer's basis in her old home was $24,000. What is the minimum amount taxpayer must reinvest in a new home if she is to avoid any recognition of taxable gain this year (assuming that she qualifies for and makes the election to exclude as much of her gain as possible)?

8. On March 19, 1956, Red inherited a home from his mother. His mother's basis in this home was $40,000; it was valued at $50,000 for estate tax purposes. Red immediately occupied the home as his own primary residence.

   On May 15, 1964, Red sold this home for $60,000. Broker's commission on the sale was $3,600. Two weeks prior to making this sale, Red purchased a new primary residence for $55,000.

   On July 24, 1971, Red's residence was condemned by the State Highway Commission. Red received a condemnation award of $60,000. On November 22, 1971, Red purchased his next primary residence for $56,000 and elected to pay the minimum possible tax for 1971.

   On February 14, 1975, Red gave his primary residence to his daughter as a wedding gift. On the day of the gift, the home was valued at $60,000. Red paid a gift tax of $1,500 before leaving for a round-the-world cruise.

   On December 15 of this year, Red's daughter sold the home, which she had occupied as her primary residence since February 15, 1975, for $65,000. Because she sold the home herself, there was no commission on this sale. She moved into a rented apartment and has no intention of returning to home ownership in the near future. What gain or loss must Red's daughter recognize on the sale she made this year?

9. Taxpayer purchased a primary residence in 1965 for $18,000. She sold that same residence for $38,000 this year. To sell the home, however, taxpayer incurred and paid fixing-up expenses of $400 and a real estate commission of $2,280. Three months after this sale, but within the current year, taxpayer purchased a new home for $35,500. Taxpayer is 40 years old.
   a. What amount of gain did taxpayer realize because of the home sale?

    b. What minimum amount of gain must taxpayer recognize because of the home sale?

    c. If taxpayer recognizes only the minimum amount of gain, what is the tax basis of the new home?

10. Plush resides in his palatial home in Austin, Texas. During the year, Plush sold his Lake Travis cottage for $40,000. Plush has occupied this cottage for four to six weeks each year since building it for $28,000 four years ago. Plush paid fixing-up expenses of $200 and a real estate commission of $2,400 to sell the cottage. Two months later, Plush purchased a mobile land cruiser for $42,000, which he intends to use as his "vacation home."

    a. What amount of gain did Plush realize because of the sale of his Lake Travis cottage?

    b. What minimum amount of gain must Plush recognize because of the sale of his Lake Travis cottage?

    c. If Plush recognizes only the minimum amount of gain, what is the tax basis of his new mobile land cruiser?

11. Embryo, Inc., suffered a net operating loss of $10,000 in 19x4. The loss was attributable to circumstances that management does not expect to recur. Embryo, Inc., has reported taxable income since its inception in 19x1 as follows:

Year	Taxable Income
19×1	$ 5,000
19×2	30,000
19×3	90,000
19×4	(10,000)

Management projects Embryo's taxable income to be $150,000 in 19x5. Using current corporate tax rates in all years (19x1 through 19x5), explain the potential value of the 19x4 corporate net operating loss by completing the following blanks: Management has a choice; it may elect to receive a refund of $_____ immediately or hope for a deduction worth as much as $_____ next year.

12. On December 12 of last year, the board of directors of Schmart Shops, Inc., voted to sell its 500 shares of Inland Steel for $35,000. These 500 shares had been purchased 14 months earlier at a cost of $42,000. On its tax return for last year, Schmart Shops deducted the $7,000 long-term capital loss on the 500 Inland Steel shares from a $10,000 short-term capital gain it had recognized on another investment sold earlier in the year. On January 8, this year, the board reviewed its earlier action and, believing the market for Inland Steel was going to increase, voted to purchase 600 shares of Inland Steel at the market price of $71 per share.

    a. Was the tax treatment of the Inland Steel investment correctly reported for last year by Schmart Shops, Inc.? Explain.

    b. What is Schmart Shops' tax basis in the 600 shares of Inland Steel it acquired on January 8? Explain briefly.

    c. If the board had invested in U.S. Steel on January 8, rather than Inland Steel, would your answer to part a have been different? Explain.

13. Discuss the problems that arise from applying the general rules to determine the tax consequences of a particular transaction in each of the following fact situations. How has each problem been "resolved"?

    a. Henry Dee had operated a corner grocery store as a sole proprietorship for several years. Because the store had grown to reasonable size, Henry incorporated his business as Henry's Groceries, Inc. To accomplish this, Henry transferred all business assets to the new corporation in exchange for all 1,000 shares of the corporation's voting stock. (Consider both Henry's tax problems and those of Henry's Groceries, Inc.; discuss questions of "basis" as well as problems in "recognition of gain or loss.")

b. After operating and expanding this grocery business for another 10 years, Henry "merged" his corporation with Giant Corporation, a national chain of food stores. Giant gave Henry the three options detailed below. (Discuss the tax consequences of each option.)

   (1) A cash purchase of all operating assets for $300,000
   (2) An exchange of 500 shares of Giant voting stock for all the operating assets of Henry's Groceries, Inc
   (3) A statutory merger of Henry's Groceries, Inc. into Giant Corporation by an exchange of 400 shares of Giant for all 1,000 shares of Henry's (after which Henry's Groceries, Inc. would be liquidated)

c. Assume that Henry accepted option 3 and that five years later Giant Corporation was consolidated with 10 other firms engaged in various businesses into a new corporation, Conglomerate American. Thus, Henry ended up holding a small interest in a new and highly diversified corporate entity. Do the tax consequences of this series of transactions square with the idea that Henry has experienced only an insignificant change in the "form" of his investment? Do they square with a wherewithal-to-pay concept? Explain.

14. Susan purchased 100 shares of DEF common on February 12, 19x1, for $4,800. On October 1, 19x4, she received 20 additional shares of DEF common as a nontaxable stock dividend.

a. What is Susan's cost basis per share after receipt of the stock dividend?
b. What is Susan's "date basis" in each of the 20 "dividend shares"?
c. Suppose that instead of 20 additional shares of DEF common, Susan had received 20 shares of GHI common (which had been held by DEF corporation as an investment).

   (1) Would Susan report the receipt of the 20 shares of GHI as ordinary income (dividend), as capital gain, or as a nontaxable distribution?
   (2) Assume that DEF had paid $50 per share for the GHI stock two years prior to distributing it and that at distribution it had a fair market value of $60 per share. Would DEF have to recognize the $10 per share gain inherent in the GHI stock when it distributes the stock to its shareholders?

15. John Doe purchased 100 shares of ABC common on October 30, 19x3, for $680. On March 1, 19x4, John received 100 stock rights. The provision of the rights agreement authorized John to purchase one new share of ABC common for $5 and four rights. Immediately following issuance of these rights, ABC common is selling ex-rights at $8 per share; the rights are selling for 50 cents each.

a. Does John have to report taxable income in 19x4 because he received this right to purchase additional shares of stock?
b. What is John's cost basis for his 100 stock rights, assuming the distribution was nontaxable?
c. Assuming that John elects to allocate basis of the rights and that he exercises his option and purchases the shares:

   (1) What is his cost basis for each newly acquired share?
   (2) What is his "date basis" in each of the new shares?
   (3) What is his cost basis in each of his old shares?

16. James Madison and Henry Clay formed a corporation on July 1 of this year.

Madison transferred to the corporation the assets of his existing hardware business, which had a basis of $8,000, and Clay transferred assets that had a basis of $18,000. Each individual received 200 shares of stock in the new corporation; each share had a fair market value of $80. In addition, Madison's wife was issued one share of stock on the investment of $80 cash. Discuss the tax consequences of this transaction, including the basis of shares received and the basis of the corporation in the property.

17. State briefly the underlying rationale for the "nontaxability" of certain corporate reorganizations.

18. Taxpayer owns 100 shares of XYZ common stock, which she acquired several years ago. Her basis is $40 per share. On May 5 of the current year, when the stock was $60 and the rights $1, she received 100 nontaxable rights from the corporation. For 10 rights and a payment of $50, the stockholder may acquire an additional share of XYZ common.

    a. If the taxpayer sells the rights on November 15 of the same year for $1.50 each, what is her gain or loss, and how is it taxed (1) if she elects to allocate basis? and (2) if she does not allocate?

    b. If the taxpayer exercises her rights on November 15 and sells the 10 shares acquired thereby on December 3 of the same year for $68 per share, what is her gain or loss, and how is it taxed (1) if she allocates the basis? and (2) if she does not allocate the basis?

19. On July 1 of the current year, Arvid Corporation merged into Berrium Incorporated in a transaction that qualified under Secs. 354 and 368(a). As a result of this corporate merger, Homer exchanged 2,000 shares of Arvid stock for 500 new shares of Berrium and $1,219 cash. Homer's basis in the 2,000 shares of Arvid was $8,237; the fair market value of the 500 Berrium shares was $34,977 on the day they were received.

    a. What income did Homer realize on this exchange?

    b. How much of this realized income must Homer recognize this year?

    c. What is Homer's tax basis in the 500 shares of Berrium?

20. Kyle, Dan, and Bob decided to pool some assets in a new corporate business to be known as KDB Company. Kyle contributed $4,000 cash plus equipment with a fair market value of $26,000 and a tax basis of $15,000. Dan contributed land with a fair market value of $30,000 and a tax basis of $40,000. Bob contributed $20,000 cash and a good deal of work, which all parties agreed was worth $10,000. In exchange, each man received 1,000 shares of KDB stock.

    a. If all the contributions are made under a single plan so that the transaction qualifies under Sec. 351(a):

       (1) How much taxable income or loss does each man recognize in the year because KDB incorporated?

       (2) What is the tax basis of the 1,000 shares of KDB each man owns?

       (3) What is the tax basis of the equipment and land owned by KDB Company?

       (4) Why might Dan strongly prefer to arrange the incorporating transaction in a way that would not qualify it under Sec. 351(a)?

       (5) Why might Kyle strongly prefer to keep the transaction as it is currently arranged?

    b. If the incorporation plans were revised so that initially Dan contributed $30,000 cash and subsequently, in a wholly separate transaction, KDB Company purchased the land from Dan for $30,000, why might both Kyle and Dan be satisfied?

    c. Under either plan (a or b, above), each owner has contributed $30,000 in cash, equivalent property, and/or services to KDB Company in exchange for 1,000 shares of stock. Nevertheless, in one important sense Kyle has not contributed his fair share. Explain.

21. On March 20 of this year, Ida exchanged all of her shares of common stock in Ida Marie Cosmetics for 350,000 shares of Wellblest Corporation and $100,000 cash. Ida, the original stockholder of Ida Marie Cosmetics, had an adjusted basis of only $75,000 in the shares she gave up. Wellblest shares were selling for $8 on the day of the exchange.
    a. What amount of gain did Ida realize on this exchange?
    b. What amount of gain must Ida recognize this year if the exchange does not qualify as a reorganization under Sec. 368?
    c. What amount of gain must Ida recognize this year if the exchange qualifies as a reorganization under Sec. 368?
    d. What kind of income—ordinary or capital—is Ida's gain?
    e. If Ida's exchange qualifies as a reorganization and she does not dispose of her Wellblest shares prior to her death, who will finally pay the income tax on the taxable gain deferred at the time of this exchange? Explain briefly.

SUPPLEMENTAL PROBLEMS

22. In 1960, Ted Saldin built a new primary residence for $40,000 in Kansas City. Because he feared that a neighbor would build another home closer than he desired, Ted also bought the one vacant lot between his new residence and a neighboring home for $8,000. In 1970, Ted was transferred to New York. He sold the Kansas City home and acquired another in Greenwich, Connecticut. Ted did not, however, sell the vacant lot. He kept it as both an investment and a possible retirement site. By 1978, Ted decided that he would not retire in Kansas City and thought about retiring somewhere in Florida. Because Ted is in a high tax bracket, he is reluctant to sell the lot, which has appreciated to about $28,000 in value. Nevertheless, he has no good reason to retain ownership.
    a. Suggest a tax-saving plan that will achieve Ted's objectives.
    b. What precautions do you suggest that Ted take to be certain that the plan succeeds?

23. Should corporate financial accounting be of any significance in the determination of tax consequences of a given transaction? Explain your answer, giving some consideration to the following quotation from *Bazley* v. *Commissioner* (331 U.S. 740):

> No doubt there was a recapitalization of the Bazley Corporation in the sense that the symbols that represented its capital were changed, so that the fiscal basis of its operations would appear very differently on its books. But the form of a transaction is reflected by correct corporate accounting opens questions as to the proper application of a taxing statute; it does not close them. Corporate accounting may represent that correspondence between change in the form of capital structure and essential identity in fact which is the essence of a transaction relieved from taxation as a reorganization.

PART SIX

Tax Planning

The phenomenal proliferation of law, loophole, litigation, and juridical exegesis has spawned a huge tax industry. It gathers its capital from legal conundrums.
Peter Meyer, Harpers *(1977)*

Close the loopholes and you will not get a bunch of contented taxpayers; you will get a lot of dropouts from the rat race, and the whole economy will go to hell from sheer despair.
Larry Martz, New York *(1969)*

CHAPTER 19

The Tax-Planning Process

President Carter, speaking in the Department of Agriculture, made the offhand comment that some in his audience were living in sin. That quaint expression clearly puzzled his hearers. When he clarified it by suggesting that those who were so living should get married, the response was laughter. Did not the President know that, by congressional ukase, marriage would result in a tax penalty? That was part of a "reform" bill.
Henry M. Wriston The Christian Science Monitor *(April 13, 1977)*

A final tax liability is a function of three variables—the law, the facts, and an administrative (and sometimes judicial) process. Most of this text is an explication of the law; a few pages describe the administrative and judicial processes that operationalize the written rules or law. Except for a few problem assignments, we have given scant attention to the critical role of facts. In this chapter, we demonstrate how important the facts are to the determination of any tax liability.

Observe that facts are the one variable that almost everyone can do something about. If you are not satisfied with either the law or the administrative and judicial processes, there is relatively little that you can do (unless, of course, you are a veritable mogul in American society).[1] The facts,

---

[1] In other words, only a very few people have enough money and clout to get a tax law changed by Congress. The administrative and judicial processes are similarly resistant to personal intervention.

however, can generally be modified. If you are wise enough to understand when and how to modify them, you may very well reduce your tax liability significantly. The most highly qualified professional tax experts earn most of their lucrative fees by giving advice on alternative ways of arranging facts! In other words, most professional tax planning is little more than the prearrangement of facts in the most tax-favored way.

AVOIDANCE VERSUS EVASION

Successful tax planning, or tax *avoidance,* must be clearly distinguished from tax *evasion.* In tax jargon, the latter term refers to the *illegal* reduction of a tax liability, whereas the former term encompasses only *legal* means of achieving that same objective. For example, assume a taxpayer claims that he has ten dependent children when filing his federal income tax return even though he actually has only two such dependents. That misrepresentation of fact would constitute a simple form of tax evasion, and the guilty taxpayer would be subject to both criminal and monetary penalties. Backdating an important tax document would constitute an equally obvious form of tax evasion. Deceit, concealment, and misrepresentation are common elements in most illegal tax plans.

On the other hand, careful planning and full disclosure are common elements in tax avoidance. For example, if a taxpayer can significantly reduce income tax liability by operating a business as a corporation rather than as a sole proprietorship, there is, obviously, nothing illegal about making such a change in the facts. Perhaps the most celebrated statement made in defense of tax planning came from the pen of Judge Learned Hand in the following dissenting opinion from *Commissioner* v. *Newman:*

> Over and over again courts have said that there is nothing sinister in so arranging one's affairs as to keep taxes as low as possible. Everybody does so, rich or poor, and all do right, for nobody owes any public duty to pay more than the law demands: taxes are enforced exactions, not voluntary contributions. To demand more in the name of morals is mere cant.[2]

Although this quotation is from a dissenting opinion and, therefore, of no value as legal precedent, it is widely quoted in support of tax planning. Other judges have said essentially the same thing in majority opinions, but their choice of words is less striking.

Unfortunately, the line between avoidance and evasion is not always as clear as the earlier examples suggest. Some tax plans so distort the apparent "truth" that they approach the level of evasion. In this chapter, we are not primarily concerned with making fine-line distinctions. Nevertheless, we encourage students to develop a natural suspicion of anything that sounds too

[2]159 F.2d 848 (CCA-2, 1947).

good to be true in tax planning. As suggested in the following discussion, many apparently viable tax plans have already been curbed by statutory, judicial, or administrative action.

THE CRITICAL VARIABLES

There are alternative ways to approach tax planning systematically. One possibility is to reexamine the general formula used to determine the income tax liability of any taxable entity:

Line Number	Item
1	Income broadly conceived
2	− Exclusions
3	= Gross income
4	− Deductions
5	= Taxable income
6	× Applicable tax rate(s)
7	= Gross tax payable
8	− Tax credits (and prepayments)
9	= Net tax payable

Because the ultimate objective of income tax planning is the minimization of the bottom line—that is, the minimization of the net tax payable—the rules of simple arithmetic suggest that tax planning must necessarily involve the maximization of tax credits, the minimization of the applicable tax rate(s), and the maximization of deductions and exclusions. In other words, the items on all even-numbered lines in the above formula constitute the critical variables in tax planning. In the next few pages, we consider some fundamental tax-planning ideas implicit in the provisions already introduced in earlier chapters. In some instances, we also consider provisions that have been enacted to preclude the apparent tax plan from being successful. Finally, after considering the more isolated examples, we examine a typical tax-planning situation to see how an ordinary businessperson might reduce taxes.

Maximizing Exclusions

Simple illustrations of maximizing exclusions can be readily constructed. Assume that taxpayer Lucky is a head of household and reports a $200,000 taxable income, claims two exemption deductions, and pays a tax of $57,092 in 1988. If we assume that $100,000 of Lucky's annual income comes from interest on bank deposits or commercial loans, we can quickly see how some elementary tax planning could reduce taxes. If Lucky were to switch his investments from bank deposits or commercial loans, we can quickly see how some elementary tax planning could reduce taxes. If Lucky were to switch his investments from bank deposits or commercial loans to state government bonds, the interest could be excluded from taxable income, and Lucky's net tax payable would decrease from $57,092 per year to $26,810.50 (that is, to the tax for a head of household with two exemptions reporting $100,000 taxable income). This plan would save Lucky $30,281.50 per year in taxes. That fact alone does not, however, support a conclusion that switching investments from bank deposits to state government bonds is necessarily wise.

To determine the wisdom of proposing such a tax plan for Lucky, we must examine the after-tax rate of return on the investment. Let us keep the arithmetic as simple as possible by assuming that Lucky is earning an 8% rate of return on his original investment in bank deposits or commercial loans. To receive a $100,000 annual interest income, Lucky must have $1,250,000 invested. If the interest rate on state government bonds is only 6%, Lucky's annual interest income would drop from $100,000 per year to $75,000 per year, other things being equal. However, the sum of the $30,281.50 tax savings plus the $75,000 annual interest exceeds the original return by $5,281.50 per year. Thus, with the assumed interest rates of 8% and 6%, and with Lucky's marginal tax bracket, this tax plan is a favorable plan, assuming no change in the risk of the two investments. Further study of this example explains why tax-exempt securities are especially favorable investments to taxpayers in the highest marginal tax brackets, whereas the same securities are of little or no interest to taxpayers in the low marginal tax brackets. The after-tax rate of return on tax-exempt securities depends directly on the taxpayer's marginal tax bracket.

Another tax plan might be based on exclusions that can be thought of as "wage and salary supplements." To illustrate these opportunities briefly, let us consider the case of taxpayer Black, who has operated a small-town mortuary as a sole proprietorship for many years. He has always purchased life, health, and accident insurance from his own after-tax funds; he has always provided his own meals and lodging from the same source; and he has never had any "death benefits." What would keep Black from forming a corporation (in which he and his family own the entire equity interest) and transferring all (or most) of his assets to the new corporation, which would then "hire" Black as its principal employee? Couldn't the new corporation provide its employees (including Black) with certain supplemental benefits and get a tax deduction for the cost of the (group-term) life insurance premiums, the health and accident insurance premiums, the casualty insurance, utilities, and upkeep on the home? If Black can exclude the receipt of those benefits from his own gross income (under the conditions stipulated in the statutory authorities noted earlier), and if Black's corporation can deduct the cost of those benefits in the calculation of its own taxable income, won't Black have implemented a successful tax plan that involves both the maximization of exclusions (for himself) and the maximization of deductions (via his new corporate entity)?

Under the proper circumstances, the I.R.S. would have a difficult, if not impossible, task in challenging such a tax plan. Although many aspects of this proposal could be subject to attack, if the taxpayer were sufficiently careful in attention to detail—that is, if Black's tax advisor carefully planned, executed, and documented each step in this proposal—there is no fundamental reason that the plan could not succeed. The myriad of detail necessary to reach that happy result must remain outside the confines of this introductory text. However, the basic idea should be instructive.

Maximizing Deductions

To illustrate how tax planning can be achieved through the maximization of deductions, consider another simplified example. Suppose that Ionna Stoor is a very successful single businesswoman with an annual taxable income of $200,000. In addition, Stoor is the sole stockholder of the Stoor Corporation, which operates a small brewery. If Stoor were suddenly to inherit a large block of stock in other corporations, which paid her $100,000 in dividends per year, she would discover that Uncle Sam took 28% of her additional income by way of income taxes. Her annual taxable income would have increased from $200,000 to $300,000, and her annual tax liability would have increased from $56,546 to $84,546. In other words, after paying income taxes, Stoor would have only $72,000 of her $100,000 annual dividend income to reinvest in other property.

With a little tax planning, Stoor could transfer her newly inherited stocks to her wholly owned corporation, the Stoor Corporation. As a corporation, the latter taxpayer would be entitled to an 80% dividends-received deduction. Thus, if the Stoor Corporation were to receive an additional $100,000 in dividends each year, it could deduct $80,000 of that amount and increase its taxable income by only $20,000. The corporation's federal income tax on $20,000 would amount to $6,800 (assuming a 34% marginal corporate tax rate). Thus, by giving the title to the stocks to a corporate entity, and thereby maximizing deductions, Stoor would have reduced the income tax on the $100,000 in annual dividends from $28,000 to $6,800; at the same time, she would have increased her reinvestment potential from $72,000 to $93,200 per year!

The preceding example is a dramatic illustration of how taxes can be saved by maximizing deductions. It is also a dramatic example of how immediate tax savings may be only a part of the critical story. That is, Stoor's stocks are now tied up in a corporate entity and she may encounter major tax issues if she ever tries to get them back out of that corporation prior to her death.

Many other, sometimes equally convoluted, possibilities exist based on the same basic principle. In the discussion of maximizing exclusions, we briefly considered how an imaginary taxpayer, Black (the operator of a small-town mortuary), could decrease his tax liability through the use of such corporate fringe benefits as life, health, and accident insurance; meals and lodging; and certain death benefits. We pointed out that Black benefited from the exclusion provisions of the Code because he did not have to report as gross income the value he received in the form of group-term life, health, and accident insurance; meals and lodging; and certain death benefits. Note, however, that the real tax benefits implicit in those examples depend not only on the fact that they can be excluded from the calculation of Black's personal taxable income, but also on the fact that the cost of those same benefits can be deducted as ordinary and necessary business expenses by Black's wholly owned corporation, which pays the bills. In summary, therefore, the tax savings implicit in those examples really stem from the maximization of both exclusions and deductions. Through the use of a corporate entity, Black can convert what would otherwise largely have been nondeductible personal expenditures into tax-deductible expenses without creating any taxable income for himself (because of the statutory exclusion provisions).

Minimizing the Tax Rate

A third critical variable in tax planning is the applicable tax rate. As noted early in the text, the marginal tax rate is to business affairs what the law of gravity is to physics. Just as water seeks its lowest level (due to the laws of gravity), so also taxable income seeks its lowest marginal tax rate (due to tax planning). The tax-planning objective is achieved, of course, when the marginal tax rate is minimized. This principle can once again be readily illustrated through a simple example.

Suppose that Mr. and Mrs. Isadore Safe, a highly successful locksmith and his wife, report an annual taxable income of $200,000. If Mrs. Safe suddenly inherited $100,000 cash from her recently deceased uncle, Willis More, she might be tempted to deposit the inheritance in a bank savings account and to use the interest to finance the education of her two children. If Mrs. Safe received 7.5% interest on her savings account, she would discover that the additional $7,500 in interest each year increased the annual income tax liability payable by her and Mr. Safe by $2,100. In other words, only $5,400 would be left after taxes to apply toward the children's education. With a little planning, Mrs. Safe might give the $100,000 that she inherited equally to her two children. Each of the Safe children would now receive $3,750 per year in interest. If we assume that the children received no other income and that they were each 14 years of age or older, they would each pay an income tax of $487.50. In this way, the aggregate tax liability on the $7,500 of interest each year would have been reduced from $2,100 to $975, and the amount left toward the children's education would have increased from $5,400 to $6,525 per year.

The tax savings implicit in this simple example is attributable to the combined effect of minimizing the tax rate and maximizing deductions. Mr. and Mrs. Isadore Safe were in a 28% marginal tax bracket; their children were in a 15% marginal tax bracket. Transferring the $7,500 annual interest income from their higher marginal tax bracket to the children's lower marginal tax bracket created a tax savings. The aggregate tax savings was further increased because the children could claim an additional $500 standard deduction on their own tax returns. (As discussed in earlier chapters, the 1986 TRA largely eliminates the tax saving if the child is under 14 years old.)

A small corporate entity may also be another useful vehicle in minimizing tax rates where the corporate rate is lower than that of the shareholder. If one individual owns the entire equity interest in a corporation, that corporation is, obviously, a mere alter ego of the sole stockholder. Nevertheless, the I.R.S. and the courts recognize the existence of a separate (corporate) taxpayer as long as it has a legitimate business purpose. Unfortunately, however, if the corporation is found to hold assets such as shares of stock, it may be a personal holding company subject to severe penalties as discussed later in this chapter.

Maximizing Credits

Relative to the three other variables already discussed, the opportunity to save taxes through the maximization of credits is more limited for the "average" taxpayer. Nevertheless, a taxpayer can help maximize the value of available credits. For example, a taxpayer weighing alternative investment opportunities must consider tax credits carefully before making final decisions. An investment in the rehabilitation of a certified historic structure can give rise to a tax credit of as much as 20% of the amount expended in the rehabilitation, whereas the construction of a new building ordinarily provides no investment credit. Similarly, the purchase of a robot or other piece of industrial equipment generally does not give rise to any credit, but the employment of individuals who meet specified criteria may yield a credit. Whether or not (1) a remodeled old building is a good substitute for a new one, or (2) an employee can replace an industrial robot are difficult and separate questions. Nevertheless, neither decision can be made without giving adequate attention to tax credits.

ANOTHER VIEW OF THE OPPORTUNITIES

An alternative way of viewing tax-planning opportunities is to observe that our income tax is constrained by time, entity, and accounting method. We could, therefore, go back and review each illustration and reclassify the tax savings as being attributable to time, entity, or accounting-method manipulation rather than as maximizing deductions, minimizing tax rate, and so on. However, our objective here is not to derive the best possible classification system for tax planning. Rather, it is to emphasize fundamental ways in which we should examine routine facts to determine the tax-preferred alternative. Consequently, we examine very briefly a few additional planning ideas in this new way.

The Time Constraint

Observe that our income tax rates "start over" with each new tax year. Because very few taxpayers have a constant level of taxable income in each year, taxpayers tend to have high-tax years and low-tax years. As explained earlier, the tax value of a deduction is directly dependent on the marginal tax bracket of the party reporting it. Obviously, taxpayers tend to recognize losses and other deductions in high-tax years and to defer the recognition of taxable income to low-tax years. However, a taxpayer should control tax timing only after giving full consideration to the time value of money. Sometimes the financial cost of deferral is greater than the tax benefit.

The Accounting Method Constraint

Most taxable entities are generally free to select their own accounting methods. Sometimes a single entity may utilize more than one accounting method if it has more than one trade or business. By selecting accounting methods carefully, a taxpayer can save tax dollars. For example, many American corporations switched to the LIFO (last-in, first-out) inventory costing method in the 1970s to save taxes. Because of the rapid inflation experienced during those years, the cost of goods sold determined under the LIFO method was considerably larger than it would have been under any other method for most businesses. Accordingly, the switch was commonly made largely to save taxes because of the lower incomes that were thereby reported.

In the case of an individual taxpayer, the exact definitional distinction between accounting methods and certain tax options is sometimes blurred. To illustrate this opportunity, consider the case of the wage earner whose itemized deductions nearly always equal the standard deduction. That taxpayer would likely conclude that no tax planning can help. Actually, such a taxpayer does have one limited chance at playing the tax game. Because he or she can itemize deductions in any year and can report taxable income on a cash basis of accounting, he or she can benefit by carefully timing deductible expenditures and keeping good records. The basic idea involves itemizing deductions every other year. In years when deductions do not exceed the standard deduction, the taxpayer should defer all tax-deductible expenditures to the maximum extent possible. For example, in those years, the taxpayer should:

1. Make minimal charitable contributions
2. Defer business-related interest payments
3. Defer paying doctor and dentist bills
4. Avoid making property tax payments

In years when deductions exceed the standard deduction, the taxpayer should do just the opposite. This tax plan can be illustrated easily, as in the following diagram. In this way, the taxpayer's aggregate deductions may be greater and tax liability smaller, over several years.

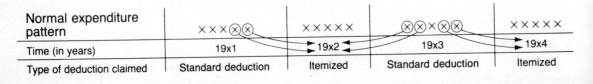

Normal expenditure pattern	× × × ⊗ ⊗	× × × × ×	⊗ ⊗ × ⊗ ⊗	× × × × ×
Time (in years)	19x1	19x2	19x3	19x4
Type of deduction claimed	Standard deduction	Itemized	Standard deduction	Itemized

Other examples of successful tax planning could be included here. Those examples would add little, if anything, to the fundamentals already introduced. Therefore, rather than belabor isolated examples, let us turn to some limitations that often constrain otherwise viable tax plans.

SOME LIMITATIONS

Tax planning is not always as simple as it has appeared in the examples in this chapter. The Internal Revenue Service, Congress, and the courts are constantly putting limitations on some of the more grandiose ideas intended to save taxes. Although we cannot explore this fascinating subject in depth, we might examine briefly two statutory limitations to some of the more obvious tax-saving opportunities. Let us return to a modified version of the facts in the example of Ionna Stoor.

The Personal Holding Company Tax

Again assume that Ionna Stoor is a very successful single businesswoman with an annual taxable income of $200,000 who inherits a large block of stock that pays her an additional $100,000 in dividends each year. However, Stoor does *not* already own the outstanding stock of a viable corporation. Having inherited this stock, and knowing about the corporate dividends-received deduction, Stoor might be tempted to create a new corporate entity and to transfer to it her interest in the newly inherited shares. She would be hoping, of course, to reduce her tax on the $100,000 in dividends from $28,000 (if received by her directly) to $3,000 (if received by her newly created corporation). The corporate tax would equal 15% of $20,000 (that is, a $100,000 dividend less an $80,000 dividends-received deduction). Such a plan could not succeed.

Unfortunately, this apparently grand tax plan is indeed too good to be true. Realizing the existence of the possibility just described, Congress long ago enacted the personal holding company tax (Secs. 541–547). Under the proposed tax plan, Stoor's new corporation would constitute a personal holding company and be subject to a separate tax (in addition to the $3,000 income tax) of $27,160 [28%($100,000 − $3,000)]. The many details of Secs. 541–547 are beyond the scope of this elementary text. We need observe only that the personal holding company tax generally applies only to corporations (1) whose stock is closely held (that is, more than 50% of its stock is owned by or for any five or fewer individuals) and (2) whose income is largely from passive sources [more technically, "at least 60% of its adjusted ordinary gross income . . . for the taxable year is personal holding company income" (Sec. 542(a)(1))]. ("Passive income" in this context includes "portfolio income.") The definitional nuances implicit in any interpretation of the Code section just quoted are substantial. Nevertheless, even the beginner can readily understand why Stoor's idea cannot succeed as proposed.

However, if Stoor could transfer these shares to a corporation that was engaged in the conduct of an *active* trade or business, as originally proposed, and if the extra dividends (along with any other personal holding company income) did not exceed 60% of that corporation's "adjusted ordinary gross income," then the annual tax savings explained above could actually be realized. To achieve this favorable result, the "active" business need not be profitable; only additional *gross* income is needed, not net income. Hence, a telephone answering service, a bowling alley, or a coin-operated laundry that just broke even could be enough to save these taxes. In other words, the basic idea suggested is viable, but only if done with proper regard for the possible limitations imposed by Secs. 541–547.

The Accumulated Earnings Tax

A second possible hindrance to the achievement of the intended tax savings suggested in this example could arise from Secs. 531–537. Those Code sections impose an accumulated earnings tax on any corporation that accumulates its earnings "beyond the reasonable needs of the business."[3] The purpose of this penalty tax is to force corporations either to use any accumulated retained earnings in reasonable business needs or to distribute those same amounts to their stockholders. For Stoor's corporation, the fact that the newly expanded brewery would be receiving $100,000 of dividend income each year makes the Stoor Corporation a prime candidate for this tax even if it could escape the personal holding company tax. Unless the corporation used the accumulated earnings for reasonable business needs, it would have to either pay the penalty tax or distribute the excess corporate funds as a dividend to Stoor.[4] The latter alternative is not satisfactory from her standpoint, because it would result in the dividends being taxed at 28% after all. Consequently, the desirable tax result *is* possible, but only if Stoor can avoid *both* the personal holding company tax and the accumulated earnings tax.

Again, we will not discuss the many complexities associated with the accumulated earnings tax. We need observe only that reasonable people frequently disagree over the reasonableness of earnings accumulated in American corporations, especially in closely held corporations. Thus, I.R.S. agents and taxpayers commonly disagree over the proper application of this tax provision to specific corporate circumstances. The question that must be answered is, ultimately, a question of *fact* (not a question of law) that can be resolved only by a court decision if the agent and the taxpayer cannot reach an earlier settlement. The value of a tax expert's assistance in the bargaining process that takes place should be obvious.

---

[3]Section 535(c)(2) provides a minimum accumulation of $250,000 for most corporations without the imposition of this tax. However, the accumulation of earnings beyond this *de minimis* amount can be retained without penalty only for "reasonable business needs."

[4]The rate of this penalty tax is 27½% of the first $100,000 of unreasonably accumulated earnings and 38½% of any additional amounts so accumulated.

TAX PLANNING FOR SMALLER BUSINESSES IN GENERAL

Successful tax plans take a variety of forms. One major, integrated set of tax plans that was common to small businesses prior to 1970, and that can still work under limited circumstances, involves the use of multiple corporate entities to gain maximum advantage of the lower tax brackets allowed corporations reporting less than $75,000 of taxable income each year. To work really well under current law, the taxable income of each corporation will have to be kept below $50,000 per year. The essential elements of this scheme are depicted in Figure 19-1. The income stream produced directly and indirectly by taxpayer O/O (an owner–operator) is depicted by the large arrow on the left side of Figure 19-1. This income can sometimes be protected from higher individual income tax rates by the creation of multiple corporate entities. In one sense, the corporation can serve as a tax fence to block the income from flowing directly and immediately to taxpayer O/O.

The owner–operator extracts from the corporations enough income to (1) satisfy personal consumption requirements and (2) keep the corporate taxable income at (ideally) $50,000 or less each year. He or she should extract income only in a form that will be deductible to the corporations and taxable to him or her. Salary, interest (on debt), and rents (on property owned by taxpayer O/O, but leased to and used by his or her corporations) are common vehicles used to extract whatever income O/O deems necessary. Obviously, to the extent available in this plan, taxpayer O/O should also have the corporations

FIGURE **19-1**　　A Common Small Business Tax Arrangement

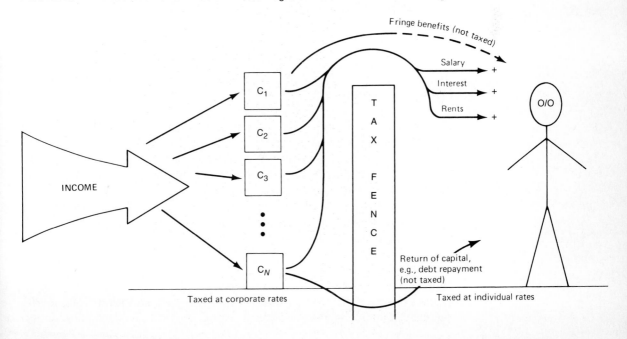

purchase items whose cost can be immediately deducted (by the corporations) and never taxed to the owner–operator as an individual. In general, the costs of certain fringe benefits fall into this category.

Many tax disputes of the past three decades, and many of the complex rules noted earlier in this text, derive naturally from this setting. For example, one tax problem that continues to plague small businesses involves the need to distinguish clearly between corporate debt and equity. Taxpayers—such as O/O in Figure 19-1—commonly create their closely held corporations with minimum equity and maximum debt. They prefer to record a $100,000 investment in, say, C_5 (that is, corporation 5) as $80,000 long-term debt and $20,000 common stock, rather than as $20,000 debt and $80,000 equity, because

1. The debt gives rise to an immediately deductible corporate interest payment (whereas dividends of an equivalent amount cannot be deducted).
2. The existence of the debt may be used to justify the accumulation of earnings (to pay off the debt at a later date) and thus to avoid the penalty tax associated with any "unreasonable" accumulations of earnings.
3. The payment of the face of the debt results only in a return of capital to the owner—an event delightfully free of any tax consequences under most circumstances.

As one would suspect however, there are many limits placed on the debt structure of the corporation in order to restrict "disguised equity."

In summary, because of our income tax laws, at least a few closely held businesses in the United States continue to operate through multiple corporate entities. The owners extract as much from those corporations as possible by way of tax-free fringe benefits and as return of capital. Beyond that, the owners satisfy personal needs and tax results through variable salary, interest, and rent payments. Retirement generally involves a tax-free reorganization.

Multiple Corporations

The reason for multiple corporations in tax planning for small businesses may not be apparent. The fundamental advantage derives from a basic concept suggested earlier in this chapter. Generally speaking, so long as the income tax rates are progressive it is desirable to spread a given amount of income over a maximum number of taxable entities. As a result, each entity can pay tax on its first dollars of income at the lowest possible marginal rate. This same idea lies behind the savings illustrated earlier for Mr. and Mrs. Isadore Safe and their interest on a $100,000 inheritance.

The potential value of splitting a $200,000 corporate taxable income equally between two corporate entities—rather than reporting all of it in one entity—is clearly demonstrated in Figure 19-2. Observe that there is, of course, no tax benefit whatsoever in multiple corporations as long as the aggregate amount of taxable income recognized within the corporation(s)

FIGURE 19-2   Tax Advantage of (Four) Multiple Corporations After 1987

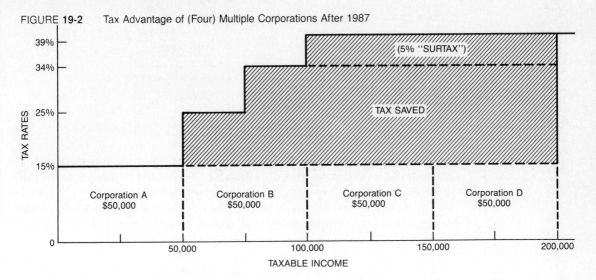

does not exceed $50,000. If the recognized income exceeds that amount, however, some tax benefit is inevitable. The larger the corporate taxable income, in general, the greater the number of corporations desired. For example, if the corporate taxable income is $300,000 each year, splitting that taxable income equally among six corporations (rather than allowing all of it to be earned by one corporation) would yield a tax saving of $55,250, or 55% of the total corporate tax liability! An annuity of $55,250 per year for 30 years, earning only 6% after taxes, is worth approximately $4.4 million! Obviously, the owners of small American businesses have a real incentive to (1) create multiple corporations and (2) divide their income within those corporations. By retaining income within multiple family corporations, and by passing ownership of those corporations from one generation to another only at the death of the prior owner, large amounts of taxable income can be sheltered from the U.S. personal income taxes. However, if multiple corporations are members of a "controlled group" of corporations, the taxable income of the several corporations will have to be combined and taxed as if the total were earned by a single taxable entity.

Controlled Groups

Is it possible for multiple corporations to exist without creating a controlled group? The answer is yes, but only at a price. A detailed analysis of the definitional nuances associated with a controlled group of corporations is beyond the confines of this text solely because of the time and space required to explain them adequately. We can, however, look at a few possible family ownership arrangements that could become increasingly typical in the years ahead.

A controlled group can exist in any one of three forms: parent–subsidiary, brother–sister, or a combination of these two. A parent–subsidiary group

FIGURE **19-3**   Simple Example of Two Controlled Corporations

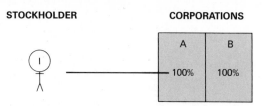

exists whenever one or more chains of corporations are connected with a common 80% corporate–parent ownership. The brother–sister form of the controlled group of corporations is defined by two tests—an 80% test *plus* a 50% test. The former test requires that five or fewer persons own 80% of the stock of the several corporations being tested. The 50% test requires that five or fewer persons own *more than* 50% of the stock of two or more corporations, "taking into account the stock ownership of each such person only to the extent such stock ownership is identical with respect to each such corporation" [Sec. 1563(a)(2)(B)]. Both the 80% test and the 50% test have created difficulties in statutory interpretation. Most of the definitional problems associated with the 50% test were resolved by Treasury Regulations; those associated with the 80% test were resolved when the U.S. Supreme Court handed down its decision in a case involving two Iowa corporations, Vogel Fertilizer and Vogel Popcorn.

To unravel the statutory syntax, we examine a few examples. Suppose that individual taxpayer I owned 100% of the outstanding stock of both Corporation A and Corporation B. This ownership arrangement is illustrated in Figure 19-3. In this illustration, both the 80 and 50% tests are obviously satisfied because one individual (taxpayer I) owns all of both corporations.

Let us complicate matters slightly by considering Figure 19-4, in which individual I owns 60% of Corporation A and 40% of Corporation B, and individual J (who is unrelated to person I) owns 40% of Corporation A and 60% of Corporation B. In this illustration, the 80% test presents no special problems of interpretation, because obviously the two individuals collectively

FIGURE **19-4**   Second Example of Two Controlled Corporations

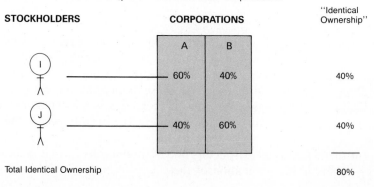

FIGURE **19-5**   Example of Noncontrolled Group

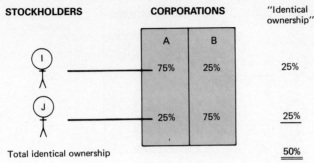

STOCKHOLDERS	CORPORATIONS		"Identical ownership"
	A	B	
I	75%	25%	25%
J	25%	75%	25%
Total identical ownership			50%

own 100% of the stock of both corporations. The meaning of the 50% identical ownership test is not as apparent because the words used in the Code to state that test are unclear. However, the Treasury Regulations state that we can make that computation simply by looking across each row in this simple matrix, finding the smallest number for each shareholder and adding these numbers. Thus, for individual I, the "identical ownership" is 40% (because taxpayer I owns only 40% of Corporation B); individual J's identical ownership is also 40% (because J owns only 40% of Corporation A). When we add (or sum) the two identical ownerships of 40%, the total (80%) obviously exceeds the *more than* 50% requirement of Sec. 1563(a)(2)(B). Consequently, corporations A and B in Figure 19-4 are also members of a controlled group of corporations.

Assume that we change the ownership, as in Figure 19-5, so that individual I owns 75% of A and 25% of B, and individual J owns 25% of A and 75% of B. In this case, corporations A and B would *not* be members of a controlled group, because the identical ownership of the two stockholders would total only 50%, and the Code requires that their identical ownership be *more than* 50%.

Are the two corporations in Figure 19-6 members of a controlled group? In this example, individual I owns 100% of Corporation A and 79% of Corporation B; individual J owns only 21% of the latter corporation. If the two shareholders can be considered together in making the Sec. 1563 tests, it appears that A and B are members of a controlled group, because two people clearly own 100% of both corporations, and the 50% identical ownership test is satisfied. In other words, in the 80% test, *must the same* (five or fewer) *stockholders own some stock in each corporation* being tested before the corporations can even be considered for controlled group status? That was the question before the Supreme Court in *Vogel Fertilizer.*[5] The Court concluded that the same stockholders must own some stock in each corporation before the corporations can be included in the 80% test to determine

[5]455 U.S. 16 (1982).

FIGURE **19-6**   Another Noncontrolled Group

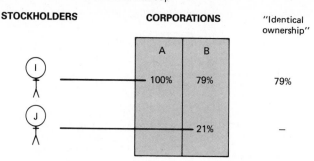

controlled group status. In other words, the Court held that corporations A and B in Figure 19-6 are *not* members of a controlled group because stockholder J owns no part of Corporation A; hence, the 80% test is *not* satisfied.

Attribution Rules

This decision by the Supreme Court opened the door for new tax avoidance possibilities. As explained above, multiple corporations can provide tax savings for any business that can divide a substantial amount of taxable income between enough different corporations each year. These tax savings are within the grasp of many closely held corporations if the owners are willing to split their stock ownership properly and if they carefully avoid the attribution rules of Sec. 1563(e). Attribution rules provide, in general, that a stockholder is deemed to own not only the stock that he or she owns directly (in his or her own name), but also indirectly the stock owned by certain other related stockholders. For example, if in Figure 19-6 individuals I and J were a parent and child, respectively, then individual I would be considered to own 100% of both corporations and individual J would also be deemed to own 100% of both corporations by operation of the family attribution rules found in Sec. 1563(e)(6). In that event, corporations A and B would be members of a controlled group, and no tax savings would be implicit in the creation of two entities.

   Because of time and space constraints, we cannot go into the details of all the attribution rules. Suffice it to note here that there is no attribution (1) between *adult* siblings (brothers and sisters) or (2) between parents and their adult children (defined as 21 years of age or older) *so long as* neither the parent nor the child owns *more than* 50% of the stock of the corporation whose shares are being imputed to the other. These technical rules allow families limited flexibility in ownership that may lead to the promised land of tax savings through multiple corporations. Persons interested in applying this idea in a real situation must obtain expert guidance before attempting the

FIGURE **19-7**   Example of Nonfamily Ownership Arrangement That Avoids Controlled Group
Status

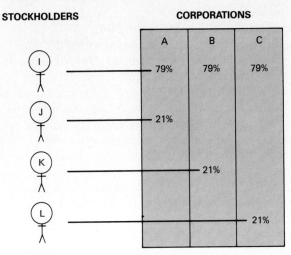

feat because the actual rules are substantially more complex than the
fragmentary observations noted here. Nevertheless, the opportunities and
rewards are sufficiently large that in some instances it will be worth the cost of
the tax adviser's guidance.

One popular arrangement involves an ownership distribution like that
depicted in Figure 19-7. One individual (I) owns 79% of the stock of three
corporations. Each of three other, unrelated individuals owns 21% of the
stock in one corporation. Individual I provides the necessary capital for the
three businesses, whereas individuals J, K, and L provide the day-to-day
management of the businesses. So long as the four stockholders are not

FIGURE **19-8**   Example of Family Ownership Arrangement That Avoids Controlled Group
Status

STOCKHOLDERS		A	B	C	D	E
P	(Parent)	100%	50%		50%	
C-1	(Adult child #1)		50%	100%		
C-2	(Adult child #2)				50%	100%

related family members, no controlled group exists per *Vogel Fertilizer*. Note also that even if J, K, and L were sons- or daughters-in-law of person I, there still would be no attribution because these relationships do not fall within the purview of *family* as defined in Sec. 1563(e)(6).

Individuals who would keep all of the stock within the family must be even more careful in distributing stock ownership. Nevertheless, multiple family corporations are possible. For example, in Figure 19-8, one parent and two adult children own all of the stock of five corporations; yet no controlled group exists. In that example, neither the 50 nor the 80% tests are satisfied; no attribution exists from parent to child (or from child to parent) because neither the parent nor the adult child owns *more than* 50% of the stock of the corporations with more than one shareholder. However, if the family in Figure 19-8 were to change its ownership ratios, however slightly, the tax results would be in jeopardy. For example, if the parent (P) were to insist on a 51% ownership in B and D corporations (and reduce the adult child's share to 49%), then corporations A, B, and D would form a controlled group and all potential family tax savings would disappear! In short, repeating an earlier observation, multiple corporations without a controlled group are possible, but only at a price. To conclude this brief glimpse into tax planning for small businesses in general, let us see how these ideas might apply to a specific family business.

A SPECIFIC EXAMPLE OF TAX PLANNING

Suppose that Mr. and Mrs. Grub have for years operated the family restaurant as a sole proprietorship. The popular restaurant produces an annual operating income of about $290,000 from the food and bar functions combined. In addition, the Grubs inherited stocks that produce about $10,000 in dividends each year. Finally, Mr. Grub owns 50% of a new "hot tub" venture that was incorporated because of its risky nature. As expected, the new business venture reported a $20,000 taxable loss this year; the owners hope it can begin to make a profit within three years.

If the Grubs are unaware of their tax opportunities, they probably report a taxable income of nearly $300,000 and pay an income tax of about $84,000 in 1988. Calculation of those amounts can be detailed as follows, assuming the Grubs do not itemize deductions:

Income from sole proprietorship	$290,000
Dividends	10,000
Adjusted gross income	$300,000
Less personal exemptions and standard deduction	(8,900)
Taxable income	$291,100
Gross tax liability (joint return) (1988 rates)	$ 82,600

Assume that the Grubs spend about $60,000 after taxes for personal comsumption expenditures each year and that they reinvest any excess funds in their family restaurant. This means, of course, that in the current year they would have approximately $160,000 available for reinvestment, calculated as follows:

Gross income received	$300,000
Less: Personal consumption expenditures	(60,000)
Income tax	(81,600)
Available for reinvestment	$158,400

If the Grubs understood our tax laws a little better, they might do the following:

1. Transfer their restaurant assets to three newly created, family-owned corporations —one for food service, another for bar service, and a third for property ownership
2. Give 50% of the stock in the bar and property corporations to their adult children
3. Transfer most of their inherited stocks to the food service corporation
4. Arrange for their corporations to pay them an $80,000 salary for their work
5. Have the new business venture make the S corporation election
6. Provide themselves with some tax-free fringe benefits

Four separate taxable entities now exist whose taxable incomes and tax liabilities might be computed as follows:

Grubs' Corporations	Food Corporation	Bar Corporation	Property Corporation
Operating income	$150,000	$80,000	$60,000
Dividends received	10,000	0	0
Less: Salary paid owners	(60,000)	(15,000)	(5,000)
Dividends-received deduction	(8,000)	0	0
Fringe Benefits	(15,000)	0	0
Taxable income	$ 77,000	$65,000	$55,000
Tax liability	$ 14,430	$11,250	$ 8,750

Mr. and Mrs. Grub	
Salary received	$80,000
Less: S corporation loss	(10,000)
Personal exemptions and standard deduction	(8,900)
Taxable income	$61,100
Gross tax liability	$13,241

Accordingly, the total "family" tax liability would be $47,581, and they would have approximately $177,000 available for reinvestment in their business. The latter amount can be determined as follows:

Grubs' Three Corporations Combined		Mr. and Mrs. Grub	
Income earned	$300,000	Income earned	$80,000*
Less: Salary paid owners	(80,000)	Less: Personal consumption	(60,000)
Fringe Benefits	(15,000)	Income tax paid	(13,241)
Income tax paid	(34,430)		
Available for reinvestment	$170,570	Available for reinvestment	$ 6,759

*Plus tax-free fringe benefits.

The treatment of the $10,000 loss deduction from the new business venture deserves further comment. S corporations are treated as conduits for tax purposes, much like partnerships. Consequently, as a 50% owner in this venture, Grub is entitled to deduct 50% of the $20,000 loss incurred by the corporation. If the new corporation does not elect S corporation treatment, the net operating loss would remain with the corporate entity. Ordinarily, a net operating loss is carried back and treated as an additional deduction against any taxable income reported by the same entity three years earlier. Because our illustration assumed a *new* venture, the corporation would have no prior years to which it could carry back its current loss. If Grub and the other owners do not elect S corporation treatment, the loss can only be carried forward and offset against future taxable income (if any is ever earned). Whether or not the S corporation election is wise from a tax standpoint depends on (1) the comparative marginal tax brackets of the entities that can claim the deduction and (2) the time value of money.

In summary, the Grub family would save over 40% of their tax bill by doing some elementary tax planning. Because of this, they could increase their reinvestment in their income-producing activity by about $20,000. Other things being equal, this should increase their income and wealth in the future. Admittedly, the story is less than 100% complete. For example, the Grubs' extra funds are now "tied up" in a corporate entity; the basis of their stock in the venture corporation is lower; they incur extra record-keeping costs with the new corporations; and their Social Security and business franchise taxes may be higher. Even with the added costs, however, the illustration demonstrates that tax planning can pay dividends in a small business without resorting to any remotely questionable practices. The question is: Are the tax savings achieved worth the trouble and potential future problems associated with achieving them?

SUMMARY

It is hoped that the discussion just completed demonstrates both the intrigue and the complexity in tax planning. Each year, the statement that "everything depends on everything" is truer than it was the year before. The utilization of tax-free fringe benefits and multiple corporations can be beneficial, but only if certain conditions are satisfied. Taxpayers will learn to use these special provisions to their best advantage, but they will also learn that doing so may require several changes in old habits and procedures. The I.R.S. will resist new plans, and their resistance will cause still further modifications. Like the ever-flowing river, the process of taxation will forever continue to modify human behavior, while human behavior will modify the process itself.

PROBLEMS

1. Many specific business transactions, as well as business operations in general, are modified significantly by our federal income tax provisions. Demonstrate your understanding of this statement by answering the following questions:
   a. Detail three specific business transactions that would be susceptible to modification for tax reasons and explain how you think the tax provision would affect the transaction.
   b. Cite two recent, major changes in the U.S. tax laws, and explain how these changes modify (or will modify) American business behavior.

2. For years, the Italians did not impose a real property tax on buildings "under construction." Discuss the effects of this rule.

3. For years, the French had a tax based on the number of windows a building had. Discuss the effects of using this tax base.

4. Esther White, M.D., owned several pieces of rental property and shares of stock in numerous corporations. A friend advised her to transfer some of the assets to a corporation to save income taxes. The doctor accepted this advice and transferred numerous properties to a newly formed corporation. The doctor gave one third of the shares to her son, one third to her daughter, and retained one third in her own name. During the first year of operations, the following income statement was prepared for the corporation:

Interest on bonds	$24,000
Dividends on stocks owned	20,000
Net rental income from properties	40,000
Total	$84,000
Deductible operating expenses	4,000
Net income	$80,000

To minimize taxes on the doctor and her children, no dividends were paid.
   a. Compute the corporation's federal tax liability using 1988 tax rates.
   b. What advice can you give the doctor?

5. Mr. and Mrs. Busy own and operate several business ventures in Boulder, Colorado. Although several of their businesses are profitable, the Busys do not distribute any cash from any of them. They prefer to accumulate all business profits within each business and reinvest them for, hopefully, still larger profits in the future. The Busys live on a $60,000 cash distribution received annually from the Busy Trust Fund, which was created by Mr. Busy's grandfather. During the current year, the Busys' businesses reported the following taxable incomes (losses are indicated by parentheses):

Busy Book Store (a sole proprietorship)	$ 5,000
Western Manufacturing Corporation (which is 100% owned by Mr. and Mrs. Busy)	(25,000)
Rocky Mountain Crater Corporation (an S corporation 80% owned by Mr. and Mrs. Busy)	10,000
Mesa Wholesale Drugs (a partnership in which Mr. Busy has a one-half interest)	20,000

Assuming that the above information constitutes all of Mr. and Mrs. Busy's business and income data for this year, and assuming that the amounts indicated represent the total income or loss for the entire business venture (not just the Busys' share):

a. What amount of gross income must Mr. and Mrs. Busy report on their joint tax return?

b. Which of these business ventures are taxable entities?

c. Which of these businesses need file only information tax returns?

d. What happens to the $25,000 loss incurred by Western Manufacturing Corporation?

e. Considering only this one year, should the Busys have elected S corporation treatment for Western Manufacturing Corporation? Explain.

6. Mr. I. M. Rich earned the following income during 19x1:

Operating income from sole proprietorship (Drag Cleaners)	$56,000
Dividends from various domestic corporate stocks (jointly owned by Mr. and Mrs. Rich)	20,000
Interest on state bonds (tax exempt)	10,000
Total income for 19x1	$86,000

Assuming that Mr. Rich is married, has one dependent child, is 45 and of good vision, does not itemize deductions, and files a joint return with his wife (who is 43 and also of good vision), determine Rich's:

a. Taxable income.

b. Gross tax liability for 19x1. (Use 1988 rates.)

c. Amount available for reinvestment in Drag Cleaners if the Riches spent $50,000 for personal consumption in 19x1.

Could the Riches reduce their income tax to provide themselves with additional capital for reinvestment in the Drag Cleaners chain? Specifically, could they gain any tax advantages by incorporating the business? Answer the above questions by answering the questions below:

d. If the Riches incorporate the business venture, should they transfer the state bonds to the new corporation? Explain.

e. If they incorporate, should they transfer the dividend-producing investments to the corporation?

Regardless of how you answered any of the questions above, *assume* that the Riches form a corporation and transfer all of their operating assets (those that comprise the chain of cleaners) and most of the corporate investments to this new corporation. The income result (assuming the same operating results as were reported in 19x1) would look something like this:

Corporation		Personal	
Operating income	$56,000	Operating income (all corporation)	$ 0
Less: Salary paid to Mr. Rich	46,000	Salary from corporation	46,000
Operating income after salary	$10,000	Tax-exempt interest on state government bonds	10,000
Dividends received	20,000	Total income	$56,000
Total income	$30,000		

(NOTE: The combined income, before income taxes, is exactly the same now as it was prior to incorporation in 19x1.) Assuming the above distribution of income and assets, determine the following:

   f. Corporation's taxable income.
   g. Corporation's tax liability. (Use 1988 rates.)
   h. Personal taxable income. (Assume all facts as before in dependents, joint return, and so on.)
   i. Personal tax liability. (Use 1988 rates.)
   j. Total taxes paid (combined personal and corporate).
   k. Amount available for reinvestment in Drag Cleaners. (Assume again, that the Riches spent $50,000 for personal consumption items.)

7. J.R. has been operating a small manufacturing business as a small proprietor for several years. For legal liability reasons, he believes it would be advisable to incorporate his business. He owns the land and building in which the business operates. What guidelines would you suggest to J.R. to be followed in forming the corporation? For example, should all the business assets be transferred to the corporation in exchange for stock?

8. In each of the following situations, state whether a controlled group exists, and if so, which corporations are part of the controlled group and what type of controlled group it is (that is, parent–subsidiary, brother–sister, or a combination). (Unless specifically stated, assume that none of the parties are related or own any other stock.)

   a. Corporation X owns 80% of Corporation Y; Individual I owns the other 20% of Corporation Y.
   b. Corporation X owns 80% of Corporation Y, Corporation Z owns the other 20% of Corporation Y, and Corporation Z does not own any stock in Corporation X.
   c. Corporation X owns 80% of Corporation Y, Corporation Z owns the other 20% of Corporation Y, and Corporation Z owns 85% of stock in Corporation X.
   d. Mr. T owns 80% of Corporation A and 80% of Corporation B. Corporation B owns 90% of Corporation C.
   e. Individual A owns 20% of Corporation X and 80% of Corporation Y. Individual B, unrelated to Individual A, owns 80% of Corporation X and 20% of Corporation Y.
   f. Individual A owns 20% of Corporation X and 80% of Corporation Y. Individual B, related to Individual A under the provision of Sec. 1563(e)(6), owns 80% of Corporation X and 20% of Corporation Y.

g. Individual A owns 51% in each of three corporations: X, Y, and Z. Individual B owns the other 49% of Corporation X; Individual C owns the other 49% of Corporation Y; and Individual D owns the remaining 49% of Corporation Z. None of the individuals are related.

h. The facts are the same as in part g, except that Individuals B, C, and D are all A's adult children.

CHAPTER 20

Corporations and Tax Planning

> *Whether the purpose be to gain an advantage under the law of the state of incorporation or to avoid or comply with the demands of creditors or to serve the creator's personal or undisclosed convenience, so long as that purpose is the equivalent of business activity or is followed by the carrying on of business by the corporation, the corporation remains a separate taxable entity.*
> Moline Properties, Inc. *v.* Commissioner, *319 U.S. 436 (1943)*

The prior chapter ended with the observation that the tax-planning process, like the ever-flowing river, continues to modify human behavior, while human behavior modifies tax planning itself. This potentially vicious circle of economic and political forces is particularly apparent in matters related to the corporate entity. The corporation has been a favorite tool of U.S. tax planners since the very beginning of the modern income tax in 1913. Whether or not it will retain this favored status after the 1986 Code is not entirely clear. Some of the tax law changes made in 1986 will very clearly reduce the viability of the corporate entity for tax-planning purposes; a few others will increase it. On balance, therefore, it seems safe to conclude that the general popularity of the corporation will not disappear, even if it does experience a decline in relative importance.

A significant reason for the popularity of corporations derives from *nontax* considerations. Most importantly, the corporation generally provides limited liability for the owners of the corporation engaged in a trade or business. That is, business creditors may generally look only to the assets of the corporation in satisfaction of any debts. The shareholder's personal assets, other than those invested to acquire the corporation's stock, remain beyond the reach of the corporation's creditors. Hence, individuals with a substantial amount of personal assets are effectively forced to utilize a corporate entity, particularly when engaging in a trade or business with significant risk.

Corporations are also popular because they are generally characterized by the free transferability of ownership interests, the centralization of management, and continuity of life. These corporate characteristics mean, of course, that corporate shareholders are free to buy and/or sell their interest in a corporation at any time, that the owners need not be personally involved in the management of the entity, and that the corporation will continue uninterrupted even though particular shareholders and managers may come and go with some regularity. These unique corporate characteristics are especially important in raising large sums of capital from diverse sources.

As we noted in Chapter 6, the importance of corporations in tax planning is evidenced by the large number of small corporations that exist, approximately 3.3 million, with only 1% of these reporting assets in excess of $10 million. The existence of this large number of small corporations can be explained by the tax advantages that accrue to incorporation.

In this chapter we attempt to explain how and why a corporation can often be useful in successful tax planning. The chapter is divided into three major parts: first, a review of a few critical tax rules; second, the broad outline of tax savings that are implicit in those fundamental rules; and third, a quick look at some of the judicial and statutory aberrations to the basic notions that must be considered when using a corporate entity for tax-planning purposes.

FUNDAMENTALS

The United States imposes only one income tax, not two or three different income taxes. The general public is frequently misled into thinking that there are at least two distinctly different income taxes because of references to "the individual income tax" and "the corporate income tax." Students are further confused by the way most college and university tax courses in the business school are organized. That is, Tax 1 is usually oriented toward the individual taxpayer; Tax 2, toward the corporate taxpayer. Because of these confusing signals, it is not surprising to find that many people do not really comprehend the fascinating interrelationship between the income tax sometimes paid by corporations, sometimes by individuals, and sometimes by both, on a single income stream.

One Tax: Three Apparent Taxable Entities

Code Sec. 1(a)–(d) reads (in part) as follows: "There is hereby imposed on the taxable income of . . . every . . . individual . . . a tax in accordance with the following table." Section 11(a) reads: "A tax is hereby imposed for each taxable year on the taxable income of every corporation." And Section 1(e) reads: "There is hereby imposed on the taxable income of—(1) every estate, and (2) every trust, . . . a tax determined in accordance with the following table." Understanding these three fundamental and deceptively simple sentences is essential to understanding the United States income tax. The words used embody at least three important notions or concepts, namely:

1. There is but one federal income tax imposed on a common tax base called taxable income,

2. That income tax must be paid by every individual, every corporation, and every estate or trust,

3. Our income tax law knows no national boundaries—it applies equally to *every* individual, corporation, estate, or trust, wherever in this galaxy they may be found.

As any intelligent reader would instinctively suspect, these three sweeping conclusions are not literally true. Indeed, the almost surreal complexity of the Code is, at least in part, due to the need to define and restrict the outer boundaries of an overzealous beginning. The Code necessarily contains exception upon exception upon exception ad infinitum, to make such a grandiose start into a workable reality.

The biggest single villain to genuine understanding of the three brief sentences, quoted at the beginning of the preceding paragraph, is to be found in the definition of the term "taxable income." For example, in the instance of fiduciary taxpayers—that is, estates and trusts—the definition of taxable income is articulated in such a manner as to make the fiduciary at best a "half-entity" or "pseudo-entity." In other words, even though the conventional wisdom is that there are three taxable entities in the U.S. federal income tax system—that is, individuals, corporations, and fiduciaries—the truth is that there are really only two (individuals and corporations) that honestly fit that description. As you will learn in the next chapter, the taxable income of an otherwise tax-recognized estate or trust is defined as only the residual income retained by the trust, if any. The taxable income distributed to a beneficiary within the year can be deducted in the determination of the fiduciary's taxable income. Hence, if a trust distributes its entire taxable income to an income beneficiary, the trust will have no taxable income and owe no income tax even though it may have earned a substantial amount of taxable income. It is doubtful, therefore, that we should classify either an estate or a trust as a true or complete taxable entity. To a lesser extent, as you will discover momentarily, this same observation is at least partially true for many small corporations.

Separate, Progressive Tax-Rate Schedules

As you discovered earlier in this text, a slightly different tax-rate schedule exists for individuals, corporations, and fiduciaries. In fact, four distinctly different schedules exist for individuals alone: one each for married persons filing a joint return, heads of households, single persons, and married persons filing separately. Although, after the 1986 Act, each of the tax rate schedules *approximates* a proportional tax rate at a sufficiently high level of taxable income, a limited degree of progression remains at lower levels of income.

The greatest amount of progression now exists for corporate taxpayers. That tax rate schedule effectively contains four steps in a progression, as shown on the rate schedule in Chapter 6 at page 6-6. This corporate tax rate is similar to that described earlier for individual taxpayers in that it, too, provides for a 5% surtax to "recapture" or "phase out" the benefit of the lower marginal rates that exist solely for those corporations recognizing relatively small amounts of taxable income. The arithmetic of the 5% phaseout or recapture is straightforward:

$$5\% \ (\$335{,}000 - \$100{,}000) = (34\% - 15\%)\$50{,}000 + (34\% - 25\%)\$25{,}000.$$

This means, of course, that corporations earning a taxable income in excess of $335,000 will ordinarily be subject to a proportional or flat tax of 34%.

Minimal progression currently exists for fiduciary taxpayers. Beginning January 1, 1988, those tax rates will be:

Tax Base	Tax Rate
$0 to $5,000	15%
$5,000 to $13,000	28%
$13,000 to $26,000	33%
Above $26,000	28%

Once again a 5% surtax serves to recapture the lower marginal rates. What is unusual in this case is the very low level of income ($13,000) at which the phaseout begins to apply. The math is as follows:

$$5\% \ (\$26{,}000 - \$13{,}000) = (28\% - 15\%) \ \$5{,}000.$$

Any fiduciary that recognizes a taxable income of only $26,000 now pays a flat tax of 28%.

General Rules and Special Provisions

The statutory rules for the computation of corporate taxable income were explained in Chapter 6, but a brief review of those rules will be helpful.

First, the same general rules for income and deductions apply to all taxpayers. However, some Code sections are restricted to individuals only (Section 212 that allows deductions for investment expenses), while others apply only to corporations (Section 248 that permits the amortization of organizational expenditures). You can usually sort out provisions that do not apply to corporations by using common sense—alimony provisions, for example.

The special provisions applicable *only* to corporations discussed in Chapter 6 were the amortization of organizational expenditures, the dividends received deduction, and the special limitation on contributions. The capital gains and losses of corporations also receive different treatment, as explained in Chapters 16 and 17.

IMPLICIT CONSEQUENCES OF FUNDAMENTAL CONCEPTS

The legal form of organization selected for any business endeavor can have important tax consequences. At least for income tax purposes, business organizations can be classified as either (1) conduits or (2) separate taxable entities. In the case of conduits, any tax attributes associated with an income stream pass directly through that entity and to the owner(s). In the case of separate taxable entities, any tax attributes associated with an income stream cease to exist beyond the entity or, stated in another way, old attributes disappear and are often transformed at the entity level. This concept is illustrated in Figure 20-1. Think of taxable income as a liquid stream that enters either a funnel or a container. If, as in a funnel, the liquid *must* pass through and simply be redirected to specific owners without basic modification—that is, whatever chemical composition the liquid had on entry must be retained and redistributed to the owners of the entity—then that legal form of business organization would be known as a conduit for federal income tax purposes. On the other hand, if, as in the entity example, the liquid might (1) enter as one thing (say, carbonated water); (2) remain there for a substantial period of time; and (3) eventually pass on as something else (say, either Diet Coke or regular Dr. Pepper), then that legal form of business organization would be known as a separate taxable entity for federal income tax purposes. Partnerships, which will be discussed further in Chapter 21, are a classic form of the tax conduit; corporations, a classic form of the separate entity.

FIGURE **20-1**   Tax Conduits Versus Tax Entities

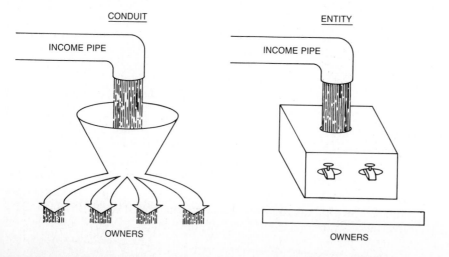

Potential for a Double Tax

The biggest income tax problem with the corporation as a separate entity is the fact that a single income stream may actually be taxed twice: once to the corporation, when it is first "earned," and a second time to the shareholders, when it is distributed by the corporation as a dividend.

Our federal income tax law could, of course, cure this apparent malady very simply by allowing corporations to deduct amounts paid to shareholders as dividends. Although often proposed, this ready solution has never gained great political momentum on Capitol Hill, apparently because the managers of our large corporations have been unwilling to face the increased pressure that such a rule would create for the distribution of substantially larger amounts of corporate dividends. U.S. corporations have, in large measure, depended on retained earnings as a source of new capital, and corporate managers apparently do not want to diminish that major opportunity.

Retained corporate earnings should be reflected in an increase in value of the corporate stock. That increase would be taxed whenever a shareholder sold or exchanged the corporation's stock in a taxable transaction. Thus, even if a corporation does not distribute its earnings as a dividend, our federal income tax law will still effectively tax a single income stream earned by a corporation twice: first, when the corporation earns the income and a second time, when the shareholder sells the appreciated stock at a gain. This potential for a double tax has long been a source of major dissatisfaction among tax scholars.

Double taxation, it is claimed, reduces the equity capital available to corporations and forces the corporations to rely heavily on debt equity. The contractual interest charges related to debt equities are tax deductions to the corporation. Interest is paid with *before-tax* dollars; dividends are paid with *after-tax* dollars. Heavy reliance on debt equities increases the risks in corporate operations because of the fixed interest charges and fixed maturities. The long-run result is an alleged unwillingness on the part of corporate management to undertake high-risk ventures and a decrease in economic stability to the extent that corporations with high debt financing must make capital adjustments because of insolvency. The bias in the tax law against equity financing results in a severe handicap to small, growing corporations, where risks are high and the supply of debt capital limited. Curtailing the economic activities of these small entrepreneurs may result in economic stagnation.

Double taxation of corporate income is presumed to work undue hardship also on shareholders with low incomes. Beginning in 1988, the total tax paid on corporate earnings distributed as dividends to individuals in the top marginal bracket is about 56%—34% tax paid by the corporation and a tax of about 22% of the original corporate income paid by the individual when the remaining 66% is distributed (66% at 33% tax rate). Observe that this total of 56% is 23 percentage points higher than the rate in the top bracket for individuals. The total tax to a shareholder in the lowest bracket is 44% (34% paid by the corporation and 15% of the remaining 66% paid by the individual); this is 29 percentage points higher than the 15% rate in the lowest bracket. The corporate tax falls proportionately on all shareholders; it reduces the earnings per share of a shareholder in the 15% bracket by the same amount as those of a shareholder in the 33% bracket. This penalty on the little person may reduce his or her willingness to invest in American industry, although it is doubtful that he or she ponders long over such an esoteric tax fact.

Critics who complain about the double taxation of corporate income assume that the tax falls on the corporation and is not shifted to suppliers and customers. However, as we discussed in Part One, the problem of tax incidence is complex, and no one can say with certainty just who bears the ultimate burden. Moreover, some empirical evidence exists that corporations are able to shift the tax. The rate of return on invested capital (using *after-tax* income) has remained fairly constant since the 1920s despite drastic changes in the tax rates on corporate income. This constant rate of return supposedly indicates a shift in the tax burden. Nevertheless, other empirical studies, using other data, have reached the opposite conclusion.[1] To the extent that the tax burden *is* shifted, there is no double taxation to the shareholders, except in their roles as consumers or as corporate employees.

The argument that double taxation penalizes the shareholder also ignores some important facts about today's securities market. The vast majority of shareholders acquired their shares in the marketplace, not by contributing to the capital of the corporation. Market values, to the extent that they are influenced by corporate income, are based not on *before-tax* income but on *after-tax* income. The prudent investor bases expectations of return on a continuation of the corporate tax and pays a price for the shares consistent with the after-tax return. To eliminate or reduce the presumed double taxation would result in a huge windfall profit to the current shareholders as the market adjusted to increased expectations. On the other hand, current shareholders are penalized whenever corporate tax rates increase unexpectedly and corporations are unable to shift the increased burden.

Finally, although the income tax law has decidedly influenced the financial structure of corporations, the principal direction of its influence has not been toward greatly increased reliance on debt equities. Generally, since World War II, the portion of all new capital raised by corporations from debt equities has not varied significantly. In some years, when the market for new stock issues is soft, corporate management turns to debt equities for new capital. The principal influence of the tax law has been to increase retention of corporate earnings, a financing policy that avoids the shareholder's recognition of income, which would be taxed at rates up to 33%. The earnings retained are reflected in increased market prices of shares, a source of income to the shareholder that is not taxed until the shares are sold. Retention of the shares until death will, of course, cause the second tax to be entirely avoided

---

[1] For a concise summary of the arguments on this point and for further references, see *The Federal Tax System*, Joint Economic Committee, 1964, pp. 54–55. See also Pechman and Okner, *Who Bears the Tax Burden?* (Washington, DC: The Brookings Institution, 1974).

because the law allows the heir a step-up in basis at the time of the original shareholder's death.

Despite the doubts just raised, the proposition that double taxation is inequitable has had strong advocates in Congress, and the law has contained various provisions to give "relief" to shareholders. From 1913 through 1936, dividends were subject only to the surtax, not to the normal tax.[2] From 1936 to 1954, no relief provisions for individuals were added, but in 1954 Congress added two—an exclusion of a limited amount of dividend income and a credit against the tax equal to 4% of most of the dividends included in taxable income. These provisions were changed again in 1964. The law currently contains only one provision directly related to the problem of double taxation. It is the dividends-received *deduction* allowed corporations.

The problem of double taxation is particularly troublesome when the shareholder is a corporation. Without some special relief, a single corporate intermediary between the corporation earning the income and the individual taxpayers would have the effect of *triple* taxation: first, when the subsidiary corporation earns the income; next, when the income is distributed to the parent corporte shareholder; and third, when the income is distributed as a dividend to individual shareholders. To partially relieve this inequity, a corporate shareholder is allowed a deduction equal to 80% of the dividends received from taxable domestic corporations. The deduction is 100% if the dividend is from small business investment companies (as specifically defined in the law). The dividend deduction is also 100% between members of an affiliated group of corporations, as explained in the prior chapter.

Potential for Tax Reduction

Corporations, from an income tax point of view, are a classic paradox. For the reasons just explained, corporations can represent the worst possible tax alternative, because what is in reality a single income stream may be subject to the federal income tax twice if it is initially "earned" by a corporate entity. For other reasons, to be explained momentarily, corporations can also represent the best possible tax alternative because they can sometimes be manipulated into causing a single income stream to disappear and not be taxed at all. As a general proposition, the former alternative is most typical for the large, publicly held corporation; the latter alternative, for the small, closely held corporation. Is it any wonder, then, why we have so few large corporations and so many small ones?

INCOME, DEDUCTION, AND EXCLUSION   To understand how a corporation can sometimes cause taxable income to vanish into thin air you must reflect on at least two basic tax concepts:

---

[2]Until the Reform Act of 1969, the tax rates for individuals contained both a normal tax and a surtax, though the distinction was not apparent in the rate schedules. The normal rate was a flat 3%, and everything else was a surtax.

1. Corporations are a separate taxable entity, entirely distinct from both owners and employees; and, as a separate taxable entity, they are subject to all of the normal rules concerning gross income, deductions, exclusions, and so on for corporate taxpayers.

2. Individuals who incorporate their trades or businesses may cause their own corporations to hire them back as corporate employees; and, as employees, those owner–employees are subject to all of the normal rules concerning gross income, deductions, exclusions, and so on for individual taxpayers.

Finally, it is necessary to recall specific Code provisions that can work to the advantage of a particular taxpayer. To illustrate, assume that farmer Brown earns a taxable income of $40,000 each year. As a sole proprietor, Brown can not deduct many of his personal living expenses—such as the depreciation on his home, the cost of his homeowner's insurance, utilities to heat, cool, and light his home, or the food he eats (see Sec. 262).

If farmer Brown were to incorporate his farming business; transfer title to his home to the corporate entity; cause the corporation to employ him to feed cattle, plant crops, and do all of the things that farmers normally do; and then cause the corporation to require that he live in the farmhouse as a condition of his employment but for the benefit of the corporation—so that he would be available to attend to emergencies with the livestock as well as provide round-the-clock security—the corporation should be eligible to deduct depreciation on the farmhouse, the insurance on the house, the utilities, food costs, and so on under either a general rule, such as Sec. 162 (for all its ordinary and necessary business expenses), or a specific rule, such as Sec. 167 (for depreciation). Farmer Brown, under the proper conditions, could exclude the value of these same items from his own personal gross income under the authority of Sec. 119 (which allows an employee to exclude the value of employer-provided meals and lodging in certain circumstances). The net effect of this tax plan, when successful, is the transmutation of what started out as taxable income for farmer Brown into "thin air," with the help of a corporate entity.[3]

The illustration just completed is, perhaps, an example of the pinnacle of federal income tax planning because it converted taxable income into nontaxable income without, in any way, reducing the enjoyment of the ultimate consumer (farmer Brown). It is a modern equivalent of ancient alchemy: that is, the conversion of base metals into gold. Because the exclusion provisions of the U.S. federal income tax law are really quite limited, there are relatively few opportunities to be this successful in tax planning. There are, however, multiple opportunities to reach somewhat lesser states of tax euphoria. In a much larger number of cases it is possible to lower the effective tax rate and/or defer the time at which the income tax is payable. Because money has a time value, the latter alternative can also have a good bit of attraction for many taxpayers.

---

[3]For recent, real-life examples of this illustration, see *J. Grant Farms Inc., et al.*, paragraph 85, 174 P-H Memo TC; *Denny L. Johnson, et al.*, paragraph 85, 175 P-H Memo TC.

LOWERING THE EFFECTIVE TAX RATE   One of the most common methods that taxpayers have used to lower their effective income tax rate has been to split up what is essentially a single income stream between multiple taxpayers. Corporations are, of course, a particularly viable vehicle to achieve this end. Anyone can create a corporation at a relatively low cost. Although the assistance of a qualified attorney in setting up a corporation is strongly recommended, it is legally possible in most states for individuals to create their own corporation with only the help of some standard forms readily available at an office-supply store.

When an individual transfers an active and profitable trade or business to a corporate entity, that individual has opened up a whole vista of new tax problems and opportunities. Because there are at least as many potential tax problems as there are tax opportunities, the act of incorporation should not be undertaken without good advice. Professors Boris Bittker and James Eustice, two leading tax scholars, have compared the corporation to a lobster pot: a thing that is easy to enter, difficult to live in, and almost impossible to escape from.[4]

As noted in the introductory remarks of this chapter, however, millions of owners of small American businesses have elected to enter this lobster pot, apparently for tax reasons. A driving force behind this incorporation of small business was the lower corporate tax rates. In every year from 1913 to 1986, the highest marginal corporate tax rate was lower than the highest marginal individual tax rate. Thus, the owners of any business producing more income than the owners needed to satisfy their own personal consumption desires had a strong incentive to incorporate their business. Doing so would have two salutary effects. First, it would split what had been a single income stream into two parts: (1) the part initially earned by the corporation but passed directly on through the corporate entity to the owners, usually as a wage or salary; and (2) the part earned and retained within the corporate entity. Observe that the first portion of income was subject to only one tax by the individual owner–employee (as compensation for services that person had rendered to the corporation) because the corporation could deduct in its own computation of corporate taxable income any reasonable salary that it paid to its employees (Sec. 162). Obviously, therefore, if a small corporation elects to distribute an amount equal to its entire taxable income as a "reasonable" wage or salary, payable to its sole owner–employee, that income will only be taxed once (to the employee) in spite of the fact that it had originally been earned by a corporation. That is why, as noted earlier, it is sometimes more accurate to think of millions of small corporations as well as trusts as quasi- or pseudo-entities from a tax point of view. Whether the taxable income earned by these small corporations will be taxed only once to the individual, only once to the corporation, or twice—to both the corporation and to the individual owner—is largely up to the managerial discretion of the owner

---

[4]See Boris I. Bittker and James S. Eustice, *Federal Income Taxation of Corporations and Shareholders,* 4th ed. (Boston: Warren, Gorham & Lamont, 1979) pp. 2–4.

–employee. It is his or her corporation, and he or she can pretty much make the calls that will determine the tax consequences, subject only to some broad and often subjective limitations such as the statutory requirement that a salary be "reasonable" in amount. That very general standard obviously leaves a lot of leeway for the tax-conscious businessperson.

In the years in which the top marginal corporate tax rate was lower than the top individual tax rate, there was a tremendous incentive to retain "excess" income (that is, income beyond the personal needs of the owner) within the corporate entity to take advantage of the lower corporate marginal rate. Today, of course, there is an equally great incentive to withdraw all corporate taxable income in excess of $75,000 per year for essentially the same (but reversed) reason. Obviously, however, this withdrawal must take the form of something that will be deductible by the corporation: dividend payments will *not* qualify; reasonable salary, interest, and rent payments will.

As another alternative, of course, the business owner today might try to create multiple corporations and split a single income stream about equally between several corporate entities, each retaining income of between $50,000 and $75,000 per year. If the owner can avoid having these several corporations being categorized as members of a controlled group, as defined in Chapter 6, then this strategy may very conveniently still serve to lower the effective marginal tax rate through the use of multiple corporate entities. In summary, even after the 1986 tax law changes, *small* corporations can still be used to reduce the effective tax rate while only slightly larger or more successful corporations may now cause the overall income tax liability to increase rather than decrease.

USING TIME TO GOOD ADVANTAGE   Corporations have also been very helpful in reducing taxes by using time to good advantage. As noted earlier, most individuals will benefit from legally deferring their payment of a federal income tax liability, because there is a positive time-value of money. One of the earliest tax plans based on this strategy simply took advantage of the fact that a corporation, as an entity that is separate and distinct from its owners, could generally make its own accounting-method elections and/or select its own fiscal year. The simplest of plans would have the corporation accrue but not pay additional amounts of salary for the owner–employees. The corporation would elect the accrual method of accounting so that it could immediately deduct the accrued salaries payable. The individual owner–employees would, of course, elect a cash method of accounting. By creating an immediate deduction for the corporation, but deferring their own need to recognize this eventual income, the owners of many small corporations were once again able to use the corporate entity to their personal advantage. The I.R.S. did not appreciate the beauty of this tax planning and soon convinced Congress to enact a Code provision that disallowed the corporation's deduction for any amount payable to a closely related party unless that amount was paid within 2½ months after the end of the corporation's tax year. Even that solution, however, allowed the business person using a corporate entity to effectively defer some limited amount of taxable income for the owner's lifetime by repeating the same procedure, at the end of each year, but paying the amount within the statutory 2½ month period. Finally, therefore, Congress closed this last tax loophole in 1984 by denying all corporations the right to deduct any expense payable to a related party until the year in which the corporation actually makes the payment, without regard for the corporation's otherwise general method of accounting.

Saving taxes through the deferral of income recognition was achieved on a much grander scale by the effective use of qualified corporate pension and profit-sharing plans. For many years prior to 1982, the tax provisions that authorized a corporation to deduct contributions made on behalf of its employees were far more generous than were the comparable provisions for self-employed taxpayers. This distinction was the motivating force behind the professional corporation movement in the 1950s and 1960s. Medical doctors, in particular, were anxious to incorporate their professional practices so that their corporations could take advantage of the immediate and comparatively large "contributions" they made to fund the qualified pension and/or profit-sharing plans created largely on behalf of the doctors who now were employees of their own professional service corporations. The corporation would be entitled to an immediate deduction for the amounts paid to the employee trust fund; that fund, as a tax-exempt entity, would invest and reinvest all proceeds free of any income tax; and the owner–employee doctors would report no amount of taxable income until they elected to receive their accumulated benefits either as a lump sum or as an annuity, usually in their retirement years. This deferral of tax often involved relatively large sums of money. It is not surprising, therefore, that the early efforts of a few medical doctors were soon copied by many other professionals including lawyers, accountants, engineers, dentists, and others.

The reaction of the I.R.S. and the Treasury Department varied widely over the years. Initially, they attempted to fight the professionals' right to incorporate. When it became apparent that they were losing that battle, they turned their attention to corrective legislation. With each major tax act passed during the last 10 to 20 years, this opportunity to use corporations to the primary advantage of the owner–employees has been slowly closed. Today the tax rules for unincorporated retirement plans (commonly known as HR-10 or Keogh plans) are generally the same as those for corporate plans. Although there is relatively little advantage in remaining incorporated for this historical reason, many doctors and other professionals have learned first-hand the truth of the lobster-pot analogy. They might today prefer to shed their corporate shells but they are unable to do so without incurring a substantial tax cost. Hence, many continue to live within the pot and add to the large number of corporate tax returns filed each year.

FAVORABLE PRESUMPTIONS   A few individuals have elected to conduct their business in corporate form, because the tax law sometimes will make a favorable presumption about a corporation that it will not make about an individual. For example, a corporation is ordinarily deemed to be engaged in a trade or business. That presumption may be particularly important for taxpayers engaged in hobby-type activities. The presumption found in Sec. 183—that a taxpayer who does not report a profit in three or more of five consecutive years is deemed not to be engaged in a business for profit —generally applies only to individuals (and S corporations).

The trade-or-business presumption common to the corporate entity may also be important to the application of other Code sections. For example, the loss deduction authorized by Sec. 165 is much more severely restricted for the individual taxpayer than it is for the corporate taxpayer. Losses incurred by individuals on purely personal (that is, nonbusiness related) properties are deductible only if due to a casualty or a theft and then only to the extent they exceed 10% of the taxpayer's A.G.I. Because corporations ordinarily are deemed to be engaged in a trade or business, no comparable limitation exists. Another example of the same advantage is found in Sec. 166(d), which requires that the *nonbusiness bad debts* of individual taxpayers be treated as capital losses. Because corporations ordinarily have only *business* bad debts, they have no comparable restriction.

Finally, corporations were often useful to tax planning before the 1986 Act because of the presumption that stock in a corporation is generally deemed to be a capital asset in the hands of the shareholder. Thus, corporations were sometimes used to convert what would have been ordinary income into capital gain for the shareholders. Because there is no longer any tax advantage associated with a capital gain, vis-a-vis ordinary income, we will not consider these old opportunities in any further detail. Instead, in the final portion of this chapter we will look briefly at a few of the more important judicial and statutory aberrations to commonsense notions about corporations.

JUDICIAL AND STATUTORY ABERRATIONS

If a student were not forewarned, it would be entirely reasonable to assume that no business organization could be treated as a corporation for federal income tax purposes unless it had legally obtained a corporate charter. It would also be reasonable to assume, based on what has been stated in this chapter, that once a business had been incorporated, the corporation would be treated as a separate taxable entity. Finally, it would be equally reasonable to assume that one corporation is like every other corporation so far as our federal income tax law is concerned. Unfortunately, however, none of these entirely reasonable assumptions are correct.

Associations Taxed As Corporations

As noted at the beginning of this chapter, Sec. 11 imposes a tax on the taxable income of *every corporation*. But precisely what is a "corporation"? The only statutory answer to that question, found in Sec. 7701(a)(3), is more likely to

FIGURE **20-2**

Characteristic	Entity		
	Corporation	Partnership	Trust
(i) Associates	Yes (but there are corporations with only one shareholder)	Yes	No
(ii) Objective: to carry on business for gain	Yes	Yes	No (the purpose of a trust is to protect a property interest)
(iii) Continuity of life	Yes	No	Yes[c]
(iv) Centralization of management	Yes	No[a]	Yes
(v) Limited liability	Yes	No[b]	Yes
(vi) Free transferability of ownership	Yes	No	Yes[d]

[a]Although the classic partnership does not have centralization of management—In other words, every partner can legally act for the entire partnership and thereby obligate every other partner—a centralized form of management is common in large partnerships. For example, consider the management structure of the "Big Eight" public accounting firms.

[b]Again, even though the garden-variety partnership is characterized by the unlimited liability of every partner, limited partnerships are quite common today.

[c]This continuity of life is subject to the rule against perpetuities.

[d]Although most interests in a trust can be freely transferred so far as the law is concerned, they are often difficult to transfer in a commercial transaction. Their value often depends on the life of one or more individuals—a difficult thing to estimate.

confuse than to clarify. It reads in its entirety: "The term 'corporation' includes associations, joint-stock companies, and insurance companies." Therefore, even without further investigation, we know that the federal income tax on corporations may be extended to *unincorporated* "associations," but the Code provides no additional help in defining an association. Judicial and administrative law, however, do help to define that term. The benchmark judicial authority is *Morrissey, et al.* v. *Commissioner*, 296 U.S. 344 (1935). The most important administrative authority is Treas. Reg. Sec. 301.7701-2(a), which expands on *Morrissey* and identifies six major characteristics of a corporate entity as follow: "(i) associates, (ii) an objective to carry on business and divide the gains therefrom, (iii) continuity of life, (iv) centralization of management, (v) liability for corporate debts limited to corporate property, and (vi) free transferability of interests."

A brief comparison of a garden-variety corporation, partnership, and trust with regard to these six characteristics is set forth in the matrix of Figure 20-2. As we can see in this matrix, a substantial amount of overlap exists among the most common forms of business organization with regard to the six characteristics. Neither the courts nor the regulations state exactly what combination of characteristics will yield a corporation for federal tax purposes. The regulations merely state:

Whether a particular organization is to be classified as an association must be determined by taking into account the presence or absence of each of these corporate characteristics. The presence or absence of these characteristics will depend upon the facts in each individual case. . . . An organization will be treated as an association if the corporate characteristics are such that the organization more nearly resembles a corporation than a partnership or trust.[5]

At this point, we need not resolve the definitional issue. It is sufficient to understand that *the federal income tax on corporations may, in unusual circumstances, be extended to an unincorporated business venture.*

The most interesting, recent, large-scale controversy in the taxation of unincorporated businesses as corporations involved the "associations" formed by medical doctors before state laws were changed to allow professional corporations. As explained earlier in this chapter, the medical doctors were the leaders in the professional incorporation movement because they wanted the then-larger pension and profit-sharing benefits that were restricted to corporate entities. The saga is doubly fascinating because the doctors were able to turn what had up until then been a major I.R.S. victory in *Morrissey* to their own advantage. Needless to say, the I.R.S. was not pleased with this judicial turn of events.[6]

Corporations Taxed As Unincorporated Businesses

On rare occasions, the courts have held that a legally incorporated entity should be ignored for federal income tax purposes. The circumstances that compel a court to reach such a drastic conclusion are, to say the least, unusual. Generally, the facts that support such a decision show beyond any doubt that the corporate shell was a mere sham. Although the stockholder went to the trouble of incorporating, he or she continued to ignore all other corporate realities. In addition, some "grand" tax plan is usually involved in these cases.[7]

The far more common situation in which a legally incorporated business is taxed as an unincorporated business venture involves the Subchapter S election. The tax rules that govern the S corporation election and taxation of S corporation income are explained in Chapter 6. Once the S election is made, the taxable items (income, gains, deductions, and so on) of the S corporation flow through to the shareholders just as taxable items flow

---

[5]Reg. Sec. 7701-2(a)(1).
[6]If you are interested in this issue, see one or all four of the following judicial decisions: *United States* v. *Kintner*, 216 F.2d 418 (CCA-9, 1954); *United States* v. *Empey*, 406 F.2d 157 (CCA-10, 1969); *O'Neill* v. *United States*, 418 F.2d 888 (CCA-6, 1969); and *Kurzner* v. *United States*, 413 F.2d 97 (CCA-5, 1969).
[7]Persons interested in the corporate-sham phenomenon might read *Johansson* v. *United States*, 336 F.2d 809 (CCA-5, 1964) or *Paymer* v. *Commissioner*, 150 F.2d 334 (CCA-2, 1945).

through a partnership to the partners. Recall, however, that for most other purposes, S corporations are treated like C corporations. For example, the S corporation recognizes gain on appreciated property distributed to its shareholders.

In summary, not every corporate entity is treated as a separate taxable entity for federal income tax purposes. A wholly unincorporated business venture may be taxed as a corporation; a legally incorporated business venture may be taxed more or less as a partnership (by making the Subchapter S election); a legal corporate entity may be completely ignored if it is considered to be a sham for tax purposes; and multiple corporate entities may be taxed to some extent as a single corporation either because they elect to file a consolidated corporate tax return or because they are members of a controlled group of corporations.

All Corporations Are Not Equal

Finally, every tax student should understand that all corporations were not created equal for federal income tax purposes. The Internal Revenue Code is replete with special provisions for certain kinds of corporations. For example, Subchapter L provides special rules for the income taxation of insurance companies; Subchapter M, for regulated investment companies; and portions of Subchapter N, for foreign corporations. In addition, there are specific Code sections and subsections that provide unique rules for more general-business type corporations. The most common corporate forms to be singled out for special treatment are the professional service corporations and closely held corporations.

A professional service corporation is defined in Sec. 269A (b)(1) as a corporation ". . . the principal activity of which is the performance of personal services and such services are substantially performed by employee –owners." As you might expect, the general import of this section is to give the Secretary of the Treasury special powers to minimize the opportunity of an individual to utilize a professional service corporation in tax avoidance or evasion. Section 441(i)(2), which places special limits on the taxable year of a professional service corporation, provides a slightly modified definition for the same type of entity. Section 535(c)(2), which authorizes an accumulated earnings tax credit, has yet a third definition of essentially the same kind of corporate entity.

If, during the last half of any year, more than 50% of a corporation's stock is owned, directly or indirectly, by five or fewer individuals, that corporation may be classified as a closely held corporation (see Sec. 465(a)(1)(B) and Sec. 542(a)(2)). That classification could provide either a potential tax limitation —as in Sec. 465(a), which limits certain loss deductions to the amount "at risk"—or a potential tax benefit—as in Sec. 2032A, which may reduce the fair market value of selected properties for estate tax purposes. Both closely held and personal service corporations may also be subject to special penalties if they underpay their federal income tax liability because of an overstatement in value (see Sec. 6659(a)).

Even in those cases where the Code provides no special treatment for the closely held corporation, the I.R.S. is often suspicious that the purely personal expenses of an owner or manager may be disguised as corporate business expenses. Therefore, supporting documentation often becomes of greater significance in the tax audit of a closely held corporation than it does in the audit of a large publicly owned and independently managed corporation in which a better system of internal checks and balances is presumed to exist. The authors do not intend to imply that large corporations may keep sloppy records for income tax purposes. Rather, we only mean to suggest that the I.R.S. is well aware that corporations owned by one or a few individuals are especially capable of manipulation, and, therefore, it deals with them accordingly.

In summary, the corporation has been a very useful vehicle in tax planning ever since 1913. Although some of the tax law changes enacted in the 1986 Tax Reform Act will limit the future of the corporate entity in tax planning, they will not eliminate that possibility. The one safe generalization is that taxpayers must be even more careful in their use of corporations today than they were in the past if they expect those plans to be successful.

PROBLEMS

1. What justification may be given for levying a tax on the corporate entity?

2. a. As two extreme alternatives to our current entity structure, (1) we could exclude corporations from the list of entities recognized for tax purposes on the grounds that all corporate income ultimately belongs to individuals and that, until such time as that income is distributed by the corporation, it ought not to be subject to tax; or (2) we could tax all corporations exactly as we tax single taxpaying individuals and then exclude from individuals' income any amounts distributed (as dividends) by the corporations. What practical consequences would follow from each of these extreme alternatives? Explain.

   b. As another alternative to our present corporate income tax, we could *currently* allocate all corporate incomes to the (ultimate) individual stockholders, whether or not the corporation distributed any income. We could then exclude corporations from any income tax. (In other words, we could treat corporations the way we treat partnerships for tax purposes.) What practical reasons preclude the general acceptance of this alternative?

   c. Finally, as another alternative to our current corporate income tax, we could recognize the corporation as a separate entity only to the extent that the corporation retained income. This could be accomplished simply by allowing the corporation a deduction for dividends paid. (In essence, this is the way we treat trusts for tax purposes.) Why do you suppose that this alternative has never been accepted by Congress?

3. Some foreign countries levy relatively high taxes on corporate earnings that are not distributed to stockholders as dividends. Compare this with the U.S. treatment of corporate income and explain the probable effects of each alternative on the source of corporate funds.

4. A U.S. taxpayer who uses a corporation to obtain lower rates for a business operation cannot afford the distribution of dividends. Why is this true? In your explanation, use the 1988 tax rates to demonstrate your conclusion.

5. Following is a summary of income and expenses of the World Corporation:

Income:

Sales of merchandise	$975,000
Interest from customers	2,300
Interest on investment in AT&T bonds	4,000
Interest on State of New York bonds	3,400
Life insurance received on death of corporation's treasurer	100,000
Refund of federal income taxes from previous year	12,000
Dividends received on investment in General Electric Company stock	22,000

Expenses:

Cost of goods sold	500,000
Salaries	122,000
Advertising, promotion, and legal services	28,000
Depreciation of property	64,000
Taxes on real estate, payroll, and so on	32,000
Interest paid	4,000
Amortization of organization expenses	500
Office expenses, postage, and computer service	80,000
Other business expenses	116,000

a. What is the corporation's gross income for the year?
b. What is the amount of routine deductions?
c. What is the amount of special "corporate-only" deductions?
d. What is the amount of total tax liability? Use 1988 rates.

6. Spinaker, Inc., a manufacturer of sailboats, had the following items in the current year (after 1987):

Revenue from sale of boats	$2,000,000
Dividends from domestic corporations	50,000
Interest on corporate bonds	20,000
Cost of goods sold	(1,400,000)
Operating expenses	200,000
Qualified contributions	50,000

a. What is Spinaker's taxable income?
b. What is Spinaker's gross tax?

7. Hardy Corporation experienced the following results from current operations (after 1987):

Revenue from sales	$250,000
Interest on State of Texas bonds	50,000
Cost of merchandise	(150,000)
Operating expenses	20,000

Using 1988 rates, what is Hardy's:
a. Marginal tax rate?

b. Average tax rate?

c. Real or effective tax rate?

8. Three unrelated individuals—Able, Baker, and Cooke—together own 100% of three corporations. Each corporation operates a separate discount store located in three different cities. Each store has annual income of $80,000.

a. If each shareholder owns 33⅓% of each corporation's stock, compute the additional tax liability due for 1988 compared with an arrangement in which Able, Baker, and Cooke each owned one of the corporations. Benefits from all brackets are allocated equally among the three companies.

b. Devise a scheme of ownership whereby Able, Baker, and Cooke could own the three corporations jointly and avoid treatment as a controlled group.

c. Discuss why the three individuals would hesitate to adopt the pattern of ownership you devised in part b. For this purpose, assume that the stores have only been in existence for a brief period.

9. Charles Goodnight owns a successful men's clothing store, which he operates as a proprietorship. Charles estimates that the net profits of the business will be $110,000. He wonders if he can gain a tax advantage by incorporation. He has no other source of income, and he would need a salary of $60,000 from the corporation. Calculate the tax savings from incorporation if Charles is single, under 65 with no dependents, and does not itemize deductions. Use the 1988 tax rates.

10. Joan Jacks is the majority shareholder of Jacks, Inc. On Joan's 1988 personal return, her marginal tax rate is 28%. After deducting Joan's salary of $320,000, the corporation had only taxable income of $50,000. When examining the 1988 corporate return, the I.R.S. agent proposed to disallow $220,000 of the salary because the salary is unreasonably high. Using 1988 rates, calculate the tax cost if the agent disallows the deduction and a court sustains this adjustment.

11. Learning, Inc., reported a taxable income of $20,000; in addition, the corporation earned $5,000 interest on its investment in municipal bonds. The corporation also paid a $25,000 dividend. The corporation had accumulated earnings and profits of $300,000.

a. On what amount of income must Learning, Inc., pay tax?

b. On what amount of income must Learning's stockholders pay tax because of the dividends distributed?

c. Based on your answers to parts a and b, what conclusions can you draw about the wisdom of a closely held corporation investing in tax-exempt securities?

12. Four years ago, ten individuals organized a new venture as a limited partnership. The general partner was a new corporation formed by the venturers. For the first two years, the venture produced total losses of $250,000, all allocated to the limited partners in equal shares, and reported by them. For the last two years, the project produced profits of $500,000 of which 10% was allocated to the general partner and the remainder reported by the limited partners in equal shares. The partnership also distributed cash of $20,000 to each limited partner in the fourth year.

a. Explain the tax effects if this venture were to be taxed as an association from inception.

b. Is this result likely? Explain.

13. Ultimately, the corporate income tax burden is borne by individuals. Name three individual economic agents who may pay the cost of corporate income tax.

14. How can double taxation of corporate income be permanently avoided?

15. What is the (1) average tax rate and (2) marginal tax rate of a corporation with taxable income of
    a. $ 90,000
    b. $180,000
    c. $360,000

16. What is the effective tax rate to a corporation with taxable income of $500,000 on:
    a. Interest income?
    b. Dividend income?

17. Would it be wholly correct to characterize an S corporation as an incorporated partnership? Explain briefly.

CHAPTER 21

Using Other Entities or Other Jurisdictions

An organization will be taxed as a corporation if, taking all relevant characteristics into account, it more nearly resembles a corporation than some other entity.
Judge Tannenwald, Phillip G. Larson v. Commissioner, *66 TC 172 (1976)*

The two preceding chapters explain some of the basic techniques used to minimize the income tax and illustrate how corporations can be useful to tax planning in certain circumstances. Other accounting entities can also play an important role. Although the entities discussed in this chapter have only marginal implications for the bulk of the nation's taxpayers, they may play a critical role in the tax plans of select taxpayers.

In this chapter, the tax-planning entity we consider first is the fiduciary. Then, we discuss the tax rules related to partnerships, with some information about how partnerships have been and are being used by those who seek to reduce their annual tax bills. Finally, we consider the possibility of moving any entity to a foreign jurisdication, at least in part, because of tax considerations.

Before turning to the tax laws relative to these other entities, the role of the individual proprietor should be clarified. In financial accounting, a sole proprietorship is treated as a separate entity, and trade or business activities are separated from the proprietor's other financial activities when financial statements are prepared. Indeed, if the same individual is engaged in several, distinct trades or businesses, accepted accounting practice generally requires a separate set of records and separate reports for each business. Tax law, however, makes no distinction between an individual and the one or more business activities in which he or she is engaged as a proprietor. A medical doctor employed as a professor in a medical school, for example, may also operate a private practice in his or her specialty and concurrently be engaged in the business of farming or ranching. Despite the three disparate activities, only one taxable entity exists—the individual. If prudent, the doctor will maintain separate records for each proprietorship. When filing a tax return, however, he or she must treat each proprietorship as a mere conduit through which all items of income, deductions, and credits flow directly to the individual.

Numerous other entities, which are not discussed in this introductory text, are subject to their own tax rules. For example, special rules apply to foreign personal holding companies, life insurance companies, banks, and savings and loan institutions. Furthermore, any organization organized for a nonprofit purpose, whether a corporation, trust, or association, may be exempt from tax law—this list includes governmental units, churches, charities, clubs, and leagues. Generally, application must be filed to establish an organization's tax-exempt status. Although these organizations are exempt from the federal income tax, many of them must file an annual information return, which is used by the I.R.S. to check their "nonprofit" status. Tax-exempt organizations may be taxed on certain prohibited transactions, and/or their entire tax-exempt status may be revoked. That possibility is also increased if the organization engages in what might be described as political activities.

THE FIDUCIARY TAXPAYER

When the income tax law was written in 1913, estates and trusts were treated as mere agents for natural persons, the beneficiaries. The income tax was levied on the beneficiary of the trust, even though in some cases the agent (that is, the estate or trust) made the actual tax payment. This manner of taxing fiduciaries, however, ignored one important question: Who should be taxed on the income of an *inter vivos* or testamentary trust when no natural person is currently designated as beneficiary—for example, when a grantor creates a trust for the benefit of individuals not yet born, with all income to accumulate until the occurrence of some subsequent event? The Revenue Act of 1916 eliminated this loophole and created a new taxable entity, the fiduciary. Before turning to discussion of the income taxation of estates and trusts, we should examine the interrelationship between the federal estate and gift taxes and the income taxation of estates and trusts. Every student should understand clearly that the taxation of *income* earned by a trust or an estate has little or nothing to do with the estate or gift tax that may impinge when an estate or trust is first created.

Estate and Gift Taxes

Beginning in 1916, the federal government levied a tax on the *transfer of wealth* at death. Responsibility for payment of that tax fell on the executor appointed in the deceased taxpayer's will, or on a court-appointed administrator when the individual died intestate (that is, without a will). The initial imposition of a tax on death transfers created a problem: given a modicum of faith on the part of the natural objects of his or her bounty, a taxpayer was able to evade the estate tax by giving away wealth before death. This rather obvious strategy prompted Congress to levy a tax on gifts. Originally passed in the early 1920s, the gift tax became a permanent feature of the federal tax structure in 1932.

The wealth-transfer taxes owe their existence to a national policy of wealth and income redistribution. A key goal of the Populist movement, redistribution had political appeal in the first decades of this century. However, the recent drift of national policy makes the original role of wealth-transfer taxes unclear. The 1976 "unification" of the wealth and gift taxes into a single donative transfers tax seemed to reinforce the importance of the transfer taxes in our tax system. Changes since 1976, particularly the lower rates and increased exemptions enacted in 1981, have signaled Congressional discontent with the redistribution policy in general and the wealth-transfer taxes in particular. Indeed, there was serious talk of complete repeal of the taxes in 1981. Despite the uncertainty of their future, the federal estate and gift taxes are still on the books, and some knowledge of how they work is essential to every student of taxation.

The determination of the unified transfer tax imposed at death begins with the calculation of the decedent's taxable estate according to the following formula:

Gross estate (fair market value of all property, wherever located, in which the decedent had an interest at death)
- (1) Funeral, administrative, and certain other expenses
- (2) Debts owed by the decedent
- (3) A marital deduction equal to the fair market value of property passing to the decedent's surviving spouse
- (4) Amounts bequeathed to charities

= Taxable estate

If a decedent has made no taxable gifts after 1976, the rates in Appendix C are applied to the taxable estate to determine his or her gross tax. The gross tax may be reduced by credits allowed for death taxes paid to states and foreign governments and for estate taxes paid on property included in the gross estate of a prior decedent within the last 10 years. Finally, the gross tax is reduced by the unified credit.

If an individual has made gifts since 1976, taxable gifts are computed using the following formula:

Gross gifts for the calendar quarter or calendar year, depending on the amount of the gifts, measured by the fair market value of the gift property on the date of the gift

- (1) An exclusion of $10,000 per donee per year. This exclusion is intended to exclude from taxation nominal gifts, and no gift tax return need be filed unless gifts to one donee exceed $10,000 for the year.
- (2) A marital deduction when the donee is the donor's spouse.
- (3) Charitable gifts

= Taxable gifts

The rates in Appendix C are used to determine the gross tax. Because of the progressive rates, however, taxable gifts during the current period must be added to all prior taxable gifts (since 1932) to obtain the total base on which a tentative tax is computed. Taxes paid on prior gifts are then subtracted from the tentative tax, and the remainder is the current tax—usually at a higher marginal rate. The unified credit must then be applied against the gift tax.

At the death of a donor who has made lifetime taxable gifts, a calculation is then made to determine the amount of the estate tax. The resulting total tax is approximately the same as that which would have been levied had the decedent's entire wealth been transferred at death.

As explained in Chapter 1, the transfer taxes affect only a small percentage of the population. Because of the large unified credit and the unlimited marital deduction, most citizens escape these taxes. For those fortunate enough to have the problem, careful planning can reduce substantially the impact of wealth-transfer taxes.

Creation of Fiduciary Taxpayers

The structure of the wealth-transfer taxes just discussed accounts for the existence of many fiduciary taxpayers. A taxpayer's death triggers the estate tax and simultaneously creates a new income tax entity—the estate. The decedent's income that arises before death must be reported on the decedent's final tax return. If the decedent is married at death, a joint return can be filed, including the income and deductions of the decedent until death and the income and deductions of the survivor for the remainder of the year. Income received or accruing to the decedent's property *after* death is reported on the estate income tax return, along with any applicable expenses. The decedent's estate reports the income and deductions related to the properties passed at death until a final distribution is made from the estate to the beneficiaries named in the will, or as identified by operation of law if no will exists. A final accounting to the probate court usually signals the end of an estate as a taxable entity.

Trusts are often created when property is distributed by an estate under the terms of a will. *Testamentary trusts* are often provided for in a decedent's will to pass property to minors and others whom the decedent does not think capable of the ownership and management of property. In other cases, the decedent merely wishes to relieve the beneficiaries of the problems of wise property management, leaving such chores in the hands of experienced trustees.

Wealthy taxpayers bent on decreasing their estate taxes may also create trusts by *inter vivos* gifts, although the extent to which the transfer taxes motivate the creation of trusts is not clear.[1] No doubt many trusts are created by *inter vivos* gifts to ensure the financial security of an elderly parent or to provide for the education of children and grandchildren. Even when the basic motivation is love or charity, the wise grantor of a trust always considers the tax consequences of his or her proposed actions.

Basic Income Tax Rules for Estates and Trusts

Once in existence, an estate or trust enjoys the mixed blessing of being an entity that *may* have to pay a tax on its income. The legal transfer of property from a decedent to his or her estate, or the transfer of property by a grantor to a trust, is not a taxable event for income tax purposes, although the transfers may be subject to the donative transfer tax. Similarly, a distribution of corpus from an estate or trust to its beneficiaries is not generally a taxable event (although there are important exceptions to this generalization). For example, the income tax problems that arise when appreciated property is transferred to a trust by *inter vivos* gift and then later sold by the trust are beyond our scope here. That dramatic event—death—leaves no doubt concerning the bona fide existence of the resulting estate as a separate taxpayer. The creation of a trust by an *inter vivos* gift, however, can create problems concerning the "tax" existence of the trust.

EFFECTIVE GRANTOR TRUSTS   To illustrate the problem of whether an *inter vivos* gift in trust results in the creation of a new taxpayer, consider the following facts: A widow with substantial wealth has taxable income derived from dividends and interest amounting to $150,000 per annum. Her top marginal rate on this taxable income is probably 28%, perhaps 33%. Assume further that she has several grandchildren with virtually no taxable income. She intends to pass her wealth to them at death. For now, however, she is not willing to make outright gifts of her property to the grandchildren. A theoretically ideal solution would be for her to create a trust for each grandchild, have each trust pay taxes at lower marginal rates, and yet retain the power to revoke the trusts and regain the property with the related income if she later needs it for her own use. This arrangement would be a nearly ideal tax situation—a lower total tax bill without giving up her claim

---

[1]For a discussion on this point, see Johnson and Vernon, "Income of Estates and Trusts," *1959 Compendium*, p. 1759. The conclusion there is that the use of trusts for tax avoidance may be greatly overestimated.

on the property. This scheme, however, violates one of the basic doctrines in our tax law.

Stated simply, the question is: Can a person effectively assign the income from property and have that income taxed to the assignee without relinquishing legal title to the property from which the income is derived? In a classic case, a father who owned corporate coupon bonds gave his son the right to clip the coupons as they matured, mail them in for payment, and retain the cash received. The son reported the interest income based on the somewhat fanciful argument that the coupons were "property" received by gift. The Supreme Court was not impressed with the argument and required that that income be reported by the father.[2] The somewhat colorful legal analogy used is that a taxpayer cannot avoid picking the fruit (recognizing income) unless he is willing to give away the entire tree (the capital that produces the income).

To make an effective transfer of an income-producing property in trust, and thus shift the income from the grantor to the trust, the grantor cannot retain any of the following powers: to revoke the trust; to control the beneficial enjoyment of the trust's income or corpus; to administer the trust property in such a manner as to benefit the grantor; or to cause the income or corpus to revert to the grantor. Detailed application of these proscribed powers must be reserved for advanced study. Prior to enactment of the Tax Reform Act of 1986, the *Clifford* trust, or short-term trust, was an important exception to the general idea that the grantor must divest himself of any interest in a trust.[3] A grantor of a trust who retained a reversionary interest in corpus was not taxed on trust income if the reversion would not occur for at least ten years after the creation of the trust. A valid short-term trust could also be created if the reversion did not occur until the death of the income beneficiary. Taxpayers made effective use of *Clifford* trusts to provide for elderly dependents, for the college education of children and grandchildren, and for other similar objectives. Unfortunately, subsequent to enactment of the Tax Reform Act of 1986, short-term trusts may no longer be used to accomplish a temporary shifting of income to taxpayers in lower marginal tax brackets.

The rules just discussed are a good example of a natural bias that exists in much of our tax law. Given the doctrine that prohibits the assignment of *income* between taxpayers—a doctrine that is clearly essential with a progressive rate structure—the individual whose only source of income is earnings cannot use the trust device to shift income to others. The "tree" of earned income is the taxpayer's body and mind; the "tree" of income that arises from property is that property. Rights to the income from the former tree cannot be assigned; income rights from the latter can be assigned if the property is also assigned.

---

[2]*Helvering* v. *Horst*, 311 U.S. 112 (1940). Earlier, in *Lucas* v. *Earl*, 281 U.S. 111 (1930), the Supreme Court had held that a lawyer could not make an anticipatory assignment of future fees and shift the income to his wife, as assignee.
[3]See *Helvering* v. *Clifford*, 309 U.S. 331 (1940).

COMPUTATIONAL RULES   Once created, estates and trusts are new taxpayers entitled to make most elections available under the law. While both estates and trusts may elect their own methods of accounting, trusts are required to adopt a calendar year for tax purposes. Estates may elect any taxable year. Availability of new elections can have good or bad results. For example, an estate may be a shareholder in an S corporation if it so elects. However, if the decedent's will provides for the transfer of stock in an S corporation to a testamentary trust, continued ownership by the trust may destroy the special election. The fact that the fiduciary is a new taxpayer can be an important consideration in establishing *inter vivos* trusts and in the timing of distributions from an estate to its beneficiaries.

Generally, estates and trusts compute their gross income, deductions, and credits under the same rules used by individuals. The many exclusions, deductions, and credits that, by their nature, are intended for individuals only, are not available to fiduciaries. On the other hand, the law contains some special deductions applicable to fiduciaries only. Instead of the individual exemption deduction, estates get an exemption of $600. Simple trusts, defined as those that *must* distribute all their income to beneficiaries currently, are allowed an exemption of $300. All other trusts get a $100 exemption. Of more importance is the deduction allowed for distributions of income to beneficiaries.

Under the simplest arrangement, estates and trusts are not taxpayers at all but mere conduits through which income and deductions flow to their beneficiaries. For example, consider the situation in which a wealthy woman transfers $200,000 cash to a trust, naming her mother as beneficiary. The trust instrument provides that all trust income as defined by the tax law, net of trust expenses, is to be paid out annually to her mother for life, with the remainder of the corpus to be distributed to the woman's children on the mother's death. This trust gives the mother an income without also imposing on her the responsibility for investing the trust corpus and without the daughter first having to pay her own income tax on the income transferred to the mother. The trust is a taxpayer, and must file a return, but it has no tax liability because it is allowed a deduction for the distribution of current income to the beneficiary. Under these circumstances, the tax burden for the trust's net income falls on the mother because the distributions are income to her.

Many estates and trusts, however, do not distribute all income currently. Executors of estates may retain some income until claims against the estate are settled. A trustee may be required to accumulate income until the beneficiaries reach a given age. The trust instrument may define income subject to current distribution in a manner different from the tax definitions; for example, capital gains on sale of property may be allocated to trust corpus, not to income. Thus, for numerous reasons, the fiduciary may have undistributed income and be subject to tax. The problems that arise when accumulated income is eventually distributed by the fiduciary are complex, and any attempt to generalize these rules for current purposes would be more dangerous than helpful.

As just explained, as estate or trust that distributes income to its beneficiaries is not taxed on that income. Instead, the beneficiaries receiving the distributed income declare it on their individual returns. What about the tax characteristics of the distributed income? Consider these facts: A complex trust realizes $3,000 of interest income on corporate bonds, $2,000 of interest on municipal bonds, and $5,000 of gain on capital assets. The trust pays various expenses of $1,000 and distributes the $9,000 remaining current income to its beneficiaries. Does the beneficiary retain the classification for the municipal bond interest and the capital gain? Yes, the character of the income items is not changed but flows through the trust to the beneficiary. Thus, ($2,000/$10,000), or ²⁄₁₀, of the $9,000 distribution is excluded by the beneficiary, and ⁵⁄₁₀ of the distribution is treated as a capital gain.

When a fiduciary has taxable income, it computes its tax using the following (1988) rate schedule:

Taxable Income	Tax Rate
$0 to $5,000	15%
$5,000 to $13,000	28%
$13,000 to $26,000	33%
Over $26,000	28%

Beginning in 1988, only $5,000 of fiduciary taxable income is subject to a 15% rate, and the benefit of this lower rate is completely recaptured through imposition of the 5% surtax when taxable income reaches $26,000. The utility of an estate or trust to shelter income from high individual marginal tax rates has been severely limited by this change in rate structure. In many cases, a complex trust that accumulates income rather than distributing it to various beneficiaries may now pay a greater amount of income tax than if the income had been totally distributed. When an income tax is levied on a fiduciary, the executor or trustee has a legal obligation to file the return and pay the tax (though the fiduciary is normally not personally liable for the tax).

Although much more could be said about the use of trusts in federal income tax planning, we will now examine some of the features of a partnership that make it useful in yet other circumstances. Recall that, unlike the corporation and the fiduciary, a partnership can never be a taxable entity.

PARTNERSHIPS

As defined in Chapter 6, a partnership exists when two or more persons join together to carry on a business or investment activity for their joint profit. A partnership is given only nominal recognition in our tax law, being treated as a mere aggregation of the proprietary interests of the partners. The tax treatment of partnerships and of transactions between partners and partnerships are covered in Chapter 6, but a brief review here will be helpful.

Review of Rules for Partnerships

As a mere aggregation of proprietary interests, all taxable items of a partnership flow through to the partners and are reported by them on their individual returns. Usually, all parties use the calendar year. Partnership items are allocated to the partners based on their agreement and the partners are given wide latitude in making allocations, so long as the allocations have substantial economic effect. Recall that taxable items are reported by the partners whether or not the partnership actually distributes cash or other property to the partners. The tax character of the items also flows through to the partners.

Transactions between partners and partnerships are not normally taxable transactions, consistent with the aggregate concept. Thus, as a general rule neither the partners nor the partnership recognizes gain or loss when property is contributed to the partnership or when property is distributed from the partnership to the partners. Exceptions to these rules exist, of course, and the exceptions can be important in limited circumstances.

Tax Planning with Partnerships

The conduit characteristic is fundamental to tax planning with partnerships. As previously discussed, this attribute has the advantage of preventing double taxation. However, partners who make little or no withdrawals must plan to meet the tax burden arising from a profitable partnership. Additional planning considerations involve ease of formation, special allocations, tax rates, the passive loss rules, and master limited partnerships.

EASE OF FORMATION   Unlike most other entities, it is very simple to form a general partnership; that is, one in which each and every partner is liable for all claims against the partnership. When two or more parties join their capital and/or efforts with the intention of earning a profit, a legal partnership comes into existence. The mere act of joint enterprise is sufficient, even if the parties have no explicit oral or written agreement, although forming a partnership without a written agreement is ill advised. In contrast, most states require a lengthy registration procedure to form a limited partnership; that is, one in which the liability of the limited partners does not exceed their capital investment in the partnership. In addition, there must be at least one general partner in a limited partnership, and limited partners are barred from management decisions.

SPECIAL ALLOCATIONS   The ability of partners to make special allocations is a long-standing tax-planning attribute that distinguishes partnerships from corporations. Unlike shareholders, partners may agree to (specially) allocate their distributive shares in a manner that is disproportionate to their contributions. Ordinary income and loss, as well as special items, may be specially allocated by the partners. While recent regulations under Sec. 704(b) attempt to clarify important limitations that apply to special allocations, unfortunately, many ambiguities remain. Nonetheless, the flexibility provided by special allocations is an attractive tax-planning attribute of partnerships.

TAX RATES   Another partnership-planning consideration was affected by the change in individual and corporate tax rates under the Tax Reform Act of 1986. Prior to the 1986 Code, as previously noted, maximum individual tax rates exceeded corporate rates. At times this difference was quite dramatic. For example, in 1936 and 1937 the maximum individual rate was 79%, while the maximum corporate rate was only 15%—a difference of 64 percentage points! While this difference continually declined over the years, the maximum individual rate still exceeded the corporate rate by 24% in 1979, dropping to just 4% in 1982. Historically, this discrepancy in the top marginal tax rates provided an incentive for individuals to adopt the corporate rather than partnership form, thereby enabling an enterprise to reinvest more after-tax dollars from profits.

However, as discussed in the preceding chapter, the top marginal rates are now higher for corporations than individuals. Therefore, the partnership conduit often results in less tax to its individual partners than a tax imposed on the same income earned by a corporation. Moreover, unlike partners, shareholders may face the problem of double taxation upon the distribution of corporate earnings. This unprecedented flip in maximum individual and corporate rates, along with double taxation, has increased the appeal of partnerships compared to corporate ownership by individuals.

MASTER LIMITED PARTNERSHIPS   The popularity of master limited partnerships (MLPs) is a recent phenomenon that has had a significant impact on corporate restructuring in America. There are two basic types of MLPs—the "roll-up" and the "drop-down" (also called a roll-down or roll-out). Recall that, under the conduit concept, contributions to form a partnership, including MLPs, are usually treated as a nontaxable event.

A roll-up MLP is generally formed by a company to consolidate numerous small limited partnerships into a "master" limited partnership. For example, an independent oil company that is a general partner in numerous and diverse small drilling partnerships may initiate a roll-up MLP to combine these operations. Typically, investors in a small partnership will contribute their interests in exchange for an interest in the larger MLP. Since most MLP units are publicly traded on major exchanges, they offer much greater liquidity for investors than interests in private, small partnership projects. In addition to liquidity, roll-up MLPs also have the potential advantage of improved internal operating efficiency and stability through diversification.

In a drop-down MLP, a company contributes some of its assets to create a new limited partnership. For example, a food services corporation may spin off its depreciable real estate and related operations into a newly created MLP. This enables owners to avoid double taxation on this segment of the business. In addition, the activity's value may be enhanced through greater flexibility in partnership management. The market also tends to place a higher value on the same assets, such as oil reserves, when held by an MLP compared to a corporation. This further enhances the owners' value and, by increasing the cost of ownership, reduces the threat of hostile takeover.

Despite the similarities between publicly traded MLP units and corporate stock, MLPs have thus far successfully avoided association status. Consequently, the reclassification of MLPs as corporations has been proposed irrespective of the judicial and administrative "association" rules. However, until such a proposal is enacted into law, this popular business form promises to continue, based on both its tax and nontax benefits.

Although no precise statistics are available, it is probably safe to conclude that most partnerships are used for small enterprises when two or three parties want to combine their talents and productive assets. Partnerships, for example, are common in agriculture; one party furnishes land and a second party conducts the actual operations. At the other extreme, we find large, publicly traded MLPs created to avoid double taxation and maximize the owners' value, while, at the same time, additional MLP units may be offered to raise capital. Finally, partnerships are a convenient vehicle for sharing risk, as, for example, in oil and gas exploration. In the latter two circumstances, the presence of a *corporate* general partner is commonplace.

In the past, promoters of tax shelters commonly used the partnership form. The aggregate concept permits losses from a tax shelter to flow through to the participants, even when the losses are financed with borrowed money. The widespread use of tax shelters forced Congress to adopt limits on the deductibility of passive losses. While these new limits apply to all passive activities, whether or not organized as a partnership, there is a close association between abusive shelters and the partnership form. The new rules limiting passive losses are explained in the following section.

PASSIVE ACTIVITIES: LOSS LIMITS AND OTHER RULES

The most effective weapon fashioned by Congress in the 1986 Act to control abusive tax shelters is the severe limit on losses from passive activities. As we will see below, the new rules go far beyond the control of tax shelters and will effect profoundly the investment patterns of many citizens. Congress was no doubt motivated to enact harsh measures because of the rapid growth of tax shelters in recent years and by the failure of earlier provisions aimed at the problem. Between 1981 and 1983, offerings of publicly-registered shelters soared from $4.9 billion to $8.4 billion. Private placements also increased dramatically. Earlier legislative solutions, such as the hobby-loss rules, the at-risk rules, and the limit on investment interest, were partial, and therefore inadequate, solutions to the problem. The new rules for passive activities should eliminate the promotion of abusive shelters. The new rules will unfortunately penalize many other investments.

We have discussed the rules for passive activities earlier in the text. Chapter 3 describes the classification of income by source—active, portfolio, and passive. Chapter 4 explains how net losses from passive activities can only be used to offset income from passive activities, not active or portfolio income. Chapter 7 covers the effects that the use of different artificial entities can have on the classification of income and the deductibility of losses. This present discussion expands on the rules explained earlier, and offers some planning solutions for taxpayers caught by the new rules.

Taxpayers Subject to the Limits

All noncorporate taxpayers are subject to the limits on passive losses, including individuals, estates and trusts. Since the limits are imposed at the taxpayer level, partnerships and S corporations that pass their tax items through to owners are not affected directly by the rules—these entities do not *deduct* losses.

The law divides C corporations into three groups for purposes of applying the passive loss limits. First, publicly-held C corporations are not affected. Closely-held C corporations are generally subject to the limits. However, Congress provided a loophole that permits a closely-held C corporation (that is not a personal-service corporation) to offset passive losses against income from the active conduct of a business, but such losses cannot be used to offset portfolio income. For this purpose, a closely-held corporation is one where 50% or more in value of its stock is owned by 5 or fewer individuals at any time during the last half of the tax year. Uses of this loophole for planning purposes are illustrated later.

C corporations that are personal-service corporations are subject to the limits, even if they are closely-held. A personal-service corporation is a corporation: (1) where the principal activity is the performance of personal services; (2) where those services are "substantially" performed by employee-owners; and (3) where more than 10% of the corporate stock is owned by all employee-owners combined. While there exists many uncertainties about the definition just given, the term personal-service corporation clearly covers all "professional" corporations employed by doctors, lawyers, accountants, and others. Without a rule that subjects personal-service corporations to the passive loss limits, an individual who earned income by performing services could incorporate, include the passive activity in the corporation, and thus avoid the limits.

To summarize, individuals, estates, trusts, and personal-service C corporations are subject to the new rules. Publicly-held C corporations are exempt. Closely-held C corporations are partly covered, but with the important exception that permits passive losses to be offset by active income.

Passive Activities Defined

The statute defines a passive activity as one that involves the conduct of any trade or business in which the taxpayer does not materially participate. To understand this new concept we must first recognize that income is first classified as either "portfolio" income or "activity" income. The later category is then classified as active or passive (giving us, courtesy of a confused legislature, the nonsense term "active activity").

Portfolio income consists of interest, dividends, and royalty income provided the asset that produces the income is held as an investment. Portfolio income also includes gains from the disposition of property that produces portfolio income. Note that interest income is not automatically portfolio. Interest earned on notes arising from the active conduct of a business is active income. Similarly, royalty income and dividends are portfolio only if the asset is held for investment and not used in a business.

Once portfolio income is distinguished from activity income, the active-passive classification generally depends on material participation.

MATERIAL PARTICIPATION   Before turning to the meaning of this critical term, we must note that Congress has arbitrarily classified the following activities:

- Rental activities are passive. A rental activity is one where payment is for the use of tangible property as opposed to payment for services. For this purpose, hotels and car rentals are active businesses because significant services are performed.
- Working interests in oil and gas deposits are always active. A working interest is that held by an operator of a property, as opposed to holding a non-active royalty interest.
- A limited partnership interest is always passive. The degree of participation by the partner or the type of activity does not affect this passive classification. Thus, a limited partner in a partnership that holds only a working interest in oil and gas has passive income or loss.
- Certain low-income housing projects are temporarily classified as active businesses in order to deter owners from abandoning these projects.

All activities other than those just listed are active or passive with respect to a taxpayer depending on whether that taxpayer meets the test of material participation. A taxpayer meets that test only if he or she is involved in the activity's operations on a *regular, continuous,* and *substantial* basis. While the statute does not specify what is meant by regular, continuous and substantial, the Committee Reports accompanying the 1986 Act identify the following factors that must be considered: whether the taxpayer's involvement makes a significant contribution to operations; whether the activity is the taxpayer's principal business; regularity of taxpayer's presence at place of business; and whether the taxpayer fulfills a significant managerial function and actually supervises agents.

Application of the test of material participation to actual facts will undoubtedly create many conflicts. At the extremes, the results are clear enough. An activity that constitutes a taxpayer's principal business is active. At the other extreme, a general partner that does nothing more than attend partners' meetings fails the test. Between these extremes, uncertainty is the usual case. For example, can a proprietor engaged in several businesses fail the test for some of those businesses? Apparently so, though surely a presumption exists that a sole proprietor materially participates in his businesses.

The foregoing discussion assumes that the taxpayer is an individual, capable of material participation. The law contains rules for application of the test with the artificial entities. For parnterships and S corporations, the partner or shareholder reporting the taxable items must meet the test. For trusts, the trustee must participate, and for estates, the executor must meet the test. For C corporations that are also personal-service corporations, the material participation test is met only if stockholders owning more than 50% in value of the corporate stock meet the test. For closely-held corporations that are not personal-service corporations, an alternate test of material participation requires that at least one employee of such corporation devotes full-time to the management of the activity, that at least three non-owner empolyees of the corporation devote full time to the activity, and that the activity has Section 162 deductions that exceed 15% of the activity's gross income. For practical purposes, these rules mean that the owner-employees must perform the requisite services for personal-service corporation. Other closely-held corporations (that are not personal service corporations) meet the test if the requisite services are performed by any employee or employees.

SEPARATION OF ACTIVITIES   The new limits on passive losses can be applied properly only if *each activity* of a taxpayer is accounted for as a separate entity. Such separation is necessary in order: (1) to apply the test of material participation to determine if the activity is active or passive; (2) to apply the limits on losses (and on tax credits); and (3) to determine when an activity is completely disposed of for purposes of deducting accumulated losses from that activity.

Congress intends that this separation of activities be made in a "realistic economic sense." In making the decision of what constitutes a separate activity, "the question to be answered is what undertakings consist of an integrated and interrelated economic unit, conducted in coordination with or reliance upon each other, and constituting an appropriate unit for the measurement of gain or loss."[4] If, for example, a taxpayer operates a farm and an apartment house, there are two activities. The taxpayer who operates two farms, geographically separated, may have two activities, but if both operations produce the same commodity and use the same employees and equipment, they may constitute a single activity. Such decisions must be made based on the facts and circumstances in each case.

Applying the Limits on Passive Losses

Once a taxpayer's activities are divided into separate activities using the above rules and it is determined that some of these activities are passive, then net losses from the passive activities may only be used to offset net income from passive activities. As explained further below, net losses from a passive activity not allowed as a current deduction are deferred to later years to offset passive income, and any deferred losses are fully deductible when the activity

[4]Senate Finance Committee Report (accompanying H.R. 3838), TRA 1986, p. 739.

is completely disposed of. Recall that for closely-held C corporations (that are not personal-service corporations), net passive losses can also be deducted against active income, but not portfolio income.

The new rules for passive activities also apply limits to the business tax credits that are allowed. Generally, a tax credit from a passive activity can only be used to reduce taxes attributable to passive activities. This rule applies to the job credit, the low-income housing credit, the incremental research credit, and the rehabilitation credit. The limits on tax credits involve complicated computational problems beyond our scope here.

ACCOUNTING FOR DISALLOWED LOSSES   Passive losses disallowed in the current year because they exceed passive income must be accounted for on an activity-by-activity basis, primarily to determine when a deferred loss is fully deductible because the activity is disposed of. The deferred loss from a given year is allowed prorata to the loss activities for that year based on the amounts of their losses. To illustrate this point, assume that a taxpayer has four passive activities that produce the results below:

Activity	Gross Income	Deductions	Net	Carryover
1	$1,000	$1,800	$ (800)	$ (214)
2	1,800	900	900	—
3	1,300	2,000	(700)	(186)
4	200	—	200	—
	$4,300	$4,700	$ (400)	$ (400)

The net losses from activities 1 and 3 are deductible to the extent of $1,100, the net income from activities 2 and 4, but the net passive loss of $400 is deferred to later years. What if activity 1 is disposed of early next year? How much of the $400 disallowed is attributable to activity 1? A pro rata allocation is necessary: for activity 1, $800/$1,500 × $400 = $214; for activity 3, $700/$1,500 × $400 =$186.

SPECIAL LIMITS FOR RENTAL OF REAL ESTATE   Because of the many taxpayers with investments in rental real estate, Congress has provided a limited relief provision that applies to most taxpayers. Individuals (and estates for two years after formation) who actively participate in the management of rental real estate may deduct net passive losses attributable to such activities, up to $25,000 per year. This rule is subject to several qualifications.

First, this provision does not create a deduction but instead excepts net passive losses on real estate rentals from the overall limit of passive income. The $25,000 is an upward limit on the real estate losses exempt from the general rule. This limit is reduced by 50% of the amount by which the taxpayer's AGI (disregarding passive losses, IRA deductions, and gross income attributable to social security) exceeds $100,000. Taxpayers with AGI of $150,000 or more therefore get no advantage from this relief measure. (If married individuals live apart throughout the year, they may use this provision on their separate returns, but the limit is $12,500 and the phase-out begins at $50,000.)

This special rule applies only to individuals (and certain estates) who own at least 10% of the property. Evidently, joint ownership can take any legal form, for example, tenants in common, general partnerships, S corporations, as long as the individual reports the taxable items. A limited partnership interest would not be subject to the provision because such an interest is specifically excepted.

In addition to the 10% ownership, the individual must actively participate in the management of the property. "Active" participation is a much less stringent test than "material" participation. The operation of rental real estate involves only limited management decisions and the taxpayer need only participate in this way. Actual work on the property can be relegated to the taxpayer's agents. On the other hand, if the taxpayer furnishes substantial services, for example, the operation of a motel, the activity may be something more than real estate rental and beyond the scope of the provision. In this instance, note that the entire activity may be active, not passive, depending on the material participation test.

To illustrate this provision, assume that an individual with AGI (as adjusted) of $90,000 owns 100% of an apartment house that the individual actively manages, his only passive activity. If the taxpayer's current loss from this activity is $20,000, the entire loss is allowed; if the loss is $30,000, $25,000 is allowed currently and the remaining $5,000 is postponed. If the taxpayer's AGI is $120,000, the limit of this special provision is $15,000 ($25,000 − .5($120,000 − $100,000), and only that amount is deductible currently.

Individuals who own low-income housing and/or utilize the credit for rehabilitation of older structures are subject to more liberal rules for the A & I phase-out (generally a $200,000 threshold) and for the degree of participation in management (generally none required).

PHASE-IN OF LIMITS FOR PREENACTMENT ACTIVITIES   These new limits on passive losses apply to all passive activities, including those begun before the 1986 Act. For Congress to restrict the deduction of losses on pre-1987 (preenactment) activities comes close to being a retroactive tax. To mitigate this problem, 65% of net losses on preenactment activities are allowed in 1987, 40% in 1988, 20% in 1989, and 10% in 1990. After 1990, the limits explained in this section apply to both pre- and postenactment activities.

To illustrate, assume that in 1987 a taxpayer has a net loss of $5,000 from a preenactment activity and no passive income. For 1987 he can still deduct $3,250 ($5,000 × .65). If the same taxpayer had a separate postenactment activity that produced a net profit of $1,000, he must first net the $5,000 loss and the $1,000 profit and apply the 65% to the net loss of $4,000 from all activities, giving a deductible loss of $2,600 in 1987 ($4,000 × .65)

Recoupment of Losses at Disposition

The rules for passive losses do not permanently disallow losses but instead defer or suspend them indefinitely until they are absorbed by passive income in later years or they finally become fully deductible when the taxpayer disposes of the passive activity that generated the suspended losses. A disposition triggers the deduction of suspended losses only if such disposition is complete, fully taxable, and not made to a related party.

To be complete, the taxpayer must dispose of his entire interest in the passive activity. If the passive activity is owned through a partnership interest, the sale of the partnership interest would be a complete disposition. On the other hand, take the case of a taxpayer engaged in several activities, one of which is passive, as a proprietor. In this case, a complete disposition presumably requires the sale of all assets used in the passive activity.

Only fully taxable dispositions cause the deduction of suspended losses. Transfers of passive activities, or assets used in such activities, to a partnership or a corporation in a non-taxable exchange or in a like-kind exchange only results in association of the suspended losses with the new property received in the non-taxable exchange. Similarly, a gift of assets used in a passive activity is not a taxable disposition. For gifts, suspended losses are allocated to and increase the basis of the property in the donee's hands, giving recognition of the deferred passive losses when the donee eventually sells the property. Transfers at death, however, though nontaxable, are effective dispositions for this purpose and the decedent's executor can deduct suspended losses on the final return. Such losses must be reduced by the amount by which the basis of the property used in the passive activity is increased by the fair-market-value rule that applies to property passed at death. If a taxpayer dies leaving to his heirs a farm classified as passive, the farm having a fair market value of $5,000,000, a basis of $4,000,000, and suspended loss of $2,500,000, only $1,500,000 passive loss is deductible on the final return, with the remaining $1,000,000 being absorbed by the increase in basis from $4,000,000 to $5,000,000.

Finally, dispositions to related parties do not trigger the deduction of suspended losses. This rule is consistent with the general rule explained in Chapter 4 that disallows losses on sales to family members, controlled corporations, and other related entities. The technical definition of relatedness, found in Section 267(b), is thorough and complex but generally gives a reasonable result.

Note that a passive activity may become an active one if the taxpayer begins to participate materially, a closely-held corporation loses that status, or some other change occurs. Mere cessation of the passive classification does not result in the allowance of suspended losses. However, the suspended passive losses from that activity can be offset against the new active income from the same activity, but not active income generally.

Planning Around These New Rules

As just explained, a taxpayer finally gets to deduct passive losses—even after death on the final return (called by economists the long-run). A taxable, complete disposition of the activity may be necessary to obtain the deduction, a move that may not be economically wise, particularly at this time when so many taxpayers may be contemplating the sale of similar assets. On the other hand, a taxpayer cannot continue to incur losses on passive activities that only increase a loss carryover. With current interest rates, losses deferred a decade or longer have only nominal value. Thus, every effort must be made to avoid the limits and, if these efforts fail, the activity must be disposed of as soon as possible without taking a distress price. Possible ways of avoiding the limits are discussed below.

ELIMINATE NET PASSIVE LOSSES   Many passive losses result because they are inherent in the investment. Thus, to say that losses can be reduced by efficient operations commonly has no meaning. In other cases, however, losses result because of the way an activity is financed, i.e., because of leverage. This is particularly true in real estate. If debt can be eliminated by using funds currently invested in portfolio items (stocks and bonds) or shifted from a passive activity to an active trade or business, the passive loss may disappear. The elimination of leverage, of course, changes the basic economic nature of many investments—a gamble using your own money takes the fun and profit out of the game.

Another solution is to create a new source of passive income. A limited parntership interest currently producing passive income is one alternative. Some evidence exists that financial markets will soon make available a wide range of "securities" in the form of interests in master limited partnerships (MLP's). Through this vehicle investments that would otherwise produce portfolio income will apparently produce passive income, at least until Congress has time to rethink this possibility.

The most direct way to get rid of passive losses is for the taxpayer to participate materially in the activity. Recall that this option is not available for rental activities (always passive) but that real estate rentals enjoy the special $25,000 limit. Just how vigorously the IRS will enforce the test of material participation remains to be seen. In any event, depending on this solution in doubtful cases before regulations, rulings, and court decisions are available may introduce intolerable risks, particularly if less risky solutions are available. The tendency of some taxpayers to create needed evidential matter on this issue will test the integrity of tax practitioners.

USE OF ARTIFICIAL ENTITIES   Proper use of the artificial entities will avoid these new rules. As mentioned before, limited partnerships can produce passive income. An active business, regardless of the current legal form, can be converted to a limited partnership of this purpose, (though the conversion may involve some current tax costs). Query: Can a limited parntership buy stocks and bonds and thereby convert the portfolio income into passive income? Certainly, loss activity currently organized as a limited partnership can be converted to a general partnership or an S corporation. Then each parnter or shareholder may be able to avoid the passive classification by materially participating in operations (or, if a real estate rental, by actively participating).

Taxpayers who have both active business income and passive losses may combine them in a closely-held "C" corporation and enjoy the loophole intended by Congress. Recall that this alternative is not available for taxpayers providing personal services. Also, the use of a C corporation after 1986 is perilous, as explained elsewhere in this Part. Any plan using C corporations must solve the double-tax problem and that is not an easy task.

MULTINATIONAL CONSIDERATIONS

The tax-planning game just may be analogous to a three-dimensional chess game. First, a player must learn the individual moves that can be made with each piece utilized in the game—a task roughly comparable to learning about each of the many tax provisions as they apply to each of the various taxable and nontaxable entities. Second, a player must learn when and how to shift business and personal transactions among and between entities for the best possible tax result—a task that could possibly be compared to a two-dimensional chess game. Third, a really advanced player must come to understand that any entity can be relocated in almost any tax jurisdiction —that is, in almost any country on planet earth—if it is sufficiently tax-advantageous to do so.

In the final section of this chapter we examine briefly the U.S. federal income tax rules that apply to multinational transactions. To begin, you should recall that the U.S. federal income tax purports to be a *global* tax. That is, in Secs. 1 and 11 the U.S. federal income tax appears (as noted in Chapter 20) to apply to *every* individual, *every* corporation, and *every* fiduciary, wherever they may be located. Many, if not most, other countries of the world are less ambitious; that is, they employ a *territorial* income tax rather than a global income tax. This means that those countries attempt to tax only the income that is derived from within their own national boundary. Income earned in any other country is, as they see it, in someone else's tax domain.

Jurisdictional Issues

The United States government quite obviously is literally incapable of taxing *every* individual, *every* corporation, and *every* fiduciary in the world, however badly it may wish to do that. A French citizen, and lifelong resident of Paris, with no business or personal nexus whatever to the U.S., is simply not going to pay alms to the U.S. government; and, if the U.S. government were so foolish as to attempt to make that French citizen pay a U.S. income tax, the French legal system would not be at all inclined to enforce the U.S. income tax efforts because the U.S. government is wholly without legal jurisdiction in that situation. Similarly, a German corporation, doing no business whatever inside the U.S., is clearly outside the U.S. taxing jurisdiction.

Therefore, even though the U.S. income tax law in Secs. 1 and 11 reads as if it imposes a tax on *every* individual, *every* corporation and *every* fiduciary, common sense should warn you not to read those statutory words literally. If you were to search the Code long and hard enough, eventually you would

FIGURE **21-1**   Individual Taxpayers

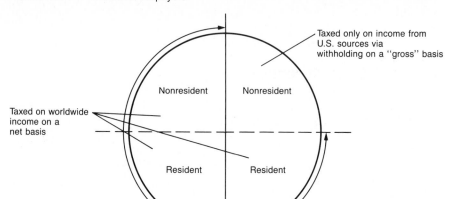

discover that all multinational transactions are subject to a whole host of special rules, *most* of which are found in Subchapter N (that is, in Secs. 861 through 999).

INDIVIDUAL TAXPAYERS   For U.S. federal income tax purposes, all of the individuals on earth can be conceptually divided between citizens and aliens. Further, each of these two categories can be further subdivided between residents and nonresidents. Thus we really have a four-way classification scheme, as depicted in Figure 21-1. In general, the U.S. taxes all U.S. citizens (resident as well as nonresident) plus all resident aliens in one manner; it taxes nonresident aliens in quite a different manner. The reason for the disparate treatment is, of course, the lack of general legal jurisdiction over the nonresident alien. In other words, one "price" of either citizenship *or* residency is the U.S. income tax obligation. If any individual wishes to wholly escape that tax obligation, he or she must remain or become a *nonresident* alien. Furthermore, he or she must refrain from doing any significant business within the United States. U.S. citizens who give up their citizenship to avoid tax are subject to special, restrictive rules (see Sec. 877).

A nonresident alien who derives any substantial amount of income from a U.S. source is likely to discover that that income stream is subject to the U.S. federal income tax. Because the U.S. government lacks legal jurisdiction over such an individual, it generally imposes an obligation on the payor of that income stream to withhold a flat tax from any payment to a nonresident alien, usually equal to 30% of the *gross income* amount otherwise payable. (The general statutory rate of 30% is subject to numerous modifications in both statutory and bilateral treaty provisions.) If the payor fails to withhold a proper tax amount, the U.S. government then has recourse against the person who made the payment if the nonresident alien refuses to pay the tax imposed by the U.S. government.

CORPORATE TAXPAYERS   Corporations, unlike people, are not classified as either citizens or aliens. Corporations can, however, be classified as either domestic or foreign. Domestic corporations are those that derive their legal authority for "being" from a U.S. government, usually one of the 50 state governments. Foreign corporations are those chartered under the laws of a "foreign" (or non-U.S.) government.

Although the foreign-versus-domestic classification is a useful starting point, it is not the sole issue of concern to corporations for federal income tax purposes. Both U.S. citizens and domestic corporations can, of course, create controlled "foreign" corporations in most countries of the world. The basic conceptual question for U.S. income tax policy is whether a controlled foreign corporation (or CFC) should be treated more like (1) a foreign corporation owned largely by foreign shareholders or (2) a mere legal extension of a taxable domestic entity. With a generous stretch of the imagination, a tax student might compare the classification of individuals to that of corporations, as illustrated in Figure 21-2

As suggested in Figure 21-2, the U.S. attempts to tax all "domestic" corporations, regardless of who owns that corporation, on its worldwide income. A CFC may also be taxed currently on at least a portion of its worldwide income largely because the U.S. government has both legal and taxing jurisdiction over at least a majority of the CFC's shareholders (hence the government can immediately force those shareholders to pay the income tax "on behalf of" the foreign corporation. The "genuine" foreign corporation—that is, the one largely owned by non-U.S. shareholders—

FIGURE **21-2**   Corporate Taxpayers

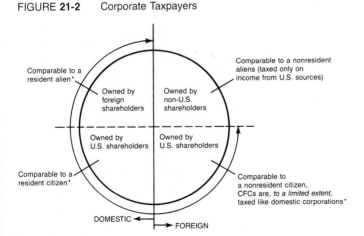

*Taxed on worldwide income on a net basis

remains largely outside the grasp of U.S. tax law (much like the nonresident alien), so the U.S. will wisely tax that entity only on the income it earns from U.S. sources.

FIDUCIARY TAXPAYERS   The multinational classification of fiduciary taxpayers is doubly difficult. Unlike individuals, estates and trusts have no "citizenship," and, unlike corporations, they really need not derive their authority for "being" from a government. For example, the biological event called death may automatically create a taxable estate. The executor of the estate of a wealthy member of the jet set, with multiple "homes" in various countries, is likely to discover that the several "home" countries will attempt to impose an estate tax on one individual decedent's estate. Because of these differences, the jurisdiction over fiduciary taxpayers depends on all the facts and circumstances of each particular case. Among the facts considered are the citizenship and/or residency of the grantor or the decedent, the citizenship and/or residency of the trustee or executor, the location of the assets, and the country under whose laws the trust indenture was created or the will is probated. Quite naturally, more than one government may attempt to achieve the primary tax jurisdiction over a single fiduciary. If the U.S. government decides that a trust or an estate is a U.S. taxable entity, it will, of course, attempt to impose a worldwide income and/or estate tax on that entity.

Double Tax Mitigation

Because the U.S. government attempts to impose a global tax—that is, to tax the worldwide income of all taxpayers deemed subject to the U.S. jurisdiction —many taxpayers are potentially subject to a double tax on a single income stream. First, it will be taxed by the government of the "host" country—that is, by the government of the country in which the income is actually earned—and then it may be taxed a second time by the U.S. government. Were there no mechanism to mitigate such a double tax, few U.S. citizens, resident aliens, or domestic corporations would find it profitable to engage in any multinational business.

To mitigate the possibility of a double income tax on a single income stream, the U.S. Code authorizes a foreign tax credit. That means, of course, that U.S. taxpayers can generally subtract as a tax credit from their gross U.S. federal income tax liability the amount of any income tax paid to a foreign country. The amount of the foreign tax credit cannot, however, exceed the maximum amount of the U.S. federal income tax liability that would have been imposed on that same amount of taxable income. In still other words, a "U.S. taxpayer" engaged in a multinational business must pay the larger of (1) the U.S. or (2) the foreign income tax on any income earned abroad. If the foreign income tax is less than the U.S. income tax on the foreign-source income, the difference must be paid immediately to the U.S. government. On the other hand, if the foreign income tax exceeds the U.S. tax on the foreign-source taxable income, the excess tax credit must (in general) be carried forward for possible offset in future years when the tax posture has reversed itself.

Although the U.S. foreign tax credit is vastly more complex than the rules stated above, that oversimplified description should serve to explain the most important single mechanism in the U.S. income taxation of multinational business.

Foreign Tax Planning

Before anyone could really understand foreign tax planning, a great number of additional Code provisions would have to be explained in detail. Unfortunately, that kind of explication must remain outside the confines of an introductory tax text. Nevertheless, it is not too early to suggest a couple of fairly obvious ways in which tax planning can be done in an international setting.

We observed earlier that a U.S. citizen who remains overseas for a specified period of time may be able to exclude from gross income for U.S. federal income tax purposes up to $70,000 per year in foreign-source *earned* income. Whether or not this will be of any real benefit to the individual depends, of course, on how the foreign country, in which the U.S. citizen is living, taxes that same income. If the host country imposes an income tax equal to or greater than the U.S. tax that ordinarily would have applied to that same income, nothing has been saved by the U.S. exclusion. On the other hand, if the foreign or host country also fails to collect (for whatever reason) any income tax whatsoever on the income earned by the U.S. expatriate taxpayer, the effect of the U.S. exclusion provision found in Sec. 911 is to convert up to $70,000 of taxable income into nontaxable income. Hence, tax planning for individual U.S. citizens working overseas will sometimes be as simple as selecting the work site carefully.

The decision to obtain a charter, for foreign corporate operations, in the right country can be equally important. In general, the U.S. will not attempt to impose an income tax on a foreign corporation unless and until it distributes that income to a U.S. shareholder. (Special rules apply to base company operations of CFCs; that is, to foreign corporations controlled by U.S. shareholders that are doing business outside the foreign country in which they are incorporated.) Therefore, tax deferral is sometimes possible for U.S. shareholders who create their foreign corporations in countries with little or no income tax. To achieve this deferral, however, they must also confine most of their foreign business to that same country of incorporation.

Prior to 1976, U.S. citizens were also able to achieve major savings in U.S. income taxes by the creation of fiduciary (trust) entities in various tax-haven countries. The rules permitting this advantage were closed, however, and today there is little or no remaining advantage for a U.S. citizen or a resident alien to create a foreign trust.

Although this brief introduction to multinational tax considerations is insufficient to allow the reader to understand very much about tax planning in the international setting, hopefully it illustrates why the decision to do business in a particular form in any foreign country may be an important consideration from a tax point of view.

PROBLEMS

1. Explain briefly how the U.S. will tax a:
   a. U.S. citizen living in the U.S.
   b. U.S. citizen living abroad.
   c. resident alien.
   d. nonresident alien.
   e. domestic corporation.
   f. foreign corporation.

2. The Maturity Trust Fund is qualified as a "complex" trust, which is not required to distribute all income currently. During 1988, it had the following transactions:

Income received (all taxable)	$4,200
Expenses of administration and other expenses relating to income	1,000
Distributions of income taxable to beneficiaries	2,600

   Compute the trust's federal income tax for the year.

3. Herman and Betty Irish have two small children who are dependent on them for support. For the current year, they expect to receive the following income:

Salaries	$80,000
Dividends from taxable domestic corporations	6,000

   The dividends are paid on stock owned jointly by Herman and Betty. They expect the following deductions:

Unreimbursed travel and transportation related to Herman's employment	$4,000
Other itemized deductions (not subject to 2% of A.G.I. floor)	6,000

   Their tax consultant has recommended that the stock owned by Herman and Betty be transferred to two trusts, one for each child. The trustees would be instructed to accumulate income and pay the accumulated income, as needed, for the college education of the children after they reach their majority. (This arrangement is a complex trust, and the annual exemption is $100 per trust.) The trust corpus, plus any accumulated income, would be paid to each child when he or she reaches the age of 30.
   a. Compute Herman and Betty's tax liability for the current year, assuming they do *not* create the trusts.
   b. Compute the combined liabilities of Herman and Betty and the two trusts, assuming the trusts are established on January 1 of the current year (ignore any federal gift taxes).
   c. How much tax is saved by the trust arrangement?

4. a. Max and Ruth Colter operate an interior decorating service in Texas. In 1988 they had the following items of income and deductions:

Profits from the business	$80,000
Dividend income from taxable domestic corporations	3,000
Interest on savings	9,000
	$92,000

Max and Ruth have two children, ages 3 and 4, and are therefore entitled to four exemption deductions. Their itemized deductions were $5,500 (after deducting the 2% A.G.I. floor). Compute their gross tax liability for 1988, assuming the children are dependents and that the business is not incorporated.

b. Devise a tax plan that minimizes the income tax of Max and Ruth. In your plan, assume that Max and Ruth have no particular need for interest income but that they would like to arrange for the maximum after-tax income in the corporation to provide for expected expansion. (For simplicity, assume that Max and Ruth need a combined income of $40,000 before taxes from the decorating service for personal living expenses.)

5. James Hampton, a client of yours, owns a large city lot that cost him $15,000 several years ago. He has been leasing the lot, which has a fair market value of $250,000, to a used car dealer. James has been approached by Henry Simon about building an office building on the property. Simon proposes to put $250,000 cash into the deal and then obtain a mortgage loan of $12 million to cover the building costs. James and Henry would operate the office building for five or six years and then sell it for a profit. List the advantages and disadvantages of using (a) a corporation, (b) an S corporation, and (c) a partnership for the new venture.

6. Tim Wortman died this year. His gross estate was valued at $2,500,000. He owed debts of $350,000, and the estate incurred administrative expenses of $50,000. There were no other estate deductions. During his life, Tim made taxable gifts totaling $550,000 and paid a gift tax of $127,300 on these gifts. Calculate the estate tax due the federal government, using current rates.

7. Briefly described below are some prospective new business ventures. For each you must decide which legal entity is best suited, giving your reasons. Consider tax rules, primarily.

a. Father and son will operate an active business that will produce good profits from the first year. Both will be actively engaged in the business, and their goal is to build a family "nest egg" by expanding this business.

b. Three business executives will buy an apartment house using borrowed funds. Because of interest and depreciation, losses will result in the early years, though they expect the property to appreciate in value. They will manage the property together.

c. Grandparents want to provide for the education of grandchildren.

8. Susan Kemp is 65 years old and in good health. Kemp has about $5,000,000 invested in corporate stocks and bonds that produce an income of approximately $300,000 per year. She has one child, a married son, who is quite wealthy in his own right, being the sole stockholder of a company that earns about $500,000 per year. However, her son has three children (ages 14, 16, and 17) who have no

current taxable income. Susan talked with her son and decided that her wealth should pass directly to her grandchildren. She has come to you for advice on the wisdom of several plans that have been recommended by other advisers. Evaluate each plan and suggest alternatives.

a. One adviser told her that she might as well wait and pass her property at death because the tax law has equalized the tax treatment of *inter vivos* gifts and death transfers.

b. Another counselor suggested that she make a gift of the bulk of her securities in trust, keeping only enough to ensure sufficient income. One trust would be created with the trustee given the power to distribute income as needed for the welfare of the grandchildren. She was told to reserve the power to revoke the trust in the event the children did not "turn out well."

c. Yet another adviser suggested that she make a series of gifts every two years to a single trust for the benefit of the three grandchildren.

9. James Whitson owns 25% of the common stock of Prism, Inc., a calendar-year taxpayer. The corporation operated for several years before making an S corporation election for 1988. In 1988, the corporation had taxable income of $100,000 and made no distributions to its shareholders. Whitson properly reported $25,000 as his share of the corporate income on his individual return. In 1989, Prism distributed the following amounts in cash to Whitson: March 1, $15,000; June 1, $20,000; October 1, $40,000. Corporate taxable income for 1989 was $120,000.

a. Why might a profitable corporation such as Prism make an S corporation election?

b. How much income must Whitson report as a result of the distributions received in 1989 and the corporation's taxable income?

10. One of the attractive features of oil and gas investments is that most of the drilling costs are immediately deductible. Why are most of these ventures structured as limited partnerships instead of S corporations?

11. List three reasons why an owner of a limited partnership interest may be unable to currently deduct his share of the partnership's losses.

12. The trading of interests in master limited partnerships (MLP) on major exchanges has made such entities very similar to corporations. Other than tax treatment, what is the major difference between a corporation and an MLP?

13. Many tax experts expect MLPs to become more popular in the future. What recent tax change could explain this trend?

14. Korpco is a U.S. corporation with international operations in Atlantis. Atlantis imposes an income tax only on Atlantis-based income. Compute Korpco's worldwide tax liability in the following independent situations.

a. U.S. earnings: $900,000; Atlantis earnings, $100,000; Atlantis tax rate, 30%.

b. U.S. earnings: $900,000; Atlantis earnings, $100,000; Atlantis tax rate, 40%.

15. Homer and Amy Wagner operate a sporting goods store and engage in various other economic activities listed below. Income (losses) for the current year appear at the right.

Net profit—sporting goods store	$50,000
Dividends on stock held as investment	3,100
Loss on rental house managed by Homer	(1,500)

Limited partnership interest in an apartment house	(4,500)
General partnership interest in a cattle operation—managed by agent	3,000
Working interest in oil well	(3,500)
Amy's loss on Tupperware sales	(1,000)

a. Calculate the Wagner's AGI, ignoring any transitional rules.

b. What is the AGI if Homer materially participates in the cattle operation?

16. John Witte engaged in the following passive activities during the current year (no rental real estate):

Activity	Gross income	Deductions	Net
1	$8,000	$11,000	($3,000)
2	15,000	10,000	5,000
3	16,000	20,000	(4,000)
	$39,000	$41,000	($2,000)

a. How much may Witte deduct against active income this year?

b. If Witte disposes of his interest in Activity 3 on the first day of next year, how much of the suspended loss is deductible?

17. Several years ago, Norma Lisa purchased an interest in a limited partnership for $40,000. Accumulated suspended losses relative to this interest amount now to $30,000. What are the tax consequences if Norma:

a. Sells the interest of $25,000 to an unrelated party?

b. Dies, leaving the interest to her friend, Tammy, when the interest has a FMV of $45,000?

c. Contributes the interest to a general partnership in a transaction where no gain or loss is recognized?

CHAPTER 22

The Alternative Minimum Tax

Alaska Air Group Inc. will lease as many as 10 commuter aircraft instead of buying them, thereby saving $4 million or more in 1987 taxes.
Lee Berton, *Wall Street Journal*, March 11, 1987, p. 1.

The tax planning process is inherently self-destructive. The life cycle of the process typically both begins and ends with the passing of a new tax law. Even before the ink of the president's signature on a new tax bill has had a chance to dry, taxpayers and their advisers are already hard at work trying to determine exactly what they can do to minimize their own tax liability under the new rules. Inevitably a number of tax-saving opportunities are identified. At first only a few people may see some of the more subtle opportunities, while other new "loopholes" become almost immediately evident to everyone. Responsible taxpayers then adjust both their business and personal transactions to comply with the new rules but still minimize their tax liability. Eventually tax returns are filed and the I.R.S. observes what has happened to cause tax revenues to be less than they might otherwise have been and, very often, to be less than they were projected to be. (Note: it is almost impossible to program the computer to reflect all of the "adjustments" that will be made in taxpayers' adaptive behavior; hence, one should not be too hasty to criticize the inaccuracy of the revenue projectors previously submitted.) Initially the I.R.S. may attempt to stem this tide and to "protect the revenue" by issuing administrative pronouncements that are intended to curtail at least the more aggressive tax plans. That action, in turn, often leads to litigation, which typically requires many years to be resolved. Finally, whenever the tax revenue losses from any particular tax-planning opportunity become sufficiently widespread, the Treasury Department urges Congress to enact remedial legislation, and the federal tax process begins all over again. In this chapter we first look briefly at the general process known as tax reform, and we then examine in somewhat greater detail the alternative minimum tax, which is a very good example of both how tax laws have changed because of tax planning and how tax planning must change because of this law.

THE TAX-REFORM PROCESS

The federal tax-reform process is rather complex. Like most processes involving many people, the process tends to resist change. This tendency to inertia is due in part to the reluctance with which people approach changes in their behavior patterns. In the case of the tax law, this understandable human tendency is strengthened by the network of vested interests that segments of the population have in the law as it stands at any point in time. It would be a peculiar world indeed if proposals to change these rules, which could result in higher taxes for the people involved, were not resisted vigorously.

Yet another, and perhaps more important, reason exists for the resistance to change in the taxing process. Once a tax law is passed and remains in effect for several years, financial transactions are modified to "fit" the law; that is, our ways of "doing business" change to accommodate the law. Our financial transactions, in turn, affect the distribution of the nation's wealth, the level of employment of the nation's resources, and other facets of our daily existence. In short, the taxing process is a major thread in our socioeconomic fabric. To propose a change in the tax process is to propose a change in that fabric. No one can guarantee what the end result will be when he or she begins to think about changing the apparently stable world.

For all these reasons, a literal translation of the word *reform* relative to our tax laws is usually inappropriate. To reform means literally "to form again." Yet, when we study the changes made in the federal income tax law, we find that the changes typically are either alterations or extensions of some concept already in the law or a very tentative trial of some new concept. The usual tax "reform" is not a repeal of some old law and a bold adventure with some new one. Instead, we find changes that are akin to tactical military probes to observe the foe's reaction. In the taxing process, most maneuvers are made cautiously and the political, social, and economic reactions carefully noted. Perhaps we should not quarrel with this type of reform. Considering the complexity of the problem of predicting the results of sweeping reforms, the wiser course may be that generally followed. A more adventuresome approach could lead to chaos. The next few years will determine whether or not we exceeded those boundaries of reasonableness in the 1986 Act.

Given the several reasons for inertia in the process, what countervailing forces cause the seemingly continuous, usually gradual, changes in tax law? Three general causes for change are apparent. The process itself contains built-in safeguards against complete stagnation. Tax specialists, in and out of government, continually study the law and its effect and recommend changes. Their objectives cover the entire spectrum from relieving gross inequities to securing special benefits for a select group to increasing the revenue.

On rare occasions, Congress undertakes a reform of the tax law due to massive public discontent. The Tax Reform Act of 1986 was in part a response to a wave of articles in the popular press and books that enjoyed unusual notoriety. These articles and books pictured a tax system that amounted to a federal subsidy for the very rich at the expense of the remaining citizenry. Often, the politicians and the authors implied that if the rich only paid their fair share, there would be enough additional revenue to support needed social programs. Although much of what appeared in the popular press bordered on "yellow" journalism, Congress did feel compelled to react to both public sentiment and to pressures from the White House.

Finally, many changes in our tax law occur because of changing economic conditions. During periods of economic downturn it is particularly likely that Congress will change the tax law hoping and believing that the changes will stimulate economic activity and get the country back on the road to recovery. Such an adaptive tax mechanism is almost inevitable in a democracy, because any politician foolish enough to be unconcerned about the issues that are uppermost in the minds of his or her constituency will soon be a *former* congressman, senator, or president.

In the remainder of this chapter we will examine the alternative minimum tax (or AMT), which is a classic example of tax-reform legislation. It is also a textbook example of the complexity involved in successful tax planning. The AMT rules to be described here include only the general rules of most common interest. Anyone concerned with solving a real-life problem involving the minimum tax must get additional help from another source. Hopefully, however, even this cursory review of AMT provisions will illustrate how and why too much "regular" income tax planning can inadvertently lead to an unanticipated tax increase rather than a planned tax reduction.

THE ALTERNATIVE MINIMUM TAX

Congress is generally reluctant to repeal major provisions of the law that favor certain segments of our society. Noting this tendency, the tax specialists in the Treasury and on the staff of the Joint Committee on Taxation apparently decided in the late 1960s that a tactic other than direct repeal was needed to increase the tax burden of taxpayers who had managed to reduce their tax liability significantly by taking advantage of the several favorable provisions that were then part of the law. The tactic adopted was a new concept—a tax on tax preferences or loopholes. According to one source, the original idea to levy a tax on loopholes is credited to Joseph A. Pechman, a well-known tax scholar of the Brookings Institution.[1] The idea was first

---

[1]"Returns Roll in for Tax Reform," *Business Week*, February 8, 1969, p. 34.

enacted into the law in 1969, but several major modifications of the original idea have been made since then. Nevertheless, the original objective remains intact; that is, no taxpayer may reduce a substantial economic income to little or no taxable income by using the various exclusions, deductions, and credits without running afoul of the minimum tax provisions.

The alternative minimum tax is just exactly what the words suggest: that is, (1) it is an *alternative* to the federal income tax computed in the "regular" or "normal" way *and* (2) it is the *minimum* federal income tax that any taxpayer can pay for a year. Hence, if the AMT is larger than the regular tax, the AMT is the amount that must be paid; but if the regular tax is larger than the AMT, the AMT is simply ignored. The computations that every taxpayer must make in order to determine the AMT payable require, for all practical purposes, a set of accounting records that is separate and distinct from both the records that must be maintained for "ordinary" federal income tax purposes and those required for financial reporting purposes. Prior to 1987, two sets of accounting records would generally suffice; today, at least three are required. (In fact, today a fourth set—to keep track of earnings and profits—is required for most corporations.) The added cost of this new complexity will be substantial. However, the AMT was the technique selected by Congress in 1986 to put an end to frequent news reports that some of the largest corporations and some of the wealthiest citizens in America had legally paid less in U.S. federal income taxes than did the legendary "widow in Dubuque."

The rejuvenated AMT was also viewed in the 1986 tax deliberations as an important element in tax-revenue generation. Under prior law, relatively little tax revenue was generated by the minimum-tax provisions; in the years between 1987 and 1991, it is expected to provide the federal treasury with over $30 billion. Some early activity in the area of equipment leasing suggests that the 1986 revenue estimates for this provision may once again prove to be unduly optimistic. As will be explained below, the difference between depreciation deductions as calculated for regular tax and for AMT purposes was intended to be a mainstay in the AMT base. Large corporate taxpayers quickly determined, however, that they might be able to reduce the AMT that would otherwise be payable in 1987 and beyond by leasing rather than buying certain depreciable equipment because, under a lease arrangement, there would be no "depreciation" per se. The apparent movement to leasing was sufficiently widespread by March 1987 to cause at least a few of the tax reformers left on Capitol Hill to comment that further changes in the AMT law might have to be made quickly to stop the eroding effect of this trend in leasing.

Basic Computation

The technical term used in Sec. 55(b) to describe the tax base for the AMT is "alternative minimum taxable income" (or AMTI). It is a numerical quantity derived from a prescribed computation that begins with taxable income (TI)

FIGURE **22-1**   Computation of the AMT

Taxable income (TI)	\$xxxxx
Plus and/or minus net "adjustments"	xxxx*
Plus "tax preferences"	xxxx
Equals net AMTI	\$xxxxx
Less "exemption" (if any)	(xxx)
Equals net AMTI	\$xxxxx
Times tax rate	(times) xx**
Equals gross AMT	\$ xxxx
Less tax credits	(minus) xxx
Equals net AMT payable	\$ xxxx

*Note that this net amount can be either positive or negative.
**The tax rate is 20% for corporations, 21% for other taxpayers.

defined in the normal way; that is, taxable income as defined in most of the prior 21 chapters of this text. A broad outline of the prescribed computation is summarized in Figure 22-1. As noted there, the basic modifications to ordinary taxable income can be subdivided between some items described as "adjustments" and other items described as "tax preferences." The only real difference between these two groups is that adjustments require the substitution of one tax number for another—a procedure that can either increase or decrease the tax base on an item-by-item basis—whereas tax preferences necessarily involve an *addition to* TI in the determination of AMTI. The details of the adjustments can be found in Secs. 56 and 58; the details of preferences, in Sec. 57. Those statutory details are unfortunately complex and the syntax unbelievably convoluted. Furthermore, some adjustments and preferences apply equally to all taxpayers; some, to individuals and fiduciaries but not to corporations; some, to corporations but not to noncorporate taxpayers; a few, to individuals and only certain kinds of corporations; and yet others, to only very special organizations.[2] In lieu of extensive statutory quotation, therefore, we will substitute a risky paraphrasing of the most widely applicable portions of the Code and hope that the reader will understand the general thrust of the law.

Adjustments and Preferences

The 1986 Code actually requires a taxpayer to compute many items in two very different ways: one way in the determination of TI, and quite another way in the determination of AMTI. These required differences are, of course, the explanation for the two different tax accounting systems noted earlier in

[2]For example, see Sec. 56(c)(2), which applies only to merchant marine capital construction funds; Sec. 56(c)(3), to Blue Cross, Blue Shield, and similar organizations; and Sec. 56(f)(2)(G), to Alaska Native Corporations.

this chapter. Differences exist for selected items of gross income, deduction, and credit. For example, even though Secs. 453 and 453A authorize the installment sale method of revenue recognition for regular income tax purposes, Sec. 56(a)(6) denies a taxpayer the right to use it in the determination of AMTI. Sec. 56(a)(1) similarly requires a different depreciation deduction calculation for AMT purposes than Sec. 167 authorizes for regular tax purposes. And Sec. 59(a) modifies, for AMT purposes, the foreign tax credit otherwise provided by Sec. 27(a).

Table 22-1 includes a very terse description of the most common adjustments and preferences, indicates their general applicability, and identifies a Code reference that provides at least a starting place for those students desiring to locate and read additional detail. Because of the differences detailed in Table 22-1, a taxpayer may also have different carryover amounts that can change both TI and AMTI in any year.

Predicting the impact of the revised AMT is difficult because of the diversity of the provisions encompassed in Secs. 55 through 59. It would appear to have its most severe impact on: (1) business ventures that use one accounting method for financial accounting purposes and a different method for tax purposes (because of the book-tax adjustment); (2) capital intensive industries, unless they lease the properties used in their trade or business (because of the TI/AMTI differences in depreciation deductions); and (3) individuals realizing large losses from passive activities. This is a distinctly different set of taxpayers from those typically subject to a minimum tax before 1987; they were usually characterized by large amounts of capital gains and/or investment credits.

As noted in the preceding paragraph, the individual taxpayers at greatest risk are those with large passive activity losses. These and other persons will also be impacted by the fact that many of the deductions that an individual taxpayer can claim in the computation of taxable income are either completely disallowed or modified in the determination of AMTI per Sec. 56(b)(1). A partial list of those differences would include:

Items totally disallowed:

1. The standard deduction
2. All "miscellaneous itemized deductions" subject to the 2% of A.G.I. floor
3. Most state, local, and foreign income taxes if deducted from A.G.I.
4. State and local property taxes if deducted from A.G.I.

Items that are allowed in a modified amount:

1. Medical expenses only to the extent they exceed 10% of the taxpayer's A.G.I.
2. Personal interest but, in general, only if paid on the taxpayer's principal residence (with a further possible limitation even in that case) and, sometimes, on one other residence
3. Net investment interest determined using special AMT rules but with no "phasein" amount for the years 1987–1990

TABLE 22-1   AMT ADJUSTMENTS AND PREFERENCES

Brief General Description	Applicable to		Code Reference
	Individuals	Corporations	
Depreciation of tangible property placed in service after 12/31/86 (requires a longer life and sometimes a less rapid method)	Yes	Yes	Sec. 56(a)(1)
Mining exploration and development costs other than oil and gas properties (requires capitalization with 10-year amortization)	Yes	Yes	Sec. 56(a)(2)
Long-term contracts entered into after 12/31/86 (requires use of percentage-of-completion method of accounting)	Yes	Yes	Sec. 56(a)(3)
Net operating loss deduction (limited to 90% of AMTI)	Yes	Yes	Secs. 56(a)(4) and 56(d)
Amortization of pollution-control facilities placed in service after 12/31/86 (requires a longer amortization period)	Yes	Yes	Sec. 56(a)(5)
Installment sale method of accounting for sales after 3/1/86 (this accounting method election denied for AMT purposes)	Yes	Yes	Sec. 56(a)(6)
Gain or loss on sale of certain properties (redetermine basis and, therefore, amount of gain or loss, using AMT rules)	Yes	Yes	Sec. 56(a)(7)
Limitations on certain "from AGI" deductions (some deductions—such as miscellaneous itemized deductions and the standard deduction—disallowed; others, modified—such as medical expense and interest)	Yes	No	Sec. 56(b)(1)
Circulation and research and experimental expenditures incurred after 12/31/86 (requires capitalization and amortization over 3 and 10 years, respectively)	Yes	No	Sec. 56(b)(2)
One half the difference between the excess of pre-tax "book income" (that is, income as reported for financial accounting purposes) over AMTI (for years beginning in 1987, 1988, and 1989; thereafter a similar adjustment will be based on "adjusted current earnings" rather than "book income")	No	Yes	Sec. 56(c), (f), and (g)
Percentage depletion in excess of adjusted basis (disallowed)	Yes	Yes	Sec. 57(a)(1)
Intangible drilling costs on oil and gas properties (may be limited to a smaller deduction)	Yes	Yes	Secs. 57(a)(2) and 57(b)
Exercise of an incentive stock option (excess of fair market value over option price is included in AMTI)	Yes	No	Sec. 57(a)(3)
Tax-exempt interest from specified "private activity bonds" (included in AMTI)	Yes	Yes	Sec. 57(a)(5)
Charitable contribution of appreciated property (unrealized gain is included in AMTI)	Yes	Yes	Sec. 57(a)(6)
Excess of rapid depreciation over straight-line depreciation on property placed in service before 1/1/87	Yes	Yes	Sec. 57(a)(7)
Deduction of losses from certain "tax shelter farm activities" (denied for AMT purposes)		No (unless a personal service corporation)	Sec. 58(a)
Deduction of passive activity losses (no "phasein" amounts allowed for years from 1987 to 1990)	Yes	No (unless a closely held C corporation or a personal service corporation)	Secs. 58(b) and 469(a)(2)

4. Charitable contributions reduced by any unrealized appreciation in capital gain properties donated to a qualifying organization

Stated in a positive, rather than negative, way, this means that the only "from-A.G.I. deductions" that most individuals can claim for AMTI purposes are:

1. Home mortgage interest
2. Charitable contributions
3. Gambling losses
4. Medical expenses and casualty losses (in relatively rare situations)

Before we consider further the impact of the AMT, let us complete our discussion of the basic AMT computation as detailed earlier in Figure 22-1.

The AMT Exemption

In order to exempt literally millions of "average" taxpayers from the need to make all of the complex AMT calculations, Congress provided a relatively generous exemption. The amount of the initial (or tentative) exemption varies from one taxpayer to another, based on both entity and filing-status differences. The initial exemptions are phased out (at the rate of 25 cents on the dollar) for taxpayers with a sufficiently large AMTI. The phaseout range begins at an AMTI of $150,000 for both corporations and individuals filing a joint return (as well as surviving spouses); at $112,500 for single persons (including heads of households); and at $75,000 for fiduciaries and married persons filing separately. This means, of course, that there is no exemption remaining for corporations and married persons filing jointly if their AMTI exceeds $310,000; for single persons, $232,500; and for fiduciaries and married persons filing separately, $155,000. These general rules can be summarized as follows:

Entity	Filing Status	Initial Exemption	Phaseout Begins at AMTI of	No Exemption if AMTI Exceeds
Corporation	N.A.	$40,000	$150,000	$310,000
Fiduciary	N.A.	20,000	75,000	155,000
Individual	Single persons and heads of households	30,000	112,500	232,500
Individual	Married persons filing jointly and surviving spouses	40,000	150,000	310,000
Individual	Married persons filing separate returns	20,000	75,000	155,000

As a practical matter, these numbers mean that even though the "average" individual taxpayer may still be able to totally ignore the AMT provisions with little risk, individuals in the upper-middle income group, as well as many corporations, will have to give them a considerable amount of time and attention. For most of these taxpayers, a competent tax adviser is no longer a luxury; one is now a virtual necessity.

AMT Credits

In general the only tax credit that can be used by all taxpayers to reduce the gross AMT liability is the foreign tax credit. C corporations may, however, also be able to utilize an investment tax credit carryforward to partially reduce their gross AMT. In addition, a new AMT credit may be used to reduce a taxpayer's *regular* income tax in future years. Each of these three credits will be explained very briefly below.

FOREIGN TAX CREDIT   The United States allows citizens, resident aliens, and domestic corporations the right to claim a foreign tax credit on income earned abroad to avoid the double taxation of a single earnings stream, as explained in Chapter 21. This provision generally applies equally to the regular tax liability and the AMT liability. However, when the foreign tax credit is used to reduce a taxpayer's AMT, a special maximum is imposed. The limit is equal to 90% of a "tentative AMT" (defined as the gross AMT liability determined without regard to either a foreign tax credit or the AMT net operating loss deduction). This 90% limit was specifically designed to keep a U.S. taxpayer, earning a substantial amount of foreign-source income, from using the foreign tax credit to totally avoid any U.S. federal income tax liability. Persons interested in additional details should read Sec. 59(a).

INVESTMENT TAX CREDIT   The "regular" investment tax credit (ITC) was generally terminated as of January 1, 1986. A significant number of taxpayers, however, still have an ITC carryforward available to reduce their current federal income tax liability. The amount of ITC that can be utilized to offset a current tax liability may depend, in the case of C corporations, on the AMT liability. In schematic form, the C corporation limit can be expressed as the *larger* of A or D, where A is the *lesser* of B or C and, in words:

B equals $25,000 + 75\% (net regular tax liability *less* $25,000); C equals net regular tax liability *less* 75% of the net AMT liability; and D equals 25% of the net AMT liability

(NOTE: in this calculation, the phrase "net AMT liability" is meant to describe the amount remaining after the foreign tax credit is subtracted from the gross AMT liability.)

Even a C corporation can use the ITC carryforward as a credit for AMT purposes only if, and to the extent that, it was derived from "regular" as opposed to "energy" or "rehabilitation" expenditures. Individuals interested in additional details should see Sec. 38(c)(3). Incidentally, like the foreign tax credit, the ITC credit may be further restricted because of the 90% rule noted earlier. That is, the combined effect of the AMT net operating loss deduction, foreign tax credit, and ITC can not exceed 90% of the gross AMT.

THE AMT CREDIT AGAINST THE REGULAR TAX   In many instances, a taxpayer will be required to pay the AMT solely because of "timing differences." In other words, many of the AMT adjustments and preferences, detailed earlier in Table 22-1, will balance themselves out over enough years. In general, the AMT provisions require a taxpayer (1) to accelerate the recognition of gross income and (2) to defer the recognition of deductions, as compared to the regular income tax provisions. If, because of these provisions, a taxpayer must pay the AMT (because it is larger than the regular tax), that taxpayer might eventually be subject to a second tax on the same item when the situation is reversed and the regular tax exceeds the AMT. This unfortunate consequence can be illustrated easily by reference to the installment sales rule. Suppose that in 1987 a taxpayer's $300,000 income was derived solely from an installment sale that was collected in 1988 and that this taxpayer had no other source of income in the latter year. Under these circumstances, if there were no AMT credit available to the taxpayer to reduce the 1988 regular tax, a single source of income would very clearly have been subject to tax twice because of the AMT rule that denies a taxpayer the right to use this accounting method for AMT purposes.

To eliminate (or minimize) this result, Sec. 53 was added to the Code in 1986. It creates an AMT credit that can be used in subsequent years to reduce *only* the regular tax liability; that is, it cannot be used to reduce the AMT payable in subsequent years. Although this credit cannot be carried back, it can be carried forward indefinitely. Without this credit Congress would have been unable to introduce the dual tax system—that is, the regular tax and the AMT—that it created in the 1986 Tax Reform Act. Individuals wanting more details concerning the AMT credit should study Sec. 53 carefully. As such an exercise would quickly prove, only certain ("deferral") adjustments and preferences can be used to determine the amount of an AMT credit.

Other AMT Issues

Even in this cursory examination of the AMT provisions, two additional observations are necessary. One concerns the amount of the AMT; the other, the potential it creates for additional interest and penalties. The wording of Sec. 55(a) can easily mask the real significance of the AMT. It reads as follows:

> There is hereby imposed (in addition to any other tax imposed by this subtitle) a tax equal to the excess (if any) of—
> (1) the tentative minimum tax for the taxable year, over
> (2) the regular tax for the taxable year.

These words imply that the AMT is only the amount added to the regular tax in a year in which the AMT exceeds the regular tax. To illustrate, assume that two taxpayers report the following for 1988:

	Taxpayer A	*Taxpayer B*
Tentative AMT	$500,000	$600,000
Regular tax	600,000	500,000
Tax imposed by Sec. 55(a)	$ 0	$100,000

Taxpayer A does not have to pay any AMT, because the $600,000 regular tax exceeds the $500,000 tentative AMT. Taxpayer B, on the other hand, must obviously pay a tax of $600,000. The questions is, what is the amount of the real AMT: only the $100,000 net amount described in Sec. 55(a) or the entire $600,000? To emphasize the significance of both (1) the dual tax system created by the AMT and (2) the impact that it could have on business practices, the authors would argue that the better answer is $600,000. Although the former answer may be literally correct, that ($100,000) alternative implies that the AMT is really an *add-on* tax rather than an *alternative* tax. Even though that conclusion was both literally and figuratively correct for corporate taxpayers prior to 1987, it is clearly incorrect today. Unfortunately, the format of the I.R.S. forms to report the AMT is also likely to endorse the $100,000 answer.

Although the AMT is an alternative to the regular federal income tax, the interest and penalty provisions applicable to the regular tax apply equally to the AMT. In other words, if, at the end of a year, a taxpayer discovers that he or she has grossly underpaid his or her tax liability because of the AMT provisions, that taxpayer will *not* be able to determine any interest and penalty amounts payable based on the lesser amount of regular tax. Unfortunately all estimated quarterly payments are supposed to be based on the larger of the two amounts, even though a taxpayer may not know until sometime after the end of the year which amount is actually payable.

THE AMT AND TAX PLANNING

The very existence of the AMT is a tribute to the success of tax planning in years past. As explained in Chapter 2, at least in part because of some of the more dramatic of those earlier success stories, Congress decided in 1986 to (1) eliminate many of the advantageous provisions that had been part of the Code for years and (2) tighten up the provisions of the AMT. The overall impact of the 1986 changes is clearly to make tax planning more difficult; it will not, however, put an end to those activities. Although the general objective may still be the maximization of wealth via, other things being equal, the minimization of taxes, today's tax planner understands that the price of too large a reduction in the regular income tax may well be an increase in the AMT. Therefore, successful tax planning now requires a careful consideration of both the ordinary and the AMT rules, as well as economic impact more generally. In other words, the general rules suggested in Chapter 19—such as the minimization of gross income and the maximization of deductions, for regular tax purposes—are overly simplistic and must now be reconsidered in light of the additional information contained in this chapter. To better understand the current milieu, in the final pages of this chapter we examine just two examples of how the recent changes in the AMT are likely to impact business behavior in the future.

Example 1: Lease or Buy?

The basic depreciation rules were explained in some detail in Chapter 15. As noted there, the Code currently provides for both (1) an accelerated cost recovery system (ACRS) and (2) an alternative cost recovery system. (Since the acronyms for both depreciation systems are identical, in this chapter we will accept common usage and refer to the former as ACRS and the latter as the "alternative system.") Most taxpayers will elect to use ACRS for "regular" tax purposes because it generally provides the largest possible deduction at the earliest possible date. Sec. 56(a)(1) requires, however, that any difference between an ACRS depreciation deduction and the alternative-system depreciation deduction for any asset placed in service after 1986 be treated as an adjustment in the AMT calculation.

To illustrate the potential impact of this one provision alone, let us consider the plight of an imaginary fledgling commuter airline, FCA, a calendar-year taxpayer. Suppose that in 1987 FCA purchased 10 new aircraft at a cost of $4 million each and elected to use ACRS in the determination of its ordinary income tax. The 10 aircraft would be classified in the 7-year property class because the midpoint guideline life for commercial aircraft (class 45.0) is 12 years. Assuming the midyear convention applied, FCA would claim a 1988 depreciation deduction of $9,795,510 on these 10 aircraft.[3] For AMT purposes, the depreciation deduction would be based on a 12-year life and a 150% declining-balance depreciation method. Hence, under the alternative system, the 1988 depreciation deduction for the 10 aircraft would total only $4,687,500.[4] The 1988 adjustment required by Sec. 56(a)(1) for FCA is,

---

[3] The ACRS depreciation deduction would be determined as follows:
a. The 7-year life implies a straight-line rate of .142857;
b. Hence the double-declining balance rate is .2857;
c. Depreciation for 1987 would have been $5,714,000 ($40 million × .2857 × ½ year); and
d. Depreciation for 1988 would be $9,795,510 for the entire year; $5,714,000 (for last half of the first year's depreciation) plus $4,081,510 (for the first half of the second year's depreciation); that is, [($40 million − $11,428,000) × .2857 × ½ year].

[4] The alternative depreciation deduction would be determined as follows:
a. A 12-year life implies a straight-line rate of .0833;
b. Hence the 150% declining-balance rate is .125;
c. Depreciation for a half year in 1987 would have been $2,500,000 (that is, $40 million × .125 × ½ year); and
d. Depreciation for 1988 would have been $4,687,500 [or $2,500,000 + ½ ($35 million × .125)].

therefore, $5,108,010 (that is, $9,795,510 − $4,687,500). If we assume that FCA recognizes a $1,500,000 regular taxable income in 1988 and has no other items of tax preference—a heroic assumption—FCA's regular income tax will be $510,000 (or 34% × $1,500,000). FCA's AMTI would be $6,608,010 (or $1,500,000 + $5,108,010) and the net AMT payable, $1,321,602 (that is, 20% of $6,608,010). In short, FCA would clearly have fallen victim to too much regular tax planning and too little AMT planning in 1988.

The question is, what could FCA have done differently to avoid this increase in its 1988 federal income tax liability? Observe that this is a much more difficult question to answer than is answering the question of how FCA could avoid paying the AMT. To do that, FCA could have either adopted the alternative depreciation system (rather than ACRS) for regular tax purposes or simply elected a "slower" regular depreciation method. Each of those alternatives, however, would simply have increased FCA's 1988 regular income tax liability. At some point, of course, the AMT would be less than the regular tax.

The tax-planning strategy, therefore, should be to keep FCA's federal income liability as low as possible and still achieve the company's other objectives. This statement of FCA's objectives may better explain why—as noted in the headnote to this chapter—leasing immediately became somewhat more popular after the 1986 Act was signed. With the right lease agreement for at least some of the 10 aircraft, FCA can do essentially what it wants to do; deduct lease payments generally comparable in amount to ACRS deductions; and (perhaps) eventually end up with the title to the aircraft, all without increasing its 1988 federal income tax liability above the $510,000 regular figure. In order for this plan to work, the apparent lessor must be in a position where the AMT represents no problem; that is, the lessor corporation will pay the regular tax. Note also that FCA need not lease all 10 of the aircraft. Because the marginal AMT rate for corporate taxpayers is 20%, FCA's AMT will not exceed its regular tax until its AMTI exceeds $2,550,000 (that is, 20% × $2,550,000 = $510,000). Hence, tax preferences (or positive adjustments) will not "harm" FCA until they exceed about $1 million (that is, AMTI could exceed TI by $1,050,000 without increasing FCA's tax liability). Because the amount of the 1988 Sec. 56(a)(1) adjustment is about $510,800 per aircraft (that is, $5,108,010/10), FCA could—in the example described here—purchase 2 planes and lease 8 with little or no negative tax impact. The reason for buying some aircraft is based on the assumption that a lease will be more costly than an outright purchase because of the need to include a profit margin for the lessor. If that profit can come from differences in the effective tax rates of the lessor and the lessee, it need not show up in the cost of the equipment lease to FCA.

Example 2: Go Public, Go Private or Merge?

The difference between income as reported for federal income tax purposes and that reported for financial accounting purposes has been substantial for many years. Prior to enactment of the 1986 Tax Reform Act, however, no one was very concerned about those differences because neither income figure impacted unduly on the other. For the years 1987 through 1989 that conclusion is no longer valid. Sec. 56(c)(1), buttressed by Sec. 56(f), requires that during this three-year period one half of the excess of an "adjusted net book income" over AMTI (before making this adjustment and ignoring any NOL deduction) will be treated as an adjustment in the determination of AMTI for all corporate taxpayers. Sec. 56(f)(3) specifically prescribes a statutory hierarchy for the financial accounting statements that are to be used in making the adjustment. That hierarchy, in a decreasing order of acceptability, is as follows:

1. Required statements filed with the Securities and Exchange Commission (SEC);
2. Certified, audited income statements prepared for creditors or shareholders or for any other "substantial nontax purpose";
3. Required income statements provided to any federal, state, or local government, or any agency thereof (other than the SEC); or
4. Any other income statement prepared for creditors or shareholders or for some other substantial nontax purpose.

Corporate taxpayers having no income statement whatsoever—as well as those described only by category 4, above, if they so elect—may use earnings and profits rather than "book income" to make the Sec. 56(c)(1) adjustment.

Any privately held corporation debating whether or not to "go public" during the period from 1987 to 1989 will have to weigh carefully the potential impact of this section on the corporation's federal income tax liability. In general, most public or listed corporations prefer to report as large an income as possible to their stockholders because of the potential, positive influence a favorable earnings report may have on the value of the corporation's stock.[5] Going public has always meant that a corporation had to have its annual financial statements audited and had to file audited statements with the SEC. Today it may also mean an increase in the federal income tax liability of the corporation.

For those corporations already listed with the SEC, Sec. 56(c)(1) may present a new incentive to "go private." That is, if the corporation's federal income tax liability will be significantly increased by this new tax provision, the corporation's board will have to consider the added tax saving—among other factors—that could be achieved with less stringent financial accounting requirements.

Finally, this new twist in our federal income tax laws may cause two rather diverse but SEC-listed corporations to consider merger largely for tax reasons. To illustrate, assume that Corporation R has a $10 million regular taxable income and an AMTI of $12 million. R would, of course, pay a tax of

[5]Obviously not all individuals believe the association between reported earnings and stock prices is so direct. With all due respect, the authors would prefer to ignore the efficient markets controversy in this discussion.

$3.4 million (or 34% × $10 million) because that is greater than the AMT of $2.4 million (or 20% × $12 million). Assume also that another corporation, A, has a $10 million regular taxable income but an AMTI of $22 million. A would, in these circumstances, have to pay the AMT of $4.4 million (that is, $22 million × 20%) because it is larger than the regular tax of $3.4 million (that is, $10 million × 34%). If corporations R and A were to merge, with no change in their reported incomes, the tax liability of the combined entity would be $6.8 million (that is, either 34% of $20 million or 20% of $34 million). This is, obviously, $1 million less than the total tax liability for both corporations before the merger [that is, ($3.4 + $4.4) − $6.8] in millions.

In summary, successful tax planning requires that a taxpayer consider the impact of generally accepted accounting principles as well as federal income tax laws and economic forces. Today, more than ever before, everything does indeed depend on everything else. Thus, in tax planning, as in many other activities, there are no more simple answers.

PROBLEMS

1. For the following items, identify whether it involves an "adjustment," a "preference," or neither.
   a. Tax-exempt interest from private activity bonds.
   b. Net operating loss deduction.
   c. Personal exemption deductions.
   d. Gains reported on the installment method.
   e. Percentage depletion in excess of cost.
   f. Tax-exempt interest from public activity bonds.
   g. Depreciation on assets acquired before 1/1/87.
   h. Depreciation on assets acquired after 12/31/86.
   i. Passive activity losses allowed under phase-in rules.
   j. Charitable contribution deduction.

2. Compute the tentative minimum tax (gross AMT) for
   a. A corporation with gross AMTI of $100,000.
   b. A corporation with gross AMTI of $200,000.
   c. A corporation with gross AMTI of $400,000.
   d. A married couple with gross AMTI of $150,000.
   e. A single individual with gross AMTI of $150,000.
   f. A fiduciary with gross AMTI of $30,000.

3. Dagny Taggart, a single individual, had the following taxable income and other tax information for 1988:

Salary	$130,000
Home mortgage interest expense	12,000
State income tax	6,000
Charitable contribution of stock (basis, $10,000)	50,000

Compute Dagny's 1988 tax liability.

4. Korpco had taxable income of $1,000,000 before subtracting an NOL carryover of $975,000. Korpco had no AMT adjustments or preferences other than the NOL carryover. Compute Korpco's 1988 corporate tax liability.

5. Korpco had the following tax information for 1988:

Sales revenue	$1,000,000
Cost of sales	550,000
Operating expenses	150,000
Depreciation expense	200,000
AMT depreciation expense	140,000
Pre-tax book income	300,000

   Compute Korpco's 1988 corporate tax liability.

6. Dr. Julie Erving and her husband, Tyrone, had the following tax information for 1988:

Net taxable income from Julie's practice	$300,000
Tyrone's salary	20,000
Passive activity losses from tax-shelters	(200,000)

   The Erving's do not itemize deductions. Compute their 1988 tax liability.

7. The minimum tax credit is the difference between the tax imposed by §55(a) (see page 22-10) and what the tax imposed by §55(a) would have been if only certain preferences and adjustments (such as tax-exempt interest on private activity bonds) had been taken into account.

   In 1988, Korpco had taxable income of $40,000, AMT depreciation adjustments of $50,000, and tax-exempt interest from private activity bonds of $60,000.
   a. Compute Korpco's 1988 tax liability.
   b. Compute Korpco's 1989 minimum tax credit.
   c. Explain how the purpose of the minimum tax credit is achieved by justifying the credit computed in "b".

8. In 1989, Jorge Valasquez had a regular tax liability of $42,000 and a gross AMT of $35,000. Jorge's minimum tax credit from 1988 is $10,000.
   a. What is Jorge's 1989 tax liability?
   b. How much minimum tax credit will be available to Jorge in 1990?

9. Korpco had the following tax information for 1988:

Taxable income	$40,000
AMT depreciation adjustment	55,000
Pre-tax book income	35,000

   (Korpco had substantial inventory writedowns which were not deductible for tax purposes.)

   Compute Korpco's 1988 corporate tax liability.

10. Midwestern Airlines estimates that its 1988 regular tax liability will be $800,000, while its gross AMT will be $1,300,000, due to the substantial depreciation expense on the planes that it plans to purchase. Louisiana Leasing, Inc. estimates that its regular tax liability will be $450,000 and its gross AMT will be $500,000. Ferguson's Storm Door Corporation estimates that its regular tax liability will be $1,700,000, and its gross AMT will be $1,000,000. If you were advising Midwestern, what might you suggest they do to avoid the AMT?

11. Hugh Akston, a retired single individual, had the following investment income in 1988:

Dividends	$20,000
Tax-exempt interest from public activity bonds	40,000
(Face value $500,000, paying 8% interest)	
Tax-exempt interest from private activity bonds	40,000
(Face value $500,000, paying 8% interest)	

a. What is Akston's after-tax rate of return on the public activity bonds?
b. What is Akston's after-tax rate of return on the private activity bonds?

12. The list of tax preferences subject to the minimum tax does not include most interest on state and local government bonds.
a. Why not?
b. What would be the effect of including these items as preferences?

13. Except for the book-tax income adjustment, adjustments (but not preferences) can be either positive or negative. Explain how each of the following adjustments might be negative.
a. Depreciation on tangible property.
b. A gain or loss on the sale of depreciated property.
c. Use of the installment sale method.
d. Net operating loss deduction.
e. Mining development costs (other than oil and gas).
f. Deduction of passive loss activities in 1987–1990.

14. The passive activity loss limitations are being phased in over a four-year period in order to mitigate the effect of the provisions on heavily sheltered taxpayers who made investments under prior law. Why are these phasein provisions of little benefit to many heavily sheltered taxpayers?

PART SEVEN

Process and Research

Except as otherwise provided in this subchapter, when a return of tax is required under this title or regulations, the person required to make such return shall, without assessment or notice and demand from the Secretary, pay such tax to the internal revenue officer with whom the return is filed, and shall pay such tax at the time and place fixed for filing the return (determined without regard to any extension of time for filing the return).
Section 6151 (a)

Taxation is the most difficult function of government, and that against which their citizens are most apt to be refractory. The general aim is, therefore, to adopt the mode most consonant with the circumstances and sentiments of the country.
Thomas Jefferson

CHAPTER 23

The Federal Tax Process

Clutching a bundle of odd receipts, canceled checks and a couple of penciled lists, the taxpayer plods timidly in to do battle with the tax agent. Bureaucrats make him nervous. He recalls vague stories about criminal tax prosecutions.
Senator Magnuson, Congressional Record (1966)

The uninitiated may assume that taxation is a static body of written law. For most introductory purposes, this assumption is acceptable, because the first order of business must be to gain familiarity with the words of the Code. Nevertheless, such an assumption about the tax law is unrealistic and may even be harmful. If the law *exists* in any significant meaning of that term, its existence must be in the relationships between government, persons, and property. We must not think of the tax law as simply words in a Code, for it is a composite of the legislative actions of Congress, the administrative actions of the I.R.S., the filing of returns, the payment of taxes, and the litigation of disputes. We can understand the law only when we give up the attempt to separate its content from the human *process* of taxation; content has real significance only when viewed from the perspective of the taxing process.

In this chapter we will discuss the various sources of legal pronouncements known as the tax law. Our concern will not be with what the law is; rather, the discussion will focus on how the various legal pronouncements come into existence. We will examine the tax process in Congress, the administrative interpretation of the acts, the compliance process, and the review of tax returns by the administration.

Chapters 24 and 25 will introduce you to the necessary steps a tax advisor must learn to skillfully locate, from among the volumes of legal pronouncements, a defensible solution to a tax question that may arise during the compliance process.

CONGRESSIONAL ENACTMENT AND ADMINISTRATIVE INTERPRETATION

The initial major step in the federal taxing process is passage of a revenue bill by Congress and its approval by the president. Following this legislative action, the I.R.S. makes and releases its interpretation of the statute, primarily in the form of Treasury Regulations. The taxpayer must then accept the responsibility for knowing what the tax laws require and for complying with them.

Congressional Action

The Constitution provides that all revenue measures must originate in the House of Representatives.[1] Once passed by the House, revenue measures are considered by the Senate. The committee of the House that is concerned with revenue bills is the Committee on Ways and Means.

COMMITTEE ON WAYS AND MEANS   The formal procedures of the House of Representatives provide that all bills must be introduced by a member of the House. Technically, representatives initiate tax bills by placing them in the legislative "hopper." Once introduced, all revenue bills are referred to the Committee on Ways and Means; unless the chairman is willing to have the committee consider a bill, referral to the committee amounts to an unceremonious burial. Through various stratagems, the chairman can block effectively all action on a measure, because no action by the House of Representatives is possible until the bill is reported to the floor of the House by the committee. On occasion, committee chairmen may block action on a measure that has both administrative backing and majority support in Congress. Historically, therefore, the chairman of the Committee on Ways and Means effectively initiates legislative action on revenue bills.

The idea that proposals for changes in our tax laws originate with our elected legislators placing a bill in the legislative "hopper" is a gross oversimplification of a very involved part of the tax process. Historically, most major proposals for change are presented to Congress by the Secretary of the Treasury. New proposals are often a major component of an administration's fiscal policy and reflect the economic philosophy of the

---

[1]For a thorough explanation of legislative action on tax bills, see Roy Blough, *The Federal Taxing Process* (Englewood, Cliffs, NJ: Prentice-Hall, 1952).

president and his economic advisors. Most long-run policies, however, originate in what is best described as a "kitchen" bureau, which advises both the administration and Congress. The important characteristic of this unofficial part of the process is that the influential policy makers in the bureau are not elected and generally have a long tenure.

The "kitchen" bureau is made up of economists and lawyers who serve in nonappointive posts in higher echelons of the Treasury Department, on the staff of the Joint Committee on Taxation in Congress, and as research fellows at various nonprofit organizations concerned primarily with national economic policy. Communications among members of this group are quite close, and their influence on the changes in the tax law is substantial. The chief of staff of the Joint Committee advises both the chairman of the House Ways and Means Committee and the chairman of the Senate Finance Committee on tax matters. The civil servants in the Treasury Department advise the Secretary. The research fellows appear before congressional committees regularly to offer advice. The influences of the "kitchen" bureau obviously vary from one administration to the next, depending on the general economic policy of the two groups. However, the important point is that this group of unofficial policy makers will still be around after the next election.

SENATE AND CONFERENCE ACTIONS   On passage by the House, a bill goes to the Senate, where it is referred to the Committee on Finance. Here, as in the House, public hearings are usually held. After those hearings, a bill may be reported out of committee to the Senate floor. The Senate has no "closed" rule comparable to that in the House; that is, there is no limit on debate, and amendments may be offered freely from the floor. When the party of the current administration has a strong majority in Congress (and good relations with the chairmen of the Committee on Ways and Means and the Committee on Finance), the Senate floor is often the first place that "outsiders" may directly influence the content of the bill.

The bill finally passed by the Senate normally is different from that passed by the House. The House may, of course, simply accept the Senate version, but the two versions of the bill are usually referred to a conference committee for compromise of these differences. If a compromise is reached in this committee, the revised bill is reported back to both bodies for final ratification. If both houses adopt the conference bill (which must be accepted or rejected without change), it goes to the president for signature or veto.

The conference procedure increases the power of the committee chairmen, particularly that of the chairman of the Senate Finance Committee. In conference, the chairman can readily dispose of any amendments added on the floor by the Senate. The chairmen of the committees effectively select the members from the full committee who make up the conference committee, and each house votes as a unit in conference. On rare occasions, members selected by a chairman may disagree with his position. Even then the chairman is not necessarily thwarted; he may increase the membership of the conference committee until he has a majority on the committee who favor his position.

The "kitchen" bureau can have considerable impact on legislation during the conference procedures, especially the staff of the Joint Committee on Taxation (and indirectly through this group, other members of the bureau). In conference, the compromises reached are put in writing by the staff of the Joint Committee. This group cannot write new "law" that runs counter to decisions made by the legislative conferees, but their interpretation of the agreements reached by the legislators on complex provisions do become part of the law—Representatives and Senators typically do not have the needed expertise to write the tax law in many complicated areas.

When a substantial tax measure that includes many technical provisions is considered by Congress, the committee's staff members are often the only ones with a firm grasp of the purposes behind the proposed changes. As a result, the explanations prepared by the staffs are often indispensable.

The president, of course, has the final power of the veto, but this veto is exercised sparingly in tax matters.

The process just described is certainly less than perfect. The committee chairmen have a great deal of power, and appointments to the key committees can result in tax legislation that is not responsive to the desires of a majority of Congress. Further, due to the complexity of the law, elected politicians must often depend on the advise of the "kitchen" bureau, which is never accountable to the electorate directly. Without passing judgment on it, we can only note that the legislative process just described is one with which we must live. It exists as described, and no serious proposals exist for major changes in it.

Administrative Interpretation

Once Congress enacts a new tax provision, the Treasury Department is responsible for its interpretation and enforcement. The important administrative interpretations of the law are Treasury Regulations and Revenue Rulings.

TREASURY REGULATIONS   A provision of the Internal Revenue Code requires that the Treasury Department issue regulations interpreting every section of the law. Federal administrative procedures specify the process to be used in promulgating new regulations. New regulations usually appear first as proposed regulations, about which Treasury invites the comments and criticism, either in writing or at hearings, of interested parties. The American Bar Association, the American Institute of Certified Public Accountants, and other groups frequently provide critical analysis at this point. Proposed regulations sometimes excite widespread reactions from individual taxpayers, and legislators may criticize proposals either individually or through congressional action. Based on the comments received, the Treasury acts on its proposal after the specified time period has elapsed, usually by issuing final regulations as a Treasury Decision.

A regulation generally has the same force and effect as the Internal Revenue Code. Initially, however, its standing as law is only presumptive, and taxpayers may challenge it. An appraisal of the relative strength or standing of a regulation should consider several factors. First, has the regulation been tested in a court action? A court finding that the regulation is consistent with congressional intent usually settles the matter. Second, how long has the regulation been in existence? Age lends respectability to a regulation, presumably because Congress itself would have changed the regulation if it violated congressional intent. Third, was the regulation issued soon after passage of the law? Contemporaneous issuance of the law and the Treasury interpretation enhances the likelihood that the regulation's draftsman has followed the measure through Congress and therefore understands its purpose. Judges are less likely to upset regulations promulgated on a timely basis.

New regulations usually do nothing more than elaborate on, or give examples of, the rules taken directly from the statutory language or the accompanying committee report. In some instances, the statute specifically relegates its rule-making power to the Treasury, and the resulting "statutory" regulations have clear authority. On occasion, however, the Treasury goes beyond the clear intent of Congress. For example, consider the proposed regulations on Sec. 280A, which limits the deductions allowed relative to rental income realized from vacation homes. The Code provision was enacted in 1976; the proposed regulations did not appear until 1980. The regulations sought to extend the limitation to residences rented to the taxpayer's relatives, even though the residence in question was not a "vacation" home. Prior to proposed regulations, taxpayers could rent homes to relatives and deduct the tax "loss" provided the rentals paid were fair market rentals. Although the Treasury interpretation was technically within the statutory language, the committee reports do not specifically mention rentals to relatives as a proscribed activity. The press ran stories on the problem in the fall of 1980; unhappy taxpayers alerted their Congressmen, who reacted predictably, given that general elections were on the horizon; and the Treasury Department beat a hasty retreat. Such instances are rare, and most regulations faithfully interpret congressional intent and are dependable rules. Nevertheless, when researching a case, many practitioners do not turn to the Regulations until other sources have been consulted. They feel that early reference to the Regulations may reduce their capacity to conceive of other interpretations of congressional intent that are more favorable to their clients.

REVENUE RULINGS AND OTHER PRONOUNCEMENTS   Taxpayers who are concerned about the tax treatment of a prospective transaction may ask the I.R.S. for a ruling on how the transaction will be taxed. (Under certain circumstances, the I.R.S. issues rulings on past transactions, but we will not discuss these determinations here.) The I.R.S. has no legal obligation to make advanced rulings on prospective transactions, but their policy is to offer guidance when requested, except for certain sensitive areas of the law.

The I.R.S. issues about 12,000 private letter rulings each year. In many cases, taxpayers ask for rulings not because application of the law is particularly doubtful but because the transaction involves large amounts of money and affects large numbers of taxpayers. Proposed corporate reorganizations and changes in employee pension plans are common subjects covered by letter rulings. From the several thousand issued each year, the Internal Revenue Service selects the ones that may offer guidance to the public generally and, after deleting facts that might identify the taxpayer, publishes them as Revenue Rulings. Published Revenue Rulings are reliable statements of I.R.S. interpretation of the subject provision. They do not, however, have the same standing in law as the Regulations. Taxpayers may treat transactions in a manner contrary to a revenue ruling, though such action usually results in a conflict with the I.R.S.

A taxpayer who receives a private letter ruling can be sure that it is a statement of the I.R.S. position, provided the transaction is consummated in the manner described in the request. Private rulings cannot be used as precedents by other taxpayers. Actually, the term *private ruling* is a misnomer; since 1976, by law the I.R.S. has made all rulings available to the public, and private publishers print them for resale in services. This publication notwithstanding, only those rulings published by the I.R.S. and designated as Revenue Rulings have value as precedents. Some day, a taxpayer will rely on a "private" ruling received by someone else and will probably convince the courts that the tax treatment granted by the I.R.S. in the ruling should also prevail in his or her case. Until that time, the now published rulings are still private; that is, they apply only to taxpayers who requested them.

Chapter 24 discusses other pronouncements from the Internal Revenue Service. Excepting Revenue Rulings, the most important pronouncements are Revenue Procedures, published in the same manner as rulings. Revenue Procedures also state the position of the I.R.S., but they usually deal with "procedural," as opposed to "interpretive," questions. For example, acceptable estimated lives for depreciation and other technical rules about depreciation might be the subject of a revenue procedure.

Taken together, I.R.S. pronouncements constitute a sizable body of rules. Their purpose is to give guidance to taxpayers about the interpretation of the law by the I.R.S. and thereby to avoid disputes. The Treasury Department could not administer our revenue law without extensive rule-making powers. Except for the Regulations, however, Treasury pronouncements do not have the force and effect of the basic statute.

TAXPAYER COMPLIANCE AND ADMINISTRATIVE REVIEW

The federal income tax is a self-assessed tax. Every taxpayer has the responsibility for calculation of his or her tax, completion and submission of a return form, and payment of the tax. Once a return is filed, the I.R.S. has the responsibility of reviewing and auditing returns. The purpose of this administrative review is to ensure that the tax is computed properly and that the correct tax is paid.

Responsibilities of Taxpayers

As stated above, the basic responsibilities of taxpayers are computation of their tax, completion and submission of the proper return form, and payment of the tax. The first of these duties is the really complicated part. Completion of returns, filing, and payment are more procedural questions. These duties, nevertheless, are important, and failure to comply with procedural requirements can result in financial penalties.

INDIVIDUALS   All individuals must make their tax computations on Form 1040EZ, Form 1040A, or Form 1040. In many situations, one or more schedules accompanying Form 1040 must be filed, depending on the sources of the taxpayer's income and the nature of his or her deductions. Individual taxpayers are on a pay-as-you-go system through withholding from wages and payments of estimated taxes. A final payment (or refund) is made when the annual return is filed.

Annual returns of individuals are due on the fifteenth day of the fourth month following the end of the taxable year. For calendar-year taxpayers, this means April 15. When the due date of any return (or other prescribed act) falls on a Saturday, Sunday, or legal holiday, the due date is the following work day.[2] A return is timely filed by mail if it is postmarked on the due date. The taxpayer may obtain an automatic extension of 90 days by filing Form 4868 on or before the due date of the return and paying at least 90% of the tax due with the extension. Further extensions for reasonable cause can be obtained by filing Form 2688; however, these extensions should be filed in time for approval by the I.R.S.

FIDUCIARIES   Returns of fiduciaries are filed on Form 1041. Returns are due on the fifteenth day of the fourth month after the close of the taxable year. Fiduciaries are not required to pay the tax in advance, so the entire amount is due with the return. Estates may elect to pay their taxes in four equal installments—one with the return, and one before the end of each of the three succeeding three-month periods.

CORPORATIONS   Corporations report their incomes on Form 1120. Their returns are due on the fifteenth day of the *third* month after year-end (March 15 for a calendar-year corporation). Corporations may obtain an automatic 90-day extension by filing a tentative return or by filing Form 7004. Corporations are also on a pay-as-you-go basis and must declare their estimated tax and pay the tax on a quarterly basis during the taxable year.

[2]Section 7503 and Reg. 301.7503-1(a).

Penalties and Interest

The Internal Revenue Code includes a number of penalties intended to encourage taxpayers to file a timely and accurate return and to pay their tax. The more important penalties are

1. *Failure to file annual return.*   If the taxpayer fails to file a timely return, 5% of the net tax liability is added for each month or part of month the return is delayed. The maximum added is 25%. This penalty is not imposed if the taxpayer's failure is due to a reasonable cause.

2. *Failure to pay tax.*   If the taxpayer fails to pay his or her tax on time, interest is added to the tax. The interest runs from the due date of the return without considering extensions of time for filing. The Tax Reform Act of 1986 tied the interest rate for underpayment of taxes to the Federal short-term rate plus three percentage points, rounded to the nearest full percentage. The Federal short-term rate is based on the average market yield on outstanding U.S. marketable obligations with remaining maturity dates of three years or less. The interest rate is adjusted quarterly based on the rate in effect for the first month of the previous quarter. Thus, the rate for the last quarter for calendar year 1987 is based on the July Federal short-term rate.

   In addition to the interest on underpayments, the statute provides a penalty of 0.5% per month (or part thereof) for any underpayment. The penalty is not imposed if the taxpayer can show that the payment deficiency was due to a reasonable cause and was not willful neglect.

3. *Deficiencies in tax paid.*   If the tax computation is incorrect and the tax payment is less than the tax owed, a penalty of 5% of the understatement is added to the tax when the deficiency is due to negligence. If the deficiency is due to willful negligence or fraud, a penalty of 75% of the deficiency is added to the tax. When the fraud penalty is imposed, the penalty for failure to file and the 5% penalty for negligence are not imposed.

4. *Criminal penalties.*   The willful failure to pay the tax, to file a return, to keep adequate records, or the attempt to evade or defeat the tax, and willful making and subscribing to a false return are criminal acts, misdemeanors, or felonies. Fines up to $100,000 and imprisonment of up to five years are the punishment for these criminal acts.

The criminal penalties are imposed only after the taxpayer is found guilty in criminal proceedings. The other penalties, however, are imposed by the I.R.S. The assessment of penalties by the I.R.S. is subject to administrative and judicial review, which is explained later in this chapter.

The list of penalties above is by no means complete. Penalties for underpayment of estimated taxes, for failure to file information returns, and for numerous other acts or failure to act are all aimed at improving the equitable administration of our tax laws. The Economic Recovery Tax Act of 1981 and the Tax Reform Act of 1986 added or increased several penalties aimed at tax "protesters" and others who defy the laws. For example, "protesters" who file false statements with respect to withholdings can be penalized $500 for each false statement, not to mention more severe criminal penalties, including a one-year imprisonment.

Perhaps the most significant new penalty was added in 1982, when a 10% penalty was imposed for "substantial" understatements of tax liability when taxpayers do not have *substantial authority* for their positions. This penalty was further increased to 20% by the Tax Reform Act of 1986. Prior to this penalty, tax practitioners could recommend a course of action to clients provided a "reasonable basis" existed in law for such action. The term "substantial authority" implies a higher standard than "reasonable basis." Tax practitioners must exercise more caution in the future as a result of this change.

Role of the Tax Expert

The preceding list of taxpayers' responsibilities leads to an obvious conclusion: many taxpayers are unable to fulfill their duties personally. Rules governing unusual or complex transactions are often beyond the scope of the average citizen's knowledge. Many taxpayers are unable to comprehend the instructions on the return forms. Certainly a high-income taxpayer will do everything possible to reduce tax liability. For all these reasons, a group of specialists or experts is willing to assist a taxpayer for a fee.

The number of tax experts offering their services to the public probably exceeds 200,000. Unfortunately, no comprehensive system of regulation exists to ensure that persons engaged in tax practice meet reasonable standards of competence. In the past, the only effective regulation of tax practice has come from the Treasury Department. The department issues Treasury cards to practitioners, which entitle them to represent taxpayers before the I.R.S. However, few individuals have taken the exams and obtained Treasury cards. Licensed lawyers and certified public accountants can practice before the I.R.S. without a Treasury card. In general, the groups in our society best qualified to give taxpayers advice on tax matters are licensed attorneys and accountants. Yet they are in the minority when it comes to the number of "tax experts" advising taxpayers. This fact raises a serious question: What training and qualifications do the unlicensed "experts" have?

Beyond a doubt, many people who present themselves to the public as tax practitioners have little or no expertise in tax matters. State laws are silent on who may engage in tax practice. Practitioners authorized to practice before the I.R.S. must observe the provisions of Treasury Circular 230, but other practitioners have no similar restrictions on their activities. They are free to advertise, to represent themselves as "experts," and to make any sort of arrangement regarding fees. It is all too common for a practitioner to rent a vacant building during tax season, engage in extensive advertising, charge a fee based on the "refund" obtained, and then close shop before the I.R.S. has an opportunity to review the returns filed. As an advertising gimmick, some practitioners "guarantee" their returns, promising to pay deficiencies assessed on the returns they prepare. Normally such a guarantee is worthless. Some practitioners with Treasury cards are not above doubt either, and many others look on the practice as just another business, paying maximum attention to efficient return preparation and minimum attention to equitable administration of the law.[3]

The Tax Reform Act of 1976 gave the Treasury some needed powers to ensure that all individuals involved in the preparation of tax returns for remuneration observe some nominal rules of conduct. These new rules have had little impact on attorneys and licensed accountants, because most of the actions proscribed by the new law are rules of conduct that most knowledgeable practitioners had previously observed. The new rules make it a misdemeanor subject to a $1,000 fine and/or imprisonment up to one year for the unauthorized disclosure of information obtained during the preparation of a return. However, the practitioner can, and often must, disclose information to I.R.S. agents and to related taxpayers under certain conditions. The rules also assess civil penalties ranging from $25 to $500 for each wrongful act related to the preparation of returns. Acts that result in a penalty are (1) failure to sign a return as preparer or failure to provide the preparer's identification number; (2) failure to retain copies of returns filed for a three-year period; (3) failure to provide the I.R.S. with certain information about employees who prepare returns; (4) failure of the preparer to provide the taxpayer with a copy of his or her return; (5) understatement of the tax liability due to negligent or intentional disregard for the tax laws; and (6) endorsement or negotiation of any check issued to the taxpayer. These new penalties do not give the Treasury powers to improve the technical qualifications of return preparers. The criminal and civil penalties only increase the risks for the unscrupulous or uninformed preparer.

The tax law is indeed complex. Many taxpayers need professional assistance in fulfilling their responsibilities and, incidentally, in minimizing their tax liability. In view of the preceding facts, however, the taxpayer should be cautious when seeking "expert" assistance. Individuals who publicly claim the status of expert may be the least qualified because persons with at least the minimal qualifications may be forbidden by their professions to claim any such status. Recently, some state bar associations have allowed lawyers specializing in tax matters to identify themselves in advertisements. In 1978, the American Institute of Certified Public Accountants changed its code of ethics, permitting limited advertising by CPAs. Under the new rules, members can advertise, including the firm name and members, services offered, fees charged, and general information about qualifications. The new rules prohibit self-laudatory statements, invidious comparisons with other professionals, and testimonials or endorsements. Although a CPA cannot list the "24 reasons" why he or she should file your return, members can get their names before the public. Despite this limited advertising by lawyers and accountants, it remains true that those "experts" who make public pronouncements about their expertise are generally the least qualified to give taxpayers assistance.

---

[3]For a good description of how one national tax service operates, see "Storefront Tax Service Earns a Good Return," *Business Week* (March 25, 1967), pp. 196–202.

Review by the Internal Revenue Service

Taxpayers file their returns at an I.R.S. regional service center. The United States is divided into seven regions, and there is an I.R.S. service center in each region. These centers utilize the latest data-processing equipment in handling returns. The United States is also divided into 58 districts. In recent years, the mechanical processing of returns has been shifted from district offices to the service centers. Personnel in the district offices, however, still perform most of the important review work.

AUDITING PROCEDURES   All returns received by the I.R.S. are checked for mechanical accuracy, which includes the following:

1. Arithmetic, including computation of tax.
2. Transfer of amounts from supporting schedules to return.
3. Matching information returns filed with the income reported on the return. For example, the employer submits a copy of each employee's Form W-2 (withholding) to the I.R.S. The I.R.S. also receives a veritable mountain of Forms 1099 showing the amounts of interest paid to taxpayers by financial institutions, the dividends paid to shareholders by corporations, and certain other payments. Because of budgetary constraints, the I.R.S. has never matched all information returns to the relevant tax returns. Congress has exerted constant pressure on the I.R.S. to use the information returns. As a result, the I.R.S. expects to match up all returns in the near future.

The service centers, using automated equipment, do most of this mechanical work. If a mechanical error that results in an understatement of tax is discovered, a bill for the deficiency is sent to the taxpayer. If an error has resulted in an overpayment, the excess payment is credited to the taxpayer or refunded.

In addition to the mechanical processing just described, the computers are programmed to select certain returns for further examination. Using multiple linear discriminant analysis, the program selects those returns that, on audit, are most likely to yield additional taxes. In addition, certain returns are automatically tagged for examination based on arbitrary criteria such as large refunds and reported income in excess of a certain amount. Finally, the computer randomly selects returns for examination. These returns are used in the "compliance program," in which the error rate on the sample selected is used to infer statistically the error rate on all returns. The number of returns selected for examination varies from year to year based mainly on the personnel available to conduct audits.

The returns selected for audit by the service centers are forwarded to the appropriate district office. There, the returns are eventually assigned to revenue agents for audit. This examination may be an "office audit" or a "field audit." For the office audit, the taxpayer is notified of the items under examination and is requested to bring to the district office the necessary records and supporting documents. For taxpayers with extensive records, the agents perform a field audit at the taxpayer's place of business.

On completion of the agent's examination, the agent normally confers with the taxpayer about his or her findings. In some cases, the agent communicates the findings to the taxpayer by letter. The smart taxpayer has expert help during these conversations if any material amounts are involved. Technically, only practitioners with Treasury cards, lawyers, and accountants can represent taxpayers; most agents, however, are willing to work with the taxpayer's "preparer" or advisor, even if the person does not have a Treasury card or is not a lawyer or a certified public accountant.

This contact between taxpayers and the examining agents can have any one of three results:

1. The agent may find that the return is correct as filed. In this event, the findings of the agent are reviewed by the audit division and, if the reviewer agrees with the findings, the audit is finished.

2. The agent may propose adjustments, which normally increase the tax, and the taxpayer may agree. The agent then makes an assessment of the deficiency on Form 870. After review of the findings by the review staff, the taxpayer signs Form 870 and pays the deficiency. The payment normally closes the return, which means that no subsequent adjustments are made to the tax for that year. In a few cases, the adjustments may result in a refund to the taxpayer.

3. The agent may propose adjustments resulting in a deficiency, and the taxpayer may disagree. When no agreement is reached between the agent and the taxpayer, the taxpayer may obtain either a conference in the Appeals office or judicial review. These alternatives are explained later. The I.R.S. auditing process is depicted in Figure 23-1.

Taxpayers experiencing their first tax return examination are often apprehensive when they are notified of the impending audit. Some undoubtedly have visions of a merciless inquisition that finally wrings out the last possible tax dollar. Taxpayers with this notion are sometimes surprised to find that the agents are reasonable persons who are trying to administer fairly a complex law. Only taxpayers guilty of fraud or gross negligence have anything to fear. This does not mean, of course, that the taxpayer will necessarily win his or her case. One serious criticism of the tax process at the audit level is the lack of training and expertise of many agents. This criticism is more frequently valid for I.R.S. personnel who conduct office audits. Because of lower pay and a somewhat limited opportunity for rapid advancement, many graduates from strong accounting and law programs in colleges and universities do not consider careers with the I.R.S. Given a national shortage of individuals with training and expertise in the tax law, the I.R.S. has been forced to hire some individuals without strong qualifications. We believe that beginning salaries for agents should be increased and that promotion policies in the I.R.S. should emphasize merit. These changes would place the I.R.S. in a better position to compete for the limited talent available.

APPEALS CONFERENCES   When the taxpayer refuses to agree to the agent's proposed adjustments, the agent prepares a complete report of the findings,

FIGURE 23-1   Income Tax Audit Procedure of the Internal Revenue Service

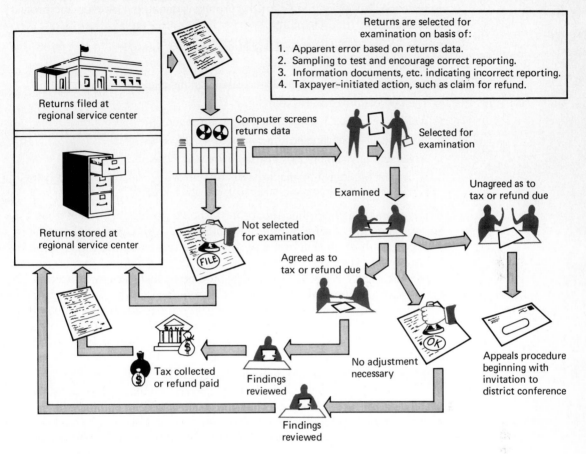

which is submitted to the review staff in the district office. After review (and changes, if required), the report on the examination is mailed to the taxpayer. The covering letter, called the *30-day letter,* notifies the taxpayer of the proposed deficiency and normally gives the taxpayer a 30-day period in which to decide on a course of action. Three avenues are open to the taxpayer at this point:

1. Taxpayer may accept the examiner's findings, sign Form 870, and close the case.
2. Taxpayer may request a conference with the Appeals office. The conferees in this office are organized on a regional basis, and they have broad powers to settle disputes with taxpayers as explained below.
3. Taxpayer may ignore the 30-day letter and wait for the formal deficiency notice, called the *90-day letter.* On receipt of the 90-day letter, the taxpayer must either pay the deficiency or take the case to the courts.

The appeals conference.   The right of appeal to the Appeals office is automatic on receipt of the 30-day letter. When the amount of the deficiency is more than $2,500, the taxpayer must file a written protest before the conference. No specific form for the protest is dictated; however, the protest must include certain elements:

1. A statement that the taxpayer wishes to appeal the assessment
2. The taxpayer's name and address
3. The date and symbols of the 30-day letter and the finding being protested
4. The tax year or years involved
5. An itemized schedule of unagreed adjustments
6. A statement supporting facts in contested factual issues
7. Arguments and authorities on which the protest is based
8. A declaration, signed by the taxpayer, that he or she believes, under penalty of perjury, that facts stated are "true, correct, and complete"

It is generally agreed that the protest should include all issues that the taxpayer intends to raise during the conference. Although no rule prohibits the taxpayer from raising new issues, surprise moves during the conference are rarely effective.

The conference is informal, and there are no formal rules for procedure. If the taxpayer is represented by an accountant or lawyer, which is the common practice, the taxpayer's agent must present a power of attorney. The points of departure are typically the revenue agent's report (RAR) and the taxpayer's protest, if one is filed. The factual and/or legal points at issue are then discussed.

Before October 1978, administrative review by the I.R.S. consisted of a two-level conference procedure. First, taxpayers had the right to a conference in the district office. This level was known as the "informal" conference, and historically the conferees from the district staff had only limited powers to settle disputes. If agreement could not be reached at the informal conference, the taxpayer next took the dispute to a "formal" conference with the regional appellate staff. These conferees traditionally could settle disputes based on the "hazards of litigation." This term refers to an assessment of the probability that the government might lose the dispute in judicial proceedings. Instead of settling disagreements on a yes–no basis, the appellate conferees could bargain for a compromise settlement. Because of this power, which the district conferees did not have, most disputes were settled at the formal conference, especially those involving large amounts.

The recent change eliminates the duplication of effort by eliminating the district or informal conference. There is now only one administrative review office, the Appeals office. The conferees here have broad powers of settlement, including the power to compromise an issue based on the hazards of litigation. The settlement authority, however, depends on whether the case is nondocketed or docketed.

Nondocketed cases are those that reach the Appeals office before the statutory deficiency notice (90-day letter) is issued. For nondocketed cases, the Appeals office has exclusive jurisdiction. The conferees are required to consider the hazards of litigation without regard to the amount involved. The purpose of the Appeals office is to keep disputes out of the courts. If the law is uncertain, the appellate conferees welcome offers to compromise the issues and themselves make such offers. However, offers of 20% or less are generally ignored because the conferees are instructed not to accept offers that have only nuisance value. After the conference, agreements reached, if any, are reviewed by the head of the Appeals office at the regional office. If, on review, the settlement is not acceptable, the taxpayer is generally given an opportunity to hold a conference with the reviewer. If agreement is reached, Form 870-AD is completed and the case, for all practical purposes, is closed. If no agreement is reached, the 90-day letter is then issued.

Docketed cases are those for which the 90-day letter has already been issued and the taxpayer has filed a petition in the Tax Court. Each petition filed is given a docket number, and the case formally becomes the responsibility of the regional counsel and is assigned to an attorney who represents the Justice Department but works at the I.R.S. regional office. In the period after a case is docketed but before a date for trial is set, settlement authority is effectively shared by the Appeals office and the regional counsel, although the latter has final jurisdiction formally. Thus, the docketed case is referred to the Appeals office, and an effort is made to reach a compromise. This is generally true even though the same dispute may have already been handled in an appeals conference. At this point, maximum pressure is on both the government and the taxpayer to reach a settlement, because neither typically wants to incur the bother and costs of court proceedings.

Taxpayers who permit their disputes to reach the docketed status are very often gambling that the regional counsel will take a more cautious stance relative to the hazards of litigation than that taken by the Appeals office. After all, some attorney in the regional counsel office must consider the actual trial. On the other hand, any offer previously made by the Appeals office before the case is docketed is no longer in effect. The taxpayer may find that regional counsel has a more optimistic outlook and be forced to accept a reduced offer, to capitulate entirely, or to go to trial.

After a case is set for trial, settlement authority rests solely with the regional counsel. From this point on, the licensed accountant can play only an advisory role. Direct negotiations with government counsel by an accountant would certainly be construed as the practice of law.

Calculating the odds.   Although the preceding discussion refers to the taxpayer as the active participant, wise taxpayers usually seek professional help for appeals conferences. Indeed, most practitioners advise their clients not to attend the proceedings unless they are knowledgeable in tax matters. Representation at the conferences by skilled professionals costs money. As a result, the betting odds favor the taxpayer with a relatively large amount in dispute, because of three factors. First, the *absolute* amount that can be gained from the conferences is greater. Second, the cost of professional representation increases as the amount in dispute increases, but less than proportionally. Third, the fees paid for professional help may be an income tax deduction, and the after-tax cost of these services declines relatively as the taxpayer's marginal tax rate increases.

Some simple arithmetic illustrates the point. Take the situation of taxpayers A and B, who are considering the wisdom of hiring a professional to represent them at an appellate conference. Relevant facts are as follows:

	A	B
Amount of tax in dispute	$9,600	$100,000
Accountant's fee for preparing protest and handling conference	$2,000	$ 5,000
Marginal tax rate	28%	28%
After-tax cost of professional service	$1,440	$ 3,600
Estimated probability of winning	50%	50%

Taxpayer A is faced with a $1,440 net cost to gain $9,600, odds of 6 to 1. B, on the other hand, is betting $3,600 to gain $100,000, odds of almost 27 to 1.

JUDICIAL REVIEW

Before turning to judicial consideration of tax conflicts, we should note that the tax process has many procedures built into it to protect the rights of taxpayers, although the system is biased in favor of affluent taxpayers. First, the law is enacted by elected officials. Before enactment, individual taxpayers and special interest groups may be given an opportunity to express their opinions of the proposals at the congressional committee hearings. After enactment, the administration must set out its interpretation of the law in regulations. Proposed regulations are circulated to interested parties before final adoption. The I.R.S. makes numerous rulings that help taxpayers assess the impact of the income tax on their financial affairs. After the taxpayer files a return, proposed adjustments to the tax calculation are considered carefully in conferences with agents and conferees. Finally, the conflict is considered by the Appeals office, whose primary function is settlement of conflicts.

This lengthy process can hardly be termed arbitrary. The government cannot be said to "run roughshod" over the taxpayer. Indeed, a fairer criticism of the process might be that it is too cumbersome, that too much time and effort are spent on safeguarding property rights. In any event, taxpayers who cannot reach an agreement with the I.R.S. may take their cases to the courts. Through appeals, each taxpayer may insist on the protection of his or her rights until a decision has been rendered by the Supreme Court.

Three avenues for judicial review are open to taxpayers. The taxpayer may have his or her case heard first by the Tax Court of the United States, or he or she may go first to a U.S. district court or to the Claims Court. Because the popular alternative is the Tax Court, we consider it first.

The Tax Court Route

Taxpayers who do not reach an agreement with the Appeals office receive the 90-day letter, which is the formal deficiency notice. The letter gives the taxpayer a 90-day period within which to file a petition with the Tax Court. If a petition is not filed, the I.R.S. assesses the additional tax and, if the taxpayer fails to pay, takes legal steps to force payment.

If a petition is filed, the conflict is heard by the Tax Court (called the Board of Tax Appeals prior to 1943). This court is specially organized to hear tax cases and is completely independent of the I.R.S. Judges are appointed to the Tax Court for a 15-year term by the president. Although the Tax Court has its headquarters in Washington, D.C., sessions are held in all major cities at various times, and the taxpayer may request a hearing in his or her general area.

The Tax Court is a trial court, at which taxpayers may represent themselves or be represented by counsel. Generally, only attorneys are admitted to practice in the Tax Court, although some CPAs have been granted this right by examination. At the hearing, depositions of witnesses and oral and written arguments of the parties are presented to the Court. There is no jury. The Court arrives at its decision and writes up its findings in an opinion. This opinion is presented to the parties.

Concern about the expense of litigation, particularly issues involving relatively small amounts of tax, prompted Congress to permit the Tax Court to set up a small claims division to handle disputes when the amount in contest does not exceed $10,000 plus any amounts conceded by the parties. Hearings are not before judges but before commissioners appointed by the Chief Judge of the Tax Court. In the small claims division, formal rules of evidence need not be followed; the Tax Court can prescribe rules of evidence it feels to be appropriate. The findings of the commissioner are not reported in formal written opinions, and the opinions cannot be used as precedent in other cases. Finally, the decisions in small claims cases cannot be appealed to a higher court—the decision is final for both parties.

Throughout the review process, the taxpayer must take the initiative. He or she must ask for the conferences with the I.R.S. and for the hearing before the Tax Court. In all conferences and hearings, the determination of the I.R.S. is presumed to be correct. The taxpayer generally must carry the burden of proving that the proposed adjustments are incorrect. The decision of the Tax Court, however, may be disputed by either party. If the decision goes against the government, the Justice Department may appeal. Taxpayers also have the right of appeal. (Decisions in the small claims division cannot be appealed by either party.)

Appeals from decisions of the Tax Court (and U.S. District Courts—see next section) are made to the U.S. Courts of Appeals based upon the geographical location of the taxpayer. There are 12 Courts of Appeals in the country as indicated in Table 23-1. Again, oral and written arguments are presented by the parties, and a decision is reached by the judges of the court. The final appeal is, of course, to the U.S. Supreme Court. Either party to the dispute may ask the Court to consider the case by asking for a writ of *certiorari*. The Supreme Court normally only hears cases when the Courts of Appeals have reached different conclusions on the same issue or when, in the Court's opinion, the constitutionality of a tax law is questionable.

If the Tax Court route is selected, the taxpayer is *not* assessed for the deficiency until the lengthy process of administrative and judicial review is

TABLE **23-1**

UNITED STATES COURTS OF APPEALS

Federal Circuit	Geographical Areas Served
First (CA-1)	Maine, New Hampshire, Massachusetts, Rhode Island, Connecticut, Puerto Rico
Second (CA-2)	New York, Vermont
Third (CA-3)	Pennsylvania, New Jersey, U.S. Virgin Islands
Fourth (CA-4)	West Virginia, Maryland, Delaware, Virginia, North Carolina, South Carolina
Fifth (CA-5)	Texas, Louisiana, Mississippi
Sixth (CA-6)	Michigan, Ohio, Kentucky, Tennessee
Seventh (CA-7)	Wisconsin, Illinois, Indiana
Eighth (CA-8)	North Dakota, South Dakota, Nebraska, Minnesota, Iowa, Missouri, Arkansas
Ninth (CA-9)	Washington, Montana, Oregon, Idaho, California, Nevada, Arizona, Alaska, Guam, Hawaii
Tenth (CA-10)	Wyoming, Utah, Colorado, Kansas, Oklahoma, New Mexico
Eleventh (CA-11)	Alabama, Georgia, Florida, Canal Zone
District of Columbia (CA-DC)	Washington, D.C.

complete. The taxpayer pays the tax according to *his* or *her* computation; additional assessments are made only at the end of the review process. However, the taxpayer must pay interest on any eventual deficiencies. Interest is calculated from the due date of the return.

The District Court Route

For reasons too sophisticated to explain here, taxpayers may wish to avoid the hearing before the Tax Court. To do so, the taxpayer merely pays the proposed deficiency at any point in the process before the petition to the Tax Court. He or she may then file a claim for refund of the deficiency paid.

The claim for refund sets in motion the administrative review procedures previously discussed. Thus, the claim is considered by the district office. If the claim is denied, as it normally is, a 30-day letter is sent, which may lead to an

Appeals office conference. If no agreement is reached in these conferences, the refund claim is denied by the I.R.S. When a claim for refund is denied, the taxpayer has a statutory right to sue the government for the tax illegally (in the eyes of the taxpayer) assessed and collected.

Most suits to force a refund are brought in U.S. district courts. In this court, the taxpayer must be represented by an attorney. A jury of peers may be used to determine the facts. A district court judge, however, decides the law. Once a decision is reached in this court, either party may appeal to the appropriate circuit court of appeals (see Table 23-1). The decision of this court may, in turn, be appealed to the Supreme Court.

The Claims Court Route

As an alternative to the district court, taxpayers can sue for a refund in the Claims Court of the United States. The Claims Court was created by the Federal Courts Improvement Act of 1982 and has assumed the duties previously handled by the trial division of the old Court of Claims. The 1982 Act also authorized the U.S. Court of Appeals for the Federal Circuit by merging the old U.S. Court of Claims and the U.S. Court of Customs and Patent Appeals, resulting in the 13th court of appeals. The Claims Court is headquartered in Washington, D.C., and is composed of sixteen judges appointed by the president of the United States for terms of fifteen years. The judges sit singly, nationwide, to hear cases involving claims against the U.S. government.

Twelve judges serve on the new Court of Appeals for the Federal Circuit. Vacancies are filled by the president with the advice and consent of the Senate. Typically, courts of appeal sit in panels of three or in banc (the entire panel of judges). The 1982 Act, however, allows this new appeals court to sit in panels of larger than three and less than twelve. The court may hear cases in any city in which the other twelve appeals courts sit. The court's primary responsibility is to review appeals from the new Claims Court.

The procedures for administrative and judicial review of conflicts are briefly summarized in Figure 23-2. Note that agreement may be reached at any step in the process. Even after the petition is filed with the Tax Court, or suit filed in a district court or the Claims Court, court conferences between the government and the taxpayer are frequent, and agreement may be reached at any time.

How the I.R.S. Plays the Judicial Game

The person not yet initiated into the subtleties of the tax process would logically assume that once a court has reached a decision and the loser does not appeal that decision, then that decision can be safely relied on by other taxpayers. For example, if a taxpayer wins a fight with the I.R.S. in the Tax Court and the I.R.S. does not appeal the Tax Court decision, then other taxpayers with the same factual situation should be able to rely on the court's

FIGURE **23-2**   Income Tax Appeal Procedure of the Internal Revenue Service

**Income Tax
Appeal
Procedure**
Internal Revenue Service

At any stage of procedure:
You can agree and arrange to pay.
You can ask the Service to issue
you a notice of deficiency so you
can file a petition with the Tax Court.
You can pay the tax and file a claim
for a refund.

**Examination of
income tax return**
District Director's Office

Preliminary notice
30-Day Letter

Protest
(when required)

Appeals Office

If you do not respond or
the 30-day period expires,
then

Notice of deficiency
90-Day Letter

Preliminary notice
30-Day Letter

**Consideration of
claim for refund**
District Director's Office

Pay tax and file
claim for refund

CHOICE
OF
ACTION

No tax payment

Petition to Tax Court

Protest
(when required)

Appeals Office

Agreed

Appeals Office

Not previously
considered by
Appeals

Tax Court
No Appeal Permitted
in Cases Handled
under Small Tax
Case Procedure

Unagreed

Reconsidered by
Appeals because of
settlement possibility

District Counsel

Trial

Statutory notice
Claim Disallowance

CHOICE
OF
ACTION

District Court

Court Of Appeals

Claims Court

**U.S. Court of
Appeals for
the Federal Circuit**

U.S. Supreme Court

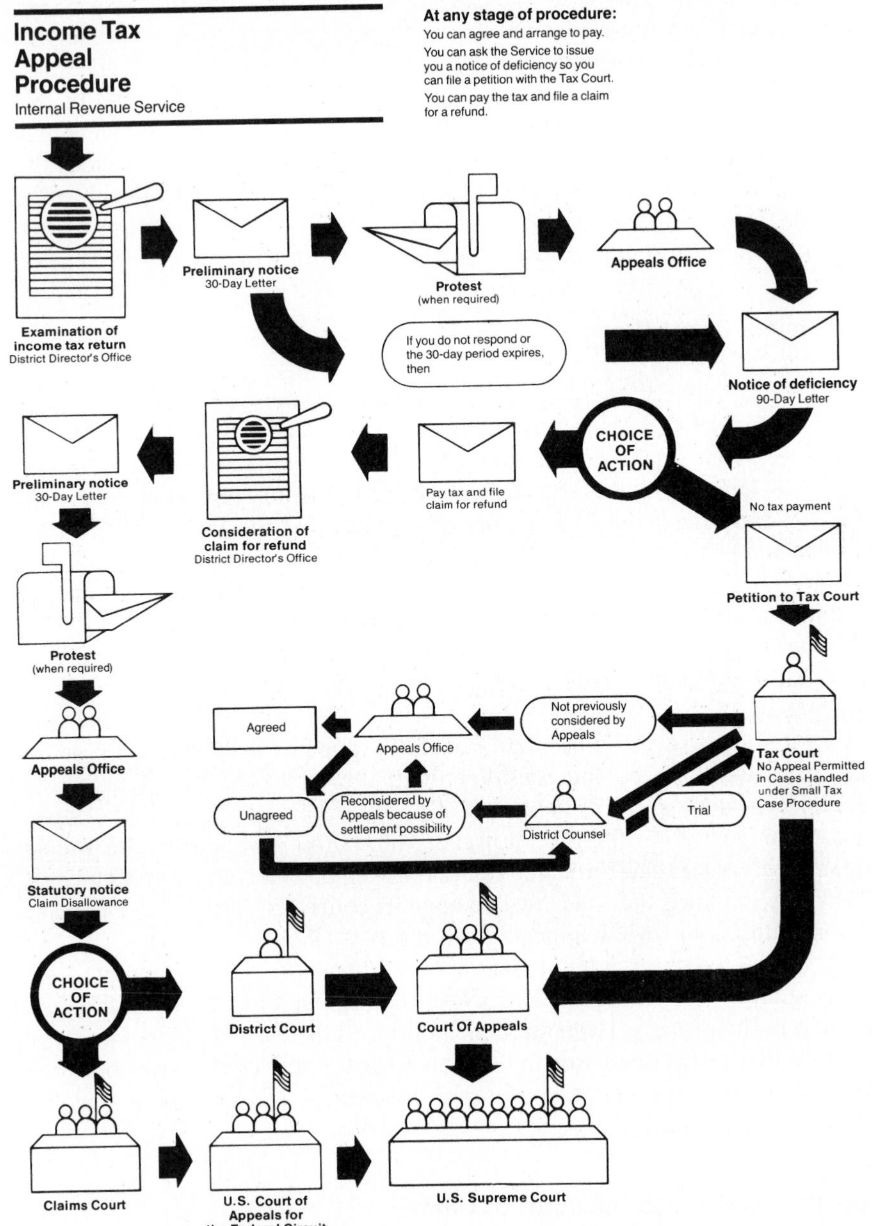

decision. Unfortunately, while logical, the game is played using more complicated rules.

When the I.R.S. loses in the Tax Court, it may follow one of four possible alternative procedures. First, it can appeal the decision as discussed earlier.

This appeal, of course, is a clear signal that the I.R.S. does not agree with the Tax Court's conclusions. Second, the General Counsel for the I.R.S. may announce an *acquiescence,* which lets everyone know that the I.R.S. will follow the decision in other situations with the same facts. Third, the I.R.S. may announce a *nonacquiescence,* a clear signal that it will not follow the decision, even though it may not choose to appeal it. Finally, it may remain silent, in which case we do not know what it will do in similar situations.

For decisions reached by district courts and by the Claims Court, the I.R.S. has two courses of action, either an appeal to the appropriate court or silence. Silence, however, cannot be interpreted as acquiescence. As with the Tax Court decisions, silence may signify agreement or disagreement. Taxpayers and their advisors may rely on a decision of a district court or the Claims Court, but this does not mean that the I.R.S. will not attempt to enforce a rule of law contrary to the decision.

What happens if the I.R.S. has appealed a Tax Court or district court decision and has lost again? Logically, this should end the matter, but, again, logic goes for naught. The I.R.S. must follow decisions of the Circuit Courts of Appeals, but *only* in that particular circuit. Often, the government applies a contrary rule in the jurisdiction of other Circuit Courts to obtain conflicting rulings. Given a conflict of opinion between Circuit Courts of Appeal, the case *may* then be heard before the Supreme Court and the question finally resolved.

The process just described seems, at first glance, grossly unfair and wasteful. However, we must remember the extraordinary measures taxpayers take to reduce their taxes, the enormous stakes involved in the annual contest, and that the I.R.S. is charged with the role of protecting the revenues by enforcing the laws passed by Congress. That the government occasionally persists beyond reason to enforce the law based on *its* interpretation is a natural result of the process.

Despite the several criticisms of the compliance process noted in this chapter, the overall process is a relatively fair one, in which citizens are safeguarded against arbitrary administration and confiscation. Maintenance of a fair, equitable process is essential if the income tax law is to play the vital role assigned to it in our political and economic system.

SOME STATISTICS ON THE TAX PROCESS

The process described above is a complicated one. To help the student place the various steps in proper perspective, it might be helpful to review some statistics on how well the taxpayer does in the process relative to the government. The statistics are restricted to the administrative and judicial review. How the taxpayer fares in the legislative process cannot be reduced to neat numbers.

In 1985, approximately 178 million returns were filed, including about 99.4 million individual income tax returns and 3.3 million corporate income tax returns.[4] Most of these returns were verified at the regional service centers, and mechanical errors were corrected through correspondence with the taxpayers. Also during 1985, the I.R.S. examined about 1.5 million returns, with over 519,000 examined by field agents. Usually, about 1.3% of the individual returns are examined compared with about 2.4% of the corporate returns. In recent years, the number of returns examined has been decreasing slightly. However, because of inflation and improved techniques for selecting returns, the total additional assessments resulting from the audits have increased. For 1985, recommended additional taxes and penalties totaled $17.1 billion, an increase of 19.4% over 1984. Additional assessments on individual and fiduciary returns amounted to about $5 billion compared with $10.7 billion on corporate returns.

The vast majority of disputes are settled at the audit level. In 1985, the I.R.S. settled over 1.3 million returns at the audit level. The Appeals office handled 91,134 cases in 1985. Nearly 90% of these cases were settled by the Appeals office or before trial in the Tax Court. In summary, most disputes are settled in the administrative review procedures, and in a typical year taxpayers eventually pay about 50% of original assessments for additional taxes and penalties. This percent varies significantly, however, at different levels of income. Unfortunately, the settlement ratio is disproportionately high at the low end of the income scale. This could be due to poor representation in behalf of the low-income taxpayer; a realization that it does not "pay" to dispute small amounts of tax; an unreasonable attitude of agents in small cases; or any of several other factors. In any event, the fact bears further investigation.

Taxpayers who can afford to take their disputes with the I.R.S. to court also fare reasonably well. In 1985, for example, the government was able to enforce 51.7% of its additional assessments in the Tax Court. In the same year, the government won on over 65% of the claimed refunds in the district courts and over 66% in the Claims Court.

The number of litigated decisions is very small relative to disputes settled in the administrative review procedures. On the other hand, nearly 34,000 cases related to the federal tax laws were filed in 1985 in the Tax Court alone. That amounts to a sizable body of "new" law and underscores the point that taxation is a human process—never static, but always in a state of flux.

PROBLEMS

1. a. What are the three courts in which legal action may be initiated in income tax matters?
   b. Which of these courts may include a jury trial?
   c. To which court are the majority of tax disputes taken?
   d. What is the appeal route from each court?

[4]Annual Report of the Commissioner and Chief Council of the Internal Revenue Service (Washington, DC: U.S. Government Printing Office, 1982).

2. In addition to his salary, Tom Tulle has a substantial amount of income from dividends and interest. Income tax withheld from his salary in 1986 will amount to only 60% of the estimated total tax. Prior to 1986, Tom had not filed and paid quarterly estimates. Would you advise him to follow the same procedures in 1986? Explain.

3. What alternatives are available to a taxpayer on receipt of the 30-day letter? The 90-day letter?

4. Assume that a calendar-year taxpayer fails to file a return until December 30. Outline the statutory (as opposed to criminal) penalties that might be imposed by the I.R.S., assuming:
   a. The failure was willful (but not fraudulent).
   b. The failure was fraudulent.

5. The text describes the different levels of administrative and judicial review. What requirements must a tax practitioner meet to represent taxpayers at the different levels?

6. Below are statements about the tax process. State whether each is true or false. If false, explain why.
   a. The statutory notice of a tax deficiency is issued following the completion of the audit process.
   b. A taxpayer cannot obtain court action on a tax case until he or she has exhausted all procedures for relief within the I.R.S.
   c. Taxpayers have an undisputed right to a hearing before the Supreme Court after proper actions have been brought at the appropriate lower courts.
   d. Most tax disputes between the I.R.S. and taxpayers are settled at the appeals conference.
   e. Taxpayers must have a formal protest prepared before they are entitled to a hearing at the appeals conference.
   f. Most taxpayers elect to carry their disputes to federal district courts, if they decide to go to court.
   g. In tax matters, our system of justice is even-handed, affording equal opportunities in our society.

7. Robert McFee filed his income tax return, due April 15, on July 20. Although he had filed an automatic extension to file, he had not requested a second extension. The delay was attributable to the fact that McFee, an accountant, was simply too busy filing returns for other people. An analysis of his return showed that he had made quarterly estimated payments of $8,400, whereas the actual tax liability for the year was $9,200. Describe the penalties and other action that McFee faces.

8. Assume the same facts as in Problem 7, except that the quarterly payments totaled $9,200, whereas McFee's actual tax liability for the year was $8,400. Describe the penalties and other action that McFee faces.

9. a. In a previous year, the taxpayer reported gross income of $6,000, on which he paid a tax of $150. In reviewing his records during the current year, he discovered a "remittance advice" for $120 that he had received in the previous tax year and that he had failed to report on his tax return for that year. What is your advice to him? What types of liabilities will he have if he follows your advice?
   b. A friend of the taxpayer in part a, above, suggests to the taxpayer that he should "just forget that $120. They [the I.R.S.] never audit returns with incomes as low as yours." Reply to this, including in your answer a review of the procedures by which returns are selected for audit.

10. On his tax return for 19x1, Omar claimed a dependency exemption for his mother. His return was audited, and an agent disallowed the dependency exemption. Omar received a 30-day letter notifying him of a proposed additional tax liability of $182. Omar is very perturbed over this assessment and says to you, a tax expert, "I'll take it to court. I'm just not going to pay this $182."

    a. What procedure do you suggest that Omar follow?

    b. What procedure would be necessary to literally "take it to court"?

11. In researching a tax case, you find a decision of the Fifth Circuit Court of Appeals that supports a favorable outcome of your situation. Is it certain that the I.R.S. will follow this decision? What if you reside in California (Ninth Circuit)?

12. a. Explain the difference between a *nondocketed* case and a *docketed* case.

    b. Why might a taxpayer refuse an offer of compromise from the appelate conferee and file a petition with the Tax Court, even when he or she does not anticipate actual litigation?

    c. Who has settlement jurisdiction for nondocketed cases? For docketed cases? For cases scheduled for trial?

13. List three factors that bias the compliance process in favor of wealthy taxpayers.

14. a. When can a taxpayer unquestionably rely on a Tax Court decision, given the same facts?

    b. What signal or signals does the I.R.S. give taxpayers to indicate that a Tax Court decision will not be followed?

15. John Price recently received a letter from the I.R.S. stating that John's return for a recent year is being examined. John, an engineer, prepared the return himself. The letter asks John to bring his records for the year under examination when he appears for the office audit. John is convinced that he has made some terrible mistake in the computation of his tax and is worried. What can you tell him that will ease his mind?

SUPPLEMENTAL PROBLEMS

16. The Alpha Company is engaged in the business of manufacturing hot and cold patches for automobile tires. The company began business as a partnership in 1936 and has just incorporated under Sec. 351. In years past, the company had been moderately successful, due in a large part to its patented Hot Patch. The advent of the tubeless tire has adversely affected its sales, however, and the company is short of working capital and in need of financing. The owners of Alpha Company have been approached by Vinnie Vez, a business promoter and financial consultant, who has recently acquired all the stock of Omega Company, a Cleveland-based corporation engaged in the manufacture of rubber floor mats for automobiles. Omega was a closely held family corporation that was sold when the founder and head of the family died. Omega also needs working capital because it has invested most of its profits in acquiring special-order rubber fabrication machinery. Vez has proposed that Alpha buy Omega and thus obtain much-needed diversification. As a part of the deal, Vez proposes to arrange the requisite financing for both companies.

    After due consideration, Alpha's board of directors has authorized and issued $4,500,000 in 20-year 7% monthly payment registered bonds secured by Alpha's cash flow and by a $6,800,000 secured negotiable note of Air & Earth Investment

Company, payable to Alpha. (This note was given to Alpha when it sold to and then leased back all its operating equipment from Air & Earth.) The bonds are to be purchased by Vez from Alpha for less than their face value (hereinafter referred to as discount) in exchange for the following: (1) All the capital stock of Omega Company (having a value of $1,750,000); (2) $1,375,000 cash (borrowed by Vez from the bank); and (3) Vez's five-year 5% negotiable note in the face amount of $250,000. Vez will pledge Alpha bonds having a face value of $2,750,000 to a bank for a five-year loan of $1,750,000. As described in (2), $1,375,000 of the loan proceeds will be delivered to Alpha by Vez. The remaining $1,750,000 in bonds will be delivered by Vez to the family owners of Omega to secure Vez's payment of the purchase price of Omega's stock.

a. What are the federal income tax consequences to Alpha?

b. What are the federal income tax consequences to Vinnie Vez?

17. During his lifetime, Sam Jones has amassed a great deal of wealth, consisting of property, stocks, and cash. A number of years ago, Sam came to you with an idea about setting up a trust to take care of his brothers and sisters in the event of his death. The two of you worked out a plan to his satisfaction.

When Sam died several years ago, all the properties except the stock were sold and all the cash was divided among two brothers, two sisters, three daughters, and assorted grandchildren.

The stock, which constituted controlling interests in Jones Van Lines, Inc. and J&L Management Company, Inc., was to be held in a trust. Income from the stock would go to the two sisters, aged 63 and 68, and the two brothers, 60 and 64, for the remainder of their lives.

Each beneficiary received a certain sum per month. Any excess amount not paid would accumulate as part of the corpus. With the death of the last brother or sister, the trust would terminate and equal shares would be distributed to Ralph, Waldo, and Emmett, three of Sam's grandchildren.

The two companies' earnings and dividends for 19x1–19x3 were as follows:

| | Jones Van Lines | | J&L Management | |
	Earnings	Dividends	Earnings	Dividends
19x1	$764,890.06	$37,550	$66,482.57	$11,675
19x2	687,934.50	29,500	65,994.60	11,550
19x3	701,650.35	32,400	66,891.66	12,045

In early 19x4, Ralph, Waldo, and Emmett came to you for help, because you are the family's tax advisor and consultant. With the two companies' stock tied up in the trust, they cannot run the businesses with the flexibility they would like. Although they will eventually receive the stock, they would like to have it now so that they might run the businesses as they would like.

a. Can the three men gain possession of the stock immediately?

b. If they can obtain the stock, will any tax advantage be available to them?

CHAPTER 24

The Nature and Techniques of Tax Research

I still feel deeply indebted to an old, experienced lawyer who was one of my teachers in law school. —I have never forgotten what he laid down as the first and fundamental rule of practicing law: "Get the facts and the law will usually take care of itself."—It is a rule that is frequently ignored by young lawyers and accountants who are not experienced in advocacy. They get so wrought up over "The law" that they forget the primary importance of the facts—all the facts. As a matter of fact, nearly all disputed tax cases, either before the Service or in the courts, involve questions of fact rather than questions of law.
Hugh C. Bickford, *Successful Tax Practice* (1967)

Defining tax law: . . . a composite of constitutional doctrine and changing statutory provisions each having its history.
Judge Jerome Frank (1889–1957)

We have assumed in this book that you have had no prior exposure to the field of income taxation. During this first tax course, you should have observed numerous limitations in the wording of the Internal Revenue Code. Frequently, even after you have located and read the pertinent code section, the tax answer relevant to a specific set of facts is not obvious. The architects of a tax statute and the related regulations are unable to predict all the situations that may arise in connection with the affairs of millions of taxpayers. Consequently, attempts are made continually by Congress, the Treasury Department, the I.R.S., and the courts to clarify and interpret the statute, adding volumes of authority to the already complex maze of the Code. Thus, every successful tax advisor must be proficient in quickly locating, from among the volumes upon volumes of potential authority, a defensible solution to the tax questions that arise from specific facts. The process of locating and articulating good tax answers is called tax research.

This chapter serves as an introduction to tax research as defined in the above paragraph. We shall introduce you to the research methodology commonly used by accountants and lawyers as they perform tax-related work. Upon completion of this chapter and the associated problems, you should be able to perform basic tax research by yourself. At the same time, however, you should realize that the ability to do good tax research quickly is a skill; and, as with every other skill, your ability to perform well will increase with practice. This introduction can be a good starting point for years of experience.

In compliance work, a tax advisor's primary objective is to be certain that the client has done whatever the law demands, that is, has complied with the law. In planning engagements, an advisor's primary objective generally is to arrange the client's affairs in such a way as to minimize the tax liability. The research methodology used for both tax compliance and tax planning is basically the same. It consists of locating, interpreting, and applying the appropriate tax laws to particular facts. Unfortunately, these are not easy tasks. Although much publicity has been given to the simplification of our tax laws, the opposite has occurred. Every recent tax act, including the Tax Reform Act of 1986, has, in fact, added complexities to laws that are already quite complex. Consequently, more and more taxpayers seek assistance from "tax experts" to ensure correct compliance at minimum tax costs.

Tax research consists of five basic steps: (1) determining accurate facts; (2) identifying the issues or questions; (3) searching for defensible and authoritative solutions; (4) resolving incomplete and sometimes conflicting authority, evaluating that authority, and reaching a conclusion; and (5) communicating the conclusion. In this chapter we shall consider the process of gathering sufficient and accurate facts in conjunction with a tax problem. Identifying the pertinent question or questions from a set of facts will also be discussed. In addition we shall deal with the creation, location, and interpretation of appropriate authority. In Chapter 25 we shall examine the proper methods of communicating research conclusions.

THE IMPORTANCE OF FACTS

The first task that a tax advisor must master is that of properly gathering facts. The assimilation of facts is a skill that can only be learned with experience. An inexperienced tax advisor may be embarrassed upon returning from a conference with a client and realizing that one or more pertinent questions were never raised. Sometimes obtaining the necessary facts can be costly. For example, assume that you have a client who entered the United States on an immigrant visa and subsequently returned to his native country to oversee personal business matters. He remains outside the United States for a period in excess of 12 months, including one complete tax year. Because your client is not a U.S. citizen and because he was absent from the United States during a complete tax year, it might appear that, for that tax year, he should be considered a *nonresident* alien. Judicial law, however, seems to imply that his status may be that of a resident alien if he intends to return to the United States at some future date on his immigrant visa.[1] The fact that his absence is temporary and that he intends to return to the United States as an immigrant could account for such a status. The tax consequences of such a situation could be far reaching. Income earned by the taxpayer from services rendered in his native country and potential disposition of property in that country just could be taxable under U.S. tax laws. Obviously, therefore, your ability to reach a correct tax answer will depend to a great degree on your understanding of all the facts. And gathering those facts, especially from an overseas client, may be quite expensive. Knowledge of the law is important, but without a full knowledge of the facts, even a thorough knowledge of the law may be of little value in specific cases.

The critical role of facts can also be demonstrated in less exotic areas such as computing bad debts, receiving a gift, deducting losses, and determining travel and entertainment expenses. In each area, the tax statutes appear to be precise. Consequently, specific facts are frequently the most relevant criteria to tax situations. Section 165(c) of the Internal Revenue Code, for example, limits loss deductions by an individual taxpayer to those incurred in a trade or business, those arising from a transaction entered into for profit, and those considered to be a casualty or theft loss. Assume that your client intends to claim a theft loss deduction. In order to satisfy the definition of theft loss given in the Code, your client must establish that a theft actually occurred. The courts have held on a number of occasions that a mysterious disappearance of property does not constitute a casualty or theft loss.[2] Thus, an actual police report verifying the theft, depositions of witnesses who observed a break-in, or photographs helping to establish that a break-in occurred may be needed to provide sufficient factual evidence of a casualty loss to sustain the deduction claimed. Once again, the *facts* are important.

Documentation of facts, as indicated by the foregoing example, is another important skill to be learned by every tax advisor. In the case of a casualty loss deduction, the tax advisor should impress on the client the importance of gathering and retaining such documents as accident reports and written statements of witnesses. Purchase invoices and insurance policies can also serve as evidence that the damaged or stolen property existed and belonged to the taxpayer. An appraisal report or pictures or both can help to establish the condition of property before and after a casualty.

[1]*J. J. Friedman,* 37 TC 539 (1961).
[2]See, for example, *Edgar F. Stevens,* 6 TCM 805 (1947).

A closely related question concerns the proper time to prepare documentation in support of a deduction. Should documentation be made in the year in which the loss is claimed, or should the tax advisor wait to see if the deduction is challenged by the Internal Revenue Service? Audits are usually made two to three years after a return is filed. It may be quite cumbersome to assemble evidence and documentation to support a deduction after considerable time has elapsed. Often prospective witnesses have died or moved, and important documents are no longer available. On the other hand, collecting documents does cost something, and the I.R.S. may never challenge the return. After all, fewer than 3% of all returns filed are audited. In sum, needed documentation generally will be much less costly to gather and preserve at an early date; therefore, some effort to do so is warranted because the risk of an I.R.S. challenge is always present.

TWO CASES OF FACT COMPARED

To further illustrate the important role of facts in the resolution of tax questions, let us examine two court decisions. Both cases deal with the same question: Does the invasion of a house by termites and the resulting destruction constitute a deductible casualty loss under Sec. 165(c)? Although neither case is a benchmark decision, each one demonstrates the importance of facts in the resolution of a tax question.

As you read the decisions of both cases, note the similarities and differences. The first case, involving Joseph and Roselle Shopmaker, was decided in 1953 by the U.S. District Court for the Eastern District of Missouri. The decision, rendered by District Judge Hulen, reads in part as follows:

FINDINGS OF FACT

In December, 1949, plaintiffs purchased the residence which is the subject matter of the claim. It had been constructed some twelve years prior. Its expectancy is fifty years. At time of purchase, plaintiff, Joseph Shopmaker, and the real estate agent testified that he had made a number of inspections of houses and knew how to detect termites. No evidence of termites was found at the time plaintiffs purchased the residence. No termites were found during the year 1950. On February 8, 1951, termites swarmed in the kitchen. Witness Ralph Hoener examined the house and found extensive damage from termites. He has been in the termite business for twenty-one years. As an expert he testified he could not tell when the termites invaded the house for the first time. On February 8 he found swarms in two locations.

Installation of termite controls is an occupation for experts, but the presence of termites can be determined by non-experts. They are detected by the runways on the ground and across material that they do not attack, by swarming and piercing the wood, which after termite destruction remains only a hollow shell. The real estate agent who examined the property at the time plaintiffs made the purchase testified he was informed on the manner of detecting termites. He found no runways or swarms at the time of his inspection. He used a penknife to pierce the wood joints in the basement. This is substantial evidence that the residence was free of termites at the time plaintiffs purchased in December, 1949. The facts bring this case within the *Rosenberg* case.

OPINION

We are impressed with the argument of plaintiffs that the casualty is the invasion of the premises by termites. This is a comparatively quick or sudden operation. The resultant damage which may extend over a period of months or years flows from the casualty. The damage and the time it takes for the termites to effect it should not be confused with their initial invasion and determining what is the casualty. The case of *Burkett* 10 TCM 948, (1951), referred to in the *Rosenberg* opinion, illustrates this observation. In the Burkett case, sand from wooden foundations under a house was washed away during a hurricane. The result was that foundation posts gradually sank over a period of two years, eventually requiring the replacement of many of the posts in order to level the floors. The commissioner held this was a loss by casualty. The casualty was the washing away of the sand during the hurricane. The damage developed over a period of years from that casualty.

The evidence is undisputed that if plaintiffs are entitled to recover, judgment should be for a refund of $1,476.56.

Let judgment be settled and submitted accordingly.[3]

The second case, involving Joseph and Margaret Austra, was heard by the Tax Court in 1966. The decision, rendered by Judge Tannenwald, reads in part as follows:

FINDINGS OF FACT

The petitioners are husband and wife and reside in Germantown, Maryland. They filed their joint federal income tax return for the year 1960 with the district director of internal revenue, Baltimore, Maryland.

Petitioners completed construction of a home in Germantown in 1954. They lived in the house through the taxable year involved herein.

The house was one-story and of wood frame construction. There was an open or "crawl" between the ground and the base of the house under the kitchen and dining area.

In July 1958, termite infestation was discovered in supporting wooden beams and posts in the crawl space, and the damage was repaired. The repairs consisted of replacing the damaged wooden posts which had been in contact with the ground with posts of steel and adding a cement wall capped with concrete to the base of the house under the kitchen and dining area. The contractor who made the repairs did not check the remainder of the house for termite infestation.

After the repairs in 1958 and through May 1960, no exterminator inspected the house for termites, although petitioners themselves made periodic examinations of the house. The contractor who made the 1958 repairs applied preventative spray to the house twice in 1959.

[3]*Shopmaker*, 54-1 USTC 9195 (DC, ED MO; 1953).

In June 1960, termite infestation, consisting of both live and dead channels, were discovered in the portion of the house not checked for infestation in 1958. There was no infestation discovered in the primary supports of the house which the contractor had checked and repaired in 1958. The damage was repaired and the repairs were paid for in 1960.

Termite infestation may be present notwithstanding the absence of outward signs of such infestation. It may not be apparent from visual inspection of the interior and exterior of a building.

Petitioners in 1960 had the house repaired and remodeled and paid therefor a total of $4,200. Of this amount, $2,565 represented the cost of repairing the termite damage.

In their 1960 return petitioners deducted $2,500 as a loss from termite damage. In an amended return for that year they increased the amount of the claim deduction to $2,789.22.

OPINION

The sole issue in the instant case is whether the hole drilled in the petitioners' pocketbook by termites in 1960 gave rise to a deductible casualty loss. Petitioners contend that the termite infestation occurred between 1958 and 1960 and thus met the requirement of "suddenness" which the decisions have incorporated in subsection (c)(3). Respondent argues that petitioners have not proved that the infestation discovered in 1960 had not begun before July 1958, and, even if the infestation began on or after July 1958, petitioners have still not established the requisite suddenness. We agree with respondent.

In prior cases, we have construed "casualty" as used in section 165(c)(3) to mean "an accident, a mishap, some sudden invasion of a hostile agency; it excludes the progressive deterioration of property through a steadily operating cause."

The instant case is strikingly similar to *Rudolph Lewis Hoppy,* supra. In that case, a professional exterminator in 1956 discovered and repaired damage to the substructure of the taxpayer's residence caused by a fungus infestation commonly known as "dry rot." The exterminator's inspection of the premises was limited to the substructure.

After the repairs and through November 1959, taxpayer, from time to time, personally inspected the substructure of the house. In November 1959, infestation was discovered entirely above the substructure. We held that the taxpayer had failed to prove that the areas first discovered in 1959 to be infested were free of such infestation at the time of the exterminator's inspection in 1956 and that, as a consequence, he had not shown the suddenness necessary to support a deduction in 1959. Compare *E. G. Kilroe,* supra.

Although the instant case involves termite damage and Hoppy involved damage from dry rot, petitioners in both cases failed to prove that the damage did not occur substantially earlier than its discovery, and the decision in Hoppy is controlling in the instant case.[4]

Comparing these cases, we find a number of identical facts. In both instances the taxpayers claimed a casualty loss deduction in their income tax

[4]*Joseph A. Austra,* 66,028 P-H Memo TC (1966).

returns for a loss incurred through the invasion of their personal residences by termites. The question, therefore, is whether or not the invasion of a personal residence by termites constitutes a casualty loss. In *Shopmaker,* the taxpayers were able to establish to the satisfaction of the court that their home had been free of termites at a specific date. The taxpayers' proof relied heavily on the testimony of two expert witnesses. A real estate agent testified that he had made an inspection in December of 1949 and had found the home free of termites. Further evidence was introduced to show that a termite inspection can be performed by one not regularly in the business of pest extermination. Detailed procedures of the initial inspection were explained. These facts were corroborated by a second expert witness whose profession was that of termite control. This evidence indicated that termites were first discovered in February 1951. Finally, the period from December 1949 to February 1951 was determined by the courts to satisfy the suddenness test, which is an essential ingredient for a casualty loss deduction.

In *Austra,* the facts presented did not prove to the satisfaction of the court that in July 1958, when a termite infestation was first discovered in a portion of the house, the rest of the home was completely free of termites. In fact, the findings indicate that in June of 1960 termites were discovered in a portion of the house that had not been checked for infestation in 1958. Observe also that no expert testimony was presented; hence, many of the facts introduced by the taxpayers were not independently corroborated.

As indicated previously, neither of these decisions is a particularly important judicial determination. In fact, the Internal Revenue Service has announced that a deduction for termite damage will be routinely challenged. In the opinion of the I.R.S., termite infestation cannot meet the suddenness test. Nevertheless, these two cases demonstrate the importance of facts. They also suggest the importance of presenting facts; the way facts are assembled and substantiated frequently influences a court's decision. An expert understanding of the tax laws alone will not make anyone a good tax advisor. The ability to delineate, assimilate, and interpret the facts in each situation is an equally necessary and important quality for a successful tax researcher.

IDENTIFYING THE QUESTIONS

Once the researcher has gathered and identified all the pertinent facts, he or she must then enumerate the appropriate questions so that the necessary authority can be located. Consider the following example. Tim Wright, age 46, lost his job in San Antonio, Texas during the summer of 19X1. Despite considerable efforts on his part, he was unable to find employment in his accustomed salary range. He, therefore, expanded his search to other Texas cities and eventually accepted a new position in Houston. Since immediate attempts to sell his residence failed, Tim instructed his realtor to list the home as being for "sale or lease." He had purchased the home three years earlier for $72,000.

In the meantime, Tim searched for housing in the Houston area. His new job kept him away from home during the week on a regular basis. Since Tim's wife did not enjoy yard work and would not perform even minor maintenance work, they decided to purchase a condominium, which allowed them to obtain, for a fee, regular maintenance and yard care. They agreed with the seller on a price of $93,000 and occupied their new condominium on October 1, 19X1.

The former residence in San Antonio remained unsold but was finally leased in November 19X1. Throughout 19X2 the home remained leased, except for the month of December. A new lessee occupied the home in January 19X3, who also signed a 90-day option to purchase the home provided he could find suitable financing. The option was exercised in March 19X3, and final closing occurred on April 30, 19X3, for an adjusted sales price of $89,000.

Generating the appropriate questions (or "issues") is another critical tax skill that can be developed through practice. Typically, the form in which the issues are stated varies with experience. A tax advisor with limited experience and only a passing knowledge of the Internal Revenue Code might assemble the following questions from the example:

1. May Tim Wright defer the gain on the sale of his San Antonio residence?
2. What are the conditions of a tax deferral?
3. What type of domicile qualifies as a replacement residence?

The initial search for satisfactory conclusions to tax questions ordinarily raises additional questions (issues) in the mind of the tax advisor. Sometimes questions that should be raised completely escape the attention of an inexperienced researcher. In order to reach a supportable solution to this example problem, the researcher must enumerate all of the requirements for a tax deferral on the sale of the old residence. Thus, even if overlooked initially, a tax advisor should eventually reach at least one additional question, namely:

4. May the Wrights lease the San Antonio residence before finally selling it?

This question must be examined before the Wrights can be assured that deferral treatment applies.

A more experienced tax advisor might phrase the original questions in an entirely different way. The fact that he or she has greater knowledge of the Code is likely to result in a question that includes a direct reference to a specific Code section. For instance, a more seasoned advisor might ask the following question:

1. Does the sale of the San Antonio residence and the purchase of the Houston condominium qualify for a tax deferral under Sec. 1034?

The advisor's familiarity with Sec. 1034 quite possibly includes an implicit recognition of the significance of the facts that this transaction meets the following requirements:

a. A new residence was acquired within a time period which begins two years before and ends two years after the sale of the old residence.
b. The cost of the new residence exceeds the adjusted sales price of the old residence.

Experience and careful attention to detail may lead the researcher to wonder, however, whether the proceeds from the sale of a family home qualifies for a tax-free rollover into a condominium. Thus, the researcher will formulate this pertinent question:

2. Does a condominium qualify under Sec. 1034(a) as a new principal residence?

Anyone with reasonable business acumen will soon realize that a conversion of a personal residence to rental property is typically accompanied by a host of tax consequences such as a basis determination, depreciation computation, and potential recapture problems. Thus, the sophisticated researcher will arrive at this key question:

3. Does the temporary leasing of a personal residence disqualify a former principal residence from coverage under the provisions of Sec. 1034?

The seasoned tax researcher realizes that lengthy periods of contemplative thought may be necessary before the complex tax issues implicit in many business transactions become obvious. In addition, a good imagination and considerable creativity are important traits of every successful tax advisor. Experience, of course, cannot be overrated. Familiarity with tax provisions enables a researcher to ignore potential issues for which he or she already knows the answers. Research of similar issues on previous occasions is an important item of inventory to the tax advisor. On the other hand, too much experience can sometimes stunt one's ability to be imaginative. Too often a researcher may simply say, "Yes, that looks familiar. We'll handle it the same way we did in previous situations." Whenever that happens, the tax advisor obviously forfeits the opportunity to investigate alternatives that may be even more advantageous to a particular client.

BEFORE-THE-FACTS RESEARCH

In the foregoing discussion we have emphasized the methodology appropriate for after-the-fact research. Research before all of the critical events of a transaction have actually occurred is known as tax planning. Tax planning involves carefully structuring facts before they have occurred. As a first step, the tax advisor must determine what desired outcome the client has in mind. Once the desired result is established, the question is one of identifying the alternatives available to reach the desired outcome. The process is much the same as identifying a point on a road map and then examining the various ways of getting there. Some routes will turn out to be more efficient; that is, they may be shorter or have fewer obstacles such as rugged mountains, narrow bridges, or roads in need of repair. Tax planning carries with it considerable risk; seldom will the tax advisor find a client situation that duplicates, in every respect, the facts implicit in prior authority. Thus, the objective of the tax planner is to reduce the risk inherent in the plan proposed to a client. An advisor should explain to the client any risks involved in each alternative. Because nontax considerations may frequently outweigh tax objectives, the client may not always elect the safest and most efficient alternative. In the end, the client must make the final decision as to which alternative should be pursued.

After a decision has been made to adopt a particular course of action to achieve a desired tax result, the advisor should exercise sufficient care and offer constant encouragement to implement the facts assumed in the original plan. Even a slight variation in facts can often introduce additional issues and undesired results. Sufficient documentation should be preserved to substantiate that the desired course of action was followed. Finally, every tax plan must have as an underlying objective a business purpose other than that of tax avoidance. If no business purpose exists, the I.R.S. is likely to challenge the plan and invoke the judicial "substance over form" doctrine. Accordingly, the good tax advisor will also ensure that every tax plan has a well-documented business purpose.

So far in this chapter we have examined the critical role that facts play in tax research. Appropriate issue(s) can be identified only if all the facts are known and can be substantiated. In the next section, we examine the task of locating appropriate authority to prepare a defensible position for specific tax questions.

TAX RESEARCH: LOCATING AND ASSESSING AUTHORITY

In resolving tax issues or questions, a researcher must locate, interpret, and evaluate all the numerous authorities relevant to a particular fact situation, including the statutes and interpretations by the I.R.S. and the courts. Ordinarily, the search should begin with statutory authority. From that point, the procedures become less well defined. Some good researchers go next to administrative authority, then to judicial authority, and finally to secondary references. Other good researchers contend that one should avoid reading administrative authority as long as possible because it represents the I.R.S.'s point of view. They argue that it is too easy to become closed-minded early in the research process, and, hence, they would defer the government's position until the end.

Regardless in which order the researcher seeks out relevant authority to sustain a defensible position, once a conclusion has been reached the job is not complete until the findings have been communicated to the interested and involved parties.

In the remainder of this chapter we discuss how and where a tax advisor may locate pertinent authority to support an answer to a tax question. We also examine how to assess and interpret potential authority. (In the following chapter, we address the importance of effectively communicating the findings and conclusions reached by the researcher.

SOURCES OF FEDERAL INCOME TAX LAW

In tax law, as elsewhere, some rules are more important than others, with the weight or force of each rule depending on its *source*. You can read and learn the tax law more intelligently if you understand roughly the weight that should be given to any particular source. In addition, your instructor may ask you to research the answers to problems that go beyond the rules included in this text. To do this you must know how the various sources of law are organized into a cohesive library. The remainder of this chapter is therefore devoted to an outline of the sources of income tax law and to the organization of these sources in a typical tax library.

Chapter 23, "The Federal Tax Process," also dealt with the sources of our income tax law, but from a different perspective. That chapter emphasized the internal workings of Congress, the administration, and the judiciary. In this chapter, we concentrate on *what* the tax-writing agencies produce; in Chapter 23, we concentrated on *how* these agencies produce tax law. You may choose to reread Chapter 23 in conjunction with your study of the sources below.

Sources of Law from Congressional Action

The legislative process described in Chapter 23 produced our basic tax law, the Internal Revenue Code of 1986. Congress passes new tax laws of some sort each year. A tax bill passed by Congress is usually issued as a Revenue Act that amends the existing Internal Revenue Code. The most recent exception to this practice occurred in 1986, when the Tax Reform Act of 1986 also created the Internal Revenue Code of 1986. From 1954 to 1986, tax legislation simply amended the Internal Revenue Code of 1954. Before 1954, Revenue Acts amended the tax laws codified in the 1939 Revenue Code. Prior to the 1939 Code, the tax provisions consisted of an accumulation of separate Revenue Acts, passed at irregular intervals since 1913. A public outcry for a more systematic organization of the tax laws passed since 1913 convinced Congress to authorize the creation of the first Revenue Code in 1939.

Some Revenue Acts are named to reflect a specific objective of Congress, such as the Tax Reform Act of 1986, the Economic Recovery Tax Act of 1981, and the Tax Reduction and Simplification Act of 1977. Officially, however, a revenue bill is signed into law as a public law. For example, the Tax Reduction and Simplification Act of 1977 is officially known as Public Law 95-30, and the Tax Reform Act of 1986 was passed as Public Law 99-514.

The Internal Revenue Code is the primary source for all research and planning in taxation. All other laws from other sources play only secondary roles.

Once Congress passes a new provision, the other sources generally try to interpret the *intent* of Congress relative to that provision. The legislative process itself results in some sources that are widely used to indicate congressional intent.

1. The most important sources for interpretation are the committee reports that accompany the revenue acts when they are submitted to the House or Senate. Each revenue bill from the Committee on Ways and Means is accompanied by a House Report that explains the problem as well as the changes in the law proposed in response to the problem. Reports also accompany the bills reported by the Senate Finance Committee and the conference committee.

2. Hearings before the Committee on Ways and Means and the Committee on Finance are often published. These hearings provide invaluable insights into the political, economic, and social problems the legislators must confront.

3. The *Congressional Record* contains the floor debates in the House and Senate on revenue bills. Often the responses to questions raised shed some light on congressional intent.

These sources exist before final passage of an amendment to the Code and often relate in plain language just what Congress hopes to accomplish with the amendment. Although these sources may help to interpret the law, the starting point for any investigation into our tax law must be the Code.

The Internal Revenue Code of 1986 has an elaborate organizational scheme that can be depicted as follows:

(9) SUBTITLES—designated by uppercase English letters A–G; Subtitle A is titled "Income Taxes."

(60) CHAPTERS—designated by Arabic numerals 1–98 (some numbers unused); Chapter 1 is titled "Normal Taxes and Surtaxes."

SUBCHAPTERS—designated by uppercase English letters, as required; Chapter 1 has 20 Subchapters (Subchapters R and U repealed), A–V.

PARTS—designated by Roman numerals, as required; Chapter 1, Subchapter A, has 6 Parts, I–VII (Part V repealed).

SUBPARTS—designated by uppercase English letters, as required.

SECTIONS—designated by Arabic numerals, as required. See text below for important details of this subdivision of the Code.

SUBSECTIONS—designated by lowercase English letters in parentheses, as required.

PARAGRAPHS—designated by Arabic numerals in parentheses, as required.

SUBPARAGRAPHS—designated by uppercase English letters in parentheses, as required.

SUB-SUBPARAGRAPHS—designated by lowercase Roman numerals in parentheses, as required.

As shown in Table 24-1, Chapter 1 is titled "Normal Taxes and Surtaxes" and contains Subchapters A through V. Because Subchapter R and U were repealed in 1969 and 1986 respectively, only 20 Subchapters are currently operative.

Nearly all the "popular" income tax literature refers only to the "Sections" or lower subdivision of the Code. Thus, for example, "Sec. 301" refers (without specific mention) to the 1986 Code, Subtitle A, Chapter 1, Subchapter C, Part I. The reference is definitive because the sections are numbered progressively from Subtitle A, Chapter 1. There is only one Sec. 301. Also, not all numbers were used originally, enabling Congress to add sections at the end of any subchapter or part. In a sense, the Code is like a chart of accounts in an accounting system. To illustrate, Subchapter A, Part I, uses section numbers 1 through 5—currently, no sections numbered 6 through 10 exist; Part II uses section numbers 11 and 12; Part III uses number 15 only; Part IV uses a further organizational division, namely Subparts. Subpart A uses section numbers 21 through 26; Subpart B uses sections 27 through 29; Subpart C uses section numbers 32 through 35; and so on.

Because most of the tax literature refers only to a section number, it is important to understand what a reference, such as "Sec. 301(b)(1)(A)," means. Suppose you read this citation in connection with a discussion on "distribution by a corporation to individual shareholders." To learn more about the topic you would have to (1) have access to the 1986 Code and (2) know how to locate the specific reference. A few instructors require even their introductory tax students to purchase a paperback copy of the current Code. Other students can locate the Code volume of almost any tax reference service in a library. Still others may be satisfied with frequently reprinted excerpts from the Code, such as those included in this text.

Commercial companies—such as Commerce Clearing House (CCH), Prentice-Hall (P-H), Research Institute of America (RIA), and West Publishing Company—publish paperback editions of the Code, which are typically used by tax professionals as their working copy. The official copy of the Internal Revenue Code is found in Title 26 of the United States Code. Regardless of where and how you find the Code, any reference to Sec. 301(b)(1)(A) should lead you to the words shown in Figure 24-1 (page 24/16).

TABLE 24-1

SUBTITLE A—INCOME TAXES

Chapter 1 Normal Taxes and Surtaxes

Subchapter A Determination of tax liability
Part I   Tax on individuals
Part II   Tax on corporations
Part III   Changes in rates during a taxable year
Part IV   Credits against tax
Part V   Repealed
Part VI   Alternative Minimum Tax
Part VII   Environmental Tax

Subchapter B Computation of taxable income
Part I   Definition of gross income, adjusted gross income, taxable income, etc.
Part II   Items specifically included in gross income
Part III   Items specifically excluded from gross income
Part IV   Tax exemption requirements for state and local bonds
Part V   Deductions for personal exemptions
Part VI   Itemized deductions for individuals and corporations
Part VII   Additional itemized deductions for individuals
Part VIII   Special deductions for corporations
Part IX   Items not deductible
Part X   Terminal railroad corporations and their shareholders
Part XI   Special rules relating to corporate preference items

Subchapter C Corporate distributions and adjustments
Part I   Distributions by corporations
Part II   Corporate liquidations
Part III   Corporate organizations and reorganizations
Part IV   Insolvency reorganizations
Part V   Carryovers
Part VI   Treatment of certain interests as stock or indebtedness
Part VII   Miscellaneous Corporate Provisions

Subchapter D Deferred compensation, etc.
Part I   Pension, profit-sharing, stock bonus plans, etc.
Part II   Certain stock options

Subchapter E Accounting periods and methods of accounting
Part I   Accounting periods
Part II   Methods of accounting
Part III   Adjustments

Subchapter F Exempt organizations
Part I   General rule
Part II   Private foundations
Part III   Taxation of business income of certain exempt organizations
Part IV   Farmers' cooperatives
Part V   Shipowners' protection and indemnity associations
Part VI   Political organizations
Part VII   Certain homeowners associations

Subchapter G Corporations used to avoid income tax on shareholders
Part I   Corporations improperly accumulating surplus
Part II   Personal holding companies
Part III   Foreign personal holding companies
Part IV   Deduction for dividends paid

Subchapter H Banking institutions
Part I   Rules of general application to banking institutions
Part II   Mutual savings banks, etc.

TABLE **24-1** Continued

Subchapter I Natural resources
  Part I   Deductions
  Part II   Exclusions from gross income
  Part III   Sales and exchanges
  Part IV   Mineral production payments
  Part V   Continental shelf areas

Subchapter J Estates, trusts, beneficiaries, and decedents
  Part I   Estates, trusts, and beneficiaries
  Part II   Income in respect of decedents

Subchapter K Partners and partnerships
  Part I   Determination of tax liability
  Part II   Contributions, distributions, and transfers
  Part III   Definitions

Subchapter L Insurance companies
  Part I   Life insurance companies
  Part II   Other insurance companies
  Part III   Provisions of general application

Subchapter M Regulated investment companies and real estate investment trusts
  Part I   Regulated investment companies
  Part II   Real estate investment trusts
  Part III   Provisions which apply to both regulated investment companies and real estate
               investment trusts
  Part IV   Real estate mortgage investment conduits

Subchapter N Tax based on income from sources within or without the United States
  Part I   Determination of sources of income
  Part II   Nonresident aliens and foreign corporations
  Part III   Income from sources without the United States
  Part IV   Domestic international sales corporations
  Part V   International boycott determinations

Subchapter O Gain or loss on disposition of property
  Part I   Determination of amount of and recognition of gain or loss
  Part II   Basis rules of general application
  Part III   Common nontaxable exchanges
  Part IV   Special rules
  Part V   Changes to effectuate F.C.C. policy
  Part VI   Exchanges in obedience to S.E.C. orders
  Part VII   Wash sales, straddles
  Part VIII   Distributions pursuant to Bank Holding Company Act

Subchapter P Capital gains and losses
  Part I   Treatment of capital gains
  Part II   Treatment of capital losses
  Part III   General rules for determining capital gains and losses
  Part IV   Special rules for determining capital gains and losses
  Part V   Special rules for bonds and other debt instruments
  Part VI   Treatment of certain passive foreign investment companies

Subchapter Q Readjustment of tax between years and special limitations
  Part I   Repealed
  Part II   Mitigation of effect of limitations and other provisions
  Part III   Repealed
  Part IV   Repealed
  Part V   Claim of right
  Part VI   Repealed
  Part VII   Recoveries of foreign expropriation losses

TABLE 24-1 Continued

Subchapter R Repealed
Subchapter S Tax treatment of S corporations and their shareholders
Subchapter T Cooperatives and their patrons
    Part I   Tax treatment of cooperatives
    Part II   Tax treatment by patrons of patronage dividends and per-unit retain allocations
    Part III   Definitions; special rules
Subchapter U Repealed
Subchapter V Title 11 cases

Section 301, Subsection (b), Paragraph (1), Subparagraph (A), Sub-Subparagraphs (i) and (ii) indicate that a distribution by a corporation to a noncorporate shareholder includes the amount of money distributed plus the fair market value of any additional property received by the shareholder.

Interpretation by the Treasury Department

The Internal Revenue Code authorizes and instructs the Secretary of the Treasury or his or her delegate to issue regulations interpreting the tax law. The I.R.S., a subdivision of the Treasury Department, also issues many pronouncements under the generic class of *rulings* dealing with the administration and interpretation of our tax laws.

REGULATIONS   The Regulations, which contain the Secretary's interpretation of the Internal Revenue Code, have the force and effect of the Code, unless they are shown to be in conflict with congressional intent.[5] Instructions

FIGURE 24-1

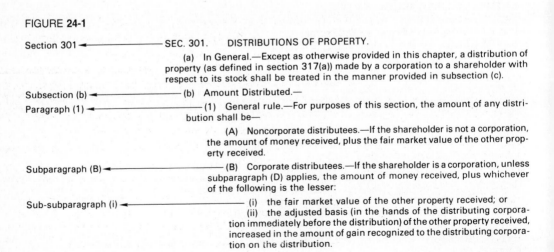

Section 301 ◄————————— SEC. 301.   DISTRIBUTIONS OF PROPERTY.
    (a) In General.—Except as otherwise provided in this chapter, a distribution of property (as defined in section 317(a)) made by a corporation to a shareholder with respect to its stock shall be treated in the manner provided in subsection (c).
Subsection (b) ◄————————— (b) Amount Distributed.—
Paragraph (1) ◄————————— (1) General rule.—For purposes of this section, the amount of any distribution shall be—
    (A) Noncorporate distributees.—If the shareholder is not a corporation, the amount of money received, plus the fair market value of the other property received.
Subparagraph (B) ◄————————— (B) Corporate distributees.—If the shareholder is a corporation, unless subparagraph (D) applies, the amount of money received, plus whichever of the following is the lesser:
Sub-subparagraph (i) ◄————————— (i)   the fair market value of the other property received; or
    (ii) the adjusted basis (in the hands of the distributing corporation immediately before the distribution) of the other property received, increased in the amount of gain recognized to the distributing corporation on the distribution.

---

[5]*Maryland Casualty Co.* v. *U.S.*, 251 U.S. 342 (1920).

printed on and accompanying official tax return forms also constitute part of the regulations. Regulations contain helpful amplifications of the Code and many useful examples. Before regulations are officially released on a new or amended provision, *proposed* regulations are published and circulated. The Treasury Department invites comments and suggestions on the proposed regulations from all interested parties. After a period specified in the proposed regulations, final regulations are adopted, incorporating changes necessitated by the comments received. The Secretary revises and expands the Regulations when Congress amends the Code and adds new provisions to it.

Regulations and amendments or revisions to regulations are first issued as Treasury Decisions (TD). These releases must have the approval of the Treasury Department, and after release they may be relied on as a precedent; that is, they are binding on the government.

When adopted, regulations for all federal taxes are printed in Title 26 of the Code of Federal Regulations. Title 26 is divided into parts that correspond with the subtitles in the Internal Revenue Code. Thus, Part 1 of the Regulations deals with Subtitle A of the Code, the income tax. In addition, the parts are subdivided into sections that correspond with sections of the Code. Thus, Part 1, Section 162, of the Regulations deals with the ordinary and necessary expenses of carrying on a trade or business. The complete citation for that section of the Regulations is 26 CFR 1.162, which means Title 26, Code of Federal Regulations, Part 1, Section 162. For brevity, the citation often is reduced to Treas. Reg. Sec. 1.162-x, or even Reg. 1.162-x. A complete citation to any Treasury regulation has four distinct parts, as follows:

1. The number to the left of the decimal point indicates that the regulation deals either with a specific tax or with a procedural rule, as follows:

> 1. Income tax
> 20. Estate tax
> 25. Gift tax
> 31. Employment tax
> 48. or 49. Excise tax
> 301. Administrative and procedural rule
> 601. Statement of procedural rules

2. The number between the decimal point and the dash (-) indicates the Code section that the regulation is interpreting.

3. The first number to the right of the dash indicates the sequential number of the regulation interpreting the Code section already identified.

4. The letters and/or numbers following the first number to the right of the dash indicate subreferences within a regulation to help the reader find a particular point of interpretation.

For example, Treas. Reg. Sec. 1.162-3(b)(2) refers to an income tax regulation (denoted by the 1.); interpreting Code Sec. 162 (denoted by the numbers between the decimal point and the dash); specifically to Regulation number 3 (denoted by the 3 immediately following the dash); and to part (b)(2) of that regulation.

As stated above, most regulations have the same force and effect as the Code. Newly issued regulations, however, may not reflect congressional intent and occasionally the courts hold a regulation invalid. However, a few years after the promulgation of a regulation, judges generally are reluctant to overrule the interpretive powers of the Treasury Department.

The *Internal Revenue Bulletin,* which is published weekly by the Internal Revenue Service, contains much of the information referred to in the preceding pages. For example, the *Bulletin* includes copies of the Internal Revenue Acts, committee reports on these acts, and all Treasury Decisions. It also includes all revenue rulings.

REVENUE RULINGS   The Commissioner's interpretation of certain provisions of the law in relation to a specific fact case is released from time to time as a revenue ruling. These rulings do not constitute a comprehensive coverage of the Internal Revenue Code. The Commissioner is not required by law to follow his interpretation in a revenue ruling in all cases, although a ruling generally is binding on the government with respect to the facts on which the ruling was requested. Revenue rulings are consecutively numbered each calendar year and are cited Rev. Rul. 1980-1, etc.[6] Revenue rulings originate with taxpayers who have asked the Commissioner to rule on how a prospective transaction will be taxed. The form used to request a ruling is specified by the Commissioner. The I.R.S., however, is not compelled to make the ruling.

Each year, the I.R.S. issues a large number of rulings, but until recently, it selected only a small number for publication in the *Bulletin.* Determination of which rulings to publish historically was made by the I.R.S. based on its opinion of the ruling's usefulness to taxpayers generally. The Tax Reform Act of 1976, however, contained a provision that requires the I.R.S. to make private rulings and certain other written determinations available to the public.

OTHER RELEASES   Tax information releases deal with timely topics of general interest and are released to the popular press. Revenue procedures (Rev. Proc.) explain procedures and other duties of taxpayers. There are various other forms of releases. On occasion these releases can be very important to taxpayers—for example, the depreciation guidelines were originally published as a revenue procedure.

The material in the *Bulletin* is reorganized and printed in a bound volume on a semiannual basis. The bound volumes are called *Cumulative Bulletins* and are cited C.B. Thus, 1980-1 C.B. would contain Rev. Rul. 1980-1, as well as other information.

---

[6]Prior to 1953, citations for rulings identified the source of the ruling. There were many different series, each with its own alphabetic identification. A list of the varied citations is available in most tax services.

Statutory Interpretation by Courts

As suggested above, the Treasury Department and the Internal Revenue Service both publish "official" interpretations of the Code in such pronouncements as Treasury Regulations and Revenue Rulings, respectively. But, as you may already suspect, not everyone agrees with the government's interpretations of the Code. Hence, disputes frequently develop between I.R.S. agents and taxpayers. If these two parties cannot otherwise agree, the only way to resolve a disputed interpretation of the Code is through a court; that is, through a judicial interpretation of the statutory law. Taxpayers may obtain a judicial review of their disputes with the government either by filing a petition with the Tax Court of the United States or by suing the government in a U.S. District Court or the Claims Court.

TAX COURT ROUTE   When the I.R.S. claims that a taxpayer owes a tax greater than that on the return filed, and the I.R.S. and the taxpayer cannot reach a compromise, the taxpayer can petition the Tax Court of the United States for a judicial review of the dispute before the I.R.S. officially assesses the additional tax. The Tax Court exists solely to resolve disputes over the internal revenue laws, and its 19 judges are therefore tax specialists. Prior to 1943, the Tax Court was known as the Board of Tax Appeals. Lawyers for the government and the taxpayer present written and oral arguments and other evidence to the court, which then decides all questions of fact and law. The court is headquartered in Washington, D.C., but it hears cases throughout the country.

The Chief Justice of the Tax Court classifies the court's decisions as either *regular* decisions or *memorandum* decisions, both of which are valid precedents. Regular decisions are reported by the U.S. Government Printing Office in *Tax Court Reports,* commonly cited—T.C.—. Memorandum decisions are redundant decisions that, in the Chief Justice's opinion, add nothing to the tax law.

Tax Court Memorandum Decisions are published by the government only in mimeograph form. Because these decisions do have precedential value, two publishing companies (CCH and P-H) publish all memorandum decisions, first in loose-leaf "advance sheets" and, at the end of each year, in hard-bound copy. The CCH publication is titled *Tax Court Memorandum Decisions* (cited _____ TCM _____); the P-H edition is titled *Prentice-Hall Memorandum Decisions* (cited _____ PH Memo TC).

The losing party in a dispute before the Tax Court can appeal the decision to the U.S. Circuit Courts of Appeal. Twelve Courts of Appeal exist for the District of Columbia and the 11 appellate regions of the country. Here also, attorneys for the taxpayer and for the government present oral and written arguments to the court. Current decisions of these courts are reported in the *Federal Reporter,* Second Series, commonly cited—F.2d—.

Appeals from Circuit Court decisions are made to the Supreme Court of the United States. However, the Supreme Court grants *certiorari* (that is, agrees to hear appeals) in only a limited number of tax cases each year, usually when a conflict exists in the decisions of two or more of the Circuit Courts of Appeal. Decisions of the U.S. Supreme Court are published in several different reporters.

When a taxpayer takes a dispute to the Tax Court, additional taxes, if any, are not assessed until the appeals procedures are complete. Interest on the underpayment of the tax is calculated from the due date of the return (as explained in Chapter 23).

DISTRICT COURT ROUTE   A second line of legal redress available to taxpayers involves the U.S. District Courts. When disagreements arise, taxpayers can pay the additional taxes assessed by the I.R.S. and then file a claim for a refund of that tax. The I.R.S. usually disallows the refund claim, and the taxpayer can then sue the government in a District Court for the tax illegally collected. This right to sue for taxes collected illegally is specifically provided for in the Internal Revenue Code.

Numerous District Courts are located throughout the United States. In these courts, the taxpayer may have a jury make a determination of factual issues and the judge decide the questions of law. In tax matters, however, the usual procedure is to have the court decide both questions of fact and law. Judges in the U.S. District Courts hear and decide all manner of legal questions, not just questions related to the Internal Revenue Code. District Court decisions are reported in the *Federal Supplement,* commonly cited— F.Supp.—.

Appeals from decisions of the District Courts are the same as from the Tax Court—first to the Circuit Courts of Appeal and then, if *certiorari* is granted, to the Supreme Court. If at the end of the process, the taxpayer's claim for refund is allowed, the government pays the taxpayer interest computed from the date of the overpayment.

CLAIMS COURT ROUTE   Taxpayers may also bring suits for taxes collected illegally in the Claims Court. This court holds proceedings nationwide, and it specializes in suits against the government. Appeals from Claims Court decisions are made first to the Court of Appeals for the Federal Circuit and then, possibly, to the Supreme Court. Decisions of the Claims Court are published in the *U.S. Claims Court Reports,* typically cited—Cl.Ct.—. Cases heard before the Court of Appeals for the Federal District appear, along with the cases of the U.S. Circuit Courts of Appeals, in the *Federal Reporter, Second Series,* cited —F.2d—.

Identifying Court Decisions

A record of most judicial interpretations is—like an administrative interpretation by the Treasury Department or the I.R.S.—published and made available to the general public. The common form of citation for any judicial proceeding consists of two sets of numbers and one set of letters, as follows:

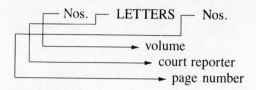

The first set of numbers refers to the volume number of a particular reporter series. The letters tell you which reporter series is cited. Finally, the last set of numbers *usually* refers to the exact page number on which that particular judicial interpretation may be located. For example,

54 AFTR 2d 310

refers to

1. Volume 54 of
2. The American Federal Tax Reporter, second series
3. At page 310

Immediately preceding such a citation is ordinarily the "name" of the case. Additional information—such as the court and, possibly, the year in which the opinion was rendered—follows the citation. Thus, for example, you might see the following citation:

Tax Students, Inc. v. *Comm'r. of Internal Revenue,* 54 AFTR 2d 310 (CA-5, 1980).

This fictitious citation refers to litigation between a corporation titled Tax Students and the Commissioner of the Internal Revenue Service; the decision in the case could be found at page 310 of the 54th volume of the American Federal Tax Reporter (second series). The opinion found there would be that of the Fifth Circuit Court of Appeals, an opinion rendered in 1980. Since the adversaries in all cases dealing with tax matters are taxpayers and the government, the names of cases are commonly shortened to include only the taxpayers' names.

   Many commercially competitive court reporter series are published. The ones that you are most likely to encounter in researching a tax problem are summarized in Table 24-2. A good deal of overlap exists among the various court reporters, and each has unique features too numerous to mention or explain here.[7] In general, however, you may use any one of the court reporters in basic tax research. Use whatever is available in your library.

[7]For additional details, see Ray M. Sommerfeld and G. Fred Streuling, *Tax Research Techniques,* 2d ed. (AICPA Tax Study No. 5), New York: American Institute of Certified Public Accountants, 1981, Chap. 4.

TABLE 24-2

PUBLICATION SUMMARY OF COURT DECISIONS

Courts		Publisher	Title	Citations
Tax Court				
Regular Decisions:				
1924–1942	P[a]	GPO	U.S. Board of Tax Appeals Reports	*Nellie G. Dodge,* 40 BTA 209 (1939)
1943–present	P	GPO	Tax Court of U.S. Reports[b]	*Lester Crown,* 67 TC 1060 (1977)
Memorandum Decisions:				
1924–1942	P	P–H	P-H BTA Memorandum Decisions	*R. Olsen,* 38 BTA 1531, Dock 86970 (Memo) Aug. 16, 1938, 1938 P–H ¶ 6.413
1943–present	P	P–H	P-H TC Memorandum Decisions	*John C. Kenny,* 1966, P–H TC Memo 66-1027
1942–present	P	CCH	Tax Court Memorandum Decisions	*John C. Kenny,* 25 TCM 913 (1966)
District Court				
1924–1932	P	West	Federal Reporter 2nd	*Obispo Oil Co.* v. *Welch,* 48 F.2d 872 (DC Cal., 1931)
1932–present	P	West	Federal Supplement	*Armstrong* v. *O'Connell,* 451 F.Supp 817 (DC Wisc., 1978)
1900–present	S	P–H	American Federal Tax Reports	*Nickerson* v. *Gilbert,* 42 AFTR2d 78-5886 (DC RI, 1978)
1913–present	S	CCH	United States Tax Cases	*Nick* v. *Dunlap,* 50-2 USTC ¶ 9436 *(DC Tex., 1950)*
Claims Court[c]				
1982–present	P	West	U.S. Claims Court Reports	*Raphan* v. *U.S.,* 3 Cl.Ct. 457 (1983)
1982–present	S	P–H	American Federal Tax Reports 2nd	*Raphan* v. *U.S.,* 52 AFTR2d 83-5984 (Cl.Ct., 1983)
1982–present	S	CCH	United States Tax Cases	*Raphan* v. *U.S.,* 83-2 USTC ¶ 9613 (Cl.Ct., 1983)
Circuit Court of Appeals[d]				
1900–present	P	West	Federal Reporter 2nd	*Vishnevsky* v. *U.S.,* 581 F.2d 1249 (CA-7, 1978)
1900–present	S	P–H	American Federal Tax Reports 2nd	*Vishnevsky* v. *U.S.,* 42 AFTR2d 78-5681 (CA-7, 1978)
1913–present	S	CCH	United States Tax Cases	*Vishnevsky* v. *U.S.,* 78-2 USTC ¶ 9640 (CA-7, 1978)
Supreme Court				
1900–present	P	West	Supreme Court Reporter	*Commr.* v. *Kowalski,* 984 S.Ct. 315 (1977)
1900–present	P	GPO	United States Reports	*Commr.* v. *Kowalski,* 434 US 77 (1977)
1900–present	S	P–H	American Federal Tax Reports 2nd	*Commr.* v. *Kowalski,* 40 AFTR2d 78-5681 (S.Ct., 1977)
1913–present	S	CCH	United States Tax Cases	*Commr.* v. *Kowalski,* 77–2 USTC ¶ 9748 (S.Ct., 1977)

[a]"P" = Primary Citation; "S" = Secondary Citation.
[b]After 1969, "Tax Court of the U.S. Reports" is referred to as "United States Tax Court Reports."
[c]In 1982, the predecessor Court of Claims was merged into the new U.S. Court of Appeals for the Federal District. In its place the Claims Court was created. Cases of the old Court of Claims can be found in the following services:
    F. Supp (West) 1932–60
    F.2d (West) 1929–32; 1960–82
    AFTR2d (P–H) 1900–82
    USTC (CCH) 1913–82
[d]Includes since 1982 the new U.S. Court of Appeals for the Federal District.

Rather than deciding which court reporter to use, your first big problem is more likely to be locating an appropriate citation to a pertinent administrative or judicial interpretation of the Code.

Locating Court Decisions

The researcher frequently relies on a citator to locate pertinent judicial authority. A citator is a reference that directs a researcher to the appropriate judicial reporter service in which a particular case can be located. The most important function of a citator, however, is to identify subsequent cases that are related with respect to facts and issues to the primary case.

Three major citator services are available. Shepard's Citations, Inc., publishes a comprehensive legal citator that references all federal and state cases, tax and nontax alike. Consisting of numerous volumes requiring extensive space, *Shepard's Citations* is not found in the typical tax library. Both CCH and P-H publish citator services that focus entirely on tax cases. The CCH edition is a two-volume, loose-leaf service that contains case names in alphabetical order. The judicial history of each case is shown, including the court of original jurisdiction and subsequent appeals. In addition, most subsequent cases in which the original case was cited are listed after that specific case. The CCH citator does not, however, communicate the disposition of the subsequent cases. If a later case deals with an issue considered in the original case, the researcher must actually read the later case to determine whether or not the subsequent case followed the former case, overruled the former case, or was distinguished from the former case.

The P-H citator consists of four bound volumes and two loose-leaf binders. Each volume covers a specific period of time. The two most recent volumes, the loose-leaf, cover cases handed down from 1978 to the present. Thus, the judicial history of relatively current cases (those handed down after 1977) can be determined by referring only to the current volume. The judicial history of cases that were adjudicated before 1942, however, requires an examination in each of the six volumes, because Volume 1 covers all citations made during the period 1796 to 1941, Volume 2 covers citations from 1942 to 1948, and so on. For example, a case decided in 1948 will initially be cited in Volume 2. Subsequent developments regarding the case—such as appeals to a higher court, use as precedent in a new case, or a new case with similar facts for which a court renders an opposing opinion and effectively overrules the original case—will be located in subsequent volumes of the citator. Disclosure of each case citation is similar to that found in the CCH citator with two major exceptions. Case citations of subsequent cases in the P-H citator disclose whether they followed, overruled, or modified the original case or issue. In addition, subsequent cases in which the original case is cited are listed in order of specific issues enumerated in the original case. Consequently, even though the CCH citator is more convenient to work with, the P-H citator provides more complete information pertaining to a particular case.

TABLE **24-3**

LIST OF MAJOR TAX SERVICE PUBLICATIONS

Title of Service	Publisher	Organization According to—	Arrangement of Content
Federal Taxes	Prentice-Hall	Code Section	Code Section, Regs., Editorials, Synopsis of Cases & Rev. Rul.
Mertens Law of Federal Income Taxation	Callaghan & Co.	Topic	Editorial treatise with footnotes
Rabkin & Johnson, Federal Income, Gift & Estate Taxation	Matthew Bender & Co.	Code Section	Editorial discussion with references in body of text
Standard Federal Tax Reporter	Commerce Clearing House, Inc.	Code Section	Code Section, Regs., Editorials, Synopsis of Cases & Rev. Rul.
Tax Coordinator 2d	Research Institute of America	Topic	Editorial discussion with footnotes
Tax Management Portfolios	Bureau of National Affairs	Topic	Editorial discussion with footnotes

Editorial Sources

Several publishing companies have created tax services that conveniently assemble, in one set of reference works, the necessary research materials relating to a specific tax topic. Table 24-3 identifies the most popular services currently available.

All the tax services mentioned in Table 24-3 are published in a loose-leaf format. Source materials are found in each service either through a topical index or by reference to a Code section. Learning to use the index of a particular service is the key to using it effectively. A good tax library necessarily includes more than one tax service and possibly contains all available services. Because each service may emphasize a different facet of a particular tax law and each service has a unique indexing system, a researcher should check a tax problem through several services to ensure that he or she has located and defined all aspects of a defensible position.

Other potential editorial sources for locating answers to tax research problems are books, magazines, and newsletters. One example of a widely respected treatise is Bittker and Eustice's *Federal Income Taxation of Corporations and Shareholders,* published by Warren, Gorham & Lamont. Numerous other reference works can be found in any tax library.

Tax magazines (for example, *The Journal of Taxation, The Tax Adviser, TAXES—The Tax Magazine, Taxation for Accountants*)—as well as various law journals are an excellent source of discussion on current tax topics that can assist a researcher in finding a solution to a difficult tax issue. Most tax professionals personally subscribe to one or more of these journals; all of them are standard items in a good tax library.

A number of tax newsletters are also published on a monthly, biweekly, weekly, and even daily basis. For instance, both CCH and P-H provide weekly updates titled *Taxes on Parade* and *Accountant's Weekly Report,* respectively. Because tax advisors work in a dynamic field, newsletters are an important means of keeping informed of recent developments at the congressional, administrative, and judicial levels.

Computer-Assisted Research

Since computers have the ability to store large quantities of information and to retrieve such information quickly, it is not surprising that their capability has been utilized to assist tax advisors with their research. Two companies, Mead Data Central, Inc., and West Publishing Company, are marketing their computer libraries under the brand names LEXIS and WESTLAW respectively. Both libraries contain all types of statutory, administrative, judicial, and editorial source documents. Since these legal libraries are not limited to tax-related materials, they are especially popular with attorneys. However, large CPA firms also subscribe to LEXIS for most of their major offices. Computer libraries, such as LEXIS and WESTLAW, are still relatively expensive to use. Therefore, many CPA firms limit access to LEXIS in each office to a few designated experts.

Commerce Clearing House (CCH) and Prentice Hall (P-H) have also begun to market their respective tax services as a computer library. CCH uses the title CCH ACCESS, while P-H markets its product under the name PHINET. Since this is an introductory tax course, it is not practical to give an in-depth explanation of each computer library. Suffice it to say that to efficiently utilize the computer to do tax research, one must first become a proficient manual researcher. Only then will it become cost efficient to use the computer.

INTERPRETING AND ASSESSING POTENTIAL AUTHORITY

In searching for a defensible solution to a tax problem, the researcher must keep in mind that the primary authority ordinarily consists of the tax statute—the Internal Revenue Code of 1986 as amended. Frequently, however, the specific problem with which the researcher is wrestling is not explicitly addressed in the Code. Consequently, the next line of authority to be considered might be the Treasury Regulations. Yet, as students soon discover, even the regulations are limited in many respects when explaining the application of the law. Another step in seeking a solution is to consider Revenue Rulings or Revenue Procedures. If the researcher is unable to locate a ruling or procedure that is "on all fours" (that is, identical with the given facts), potential judicial authority might be investigated. Note that the sequence suggested here agrees with the format found in both the CCH and

P-H tax services; that is, statute first, regulations next, and other administrative and judicial authority last.

Consideration of judicial decisions should include a review of the court that rendered the decision, the year in which the decision was rendered, and subsequent cases on similar facts. Because Supreme Court decisions cannot be appealed further, they are final authority and may even hold that the statute and regulations are unconstitutional. A decision by one of the circuit courts of appeals is controlling only in that respective circuit. That is, neither the I.R.S. nor the Tax Court is obliged to follow a fifth circuit decision in a ninth circuit dispute. Any taxpayer may attempt to take a position contrary to that rendered by a circuit court in a circuit in which he or she does not reside. Obviously, however, the risks are high that in the event of litigation, the local circuit court may follow its sister court. A similar philosophy applies to district court decisions. No general application of a district court decision is required outside its immediate jurisdiction. Claims court decisions are hard to assess; unless a conflicting decision by one or more of the circuit courts exists, however, a request to the Supreme Court for *certiorari* is not likely to be granted. Thus, a Claims Court decision may constitute a final authority—at least for the taxpayer involved in that litigation.

Tax Court decisions have general application. The commissioner, through his acquiescence policy, however, has taken the liberty of putting taxpayers on notice that he will either follow a decision or take a hard-line position in opposing a Tax Court decision. A Tax Court case to which the commissioner has not publicly announced an acquiescence or nonacquiescence is nevertheless an important precedent. The Tax Court is not required to universally follow a circuit court decision that overturned an earlier Tax Court decision. The Tax Court has held in *Jack E. Golsen,* 54 TC 742 (1970), however, that it will consider itself bound by a circuit court decision, *but only for other cases litigated in that particular circuit.*

A formal citation to a judicial decision should specify the year in which the case was litigated. The age of a case may signal to the researcher that the authority may be outdated. In a few instances, however, older cases have become benchmark decisions, and such cases have unusually strong precedential authority. One can usually detect the importance of a case by noting how often it has been cited in subsequent decisions. (The CCH citator can furnish such information to the researcher at a glance.) As indicated earlier, it is also essential to trace a case through a citator to ensure that subsequent court decisions did not overturn the law on which the researcher intends to rely.

On relatively rare occasions, a tax researcher may encounter a situation for which he or she is absolutely unable to locate any applicable authority. In such cases, authority from a set of related but not identical facts may be used. For example, a Tax Court decision or revenue ruling dealing with the valuation process of stock in a closely held corporation may help to determine the value of a partnership interest. Without any authority, a researcher may need to apply creativity or some logical methodology from another related field, such as accounting. In this way, if the I.R.S. accepts the treatment, new authority may be created.

Another obstacle may be encountered when the researcher finds conflicting authority. This can happen in the form of disagreements between courts or between the courts and the I.R.S. Disagreements between courts are usually resolved in favor of the conclusion rendered by the court of highest authority. Conflicting decisions between the Tax Court and a district court, between two district courts, or between the Tax Court and a circuit court of appeals must be considered temporary authority. In those instances there is a high probability of further litigation on similar facts that will be appealed to a higher court for clarification. The risk of receiving an adverse decision, therefore, is higher than normal.

Finally, a researcher may be faced with a situation such as the two cases dealing with casualty losses that resulted in opposing judicial opinions that we presented earlier in this chapter. Because the law pertaining to casualty losses is well established, the divergent opinions resulted from a difference in the underlying facts. Thus, if the law is specific and clear but the facts are uncertain or unsubstantiated, the tax advisor must do everything possible to bring order to whatever factual information is available. The researcher must be careful, however, that in a desire to create a favorable situation for a client, he or she does not modify any existing facts. Facts can only be changed in a planning situation, that is, before they occur. Changing facts after an event has occurred could constitute fraud. Thus, the advisor must try to clarify and substantiate facts through verifiable evidence such as testimony, pictures, appraisals, and so on.

PROBLEMS

1. As defined in Chapter 24, tax research involves a sequence of five steps. List them in order.

2. Research in connection with tax planning is frequently referred to as before-the-fact research. Explain what is meant by tax planning and contrast it with after-the-fact research.

3. a. Locate and read the two cases cited below. How to locate tax court cases and the format of judicial citations is discussed in detail on pages 24-19 to 24-21. Table 24-2 (page 24-22) should also be helpful.
   Robert N. Hewitt, 16 TCM 468, TC Memo 1957–112.
   John Thomas Blake, 29 TCM 513, TC Memo 1970–117.
   b. Enumerate, in outline form, the important facts of each case.
   c. Suggest, in outline form, the facts that you feel most influenced the judges to reach opposite conclusions in the two cases.

4. a. Locate and read the two cases cited below:
   FS Services, Inc., 413 F.2d 548, 69-2 USTC ¶9539 (Ct.Cls., 1969).
   Dearborn Company, 444 F.2d 1145, 71-1 USTC ¶9478 (Ct.Cls., 1971).

  b. Enumerate, in outline form, the important facts of each case.
  c. Suggest, in outline form, those facts that you feel most influenced the judges to reach opposite conclusions in the two cases.

5. a. Locate and read the two cases cited below:
     Martha S. Cowarde, 35 TCM 1066, TC Memo 1976-246.
     C.E.R. Howard, 28 TCM 1435, TC Memo 1969-277.
  b. Enumerate, in outline form, the important facts related to casualty losses in each case.
  c. Suggest, in outline form, those facts that you feel most influenced the judges to reach opposite conclusions in the two cases.

6. On January 2, 19x1, Paul Daniels sold a parcel of land to John Pope. Paul acquired the parcel several years ago at a cost of $6,200. At the time of the acquisition, his intentions were to hold the land for appreciation. The city commission, however, recently voted to locate the new city dump adjacent to his property. Fortunately, Paul heard that John, who operates a scavenger and antique business, was searching for a piece of land near the new dump site. Paul arranged the sale on an installment contract. The arrangement called for four $15,000 installment notes (noninterest bearing) due in consecutive years on the last day of the year. The first note is due on December 31, 19x1. In connection with the filing of Paul Daniel's 19x1 tax return, what questions should be raised based on the foregoing facts? Do not search for solutions at this time. Just enumerate those issues that you feel require further investigation.

7. A CPA firm reimburses its employees for expenses related to educational pursuits that are either directly or indirectly related to the performance of their duties in the firm. As a result, two of its employees are working toward law degrees at two different institutions. Tom Layton is enrolled at Future State University and will graduate next year with a law degree. He plans to sit for the bar exam at that time but intends to remain with his present employer. Rick Simpson did not do well on the LSAT exam and, therefore, could not obtain acceptance at Future State. He enrolled at Night Tech College. The college is not accredited; consequently, Rick will not be able to sit for the bar exam. After graduation, however, he plans to look for a position as an assistant controller or controller and feels that the law degree will make him more marketable. Also, the firm wishes to further formalize the educational benefits program and plans to publish a pamphlet that will answer questions employees such as Tom and Rick may raise concerning the tax treatment of the educational benefits. What questions should be examined relative to the payments made by the CPA firm? Do not search for solutions at this time. Simply enumerate those issues you feel require further investigation.

8. Alice Mariyou is a junior at Golden West University, where she has been enrolled on a full-time basis since her freshman year. Alice is employed on a part-time basis by the student bookstore. According to the W-2 form issued by the bookstore, she earned gross wages of $3,400 for 19x1, which she used entirely for her own support. In November of 19x1 Alice married Tom Ready, a first-year law student. For 19x1 Tom earned $1,200 from a summer job. Tom and Alice filed a joint return and were refunded all income taxes withheld.

   Alice's parents have assisted with her educational expenses. In past years, however, Alice has usually earned more at the bookstore than the total amount furnished by her parents. For example, in 19x1 Alice's parents paid $800 toward tuition and $200 for books. Tom and Alice have moved into a one-bedroom apartment located within walking distance of campus. The monthly rent, including utilities, totals $300. Before her marriage, when school was in session, Alice lived in her sorority house. During the summer and on weekends, however, she usually stayed with her parents. Even now, Tom and Alice frequently visit Alice's parents on weekends. Alice's parents have stated that her former bedroom will always be available for them to use. Recently, someone inquired about the possibility of renting Alice's bedroom as a sleeping room and offered $100 per month. Although Alice's parents are not wealthy and could use the extra income at this time, the offer was declined. They are still smarting from the November wedding which cost a total of $2,400 (wedding dress, $280; flowers, $220; reception, $1,800; contribution to the minister, $100). Alice's parents feel that taking in a renter would jeopardize the visits from Tom and Alice, which they look forward to.

List all possible tax questions that come to mind for the tax year 19x1. Do not search for solutions at this time, but enumerate those issues that you feel require further investigation.

9. Earl and Ellice are married but have for various good reasons filed separate tax returns during the last five years. Recently, an early winter storm caused considerable damage to their personal residence. Earl paid all the expenses necessary to restore the property to its condition immediately before the casualty. The storm had been forecast by the National Weather Service, and Earl and Ellice had plenty of time to prepare for the onslaught. Despite all their preparations, however, the storm caused approximately $12,400 in damages, which were not covered by insurance. Earl and Ellice own their personal residence under state law as tenants by the entireties. You have been asked to prepare Earl and Ellice's separate returns for the current year. List the tax questions that you feel warrant research. Do not search for solutions at this time. Just enumerate those issues that you feel require further investigation.

10. Indicate whether each of the following statements is true (T) or false (F). If you feel the statement is false, explain why it is false.

   a. Tax proposals for consideration by Congress may be introduced in either the House or Senate.
   b. The House Ways and Means Committee and the Senate Finance Committee hold separate hearings on the same proposed tax bill.
   c. Committee Reports are the only general source from which interested parties can obtain an understanding of the underlying reasons for passage of a particular tax provision.
   d. Amendments to a tax bill, made during the bill's debate on the floor of either the House or Senate, are reported in the Congressional Committee Reports.
   e. Treasury Regulations are published by the Treasury Department to assist taxpayers with a general interpretation of the Internal Revenue Code.
   f. Since passage of the Sixteenth Amendment, Congress has passed only two Internal Revenue Codes. The most recent Code is known as the Internal Revenue Code of 1954.
   g. Revenue Rulings are issued regularly by the I.R.S. Taxpayers may rely on rulings when their fact situations are identical with those mentioned in the published rulings.
   h. Revenue Rulings are similar to Revenue Procedures except that rulings apply to income tax issues while procedures apply to gift and estate tax issues.
   i. Private letter rulings issued to taxpayers by the I.R.S. are published by commercial publishers like CCH and P-H. They have no precedential value,

however, other than for the taxpayer by whom the ruling was requested and only for the identical fact situation mentioned in the ruling request.

j. If a taxpayer cannot reach an agreement through the normal appeals process with the I.R.S. over a tax issue, he or she must pay the contested tax liability. The taxpayer may then file suit in the United States Tax Court and request a refund.

k. Decisions rendered by the United States Tax Court are published by CCH in a publication titled *U.S. Tax Cases.*

l. The I.R.S. publishes Revenue Rulings and Revenue Procedures in a weekly publication titled *Internal Revenue Bulletin.* The weekly bulletins are then compiled in an annual publication of two to three volumes under the title *Cumulative Bulletin.*

m. The Tax Court issues both regular and memorandum decisions. Only the regular decisions are published, however, while *memorandum* decisions are only informally announced to interested parties. Memorandum decisions therefore have no precedential value.

n. A number of commercial publishers produce tax services that are a helpful tool to tax professionals.

o. Each publisher uses a unique system of organizing the various tax resource materials. Consequently, most tax professionals subscribe to that one tax service with which they can most readily identify. Subscription to more than one tax service is an unnecessary expense that most tax professionals can ill afford.

p. The I.R.S. is required by law to comply with decisions handed down by the Tax Court and to dispose of subsequent fact situations by other taxpayers in the same manner.

q. Decisions by the Tax Court can be appealed by either the taxpayer or the I.R.S. to a Circuit Court of Appeals.

r. *The Journal of Taxation* is a highly respected tax magazine read by most competent tax professionals.

s. Most tax services are updated weekly. It is therefore a waste of money to subscribe to any of the many tax newsletters available on a weekly, biweekly, or monthly basis.

t. The sign of a true professional is her desire to keep up to date with knowledge developed in her field. It is therefore understood that a tax advisor must maintain her professional competence by being aware of new developments and changes in the law that may be of importance to clients even if it means that she has to do it on her own time.

11. Visit your campus library and determine which of the following publications it includes:
    a. Standard Federal Tax Reporter (CCH)
    b. Federal Taxes (P-H)
    c. Law of Federal Income Taxation (Mertens)
    d. Tax Management Portfolios (BNA)
    e. United States Tax Court Reports (GPO)
    f. United States Tax Cases (CCH)
    g. The American Federal Tax Reports (P-H)
    h. Prentice-Hall T.C. Memorandum Decisions (P-H)
    i. Tax Court Memorandum Decisions (CCH)
    j. Cumulative Bulletin (GPO)

12. Locate the case cited at 77-2 USTC ¶9536.
    a. What court heard the case?
    b. Name the judge who issued the opinion.
    c. How many issues were enumerated in this case?
    d. Can you give a primary citation for the case?

13. Locate Volume 67 of the *Tax Court of the United States Reports* (TC).
    a. What is the time period covered by this volume?
    b. How many regular judges served on the Tax Court for the period covered by Volume 67?
    c. List the various indexes found in Volume 67.
    d. Locate the case cited at 67 TC 352 and indicate how many issues were presented in the case.

14. Locate *1976-1 Internal Revenue Cumulative Bulletin (CB)*.
    a. What time period is covered by Volume 1?
    b. What do you find on page 1?
    c. What items are printed in Part I of the bulletin?
    d. In what order are the items presented in Part I?
    e. What items are printed in Part II?
    f. What items are printed in Part III?

15. Locate the case cited at 28 AFTR2d 71-5676.
    a. What court heard the case?
    b. List the judge(s) who heard the case.
    c. Who wrote the opinion?
    d. Name the court of original jurisdiction.
    e. What is the primary citation for this case?
    f. Where did you find the primary citation?
    g. Write the complete citation to a CCH publication in which the same case is located.

16. Locate the *Tax Management Portfolios* (BNA) in your library.
    a. Examine Volume 274 and list the title of the portfolio.
    b. Examine Volume 5 and list the title of the portfolio.
    c. Examine Volume 132 and list the title of the portfolio.
    d. Notice that a different color ink was used for the title of each of the portfolios you examined. Of what significance are the following colors?
       (1) Red
       (2) Black
       (3) Green
    e. Each portfolio is organized in three main sections. List the three sections.
    f. How can the researcher find material in the respective portfolios?

17. Locate Prentice-Hall's *Federal Taxes* and Commerce Clearing House's *Standard Federal Tax Reporter*. Then for each tax service, answer the following questions:
    a. In which volume is the index located?
    b. Is the index arranged by topic or Code section?
    c. If all you have is a Code section, how do you locate additional material?
    d. Each service has a volume designated as New Matters. What does it contain?
    e. Each service uses tabs to facilitate indexing. How is the material between the tabs organized?

18. Locate Merten's Law of Federal Income Taxation in your library.
    a. Which volume contains the index?

    b. Is the index arranged by Code section or topic?

    c. Can access be obtained to the treatise volumes if the researcher only knows a Code section?

    d. Examine the loose-leaf "Rulings" volume and indicate what is found under the tab designated "Code-Rulings Table."

    e. What type of information is available under the tab designated "Rulings Status Table"?

    f. Examine one of the treatise volumes. In what form is the material in the volumes presented?

    g. Can you locate the complete text of the Internal Revenue Code of 1986 in any of the treatise volumes or in one of the other volumes?

19. In your library locate the bound volumes that contain the Tax Court Memorandum Decisions.

    a. Indicate the publisher of the service in your library:

        (1) CCH

        (2) P-H

        (3) Both

    Answer the remaining questions with respect to either the CCH or P-H publication and indicate which publication you used.

    b. How are Tax Court Memorandum Decisions cited?

    c. What time period is covered by Volume 35?

    d. In what order are the cases presented in each volume?

CHAPTER 25

Tax Research: Communicating the Results

Not only do we live in a world of communication (or overcommunication) but more and more we find that the quality of the communication plays a vital role in our evaluation of the communicator.

As a result, we sometimes hire the best communicator rather than the best accountant, the best communicator rather than the best engineer, the best communicator rather than the best manager, and perhaps even the best communicator rather than the best statesman!

Norman B. Sigband, *Communication for Management and Business,* 1982.

Knowledge can benefit society only if it is properly communicated. This fact is particularly critical for persons engaged in a service profession. For example, the most competent physician will never build more than a mediocre practice unless he or she learns to communicate with patients. Similarly, a tax researcher has gained little after locating a defensible answer to a research problem unless the conclusion can be communicated to associates, clients, and the I.R.S.

Communication, of course, consists of both verbal and written forms of disseminating information. In this chapter, we limit ourselves to the methodology employed by tax professionals as they convey in writing the facts and conclusions of their tax research.

THE CLIENT FILE

Law firms and CPA firms typically maintain files on their clients in which they retain copies of correspondence, selected documents, and possibly tax returns. In some instances, tax returns are kept in annual files, while other documents—such as articles of incorporation, partnership agreements, and special research projects—are retained in a master file spanning a number of years. Regardless of the system employed, client files are an important source for storing and disseminating information.

The starting point for a tax research project is a set of facts. A tax researcher may receive the necessary facts directly from the client or through a superior. If the information is obtained orally, the researcher should prepare a memo setting forth his or her understanding of the facts and place that memo in the client file. Of course, information obtained in written form, either from a superior or directly from the client, is also filed in the client file. Additional communications elaborating or clarifying existing information are retained in the same manner.

As a researcher begins the task of locating authority for the pertinent questions identified from the facts, copies of relevant source material—Code sections, regulations, judicial decisions, and revenue rulings—are systematically arranged by issue in the client file. The process of organizing the pertinent materials is demonstrated at the end of this chapter and will prove helpful in solving research problems.

When the researcher has reached a defensible solution to a research problem, that conclusion is usually communicated via an office memorandum to the researcher's superior or superiors or to a colleague who has authority for review and approval. Frequently, a partner or manager may request that all pertinent information be set forth in the form of a draft client letter (or protest letter to the I.R.S.). These letters also become part of the client file.

A properly maintained client file is extremely important to a smoothly operating tax practice. The file should be systematically indexed and cross-referenced, as illustrated at the end of this chapter, to allow the reviewing authority to move quickly through the material. The old adage "time is money" is especially true for the tax professional. In preparing a client file, therefore, the researcher must leave sufficient tracks so that persons who follow can easily understand the methodology employed and line of reasoning pursued.

In addition to facilitating the reviewing process, a client file is important for subsequent I.R.S. audits, which usually occur several years after the research was performed. At that time, the client research file becomes a significant source of information for purposes of recalling the authority used in support of the position taken on the tax return under audit.

Because staff assignments in both CPA and law firms change frequently due to promotion and personnel turnover, a client file is an important source of information for the newly assigned staff person. The file reveals all prior research performed and the authority on which conclusions were based. Without a good client file, each new staff person would have to repeat much of the work previously performed in order to be comfortable with the treatment of certain transactions on a current tax return. A client file can also save significant time when another client of the same office of the same firm presents a fact situation similar to one already researched for another client.

THE CLIENT LETTER

A tax advisor can sell only time and expertise. Clients frequently measure the quality of the service they receive on the basis of a tangible end product. In connection with a tax compliance engagement, such a product may constitute the completed tax return and possibly the amount of additional tax the client must pay (or the size of the refund the client will receive). In tax planning engagements, the end product is usually a conference and a letter to the client summarizing the research undertaken. Thus, because the client letter is the product for which the client is billed, it should be representative of the effort expended.

The style of a client letter will vary from firm to firm. Some firms believe that the contents of a client letter should depend on the degree of the client's sophistication in the field of taxation or law. Other firms feel that the letter should contain considerable detail—including citations to appropriate Code sections, regulations, court decisions, and revenue rulings—regardless of the client's expertise, in order to demonstrate the degree of research performed. Some firms prepare two letters: one letter spells out the technical detail of the research findings, complete with citations, and the second serves as a transmittal letter, conveying in layperson's terms the gist of the research findings and recommendations.

The reasons for preparing both a technical and a transmittal letter may be twofold. First, if a firm espouses the philosophy that a client letter should be written with the technical expertise of the client in mind, more often than not it becomes a document that deals in generalities rather than specific technical details. If the research conclusions are subsequently challenged by an I.R.S. audit, a technical letter containing the basis for the conclusion will serve to substantiate the original advice given. In a more serious situation, such as a potential lawsuit from a client who claims that the tax advisor gave erroneous advice, a technical letter may be the only evidence the tax advisor has to protect his or her reputation. A second reason for preparing two separate letters is that client letters have a tendency of falling into the wrong hands at the wrong time. If a client letter is examined during an I.R.S. audit, the agent has the advantage of preparing a case based on the specific authority set forth in the client letter. Consequently, some firms feel that the technical letter should be kept in the client file in the tax advisor's vault. If a firm sends both the transmittal and technical letter to the client, the tax advisor may request that the client return or destroy the technical letter.[1]

Every client letter should follow a specific format. The letter should include a restatement of the facts on which the research was based. Applicable facts should be accompanied by a disclaimer similar to the following:

> The conclusions reached in our research are based on the above facts. If these facts are incorrect or incomplete, no matter how insignificant they may appear to you, please bring it to our attention immediately, because different facts may require a different conclusion.

The foregoing statement is appropriate in conjunction with an "after-the-fact" engagement. In a planning engagement, the wording may cover the following points:

> The conclusions reached in our research are based on the above facts. It is, therefore, important that you implement the tax plan exactly as stated. Any deviation from the suggested plan, no matter how insignificant it may appear to you, may jeopardize the result. In addition, future changes in the tax law may also adversely affect our conclusion.

After a concise restatement of facts and the appropriate disclaimer, the client letter should enumerate the various issues that were examined. Conclusions are then presented. The letter may end with a summary, which can range from a brief statement to a detailed discussion, setting forth reasons and authorities on which the conclusions are based (see Figure 25-2).

PROTEST LETTERS, DETERMINATION LETTERS, AND REQUESTS FOR RULINGS

A considerable portion of the services rendered by a tax advisor consists of the settlement of disagreements between taxpayers and the I.R.S. The tax laws are replete with areas of uncertainty, which frequently result in divergent interpretations. If a revenue agent, as a result of an audit, makes a deficiency assessment to which the taxpayer and the advisor take exception, in most cases a written protest must be prepared. The format of a *protest letter* is similar to that of a technical client letter. The protest should contain an accurate summary of the facts and an enumeration of the issues contested. In addition, the protest should set forth the reasons why the taxpayer is taking issue with the revenue agent's report (RAR) as well as the authority on which the taxpayer relies.

---

[1]Tax accountants, unlike attorneys, are not protected by privileged communication. Thus, the I.R.S. may issue a summons for specific documents in the possession of the accountant that are pertinent to an examination. Sometimes, however, a district court judge will not enforce the I.R.S. summons unless serious violations on the part of the client are suspected.

A *determination letter* is a request for technical advice on an issue raised by a revenue agent during an audit. The taxpayer and the revenue agent may seek advice from the national I.R.S. office with respect to a specific issue for which little or no authority is available. Again, the format of a determination letter varies little from that of a technical client letter or a protest letter. It will contain facts, issues or points of disagreement, authoritative discussion, and tentative conclusions reached by the opposing parties.

Both the protest letter and the determination letter result from after-the-fact situations. Frequently, however, a taxpayer wishes to understand the full impact of potential tax considerations before the events have occurred. In such a case, the taxpayer—through a tax advisor—may request an advance ruling from the I.R.S. A request for an advance ruling sets forth all the facts and circumstances surrounding the proposed transaction, the possible issues for which additional advice is needed, the tentative conclusion the client or the advisor has reached, and the appropriate supporting authority. It can be seen that a ruling request resembles both a protest letter and a determination letter in format and content.

THE TAX RESEARCH FILE

In the remaining pages of this chapter, we present an example showing the general format of a client file. Certain features, such as the indexing, will vary from firm to firm. The general concept, however, should be universal in application. The importance of a well-organized client file cannot be overstated.

Since this text is designed for an introductory course, the example is, out of necessity, rather simple. Experienced tax advisors may know the solution to this problem example without further research, and the conclusion would likely be orally communicated. Nevertheless, it is quite possible that for a general practitioner, who does not limit his or her practice exclusively to taxation, this example case may represent a true challenge.

The fact situation we use in our example is that depicted in Chapter 24: Tim Wright has sold his family residence in San Antonio and moves to Houston. Notice that we are dealing with an after-the-fact situation, since the transaction has already been culminated. The facts of the case are restated below:

> *Example:* Tim Wright, age 46, lost his job in San Antonio, Texas, during the summer of 19X1. Despite considerable efforts on his part, he was unable to find employment in his accustomed salary range. He, therefore, expanded his search to other Texas cities and eventually accepted a new position in Houston. Since immediate attempts to sell his residence failed, Tim instructed his realtor to list the home as being for "sale or lease." He had purchased the home three years earlier for $72,000.
>
> In the meantime, Tim searched for housing in the Houston area. His new job kept him away from home during the week on a regular basis. Since Tim's wife did not enjoy yard work and would not perform even

minor maintenance work, they decided to purchase a condominium, which allowed them to obtain, for a fee, regular maintenance and yard care. They agreed with the seller on a price of $93,000 and occupied their new condominium on October 1, 19X1.

The former residence in San Antonio remained unsold but was finally leased in November 19X1. Throughout 19X2 the home remained leased, except for the month of December. A new lessee occupied the home in January 19X3, who also signed a 90-day option to purchase the home provided he could find suitable financing. The option was exercised in March 19X3, and final closing occurred on April 30, 19X3, for an adjusted sales price of $89,000.

The client file in this case contains a client letter, a memo to the file, a general summary of the tax research problem, and a detailed summary of the problem. An index to the file appears in Figure 25-1.

Note that the client letter, shown in Figure 25-2, contains a disclaimer before the restatement of facts. The memo to the file (Figure 25-3) records information received by telephone.

Figure 25-4 is the general summary of research questions, and Figure 25-5 is a detailed summary containing copies of and citations to relevant authoritative documents.

The detailed summary (Figure 25-5) should be assembled in successive steps as the researcher identifies issues and subissues and locates solutions to the issues raised. Producing the detailed summary entails a lot of cutting and pasting; that is, pertinent authority such as Code sections, regulations, revenue rulings, and court decisions are located, and selected segments are then xeroxed and pasted into the working papers. Subsequently, key words or phrases are highlighted to focus attention on their significance to the conclusion reached.

As mentioned in Chapter 5, the technique used to identify the important issues or questions for a tax problem cannot be taught in a textbook. To a large extent, the questions that you feel should be investigated will depend on your background and understanding of the tax statutes. Obviously, your ability to think analytically and creatively will play an important role in arriving at satisfactory solutions to a research problem. The example demonstrates some typical questions a researcher might raise and the sequence in which such questions should come to mind.

The pressures of a tax practice to complete the work in the least amount of time often tempts the researcher to take shortcuts, especially in the preparation of the client file. However, if an answer to a question had to be researched, the findings should be documented in the client file. For the experienced practitioner, the foregoing detail of documentation could perhaps be considered too idealistic. However, to a "rookie" the example demonstrates the proper approach to a tax question. Once the researcher becomes seasoned, he or she will intuitively ignore the more obvious issues, reduce the amount of cutting and pasting for the file, and adapt to the standard operating procedures for research files in his or her office.

FIGURE **25-1**

Tim Wright
Tax File
March 19X4

Index to Working Papers

Item	Page Ref.
Client Letter	I-1, I-2
Memo to File--Paul Advisor	I-3
General Summary--Tax Research Problem	A-1
Detailed Summary--Tax Research Problem	B-1 thru B-6

FIGURE **25-2**

PAUL ADVISOR & CO.
CERTIFIED PUBLIC ACCOUNTANTS
1313 High Rise Court
Professional City, USA 11111

March 25, 19X4

Mr. Tim Wright
1319 Arroyo Drive
Houston, TX 77000

Dear Mr. Wright:

This letter acknowledges our oral agreement of March 18, 19X4, to prepare
your 19X3 income tax returns and to investigate the tax implications of your
sale of the San Antonio residence and purchase of your Houston condominium.
Set forth in this letter are the results of the research we performed
concerning the sale and purchase of these residences.

Before stating the results of our investigation, I would like to restate
the important facts as we understand them. Please review them carefully.
If any of the following facts are incomplete or incorrect, please bring
it to my attention immediately, no matter how insignificant the difference
may appear to you.

In 19X1 you moved from San Antonio to Houston. You purchased as your
new residence in Houston a condominium on October 1, 19X1, for $93,000.
Immediate efforts to sell your home in San Antonio were unsuccessful.
Consequently, your realtor listed the home as being for sale or lease. With
the exception of a few months, the house was rented for the remainder of
19X1 and during 19X2. In January 19X3, a new lessee occupied the San
Antonio residence on a lease with a 90-day option to purchase the home. The
option was exercised in March 19X3, and final closing occurred on April 30,
19X3. The adjusted sales price totaled $89,000, which represented a
significant appreciation of the home for which you had paid $72,000 in 19W8.

Assuming that the foregoing facts are complete and accurate, we have
reached the following conclusion. The gain realized on the sale of your
San Antonio house will qualify for a tax-free rollover into your Houston
condominium. One basic condition--that the proceeds must be reinvested
within a time period beginning two years before and ending two years after
the sale of the old residence--has been satisfied. Another requirement,
that the cost of the new residence must equal or exceed the adjusted sales
price of the old residence, has also been met. In addition, our two major
areas of concern appear to favor a tax-free resolution. First, the I.R.S.
has ruled that a condominium does qualify as a legitimate replacement residence.
Finally, the fact that your San Antonio residence did not immediately sell
due to the exigencies of the real estate market and that, consequently,

I-1

FIGURE **25-2**   (continued)

Mr. Tim Wright
Page 2
March 25, 19X4

you leased the residence until a suitable buyer was found, has been addressed
on several occasions by the courts. Since the facts of your transaction
are similar to those of the most recently litigated case, we have concluded
that the I.R.S. will most likely not challenge your tax-free rollover.

    If you have additional questions, please contact me. As soon as your
19X3 tax returns are completed, I will contact you.

                    Sincerely,

                    Paul Advisor

PA:11

I-2

FIGURE **25-3**

PAUL ADVISOR & CO.
CERTIFIED PUBLIC ACCOUNTANTS
1313 High Rise Court
Professional City, USA 11111

March 19, 19X4

MEMO TO FILE

FROM: Paul Advisor

SUBJECT: Tim Wright--Sale of Personal Residence

    While gathering the necessary information for Mr. Wright's 19X3
tax returns, the following facts came to light regarding his 19X1 move
from San Antonio to Houston:

1. Mr. Wright did not sell his San Antonio residence until April 30, 19X3.
    From October 1, 19X1 to April 30, 19X3, the former residence was held for
    sale or lease and, with the exception of approximately two months,
    was actually leased during that time.

2. Mr. Wright's new residence was acquired on October 1, 19X1, for a total
    cost of $93,000.

3. Mr. Wright's former residence was sold on April 30, 19X3, for an
    adjusted sales price of $89,000.

4. Mr. Wright's new residence is a condominium located at 1319 Arroyo
    Drive, Houston, TX 77000.

    The transaction appears to qualify for the rollover treatment under
Section 1034. However, I am not altogether certain concerning a couple of
issues, which I mentioned to Mr. Wright. First, does a condominium qualify
for the rollover? Second, does the fact that the former residence was leased
until a buyer was finally found prevent the tax-free rollover? These issues
should be researched prior to the 19X3 return preparation. Since Mr. Wright
is anxious to know the results of our research, I have promised him a formal
letter which will convey our findings.

I-3

FIGURE **25-4**

Tim Wright
General Summary of Research Questions

March 19X4

W.P. Index

I. Does the sale of the San Antonio
    residence and the purchase of the
    Houston condominium qualify for
    the rollover provisions of
    Section 1034?

    Conclusion: Yes; Section 1034
    conditions are all met. In
    addition, the question of
    whether a condominium qualifies   B-1 thru B-6
    as a principal residence and
    whether a temporary rental of
    the former residence before
    sale disqualifies the
    transaction was also
    investigated and resolved
    in favor of Mr. Wright.

A-1

FIGURE 25-5

Tim Wright
Detailed Summary of Research Questions

March 19X4

W.P. Index

Question 1-1: Was a new residence acquired
within the statutory replacement
period?

Conclusion: Yes; see Section 1034(a) below:

(a) Nonrecognition of Gain.-- If property (in
this section called "old residence")
used by the taxpayer as his principal
residence is sold by him, and, within a
period beginning 2 years before the date
of such sale and ending 2 years after
such date, property (in this section
called "new residence") is purchased
and used by the taxpayer as his principal
residence, gain (if any) from such sale
shall be recognized only to the extent
that the taxpayer's adjusted sales
price (as defined in subsection (b)) of
the old residence exceeds the taxpayer's
cost of purchasing the new residence.

New home bought
10-1-X1

Old home sold
4-30-X3

w/in 2 yrs

Question 1-2: Were the proceeds from the sale of
the old residence reinvested in
accordance with the requirements
of Section 1034(a)?

Conclusion: Yes; see below:

Cost of condominium $93,000   *— Greater than*
                                     adjusted sales price

Adjusted sales price
of San Antonio
home $89,000

B-1

FIGURE **25-5** (continued)

Tim Wright
Detailed Summary of Research Questions

March 19X4

W.P. Index

Question 1-3:   *Does a condominium qualify under Section 1034(a) as a new principal residence?*

Conclusion: *Yes; see Rev. Rul. 64-31, 1964-1 CB 300*

In 1961, the taxpayer sold his principal residence at a gain. Within one year from the date of sale, he purchased and occupied an apartment in a so-called "condominium" apartment project. He received the legal title in fee simple to a one-family unit in a multi-unit structure coupled with ownership of an undivided interest in the land and all other parts of the structure held in common with the other owners of the individual units.

Condominium acquisition

The procedure for organizing the apartment project and conveying ownership in fee simple of the individual apartments was accomplished by (1) the execution and recording of a declaration that described the land comprising the entire project area, each apartment space, the land space and property owned in common, and the percentage of common elements pertaining to each apartment space, along with administrative regulations governing the relationship between the owners; (2) the recording of an apartment survey describing the various apartment spaces and identifying each apartment space by number; and (3) the execution and recording of individual deeds for each apartment space and the common elements pertaining thereto.

None of the administrative regulations contained in the declaration can deprive the taxpayer of his title to the apartment space and the rights in common attached to it. The taxpayer is free to sell or lease his apartment space at any price, subject only to the limitation that he give first option

Mr. Wright met this requirement

B-2

FIGURE **25-5**   (continued)

Tim Wright
Detailed Summary of Research Questions

March 19X4

W.P. Index

> to buy or lease on equal terms to the
> other owners.
>
> The taxpayer is liable to the local tax
> authority for the tax assessment with
> respect to his interest in the land and
> all other parts of the structure.
>
> *
>
> Based on the facts and circumstances
> presented, it is held that the taxpayer
> purchased a new residence, within the
> meaning of section 1034(a) of the Code,
> and is entitled to the relief provided
> for by section 1034(a) with respect to
> the gain from the sale of his old
> residence.

Mr. Wright met
this requirement.

I.R.S.
conclusion

Question 1-4:   *Does the temporary leasing of*
a personal residence before its
sale disqualify a former principal
residence from coverage under the
provisions of Section 1034?

Conclusion: *No; according to the most recent*
litigation of the issue,
temporary leasing will not
disqualify a former principal
residence. However, each case is
determined on its own facts and
circumstances. Mr. Wright's
facts seem to be similar to those
found in Clapham, *63 TC 46 (1975):*

> In determining whether a temporary rental deprives
> a home of its character as a principal residence
> Congress deliberately provided latitude to
> effectuate the remedial policy of the statute by
> making a determination depend on the "facts and
> circumstances" of each case. Petitioners
> habitually used their Mill Valley residence as
> their principal residence as required by the
> statute. The parties have stipulated that the

Note!

B-3

FIGURE **25-5** (continued)

Tim Wright
Detailed Summary of Research Questions

March 19X4

W.P. Index

petitioners had no plans for this former
residence other than to dispose of it as
soon as an offer was received; that they
received no offers to purchase the house
until the time of sale in 1969; that
financial circumstances dictated
acceptance of an offer to rent in the
spring of 1967 and again in the fall of
1968; and that the primary wish of
petitioners was to sell their old residence.
Additionally, the earlier lease included
an option to purchase and the property
was left vacant for substantial periods
in order to facilitate sales efforts
by the real estate broker with whom
petitioners had listed the property.

Same with Mr. Wright

We believe these rentals were necessitated
by the exigencies of the real estate
market, were ancillary to sales efforts,
and arise from petitioners' use of the
Mill Valley property as their principal
residence. The rental activities and
the sale of the property were precipitated
by the change in Mr. Clapham's employment
location that Congress viewed as an
"involuntary conversion" situation where
the need for relief is "especially
clear." In leasing the premises,
petitioners' dominant motive was to sell
the property at the earliest possible
date rather than to hold the property
for the realization of rental income.
Under the facts and circumstances here
present, the lease was therefore for a
temporary period contemplated by the
legislative history and the regulations,
and petitioners are entitled to the benefits
of section 1034.

Dicta of Court

Same with Mr. Wright

Conclusion

B-4

FIGURE **25-5**   (continued)

Tim Wright
Detailed Summary of Research Questions

March 19X4

W.P. Index

However, the courts have also ruled to the contrary in:

1. <u>Stolk</u>, 40 TC 345 (1963), acq., aff'd 326 F.2d 760(2nd Cir., 1964). The taxpayer was considered to have "abandoned" his former principal residence when he occupied a rented apartment during the week, returning to his former residence only on weekends.

2. <u>Houlette</u>, 48 TC 350 (1967). The taxpayer was deemed to have "abandoned" his former principal residence when he rented it for six years prior to sale.

Note, however, that the <u>Clapham</u> Court said about the two cases <u>cited</u> above:

Respondent misinterprets these cases. Both <u>Stolk</u> and <u>Houlette</u> make it clear that whether or not property is the principal residence of the taxpayer depends on all the facts and circumstances in each individual case.

See also Regs. 1.1034-1(c)(3)(i):

(3) Property used by the taxpayer as his principal residence. (i) <u>Whether or not property is used by the taxpayer as his residence, and whether or not property is used by the taxpayer as his principal residence (in the case of a taxpayer using more than one property as a residence), depends upon all the facts and circumstances in each case, including the good faith of the taxpayer</u>. The mere fact that property is, or has been, rented is not determinative that such property is not used by the taxpayer as his principal residence. For example, if

Supports Mr. Wright's decision

B-5

FIGURE **25-5**   (continued)

Tim Wright
Detailed Summary of Research Questions

March 19X4

W.P. Index

the taxpayer purchases his new residence
before he sells his old residence, the fact
that he temporarily rents out the new
residence during the period before he
vacates the old residence may not, in the
light of all the facts and circumstances in
the case, prevent the new residence from
being considered as property used by the
taxpayer as his principal residence.

B-6

SUMMARY

The product a tax advisor markets is his or her ability to reach conclusions relative to the tax laws based on a given set of facts. Research in connection with tax compliance, or after-the-facts research, is tax research that is initiated after the facts have transpired in order to sustain the proper treatment of an item on a tax return that is challenged as the result of an audit, for example. Tax research performed to determine how facts should transpire before they occur in order to achieve the most advantageous tax result is known as tax planning, or before-the-facts research.

To ensure that the conclusions reached by the tax advisor are defensible, he or she must learn to identify, based on a set of facts, the pertinent issues (or questions) and then locate and interpret relevant authority in support of the conclusion. However, the task is not complete until the findings and recommendations have been effectively communicated to the parties involved. Mastering the skills needed to efficiently perform the research steps—(1) gathering the facts, (2) identifying the relevant questions, (3) locating and interpreting the authority, (4) reaching a conclusion, and (5) communicating the results—can be fully appreciated only through experience in a tax library. It is critical, therefore, that you supplement your reading with considerable time in a tax library. Only in that way will the foregoing pages come to life.

PROBLEMS

1. Phillip Hardluck collects antique rugs and wall coverings. Many of his artifacts were acquired years ago at bargain prices and have since increased substantially in value. Recently, the drain-hose of his water softener became disconnected during the softening cycle, flooding both the utility room and Phil's study. As a result, a Chinese rug, constructed of paper cords, was partially immersed in water and completely destroyed. Phil bought the rug 15 years ago for $250. In two recent art shows, however, the rug was appraised by three independent experts at $2,250, $2,500, and $2,450, respectively.

   The loss is covered via a rider on Phil's homeowner's insurance policy, which is written for $200 deductible. Because Phil has already made three claims against his policy during the current calendar year, however, he has decided not to place the claim for the rug. Instead, he wants to deduct the loss on his federal income tax return. For this reason, he has contacted you to assist him in the interpretation of the appropriate casualty loss provisions.

   a. Identify the pertinent issue(s) to be researched.
   b. Compute the appropriate casualty loss deductions.
   c. Write a client letter to Mr. Hardluck in which you set forth the reasons for your conclusions reached in part b.
   d. Prepare a client file that contains the support necessary to substantiate your claim computed in part b.

2. You live in a state that has stiff usury laws. As is the case in most other states, however, corporations are not governed by usury laws. One of your clients, Richard Green, needs a loan for his partnership to develop a new line of business. Several banks are interested lenders but have requested that Green create a corporation for purposes of effecting the loan. One of the bank loan officers, who has a law degree, has suggested that if a corporation is formed to circumvent the usury laws, it will undoubtedly be considered a sham for tax purposes and thus losses sustained by the corporation will still be available as a pass-through to the individual partners.

    The creation of a straw corporation is a commonly used mechanism, and all parties, including the lender, are usually aware of the real intent of the scheme. The new business venture planned by Richard Green and his partners will produce losses for at least four years, and it is important to them that such losses can be offset against other partnership income. A significant portion of the early losses will be the interest expense on the loan.

  a. Identify the pertinent issue(s) to be researched.

  b. State your conclusion reached regarding the issue(s) identified above.

  c. Write a client letter to Richard Green in which you set forth the reasons for your conclusion reached in part b.

  d. Prepare a client file that contains the support necessary to substantiate your conclusion reached in part b.

3. Paul Schussbummer, your client, owns a ski cabin near the Sundance Ski Resort in the Utah Rockies. His permanent residence is in Dallas, Texas, where he is a top-level executive for a manufacturing company that is also your client. Paul and his family take annual skiing vacations in Utah.

    During the vacation, the Schussbummers reside exclusively in the ski cabin. Over the years, Paul has enjoyed the annual ski vacations except for one thing. Because the cabin is usually unoccupied for the remainder of the year, a considerable portion of the first week in Utah is wasted on repairs and maintenance to place the cabin into a livable condition. Recently, Paul talked to a cabin neighbor who explained that years ago he had transferred his cabin as a charitable gift to Brigham Young University. Now BYU maintains the cabin year round and uses the cabin for research projects and alumni guests. In addition, BYU guarantees the neighbor use of the cabin for thirty days each year and will not sell the cabin during his or his spouse's lifetime. Paul explained this scheme to his brother-in-law, currently attending law school, whose recollection from his income tax course seemed to be that a taxpayer cannot make a property gift of less than the entire interest. Paul's brother-in-law feels that a guarantee to use the cabin for a specified period of time during the year would constitute a remainder interest, which would disqualify the cabin as a charitable contribution. Paul contacts you for a clarification.

  a. Identify the pertinent issue(s) to be researched.

  b. State your conclusion reached regarding the issue(s) identified above.

  c. Write a client letter to Paul Schussbummer in which you set forth the reasons for your conclusions reached in part b.

  d. Prepare a client file that contains the support necessary to substantiate your conclusions reached in part b.

4. Reed and Susan Jamison were both previously married. Each brought separate property into their current marriage. At the present time, they are both employed in high-paying executive positions and file joint annual federal tax returns. During

19X1 Reed sold some of his separately owned stock to Susan. The broker's advice discloses the following information.

| | Date | | | Net |
Type	Acquired	Sold	Cost	sales price
100 Shares ABC common	12-15-U1	1-10-X1	$ 2,200	$ 1,000
2000 Shares XYZ common	6-13-U3	1-12-X1	11,600	32,800

To reduce the immediate tax liability, Reed decided to arrange the second transaction so that it would qualify as an installment sale. Susan has retained the stock from the first transaction but sold the XYZ stock on January 15, 19X1 for $32,900 and later deposited the proceeds in a real estate tax shelter. The agreement between Reed and Susan calls for the transfer of the annual cash flow from the real estate investment to Reed as payment for principal and interest on the installment contract. Reed projects that it will take approximately 10 years to complete the payments for the installment contract.

Because Susan did not buy into the real estate project until January 19X2, she made no payments to Reed until 19X2.

You have been asked to prepare Reed and Susan's joint return for 19X1.

a. Which issue(s) do you wish to examine in connection with the above transactions?

b. Compute the net capital gain or loss to be reported on the 19X1 joint return.

c. Write an office memorandum to the files in which you set forth the reasons for your conclusions reached in part b.

d. Prepare a client file in which you set forth the support necessary to substantiate your conclusions reached in part b.

5. Reacquaint yourself with the facts of Problem 7 in Chapter 24.
   a. Determine which issue(s) you wish to examine in connection with the facts of Problem 7.
   b. State your conclusions reached regarding the issue(s) identified in part a, above.
   c. Write a memo to the files in which you set forth the reasons for your conclusions reached in part b.
   d. Prepare a client file that contains the support necessary to substantiate your conclusions reached in part b.

6. Reacquaint yourself with the facts of Problem 8 in Chapter 24.
   a. Determine which issue(s) you wish to examine in connection with the facts of Problem 8.
   b. State your conclusion reached regarding the issue(s) identified in part a, above.
   c. Write a letter to Alice's parents in which you set forth the reasons for your conclusions reached in part b.
   d. Prepare a client file that contains the support necessary to substantiate your conclusions reached in part b, above.

7. Reacquaint yourself with the facts of Problem 9 in Chapter 24.
   a. Assuming the damage caused to the home qualifies as a legitimate casualty loss and that the I.R.S. will accept the $12,400 as a reasonable amount for the loss sustained, determine which issue(s) you wish to examine in connection with the facts of Problem 9.

b. State your conclusion reached regarding the issue(s) identified in part a, above.

c. Write a memo to the files in which you set forth the reasons for your conclusions reached in part b.

d. Prepare a client file that contains the support necessary to substantiate your conclusions reached in part b, above.

Appendixes

Appendix A:
1987 Tax Rate Schedules

INDIVIDUAL TAXPAYERS

Caution: For individual taxpayers earning a taxable income of $50,000 or less, the I.R.S. will (in December 1987) publish a series of "Tax Tables" that should be used to determine an actual tax liability for most persons for calendar-year 1987. Use of the tax rate schedules, below, will yield a tax liability very close to that determined by using the tax tables which will be available later this year.

Single Taxpayers

If taxable income is:

Over	But not over	The tax is:	+	Rates	Of the Amount over:
$ -0-	$ 1,800	$ -0-		11%	$ -0-
1,800	16,800	198		15%	1,800
16,800	27,000	2,448		28%	16,800
27,000	54,000	5,304		35%	27,000
54,000	—	14,754		38.5%	54,000

Heads of Households

Over	But not over	The tax is:	+	Rates	Of the Amount over:
$ -0-	$ 2,500	$ -0-		11%	$ -0-
2,500	23,000	275		15%	2,500
23,000	38,000	4,350		28%	23,000
38,000	80,000	8,550		35%	38,000
80,000	—	23,250		38.5%	80,000

Married Persons Filing Jointly

Over	But not over	The tax is:	+	Rates	Of the Amount over:
$ -0-	$ 3,000	$ -0-		11%	$ -0-
3,000	28,000	330		15%	3,000
28,000	45,000	4,080		28%	28,000
45,000	90,000	8,840		35%	45,000
90,000	—	24,590		38.5%	90,000

Married Persons Filing Separate Returns

Over	But not over	The tax is:	+	Rates	Of the Amount over:
$ -0-	$ 1,500	$ -0-		11%	$ -0-
1,500	14,000	165		15%	1,500
14,000	22,500	2,040		28%	14,000
22,500	45,000	4,420		35%	22,500
45,000	—	12,295		38.5%	45,000

ESTATES AND TRUSTS

$ -0-	$ 500	$ -0-	11%	$ -0-
500	4,700	55	15%	500
4,700	7,550	685	28%	4,700
7,550	15,150	1,483	35%	7,550
15,150	—	4,143	38.5%	15,150

CORPORATIONS

Caution: A new corporate tax rate schedule became effective for tax years beginning on or after July 1, 1987. For all tax years that only include July 1, 1987, a "blended" rate must be used. The blended rate prescribed by Sec. 15 is determined on a time-allocation basis. That is, every corporate taxpayer will: (1) determine the corporation's gross tax for the entire year's income using the "old" tax rates; (2) determine the corporation's gross tax for the entire year's income using the "new" tax rates; (3) multiply the gross tax determined in step #1, above, by the number of days in the corporation's tax year before July 1, 1987, and divide this amount by 365 days; (4) multiply the gross tax determined in step #2, above, by the number of days in the corporation's tax year after June 30, 1987 and divide this amount by 365 days; and (5) add together the two amounts determined in steps #3 and #4, above. In completing steps #1 and #2 the corporation should use the following tax rate schedules:

For Years Beginning **Before** 7/1/87 (i.e., the "old" rates)—

$ -0-	$ 25,000	$ -0-	15%	$ -0-
25,000	50,000	3,750	18%	25,000
50,000	75,000	8,250	30%	50,000
75,000	100,000	15,750	40%	75,000
100,000	1,000,000	25,750	46%	100,000
1,000,000	1,405,000	439,750	51%	1,000,000
1,405,000	—	646,300	46%	1,405,000

For Years Beginning **After** 6/30/87 (i.e., the "new" rates)—

$ -0-	$ 50,000	$ -0-	15%	$ -0-
50,000	75,000	7,500	25%	50,000
75,000	100,000	13,750	34%	75,000
100,000	335,000	22,250	39%	100,000
335,000	—	113,900	34%	335,000

Appendix B:
1988 Tax Rate Schedules

INDIVIDUAL TAXPAYERS

Caution: For individual taxpayers earning a taxable income of $50,000 or less, the I.R.S. will (in December 1988) publish a series of "Tax Tables" that should be used to determine an actual tax liability for most persons for calendar-year 1988. Use of the tax rate schedules, below, will yeild a tax liability very close to that determined by using the tax tables which will be available late in 1988.

Single Taxpayers

If taxable income is: Over	But not over	The tax is:	+	Rates	Of the amount over:
$ -0-	$ 17,850	$ -0-		15%	$ -0-
17,850	43,150	2,677.50		28%	17,850
43,150	89,560	9,761.50		33%	43,150
89,560	—	25,076.80*		28%	89,560

*PLUS the lesser of (1) 5% (taxable income—$89,560) or (2) 28% (the total amount claimed for personal and dependent exemption deductions).

Heads of Households

$ -0-	$ 23,900	$ -0-	15%		$ -0-
23,900	61,650	3,585.00	28%		23,900
61,650	123,790	14,155.00	33%		61,650
123,790	—	34,661.20*	28%		123,790

*PLUS the lesser of (1) 5% (taxable income—$123,790) or (2) 28% (the total amount claimed for personal and dependent exemption deductions).

Married Persons Filing Jointly

$ -0-	$ 29,750	$ -0-	15%		$ -0-
29,750	71,900	4,462.50	28%		29,750
71,900	149,250	16,264.50	33%		71,900
149,250	—	41,790.00*	28%		149,250

*PLUS the lesser of (1) 5% (taxable income—$149,250) or (2) 28% (the total amount claimed for personal and dependent exemption deductions).

Married Persons Filing Separate Returns

$ -0-	$ 14,875	$ -0-	15%		$ -0-
14,875	35,950	2,231.25	28%		14,875
35,950	113,300	8,132.25	33%		35,950
113,300	—	31,724.00*	28%		113,300

*PLUS the lesser of (1) 5% (taxable income—$113,300) or (2) 28% (the total amount claimed for personal and dependent exemption deductions).

ESTATES AND TRUSTS

$ -0-	$ 5,000	$ -0-	15%	$ -0-
5,000	13,000	750	28%	5,000
13,000	26,000	2,990	33%	13,000
26,000	—	7,280	28%	26,000

CORPORATIONS

(For all tax years beginning on or after July 1, 1987)

$ -0-	$ 50,000	$ -0-	15%	$ -0-
50,000	75,000	7,500	25%	50,000
75,000	100,000	13,750	34%	75,000
100,000	335,000	22,250	39%	100,000
335,000	—	113,900	34%	335,000

Appendix C:
Unified Estate and Gift Tax Rates

(A) Taxable transfer equal to or less than	(B) Taxable transfer less than	(C) Tax on amount in Col. (A)	1987 rate of tax on excess over amount in Col. (A) Percent	(D) 1988 (and after) rate of tax on excess over amount in Col. (A) Percent
$ -0-	$ 10,000	$ -0-	18	18
10,000	20,000	1,800	20	20
20,000	40,000	3,800	22	22
40,000	60,000	8,200	24	24
60,000	80,000	13,000	26	26
80,000	100,000	18,200	28	28
100,000	150,000	23,800	30	30
150,000	250,000	38,800	32	32
250,000	500,000	70,800	34	34
500,000	750,000	155,800	37	37
750,000	1,000,000	248,300	39	39
1,000,000	1,250,000	345,800	41	41
1,250,000	1,500,000	448,300	43	43
1,500,000	2,000,000	555,800	45	45
2,000,000	2,500,000	780,800	49	49
2,500,000	3,000,000	1,025,800	53	50
3,000,000	—	1,290,800	55	

APPENDIX D

1986 Tax Table

Based on Taxable Income

For persons with taxable incomes of less than $50,000.

Your zero bracket amount has been built into the Tax Table.

Example: Mr. and Mrs. Brown are filing a joint return. Their taxable income on line 37 of Form 1040 is $25,325. First, they find the $25,300-25,350 income line. Next, they find the column for married filing jointly and read down the column. The amount shown where the income line and filing status column meet is $3,470. This is the tax amount they must write on line 38 of their return.

At least	But less than	Single	Married filing jointly *	Married filing separately	Head of a household
			Your tax is—		
25,200	25,250	4,406	3,448	5,468	4,075
25,250	25,300	4,419	3,459	5,487	4,087
25,300	25,350	4,432	(3,470)	5,506	4,099
25,350	25,400	4,446	3,481	5,525	4,112

If line 37 (taxable income) is—		And you are—				If line 37 (taxable income) is—		And you are—				If line 37 (taxable income) is—		And you are—			
At least	But less than	Single	Married filing jointly *	Married filing separately	Head of a household	At least	But less than	Single	Married filing jointly *	Married filing separately	Head of a household	At least	But less than	Single	Married filing jointly *	Married filing separately	Head of a household
			Your tax is—						Your tax is—						Your tax is—		
$0	$1,850	$0	$0	$0	$0	2,400	2,425	0	0	64	0	3,400	3,450	104	0	179	104
1,850	1,875	0	0	3	0	2,425	2,450	0	0	66	0	3,450	3,500	109	0	185	109
1,875	1,900	0	0	6	0	2,450	2,475	0	0	69	0	3,500	3,550	115	0	191	115
						2,475	2,500	a1	0	72	a1	3,550	3,600	120	0	197	120
1,900	1,925	0	0	9	0	2,500	2,525	4	0	75	4	3,600	3,650	126	0	203	126
1,925	1,950	0	0	11	0	2,525	2,550	6	0	77	6	3,650	3,700	132	b1	209	131
1,950	1,975	0	0	14	0	2,550	2,575	9	0	80	9	3,700	3,750	138	6	215	137
1,975	2,000	0	0	17	0	2,575	2,600	12	0	83	12	3,750	3,800	144	12	221	142
2,000						2,600	2,625	15	0	86	15	3,800	3,850	150	17	227	148
						2,625	2,650	17	0	88	17	3,850	3,900	156	23	233	153
						2,650	2,675	20	0	91	20	3,900	3,950	162	28	239	159
						2,675	2,700	23	0	94	23	3,950	4,000	168	34	245	164
2,000	2,025	0	0	20	0	2,700	2,725	26	0	97	26	**4,000**					
2,025	2,050	0	0	22	0	2,725	2,750	28	0	99	28						
2,050	2,075	0	0	25	0	2,750	2,775	31	0	102	31	4,000	4,050	174	39	251	170
2,075	2,100	0	0	28	0	2,775	2,800	34	0	105	34	4,050	4,100	180	45	257	175
						2,800	2,825	37	0	108	37	4,100	4,150	186	50	264	181
						2,825	2,850	39	0	110	39	4,150	4,200	192	56	271	186
						2,850	2,875	42	0	113	42	4,200	4,250	198	61	278	192
						2,875	2,900	45	0	116	45	4,250	4,300	204	67	285	197
2,100	2,125	0	0	31	0							4,300	4,350	210	72	292	203
2,125	2,150	0	0	33	0	2,900	2,925	48	0	119	48	4,350	4,400	216	78	299	208
2,150	2,175	0	0	36	0	2,925	2,950	50	0	121	50						
2,175	2,200	0	0	39	0	2,950	2,975	53	0	124	53	4,400	4,450	222	83	306	214
						2,975	3,000	56	0	127	56	4,450	4,500	228	89	313	219
						3,000						4,500	4,550	234	94	320	225
2,200	2,225	0	0	42	0							4,550	4,600	240	100	327	230
2,225	2,250	0	0	44	0	3,000	3,050	60	0	131	60	4,600	4,650	246	105	334	236
2,250	2,275	0	0	47	0	3,050	3,100	65	0	137	65	4,650	4,700	252	111	341	241
2,275	2,300	0	0	50	0	3,100	3,150	71	0	143	71	4,700	4,750	258	116	348	247
						3,150	3,200	76	0	149	76	4,750	4,800	264	122	355	253
2,300	2,325	0	0	53	0	3,200	3,250	82	0	155	82	4,800	4,850	271	127	362	259
2,325	2,350	0	0	55	0	3,250	3,300	87	0	161	87	4,850	4,900	278	133	369	265
2,350	2,375	0	0	58	0	3,300	3,350	93	0	167	93	4,900	4,950	285	138	376	271
2,375	2,400	0	0	61	0	3,350	3,400	98	0	173	98	4,950	5,000	292	144	383	277

* This column must also be used by a qualifying widow(er).

Continued on next page

a If your taxable income is exactly $2,480 or less, your tax is zero.

b If your taxable income is exactly $3,670 or less, your tax is zero.

1986 Tax Table—*Continued*

5,000 / 6,000 / 7,000

If line 37 (taxable income) is— At least	But less than	Single	Married filing jointly *	Married filing separately	Head of a household
5,000					
5,000	5,050	299	149	390	283
5,050	5,100	306	155	397	289
5,100	5,150	313	160	404	295
5,150	5,200	320	166	411	301
5,200	5,250	327	171	418	307
5,250	5,300	334	177	425	313
5,300	5,350	341	182	432	319
5,350	5,400	348	188	439	325
5,400	5,450	355	193	446	331
5,450	5,500	362	199	453	337
5,500	5,550	369	204	460	343
5,550	5,600	376	210	467	349
5,600	5,650	383	215	474	355
5,650	5,700	390	221	481	361
5,700	5,750	397	226	488	367
5,750	5,800	404	232	495	373
5,800	5,850	411	237	502	379
5,850	5,900	418	243	509	385
5,900	5,950	425	248	516	391
5,950	6,000	432	254	523	397
6,000					
6,000	6,050	439	260	530	403
6,050	6,100	446	266	537	409
6,100	6,150	453	272	544	415
6,150	6,200	460	278	551	421
6,200	6,250	467	284	558	427
6,250	6,300	474	290	565	433
6,300	6,350	481	296	572	439
6,350	6,400	488	302	579	445
6,400	6,450	495	308	586	451
6,450	6,500	502	314	594	457
6,500	6,550	509	320	602	463
6,550	6,600	516	326	610	469
6,600	6,650	523	332	618	475
6,650	6,700	530	338	626	481
6,700	6,750	537	344	634	487
6,750	6,800	544	350	642	493
6,800	6,850	551	356	650	499
6,850	6,900	558	362	658	505
6,900	6,950	565	368	666	511
6,950	7,000	572	374	674	517
7,000					
7,000	7,050	579	380	682	523
7,050	7,100	587	386	690	530
7,100	7,150	594	392	698	537
7,150	7,200	602	398	706	544
7,200	7,250	609	404	714	551
7,250	7,300	617	410	722	558
7,300	7,350	624	416	730	565
7,350	7,400	632	422	738	572
7,400	7,450	639	428	746	579
7,450	7,500	647	434	754	586
7,500	7,550	654	440	762	593
7,550	7,600	662	446	770	600
7,600	7,650	669	452	778	607
7,650	7,700	677	458	786	614
7,700	7,750	684	464	794	621
7,750	7,800	692	470	802	628
7,800	7,850	699	476	810	635
7,850	7,900	707	482	818	642
7,900	7,950	714	488	826	649
7,950	8,000	722	494	834	656

8,000 / 9,000 / 10,000

If line 37 (taxable income) is— At least	But less than	Single	Married filing jointly *	Married filing separately	Head of a household
8,000					
8,000	8,050	729	500	842	663
8,050	8,100	737	506	850	670
8,100	8,150	744	512	858	677
8,150	8,200	752	518	866	684
8,200	8,250	759	524	874	691
8,250	8,300	767	531	882	698
8,300	8,350	774	538	890	705
8,350	8,400	782	545	898	712
8,400	8,450	789	552	906	719
8,450	8,500	797	559	914	726
8,500	8,550	804	566	922	733
8,550	8,600	812	573	930	740
8,600	8,650	819	580	938	747
8,650	8,700	827	587	947	754
8,700	8,750	834	594	956	761
8,750	8,800	842	601	965	768
8,800	8,850	849	608	974	775
8,850	8,900	857	615	983	782
8,900	8,950	864	622	992	789
8,950	9,000	872	629	1,001	796
9,000					
9,000	9,050	879	636	1,010	803
9,050	9,100	887	643	1,019	810
9,100	9,150	894	650	1,028	817
9,150	9,200	902	657	1,037	824
9,200	9,250	910	664	1,046	831
9,250	9,300	918	671	1,055	838
9,300	9,350	926	678	1,064	845
9,350	9,400	934	685	1,073	852
9,400	9,450	942	692	1,082	860
9,450	9,500	950	699	1,091	869
9,500	9,550	958	706	1,100	877
9,550	9,600	966	713	1,109	886
9,600	9,650	974	720	1,118	894
9,650	9,700	982	727	1,127	903
9,700	9,750	990	734	1,136	911
9,750	9,800	998	741	1,145	920
9,800	9,850	1,006	748	1,154	928
9,850	9,900	1,014	755	1,163	937
9,900	9,950	1,022	762	1,172	945
9,950	10,000	1,030	769	1,181	954
10,000					
10,000	10,050	1,038	776	1,190	962
10,050	10,100	1,046	783	1,199	971
10,100	10,150	1,054	790	1,208	979
10,150	10,200	1,062	797	1,217	988
10,200	10,250	1,070	804	1,226	996
10,250	10,300	1,078	811	1,235	1,005
10,300	10,350	1,086	818	1,244	1,013
10,350	10,400	1,094	825	1,253	1,022
10,400	10,450	1,102	832	1,262	1,030
10,450	10,500	1,110	839	1,271	1,039
10,500	10,550	1,118	846	1,280	1,047
10,550	10,600	1,126	853	1,289	1,056
10,600	10,650	1,134	860	1,298	1,064
10,650	10,700	1,142	867	1,307	1,073
10,700	10,750	1,150	874	1,316	1,081
10,750	10,800	1,158	881	1,325	1,090
10,800	10,850	1,166	888	1,334	1,098
10,850	10,900	1,174	895	1,343	1,107
10,900	10,950	1,182	902	1,353	1,115
10,950	11,000	1,190	909	1,364	1,124

11,000 / 12,000 / 13,000

If line 37 (taxable income) is— At least	But less than	Single	Married filing jointly *	Married filing separately	Head of a household
11,000					
11,000	11,050	1,198	916	1,375	1,132
11,050	11,100	1,206	923	1,386	1,141
11,100	11,150	1,214	930	1,397	1,149
11,150	11,200	1,222	937	1,408	1,158
11,200	11,250	1,230	944	1,419	1,166
11,250	11,300	1,238	951	1,430	1,175
11,300	11,350	1,246	958	1,441	1,183
11,350	11,400	1,254	965	1,452	1,192
11,400	11,450	1,262	972	1,463	1,200
11,450	11,500	1,270	979	1,474	1,209
11,500	11,550	1,278	986	1,485	1,217
11,550	11,600	1,286	993	1,496	1,226
11,600	11,650	1,294	1,000	1,507	1,234
11,650	11,700	1,302	1,007	1,518	1,243
11,700	11,750	1,311	1,014	1,529	1,251
11,750	11,800	1,320	1,021	1,540	1,260
11,800	11,850	1,329	1,028	1,551	1,268
11,850	11,900	1,338	1,035	1,562	1,277
11,900	11,950	1,347	1,042	1,573	1,285
11,950	12,000	1,356	1,049	1,584	1,294
12,000					
12,000	12,050	1,365	1,056	1,595	1,302
12,050	12,100	1,374	1,063	1,606	1,311
12,100	12,150	1,383	1,070	1,617	1,319
12,150	12,200	1,392	1,077	1,628	1,328
12,200	12,250	1,401	1,084	1,639	1,336
12,250	12,300	1,410	1,091	1,650	1,345
12,300	12,350	1,419	1,098	1,661	1,353
12,350	12,400	1,428	1,105	1,672	1,362
12,400	12,450	1,437	1,112	1,683	1,370
12,450	12,500	1,446	1,119	1,694	1,379
12,500	12,550	1,455	1,126	1,705	1,387
12,550	12,600	1,464	1,133	1,716	1,396
12,600	12,650	1,473	1,140	1,727	1,404
12,650	12,700	1,482	1,147	1,738	1,413
12,700	12,750	1,491	1,154	1,749	1,421
12,750	12,800	1,500	1,161	1,760	1,430
12,800	12,850	1,509	1,168	1,771	1,439
12,850	12,900	1,518	1,176	1,782	1,448
12,900	12,950	1,527	1,184	1,793	1,457
12,950	13,000	1,536	1,192	1,804	1,466
13,000					
13,000	13,050	1,545	1,200	1,815	1,475
13,050	13,100	1,554	1,208	1,826	1,484
13,100	13,150	1,563	1,216	1,837	1,493
13,150	13,200	1,572	1,224	1,848	1,502
13,200	13,250	1,581	1,232	1,859	1,511
13,250	13,300	1,590	1,240	1,870	1,520
13,300	13,350	1,599	1,248	1,882	1,529
13,350	13,400	1,608	1,256	1,895	1,538
13,400	13,450	1,617	1,264	1,907	1,547
13,450	13,500	1,626	1,272	1,920	1,556
13,500	13,550	1,635	1,280	1,932	1,565
13,550	13,600	1,644	1,288	1,945	1,574
13,600	13,650	1,653	1,296	1,957	1,583
13,650	13,700	1,662	1,304	1,970	1,592
13,700	13,750	1,671	1,312	1,982	1,601
13,750	13,800	1,680	1,320	1,995	1,610
13,800	13,850	1,689	1,328	2,007	1,619
13,850	13,900	1,698	1,336	2,020	1,628
13,900	13,950	1,707	1,344	2,032	1,637
13,950	14,000	1,717	1,352	2,045	1,646

* This column must also be used by a qualifying widow(er).

Continued on next page

1986 Tax Table—*Continued*

If line 37 (taxable income) is—		And you are—			
At least	But less than	Single	Married filing jointly *	Married filing separately	Head of a household
		Your tax is—			

14,000

At least	But less than	Single	Married filing jointly	Married filing separately	Head of a household
14,000	14,050	1,727	1,360	2,057	1,655
14,050	14,100	1,737	1,368	2,070	1,664
14,100	14,150	1,747	1,376	2,082	1,673
14,150	14,200	1,757	1,384	2,095	1,682
14,200	14,250	1,767	1,392	2,107	1,691
14,250	14,300	1,777	1,400	2,120	1,700
14,300	14,350	1,787	1,408	2,132	1,709
14,350	14,400	1,797	1,416	2,145	1,718
14,400	14,450	1,807	1,424	2,157	1,727
14,450	14,500	1,817	1,432	2,170	1,736
14,500	14,550	1,827	1,440	2,182	1,745
14,550	14,600	1,837	1,448	2,195	1,754
14,600	14,650	1,847	1,456	2,207	1,763
14,650	14,700	1,857	1,464	2,220	1,772
14,700	14,750	1,867	1,472	2,232	1,781
14,750	14,800	1,877	1,480	2,245	1,790
14,800	14,850	1,887	1,488	2,257	1,799
14,850	14,900	1,897	1,496	2,270	1,808
14,900	14,950	1,907	1,504	2,282	1,817
14,950	15,000	1,917	1,512	2,295	1,826

15,000

At least	But less than	Single	Married filing jointly	Married filing separately	Head of a household
15,000	15,050	1,927	1,520	2,307	1,835
15,050	15,100	1,937	1,528	2,320	1,844
15,100	15,150	1,947	1,536	2,332	1,853
15,150	15,200	1,957	1,544	2,345	1,862
15,200	15,250	1,967	1,552	2,357	1,871
15,250	15,300	1,977	1,560	2,370	1,880
15,300	15,350	1,987	1,568	2,382	1,889
15,350	15,400	1,997	1,576	2,395	1,898
15,400	15,450	2,007	1,584	2,407	1,907
15,450	15,500	2,017	1,592	2,420	1,916
15,500	15,550	2,027	1,600	2,432	1,925
15,550	15,600	2,037	1,608	2,445	1,934
15,600	15,650	2,047	1,616	2,457	1,943
15,650	15,700	2,057	1,624	2,470	1,952
15,700	15,750	2,067	1,632	2,482	1,961
15,750	15,800	2,077	1,640	2,495	1,970
15,800	15,850	2,087	1,648	2,507	1,979
15,850	15,900	2,097	1,656	2,520	1,988
15,900	15,950	2,107	1,664	2,532	1,997
15,950	16,000	2,117	1,672	2,545	2,006

16,000

At least	But less than	Single	Married filing jointly	Married filing separately	Head of a household
16,000	16,050	2,127	1,680	2,557	2,015
16,050	16,100	2,137	1,688	2,570	2,024
16,100	16,150	2,147	1,696	2,582	2,033
16,150	16,200	2,157	1,704	2,596	2,042
16,200	16,250	2,168	1,712	2,610	2,052
16,250	16,300	2,180	1,720	2,624	2,062
16,300	16,350	2,191	1,728	2,638	2,072
16,350	16,400	2,203	1,736	2,652	2,082
16,400	16,450	2,214	1,744	2,666	2,092
16,450	16,500	2,226	1,752	2,680	2,102
16,500	16,550	2,237	1,760	2,694	2,112
16,550	16,600	2,249	1,768	2,708	2,122
16,600	16,650	2,260	1,776	2,722	2,132
16,650	16,700	2,272	1,784	2,736	2,142
16,700	16,750	2,283	1,792	2,750	2,152
16,750	16,800	2,295	1,800	2,764	2,162
16,800	16,850	2,306	1,808	2,778	2,172
16,850	16,900	2,318	1,816	2,792	2,182
16,900	16,950	2,329	1,824	2,806	2,192
16,950	17,000	2,341	1,832	2,820	2,202

17,000

At least	But less than	Single	Married filing jointly	Married filing separately	Head of a household
17,000	17,050	2,352	1,840	2,834	2,212
17,050	17,100	2,364	1,848	2,848	2,222
17,100	17,150	2,375	1,856	2,862	2,232
17,150	17,200	2,387	1,864	2,876	2,242
17,200	17,250	2,398	1,872	2,890	2,252
17,250	17,300	2,410	1,880	2,904	2,262
17,300	17,350	2,421	1,889	2,918	2,272
17,350	17,400	2,433	1,898	2,932	2,282
17,400	17,450	2,444	1,907	2,946	2,292
17,450	17,500	2,456	1,916	2,960	2,302
17,500	17,550	2,467	1,925	2,974	2,312
17,550	17,600	2,479	1,934	2,988	2,322
17,600	17,650	2,490	1,943	3,002	2,332
17,650	17,700	2,502	1,952	3,016	2,342
17,700	17,750	2,513	1,961	3,030	2,352
17,750	17,800	2,525	1,970	3,044	2,362
17,800	17,850	2,536	1,979	3,058	2,372
17,850	17,900	2,548	1,988	3,072	2,382
17,900	17,950	2,559	1,997	3,086	2,392
17,950	18,000	2,571	2,006	3,100	2,402

18,000

At least	But less than	Single	Married filing jointly	Married filing separately	Head of a household
18,000	18,050	2,582	2,015	3,114	2,412
18,050	18,100	2,594	2,024	3,128	2,422
18,100	18,150	2,605	2,033	3,142	2,432
18,150	18,200	2,617	2,042	3,156	2,442
18,200	18,250	2,628	2,051	3,170	2,452
18,250	18,300	2,640	2,060	3,184	2,462
18,300	18,350	2,651	2,069	3,198	2,472
18,350	18,400	2,663	2,078	3,212	2,482
18,400	18,450	2,674	2,087	3,226	2,492
18,450	18,500	2,686	2,096	3,240	2,502
18,500	18,550	2,697	2,105	3,254	2,512
18,550	18,600	2,709	2,114	3,268	2,522
18,600	18,650	2,720	2,123	3,282	2,532
18,650	18,700	2,732	2,132	3,296	2,542
18,700	18,750	2,743	2,141	3,310	2,552
18,750	18,800	2,755	2,150	3,324	2,562
18,800	18,850	2,766	2,159	3,338	2,572
18,850	18,900	2,778	2,168	3,352	2,582
18,900	18,950	2,789	2,177	3,366	2,592
18,950	19,000	2,801	2,186	3,380	2,602

19,000

At least	But less than	Single	Married filing jointly	Married filing separately	Head of a household
19,000	19,050	2,812	2,195	3,396	2,612
19,050	19,100	2,824	2,204	3,412	2,622
19,100	19,150	2,835	2,213	3,429	2,632
19,150	19,200	2,847	2,222	3,445	2,642
19,200	19,250	2,858	2,231	3,462	2,652
19,250	19,300	2,870	2,240	3,478	2,662
19,300	19,350	2,881	2,249	3,495	2,672
19,350	19,400	2,893	2,258	3,511	2,682
19,400	19,450	2,904	2,267	3,528	2,692
19,450	19,500	2,916	2,276	3,544	2,702
19,500	19,550	2,927	2,285	3,561	2,712
19,550	19,600	2,939	2,294	3,577	2,722
19,600	19,650	2,950	2,303	3,594	2,732
19,650	19,700	2,963	2,312	3,610	2,743
19,700	19,750	2,976	2,321	3,627	2,755
19,750	19,800	2,989	2,330	3,643	2,767
19,800	19,850	3,002	2,339	3,660	2,779
19,850	19,900	3,015	2,348	3,676	2,791
19,900	19,950	3,028	2,357	3,693	2,803
19,950	20,000	3,041	2,366	3,709	2,815

20,000

At least	But less than	Single	Married filing jointly	Married filing separately	Head of a household
20,000	20,050	3,054	2,375	3,726	2,827
20,050	20,100	3,067	2,384	3,742	2,839
20,100	20,150	3,080	2,393	3,759	2,851
20,150	20,200	3,093	2,402	3,775	2,863
20,200	20,250	3,106	2,411	3,792	2,875
20,250	20,300	3,119	2,420	3,808	2,887
20,300	20,350	3,132	2,429	3,825	2,899
20,350	20,400	3,145	2,438	3,841	2,911
20,400	20,450	3,158	2,447	3,858	2,923
20,450	20,500	3,171	2,456	3,874	2,935
20,500	20,550	3,184	2,465	3,891	2,947
20,550	20,600	3,197	2,474	3,907	2,959
20,600	20,650	3,210	2,483	3,924	2,971
20,650	20,700	3,223	2,492	3,940	2,983
20,700	20,750	3,236	2,501	3,957	2,995
20,750	20,800	3,249	2,510	3,973	3,007
20,800	20,850	3,262	2,519	3,990	3,019
20,850	20,900	3,275	2,528	4,006	3,031
20,900	20,950	3,288	2,537	4,023	3,043
20,950	21,000	3,301	2,546	4,039	3,055

21,000

At least	But less than	Single	Married filing jointly	Married filing separately	Head of a household
21,000	21,050	3,314	2,555	4,056	3,067
21,050	21,100	3,327	2,564	4,072	3,079
21,100	21,150	3,340	2,573	4,089	3,091
21,150	21,200	3,353	2,582	4,105	3,103
21,200	21,250	3,366	2,591	4,122	3,115
21,250	21,300	3,379	2,600	4,138	3,127
21,300	21,350	3,392	2,609	4,155	3,139
21,350	21,400	3,405	2,618	4,171	3,151
21,400	21,450	3,418	2,627	4,188	3,163
21,450	21,500	3,431	2,636	4,204	3,175
21,500	21,550	3,444	2,645	4,221	3,187
21,550	21,600	3,457	2,654	4,237	3,199
21,600	21,650	3,470	2,663	4,254	3,211
21,650	21,700	3,483	2,672	4,270	3,223
21,700	21,750	3,496	2,681	4,287	3,235
21,750	21,800	3,509	2,690	4,303	3,247
21,800	21,850	3,522	2,700	4,320	3,259
21,850	21,900	3,535	2,711	4,336	3,271
21,900	21,950	3,548	2,722	4,353	3,283
21,950	22,000	3,561	2,733	4,369	3,295

22,000

At least	But less than	Single	Married filing jointly	Married filing separately	Head of a household
22,000	22,050	3,574	2,744	4,386	3,307
22,050	22,100	3,587	2,755	4,402	3,319
22,100	22,150	3,600	2,766	4,419	3,331
22,150	22,200	3,613	2,777	4,435	3,343
22,200	22,250	3,626	2,788	4,452	3,355
22,250	22,300	3,639	2,799	4,468	3,367
22,300	22,350	3,652	2,810	4,485	3,379
22,350	22,400	3,665	2,821	4,501	3,391
22,400	22,450	3,678	2,832	4,518	3,403
22,450	22,500	3,691	2,843	4,534	3,415
22,500	22,550	3,704	2,854	4,551	3,427
22,550	22,600	3,717	2,865	4,567	3,439
22,600	22,650	3,730	2,876	4,584	3,451
22,650	22,700	3,743	2,887	4,600	3,463
22,700	22,750	3,756	2,898	4,617	3,475
22,750	22,800	3,769	2,909	4,633	3,487
22,800	22,850	3,782	2,920	4,650	3,499
22,850	22,900	3,795	2,931	4,666	3,511
22,900	22,950	3,808	2,942	4,683	3,523
22,950	23,000	3,821	2,953	4,699	3,535

* This column must also be used by a qualifying widow(er)

Continued on next page

1986 Tax Table—*Continued*

23,000

If line 37 (taxable income) is— At least	But less than	Single	Married filing jointly *	Married filing separately	Head of a household
23,000	23,050	3,834	2,964	4,716	3,547
23,050	23,100	3,847	2,975	4,732	3,559
23,100	23,150	3,860	2,986	4,749	3,571
23,150	23,200	3,873	2,997	4,765	3,583
23,200	23,250	3,886	3,008	4,782	3,595
23,250	23,300	3,899	3,019	4,798	3,607
23,300	23,350	3,912	3,030	4,815	3,619
23,350	23,400	3,925	3,041	4,831	3,631
23,400	23,450	3,938	3,052	4,848	3,643
23,450	23,500	3,951	3,063	4,864	3,655
23,500	23,550	3,964	3,074	4,881	3,667
23,550	23,600	3,977	3,085	4,897	3,679
23,600	23,650	3,990	3,096	4,914	3,691
23,650	23,700	4,003	3,107	4,930	3,703
23,700	23,750	4,016	3,118	4,947	3,715
23,750	23,800	4,029	3,129	4,963	3,727
23,800	23,850	4,042	3,140	4,980	3,739
23,850	23,900	4,055	3,151	4,996	3,751
23,900	23,950	4,068	3,162	5,013	3,763
23,950	24,000	4,081	3,173	5,029	3,775

24,000

At least	But less than	Single	Married filing jointly *	Married filing separately	Head of a household
24,000	24,050	4,094	3,184	5,046	3,787
24,050	24,100	4,107	3,195	5,062	3,799
24,100	24,150	4,120	3,206	5,079	3,811
24,150	24,200	4,133	3,217	5,095	3,823
24,200	24,250	4,146	3,228	5,112	3,835
24,250	24,300	4,159	3,239	5,128	3,847
24,300	24,350	4,172	3,250	5,145	3,859
24,350	24,400	4,185	3,261	5,161	3,871
24,400	24,450	4,198	3,272	5,178	3,883
24,450	24,500	4,211	3,283	5,194	3,895
24,500	24,550	4,224	3,294	5,211	3,907
24,550	24,600	4,237	3,305	5,227	3,919
24,600	24,650	4,250	3,316	5,244	3,931
24,650	24,700	4,263	3,327	5,260	3,943
24,700	24,750	4,276	3,338	5,278	3,955
24,750	24,800	4,289	3,349	5,297	3,967
24,800	24,850	4,302	3,360	5,316	3,979
24,850	24,900	4,315	3,371	5,335	3,991
24,900	24,950	4,328	3,382	5,354	4,003
24,950	25,000	4,341	3,393	5,373	4,015

25,000

At least	But less than	Single	Married filing jointly *	Married filing separately	Head of a household
25,000	25,050	4,354	3,404	5,392	4,027
25,050	25,100	4,367	3,415	5,411	4,039
25,100	25,150	4,380	3,426	5,430	4,051
25,150	25,200	4,393	3,437	5,449	4,063
25,200	25,250	4,406	3,448	5,468	4,075
25,250	25,300	4,419	3,459	5,487	4,087
25,300	25,350	4,432	3,470	5,506	4,099
25,350	25,400	4,446	3,481	5,525	4,112
25,400	25,450	4,461	3,492	5,544	4,126
25,450	25,500	4,476	3,503	5,563	4,140
25,500	25,550	4,491	3,514	5,582	4,154
25,550	25,600	4,506	3,525	5,601	4,168
25,600	25,650	4,521	3,536	5,620	4,182
25,650	25,700	4,536	3,547	5,639	4,196
25,700	25,750	4,551	3,558	5,658	4,210
25,750	25,800	4,566	3,569	5,677	4,224
25,800	25,850	4,581	3,580	5,696	4,238
25,850	25,900	4,596	3,591	5,715	4,252
25,900	25,950	4,611	3,602	5,734	4,266
25,950	26,000	4,626	3,613	5,753	4,280

26,000

At least	But less than	Single	Married filing jointly *	Married filing separately	Head of a household
26,000	26,050	4,641	3,624	5,772	4,294
26,050	26,100	4,656	3,635	5,791	4,308
26,100	26,150	4,671	3,646	5,810	4,322
26,150	26,200	4,686	3,657	5,829	4,336
26,200	26,250	4,701	3,668	5,848	4,350
26,250	26,300	4,716	3,679	5,867	4,364
26,300	26,350	4,731	3,690	5,886	4,378
26,350	26,400	4,746	3,701	5,905	4,392
26,400	26,450	4,761	3,712	5,924	4,406
26,450	26,500	4,776	3,723	5,943	4,420
26,500	26,550	4,791	3,734	5,962	4,434
26,550	26,600	4,806	3,746	5,981	4,448
26,600	26,650	4,821	3,758	6,000	4,462
26,650	26,700	4,836	3,771	6,019	4,476
26,700	26,750	4,851	3,783	6,038	4,490
26,750	26,800	4,866	3,796	6,057	4,504
26,800	26,850	4,881	3,808	6,076	4,518
26,850	26,900	4,896	3,821	6,095	4,532
26,900	26,950	4,911	3,833	6,114	4,546
26,950	27,000	4,926	3,846	6,133	4,560

27,000

At least	But less than	Single	Married filing jointly *	Married filing separately	Head of a household
27,000	27,050	4,941	3,858	6,152	4,574
27,050	27,100	4,956	3,871	6,171	4,588
27,100	27,150	4,971	3,883	6,190	4,602
27,150	27,200	4,986	3,896	6,209	4,616
27,200	27,250	5,001	3,908	6,228	4,630
27,250	27,300	5,016	3,921	6,247	4,644
27,300	27,350	5,031	3,933	6,266	4,658
27,350	27,400	5,046	3,946	6,285	4,672
27,400	27,450	5,061	3,958	6,304	4,686
27,450	27,500	5,076	3,971	6,323	4,700
27,500	27,550	5,091	3,983	6,342	4,714
27,550	27,600	5,106	3,996	6,361	4,728
27,600	27,650	5,121	4,008	6,380	4,742
27,650	27,700	5,136	4,021	6,399	4,756
27,700	27,750	5,151	4,033	6,418	4,770
27,750	27,800	5,166	4,046	6,437	4,784
27,800	27,850	5,181	4,058	6,456	4,798
27,850	27,900	5,196	4,071	6,475	4,812
27,900	27,950	5,211	4,083	6,494	4,826
27,950	28,000	5,226	4,096	6,513	4,840

28,000

At least	But less than	Single	Married filing jointly *	Married filing separately	Head of a household
28,000	28,050	5,241	4,108	6,532	4,854
28,050	28,100	5,256	4,121	6,551	4,868
28,100	28,150	5,271	4,133	6,570	4,882
28,150	28,200	5,286	4,146	6,589	4,896
28,200	28,250	5,301	4,158	6,608	4,910
28,250	28,300	5,316	4,171	6,627	4,924
28,300	28,350	5,331	4,183	6,646	4,938
28,350	28,400	5,346	4,196	6,665	4,952
28,400	28,450	5,361	4,208	6,684	4,966
28,450	28,500	5,376	4,221	6,703	4,980
28,500	28,550	5,391	4,233	6,722	4,994
28,550	28,600	5,406	4,246	6,741	5,008
28,600	28,650	5,421	4,258	6,760	5,022
28,650	28,700	5,436	4,271	6,779	5,036
28,700	28,750	5,451	4,283	6,798	5,050
28,750	28,800	5,466	4,296	6,817	5,064
28,800	28,850	5,481	4,308	6,836	5,078
28,850	28,900	5,496	4,321	6,855	5,092
28,900	28,950	5,511	4,333	6,874	5,106
28,950	29,000	5,526	4,346	6,893	5,120

29,000

At least	But less than	Single	Married filing jointly *	Married filing separately	Head of a household
29,000	29,050	5,541	4,358	6,912	5,134
29,050	29,100	5,556	4,371	6,931	5,148
29,100	29,150	5,571	4,383	6,950	5,162
29,150	29,200	5,586	4,396	6,969	5,176
29,200	29,250	5,601	4,408	6,988	5,190
29,250	29,300	5,616	4,421	7,007	5,204
29,300	29,350	5,631	4,433	7,026	5,218
29,350	29,400	5,646	4,446	7,045	5,232
29,400	29,450	5,661	4,458	7,064	5,246
29,450	29,500	5,676	4,471	7,083	5,260
29,500	29,550	5,691	4,483	7,102	5,274
29,550	29,600	5,706	4,496	7,121	5,288
29,600	29,650	5,721	4,508	7,140	5,302
29,650	29,700	5,736	4,521	7,159	5,316
29,700	29,750	5,751	4,533	7,178	5,330
29,750	29,800	5,766	4,546	7,197	5,344
29,800	29,850	5,781	4,558	7,216	5,358
29,850	29,900	5,796	4,571	7,235	5,372
29,900	29,950	5,811	4,583	7,254	5,386
29,950	30,000	5,826	4,596	7,273	5,400

30,000

At least	But less than	Single	Married filing jointly *	Married filing separately	Head of a household
30,000	30,050	5,841	4,608	7,292	5,414
30,050	30,100	5,856	4,621	7,311	5,428
30,100	30,150	5,871	4,633	7,330	5,442
30,150	30,200	5,886	4,646	7,349	5,456
30,200	30,250	5,901	4,658	7,368	5,470
30,250	30,300	5,916	4,671	7,387	5,484
30,300	30,350	5,931	4,683	7,406	5,498
30,350	30,400	5,946	4,696	7,425	5,512
30,400	30,450	5,961	4,708	7,444	5,526
30,450	30,500	5,976	4,721	7,463	5,540
30,500	30,550	5,991	4,733	7,482	5,554
30,550	30,600	6,006	4,746	7,501	5,568
30,600	30,650	6,021	4,758	7,520	5,582
30,650	30,700	6,036	4,771	7,539	5,596
30,700	30,750	6,051	4,783	7,558	5,610
30,750	30,800	6,066	4,796	7,577	5,624
30,800	30,850	6,081	4,808	7,596	5,638
30,850	30,900	6,096	4,821	7,615	5,652
30,900	30,950	6,111	4,833	7,634	5,666
30,950	31,000	6,126	4,846	7,653	5,680

31,000

At least	But less than	Single	Married filing jointly *	Married filing separately	Head of a household
31,000	31,050	6,141	4,858	7,672	5,694
31,050	31,100	6,156	4,871	7,691	5,708
31,100	31,150	6,172	4,883	7,710	5,724
31,150	31,200	6,189	4,896	7,729	5,740
31,200	31,250	6,206	4,908	7,748	5,756
31,250	31,300	6,223	4,921	7,767	5,772
31,300	31,350	6,240	4,933	7,786	5,788
31,350	31,400	6,257	4,946	7,805	5,804
31,400	31,450	6,274	4,958	7,824	5,820
31,450	31,500	6,291	4,971	7,843	5,836
31,500	31,550	6,308	4,983	7,862	5,852
31,550	31,600	6,325	4,996	7,881	5,868
31,600	31,650	6,342	5,008	7,900	5,884
31,650	31,700	6,359	5,021	7,919	5,900
31,700	31,750	6,376	5,033	7,938	5,916
31,750	31,800	6,393	5,046	7,957	5,932
31,800	31,850	6,410	5,058	7,976	5,948
31,850	31,900	6,427	5,071	7,995	5,964
31,900	31,950	6,444	5,083	8,014	5,980
31,950	32,000	6,461	5,096	8,033	5,996

* This column must also be used by a qualifying widow(er).

Continued on next page

1986 Tax Table—*Continued*

If line 37 (taxable income) is— At least	But less than	Single	Married filing jointly *	Married filing separately	Head of a household
32,000					
32,000	32,050	6,478	5,108	8,052	6,012
32,050	32,100	6,495	5,121	8,071	6,028
32,100	32,150	6,512	5,133	8,090	6,044
32,150	32,200	6,529	5,146	8,109	6,060
32,200	32,250	6,546	5,158	8,128	6,076
32,250	32,300	6,563	5,171	8,147	6,092
32,300	32,350	6,580	5,185	8,166	6,108
32,350	32,400	6,597	5,199	8,185	6,124
32,400	32,450	6,614	5,213	8,206	6,140
32,450	32,500	6,631	5,227	8,227	6,156
32,500	32,550	6,648	5,241	8,248	6,172
32,550	32,600	6,665	5,255	8,269	6,188
32,600	32,650	6,682	5,269	8,290	6,204
32,650	32,700	6,699	5,283	8,311	6,220
32,700	32,750	6,716	5,297	8,332	6,236
32,750	32,800	6,733	5,311	8,353	6,252
32,800	32,850	6,750	5,325	8,374	6,268
32,850	32,900	6,767	5,339	8,395	6,284
32,900	32,950	6,784	5,353	8,416	6,300
32,950	33,000	6,801	5,367	8,437	6,316
33,000					
33,000	33,050	6,818	5,381	8,458	6,332
33,050	33,100	6,835	5,395	8,479	6,348
33,100	33,150	6,852	5,409	8,500	6,364
33,150	33,200	6,869	5,423	8,521	6,380
33,200	33,250	6,886	5,437	8,542	6,396
33,250	33,300	6,903	5,451	8,563	6,412
33,300	33,350	6,920	5,465	8,584	6,428
33,350	33,400	6,937	5,479	8,605	6,444
33,400	33,450	6,954	5,493	8,626	6,460
33,450	33,500	6,971	5,507	8,647	6,476
33,500	33,550	6,988	5,521	8,668	6,492
33,550	33,600	7,005	5,535	8,689	6,508
33,600	33,650	7,022	5,549	8,710	6,524
33,650	33,700	7,039	5,563	8,731	6,540
33,700	33,750	7,056	5,577	8,752	6,556
33,750	33,800	7,073	5,591	8,773	6,572
33,800	33,850	7,090	5,605	8,794	6,588
33,850	33,900	7,107	5,619	8,815	6,604
33,900	33,950	7,124	5,633	8,836	6,620
33,950	34,000	7,141	5,647	8,857	6,636
34,000					
34,000	34,050	7,158	5,661	8,878	6,652
34,050	34,100	7,175	5,675	8,899	6,668
34,100	34,150	7,192	5,689	8,920	6,684
34,150	34,200	7,209	5,703	8,941	6,700
34,200	34,250	7,226	5,717	8,962	6,716
34,250	34,300	7,243	5,731	8,983	6,732
34,300	34,350	7,260	5,745	9,004	6,748
34,350	34,400	7,277	5,759	9,025	6,764
34,400	34,450	7,294	5,773	9,046	6,780
34,450	34,500	7,311	5,787	9,067	6,796
34,500	34,550	7,328	5,801	9,088	6,812
34,550	34,600	7,345	5,815	9,109	6,828
34,600	34,650	7,362	5,829	9,130	6,844
34,650	34,700	7,379	5,843	9,151	6,860
34,700	34,750	7,396	5,857	9,172	6,876
34,750	34,800	7,413	5,871	9,193	6,892
34,800	34,850	7,430	5,885	9,214	6,908
34,850	34,900	7,447	5,899	9,235	6,924
34,900	34,950	7,464	5,913	9,256	6,940
34,950	35,000	7,481	5,927	9,277	6,956

If line 37 (taxable income) is— At least	But less than	Single	Married filing jointly *	Married filing separately	Head of a household
35,000					
35,000	35,050	7,498	5,941	9,298	6,972
35,050	35,100	7,515	5,955	9,319	6,988
35,100	35,150	7,532	5,969	9,340	7,004
35,150	35,200	7,549	5,983	9,361	7,020
35,200	35,250	7,566	5,997	9,382	7,036
35,250	35,300	7,583	6,011	9,403	7,052
35,300	35,350	7,600	6,025	9,424	7,068
35,350	35,400	7,617	6,039	9,445	7,084
35,400	35,450	7,634	6,053	9,466	7,100
35,450	35,500	7,651	6,067	9,487	7,116
35,500	35,550	7,668	6,081	9,508	7,132
35,550	35,600	7,685	6,095	9,529	7,148
35,600	35,650	7,702	6,109	9,550	7,164
35,650	35,700	7,719	6,123	9,571	7,180
35,700	35,750	7,736	6,137	9,592	7,196
35,750	35,800	7,753	6,151	9,613	7,212
35,800	35,850	7,770	6,165	9,634	7,228
35,850	35,900	7,787	6,179	9,655	7,244
35,900	35,950	7,804	6,193	9,676	7,260
35,950	36,000	7,821	6,207	9,697	7,276
36,000					
36,000	36,050	7,838	6,221	9,718	7,292
36,050	36,100	7,855	6,235	9,739	7,308
36,100	36,150	7,872	6,249	9,760	7,324
36,150	36,200	7,889	6,263	9,781	7,340
36,200	36,250	7,906	6,277	9,802	7,356
36,250	36,300	7,923	6,291	9,823	7,372
36,300	36,350	7,940	6,305	9,844	7,388
36,350	36,400	7,957	6,319	9,865	7,404
36,400	36,450	7,974	6,333	9,886	7,420
36,450	36,500	7,991	6,347	9,907	7,436
36,500	36,550	8,008	6,361	9,928	7,452
36,550	36,600	8,025	6,375	9,949	7,468
36,600	36,650	8,042	6,389	9,970	7,484
36,650	36,700	8,059	6,403	9,991	7,500
36,700	36,750	8,076	6,417	10,012	7,516
36,750	36,800	8,093	6,431	10,033	7,532
36,800	36,850	8,111	6,445	10,054	7,548
36,850	36,900	8,130	6,459	10,075	7,566
36,900	36,950	8,149	6,473	10,096	7,583
36,950	37,000	8,168	6,487	10,117	7,601
37,000					
37,000	37,050	8,187	6,501	10,138	7,618
37,050	37,100	8,206	6,515	10,159	7,636
37,100	37,150	8,225	6,529	10,180	7,653
37,150	37,200	8,244	6,543	10,201	7,671
37,200	37,250	8,263	6,557	10,222	7,688
37,250	37,300	8,282	6,571	10,243	7,706
37,300	37,350	8,301	6,585	10,264	7,723
37,350	37,400	8,320	6,599	10,285	7,741
37,400	37,450	8,339	6,613	10,306	7,758
37,450	37,500	8,358	6,627	10,327	7,776
37,500	37,550	8,377	6,641	10,348	7,793
37,550	37,600	8,396	6,655	10,369	7,811
37,600	37,650	8,415	6,669	10,390	7,828
37,650	37,700	8,434	6,683	10,411	7,846
37,700	37,750	8,453	6,697	10,432	7,863
37,750	37,800	8,472	6,711	10,453	7,881
37,800	37,850	8,491	6,725	10,474	7,898
37,850	37,900	8,510	6,739	10,495	7,916
37,900	37,950	8,529	6,753	10,516	7,933
37,950	38,000	8,548	6,767	10,537	7,951

If line 37 (taxable income) is— At least	But less than	Single	Married filing jointly *	Married filing separately	Head of a household
38,000					
38,000	38,050	8,567	6,783	10,558	7,968
38,050	38,100	8,586	6,800	10,579	7,986
38,100	38,150	8,605	6,816	10,600	8,003
38,150	38,200	8,624	6,833	10,621	8,021
38,200	38,250	8,643	6,849	10,642	8,038
38,250	38,300	8,662	6,866	10,663	8,056
38,300	38,350	8,681	6,882	10,684	8,073
38,350	38,400	8,700	6,899	10,705	8,091
38,400	38,450	8,719	6,915	10,726	8,108
38,450	38,500	8,738	6,932	10,747	8,126
38,500	38,550	8,757	6,948	10,768	8,143
38,550	38,600	8,776	6,965	10,789	8,161
38,600	38,650	8,795	6,981	10,810	8,178
38,650	38,700	8,814	6,998	10,831	8,196
38,700	38,750	8,833	7,014	10,852	8,213
38,750	38,800	8,852	7,031	10,873	8,231
38,800	38,850	8,871	7,047	10,894	8,248
38,850	38,900	8,890	7,064	10,915	8,266
38,900	38,950	8,909	7,080	10,936	8,283
38,950	39,000	8,928	7,097	10,957	8,301
39,000					
39,000	39,050	8,947	7,113	10,978	8,318
39,050	39,100	8,966	7,130	10,999	8,336
39,100	39,150	8,985	7,146	11,020	8,353
39,150	39,200	9,004	7,163	11,041	8,371
39,200	39,250	9,023	7,179	11,062	8,388
39,250	39,300	9,042	7,196	11,083	8,406
39,300	39,350	9,061	7,212	11,104	8,423
39,350	39,400	9,080	7,229	11,125	8,441
39,400	39,450	9,099	7,245	11,146	8,458
39,450	39,500	9,118	7,262	11,167	8,476
39,500	39,550	9,137	7,278	11,188	8,493
39,550	39,600	9,156	7,295	11,209	8,511
39,600	39,650	9,175	7,311	11,230	8,528
39,650	39,700	9,194	7,328	11,251	8,546
39,700	39,750	9,213	7,344	11,272	8,563
39,750	39,800	9,232	7,361	11,293	8,581
39,800	39,850	9,251	7,377	11,314	8,598
39,850	39,900	9,270	7,394	11,335	8,616
39,900	39,950	9,289	7,410	11,356	8,633
39,950	40,000	9,308	7,427	11,377	8,651
40,000					
40,000	40,050	9,327	7,443	11,398	8,668
40,050	40,100	9,346	7,460	11,419	8,686
40,100	40,150	9,365	7,476	11,440	8,703
40,150	40,200	9,384	7,493	11,461	8,721
40,200	40,250	9,403	7,509	11,482	8,738
40,250	40,300	9,422	7,526	11,503	8,756
40,300	40,350	9,441	7,542	11,524	8,773
40,350	40,400	9,460	7,559	11,545	8,791
40,400	40,450	9,479	7,575	11,566	8,808
40,450	40,500	9,498	7,592	11,587	8,826
40,500	40,550	9,517	7,608	11,608	8,843
40,550	40,600	9,536	7,625	11,629	8,861
40,600	40,650	9,555	7,641	11,650	8,878
40,650	40,700	9,574	7,658	11,671	8,896
40,700	40,750	9,593	7,674	11,692	8,913
40,750	40,800	9,612	7,691	11,713	8,931
40,800	40,850	9,631	7,707	11,734	8,948
40,850	40,900	9,650	7,724	11,755	8,966
40,900	40,950	9,669	7,740	11,776	8,983
40,950	41,000	9,688	7,757	11,797	9,001

* This column must also be used by a qualifying widow(er).

Continued on next page

1986 Tax Table—Continued

If line 37 (taxable income) is— At least	But less than	Single	Married filing jointly *	Married filing separately	Head of a household
41,000					
41,000	41,050	9,707	7,773	11,818	9,018
41,050	41,100	9,726	7,790	11,839	9,036
41,100	41,150	9,745	7,806	11,860	9,053
41,150	41,200	9,764	7,823	11,881	9,071
41,200	41,250	9,783	7,839	11,902	9,088
41,250	41,300	9,802	7,856	11,923	9,106
41,300	41,350	9,821	7,872	11,944	9,123
41,350	41,400	9,840	7,889	11,965	9,141
41,400	41,450	9,859	7,905	11,986	9,158
41,450	41,500	9,878	7,922	12,007	9,176
41,500	41,550	9,897	7,938	12,028	9,193
41,550	41,600	9,916	7,955	12,049	9,211
41,600	41,650	9,935	7,971	12,070	9,228
41,650	41,700	9,954	7,988	12,091	9,246
41,700	41,750	9,973	8,004	12,112	9,263
41,750	41,800	9,992	8,021	12,133	9,281
41,800	41,850	10,011	8,037	12,154	9,298
41,850	41,900	10,030	8,054	12,175	9,316
41,900	41,950	10,049	8,070	12,196	9,333
41,950	42,000	10,068	8,087	12,217	9,351
42,000					
42,000	42,050	10,087	8,103	12,238	9,368
42,050	42,100	10,106	8,120	12,259	9,386
42,100	42,150	10,125	8,136	12,280	9,403
42,150	42,200	10,144	8,153	12,301	9,421
42,200	42,250	10,163	8,169	12,322	9,438
42,250	42,300	10,182	8,186	12,343	9,456
42,300	42,350	10,201	8,202	12,364	9,473
42,350	42,400	10,220	8,219	12,385	9,491
42,400	42,450	10,239	8,235	12,406	9,508
42,450	42,500	10,258	8,252	12,427	9,526
42,500	42,550	10,277	8,268	12,448	9,543
42,550	42,600	10,296	8,285	12,469	9,561
42,600	42,650	10,315	8,301	12,490	9,578
42,650	42,700	10,334	8,318	12,511	9,596
42,700	42,750	10,353	8,334	12,532	9,613
42,750	42,800	10,372	8,351	12,553	9,631
42,800	42,850	10,391	8,367	12,574	9,648
42,850	42,900	10,410	8,384	12,595	9,666
42,900	42,950	10,429	8,400	12,616	9,683
42,950	43,000	10,448	8,417	12,637	9,701
43,000					
43,000	43,050	10,467	8,433	12,658	9,718
43,050	43,100	10,486	8,450	12,679	9,736
43,100	43,150	10,505	8,466	12,700	9,753
43,150	43,200	10,524	8,483	12,721	9,771
43,200	43,250	10,543	8,499	12,742	9,788
43,250	43,300	10,562	8,516	12,763	9,806
43,300	43,350	10,581	8,532	12,784	9,823
43,350	43,400	10,600	8,549	12,805	9,841
43,400	43,450	10,619	8,565	12,826	9,858
43,450	43,500	10,638	8,582	12,847	9,876
43,500	43,550	10,657	8,598	12,868	9,893
43,550	43,600	10,676	8,615	12,889	9,911
43,600	43,650	10,695	8,631	12,910	9,928
43,650	43,700	10,714	8,648	12,931	9,946
43,700	43,750	10,733	8,664	12,952	9,963
43,750	43,800	10,752	8,681	12,973	9,981
43,800	43,850	10,771	8,697	12,994	9,998
43,850	43,900	10,790	8,714	13,015	10,016
43,900	43,950	10,809	8,730	13,036	10,033
43,950	44,000	10,828	8,747	13,057	10,051

If line 37 (taxable income) is— At least	But less than	Single	Married filing jointly *	Married filing separately	Head of a household
44,000					
44,000	44,050	10,847	8,763	13,078	10,068
44,050	44,100	10,866	8,780	13,099	10,086
44,100	44,150	10,885	8,796	13,120	10,103
44,150	44,200	10,904	8,813	13,141	10,121
44,200	44,250	10,923	8,829	13,162	10,138
44,250	44,300	10,942	8,846	13,183	10,156
44,300	44,350	10,961	8,862	13,204	10,173
44,350	44,400	10,980	8,879	13,225	10,191
44,400	44,450	10,999	8,895	13,246	10,208
44,450	44,500	11,018	8,912	13,267	10,226
44,500	44,550	11,037	8,928	13,288	10,243
44,550	44,600	11,056	8,945	13,309	10,261
44,600	44,650	11,075	8,961	13,330	10,278
44,650	44,700	11,094	8,978	13,351	10,296
44,700	44,750	11,113	8,994	13,372	10,313
44,750	44,800	11,132	9,011	13,393	10,331
44,800	44,850	11,153	9,027	13,414	10,348
44,850	44,900	11,174	9,044	13,435	10,366
44,900	44,950	11,195	9,060	13,456	10,383
44,950	45,000	11,216	9,077	13,477	10,401
45,000					
45,000	45,050	11,237	9,093	13,498	10,418
45,050	45,100	11,258	9,110	13,519	10,436
45,100	45,150	11,279	9,126	13,540	10,453
45,150	45,200	11,300	9,143	13,561	10,471
45,200	45,250	11,321	9,159	13,582	10,488
45,250	45,300	11,342	9,176	13,603	10,506
45,300	45,350	11,363	9,192	13,624	10,523
45,350	45,400	11,384	9,209	13,645	10,541
45,400	45,450	11,405	9,225	13,666	10,558
45,450	45,500	11,426	9,242	13,687	10,576
45,500	45,550	11,447	9,258	13,708	10,593
45,550	45,600	11,468	9,275	13,729	10,611
45,600	45,650	11,489	9,291	13,750	10,628
45,650	45,700	11,510	9,308	13,771	10,646
45,700	45,750	11,531	9,324	13,792	10,663
45,750	45,800	11,552	9,341	13,813	10,681
45,800	45,850	11,573	9,357	13,834	10,698
45,850	45,900	11,594	9,374	13,855	10,716
45,900	45,950	11,615	9,390	13,876	10,733
45,950	46,000	11,636	9,407	13,897	10,751
46,000					
46,000	46,050	11,657	9,423	13,918	10,768
46,050	46,100	11,678	9,440	13,939	10,786
46,100	46,150	11,699	9,456	13,960	10,803
46,150	46,200	11,720	9,473	13,981	10,821
46,200	46,250	11,741	9,489	14,003	10,838
46,250	46,300	11,762	9,506	14,025	10,856
46,300	46,350	11,783	9,522	14,048	10,873
46,350	46,400	11,804	9,539	14,070	10,891
46,400	46,450	11,825	9,555	14,093	10,908
46,450	46,500	11,846	9,572	14,115	10,926
46,500	46,550	11,867	9,588	14,138	10,943
46,550	46,600	11,888	9,605	14,160	10,961
46,600	46,650	11,909	9,621	14,183	10,978
46,650	46,700	11,930	9,638	14,205	10,996
46,700	46,750	11,951	9,654	14,228	11,013
46,750	46,800	11,972	9,671	14,250	11,031
46,800	46,850	11,993	9,687	14,273	11,048
46,850	46,900	12,014	9,704	14,295	11,066
46,900	46,950	12,035	9,720	14,318	11,083
46,950	47,000	12,056	9,737	14,340	11,101

If line 37 (taxable income) is— At least	But less than	Single	Married filing jointly *	Married filing separately	Head of a household
47,000					
47,000	47,050	12,077	9,753	14,363	11,118
47,050	47,100	12,098	9,770	14,385	11,136
47,100	47,150	12,119	9,786	14,408	11,153
47,150	47,200	12,140	9,803	14,430	11,171
47,200	47,250	12,161	9,819	14,453	11,188
47,250	47,300	12,182	9,836	14,475	11,206
47,300	47,350	12,203	9,852	14,498	11,223
47,350	47,400	12,224	9,869	14,520	11,241
47,400	47,450	12,245	9,885	14,543	11,258
47,450	47,500	12,266	9,902	14,565	11,276
47,500	47,550	12,287	9,918	14,588	11,293
47,550	47,600	12,308	9,935	14,610	11,311
47,600	47,650	12,329	9,951	14,633	11,328
47,650	47,700	12,350	9,968	14,655	11,346
47,700	47,750	12,371	9,984	14,678	11,363
47,750	47,800	12,392	10,001	14,700	11,381
47,800	47,850	12,413	10,017	14,723	11,398
47,850	47,900	12,434	10,034	14,745	11,416
47,900	47,950	12,455	10,050	14,768	11,433
47,950	48,000	12,476	10,067	14,790	11,451
48,000					
48,000	48,050	12,497	10,083	14,813	11,468
48,050	48,100	12,518	10,100	14,835	11,486
48,100	48,150	12,539	10,116	14,858	11,503
48,150	48,200	12,560	10,133	14,880	11,521
48,200	48,250	12,581	10,149	14,903	11,538
48,250	48,300	12,602	10,166	14,925	11,558
48,300	48,350	12,623	10,182	14,948	11,579
48,350	48,400	12,644	10,199	14,970	11,600
48,400	48,450	12,665	10,215	14,993	11,621
48,450	48,500	12,686	10,232	15,015	11,642
48,500	48,550	12,707	10,248	15,038	11,663
48,550	48,600	12,728	10,265	15,060	11,684
48,600	48,650	12,749	10,281	15,083	11,705
48,650	48,700	12,770	10,298	15,105	11,726
48,700	48,750	12,791	10,314	15,128	11,747
48,750	48,800	12,812	10,331	15,150	11,768
48,800	48,850	12,833	10,347	15,173	11,789
48,850	48,900	12,854	10,364	15,195	11,810
48,900	48,950	12,875	10,380	15,218	11,831
48,950	49,000	12,896	10,397	15,240	11,852
49,000					
49,000	49,050	12,917	10,413	15,263	11,873
49,050	49,100	12,938	10,430	15,285	11,894
49,100	49,150	12,959	10,446	15,308	11,915
49,150	49,200	12,980	10,463	15,330	11,936
49,200	49,250	13,001	10,479	15,353	11,957
49,250	49,300	13,022	10,496	15,375	11,978
49,300	49,350	13,043	10,512	15,398	11,999
49,350	49,400	13,064	10,529	15,420	12,020
49,400	49,450	13,085	10,546	15,443	12,041
49,450	49,500	13,106	10,565	15,465	12,062
49,500	49,550	13,127	10,584	15,488	12,083
49,550	49,600	13,148	10,603	15,510	12,104
49,600	49,650	13,169	10,622	15,533	12,125
49,650	49,700	13,190	10,641	15,555	12,146
49,700	49,750	13,211	10,660	15,578	12,167
49,750	49,800	13,232	10,679	15,600	12,188
49,800	49,850	13,253	10,698	15,623	12,209
49,850	49,900	13,274	10,717	15,645	12,230
49,900	49,950	13,295	10,736	15,668	12,251
49,950	50,000	13,316	10,755	15,690	12,272

* This column must also be used by a qualifying widow(er).

50,000 or over—use tax rate schedules

Index

A 7
B 8
C 9
D 0
E 1
F 2
G 3
H 4
I 5
J 6